The Christian History of the American Revolution

George Washington

The Character and Influence of One Man

"WHERE THE SPIRIT OF THE LORD IS, THERE IS LIBERTY." II CORINTHIANS 3:17
TM

PARTS UNKNOWN
KRISS or KILLISTINONS
BAY
CHRISTINAUX
ASSINIPOELS
NEW FRANCE or CANADA
ALGONQUINS or ADIRONDIKS
LAKE SUPERIOR
NADOUESSIS or SIOUX
OUTAOWAS
LAKE HURON
LAKE MICHIGAN or ILINOIS
MAHA and TINTONS
L. ONTARIO or CATARAQUI
PADUCAS NATION
LAKE ERIE or OKSWEGO
Great Meadows
PANIS NATION
PENSILVANIA
ILINOIS
KANSEZ NATION
PALUCAS NATION
CHIKTAGHICKS
OZAGES NATION
VIRGINIA
COUNTRY
LOUISIANA
NORTH CAROLINA
SOUTH CAROLINA
CONQUERED
GEORGIA
WEST FLORIDA
Mouths of the Missisipi or St. Louis
BAHAMA
NEW JERSEY

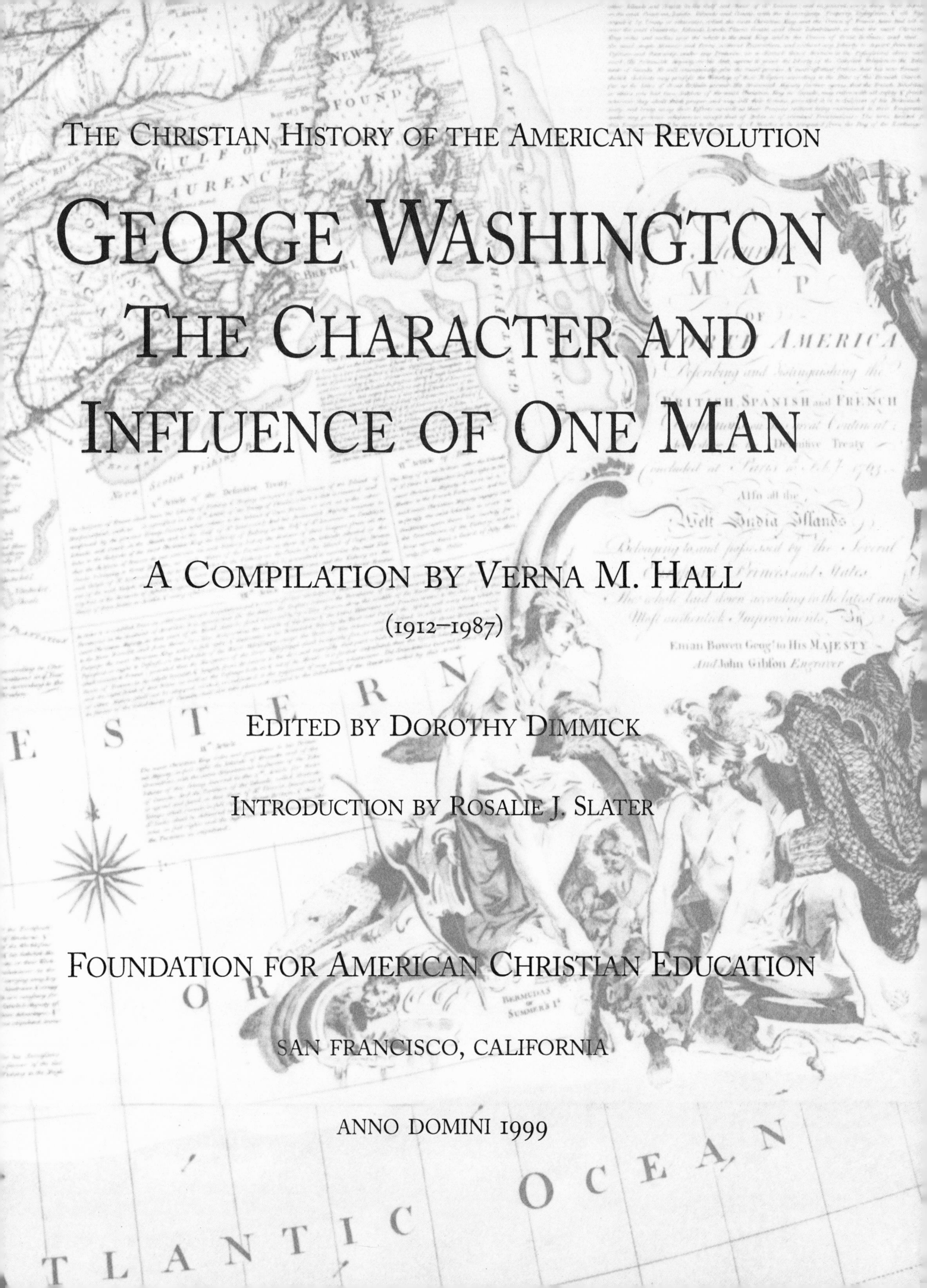

THE CHRISTIAN HISTORY OF THE AMERICAN REVOLUTION

GEORGE WASHINGTON THE CHARACTER AND INFLUENCE OF ONE MAN

A COMPILATION BY VERNA M. HALL
(1912–1987)

EDITED BY DOROTHY DIMMICK

INTRODUCTION BY ROSALIE J. SLATER

FOUNDATION FOR AMERICAN CHRISTIAN EDUCATION

SAN FRANCISCO, CALIFORNIA

ANNO DOMINI 1999

George Washington: The Character and Influence of One Man
compiled by Verna M. Hall

First Edition

Published by the

Foundation for American Christian Education
Box 27035, San Francisco, California 94127

Printed by The C. J. Krehbiel Co.
Cincinnati, Ohio

Library of Congress Catalog Card Number 00-100712
ISBN 0-912498-25-0

CHRISTIAN HISTORY SERIES
compiled by Verna M. Hall

The Christian History of the Constitution of the United States of America (Volume I): *Christian Self-Government;*

The Christian History of the Constitution of the United States of America (Volume II): *Christian Self-Government with Union;*

The Christian History of the American Revolution: Consider and Ponder

Free Catalogue & Ordering:
F. A. C. E., PO BOX 9588
CHESAPEAKE, VIRGINIA 23321
800-352-FACE • www.face.net

TITLE PAGE MAP:

AN ACCURATE MAP OF NORTH AMERICA (DETAIL)
EMAN BOWEN, GEOGRAPHER, AND JOHN GIBSON, ENGRAVER
PRINTED FOR ROBERT SAYER, LONDON, 1763.
FULL MAP: 40 X 45¾ INCHES
SCALE IN THE ORIGINAL: 1 INCH + 85.7 MILES
COURTESY OF WILLIAM L. CLEMENTS LIBRARY,
ANN ARBOR, MICHIGAN

COVER EMBOSSED PROFILE OF GEORGE WASHINGTON FROM
MEDALLION BASED ON ORIGINAL BUST BY HOUDON

THE HAND OF GOD IN AMERICA'S CHRISTIAN HISTORY: DIVINE PROVIDENCE IN THE LIFE OF GEORGE WASHINGTON

"The phrase 'America's Christian History' and the title *The Christian History of the American Revolution* is based upon the conviction that America's civil freedom, i.e., freedom for the individual, came from God through His son, Jesus Christ, and is the result or effect of Christianity's development and westward march from Asia, through Europe and England to America.

"The cause and timing of events which led to the War for American Independence, the raising up of civil and military leaders and the willingness of a diversified people to be self-governed—the cause of these aspects and many more—is attributed to the fulfillment of the promises of God to those who obey His precepts in His Word, obey His Law of Liberty in all aspects of their lives—including civil government." —Verna M. Hall

(*The Christian History of the American Revolution: Consider and Ponder,* by Verna M. Hall, 1975, p. XXIV)

"Citizens of the United States! While with grateful hearts you recollect the virtues of your Washington, carry your thoughts one step farther. On a review of his life, and of all the circumstances and the times in which he lived, you must be convinced, that a kind Providence in its beneficence raised him, and endowed him with extraordinary virtues, to be to you an instrument of great good."

(David Ramsay, *History of the American Revolution,* 1790.)

"The youthful commander had . . . a foretaste, in . . . his incipient campaigns, of the perils and complexities which awaited him from enemies in the field, and lax friends in legislative councils in the grander operations of his future years."

(Washington Irving, *The Life of Washington,* Vol. I, 1856.)

GEORGE WASHINGTON AS A BRITISH COLONIAL COLONEL IN THE VIRGINIA REGIMENT
BY CHARLES WILLSON PEALE, 1772

Painted from life; the only likeness of George Washington done before the Revolution.

Courtesy of
Washington—Custis—Lee Collection
Washington and Lee University,
Lexington, Virginia

For Mr. & Mrs. John G. Talcott, Jr.

This book is dedicated to John and Rosalin Talcott,
Christians and American Patriots,
who were early supporters of
The Foundation for American Christian Education.
Throughout the years they have never wavered
in faith and in love for America,
generously contributing their support
in every possible way.
This book on George Washington is a demonstration of
their steadfastness and Christian love.

Acknowledgments

Carole Goodman Adams

Isn't it unusual that a "compiler" of ideas, collecting selected writings from primary souces rather than presenting her own writing, would have the influence that Verna Hall has had in modern America? The writers Verna included in her books were her "carriers"—voices from the era that produced our liberties, resonant with the conscience and character of the age. Verna expected that this model of research would also "carry" the moral authority to impact the thinking of modern America.

Isn't it surprising that a woman would be the herald of a new era? While American Christians were succumbing to the lure of socialism, while the pulpit was abandoning America's Gospel purpose, and while twentieth century Christian leaders were rhetoricizing the "post-Christian" era, Verna Hall, a musical woman, a Biblical woman, a model herself of the character and influence of one individual, began rebuilding the walls.

Isn't it extraordinary that history in its pure state can revive the conscience of a generation? The acknowledgment Verna Hall wrote for the first volume in this series, *The Christian History of the American Revolution: Consider and Ponder,* begins with . . . "*When one undertakes a work to call to the attention of the American Christians the vast amount of written evidence of America's Christian history. . . .*" This opening is mighty in its humility. How astounding that the work that spawned the most hopeful movement of the twentieth century began with the mission of simply calling attention to America's Christian history. In a time when our daily mail urges support of more than one world-saving mission, Verna's mission is certainly unique. Getting our attention may be a greater challenge than Verna knew, thanks to the ravages of the video age to our attention spans. But her purpose reveals her respect for the individual American—her expectation that we can think, reason, and respond responsibly to the duties that the knowledge of America's Christian history imposes upon us. Verna makes no lofty promises and claims no spectacular numbers or miracles. She simply is calling us to attention, believing that we would know what to do. What faith.

Today, as we publish her Volume II of *The Christian History of the American Revolution* series, Verna is gone. If she were sitting in my seat, writing her own acknowledgments to this volume, she would quietly thank those who gave her encouragement and support. We endeavor here to speak that appreciation for her.

Verna's most ardent encourager was her partner, the President of the Foundation for American

Christian Education, Rosalie June Slater. Rosalie's investment of her life and energies in Verna's vision made it possible for Verna to accomplish what God told her to do. Rosalie's faith in Americans, in their resilience and idealism, and her unwavering dedication to publish these works, testify of her great heart of love for God and man. In 1995, as the F.A.C.E. Board met in San Francisco, Rosalie challenged us to publish this work. At that time, the manuscript was in dozens of notebooks, typewritten with notations in Verna's handwriting, in file boxes. Over the next four years, the research necessary to discover Verna's format, inclusions and exclusions, ideas for illustration, indexing, and technical design was directed by Rosalie Slater.

In the original list of helpers appears the name, Dorothy Dimmick. Like Verna, Dorothy is an unassuming, yet uncompromising woman. Dorothy's life as wife, mother, researcher and writer in her own right, includes a unique relationship to Verna Hall. In the 1950s, when Verna was beginning to teach the history of the American constitution in her study group in San Francisco, Dorothy and Walter held study sessions in their home in Silicon Valley. Inspired by the importance of this scholarship, Dorothy gave years as a volunteer indexer, research assistant, and steady student of Verna's work. In 1997, Dorothy picked up the challenge to complete the editing of the book, an enormous task. Dorothy is the "carrier" of this book as much as is Washington Irving through his biography, or Washington through his prolific journals and letters. Verna would hail Dorothy's efforts as essential to the final publication.

As we began to put Verna's work into book form, the Lord used Katherine Dang, one of the early students, a teacher in the first pilot school, who came to love George Washington through Verna's work. Katherine reviewed the material, wrote marginal notes, developed the chronology, and set up the Scripture references found in the appendix.

Desta Garrett, typographer and F.A.C.E. production manager, is also a "carrier" of the vision for this book. As a research assistant to Verna and Rosalie, Desta developed an abiding love for America's Christian history. In the production of the book, she has held the technical standard and ideals of all F.A.C.E. publications high for those who have been involved,—editors, production staff, proofreaders, and printers. Desta maintains the spirit and intent of the compiler faithfully and diligently.

From the beginning of Verna's mission, Mary-Elaine Adams Swanson was there to assist with research and teaching. She was one of the co-leaders in Verna's study group in San Francisco. Mary-Elaine is the gifted writer who produced the author biographies for Verna's compilations. She provides the biographies of the writers and artists for this volume.

This volume has the distinction of being the fruit of half a century of consistently shared ideals and constant friendship of many individuals, demonstrating again the timelessness and unifying effect of truth. In Verna's list of additional encouragers for this volume would be the following who have given financially and personally to the effort:

John and Rosalin Talcott,
  to whom the volume is dedicated
Janet Havard Mosser
Thomas and Christi Moorman
Walter Franklin Dimmick
Martha Shirley
Al Vipiano
Elizabeth Youmans
Maxwell Lyons
John and Carole Adams
Mrs. Lincoln Edward Gould
Mrs. Ruth Schneider
And dozens of individuals whose
financial support made the
publication possible.

It is the hope of the Foundation for American Christian Education that this book will add truth and grace to the rich repository of character that is our rightful heritage as American Christians.

Carole Goodman Adams, Ph.D.
Secretary-Treasurer,
Foundation for American Christian Education

San Francisco, California
December 14, 1999

Contents

The Dedication of the Washington National Monument 281

Rebuilding the Foundations

Appendix

A

B

Indexes

Indexing Key: Letters a, b, c, d following page numbers indicate first, second, third, fourth quarters of page—

a	c
b	d

Illustrations

Appendix

Introduction

George Washington: Establishing the Character of America

Rosalie J. Slater

While more than a million Americans visit Mount Vernon, the home of George Washington, every year, few know the details of his magnificent character or are aware of his unique contributions to our nation. When Miss Verna Hall became aware of the great gulf of ignorance which separated most Americans from knowledge of the father and founder of the American Republic, she began to search out some primary sources of his character and influence. The result was many years of gathering resources of Washington's own words as he participated in the many demands of his life. This resulted in a compilation, or gathering together of several volumes by and about George Washington. We are now preparing to publish a primary volume to set forth some highlights of his character and influence.

In the F.A.C.E. library in San Francisco is a set of 39 volumes of the *Writings of George Washington*, edited by John C. Fitzpatrick. This was a government printing in 1932 to commemorate the 200th anniversary of the birth of George Washington, 1732–1932. In the opening volume Miss Hall found the following appraisal of Washington by President Herbert Hoover who was President of the United States at that time.

Hoover's Foreword defined George Washington as "the most voluminous American writer of this period." He also stated that "his principles of government have had more influence on the development of the American commonwealth than those of any other man."

Hoover also indicated that biographical studies had failed to communicate that Washington was "the most potent human and intellectual force in a firmament of American intellect." (p. iii)

As we study this volume we find George Washington's character presented two ways: first, through seeing the many demands upon him in his "activity as man of affairs" as Commander-in-Chief of the Continental Army, and as the first President of our American Constitutional Republic; and, second, through the regard of his cotemporaries who lived with him in the same century, for the integrity and consistency of his high moral character in public and in private life.

It took a man of President Herbert Hoover's unique background to discern Washington as an engineer. "His countrymen have not realized how modern he was in his engineering operations—as reclaimer of the Dismal Swamp; as advisor and engineer of the Potomac and James River Canal; as the first advocate of a combined highway and waterway from the Atlantic Coast to the Ohio River; as a bank director; as an investor; as one of the earliest Americans to recognize the possibilities of power transportation by water; and the first to suggest that air navigation might be very useful to the people of the United States." (p. v)

Douglas Southall Freeman, one of America's most scholarly biographers, spent the last years of his professional life researching and writing six volumes on the life and services of George Washington. Dr. Freeman, who had spent 29 years on Robert E. Lee and Lee's Lieutenants, calculated that the eight and a half years he spent on George Washington, some "15,693 hours" was "roughly equivalent" to his earlier "historical task" with Lee. (Douglas Southall Freeman, *George Washington, A Biography,* in six volumes. New York: Charles Scribner's Sons, 1954, Vol. Six, p. xxiii)

Dr. Freeman's assessment of George Washington can first be found in his joy in the work—even at an age when many historians would have not taken on such an immense task. Several times he wrote in his Diary: "Rejoiced to get back to my beloved work."

". . . [A]t the end of six years of work on Washington he described it as 'joyous labor.'" It was, he said "the most delightful intellectual experience" of his life. (p. xxviii)

Dr. Freeman's final assessment of Washington's character was stated in these words:

"What more could I ask for myself than to make the rediscovery that in Washington this nation and the western hemisphere have a man, 'greater than the world knew, living and dying,' a man dedicated, just and incorruptible, an example for long centuries of what character and diligence can achieve?" (Preface, p. xxxviii–xxxix)

It is important to understand what Verna Hall sought to convey in her compilation of *George Washington: The Character and Influence of One Man.* While many researchers might have avoided Washington's religious background, that is one of the major concerns of Miss Hall. As an American Christian she knew how important it is for this nation, and particularly for those dealing with the rising generations, to restore the standards of character which we associate Biblically with the office of President of the United States. In the *Papers* of Herbert Hoover, his first public statement is in regard to the Office of President and his response to it:

Inaugural Address, March 4, 1929
(Delivered in person at the Capitol)

My countrymen:

"This occasion is not alone the administration of the most sacred oath which can be assumed by an American citizen. It is a dedication and consecration under God to the highest office in service of our people. I assume this trust in the humility of knowledge that only through the guidance of Almighty Providence can I hope to discharge its ever-increasing burdens." (Herbert Hoover, *Public Papers of the Presidents of the United States,* 1929, p. 1)

George Washington was humbly conscious of the tremendous responsibilities of the new office of president of the United States. He knew that the whole world would measure America by the character of the man who occupied that office. And indeed most nations identified Washington as "America" long before they were acquainted with the nation.

One of the unique Biblical features of American government has always been our election of individuals to stand as our representatives for public office. Each geographical area chose individuals whom they knew—men of character. In fact, Rev. Thomas Hooker preached the sermon May 31, 1638 in Connecticut which led to its formation of government. It was known as Fundamental Orders, our first state constitution—the first in the nation. He reminded his listeners of God's Biblical admonition regarding "the privilege of election." Hooker took his sermon from—

"Text:

Deuteronomy 1:13. *Take you wise men, and understanding, and known among your tribes, and I will make them rulers over you. Captains over thousands, and captains over hundreds—over fifties—over tens, etc.*

"Doctrine:

I. That the choice of public magistrates belongs unto the people by God's own allowance.

II. The privilege of election which belongs unto the people, therefore, must not be exercised according to their humors, but according to the blessed will and law of God.

III. They who have power to appoint officers and magistrates, it is their power, also, to set the bounds of the power and place unto which they call them.

"REASONS:

I. Because the foundation of authority is laid, firstly, in the free consent of the people.

II. Because, by a free choice the hearts of the people will be more inclined to the love of the persons (chosen), and more ready to yield (obedience).

III. Because of that duty and engagement of the people.

"USES:

The lesson taught is threefold:—

I. There is matter of thankful acknowledgment in the (appreciation) of God's faithfulness towards us and the permission of these measures that God doth commend and vouchsafe.

II. Of reproof—to dash the conceits of all those that shall oppose it.

III. Of exhortation—to persuade us as God hath given us liberty to *take* it.

"And lastly. As God hath spared our lives and given us them in liberty, so seek the guidance of God, and choose *in* God and *for* God. . . .

"Eight months later, the fundamental laws embodying these principles for the first time in human history, were 'sentenced, ordered, and decreed.' It is impossible not to recognize the Master hand. The Pastor of the Hartford Church was Connecticut's great Legislator, also."
(Verna M. Hall, compiler. *Christian History of the Constitution of the United States of America,* Volume I: *Christian Self-Government*. San Francisco: Foundation for American Christian Education, 1960, pp. 250–251)

This year of our Lord, 1999, celebrates the Bicentennial of the death of George Washington on December 14. There were many, many men and women who had lived with Washington through both the American Revolution, the Constitutional Convention, and the first two terms of the presidency. Thus the recognition of his character and worth was at a high peak. The astonishing fact is that more than 323 funeral or memorial orations were given through February 22 of 1800. George Washington was so respected, loved, and admired, that the nation wished to recall his greatness and humility to mind.

Among the many memorial orations, one of the first requested to be delivered twelve days after Washington's death, was by Henry Lee—Light Horse Harry Lee, father of Robert E. Lee, Confederate General. Light Horse Harry was born in Virginia in 1756. He entered the College of New Jersey at Princeton at age 13 where he distinguished himself in his studies. At the age of nineteen he entered the service of his country as a captain of cavalry. Light Horse Harry became an able and gallant officer and soon won the confidence of General Washington which continued through life. Light Horse Harry was called to take a number of distinguished positions; then he was elected to the legislature of Virginia in 1786, chosen as a delegate to the Continental Congress, and served as a member of the Virginia convention to ratify the Federal Constitution. In 1792 he was elected Governor of Virginia.

Lee's "Eulogy on Washington" was delivered at Philadelphia on December 26, 1799, and was so greatly admired by Lee's contemporaries that it was included by them among the great classics of American oratory. Here are a few brief excerpts:

"In obedience to your will, I rise your humble organ, with the hope of executing a part of the system of public mourning which you have been pleased to adopt, commemorative of the death of the most illustrious and most beloved personage this country has ever produced. . . .

"The founder of our federate republic—our bulwark in war, our guide in peace, is no more! O that this were but questionable! Hope, the comforter of the wretched, would pour into our agonizing hearts its balmy dew. But alas! there is no hope for us; our Washington is removed forever! . . .

"How, my fellow-citizens, shall I single to your grateful hearts his pre-eminent worth? Where shall I begin in opening to your view a character throughout sublime? Shall I speak of his war-like achievements, all springing from obedience to his country's will—all directed to his country's good? . . .

"To the horrid din of battle, sweet peace succeeded; and our virtuous chief, mindful only of the common good, in a moment tempting personal aggrandizement, hushed the discontents of growing sedition; and surrendering his power into the hands from which he had received it, converted his sword into a ploughshare, teaching an admiring world that to be truly great, you must be truly good.

"Were I to stop here, the picture would be incomplete, and the task imposed unfinished. Great as was our Washington in war, and as much as did that greatness contribute to produce the American Republic, it is not in war alone his pre-eminence stands conspicuous. His various talents, combining all the capacities of a statesman, with those of a soldier, fitted him alike to guide the councils and armies of our nation. . . .

"The finger of an overruling Providence, pointing at Washington, was neither mistaken nor unobserved; when to realize the vast hopes to which our Revolution had given birth, a change of political system became indispensable. . . .

"This arduous task devolved on citizens selected by the people, from knowledge of their wisdom and confidence in their virtue. In this august assembly of sages and patriots, Washington was of course found; and as if acknowledged to be most wise where all were wise, with one voice he was declared their chief. . . .

"To have framed a constitution, was showing only, without realizing, the general happiness. This great work remained to be done; and America, steadfast in her preference, with one voice summoned her beloved Washington, unpracticed as he was in the duties of civil administration, to execute this last act in the completion of the national felicity. Obedient to her call, he assumed the high office with that self-distrust peculiar to his innate modesty, the constant attendant of pre-eminent virtue. . . . Commencing his administration, what heart is not charmed with the recollection of the pure and wise principles announced by himself, as the basis of his political life! . . ."

Light Horse Harry Lee ended his Eulogy on Washington delivered to the Congress with this famous phrase summarizing the life and testimony of George Washington:

"First in war, first in peace, and first in the hearts of his countrymen, he was second to none in the humble and endearing scenes of private life. Pious, just, humane, temperate, and sincere; uniform, dignified, and commanding, his example was as edifying to all around him as were the effects of that example lasting. . . ."
(Henry Lee, *Orations of American Orators*, Vol. I. New York: The Colonial Press, 1900)

George Washington, Architect of America's Future

When I first visited Mount Vernon with Verna Hall in the 1960s, she pointed out to me certain features of the main building which she indicated revealed that George Washington had architecturally elevated and beautified the house. This year upon a visit back to Mount Vernon, I discovered a recent publication entitled *George Washington, Architect*, by Allen Greenberg. Published in 1999, it appears at the Bicentennial of his passing, to inspire our nation to restore the structures and character of our American Republic—internally and externally.

Just as we say "Literature reflects the character of a nation," so does architecture express a philosophy of government. In America, how often, as you drive the many streets of our many cities and towns, do you see the multitude of individual homes, individually styled, but with the features of Christian self-government. Even the idea of a front porch on the humble but popular bungalow, indicates the friendliness and openness of our neighborhoods.

Just as the idea of a class society with "nobility," was repulsive to George Washington, so was the idea of non-productive land distasteful. That is why he includes in his design of his beautiful gardens his farms, as an important area of his active contribution.

We find Mount Vernon an example of American ideals which can inspire every American homeowner to express, however humbly. Washington makes a number of references Biblically to the satisfaction and peace which comes from abiding under one's own God-given "vine and fig tree." What a remarkable goal for men, women, and children in all nations, as a significant outcome of Christianity. Many who flee to America for religious and political freedom find their ultimate satisfaction of experiencing "life, liberty, and property" in the achievement of their own individual home and family.

The Capital City of America: Washington

George Washington also made the most important contributions to the planning, building and establishing of our nation's capital city—Washington, D.C.

The great English architect, "Sir Christopher Wren, writing in England a century before the American Revolution: 'Architecture has its political Use; public building being the Ornament of a Country; it establishes a Nation, draws People and Commerce; makes the People love their native Country, which Passion is the Original of all great actions in a Commonwealth.'" (Allan Greenberg.

George Washington, Architect, Andreas Papadakis Publisher, 1999, p. 95)

". . . Washington believed that part of the architect's responsibility was to incorporate political symbolism into the design of public buildings. New architecture and city plans, he proposed, should respond to the needs of democratic forms of government so that citizens could feel that it was they who constituted the government and that elected officials and civil servants were there to serve them. For Washington, the planning and design of a new capital city was of paramount importance, for it would set an example for the states and cities to follow. While he clearly believed that Europe had little it could teach the new nation about such matters, he was well aware that democracy and republicanism were classical ideals and knew that he was working within a larger tradition of classical architecture and city planning." (p. 99)

In all the areas of life in which it was important for George Washington to make a contribution of character and influence, God prepared him through his obedience to the Biblical principles governing home, church and nation.

Let us take upon ourselves the responsibility as contributors to the architecture of our children's characters, the future generations of this nation, all that God has set forth for us in His Word:

Hear, O Israel: The Lord our God is one Lord:
And thou shalt love the Lord thy God with all thine heart, and with all thy soul, and with all thy might.
And these words, which I command thee this day, shall be in thine heart:
And thou shalt teach them diligently unto thy children, and shalt talk of them when thou sittest in thine house, and when thou walkest by the way, and when thou liest down, and when thou riseth up. (Deuteronomy 6:4–6)

An Affectionate Husband, Father, Grandfather

Of all the contributions George Washington made to this nation, that which means the most to those of us who deal with families and young people, are George Washington's tender relationships. We know of course of his devotion to his wife, Martha Custis. While Martha did not bear him children she did bring into their marriage her own two children, Jacky and Patsy. Washington was tender and fatherly to them both though they did not survive the war. Jacky, however, had married young and his four children became the grandchildren that were cherished and lived at Mount Vernon.

"When Eleanor Parke Custis Lewis died in 1852, the *Philadelphia Inquirer* reported her passing under the headline, 'Death of a distinguished lady.'. . . Her place in history was assured by her unique relationship with George Washington, her stepgrandfather, under whose roof she was raised. Nelly went to live at Mount Vernon just before General Washington returned home from the war, and the family enjoyed a peaceful interlude there before he once again answered the call of his country. As a member of the president's household, Nelly was a firsthand observer of Washington's often tumultuous eight years as the country's first chief executive. These years were Nelly's own golden years. She then returned with the Washingtons to Mount Vernon, where the former president contentedly lived out his retirement years.

"Through Nelly's eyes one sees her 'Grand-papa' in a human light as a caring father and attentive guardian rather than as an icon inscribed with the words 'Father of His Country.' A concerned father emerges who worries about his foster daughter's education and her courtships, and attempts to launch her happiness after her marriage. Nelly claimed she was never in awe of George Washington as others were. She made him laugh, she made him proud, and she showed him enormous devotion and respect throughout her life." (David L. Ribblett. *Nelly Custis: Child of Mount Vernon.* Mount Vernon, Virginia: The Mount Vernon Ladies' Association, Prologue, 1993, p. iv)

When the young Marquis de Lafayette came to America at the age of 19 to help fight for Independence, he and General Washington instantly became father and son. For both men this was a deep and tender relationship. Lafayette named his own son George Washington Lafayette. Upon his return to France and before his imprisonment in Austria, he and his wife entrusted their son to President Washington. Lafayette had never known his own father who died on the battlefield before he was born. And George Washington was blessed with the young aristocrat's devotion to the American Revolution. Not only did Lafayette shed his blood at the Battle of Brandywine, but he helped bring the French fleet to Virginia to defeat the British Navy.

An Evangelical Father of Our Country

Those who do not associate George Washington with an evangelical outreach would find this statement from *The Journals of the Rev. Henry Melchior Muhlenberg*, founder of Lutheranism in Trapp, Pennsylvania, May 7, 1778, most interesting:

"I heard a fine example today, namely, that His Excellency General Washington rode around among his army yesterday and admonished each and every one to fear God, to put away the wickedness that has set in and become so general, and to practice the Christian virtues. From all appearances this gentleman does not belong to the so-called world of society, but he respects God's Word, believes in the atonement though Christ, and bears himself in humility and gentleness. Therefore the Lord God, has also singularly, yea, marvelously, preserved him from harm in the midst of countless perils, ambuscades, fatigues, etc., and has hitherto graciously held him in his hand as a chosen vessel." (Rev. Henry Melchior Muhlenberg, "Oration at Valley Forge" Verna M. Hall, *The Christian History of the American Revolution: Consider and Ponder*. San Francisco: Foundation for American Christian Education, 1975, p. 68c)

Miss Verna Hall researched the Christian life and conviction of George Washington as the Lord led her to find many sources which had been neglected or ignored. The writings of George Washington were always a constant reminder of how deeply God had prepared him to make Biblical principles his guide and to love the Lord with all his heart. This prayer, found in his writings, indicates how closely George Washington associated the success of the American nation with the spirit and practice of the Christian religion.

"I now make it my earnest prayer, that God would have you, and the State over which you preside, in his holy protection, that he would incline the hearts of the Citizens to cultivate a spirit of subordination and obedience to Government, to entertain a brotherly affection and love for one another, for their fellow Citizens of the United States at large, and particularly for their brethren who have served in the Field, and finally, that he would most graciously be pleased to dispose us all, to do Justice, to love mercy, and to demean ourselves with that Charity, humility, and pacific temper of mind which were the Characteristicks of the Divine Author of our blessed Religion, and without an humble imitation of whose example in these things, we can never hope to be a happy Nation." (George Washington, "Circular Letter to the States," 1783; full text on pp. 208–10)

Rosalie J. Slater
President and Co-Founder.
Foundation for American Christian Education

San Francisco, California
September 17, 1999

REMEMBER

EDITOR'S PREFACE

Dorothy Dimmick

This present volume of the *Christian History of the American Revolution*, titled *George Washington: The Character and Influence of One Man*, should reveal to all mankind the Christian principles of that beloved individual, George Washington, the Father of our Country.

His deep faith in the Providence of God, as recorded in this book, should serve as a reminder to those who profess Christianity that the Bible must be lived according to Scripture: *"Train up a child in the way that he should go and when he is old, he will not depart from it."* (Proverbs 22:6)

Early in life George Washington exhibited a firm foundation in the Biblical teachings of his parents and of the Church. Seldom do we see this manifestation of Christianity in his life in printed material about him.

The era in which he lived was one in which the vital foundations of America were still strong and active in the hearts of the American people. There was still a remembrance of the faith and integrity of their ancestors in a strong dependence based upon religious teachings; a firm reliance on the God-given lawful rights of Liberty their forefathers had exhibited in the founding of our Country. As Miss Hall stated, at that time the populace was a "Bible-believing people."

Miss Verna Hall, Christian Scholar and Historian, envisioned a plan for bringing to light the truth about the history of the American Revolution. She and Miss Rosalie Slater established the Foundation for American Christian Education in San Francisco as a vehicle for restoring to Americans, the Christian foundation of their country.

For about thirty years Miss Hall collected documentation about the life and work of George Washington. Miss Hall died in 1987. The voluminous material collected by Miss Hall had been neatly stored at the Foundation for American Christian Education, which served as the home of Miss Hall and Miss Rosalie Slater, the American Christian Educator. It is the desire of Miss Slater that this volume be published in honor of the memory of Miss Hall, Compiler of *The Character and Influence of One Man.* Miss Katherine Dang initially determined most of the content of the present text from the original notes and galley sheets which had been compiled by Miss Hall. That this information should be placed in our hands is one of the great blessings of "the Author of great good."

The book begins with THE CHARACTER OF WASHINGTON. The Hon. Robert C. Winthrop wrote: ". . . what are all the noble words which Washington wrote or uttered, what are all the incidents of his birth and death, what are all the details of his marvelous career from the commencement to its close, in comparison with his own exalted character as a Man?"

In the chapter The Character and Influence of One Man, we read an observation by Rev. C. W. Upham (1851): ". . . The Revolution of the North American British Colonies, which resulted in the establishment of independent, republican, and constitutional empire, is one of the greatest and [most] momentous events in the history of the world. . . . The great and glorious event was identified most distinctly with the character and influence of one man."

The Character of Washington by his Cotemporaries gives us beautiful renditions of his character by those who knew him best, David Ramsay, John Marshall, Rev. Aaron Bancroft. In 1826, John Marshall wrote: "Without making ostentatious professions of religion, he was a sincere believer in the Christian faith, and a truly devout man."

The Christian message of this volume is contained in George Washington, His Providential Preparation. This section contains excerpts from the *The Life of George Washington* written by Washington Irving. "Just as the twig is bent, the tree's inclined," (Alexander Pope). We read of the very early influence in Washington's life of his venerated mother, Mary Ball Washington. It was her habit to read the Bible and other classical works to her children when they were little. Miss Hall and Miss Slater were delighted to find *The Great Audit* by Sir Matthew Hale published in 1679, which she read to her young children. This is reprinted for us.

Washington's frontier expeditions are written of in His Providential Preparation. In 1754 Washington discloses his *motives of action*: ". . . the motives that have led me here are pure and noble. I had no view of acquisition but that of honor, by serving faithfully my king and my country." Irving states: "Such were the noble impulses of Washington at the age of 22, and such continued to actuate him throughout life . . . (these) motives . . . in after-life carried him into the Revolution."

In 1755 Washington wrote to his brother Augustine of his wilderness experiences in the campaign against the French. At the time he was Adjutant-general of the Northern Division of Virginia province. Washington furnishes us with a brief summary of his "bitter experience." Mr. Irving states: "What a striking lesson is furnished by this brief summary! How little was he aware of the vast advantages he was acquiring in the school of bitter experience! 'In the hand of heaven he stood,' to be shaped and trained for its great purpose, and every trial and vicissitude of his early life, but fitted him to cope with one or other of the varied and multifarious duties of his future destiny."

Also is reprinted for us George Washington's *Rules of Civility* which were copied by him when about thirteen years of age. The 110th Rule reads, "*Labour to keep alive in your Breast that Little Spark of Celestial fire called Conscience.*" From his school Notebook, we view his drawings in his own hand of some of his surveying work, accurate and neat, and some of the mathematical problems he had worked out.

About the Letters from his busy pen found in Christian Conviction Statements, 1755–1789, we read: ". . . addresses, despatches, and letters to everyone, in every part of the country, was a continued exertion of reason, to save his country. When the memory of individual exertion shall be lost and history shall only speak, in general terms of the Revolutionary conflict, these letters and addresses of Washington will preserve the particular scenes of that day and bring them at once to the understanding of men." (Knapp, p. 13)

One of the military orders recorded for us deals with the Canadian Expedition of 1775. I find it interesting that General Washington is giving orders to Colonel Benedict Arnold, as well as giving him moral advice: "While we are contending for our own Liberty, we should be very cautious of violating the Rights of Conscience in others, ever considering that God alone is the Judge of the Hearts of Men, and to Him only in this case, they are answerable."

From his own Diary, we are privileged to view his own words, his own thoughts, his own decisions. We begin to understand how he internally responded to each individual, or how he handled each individual problem as it arose. His total dependence upon Providence is a lesson for us all. These letters should be read by every school child; they should be examples of the Christian character of George Washington, a man to emulate.

Washington died December 14, 1799. In our year of December 1999, the Bicentennial of his death, we read The Dedication of the Washington National Monument. On a Resolution adopted by the House of Representatives December 24, 1799 and passed by both Houses of Congress, a marble monument to Washington's memory was to be erected in the City of Washington. It was not until a call to the citizens held in the City Hall on September 26, 1833, that the Washington National Monument Society was formed, Chief Justice John Marshall being its first President. The story of the actual building of, and the final dedication of this Monument on February 21, 1885, took place over a period of eighty-five years. Here is chronicled the desire of the people to create a structure worthy of the character of one man, George Washington. This section begins with: "The Confession and Creed of Washington, which never can be forgotten by any Christian Patriot."

This present volume records for us his early life experiences. Harsh though they might have been, they were preparing him, and strengthening him, for his later experiences, guiding him through the War for Independence; using his practical influence when establishing the Constitution; and establishing laws of Liberty when, as President of a fledgling nation, the new and untried government, he became the Founder and Father of this glorious Republic. Throughout this book we witness his utter and complete dependence upon the Providence of God, from boyhood to manhood.

American Christians, let us remember to honor, respect, and learn from the life of one of God's chosen vessels—in whom there was no guile.

—Dorothy Dimmick, *Editor*

The Character of George Washington

"When I contemplate the interposition of Providence, as it was visibly manifest in guiding us through the Revolution, in preparing us for the reception of the General Government, and in conciliating the good-will of the people of America toward one another after its adoption, I feel myself oppressed and almost overwhelmed with a sence of Divine munificence."

—George Washington

(Quoted by Robert C. Winthrop in his Oration at the Dedication of the Washington National Monument, 1885)

The Battle Is the Lord's

Ephesians 6:10-18

Finally, my brethren, be strong in the Lord, and in the power of his might.

Put on the whole armour of God, that ye may be able to stand against the wiles of the devil.

For we wrestle not against flesh and blood, but against principalities, against powers, against the rulers of the darkness of this world, against spiritual wickedness in high places.

Wherefore take unto you the whole armour of God, that ye may be able to withstand in the evil day, and having done all, to stand.

Stand therefore, having your loins girt about with truth, and having on the breastplate of righteousness;

And your feet shod with the preparation of the gospel of peace;

Above all, taking the shield of faith, wherewith ye shall be able to quench all the fiery darts of the wicked.

And take the helmet of salvation, and the sword of the Spirit, which is the word of God:

Praying always with all prayer and supplication in the Spirit, and watching thereunto with all perseverance and supplication for all saints; . . .

The Character and Influence of One Man

The Life of General Washington, Edited by The Rev. C. W. Upham, 1851

The history of the world, in all its scenes, and at every period, impresses upon the thoughtful student of its records a solemn sense of the amount of good and ill that has flowed from the lives and actions of a few individual men. Much, indeed, has been owing to the force of circumstances, and there have been times, when the energy and wisdom of no single person could have withstood the general current of events. But, in a great proportion of cases, we can trace the issue of things to the conduct and character of particular prominent agents. The destinies of nations and of the race are often deposited in the hands of one man. . . .

God works through the one, not the many

We ought always to contemplate eminent men in this light, and hold them responsible to a great extent, for the influence of their conduct and character. No greater blessing can be bestowed upon a country, than a virtuous and wise ruler, no greater curse than a wicked and reckless one; and our estimate of distinguished individuals should be determined, not by the amount of their talents, or by the dazzling appearance of their actions, but by the moral influence of their lives, and with reference to the degree in which they succeeded or failed in accomplishing the good placed within their reach.

It is probable that it would be allowed, by all truly liberal and enlightened men, that the Revolution of the North American British colonies, which resulted in the establishment of an independent, republican, and constitutional empire, is one of the greatest and most momentous events in the history of the world. It is indeed, worthy of being regarded as a perfectly successful political and moral movement. The patriot and the philosophical statesman look back upon it with unmixed approval and unalloyed satisfaction. From the beginning to the end there seems to have been an overruling power guiding all things right, and bringing on the consummation steadily and surely. It is not often that human enterprises and efforts are crowned with results so completely auspicious. When we contemplate its incidents, and follow its vicissitudes to the issue towards which they all tended, we feel that never were the indications of the interposition of a favoring Providence more signal and unquestionable.

The Revolution, guided by an overruling, favoring Providence

The great and glorious event was identified most distinctly with the character and influence of one man. There were many wise, enlightened, patriotic, and powerful spirits, scattered over every part of the country, and laboring most efficiently and nobly in the cause; but whoever traces the course of things, from the commencement of the War of Independence, to the final establishment of the nation under the Federal Constitution, will not hesitate to say, that at no point could the American Revolution have dispensed with the services, or succeeded without the aid and influence, of GEORGE WASHINGTON.

★

Washington and His Generals, by Joel Tyler Headley, 1847

. . . . The American Revolution was an anomaly in the history of the world. For a feeble colony just struggling into existence,—without ships, without a regular army, and without munitions of war, to enter into open combat with the most powerful nation on the globe for the sake of a mere principle, was opening a new page to the eye of monarchs, which it is no wonder they trembled to read. Bounded on one side by a limitless forest filled with hostile savages, and on the other by the ocean, whose bosom was covered with the fleets of her foes, she nevertheless stood up in the simple majesty of justice, and offered battle to the strongest empire in the world. National weakness, internal feuds and foes, the presence and power of colonial magistrates and governors, were disregarded, or seen only to excite higher resolution; and Massachusetts stood up in the midst of the gathering storm and called aloud to Virginia, and Virginia answered her, sending her cheering voice through the gloom.

A war of principle

To bring harmony out of the discord that prevailed, produce strength from weakness, and create resources where they did not exist, was the work assigned to George Washington. How he succeeded amid the difficulties that beset his path, and for a period of seven years, filled as they were with disasters and sufferings, maintained his position, baffled his foes, and finally saved his country, will always remain a marvel to the historian of those times. Though we may now eulogize his character, we cannot estimate the fiery trial to which he was exposed. The immense burden that lay on his shoulders during those seven years of gloom and darkness, the obstacles that thickened as he advanced, the obloquy that would attend failure, and the misery that a single misstep might inflict on his country, and, more than all, the hopes of liberty intrusted to his care, combined to make him a prey to the most ceaseless anxiety, and render his life one of toil, mental activity, and fearful forebodings, sufficient to wreck the loftiest character. All the details—those petty annoyances, hopes deferred, promises broken, aid refused or plans baffled by professed friends—are left out of the account when we reckon up his qualities and estimate his virtues. Yet these are often the severest tests of a man, and those who have stood firm as a rock and pure as gold under great trials, have fallen or failed in these lesser ones.

Christian character

That was a gloomy hour for our country, when the British empire roused itself for our overthrow, and it required more than a prophet's vision to see light through the cloud that hung over our prospects. The Indian war had just closed, and the feeble colonies were beginning to emerge from the difficulties and hardships to which they had been exposed, when they were compelled to contemplate a new evil, to which all they had hitherto suffered and borne were but trifles. They had faced the dreary wilderness and lurking savage without fear, and cheerfully encountered every trial, and now, just as the night seemed past and the morning of prosperity dawning, a day so dark and appalling rose before them, that the firmest heart sunk for a moment in despondency. The little wealth they had hoarded, the new comforts they had at length succeeded in gathering around them, must be given up, and a war, the end of which no man could see, entered upon, or the liberty for which they had endured and suffered so long surrendered forever. Without arms or ammunition, without any of the means necessary to carry on hostilities, with nothing to rely upon but the justice of their cause and the protection of Heaven, they nevertheless boldly entered on the doubtful contest.

The trumpet of war sounded through all our peaceful settlements, calling the artisan from his bench, the farmer from his plow, and the man of wealth from his repose, and the shock came. Our cities were ravaged, our towns laid waste, all our strongholds taken, and our citizens butchered, yet still the nation stood firm in her integrity and her purpose. At length defeat came, and with it despondency, and privations, and sufferings unparalleled, till at last the army became almost wholly disorganized, gradually melting away, and everything trembled on the verge of ruin; yet, serene amid the storm, stood Washington, sending his clear, calm voice over the tumult, inspiring hope and courage when both seemed madness. Never before did such destinies hang on a single man, for it was not the fate of a continent which rested on the issue of the struggle, but of human liberty the world over.

History of the world is the history of liberty

The Character of Washington by His Cotemporaries

DAVID RAMSAY

To the youth of the United States, in the hope that, from the example of their common Father, they will learn to do and suffer whatever their country's good may require at their hands, the following life of George Washington, is most affectionately inscribed, by the author.

The Life of George Washington, by David Ramsay, M.D., 1811

The person of George Washington was uncommonly tall. Mountain air, abundant exercise in the open country, the wholesome toils of the chase, and the delightful scenes of rural life, expanded his limbs to an unusual, but graceful and well proportioned size. His exterior suggested to every beholder the idea of strength, united with manly gracefulness. His form was noble, and his port majestic. No man could approach him but with respect. His frame was robust, his constitution vigorous, and he was capable of enduring great fatigue. His passions were naturally strong; with them was his first contest, and over them his first victory. Before he undertook to command others, he had thoroughly learned to command himself. The powers of his mind were more solid than brilliant. Judgment was his forte.

Self-government

To vivacity, wit, and the sallies of a lively imagination, he made no pretensions. His faculties resembled those of Aristotle, Bacon, Locke, and Newton; but were very unlike those of Voltaire. Possessed of a large proportion of common sense, directed by a sound practical judgment, he was better fitted for the exalted stations to which he was called, than many others, who, to a greater brilliancy of parts, frequently add the eccentricities of genius.

Truth and utility were his objects. He steadily pursued, and generally attained them. With this view he thought much, and closely examined every subject on which he was to decide, in all its relations. Neither passion, party spirit, pride, prejudice, ambition, nor interest, influenced his deliberations. In making up his mind on great occasions, many of which occurred in which the fate of the army or nation seemed involved, he sought for information from all quarters, revolved the subject by night and by day, and examined it in every point of view. Guided by these lights, and influenced by an honest and good heart, he was imperceptibly led to decisions which were wise and judicious. Perhaps no man ever lived who was so often called upon to form a judgment in cases of real difficulty, and who so often formed a right one. Engaged in the busy scenes of life, he knew human nature, and the most proper methods of accomplish-

Biblical view of man and government

ing proposed objects. Of a thousand propositions he knew to distinguish the best, and to select among a thousand the individual most fitted for his purpose.

Military Man

As a military man, he possessed personal courage, and a firmness which neither danger nor difficulties could shake. His perseverance overcame every obstacle; his moderation conciliated all opposition; his genius supplied every resource. He knew how to conquer by delay, and deserved true praise by despising unmerited censure. Inferior to his adversary in the numbers, the equipment, and discipline of his troops, no great advantage was ever obtained over him, and no opportunity to strike an important blow was ever neglected. In the most ardent moments of the contest, his prudent firmness proved the salvation of his country.

Prudent firmness

The whole range of history does not present a character on which we can dwell with such entire unmixed admiration. His qualities were so happily blended, and so nicely harmonized, that the result was a great and perfect whole.

Integrity

The integrity of Washington was incorruptible. His principles were free from the contamination of selfish and unworthy passions. His real and avowed motives were the same. His ends were always upright, and his means pure. He was a statesman without guile, and his professions, both to his fellow-citizens and to foreign nations, were always sincere. No circumstances ever induced him to use duplicity. He was an example of the distinction which exists between wisdom and cunning; and his manly, open conduct, was an illustration of the soundness of the maxim, "that honesty is the best policy."

Statesman without guile

Learning

The learning of Washington was of a particular kind. He overstepped the tedious forms of the schools, and by the force of a correct taste and sound judgment, seized on the great ends of learning, without the assistance of those means which have been contrived to prepare less active minds for public business. By a careful study of the English language; by reading good models of fine writing, and above all, by the aid of a vigorous mind, he made himself master of a pure, elegant, and classical style. His composition was all nerve; full of correct and manly ideas, which were expressed in precise and forcible language. His answers to the innumerable addresses which on all public occasions poured in upon him, were promptly made, handsomely expressed, and always contained something appropriate. His letters to Congress; his addresses to that body on the acceptance and resignation of his commission; his general orders as Commander in Chief; his speeches and messages as president; and above all, his two farewell addresses to the people of the United States, will remain lasting monuments of the goodness of his heart, of the wisdom of his head, and of the eloquence of his pen.

The powers of his mind were in some respects peculiar. He was a great, practical, self taught genius; with a head to devise, and a hand to execute, projects of the first magnitude and greatest utility.

A self-taught genius

Spirit of Piety

There are few men of any kind, and still fewer of those the world calls great, who have not some of their virtues eclipsed by corresponding vices. But this was not the case with Gen. Washington. He had religion without austerity, dignity without pride, modesty without diffidence, courage without rashness, politeness without affectation, affability without familiarity. His private character, as well as his public one, will bear the strictest scrutiny. He was punctual in all his engagements; upright and honest in his dealings; temperate in his enjoyments; liberal and hospitable to an eminent degree; a lover of order; systematical and methodical in all his arrangements. He was the friend of morality and religion; steadily attended on public worship; encouraged and strengthened the hands of the clergy. In all his public acts, he made the most respectful mention of Providence; and, in a word, carried the spirit of piety with him both in his private life and public administration.

Will bear the strictest scrutiny

Equanimity

Washington had to form soldiers of freemen, many of whom had extravagant ideas of their personal rights. He had often to mediate between a starving army, and a high-spirited yeomanry. So great were the necessities of the soldiers under his immediate command, that he was obliged to send out detachments to seize on the property of the farmers at the point of the bayonet. The language of the soldier was, "Give me clothing, give me food, or I cannot fight, I cannot live." The language of the farmer was, "Protect my property." In this choice of difficulties, Gen. Washington not only kept his army together, but conducted with so much prudence as to command the approbation both of the army and of the citizens. He was also dependent for much of his support on the concurrence of thirteen distinct, unconnected legislatures. Animosities prevailed between his southern and northern troops, and there were strong jealousies between the states from which they respectively came. To harmonize these clashing interests, to make uniform arrangements from such discordant sources and materials, required no common share of address. Yet so great was the effect of the modest unassuming manners of Gen. Washington, that he retained the affection of all his troops, and of all the states.

Modest

He also possessed equanimity in an eminent degree. One even tenour marked the greatness of his mind, in all the variety of scenes through which he passed. In the most trying situations he never despaired, nor was he ever depressed. He was the same when retreating through Jersey from before a victorious enemy with the remains of his broken army, as when marching in triumph into Yorktown, over its demolished fortifications. The honours and applause he received from his grateful countrymen, would have made almost any other man giddy; but on him they had no mischievous effect. He exacted none of those attentions; but when forced upon him, he received them as favours, with the politeness of a well bred man. He was great in deserving them, but much greater in not being elated with them.

Balanced disposition

Patriotism

The patriotism of Washington was of the most ardent kind, and without alloy. He was very different from those noisy patriots, who, with love of country in their mouths, and hell in their hearts, lay their schemes for aggrandizing themselves at every hazard; but he was one of those who love their country in sincerity, and who hold themselves bound to consecrate all their talents to its service. Numerous were the difficulties with which he had to contend. Great were the dangers he had to encounter. Various were the toils and services in which he had to share; but to all difficulties and dangers he rose superior. To all toils and services he cheerfully submitted for his country's good.

Political Principle

In principle, Washington was a federal republican, and a republican federalist. Liberty and law, the rights of man, and the control of government, were equally dear to him; and in his opinion, equally necessary to political happiness. He was devoted to that system of equal political rights on which the constitution of his country was founded; but thought that real liberty could only be maintained by preserving the authority of the laws, and giving tone and energy to government. He conceived there was an immense difference between a balanced republic and a tumultuous democracy, or a faction calling themselves the people; and a still greater between a patriot and a demagogue. He highly respected the deliberate sentiments of the people, but their sudden ebullitions made no impression on his well balanced mind. Trusting for support to the sober second thoughts of the nation, he had the magnanimity to pursue its real interests, in opposition to prevailing prejudices. He placed a proper value on popular favour, but could never stoop to gain it by a sacrifice of duty, by artifice, or flattery. In critical times he committed his well earned popularity to hazard, and steadily pursued the line of conduct which was dictated by a sense of duty, against an opposing popular torrent.

Liberty and law, rights of man, and the control of government equally dear

Dictated by a sense of duty

Foreign Policy

While war raged in Europe, the hostile nations would scarce endure a neutral. America was in great danger of being drawn by force or intrigue into the vortex. Strong parties in the United States rendered the danger more imminent; and it required a temperate, but inflexible government, to prevent the evil. In this trying state of things, Washington was not to be moved from the true interests of his country. His object was America, and her interest was to remain in peace. Faction at home, and intrigue and menace

His object was America, and her interest was to remain in peace

from abroad, endeavoured to shake him, but in vain; he remained firm and immoveable in the storm that surrounded him. Foreign intrigue was defeated, and foreign insolence was repressed by his address and vigour; while domestic faction, dashing against him, broke itself to pieces. He met the injustice both of Britain and France by negotiation, rather than by war, but maintained toward both, that firm attitude which was proper for the magistrate of a free state. He commanded their respect, and preserved the tranquility of his country. In his public character, he knew no nation but as friends in peace, as enemies in war. Toward one he forgot ancient animosities, when the recollection of them opposed the interest of his country. Toward another, he renounced a fantastic gratitude, when it was claimed only to involve his nation in war.

With Washington it was an invariable maxim of policy, to secure his country against the injustice of foreign nations, by being in a condition to command their respect, and punish their aggressions. The defence of our commerce, the fortification of the ports, and the organization of a military force, were objects to which he paid particular attention. To the gradual formation of an American army, he was friendly; and also to military institutions, which are calculated to qualify the youth of the country for its defence. War he deprecated as a great evil, inferior only to the loss of honour and character; but thought it was most easily avoided by being ready for it, while, by the practice of universal justice, none could have any real ground of complaint. In foreign transactions, his usual policy was to cultivate peace with all the world; to observe treaties with pure and absolute faith; to check every deviation from the line of impartiality; to explain what was misapprehended, and to correct what was injurious; and then to insist upon justice being done to the nation over which he presided. In controversies with foreign nations, it was his favourite maxim so to conduct toward them, "as to put them in the wrong."

Maxim of foreign policy

War, a great evil avoided by being ready for it

Indian Tribes

In his transactions with the Indian tribes, Washington was guided by justice, humanity, and benevolence. His authority and influence were exerted to restrain the licentious white contiguous settlers, from injuring their red neighbours. To supply their wants, and prevent impositions, he strongly urged the erection of trading houses in their settlements, from which they were furnished by government with goods at first cost. The unprincipled were restrained from preying on their ignorance, by excluding all but licensed persons, with good characters, from trading with them. All this was done to pave the way for their civilization.

Justice, harmony, and benevolence

Firmness

When Washington commenced his civil administration, the United States were without any efficient government. After they had adopted one of their choice, and placed him at its head, he determined that it should be respected. By his firmness order soon took place. There was one exception. The western counties of Pennsylvania rose in arms to resist the law for raising a revenue, by an excise on domestic distilled ardent spirits. On this occasion, the fixed resolution of Washington was, that whatever expense it might cost, whatever inconvenience it might occasion, the people must be taught obedience, and the authority of the laws re-established. To secure this object, peculiarly important in the infancy of the new government, he ordered out, and put himself at the head, of an ample force, calculated to render resistance desperate, and thereby to save the lives of his fellowcitizens.

In consequence of such decided measures, the insurgents dispersed, and peace and order were restored without bloodshed. The necessity of subordination was impressed on the citizens, and the firmness of Washington's personal character was communicated to the government.

Having accomplished every object for which he re-entered public life, he gave for the second time, the rare example of voluntarily descending from the first station in the universe; the head of a free people, placed there by their unanimous suffrage. To the pride of reigning his soul was superior. To its labours he submitted only for his country.

Rulers of the world! Learn from Washington wherein true glory consists. Restrain your ambition. Consider your power as an obligation to do good. Let the world have peace, and prepare for yourselves, the enjoyment of that ecstatic pleasure which will result from devoting all your energies to the advancement of human happiness. [*All italics added.*]

Citizens of the United States! While with grateful hearts you recollect the virtues of your Washington, carry your thoughts one step farther. On a review of

Independence National Historical Park, Philadelphia, Pennsylvania

MARTHA WASHINGTON
by Charles Willson Peale (1795)

Henry E. Huntington Library & Art Gallery, San Marino, California.

GEORGE WASHINGTON
by Gilbert Stuart (1797)

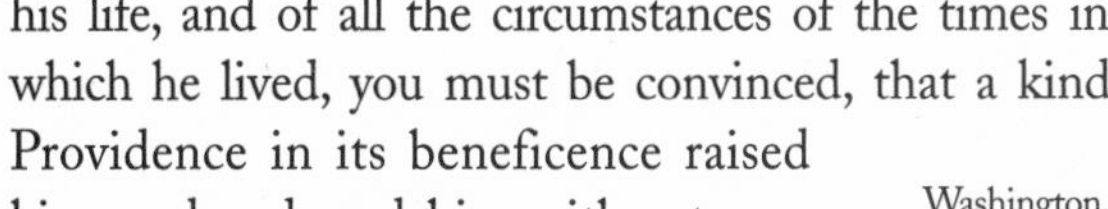

his life, and of all the circumstances of the times in which he lived, you must be convinced, that a kind Providence in its beneficence raised him, and endowed him with extraordinary virtues, to be to you an instrument of great good. None but such a man could have carried you successfully through the revolutionary times which tried men's souls, and ended in the establishment of your independence. None but such a man could have braced up your government after it had become so contemptible, from the imbecility of the federal system. None but such a man could have saved your country from being plunged into war, either with the greatest naval power in Europe, or with that which is most formidable by land, in consequence of your animosity against the one, and your partiality in favor of the other.

Washington, an instrument of Providence

Youths of the United States! Learn from Washington what may be done by an industrious improvement of your talents, and the cultivation of your moral powers. Without any extraordinary advantages from birth, fortune, patronage, or even of education, he, by virtue and industry, attained the highest seat in the temple of fame. You cannot all be commanders of armies, or chief magistrates; but you may all resemble him in the virtues of private and domestic life, in which he excelled, and in which he most delighted. Equally industrious with his plough as his sword, he esteemed idleness and inutility as the greatest disgrace of man, whose powers attain perfection only by constant and vigorous action. Washington, in private life, was as amiable as virtuous; and as great as he appeared sublime, on the public theatre of the world. He lived in the discharge of all the civil, social, and domestic offices of life. He was temperate in his desires, and faithful to his duties. For more than forty years of happy wedded love, his high example strengthened the tone of public manners. He had more real enjoyment in the bosom of his family, than in the pride of military command, or in the pomp of sovereign power.

Excelled in private and domestic virtues

On the whole, his life affords the brightest model for imitation, not only to warriors and statesmen, but to private citizens; for his character was a constellation of all the talents and virtues which dignify or adorn human nature.

> "He was a man, take him for all in all,
> We ne'er shall look upon his like again."
>
> *Shakespeare.*

The Life of George Washington, by John Marshall, 1826, 1832

JOHN MARSHALL

A desire to know intimately those illustrious personages, who have performed a conspicuous part on the great theatre of the world, is, perhaps, implanted in every human bosom. We delight to follow them through the various critical and perilous situations in which they have been placed, to view them in the extremes of adverse and prosperous fortune, to trace their progress through all the difficulties they have surmounted, and to contemplate their whole conduct, at a time when, the power and the pomp of office having disappeared, it may be presented to us in the simple garb of truth.

If among those exalted characters which are produced in every age, none can have a fairer claim to the attention and recollection of mankind than those under whose auspices great empires have been founded, or political institutions deserving to be permanent, established; a faithful representation of the various important events connected with the life of the favourite son of America, cannot be unworthy of the general regard. Among his own countrymen it will unquestionably excite the deepest interest.

As if the chosen instrument of Heaven, selected for the purpose of effecting the great designs of Providence respecting this our western hemisphere, it was the peculiar lot of this distinguished man, at every epoch when the destinies of his country seemed dependent on the measures adopted, to be called by the united voice of his fellow citizens to those high stations on which the success of those measures principally depended. It was his peculiar lot to be equally useful in obtaining the independence, and consolidating the civil institutions, of his country. We perceive him at the head of her armies, during a most arduous and perilous war on the events of which her national existence was staked, supporting with invincible fortitude the unequal conflict. That war being happily terminated, and the political revolutions of America requiring that he should once more relinquish his beloved retirement, we find him guiding her councils with the same firmness, wisdom, and virtue, which had, long and successfully, been displayed in the field. . . .

The work of Washington

It was too his peculiar fortune to afford the brightest examples of moderation and patriotism, by voluntarily divesting himself of the highest military and civil honours when the public interests no longer demanded that he should retain them. We find him retiring from the head of a victorious and discontented army which adored him, so soon as the object for which arms had been taken up was accomplished; and withdrawing from the highest office an American citizen can hold, as soon as his influence, his character, and his talents ceased to be necessary to the maintenance of that government which had been established under his auspices. . . .

The long and distressing contest between Great Britain and these states did not abound in those great battles which are so frequent in the wars of Europe. Those who expect a continued succession of victories and defeats; who can only feel engaged in the movements of vast armies, and who believe that a Hero must be perpetually in action, will be disappointed in almost every page of the following history. Seldom was the American chief in a condition to indulge his native courage in those brilliant achievements to which he was stimulated by his own feelings, and a detail of which interests, enraptures, and astonishes the reader. Had he not often checked his natural disposition, had he not tempered his ardour with caution, the war he conducted would probably have been of short duration, and the United States would still have been colonies. At the head of troops most of whom were perpetually raw because they were perpetually changing; who were neither well fed, paid, clothed, nor armed; and who were generally inferior, even in numbers, to the enemy; he derives no small title to glory from the consideration, that he never despaired of the public safety; that he was able at all times to preserve the appearance of an army, and that, in the most desperate situation of American affairs, he did not, for an instant, cease to be formidable. To estimate rightly his worth we must contemplate his difficulties. We must examine the means placed in his hands, and the use he made of those means. To preserve an army when conquest was impossible, to avoid defeat and ruin when victory was unattainable, to keep his forces embodied and suppress the discontents of his soldiers, exasperated by a long course of the most cruel privations, to seize with unerring discrimination the critical moment when vigorous offensive operations might be advantageously carried on, are actions not less valuable in themselves, nor do they require less capacity in the chief who performs them, than a continued succession of battles. But they spread less splendour over the page which recounts them, and excite weaker emotions in the bosom of the reader. . . . (Vol. I)

. . . . General Washington was rather above the common size, his frame was robust, and his constitution vigorous—capable of enduring great fatigue, and requiring a considerable degree of exercise for the preservation of his health. His exterior created in the beholder the idea of strength, united with manly gracefulness.

His manners were rather reserved than free, though they partook nothing of that dryness, and sternness, which accompany reserve when carried to an extreme; and on all proper occasions, he could relax sufficiently to show how highly he was gratified by the charms of conversation, and the pleasures of society. His person and whole deportment exhibited an unaffected and indescribable dignity, unmingled with haughtiness, of which all who approached him were sensible; and the attachment of those who possessed his friendship, and enjoyed his intimacy, was ardent, but always respectful.

His temper was humane, benevolent, and conciliatory; but there was a quickness in his sensibility to any thing apparently offensive, which experience had taught him to watch, and to correct.

In the management of his private affairs he exhibited an exact yet liberal economy. His funds were not prodigally wasted on capricious and ill examined schemes, nor refused to beneficial though costly improvements. They remained therefore competent to that expensive establishment which his reputation, added to a hospitable temper, had in some measure imposed upon him; and to those donations which real distress has a right to claim from opulence.

He made no pretensions to that vivacity which fascinates, or to that wit which dazzles, and frequently imposes on the understanding. More solid than brilliant, judgment, rather than genius, constituted the most prominent feature of his character.

A believer

Without making ostentatious professions of religion, he was a sincere believer in the Christian faith, and a truly devout man.

As a military man, he was brave, enterprising, and cautious. That malignity which was sought to strip him of all the higher qualities of a General, has conceded to him personal courage, and a firmness of resolution which neither dangers nor difficulties could shake. But candour will allow him other great and valuable endowments. If his military course does not abound with splendid achievements, it exhibits a series of judicious measures adapted to circumstances, which probably saved his country.

Judicious measures

Placed, without having studied the theory, or been taught in the school of experience the practice of war, at the head of an undisciplined, ill organized multitude, which was impatient of the restraints, and unacquainted with the ordinary duties of a camp, without the aid of officers possessing those lights which the Commander-in-chief was yet to acquire, it would have been a miracle indeed had his conduct been absolutely faultless. But, possessing an energetic and distinguishing mind, on which the lessons of experience were never lost, his errors, if he committed any, were quickly repaired; and those measures which the state of things rendered most adviseable, were seldom, if ever, neglected. Inferior to his adversary in the numbers, in the equipment, and in the discipline of his troops, it is evidence of real merit that no great and decisive advantages were ever obtained over him, and that the opportunity to strike an important blow never passed away unused. He has been termed the American Fabius; but those who compare his actions with his means, will perceive at least as much of Marcellus as of Fabius, in his character. He could not have been more enterprising, without endangering the cause he defended, nor have put more to hazard, without incurring justly the imputation of rashness. Not relying upon those chances which sometimes give a favourable issue to attempts apparently desperate, his conduct was regulated by calculations made upon the capacities of his army, and the real situation of his country. . . . (Vol. V)

Enterprising without endangering the cause

★

REV. AARON BANCROFT

The Life of George Washington, Commander of the American Army, Vol. II, Conclusion, by Aaron Bancroft, D.D., 1807, 1826

. . . . General Washington was exactly six feet in height, he appeared taller, as his shoulders rose a little higher than the true proportion. His eyes were of a gray, and his hair of a brown colour. His limbs were well formed, and indicated strength. His complexion was light, and his countenance serene and thoughtful.

His manners were graceful, manly, and dignified. His general appearance never failed to engage the respect and esteem of all who approached him.

Possessing strong natural passions, and having the nicest feelings of honour, he was in early life prone keenly to resent practices which carried the intention of abuse or insult; but the reflections of maturer age gave him the most perfect government of himself. He possessed a faculty above all other men to hide the weaknesses inseparable from human nature; and he bore with meekness and equanimity his distinguished honours.

Reserved, but not haughty, in his disposition, he was accessible to all in concerns of business, but he opened himself only to his confidential friends; and no art or address could draw from him an opinion, which he thought prudent to conceal.

He was not so much distinguished for brilliancy of genius as for solidity of judgment, and consummate prudence of conduct. He was not so eminent for any one quality of greatness and worth, as for the union of those great, amiable, and good qualities, which are very rarely combined in the same character.

Solidity of judgment, prudence of conduct

His maxims were formed upon the result of mature reflection, or extensive experience; they were the invariable rules of his practice; and on all important instances, he seemed to have an intuitive view of what the occasion rendered fit and proper. He pursued his purposes with a resolution, which, one solitary moment excepted, never failed him.

Alive to social pleasures, he delighted to enter into familiar conversation with his acquaintance, and was sometimes sportive in his letters to his friends; but he never lost sight of the dignity of his character, nor deviated from the decorous and appropriate behaviour becoming his station in society.

He commanded from all the most respectful attention, and no man in his company ever fell into light or lewd conversation. His style of living corresponded with his wealth; but his extensive establishment was managed with the strictest economy, and he ever reserved ample funds liberally to promote schemes of private benevolence, and works of publick utility. Punctual himself to every engagement, he exacted from others a strict fulfilment of contracts, but to the necessitous he was diffusive in his charities, and he greatly assisted the poorer classes of people in his vicinity, by furnishing them with means successfully to prosecute plans of industry.

In domestick and private life, he blended the authority of the master with the care and kindness of the guardian and friend. Solicitous for the welfare of his slaves, while at Mount Vernon, he every morning rode around his estates to examine their condition; for the sick, physicians were provided, and to the weak and infirm every necessary comfort was administered. The servitude of the negroes lay with weight upon his mind; he often made it the subject of conversation, and resolved several plans for their general emancipation; but could devise none, which promised success, in consistency with humanity to them, and safety to the state. . . .

Authority blended with care and kindness

He was as eminent for piety as for patriotism. His publick and private conduct evince, that he impressively felt a sense of the superintendence of God and of the dependence of man. In his addresses, while at the head of the army, and of the national government, he gratefully noticed the signal blessings of Providence, and fervently commended his country to divine benediction. In private, he was known to have been habitually devout.

Sensed the superintendence of God

In principle and practice he was a *Christian.* The support of an Episcopal church, in the vicinity of Mount Vernon, rested principally upon him, and here, when on his estate, he with constancy attended publick worship. In his address to the American people, at the close of the war, mentioning the favourable period of the world at which the independence of his country was established, and enumerating the causes which unitedly had ameliorated the condition of human society, he, above science, philosophy, commerce, and all other considerations, ranked "*the pure and benign light of Revelation.*" Supplicating Heaven that his fellow citizens might cultivate the disposition, and practise the virtues, which exalt a community, he presented the following petition to his God. "That he would most graciously be pleased to dispose us all to do justice, to love mercy, and to demean ourselves with that charity, humility and pacifick temper of mind, which were the characteristicks of the *Divine Author of our blessed religion*; without a humble imitation of whose example in these things, we can never hope to be a happy nation."

A Christian in principle and practice

Supplicated and petitioned his God

During the war, he not unfrequently rode ten or twelve miles from camp to attend publick worship; and he never omitted this attendance, when opportunity presented.

Faithful church attendance

In the establishment of his presidential household, he reserved to himself the Sabbath, free from the interruptions of private visits, or publick business; and throughout the eight years of his civil administration, he gave to the institutions of christianity the influence of his example. . . .

★

LETTERS OF WASHINGTON

The literature of the revolution is scattered throughout the history of all the transactions of that eventful period; but in no instance does it shine more conspicuously than in the productions of Washington; he was not a scholar by education or profession; his information was miscellaneous, and by no means extensive, when his early public service began. He knew something of history and mathematics, and something of the military tactics of the day. He, from his youth, saw things, at all times, through a clear medium, and expressed his thoughts with clearness, force, and honesty. His history of his journey to the Ohio, undertaken by the order of Dinwiddie, proves that his judgment was the master trait of his mind.

His first address to his army in July, 1775, is full of excellent military rules, but is wanting in that felicitous elegance which he afterwards acquired. He never suffered a sentiment to come from his pen negligently written; all was worked into ease and dignity. No commander that ever lived had so much need of this talent. Others have had to issue orders and to give an account of proceedings; Washington had not only to do these, but other things besides. He had, at times, to perform every duty incident to war, and more, from a pioneer to a field marshal; and from a sutler to a chancellor of the exchequer, at least with his pen; not only this, he had to use every argument to collect troops, and to keep them together, even for the shortest time; apathy was to be aroused; vaulting ambition to be struck down; individual bickerings to be silenced; sectional irritations to be soothed; the quarrelsome and high mettled to be controlled, that the service should not suffer; the faint and despairing to be encouraged; the living to be supported, and heaven, sometimes, knew how; and the dead were to be duly honoured, according to military usages, when the army had hardly powder enough to fire a volley at the enemy. In all this, the address of Washington was conspicuous, but the productions of his pen were more so. He wrote to all, he reasoned with all, and conquered all.

Congress was not at all times in a proper temper to render the most efficient aid; he was obliged to come upon them in all forms of entreaty; alarming them, at times, by his intimations of leaving the army, using every suggestion which could reach their pride, their patriotism, their honour, courage, or any other faculty, property, or sympathy, about them. There is not a form of reasoning that he was not obliged to assume; still, every form was pure English, good common sense, in his mother tongue. Burgoyne's letters, written in the field, are said to surpass those written in the closet; Nelson's account of the battle of the Nile is sublime; and Bonaparte's address to his soldiers under the pyramids, is full of epic grandeur. But these are momentary bursts of chivalrous feelings; while Washington's addresses, despatches, and letters, to every one, in every part of the country, was a continued exertion of reason, to save his country. When the memory of individual exertion shall be lost, and history shall only speak, in general terms, of the revolutionary conflict, these letters and addresses of Washington will preserve the particular scenes of that day, and bring them at once to the understanding of men.

Exertions of reason to save his country

THE CHARACTER OF WASHINGTON BY HIS COTEMPORARIES

The History and Topography of the United States, by Samuel L. Knapp, 1834

George Washington: His Providential Preparation

O God, thou hast taught me from my youth:
and hitherto have I declared thy wondrous works.

Psalm 71:17

Apply thine heart unto instruction,
and thine ears to the words of knowledge.

Proverb 23:12

Let your light so shine before men,
that they may see your good works,
and glorify your Father which is in heaven.

Matthew 5:16

WASHINGTON'S BOYHOOD HOME
by Benson J. Lossing

THE LIFE OF GEORGE WASHINGTON

WASHINGTON IRVING

ONE MAN'S PROVIDENTIAL PREPARATION

The Life of George Washington, Vol. I, by Washington Irving, 1856

GENEALOGY OF THE WASHINGTON FAMILY

The Washington family is of an ancient English stock, the genealogy of which has been traced up to the century immediately succeeding the Conquest. . . .

England, during the protectorate, became an uncomfortable residence to such as had signalized themselves as adherents to the house of Stuart. In 1655, an attempt at a general insurrection drew on them the vengeance of Cromwell. Many of their party who had no share in the conspiracy, yet sought refuge in other lands, where they might live free from molestation. This may have been the case with two brothers, John and Andrew Washington, great-grandsons of the grantee of Sulgrave, and uncles of Sir Henry the gallant defender of Worcester. John had for some time resided at South Cave, in the East Riding of Yorkshire;* but now emigrated with his brother to Virginia; which colony, from its allegiance to the exiled monarch and the Anglican Church, had become a favorite resort of the Cavaliers. The brothers arrived in Virginia in 1657, and purchased lands in Westmoreland County, on the northern neck, between the Potomac and Rappahannock rivers. John married a Miss Anne Pope, of the same county, and took up his residence on Bridges Creek, near where it falls into the Potomac. He became an extensive planter, and, in process of time, a magistrate and member of the House of Burgesses. Having a spark of the old military fire of the family, we find him, as Colonel Washington, leading the Virginia forces, in co-operation with those of Maryland, against a band of Seneca Indians, who were ravaging the settlements along the Potomac. In honor of his public and private virtues, the parish in which he resided was called after him, and still bears the name of Washington. He lies buried in a vault on Bridges Creek, which, for generations, was the family place of sepulture.

American immigrants, John and Andrew Washington

Civil and military leadership of John Washington

The estate continued in the family. His grandson Augustine, the father of our Washington, was born there in 1694. He was twice married; first (April 20th, 1715), to Jane, daughter of Caleb Butler, Esq., of Westmoreland County, by whom he had four

Grandson, Augustine

* South Cave is near the Humber. "In the vicinity is Cave Castle, an embattled edifice. It has a noble collection of paintings, including a portrait of General Washington, whose ancestors possessed a portion of the estate."—*Lewes, Topog. Dict.*, Vol. I, p. 530.

children, of whom only two, Lawrence and Augustine, survived the years of childhood; their mother died November 24th, 1728, and was buried in the family vault.

On the 6th of March, 1730, he married in second nuptials, Mary, the daughter of Colonel Ball, a young and beautiful girl, said to be the belle of the Northern Neck. By her he had four sons, George, Samuel, John Augustine, and Charles; and two daughters, Elizabeth, or Betty, as she was commonly called, and Mildred, who died in infancy.

Mary Ball

George, the eldest, the subject of this biography, was born on the 22d of Feb. (11th, O.S.), 1732, in the homestead on Bridges Creek. This house commanded a view over many miles of the Potomac, and the opposite shore of Maryland. It had probably been purchased with the property, and was one of the primitive farm-houses of Virginia. The roof was steep, and sloped down into low projecting caves. It had four rooms on the ground floor, and others in the attic, and an immense chimney at each end. Not a vestige of it remains. Two or three decayed fig-trees, with shrubs and vines, linger about the place, and here and there a flower grown wild serves "to mark where a garden has been.". . . A stone (placed there by George W. Custis, Esq.) marks the site of the house, and an inscription denotes its being the birthplace of Washington. . . .

February 22, 1732

The Home of Washington's Boyhood

Not long after the birth of George, his father removed to an estate in Stafford County, opposite Fredericksburg. The house was similar in style to the one at Bridges Creek, and stood on a rising ground overlooking a meadow which bordered the Rappahannock. This was the home of George's boyhood; the meadow was his playground, and the scene of his early athletic sports; but this home, like that in which he was born, has disappeared; the site is only to be traced by fragments of bricks, china, and earthenware.

His Early Education

In those days the means of instruction in Virginia were limited, and it was the custom among the wealthy planters to send their sons to England to complete their education. This was done by Augustine Washington with his eldest son Lawrence, then about fifteen years of age, and whom he no doubt considered the future head of the family. George was yet in early childhood: as his intellect dawned he received the rudiments of education in the best establishment for the purpose that the neighborhood afforded. It was what was called, in popular parlance, an "old field schoolhouse;" humble enough in its pretensions, and kept by one of his father's tenants named Hobby, who moreover was sexton of the parish. The instruction doled out by him must have been of the simplest kind, reading, writing, and ciphering, perhaps; but George had the benefit of mental and moral culture at home, from an excellent father. . . .

Lawrence Washington and His Campaign in the West Indies

When George was about seven or eight years old his brother Lawrence returned from England, a well-educated and accomplished youth. There was a difference of fourteen years in their ages, which may have been one cause of the strong attachment which took place between them. Lawrence looked down with a protecting eye upon the boy, whose dawning intelligence and perfect rectitude won his regard; while George looked up to his manly and cultivated brother as a model in mind and manners. . . .

1740

Lawrence Washington had something of the old military spirit of the family, and circumstances soon called it into action. Spanish depredations on British commerce had recently provoked reprisals. Admiral Vernon, commander-in-chief in the West Indies, had accordingly captured Porto Bello, on the Isthmus of Darien. The Spaniards were preparing to revenge the blow; the French were fitting out ships to aid them. Troops were embarked in England for another campaign in the West Indies; a regiment of four battalions was to be raised in the colonies and sent to join them in Jamaica. There was a sudden outbreak of military ardor in the province; the sound of drum and fife was heard in the villages with the parade of recruiting parties. Lawrence Washington, now twenty-two years of age, caught the infection. He obtained a captain's commission in the newly raised regiment, and embarked with it for the West Indies in 1740. He served in the joint expeditions of Admiral Vernon and General Wentworth, in the land forces commanded by

Military spirit of the family

the latter, and acquired the friendship and confidence of both of those officers. . . .

We have here the secret of that martial spirit so often cited of George in his boyish days. He had seen his brother fitted out for the wars. He had heard by letter and otherwise of the warlike scenes in which he was mingling. All these amusements took a military turn. He made soldiers of his schoolmates; they had their mimic parades, reviews, and sham fights. A boy named William Bustle was sometimes his competitor, but George was commander-in-chief of Hobby's school.

Boyhood martial spirit

Death of Washington's Father

Lawrence Washington returned home in the autumn of 1742, the campaigns in the West Indies being ended, and Admiral Vernon and General Wentworth being recalled to England. It was the intention of Lawrence to rejoin his regiment in that country, and seek promotion in the army, but circumstances completely altered his plans. He formed an attachment to Anne, the eldest daughter of the Honorable William Fairfax, of Fairfax County; his addresses were well received, and they became engaged. Their nuptials were delayed by the sudden and untimely death of his father, which took place on the 12th of April, 1743, after a short but severe attack of gout in the stomach, and when but forty-nine years of age. George had been absent from home on a visit during his father's illness, and just returned in time to receive a parting look of affection.

1743

Augustine Washington left large possessions, distributed by will among his children. To Lawrence, the estate on the banks of the Potomac, with other real property, and several shares in iron works. To Augustine, the second son by the first marriage, the old homestead and estate in Westmoreland. The children by the second marriage were severally well provided for, and George, when he became of age, was to have the house and lands on the Rappahannock.

In the month of July the marriage of Lawrence with Miss Fairfax took place. He now gave up all thoughts of foreign service, and settled himself on his estate on the banks of the Potomac, to which he gave the name of Mount Vernon, in honor of the admiral.

Lawrence's estate named Mt. Vernon

Augustine took up his abode at the homestead on Bridges Creek, and married Anne, daughter and coheiress of William Aylett, Esquire, of Westmoreland County. George, now eleven years of age, and the other children of the second marriage, had been left under the guardianship of their mother, to whom was intrusted the proceeds of all their property until they should severally come of age. She proved herself worthy of the trust. Endowed with plain, direct good sense, thorough conscientiousness, and prompt decision, she governed her family strictly, but kindly, exacting deference while she inspired affection. George, being her eldest son, was thought to be her favorite, yet she never gave him undue preference, and the implicit deference exacted from him in childhood continued to be habitually observed by him to the day of her death. He inherited from her a high temper and a spirit of command, but her early precepts and example taught him to restrain and govern that temper, and to square his conduct on the exact principles of equity and justice.

The Widowed Mother* and Her Children

Tradition gives an interesting picture of the widow, with her little flock gathered round her, as was her daily wont, reading to them lessons of religion and morality out of some standard work. Her favorite volume was Sir Matthew Hale's *Contemplations, Moral and Divine*. The admirable maxims therein contained, for outward action as well as self-government, sank deep into the mind of George, and, doubtless, had a great influence in forming his character. They certainly were exemplified in his conduct throughout life. This mother's manual, bearing his mother's name, Mary Washington, written with her own hand, was ever preserved by him with filial care, and may still be seen in the archives of Mount Vernon. A precious document! Let those who wish to know the moral foundation of his character consult its pages.

Foundations of character laid

School Exercises

Having no longer the benefit of a father's instructions at home, and the scope of tuition of Hobby, the sexton, being too limited for the growing wants of his pupil, George was now sent to reside with Augustine Washington, at Bridges Creek,

* See article on Mary Washington by Elizabeth F. Ellet on pp. 119, and Matthew Hale excerpt, p. 123.

and enjoy the benefit of a superior school in that neighborhood, kept by a Mr. Williams. His education, however, was plain and practical. He never attempted the learned languages, nor manifested any inclination for rhetoric or belles-lettres. His object, or the object of his friends, seems to have been confined to fitting him for ordinary business. His manuscript school books still exist, and are models of neatness and accuracy. One of them, it is true, a ciphering book, preserved in the library at Mount Vernon, has some school-boy attempts at caligraphy; nondescript birds, executed with a flourish of the pen, or profiles of faces, probably intended for those of his schoolmates; the rest are all grave and business like. Before he was thirteen years of age, he had copied into a volume forms for all kinds of mercantile and legal papers; bills of exchange, notes of hand, deeds, bonds, and the like. This early self-tuition gave him throughout life a lawyer's skill in drafting documents, and a merchant's exactness in keeping accounts; so that all the concerns of his various estates; his dealings with his domestic stewards and foreign agents; his accounts with government; and all his financial transactions are to this day to be seen posted up in books, in his own handwriting, monuments of his method and unwearied accuracy.*

Plain and practical education

He was a self-disciplinarian in physical as well as mental matters, and practised himself in all kinds of athletic exercises, such as running, leaping, wrestling, pitching quoits and tossing bars. His frame even in infancy had been large and powerful, and he now excelled most of his playmates in contests of agility and strength. As a proof of his muscular power, a place is still pointed out at Fredericksburg, near the lower ferry, where, when a boy, he flung a stone across the Rappahannock. In horsemanship too he already excelled and was ready to back, and able to manage the most fiery steed. Traditional anecdotes remain of his achievements in this respect.

Above all, his inherent probity, and the principles of justice on which he regulated all his conduct, even at this early period of life, were soon appreciated by his schoolmates; he was referred to as an umpire in their disputes, and his decisions were never reversed. As he had formerly been military chieftain, he was now legislator of the school; thus displaying in boyhood a type of the future man.

* See articles on George Washington's "Rules of Civility" and "School Subjects" on pp. 144 and 149, and sample facsimile pages from both in Appendix A.

Paternal Conduct of an Elder Brother

The attachment of Lawrence Washington to his brother George, seems to have acquired additional strength and tenderness on their father's death; he now took a truly paternal interest in his concerns, and had him as frequently as possible a guest at Mount Vernon. Lawrence had deservedly become a popular and leading personage in the country. He was a member of the House of Burgesses, and adjutant-general of the district, with the rank of major and a regular salary. A frequent sojourn with him brought George into familiar intercourse with the family of his father-in-law, the Hon. William Fairfax, who resided at a beautiful seat called Belvoir, a few miles below Mount Vernon, and on the same woody ridge bordering the Potomac.

The Fairfax Family

William Fairfax was a man of liberal education and intrinsic worth; he had seen much of the world, and his mind had been enriched and ripened by varied and adventurous experience. Of an ancient English family in Yorkshire, he had entered the army at the age of twenty-one; had served with honor both in the East and West Indies, and officiated as governor of New Providence, after having aided in rescuing it from pirates. For some years past he had resided in Virginia, to manage the immense landed estates of his cousin, Lord Fairfax, and lived at Belvoir in the style of an English country gentleman, surrounded by an intelligent and cultivated family of sons and daughters.

Washington's Code of Morals and Manners

An intimacy with a family like this, in which the frankness and simplicity of rural and colonial life were united with European refinement, could not but have a beneficial effect in moulding the character and manners of a somewhat homebred school-boy. It was probably his intercourse with them, and his ambition to acquit himself well in their society, that set him upon compiling a code of morals and manners, which still exists in a manuscript in his own handwriting, entitled "rules for behavior in company and conversation." It is extremely minute and circumstantial. Some of the rules for personal deportment extend to such trivial matters, and are so quaint and formal, as almost to provoke a smile; but in the main, a better manual of conduct could not be put into the hands of a youth. The whole code evinces that rigid propriety and self-control to which he subjected himself, and by which he brought all the impulses of a somewhat ardent temper under conscientious government.

An ardent temper under government

Soldiers' Tales

Other influences were brought to bear on George during his visit at Mount Vernon. His brother Lawrence still retained some of his military inclinations, fostered no doubt by his post of adjutant-general. William Fairfax, as we have shown, had been a soldier, and in many trying scenes. Some of Lawrence's comrades of the provincial regiment, who had served with him in the West Indies, were occasional visitors at Mount Vernon: or a ship of war, possibly one of Vernon's old fleet, would anchor in the Potomac, and its officers be welcome guests at the tables of Lawrence and his father-in-law. Thus military scenes on sea and shore would become the topics of conversation. The capture of Porto Bello; the bombardment of Carthagena; old stories of cruisings in the East and West Indies, and campaigns against the pirates.

Washington Prepares for the Navy

We can picture to ourselves George, a grave and earnest boy, with an expanding intellect, and a deep-seated passion for enterprise, listening to such conversations with a kindling spirit and a growing desire for military life. In this way most probably was produced that desire to enter the navy which he evinced when about fourteen years of age. The opportunity for gratifying it appeared at hand. Ships of war frequented the colonies, and at times, as we have hinted, were anchored in the Potomac. The inclination was encouraged by Lawrence Washington and Mr. Fairfax. Lawrence retained pleasant recollections of his cruisings in the fleet of Admiral Vernon, and considered the naval service a popular path to fame and fortune. George was at a suitable age to enter the navy. The great difficulty was to procure the assent of his mother. She was brought, however, to acquiesce; a midshipman's warrant was obtained, and it is even said that the luggage of the youth was actually on board of a man of war, anchored in the river just below Mount Vernon.

Fourteen years of age

A Mother's Objections

At the eleventh hour the mother's heart faltered. This was her eldest born. A son, whose strong and steadfast character promised to be a support to herself and a protection to her other children. The thought of his being completely severed from her, and exposed to the hardships and perils of a boister-

WASHINGTON'S INTERVIEW WITH HIS MOTHER

BY ALONZO CHAPPEL

ous profession, overcame even her resolute mind, and at her urgent remonstrances the nautical scheme was given up.

To school, therefore, George returned, and continued his studies for nearly two years longer, devoting himself especially to mathematics, and accomplishing himself in those branches calculated to fit him either for civil or military service.

Among these, one of the most important in the actual state of the country was land surveying. In this he schooled himself thoroughly, using the highest processes of the art; making surveys about the neighborhood, and keeping regular field books, some of which we have examined, in which the boundaries and measurements of the fields surveyed were carefully entered, and diagrams made, with a neatness and exactness as if the whole related to important land transactions instead of being mere school exercises. Thus, in his earliest days, there was perseverance and completeness in all his undertakings. Nothing was left half done, or done in a hurried and slovenly manner. The habit of mind thus cultivated continued throughout life; so that however complicated his tasks and overwhelming his cares, in the arduous and hazardous situations in which he was often placed, he found time to do every thing, and to do it well. He had acquired the magic of method, which of itself works wonders.

Self-taught surveyor

A School-Boy Passion

In one of these manuscript memorials of his practical studies and exercises, we have come upon some documents singularly in contrast with all that we have just cited, and with his apparently unromantic character. In a word, there are evidences in his own hand-writing, that, before he was fifteen years of age, he had conceived a passion for some unknown beauty, so serious as to disturb his otherwise well-regulated mind, and to make him really unhappy. Why this juvenile attachment was a source of unhappiness we have no positive means of ascertaining. Perhaps the object of it may have considered him a mere school-boy, and treated him as such; or his own shyness may have been in his way, and his "rules for behaviour and conversation" may as yet have sat awkwardly on him, and rendered him formal and ungainly when he most sought to please. Even in later years he was apt to be silent and embarrassed in female society. "He was a very bashful young man," said an old lady, whom he used to visit when they were both in their nonage. "I used often to wish that he would talk more."

Whatever may have been the reason, this early attachment seems to have been a source of poignant discomfort to him. It clung to him after he took a final leave of school in the autumn of 1747, and went to reside with his brother Lawrence at Mount Vernon. Here he continued his mathematical studies and his practice in surveying, disturbed at times by recurrences of his unlucky passion. Though by no means of a poetical temperament, the waste pages of his journal betray several attempts to pour forth his amorous sorrows in verse. They are mere commonplace rhymes, such as lovers at his age are apt to write, in which he bewails his "poor restless heart, wounded by Cupid's dart" and "bleeding for one who remains pitiless of his griefs and woes."

1747

The tenor of some of his verses induces us to believe that he never told his love; but, as we have already surmised, was prevented by his bashfulness.

> "Ah, woe is me, that I should
> love and conceal;
> Long have I wished and
> never dare reveal."

It is difficult to reconcile one's self to the idea of the cool and sedate Washington, the great champion of American liberty, a woe-worn lover in his youthful days, "sighing like furnace," and inditing plaintive verses about the groves of Mount Vernon. We are glad of an opportunity, however, of penetrating to his native feelings, and finding that under his studied decorum and reserve he had a heart of flesh, throbbing with the warm impulses of human nature.

A heart of flesh

Lord Fairfax

Being a favorite of Sir William Fairfax, he was now an occasional inmate of Belvoir. Among the persons at present residing there, was Thomas Lord Fairfax, cousin of William Fairfax, and of whose immense landed property the latter was the agent. As this nobleman was one of Washington's earliest friends, and in some degree the founder of his fortunes, his character and history are worthy of especial note.

Lord Fairfax was now nearly sixty years of age, upwards of six feet high, gaunt and raw-boned, nearsighted, with light gray eyes, sharp features, and an aquiline nose. However ungainly his present appearance, he had figured to advantage in London life in his younger days. He had received his education at the university of Oxford, where he acquitted himself with credit. He afterwards held a commission, and remained for some time in a regiment of horse called the Blues. . . .

He made a voyage to Virginia about the year 1739, to visit his vast estates there. These he inherited from his mother, Catharine, daughter of Thomas, Lord Culpepper, to whom they had been granted by Charles II. The original grant was for all the lands lying between the Rappahannock and Potomac rivers; meaning thereby, it is said, merely the territory on the northern neck, east of the Blue Ridge. His lordship, however, discovering that the Potomac headed in the Allegany Mountains, returned to England and claimed a correspondent definition of his grant. It was arranged by compromise; extending his domain into the Allegany Mountains, and comprising, among other lands, a great portion of the Shenandoah Valley.

Lord Fairfax had been delighted with his visit to Virginia. The amenity of the climate, the magnificence of the forest scenery, the abundance of game,—all pointed it out as a favored land. He was pleased, too, with the frank, cordial character of the Virginians, and their independent mode of life; and returned to it with the resolution of taking up his abode there for the remainder of his days. . . .

The Lowland Beauty

Another inmate of Belvoir at this time was George William Fairfax, about twenty-two years of age, the eldest son of the proprietor. He had been educated in England, and since his return had married a daughter of Colonel Carey, of Hampton, on James River. He had recently brought home his bride and her sister to his father's house.

The merits of Washington were known and appreciated by the Fairfax family. Though not quite sixteen years of age, he no longer seemed a boy, nor was he treated as such. Tall, athletic, and manly for his years, his early self-training, and the code of conduct he had devised, gave a gravity and decision to his conduct; his frankness and modesty inspired cordial regard, and the melancholy, of which he speaks, may have produced a softness in his manner calculated to win favor in ladies' eyes. According to his own account, the female society by which he was surrounded had a soothing effect on that melancholy. The charms of Miss Carey, the sister of the bride, seem even to have caused a slight fluttering in his bosom; which, however, was constantly rebuked by the remembrance of his former passion —so at least we judge from letters to his youthful confidants, rough drafts of which are still to be seen in his tell-tale journal.

Qualities of character at age sixteen

To one whom he addresses as his dear friend Robin, he writes: "My residence is at present at his lordship's, where I might, was my heart disengaged, pass my time very pleasantly, as there's a very agreeable young lady lives in the same house (Col. George Fairfax's wife's sister); but as that's only adding fuel to fire, it makes me the more uneasy, for by often and unavoidably being in company with her, revives my former passion for your Lowland Beauty; whereas was I to live more retired from young women, I might in some measure alleviate my sorrows, by burying that chaste and troublesome passion in the grave of oblivion," &c.

Similar avowals he makes to another of his young correspondents, whom he styles, "Dear friend John:" as also to a female confidant, styled "Dear Sally," to whom he acknowledges that the company of the "very agreeable young lady, sister-in-law of Col. George Fairfax," in a great measure cheers his sorrow and dejectedness. The object of this early passion is not positively known. Tradition states that the "lowland beauty" was a Miss Grimes, of Westmoreland, afterwards Mrs. Lee, and mother of General Henry Lee, who figured in revolutionary history as Light Horse Harry, and was a favorite with Washington, probably from the recollections of his early tenderness for the mother.

Whatever may have been the soothing effect of the female society by which he was surrounded at Belvoir, the youth found a more effectual remedy for his love melancholy in the company of Lord Fairfax. His lordship was a stanch fox-hunter, and kept horses and hounds in the English style. The hunting season had arrived. The neighborhood abounded with sport; but fox-hunting in Virginia required bold and skilful horsemanship. He found Washington as bold as himself in the saddle, and as eager to follow the hounds. He forthwith took him into peculiar favor; made him his hunting companion; and it was probably under the tuition of this hard-riding old nobleman that the youth imbibed that fondness for the chase for which he was afterwards remarked.

Proposition for a Surveying Expedition

Their fox-hunting intercourse was attended with more important results. His lordship's possessions beyond the Blue Ridge had never been regularly settled nor surveyed. Lawless intruders—squatters, as they were called—were planting themselves along the finest streams and in the richest valleys, and virtually taking possession of the country. It was the anxious desire of Lord Fairfax to have these lands examined, surveyed, and portioned out into lots, preparatory to ejecting these interlopers or bringing them to reasonable terms. In Washington, notwithstanding his youth, he beheld one fit for the task—having noticed the exercises in surveying which he kept up while at Mount Vernon, and the aptness and exactness with which every process was executed. He was well calculated, too, by his vigor and activity, his courage and hardihood, to cope with the wild country to be surveyed, and with its still wilder inhabitants. The proposition had only to be offered to Washington to be eagerly accepted. It was the very kind of occupation for which he had been diligently training himself. All the preparations required by one of his simple habits were soon made, and in a very few days he was ready for his first expedition into the wilderness.

Well-suited for his first wilderness expedition

Expedition beyond the Blue Ridge

> To exercise him in the wilderness;
> There he shall first lay down the rudiments
> Of his great warfare, ere I send him forth
> To Conquer!
> —Milton

It was in the month of March (1748), and just after he had completed his sixteenth year, that Washington set out on horseback on this surveying expedition, in company with George William Fairfax. Their route lay by Ashley's gap, a pass through the Blue Ridge, that beautiful line of mountains which, as yet, almost formed the western frontier of inhabited Virginia. Winter still lingered on the tops of the mountains, whence melting snows sent down torrents, which swelled the rivers, and occasionally rendered them almost impassable. Spring, however, was softening the lower parts of the landscape and smiling in the valleys.

March, 1748

They entered the great valley of Virginia, where it is about twenty-five miles wide; a lovely and temperate region, diversified by gentle swells and slopes, admirably adapted to cultivation. The Blue Ridge bounds it on one side, the North Mountain, a ridge of the Alleganies, on the other; while through it flows that bright and abounding river, which, on account of its surpassing beauty, was named by the Indians the Shenandoah—that is to say, "the daughter of the stars."

The first station of the travellers was at a kind of lodge in the wilderness, where the steward or land-bailiff of Lord Halifax resided, with such negroes as were required for farming purposes, and which Washington terms "his lordship's quarters." It was situated not far from the Shenandoah, and about twelve miles from the site of the present town of Winchester.

In a diary kept with his usual minuteness, Washington speaks with delight of the beauty of the trees and the richness of the land in the neighborhood, and of his riding through a noble grove of sugar-maples on the banks of the Shenandoah; and at the present day, the magnificence of the forests which still exist in this favored region justifies his eulogium.

Diary kept

He looked around, however, with an eye to the profitable rather than the poetical. The gleam of poetry and romance, inspired by his "lowland beauty," occurs no more. The real business of life has commenced with him. His diary affords no food for fancy. Every thing is practical. The qualities of the soil, the relative value of sites and localities, are faithfully recorded. In these early habits of observation and his exercises in surveying had already made him a proficient.

His surveys commenced in the lower part of the valley, some distance above the junction of the Shenandoah with the Potomac, and extended for many miles along the former river. Here and there partial "clearings" had been made by squatters and hardy pioneers, and their rude husbandry had produced abundant crops of grain, hemp, and tobacco; civilization, however, had hardly yet entered the valley, if we may judge from the note of a night's lodging at the house of one of the settlers—Captain Hite, near the site of the present town of Winchester. Here, after supper, most of the company stretched themselves in backwood style, before the fire; but Washington was shown into a bedroom. Fatigued with a hard day's work at surveying, he soon undressed; but instead of being nestled between sheets in a comfortable bed, as at the maternal home, or at Mount Vernon, he found himself on a couch of matted straw, under a threadbare blanket, swarm-

BY BENSON J. LOSSING

WASHINGTON AND FAIRFAX AT A WAR-DANCE

ing with unwelcome bedfellows. After tossing about for a few moments, he was glad to put on his clothes again, and rejoin his companions before the fire.

Such was his first experience of life in the wilderness; he soon, however, accustomed himself to "rough it," and adapt himself to fare of all kinds, though he generally preferred a bivouac before a fire, in the open air, to the accommodations of a woodman's cabin. Proceeding down the valley to the banks of the Potomac, they found that river so much swollen by the rain which had fallen among the Alleganies, as to be unfordable. To while away the time until it should subside, they made an excursion to examine certain warm springs in a valley among the mountains, since called the Berkeley Springs. There they camped out at night, under the stars; the diary makes no complaint of their accommodations; and their camping-ground is now known as Bath, one of the favorite watering-places of Virginia. One of the warm springs was subsequently appropriated by Lord Fairfax to his own use, and still bears his name.

Accustomed himself to wilderness living

After watching in vain for the river to subside, they procured a canoe, on which they crossed to the Maryland side, swimming their horses. A weary day's ride of forty miles up the left side of the river, in a continual rain, and over what Washington pronounced the worst road ever trod by man or beast, brought them to the house of a Colonel Cresap, opposite the south branch of the Potomac where they put up for the night.

Here they were detained three or four days by inclement weather. On the second day they were surprised by the appearance of a war party of thirty Indians, bearing a scalp as a trophy. A little liquor procured the spectacle of a war-dance. A large space was cleared and a fire made in the centre, round which the warriors took their seats. The principal orator made a speech, reciting their recent exploits, and rousing them to triumph. One of the warriors started up as if from sleep, and began a series of movements half-grotesque, half-tragical; the rest followed. For music, one savage drummed on a deerskin, stretched over a pot half filled with water; another rattled a gourd, containing a few shot, and decorated with a horse's tail. Their strange outcries, and uncouth forms and garbs, seen by the glare of the fire, and their whoops and yells, made them appear more like demons than human beings. All this savage gambol was no novelty to Washington's companions, experienced in frontier life; but to the youth, fresh from school, it was a strange spectacle, which he sat contemplating with deep interest, and carefully noted down in his journal. It will be found that he soon made himself acquainted with the savage character, and became expert at dealing with these inhabitants of the wilderness.

Became an expert at dealing with the Indians

From this encampment the party proceeded to the mouth of Patterson's Creek, where they recrossed the river in a canoe, swimming their horses as before. More than two weeks were now passed by them in the wild mountainous regions of Frederick County, and about the south branch of the Potomac, surveying lands and laying out lots, camped out the greater part of the time, and subsisting on wild turkeys and other game. Each one was his own cook; forked sticks served for spits, and chips of wood for dishes. The weather was unsettled. At one time their tent was blown down; at another they were driven out of it by smoke; now they were drenched with rain, and now the straw on which Washington was sleeping caught fire, and he was awakened by a companion just in time to escape a scorching.

The only variety to this camp life was a supper at the house of one Solomon Hedge, Esquire, his majesty's justice of the peace, where there were no forks at table, nor any knives, but such as the guests brought in their pockets. During their surveys they were followed by numbers of people, some of them squatters, anxious, doubtless, to procure a cheap title to the land they had appropriated; others, German emigrants, with their wives and children, seeking a new home in the wilderness. Most of the latter could not speak English; but when spoken to answered in their native tongue. They appeared to Washington ignorant as Indians, and uncouth, but "merry, and full of antic tricks." Such were the progenitors of the sturdy yeomanry now inhabiting those parts, many of whom still preserve their strong German characteristics. . . .

Having completed his surveys, he set forth from the south branch of the Potomac on his return homeward; crossed the mountains to the great Cacapehon; traversed the Shenandoah valley; passed through the Blue Ridge, and on the 12th of April found himself once more at Mount Vernon. For his services he received, according to his note-book, a doubloon per day when actively employed, and sometimes six pistoles.*

The manner in which he had acquitted himself in this arduous expedition, and his accounts of the country surveyed, gave great satisfaction to Lord Fairfax, who shortly afterwards moved across the Blue Ridge, and took up his residence at the place heretofore noted as his "quarters." Here he laid out a manor, containing ten thousand acres of arable grazing land, vast meadows, and noble forests, and projected spacious manor-house giving to the place the name of Greenway Court.

* A pistole is $3.60. A doubloon is double that sum.

George Washington as Public Surveyor

"[*Washington's surveying*] . . . *inspired a confidence in himself, kindled fresh hopes, and prepared the way for new successes. He had moreover acquired a knowledge of parts of the country hitherto little known, which were to be the scene of his first military operations; and had witnessed modes of life, with which it was necessary for him to become familiar in fulfilling the high trusts that awaited him. During this expedition he was also present at an Indian war dance, and had his first interview with a race on whose condition in peace and war he was to have a wider influence than any other man.*"

—Jared Sparks

★

It was probably through the influence of Lord Fairfax that Washington received the appointment of public surveyor. This conferred authority on his surveys, and entitled them to be recorded in the county offices; and so invariably correct have these surveys been found, that, to this day, wherever any of them stand on record, they receive implicit credit.

For three years he continued in this occupation, which proved extremely profitable, from the vast extent of country to be surveyed and the very limited number of public surveyors. It made him acquainted, also, with the country, the nature of the soil in various parts, and the value of localities; all which proved advantageous to him in his purchases in after years. Many of the finest parts of the Shenandoah valley are yet owned by members of the Washington family.

1748–1750

The Life of George Washington, Vol. I, by Washington Irving, 1856

While thus employed for months at a time surveying the lands beyond the Blue Ridge, he was often an inmate of Greenway Court. The projected manor-house was never even commenced. On a green knoll overshadowed by trees was a long stone building, one story in height, with dormer windows, two wooden belfries, chimneys studded with swallow and martin coops, and a roof sloping down in the old Virginia fashion, into low projecting eaves that formed a verandah the whole length of the house. It was probably the house originally occupied by his steward or land agent, but was now devoted to hospitable purposes, and the reception of guests. As to his lordship, it was one of his many eccentricities, that he never slept in the main edifice, but lodged apart in a wooden house not much above twelve feet square. In a small building was his office, where quitrents were given, deeds drawn, and business transacted with his tenants.

About the knoll were out-houses for his numerous servants, black and white, with stables for saddle-horses and hunters, and kennels for his hounds, for his lordship retained his keen hunting propensities, and the neighborhood abounded in game. Indians, half-breeds, and leathern-clad woodsmen loitered about the place, and partook of the abundance of the kitchen. His lordship's table was plentiful but plain, and served in the English fashion.

Here Washington had full opportunity, in the proper seasons, of indulging his fondness for field sports, and once more accompanying his lordship in the chase. The conversation of Lord Fairfax, too, was full of interest and instruction to an inexperienced youth, from his cultivated talents, his literary taste, and his past intercouse with the best society of Europe, and its most distinguished authors. He had brought books, too, with him into the wilderness, and from Washington's diary we find, that during his sojourn here he was diligently reading the history of England, and the essays of *The Spectator*.

A diligent, wilderness reader

Such was Greenway Court in these its palmy days. . . .

Three or four years were thus passed by Washington, the greater part of the time beyond the Blue Ridge, but occasionally with his brother Lawrence at Mount Vernon. His rugged and toilsome expeditions in the mountains, among rude scenes and rough people, inured him to hardships, and made him apt at expedients; while his intercourse with his cultivated brother, and with the various members of the Fairfax family, had a happy effect in toning up his mind and manners, and counteracting the careless and self-indulgent habitudes of the wilderness.

Ready to take his place in the contest for the Ohio Valley

English and French Claims to the Ohio Valley

During the time of Washington's surveying campaigns among the mountains, a grand colonizing scheme had been set on foot, destined to enlist him in hardy enterprises, and in some degree to shape the course of his future fortunes.

The treaty of peace concluded at Aix-la-Chapelle, which had put an end to the general war of Europe, had left undefined the boundaries between the British and French possessions in America; a singular remissness, considering that they had long been a subject in dispute, and a cause of frequent conflicts in the colonies. Immense regions were still claimed by both nations, and each was now eager to forestall the other by getting possession of them, and strengthening its claim by occupancy.

The most desirable of these regions lay west of the Allegany Mountains, extending from the lakes to the Ohio, and embracing the valley of that river and its tributary streams. An immense territory, possessing a salubrious climate, fertile soil, fine hunting and fishing grounds, and facilities by lakes and rivers for a vast internal commerce.

The French claimed all this country quite to the Allegany Mountains, by the right of discovery. . . .

To this illimitable claim the English opposed a right derived, at second hand, from a traditionary Indian conquest. A treaty they said, had been made at Lancaster, in 1744, between commissioners from Pennsylvania, Maryland, and Virginia, and the Iroquois, or Six Nations, whereby the latter, for four hundred pounds, gave up all right and title to the land west of the Allegany Mountains, even to the Mississippi, which land, *according to their traditions,* had been conquered by their forefathers. . . .

As yet in the region in question there was not a single white settlement. Mixed Iroquois tribes of Delawares, Shawnees, and Mingoes, had migrated into it early in the century from the French settlements in Canada, and taken up their abodes about the Ohio and its branches. The French pretended to hold them under their protection; but their allegiance, if ever acknowledged, had been sapped of late years by the influx of fur traders from Pennsylvania. These were often rough, lawless men; half Indians in dress and habits, prone to brawls, and sometimes deadly in their feuds. They were generally in the employ of some trader, who, at the head of his retainers and a string of packhorses, would make his way over mountains and through forests to the banks of the Ohio, establish his head-quarters in some Indian town, and disperse his followers to traffic among the hamlets, hunting-camps and wigwams, exchanging blankets, gaudy colored cloth, trinketry, powder, shot, and rum, for valuable furs and peltry. In this way a lucrative trade with these western tribes was springing up and becoming monopolized by the Pennsylvanians.

French claims unsubstantiated

The Ohio Company

To secure a participation in this trade, and to gain a foothold in this desirable region, became now the wish of some

1749

Courtesy of The Via Department of the Civil and Environmental Engineering Dept., Virginia Tech

GEORGE WASHINGTON — THE SURVEYOR
by Frank E. Schoonover, 1925

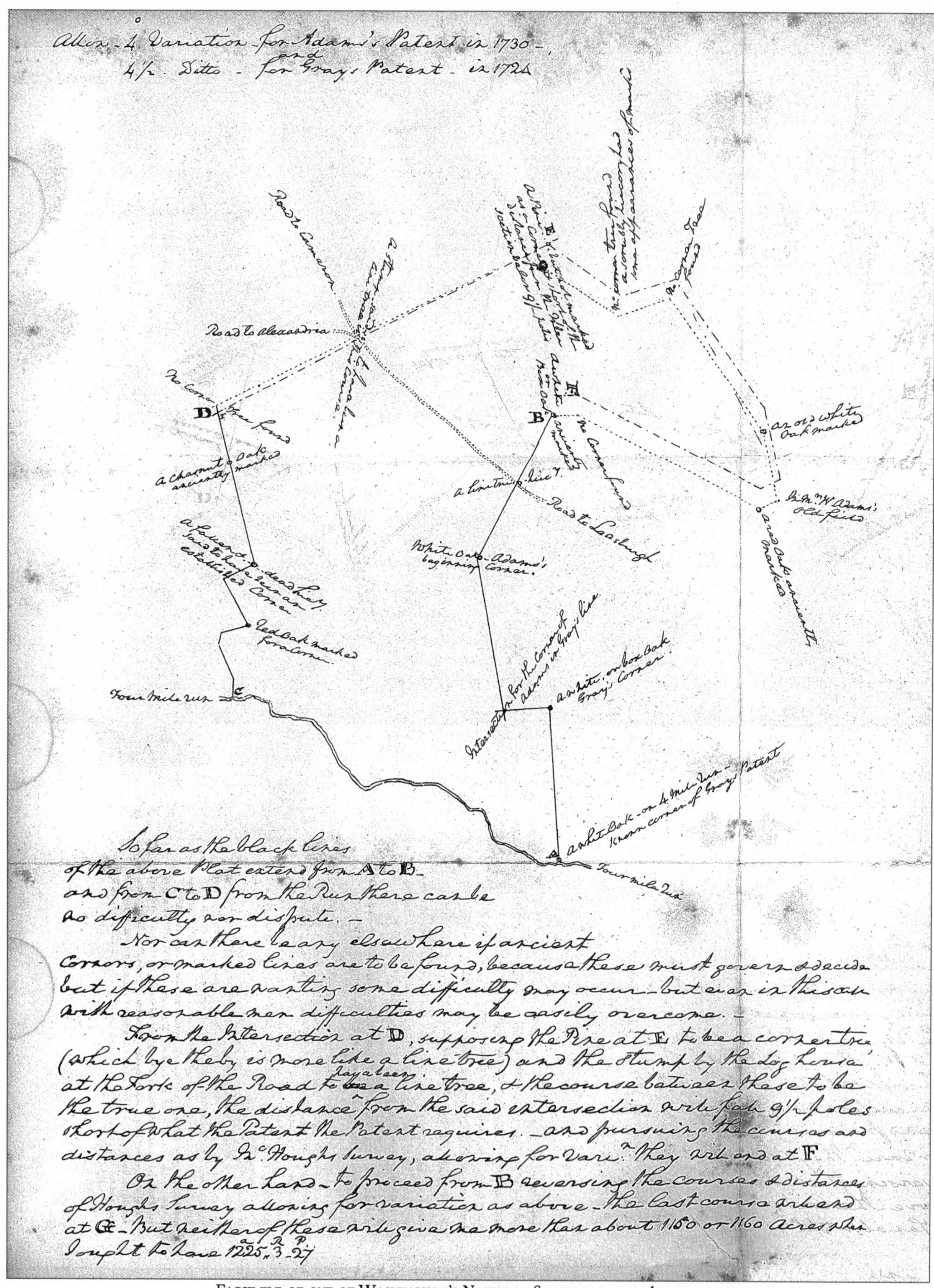

Allow 4° Variation for Adam's Patent in 1730 — and
4½ Ditto — for Grays Patent — in 1724

So far as the black lines of the above Plat extend from A to B — and from C to D from the Run there can be no difficulty nor dispute. —

Nor can there be any elsewhere if ancient Corners, or marked lines are to be found, because these must govern & decide but if these are wanting some difficulty may occur — but even in this case with reasonable men difficulties may be easily overcome. —

From the Intersection at D, supposing the Pine at E to be a corner tree (which bye the by is more like a line tree) and the Stump by the Log house at the Fork of the Road to Payabeen a line tree, & the course between these to be the true one, the distance from the said intersection will fall 9½ poles short of what the Patent the Patent requires. — and pursuing the courses and distances as by Mr. Hough's Survey, allowing for varn. they will end at F

On the other hand — to proceed from B reversing the courses & distances of Hough's Survey allowing for variation as above — the last course will end at G — But neither of these will give me more than about 1150 or 1160 Acres when I ought to have 1225 a. 3 R. 27 P.

FACSIMILE OF ONE OF WASHINGTON'S NOTES OF SURVEY MADE IN APRIL, 1799

of the most intelligent and enterprising men of Virginia and Maryland, among whom were Lawrence and Augustine Washington. With these views they projected a scheme in connection with John Hanbury, a wealthy London merchant, to obtain a grant of land from the British government, for the purpose of forming settlements or colonies beyond the Alleganies. Government readily countenanced a scheme by which French encroachments might be forestalled, and prompt and quiet possession secured of the great Ohio valley. An association was accordingly chartered in 1749, by the name of "the Ohio Company," and five hundred thousand acres of land were granted to it west of the Alleganies; between the Monongahela and Kanawha rivers; though part of the land might be taken up north of the Ohio, should it be deemed expedient. The company were to pay no quitrent for ten years; but they were to select two fifths of their lands immediately; to settle one hundred families upon them within seven years; to build a fort at their own expense, and maintain a sufficient garrison in it for defence against the Indians.

Mr. Thomas Lee, president of the council of Virginia, took the lead in the concerns of the company at the outset, and by many has been considered its founder. On his death, which soon took place, Lawrence Washington had the chief management. His enlightened mind and liberal spirit shone forth in his earliest arrangements. He wished to form the settlements with Germans from Pennsylvania. Being dissenters, however, they would be obliged, on becoming residents within the jurisdiction of Virginia, to pay parish rates, and maintain a clergyman of the church of England, though they might not understand his language nor relish his doctrines. Lawrence sought to have them exempted from this double tax on purse and conscience.

No tax on conscience

Enlightened Views of Lawrence Washington

"It has ever been my opinion," said he, "and I hope it ever will be, that restraints on conscience are cruel in regard to those on whom they are imposed, and injurious to the country imposing them. England, Holland, and Prussia, I may quote as examples, and much more Pennsylvania, which has flourished under that delightful liberty, so as to become the admiration of every man who considers the short time it has been settled. . . . This colony (Virginia) was greatly settled in the latter part of Charles the First's time, and during the usurpation, by the zealous church-men; and that spirit, which was then brought in, has ever since continued; so that, except a few Quakers, we have no dissenters. But what has been the consequence? We have increased by slow degrees, whilst our neighboring colonies, whose natural advantages are greatly inferior to ours, have become populous."

Colonies flourish where there is liberty

Such were the enlightened views of this brother of our Washington, to whom the latter owed much of his moral and mental training. The company proceeded to make preparations for their colonizing scheme. Goods were imported from England suited to the Indian trade, or for presents to the chiefs. Rewards were promised to veteran warriors and hunters among the natives acquainted with the woods and mountains, for the best route to the Ohio.

French Rivalry—Celeron De Bienville

Before the company had received its charter, however, the French were in the field. Early in 1749, the Marquis de la Galisonniere, Governor of Canada, despatched Celeron de Bienville, an intelligent officer, at the head of three hundred men, to the banks of the Ohio, to make peace, as he said, between the tribes that had become embroiled with each other during the late war, and to renew the French possession of the country. Celeron de Bienville distributed presents among the Indians, made speeches reminding them of former friendship, and warned them not to trade with the English.

He furthermore nailed leaden plates to trees, and buried others in the earth, at the confluence of the Ohio and its tributaries, bearing inscriptions purporting that all the lands on both sides of the rivers to their sources appertained, as in foregone times, to the crown of France. The Indians gazed at these mysterious plates with wondering eyes, but surmised their purport. "They mean to steal our country from us," murmured they; and they determined to seek protection from the English.

French claims drive Indians to befriend the English

Celeron, finding some traders from Pennsylvania trafficking among the Indians, summoned them to depart, and wrote by them to James Hamilton, Governor of Pennsylvania, telling him the object of his errand to those parts, and his surprise at meeting with English traders in a country to which England had no pretensions; intimating that, in future, any intruders of the kind would be rigorously dealt with.

His letter, and a report of his proceedings on the Ohio, roused the solicitude of the governor and council of Pennsylvania, for the protection of their Indian trade. Shortly afterwards, one Hugh Crawford, who had been trading with the Miami tribes on the Wabash, brought a message from them, speaking of the promises and threats with which the French were endeavoring to shake their faith, but assuring the governor that their friendship for the English "would last while the sun and moon ran round the world." This message was accompanied by three strings of wampum.

George Croghan, a Veteran Trader, and Christopher Gist, Pioneer

Governor Hamilton knew the value of Indian friendship, and suggested to the Assembly that it would be better to clinch it with presents, and that as soon as possible. An envoy accordingly was sent off early in October, who was supposed to have great influence among the western tribes. This was one George Croghan, a veteran trader, shrewd and sagacious, who had been frequently to the Ohio country with pack-horses and followers, and made himself popular among the Indians by dispersing presents with a lavish hand. He was accompanied by Andrew Montour, a Canadian of half Indian descent, who was to act as interpreter. They were provided with a small present for the emergency; but were to convoke a meeting of all the tribes at Logstown, on the Ohio, early in the ensuing spring, to receive an ample present which would be provided by the Assembly.

It was some time later in the same autumn that the Ohio company brought their plans into operation, and despatched an agent to explore the lands upon the Ohio and its branches as low as the Great Falls, take note of their fitness for cultivation, of the passes of the mountains, the courses and bearings of the rivers, and the strength and disposition of the native tribes. The man chosen for the purpose was Christopher Gist, a hardy pioneer, experienced in woodcraft and Indian life, who had his home on the banks of the Yadkin, near the boundary line of Virginia and North Carolina. He was allowed a woodsman or two for the service of the expedition. He set out on the 31st of October, from the banks of the Potomac, by an Indian path which the hunters had pointed out, leading from Wills' Creek, since called Cumberland River, to the Ohio. . . .

Gist was well received by the people of Muskingum. They were indignant at the French violation of their territories, and the capture of their "English brothers." They had not forgotten the conduct of Celeron de Bienville in the previous year, and the mysterious plates which he had nailed against trees and sunk in the ground. "If the French claim the rivers which run into the lakes," said they, "those which run into the Ohio belong to us and to our brothers the English." And they were anxious that Gist should settle among them, and build a fort for their mutual defence.

A council of the nation was now held, in which Gist invited them, in the name of the Governor of Virginia, to visit that province, where a large present of goods awaited them, sent by their father, the great king, over the water to his Ohio children. The invitation was graciously received, but no answer could be given until a grand council of the western tribes had been held, which was to take place at Logstown in the ensuing spring.

Croghan and Gist form Indian alliances in behalf of the English

Similar results attended visits made by Gist and Croghan to the Delawares and the Shawnees at their villages about the Scioto River; all promised to be at the gathering at Logstown. From the Shawnee Village, near the mouth of the Scioto, the two emissaries shaped their course north two hundred miles, crossed the Great Moneami, or Miami River, on a raft, swimming their horses; and on the 17th of February arrived at the Indian town of Piqua.

These journeyings had carried Gist about a wide extent of country beyond the Ohio. It was rich and level, watered with streams and rivulets, and clad with noble forests of hickory, walnut, ash, poplar, sugar-maple, and wild cherry-trees. Occasionally there were spacious plains covered with wild rye; natural meadows, with blue grass and clover; and buffaloes, thirty and forty at a time, grazing on them as in a cultivated pasture. Deer, elk, and wild turkeys abounded. "Nothing is wanted but cultivation," said Gist, "to make this a most delightful country." Cultivation has since proved the truth of his words. The country thus described is the present State of Ohio.

Diplomacy at Piqua

Piqua, where Gist and Croghan had arrived, was the principal town of the Twightwees or Miamis; the most powerful confederacy of the West, combining four tribes, and extending its influence even beyond the Mississippi. A king or sachem of one or other of the different tribes presided over the whole. The head chief at present was the king of the Piankeshas.

Miami Confederacy

At this town Croghan formed a treaty of alliance in the name of the Governor of Pennsylvania with two of the Miami tribes. And Gist was promised by the king of the Piankeshas, that the chiefs of the various tribes would attend the meeting at Logstown to make a treaty with Virginia.

In the height of these demonstrations of friendship, two Ottawas entered the council-house, announcing themselves as envoys from the French Governor of Canada to seek a renewal of ancient alliance. They were received with all due ceremonial; for none are more ceremonious than the Indians. The French colors were set up beside the English, and the ambassadors opened their mission. . . .

In the end the ambassadors were assured that the tribes of the Ohio and the Six Nations were hand in hand with their brothers, the English; and should war ensue with the French, they were ready to meet it.

So the French colors were taken down; the "kegs of milk" and roll of tobacco were rejected; the grand council broke up with a war-dance, and the ambassadors departed, weeping and howling, and predicting ruin to the Miamis.

When Gist returned to the Shawnee town, near the mouth of the Scioto, and reported to his Indian friends there the alliance he had formed with the Miami confederacy, there was great feasting and speech-making, and firing of guns. He had now happily accomplished the chief object of his mission—nothing remained but to descend the Ohio to the Great Falls. This, however, he was cautioned not to do. . . .

Abandoning all idea, therefore, of visiting the Falls, and contenting himself with the information concerning them which he had received from others, he shaped his course on the 18th of March for the Cuttawa, or Kentucky River. From the top of a mountain in the vicinity he had a view to the southwest as far as the eye could reach, over a vast woodland country in the fresh garniture of spring, and watered by abundant streams; but as yet only the hunting-ground of savage tribes, and the scene of their sanguinary combats. In a word, Kentucky lay spread out before him in all its wild magnificence; long before it was beheld by Daniel Boone.

First sight of Kentucky

For six weeks was this hardy pioneer making his toilful way up the valley of the Cuttawa, or Kentucky River, to the banks of the Blue Stone; often checked by precipices, and obliged to seek fords at the heads of tributary streams; and happy when he could find a buffalo path broken through the tangled forests, or worn into the everlasting rocks.

On the 1st of May he climbed a rock sixty feet high, crowning a lofty mountain, and had a distant view of the great Kanawha, breaking its way through a vast sierra; crossing that river on a raft of his own construction, he had many more weary days before him, before he reached his frontier abode on the banks of the Yadkin. He arrived there in the latter part of May, but there was no one to welcome the wanderer home. There had been an Indian massacre in the neighborhood, and he found his house silent and deserted. His heart sank within him, until an old man whom he met near the place assured him his family were safe, having fled for refuge to a settlement thirty-five miles off, on the banks of the Roanoke. There he rejoined them on the following day.

Captain Joncaire

While Gist had been making his painful way home-ward, the two Ottawa ambassadors had returned to Fort Sandusky, bringing word to the French that their flag had been struck in the council-house at Piqua, and their friendship rejected and their hostility defied by the Miamis. They informed them also of the gathering of the western tribes that was to take place at Logstown, to conclude a treaty with the Virginians.

It was a great object with the French to prevent this treaty, and to spirit up the Ohio Indians against the English. This they hoped to effect through the agency of one Captain Joncaire, a veteran diplomatist of the wilderness, whose character and story deserve a passing notice. . . .

He appeared at Logstown accompanied by another Frenchman, and forty Iroquois warriors. He found an assemblage of the western tribes, feasting and rejoicing, and firing of guns, for George Croghan and Montour the interpreter were there, and had been distributing presents on behalf of the Governor of Pennsylvania.

Joncaire was said to have the wit of a Frenchman, and the eloquence of an Iroquois. He made an animated speech to the chiefs in their own tongue, the gist of which was that their father Onontio (that is to say, the Governor of Canada) desired his children of the Ohio to turn away the Indian traders, and never to deal with them again on pain of his displeasure; so saying, he laid down a wampum belt of uncommon size, by way of emphasis to his message.

For once his eloquence was of no avail; a chief rose indignantly, shook his finger in his face, and stamping on the ground, "this is our land," said he, "What right has Onontio here? The English are our brothers. They shall live among us as long as one of us is alive. We will trade with them, and not with you;" and so saying he rejected the belt of wampum. . . .

In the mean time, . . . Mr. Gist, under sanction of the Virginia Legislature, proceeded in the same year to survey the lands within the grant of the Ohio company, lying on the south side of the Ohio river, as far down as the great Kanawha. An old Delaware sachem, meeting him while thus employed, propounded a somewhat puzzling question. "The French," said he, "claim all the land on one side of the Ohio, the English claim all the land on the other side—now where does the Indians' land lie?"

Poor savages! Between their "father," the French, and their "brothers," the English, they were in a fair way of being most lovingly shared out of the whole country. . . .

Washington Appointed District Adjutant-General

The French now prepared for hostile contingencies. They launched an armed vessel of unusual size on Lake Ontario; fortified their trading house at Niagara; strengthened their outposts, and advanced others on the upper waters of the Ohio. A stir of warlike preparation was likewise to be observed among the British colonies. It was evident that the adverse claims to the disputed territories, if pushed home, could only be settled by the stern arbitrament of the sword.

In Virginia, especially, the war spirit was manifest. The province was divided into military districts, each having an adjutant-general, with the rank of major, and the pay of one hundred and fifty pounds a year, whose duty was to attend to the organization and equipment of the militia.

Such an appointment was sought by Lawrence Washington for his brother George. It shows what must have been the maturity of mind of the latter, and the confidence inspired by his judicious conduct and aptness for business, that the post should not only be sought for him, but readily obtained; though he was yet but nineteen years of age. He proved himself worthy of the appointment.

Age nineteen

He now set about preparing himself, with his usual method and assiduity, for his new duties. Virginia had among its floating population some military relics of the late Spanish war. Among these was a certain Adjutant Muse, a Westmoreland volunteer, who had served with Lawrence Washington in the campaigns in the West Indies, and had been with him in the attack on Carthagena. He now undertook to instruct his brother George in the art of war; lent him treatises on military tactics; put him through the manual exercise, and gave him some idea of evolutions in the field. Another of Lawrence's campaigning comrades was Jacob Van Braam, a Dutchman by birth; a soldier of fortune of the Dalgetty order; who had been in the British army, but was now out of service, and, professing to be a complete master of fence, recruited his slender purse in this time of military excitement, by giving the Virginian youth lessons in the sword exercise.

Under the instructions of these veterans Mount Vernon, from being a quiet rural retreat, where Washington, three years previously, had indited love ditties to his "lowland beauty," was suddenly transformed into a school of arms, as he practised the manual exercise with Adjutant Muse, or took lessons on the broadsword from Van Braam.

Lessons in the art of war

★ ★ ★ ★ ★

The Life of George Washington by Jared Sparks, 1837, 1902

Surveying and Appointment as Adjutant

Having received a commission or appointment, as a public surveyor, which gave authority to his surveys, and enabled him to enter them in the county offices, he devoted three years to this pursuit, without any intervals of relaxation except the winter months. Portions of each year were passed among the Alleghanies, where he surveyed lands on branches of the Potomac River, which penetrated far in a southern direction among the lofty ridges and spurs of those mountains. The exposures and hardships of these expeditions could be endured only for a few weeks together. As a relief, he would come down into the settled parts, and survey private tracts and farms, thus applying himself to the uninterrupted exercise of his profession.

There being few surveyors at that time in Virginia, and the demand for them great, the pay allowed for their services was proportionably high. By diligence and habits of despatch, the employment was lucrative; and, what was more important, his probity and talents for business were at a very early age made known to gentlemen, whose standing in society rendered their friendship and interest a substantial benefit. During these three years his home was with his brother at Mount Vernon, as being nearer the scene of his labors than his mother's residence; but he often visited her, and assisted in the superintendence of her affairs.

At the age of nineteen his character had made so favorable an impression, that he was appointed to an office of considerable distinction and responsibility by the government of Virginia. The frontiers were threatened with Indian depredations and French encroachments, and, as a precautionary measure, it was resolved to put the militia in a condition for defence. To carry this into effect, the province was divided into districts, having in each an officer called an adjutant-general with the rank of major, whose duty it was to assemble and exercise the militia, inspect their arms, and enforce all the regulations for discipline prescribed by the laws. George Washington was commissioned to take charge of one of these districts. The post was probably obtained through the influence of his brother and William Fairfax, the former a delegate in the House of Burgesses, and the latter a member of the Governor's Council. The pay was one hundred and fifty pounds a year.

His military propensities had not subsided. They rather increased with his years. In Virginia were many officers, besides his brother, who had served in the recent war. Under their tuition he studied tactics, learned the manual exercise, and became expert in the use of the sword. He read the principal books on the military art, and joined practice to theory as far as circumstances would permit. This new station, therefore, was in accordance with his inclinations, and he entered upon it with alacrity and zeal.

Voyage to Barbadoes

But he had scarcely engaged in this service, when he was called to perform another duty, deeply interesting in its claims on his sensibility and fraternal affection. Lawrence Washington, originally of a slender constitution, had been for some time suffering under a pulmonary attack, which was now thought to be approaching a dangerous crisis. The physicians recommended a voyage to the West Indies, and the experiment of a warmer climate. The necessity of having some friend near him, and his attachment to George, were reasons for desiring his company. They sailed for Barbadoes in the month of September, 1751, and landed on that island after a passage of five weeks.

The change of air, the hospitality of the inhabitants, the novelty of the scene, and the assiduous attentions of his brother, revived the spirits of the patient, and seemed at first to renovate his strength. But the hope was delusive, and the old symptoms returned. The trial of a few weeks produced no essential alteration for the better; and he determined to proceed to Bermuda in the spring, and that in the meantime his brother should go back to Virginia, and accompany his wife to that island. Accordingly, George took pasage in a vessel bound to the Chesapeake, and, after encountering a most tempestuous voyage, reached home in February, having been absent somewhat more than four months.

He had the smallpox in Barbadoes. The disease was severe, but with the aid of good medical attendance, he was able to go abroad in three weeks.

The first letter from his brother at Bermuda gave an encouraging account of his health, and expressed a wish that his wife should join him there; but it was followed by another, of a different tenor, which prevented her departure. Finding no essential relief, he came home in the summer, and sank rapidly into his grave, at the age of thirty-four, leaving a wife, an infant daughter, and a large circle of friends, to deplore a loss keenly felt by them all. Few men have been more beloved for their amiable qualities, or admired for those higher traits of character which give dignity to virtue, and a charm to accomplishments of mind and manners.

By this melancholy event, new duties and responsibilities devolved upon George. Large estates were left by the deceased brother, the immediate care of which demanded his oversight. He had likewise been appointed one of the executors of the will, in which was an eventual interest of considerable magnitude pertaining to himself. . . . His time and thoughts, for several months, were taken up with these affairs, complicated in their nature, and requiring delicacy and caution in their management.

His private employments, however, did not draw him away from his public duties as adjutant-general. Indeed, the sphere of that office was enlarged.

Soon after Governor Dinwiddie came to Virginia, the colony was portioned into four grand military divisions. Major Washington's appointment was then renewed, and the northern division was allotted to him. It included several counties, each of which was to be visited at stated times by the adjutant, in order to train and instruct the militia officers, review the companies on parade, inspect the arms and accoutrements, and establish a uniform system of manœuvres and discipline. These exercises, so congenial to his taste, were equally advantageous to himself and to the subordinate officers, who could not fail to be animated by his example, activity, and enthusiasm.

★

Ill Health of Washington's Brother Lawrence

The Life of George Washington, Vol. I, by Washington Irving, 1856

His martial studies, however, were interrupted for a time by the critical state of his brother's health. The constitution of Lawrence had always been delicate, and he had been obliged repeatedly to travel for a change of air. There were now pulmonary symptoms of a threatening nature, and by advice of his physicians he determined to pass a winter in the West Indies, taking with him his favorite brother George as a companion.

Scenes at Barbadoes

They accordingly sailed for Barbadoes on the 28th of September, 1751. George kept a journal of the voyage with logbook brevity; recording the wind and weather, but no events worth citation. They landed at Barbadoes on the 3d of November. The resident physician of the place gave a favorable report of Lawrence's case, and held out hopes of a cure. The brothers were delighted with the aspect of the country, as they drove out in the cool of the evening, and beheld on all sides fields of sugar cane, and Indian corn, and groves of tropical trees, in full fruit and foliage.

September, 1751

They took up their abode at a house pleasantly situated about a mile from town, commanding an extensive prospect of sea and land, including Carlyle bay and its shipping, and belonging to Captain Crofton, commander of James Fort.

Barbadoes had its theatre, at which Washington witnessed for the first time a dramatic representation, a species of amusement of which he afterwards became fond. It was in the present instance the doleful tragedy of George Barnwell. "The character of Barnwell, and several others," notes he in his journal, "were said to be well performed. There was music adapted and regularly conducted." A safe but abstemious criticism.

Among the hospitalities of the place the brothers were invited to the house of a Judge Maynards, to dine with an association of the first people of the place, who met at each other's house alternately every Saturday, under the incontestably English title of "The Beefsteak and Tripe Club." Washington notes with admiration the profusion of tropical fruits with which the table was loaded, "the granadilla, sapadella, pomegranate, sweet orange, water-melon, forbidden fruit, and guava." The homely prosaic beefsteak and tripe must have contrasted strangely, though sturdily, with these magnificent poetical fruits of the tropics. . . .

The brothers had scarcely been a fortnight at the island when George was taken down by a severe attack of small-pox. Skilful medical treatment, with the kind attentions of friends, and especially of his brother, restored him to health in about three weeks; but his face always remained slightly marked.

After his recovery he made excursions about the island, noticing its soil, productions, fortifications, public works, and the manners of its inhabitants. While admiring the productiveness of the sugar plantations, he was shocked at the spendthrift habits of the planters, and their utter want of management.

"How wonderful," writes he, "that such people should be in debt, and not be able to indulge themselves in all the luxuries, as well as the necessaries of life. Yet so it happens. Estates are often alienated for debts. How persons coming to estates of two, three, and four hundred acres can want, is to me most wonderful." How much does this wonder speak for his own scrupulous principle of always living within compass.

Own scrupulous principle

The residence at Barbadoes failed to have the anticipated effect on the health of Lawrence, and he determined to seek the sweet climate of Bermuda in the spring. He felt the absence from his wife, and it was arranged that George should return to Virginia, and bring her out to meet him at that island. Accordingly, on the 22d of December George set sail in the Industry, bound to Virginia, where he arrived on the 1st February, 1752, after five weeks of stormy winter seafaring. Lawrence remained through

February, 1752

the winter at Barbadoes; but the very mildness of the climate relaxed and enervated him. He felt the want of the bracing winter weather to which he had been accustomed. . . .

Death of Lawrence

He was now afflicted with painful indecision, and his letters perplexed his family, leaving them uncertain as to his movements, and at a loss how to act. . . .

He did indeed hasten back and just reached Mount Vernon in time to die under his own roof, surrounded by his family and friends, and attended in his last moments by that brother on whose manly affection his heart seemed to repose. His death took place on the 26th July, 1752, when but thirty-four years of age. He was noble-spirited, pure-minded, accomplished gentleman; honored by the public, and beloved by his friends. The paternal care ever manifested by him for his youthful brother, George, and the influence his own character and conduct must have had upon him in his ductile years, should link their memories together in history, and endear the name of Lawrence Washington to every American.

July 26, 1752

Lawrence left a wife and infant daughter to inherit his ample estates. In case his daughter should die without issue, the estate of Mount Vernon, and other lands specified in his will, were to be enjoyed by her mother during her lifetime, and at her death to be inherited by his brother George. The latter was appointed one of the executors of the will; but such was the implicit confidence reposed in his judgment and integrity, that although he was but twenty years of age, the management of the affairs of the deceased was soon devolved upon him almost entirely. It is needless to say that they were managed with consummate skill and scrupulous fidelity.

Lawrence's Legacy

GEORGE WASHINGTON AS COLONEL OF THE VIRGINIA REGIMENT

Engraved by J. B. Forrest from the painting by Charles Willson Peale

Test of Character

We have been minute in our account of this expedition, as it was an early test and development of the various talents and characteristics of Washington.

The prudence, sagacity, resolution, firmness, and self-devotion manifested by him throughout; his admirable tact and self-possession in treating with fickle savages and crafty white men; the soldier's eye with which he had noticed the commanding and defensible points of the country, and every thing that would bear upon military operations; and the hardihood with which he had acquitted himself during a wintry tramp through the wilderness, through constant storms of rain and snow; often sleeping on the ground without a tent in the open air, and in danger from treacherous foes,—all pointed him out, not merely to the governor, but to the public at large, as one eminently fitted, notwithstanding his youth, for important trusts involving civil as well as military duties. It is an expedition that may be considered the foundation of his fortunes. From that moment he was the rising hope of Virginia.

–Washington Irving, *The Life of George Washington*, Vol. I, 1856

Colonial Military Experience

Washington in the French and Indian War

The time was now at hand, when the higher destinies of Washington were to unfold themselves.
—Jared Sparks

Montcalm and Wolfe Vol. 1, by Francis Parkman, 1904

It is the nature of great events to obscure the great events that came before them. The Seven Years' War in Europe is seen but dimly through revolutionary convulsions and Napoleonic tempests; and the same contest in America is half lost to sight behind the storm-cloud of the War of Independence. Few at this day see the momentous issues involved in it or the greatness of the danger that it averted. The strife that armed all the civilized world began here. "Such was the complication of political interests," says Voltaire, "that a cannon-shot fired in America could give the signal that set Europe in a blaze," Not quite. It was not a cannon-shot, but a volley from the hunting-pieces of a few backwoodsmen, commanded by a Virginian youth, George Washington.

To us of this day, the result of the American part of the war seems a foregone conclusion. It was far from being so; and very far from being so regarded by our forefathers. The numerical superiority of the British colonies was offset by organic weaknesses fatal to vigorous and united action. Nor at the outset did they, or the mother-country, aim at conquering Canada, but only at pushing back her boundaries. . . .

The Seven Years' War made England what she is. It crippled the commerce of her rival, ruined France in two continents, and blighted her as a colonial power. It gave England the control of the seas and the mastery of North America and India, made her the first of commercial nations, and prepared that vast colonial system that has planted new Englands in every quarter of the globe. And while it made England what she is, it supplied to the United States the indispensable condition of their greatness, if not of their national existence.

The American Combatants

The French claimed all America, from the Alleghanies to the Rocky Mountains, and from Mexico and Florida to the North Pole, except only the ill-defined possessions of the English on the borders of Hudson Bay; and to these vast regions, with adjacent islands, they gave the general name of New France. They controlled the highways of the continent, for they held its two great rivers. First, they had seized the St. Lawrence, and then planted themselves at the mouth of the Mississippi. Canada at the north, and Louisiana at the south, were the keys of a boundless interior, rich with incalculable possibilities. The English colonies, ranged along the Atlantic coast, had no royal road to the great inland, and were, in a manner, shut between the mountains and the sea. . . .

The thirteen British colonies were alike, insomuch as they all had representative governments, and a basis of English law. But the differences among them were great. Some were purely English; others were made up of various races, though the Anglo-Saxon was always predominant. Some had one prevailing religious creed; others had many creeds. Some had charters, and some had not. In most cases the governor was appointed by the Crown; in Pennsylvania and Maryland he was appointed by a feudal proprietor, and in Connecticut and Rhode Island he was chosen by the people. The differences of disposition and character were greater than those of form. . . .

In the heterogeneous structure of the British colonies, their clashing interests, their internal disputes, and the misplaced economy of penny-wise and short-sighted assembly-men, lay the hope of France. The rulers of Canada knew the vast numerical preponderance of their rivals; but with their centralized organization they felt themselves more than a match for any one English colony alone. They hoped to wage war under the guise of peace, and to deal with the enemy in detail; and they at length perceived that the fork of the Ohio, so strangely neglected by the English, formed, together with the Niagara, the key of the Great West. Could France hold firmly these two controlling passes, she might almost boast herself mistress of the continent. . . .

★ ★ ★ ★ ★

Council of the Ohio Tribes at Logstown

The Life of George Washington, Vol. I, by Washington Irving, 1856

The meeting of the Ohio tribes, Delawares, Shawnees, and Mingoes, to form a treaty of alliance with Virginia, took place at Logstown, at the appointed time. The chiefs of the Six Nations declined to attend. "It is not our custom," said they proudly, "to meet to treat of affairs in the woods and weeds. If the Governor of Virginia wants to speak with us, and deliver us a present from our father (the king), we will meet him at Albany, where we expect the Governor of New York will be present."

At Logstown, Colonel Fry and two other commissioners from Virginia, concluded a treaty with the tribes above named; by which the latter engaged not to molest any English settlers south of the Ohio. Tanacharisson, the half-king, now advised that his brothers of Virginia should build a strong house at the fork of the Monongahela, to resist the designs of the French. Mr. Gist was accordingly instructed to lay out a town and build a fort at Chartier's Creek, on the east side of the Ohio, a little below the site of the present city of Pittsburg. He commenced a settlement, also, in a valley just beyond Laurel Hill, not far from the Youghiogeny, and prevailed on eleven families to join him. The Ohio Company, about the same time, established a trading post, well stocked with English goods, at Wills' Creek (now Cumberland River).

The Ohio tribes were greatly incensed at the aggressions of the French, who were erecting posts within their territories, and sent deputations to remonstrate, but without effect. The half-king, as chief of the western tribes, repaired to the French posts on Lake Erie, where he made his complaint in person. . . .

French influence was successful in other quarters. Some of the Indians who had been friendly to the English showed signs of alienation. Others menaced hostilities. There were reports that the French were ascending the Mississippi from Louisiana. France, it was said, intended to connect Louisiana and Canada by a chain of military posts, and hem the English within the Allegany Mountains.

The Ohio Company complained loudly to the Lieutenant-governor of Virginia, the Hon. Robert Dinwiddie, of the hostile conduct of the French and their Indian allies. They found in Dinwiddie a ready listener; he was a stockholder in the company.

A commissioner, Captain William Trent, was sent to expostulate with the French commander on the Ohio for his aggressions on the territory of his Britannic majesty; he bore presents also of guns, powder, shot, and clothing for the friendly Indians. Trent was not a man of the true spirit for a mission to the frontier. He stopped a short time at Logstown, though the French were one hundred and fifty miles further up the river, and directed his course to Piqua, the great town of the Twightwees, where Gist and Croghan had been so well received by the Miamis, and the French flag struck in the council-house. All now was reversed.

Indian treachery

The place had been attacked by the French and Indians; the Miamis defeated with great loss; the English traders taken prisoners; the Piankesha chief, who had so proudly turned his back upon the Ottawa ambassadors, had been sacrificed by the hostile savages, and the French flag hoisted in triumph on the ruins of the town. The whole aspect of affairs was so threatening on the frontier, that Trent lost heart, and returned home without accomplishing his errand.

Washington Sent on a Mission to the French Commander

Governor Dinwiddie now looked round for a person more fitted to fulfil a mission which required physical strength and moral energy; a courage to cope with savages, and a sagacity to negotiate with white men. Washington was pointed out, as possessed of those requisites. It is true he was not yet twenty-two years of age, but public confidence in his judgment and abilities had been manifested a second time, by renewing his appointment of adjutant-general, and assigning him the northern division. He was acquainted too with the matters in litigation, having been in the bosom councils of his deceased brother. His woodland experience fitted him for an expedition through the wilderness; and his great discretion and self-command for a negotiation with the wily commanders and fickle savages. He was accordingly chosen for the expedition.

Not yet age twenty-two

By his letter of instructions he was directed to repair to Logstown, and hold a communication with Tanacharisson, Monacatoocha, alias Scarooyadi, the next in command, and the other sachems of the mixed tribes friendly to the English; inform them of the purport of his errand, and request an escort to the head-quarters of the French commander. To that commander he was to deliver his credentials, and the letter of Governor Dinwiddie, and demand an answer in the name of his Britannic majesty; but not to wait for it beyond a week. On receiving it, he was to request a sufficient escort to protect him on his return.

He was, moreover, to acquaint himself with the numbers and force of the French stationed on the Ohio and in its vicinity; their capability of being reinforced from Canada; the forts they had erected; where situated, how garrisoned; the object of their advancing into those parts, and how they were likely to be supported.

Washington set off from Williamsburg on the 30th of October (1753), the very day on which he received his credentials. At Fredericksburg he engaged his old "master of fence," Jacob Van Braam, to accompany him as interpreter; though it would appear from subsequent circumstances, that the veteran swordsman was but indifferently versed either in French or English.

Having provided himself at Alexandria with necessaries for the journey, he proceeded to Winchester, then on the frontier, where he procured horses, tents, and other travelling equipments, and then pushed on by a road newly opened to Wills' Creek (Cumberland River), where he arrived on the 14th of November.

Here he met with Mr. Gist, the intrepid pioneer, who had explored the Ohio in the employ of the company, and whom he engaged to accompany and pilot him in the present expedition. He secured the services also of one John Davidson as Indian interpreter, and of four frontiersmen, two of whom were Indian traders. With this little band, and his swordsman and interpreter, Jacob Van Braam, he set forth on the 15th of November, through a wild country, rendered almost impassable by recent storms of rain and snow.

At the mouth of Turtle Creek, on the Monongahela, he found John Frazier, the Indian trader, some of whose people, as heretofore stated, had been sent off prisoners to Canada. Frazier himself had recently been ejected by the French from the Indian village of Venango, where he had a gunsmith's establishment. According to his account, the French general who had commanded on this frontier was dead, and the greater part of the forces were retired into winter quarters.

As the rivers were all swollen so that the horses had to swim them, Washington sent all the baggage down the Monongahela in a canoe under the care of two of the men, who had orders to meet him at the confluence of that river with the Allegany, where their united waters form the Ohio.

"As I got down before the canoe," writes he in his journal, "I spent some time in viewing the rivers, and the land at the Fork, which I think extremely well situated for a fort, as it has the absolute command of both rivers. The land at the point is twenty or twenty-five feet above the common surface of the water, and a considerable bottom of flat, well-timbered land all around it, very convenient for building. The rivers are each a quarter of a mile or more across, and run here very nearly at right angles; Allegany bearing north-east, and Monongahela south-east. The former of these two is a very rapid and swift-running water, the other deep and still, without any perceptible fall." The Ohio company had intended to build a fort about

by Alonzo Chappel, 1857

WASHINGTON ON HIS MISSION TO THE OHIO, 1753

two miles from this place, on the south-east side of the river; but Washington gave the fork the decided preference. French engineers of experience proved the accuracy of his military eye, by subsequently choosing it for the site of Fort Duquesne, noted in frontier history.

Site of Fort Duquesne through his military eye

In this neighborhood lived Shingis, the king or chief sachem of the Delawares. Washington visited him at his village, to invite him to the council at Logstown. He was one of the greatest warriors of his tribe, and subsequently took up the hatchet at various times against the English, though now he seemed favorably disposed, and readily accepted the invitation.

Indian Councils

They arrived at Logstown after sunset on the 24th of November. The half-king was absent at his hunting lodge on Beaver Creek, about fifteen miles distant; but Washington had runners sent out to invite him and all the other chiefs to a grand talk on the following day.

November 24, 1753

In the morning four French deserters came into the village. They had deserted from a company of one hundred men, sent up from New Orleans with eight canoes laden with provisions. Washington drew from them an account of the French force at New Orleans, and of the forts along the Mississippi, and at the mouth of the Wabash, by which they kept up a communication with the lakes; all which he carefully noted down. The deserters were on their way to Philadelphia, conducted by a Pennsylvania trader.

About three o'clock the half-king arrived. Washington had a private conversation with him in his tent, through Davidson, the interpreter. He found him intelligent, patriotic, and proudly tenacious of his territorial rights. . . . He stated, moreover, that the French had built two forts, differing in size, but on the same model, a plan of which he gave, of his own drawing. The largest was on Lake Erie, the other on French Creek, fifteen miles apart, with a wagon road between them. The nearest and levelest way to them was now impassable, lying through large and miry savannas; they would have, therefore, to go by Venango, and it would take five or six sleeps (or days) of good travelling to reach the nearest fort. On the following morning at nine o'clock, the chiefs assembled at the council-house; where Washington, according to his instructions, informed them that he was sent by their brother, the Governor of Virginia, to deliver to the French commandant a letter of great importance,* both to their brothers the English and to themselves; and that he was to ask their advice and assistance, and some of their young men to accompany and provide for him on the way, and be his safeguard against the "French Indians" who had taken up the hatchet. He concluded by presenting the indispensable document in Indian diplomacy, a string of wampum.

*See Letter: Gov. Dinwiddie to French Commandant, Appendix A-12

The chiefs, according to etiquette, sat for some moments silent after he had concluded, as if ruminating on what had been said, or to give him time for further remark.

The half-king then rose and spoke in behalf of the tribes, assuring him that they considered the English and themselves brothers, and one people; and that they intended to return the French the "speech-belts," or wampums, which the latter had sent them. This, in Indian diplomacy, is a renunciation of all friendly relations. An escort would be furnished to Washington composed of Mingoes, Shannoahs, and Delawares, in token of the love and loyalty of those several tribes; but three days would be required to prepare for the journey.

Schooled in Indian diplomacy, French allegiance renounced

Washington remonstrated against such delay; but was informed, that an affair of such moment, where three speech-belts were to be given up, was not to be entered into without due consideration. Besides, the young men who were to form the escort were absent hunting, and the half-king could not suffer the party to go without sufficient protection. His own French speech-belt, also, was at his hunting lodge, where he must go in quest of it. Moreover, the Shannoah chiefs were yet absent, and must be waited for. In short, Washington had his first lesson in Indian diplomacy, which for punctilio, ceremonial, and secret manœuvering, is equal at least to that of civilized life. He soon found that to urge a more speedy departure would be offensive to Indian dignity and decorum, so he was fain to await the gathering together of the different chiefs with their speech-belts.

In fact there was some reason for all this caution. Tidings had reached the sachems that Captain Joncaire had called a meeting at Venango, of the Mingoes, Delawares, and other Tribes, and made them a speech, informing them that the French, for the present, had gone into winter quarters, but intended to descend the river in great force, and fight the English in the spring. He had advised them, therefore, to stand aloof; for should they interfere, the French and English would join, cut them all off, and divide their land between them.

With these rumors preying on their minds, the half-king and three other chiefs waited on Washington in his tent in the evening, and after representing that they had complied with all the requisitions of the Governor of Virginia, endeavored to draw from the youthful ambassador the true purport of his mission to the French commandant. Washington had anticipated an inquiry of the kind, knowing how natural it was that these poor people should regard, with anxiety and distrust, every movement of two formidable powers thus pressing upon them from opposite sides; he managed, however, to answer them in such a manner as to allay their solicitude without transcending the bounds of diplomatic secrecy.

After a day or two more of delay and further consultations in the council-house, the chiefs determined that but three of their number should accompany the mission, as a greater number might awaken the suspicions of the French. Accordingly, on the 30th of November, Washington set out for the French post, having his usual party augmented by an Indian hunter, and being accompanied by the half-king, an old Shannoah sachem named Jeskakake, and another chief, sometimes called Belt of Wampum, from being the keeper of the speech-belts, but generally bearing the sounding appellation of White Thunder.

Arrival at Venango

Although the distance to Venango, by the route taken, was not above seventy miles, yet such was the inclemency of the weather and the difficulty of travelling, that Washington and his party did not arrive there until the 4th of December. The French colors were flying at a house whence John Frazier, the English trader, had been driven. Washington repaired thither, and inquired of three French officers whom he saw there where the commandant resided. One of them promptly replied that he "had the command of the Ohio." It was, in fact, the redoubtable Captain Joncaire, the veteran intriguer of the frontier. On being apprised, however, of the nature of Washington's errand, he informed him that there was a general officer at the next fort, where he advised him to apply for an answer to the letter of which he was the bearer.

December 4, 1753

In the mean time, he invited Washington and his party to a supper at head-quarters. It proved a jovial one, for Joncaire appears to have been somewhat of a boon companion, and there is always ready, though rough hospitality in the wilderness. It is true, Washington, for so young a man, may not have had the most convivial air, but there may have been a moist look of promise in the old soldier Van Braam.

Joncaire and his brother officers pushed the bottle briskly. "The wine," says Washington, "as they dosed themselves pretty plentifully with it, soon banished the restraint which at first appeared in their conversation, and gave a license to their tongues to reveal their sentiments more freely. They told me that it was their absolute design to take possession of the Ohio, and by G— they would do it; for that although they were sensible the English could raise two men for their one, yet they knew their motions were too slow and dilatory to prevent any undertaking. They pretend to have an undoubted right to the river from a discovery made by one La Salle sixty years ago, and the rise of this expedition is to prevent our settling on the river or the waters of it, as they heard of some families moving out in order thereto."

Washington retained his sobriety and his composure throughout all the rodomontade and bacchanalian outbreak of the mercurial Frenchmen; leaving the task of pledging them to his master of fence, Van Braam, who was not a man to flinch from potations. He took careful note, however, of all their revelations, and collected a variety of information concerning the French forces; how and where they were distributed; the situations and distances of their forts, and their means and mode of obtaining supplies. If the veteran diplomatist of the wilderness had intended this revel for a snare, he was completely foiled by his youthful competitor.

Washington turns the tables on Joncaire

On the following day there was no travelling on account of excessive rain. Joncaire, in the mean time, having discovered that the half-king was with the mission, expressed his surprise that he had not accompanied it to his quarters on the preceding day. Washington, in truth, had feared to trust the sachem within the reach of the politic Frenchman. Nothing would do now but Joncaire must have the sachems at head-quarters. Here his diplomacy was triumphant. He received them with open arms. He was enraptured to see them. His Indian brothers! How could they be so near without coming to visit him? He made them presents; but, above all, plied them so potently with liquor, that the poor half-king, Jeskakake, and White Thunder forgot all about their wrongs, their speeches, their speech-belts, and all the business they had come upon; paid no heed to the repeated cautions of their English friends, and were soon in a complete state of frantic extravagance or drunken oblivion.

The next day the half-king made his appearance at Washington's tent, perfectly sober, and very much crestfallen. He declared, however, that he still intended to make his speech to the French, and offered to rehearse it on the spot; but Washington advised him not to waste his ammunition on inferior game like Joncaire and his comrades, but to reserve it for the commandant. The sachem was not to be persuaded. Here, he said, was the place of the council fire, where they were accustomed to transact their business with the French; and as to Joncaire, he had all the management of French affairs with the Indians.

Washington was fain to attend the council fire and listen to the speech. It was much the same in purport as that which he had made to the French general, and he ended by offering to return the French speech-belt; but this Joncaire refused to receive, telling him to carry it to the commander at the fort.

All that day and the next was the party kept at Venango by stratagems of Joncaire and his emissaries to detain and seduce the sachems. It was not until 12 o'clock, on the 7th of December, that Washington was able to extricate them out of their clutches and commence his journey.

December 7, 1753

A French commissary by the name of La Force, and three soldiers, set off in company with him. La Force went as if on ordinary business, but he proved one of the most active, daring, and mischief-making of those anomalous agents employed by the French among the Indian tribes. It is probable that he was at the bottom of many of the perplexities experienced by Washington at Venango, and now travelled with him for the prosecution of his wiles. . . .

Fort at French Creek

After four days of weary travel through snow and rain, and mire and swamp, the party reached the fort. It was situated on a kind of island on the west fork of French Creek, about fifteen miles south of Lake Erie, and consisted of four houses, forming a hollow square, defended by bastions made of palisades twelve feet high, picketed, and pierced for cannon and small arms. Within the bastions were a guard-house, chapel, and other buildings, and outside were stables, a smith's forge, and log-houses covered with bark, for the soldiers. . . .

The reception of Washington at the fort was very different from the unceremonious one experienced at the outpost of Joncaire and his convivial messmates. When he presented himself at the gate, accompanied by his interpreter, Van Braam, he was met by the officer second in command and conducted in due military form to his superior; an ancient and silver-haired chevalier of the military order of St. Louis, courteous but ceremonious; mingling the polish of the French gentleman of the old school with the precision of the soldier.

Having announced his errand through his interpreter, Van Braam, Washington offered his credentials and the letter of Governor Dinwiddie, and was disposed to proceed at once to business with the prompt frankness of a young man unhackneyed in diplomacy. The chevalier, however, politely requested him to retain the documents in his possession until his predecessor, Captain Reparti, should arrive, who was hourly expected from the next post.

At two o'clock the captain arrived. The letter and its accompanying documents were then offered again, and received in due form, and the chevalier and his officers retired with them into a private apartment, where the captain, who understood a little English, officiated as translator. The translation being finished, Washington was requested to walk in and bring his translator, Van Braam, with him, to peruse and correct it, which he did. . . .

Transactions at the Fort

The two following days were consumed in councils of the chevalier and his officers over the letter, and the necessary reply. Washington occupied himself in the mean time in observing and taking notes of the plan, dimensions, and strength of the fort, and of every thing about it. He gave orders to his people, also, to take an exact account of the canoes in readiness, and others in the process of construction, for the conveyance of troops down the river in the ensuing spring.

Observing and taking notes

As the weather continued stormy, with much

snow, and the horses were daily losing strength, he sent them down, unladen, to Venango, to await his return by water. In the mean time, he discovered that busy intrigues were going on to induce the half-king and the other sachems to abandon him, and renounce all friendship with the English. Upon learning this, he urged the chiefs to deliver up their "speech-belts" immediately, as they had promised, thereby shaking off all dependence upon the French. They accordingly pressed for an audience that very evening. A private one was at length granted them by the commander, in presence of one or two of his officers. The half-king reported the result of it to Washington. The venerable but astute chevalier cautiously evaded the acceptance of the proffered wampum; made many professions of love and friendship, and said he wished to live in peace and trade amicably with the tribes of the Ohio, in proof of which he would send down some goods immediately for them to Logstown.

As Washington understood, privately, that an officer was to accompany the man employed to convey these goods, he suspected that the real design was to arrest and bring off all straggling English traders they might meet with. What strengthened this opinion was a frank avowal which had been made to him by the chevalier, that he had orders to capture every British subject who should attempt to trade upon the Ohio or its waters. . . .

All these circumstances showed him the mischief that was brewing in these parts, and the treachery and violence that pervaded the frontier, and made him the more solicitous to accomplish his mission successfully, and conduct his little band in safety out of a wily neighborhood.

Amidst treachery and violence, cautious and solicitous

On the evening of the 14th, the Chevalier de St. Pierre [*sic*, Piere] delivered to Washington his sealed reply* to the letter of Governor Dinwiddie. The purport of previous conversations with the chevalier, and the whole complexion of affairs on the frontier, left no doubt of the nature of that reply.

*See Letter: St. Piere to Gov. Dinwiddie, Appendix A-12

Difficulties and Delays in Parting

The business of his mission being accomplished, Washington prepared on the 15th to return by water to Venango; but a secret influence was at work which retarded every movement.

December 15, 1753

"The commandant," writes he, "ordered a plentiful store of liquor and provisions to be put on board our canoes, and appeared to be extremely complaisant, though he was exerting every artifice which he could invent to set our Indians at variance with us, to prevent their going until after our departure; presents, rewards, and every thing which could be suggested by him or his officers. I cannot say that ever in my life I suffered so much anxiety as I did in this affair. I saw that every stratagem which the most fruitful brain could invent was practised to win the half-king to their interests, and that leaving him there was giving them the opportunity they had aimed at. I went to the half-king, and pressed him in the strongest terms to go; he told me that the commandant would not discharge him until the morning. I then went to the commandant, and desired him to do their business, and complained to him of ill treatment; for, keeping them, as they were a part of my company, was detaining me. This he promised not to do, but to forward my journey as much as he could. He protested he did not keep them, but was ignorant of the cause of their stay; though I soon found it out. He had promised them a present of guns if they would wait until the morning. As I was very much pressed by the Indians to wait this day for them, I consented, on the promise that nothing should hinder them in the morning."

The next morning (16th) the French, in fulfilment of their promise, had to give the present of guns. They then endeavored to detain the sachems with liquor, which at any other time might have prevailed; but Washington reminded the half-king that his royal word was pledged to depart, and urged it upon him so closely that, exerting unwonted resolution and self-denial, he turned his back upon the liquor and embarked.

It was rough and laborious navigation. French Creek was swollen and turbulent, and full of floating ice. The frail canoes were several times in danger of being staved to pieces against rocks. Often the voyagers had to leap out and remain in the water half an hour at a time, drawing the canoes over shoals, and at one place to carry them a quarter of a mile across a neck of land, the river being completely dammed by ice. It was not until the 22nd that they reached Venango. . . .

Preserved through death defying journey

Return from Venango

On the 25th of December, Washington and his little party set out by land from Venango on their route homeward. They

December 25, 1753

had a long winter's journey before them, through a wilderness beset with dangers and difficulties. The packhorses, laden with tents, baggage, and provisions, were completely jaded; it was feared they would give out. Washington dismounted, gave up his saddle-horse to aid in transporting the baggage, and requested his companions to do the same. None but the drivers remained in the saddle. He now equipped himself in an Indian hunting-dress, and with Van Braam, Gist, and John Davidson, the Indian interpreter, proceeded on foot.

The cold increased. There was deep snow that froze as it fell. The horses grew less and less capable of travelling. For three days they toiled on slowly and wearily. Washington was impatient to accomplish his journey, and make his report to the governor; he determined, therefore, to hasten some distance in advance of the party, and then strike for the fork of the Ohio by the nearest course directly through the woods. He accordingly put the cavalcade under the command of Van Braam, and furnished him with money for expenses; then disencumbering himself of all superfluous clothing, buckling himself up in a watch-coat, strapping his pack on his shoulders, containing his papers and provisions, and taking gun in hand, he left the horses to flounder on, and struck manfully ahead, accompanied only by Mr. Gist, who had equipped himself in like manner. . . .

Struck manfully ahead on foot

At Murdering Town he found a party of Indians, who appeared to have known of his coming, and to have been waiting for him. One of them accosted Mr. Gist, and expressed great joy at seeing him. The wary woodsman regarded him narrowly, and thought he had seen him at Joncaire's. If so, he and his comrades were in the French interest, and their lying in wait boded no good. The Indian was very curious in his inquiries as to when they had left Venango; how they came to be travelling on foot; where they had left their horses, and when it was probable the latter would reach this place. All these questions increased the distrust of Gist, and rendered him extremely cautious in reply.

The route hence to Shannopins Town lay through a trackless wild, of which the travellers knew nothing; after some consultation, therefore, it was deemed expedient to engage one of the Indians as a guide. He entered upon his duties with alacrity, took Washington's pack upon his back, and led the way by what he said was the most direct course. After travelling briskly for eight or ten miles Washington became fatigued, and his feet were chafed; he thought, too, they were taking a direction too much to the northeast; he came to a halt, therefore, and determined to light a fire, make a shelter of the bark and branches of trees, and encamp there for the night. The Indian demurred; he offered, as Washington was fatigued, to carry his gun, but the latter was too wary to part with his weapon. The Indian now grew churlish. There were Ottawa Indians in the woods, he said, who might be attracted by their fire, and surprise and scalp them; he urged, therefore, that they should continue on: he would take them to his cabin, where they would be safe.

Mr. Gist's suspicions increased, but he said nothing. Washington's also were awakened. They proceeded some distance further: the guide paused and listened. He had heard, he said, the report of a gun toward the north; it must be from his cabin; he accordingly turned his steps in that direction.

Washington began to apprehend an ambuscade of savages. He knew the hostility of many of them to the English, and what a desirable trophy was the scalp of a white man. The Indian still kept on toward the north; he pretended to hear two whoops—they were from his cabin—it could not be far off.

They went on two miles further, when Washington signified his determination to encamp at the first water they should find. The guide said nothing but kept doggedly on. After a little while they arrived at an opening in the woods, and emerging from the deep shadows in which they had been travelling, found themselves in a clear meadow, rendered still more light by the glare of the snow upon the ground. Scarcely had they emerged when the Indian, who was about fifteen paces ahead, suddenly turned, leveled his gun, and fired. Washington was startled for an instant, but, feeling that he was not wounded, demanded quickly of Mr. Gist if he was shot. The latter answered in the negative. The Indian in the mean time had run forward, and screened himself behind a large white oak, where he was reloading his gun. They overtook, and seized him. Gist would have put him to death on the spot, but Washington humanely prevented him. They permitted him to finish the loading of his gun; but, after he had put in the ball, took the weapon from him, and let him see that he was under guard. Arriving at a small stream they ordered the Indian to make a fire, and took

Divine protection against Indian gun fire

Humane treatment of enemy

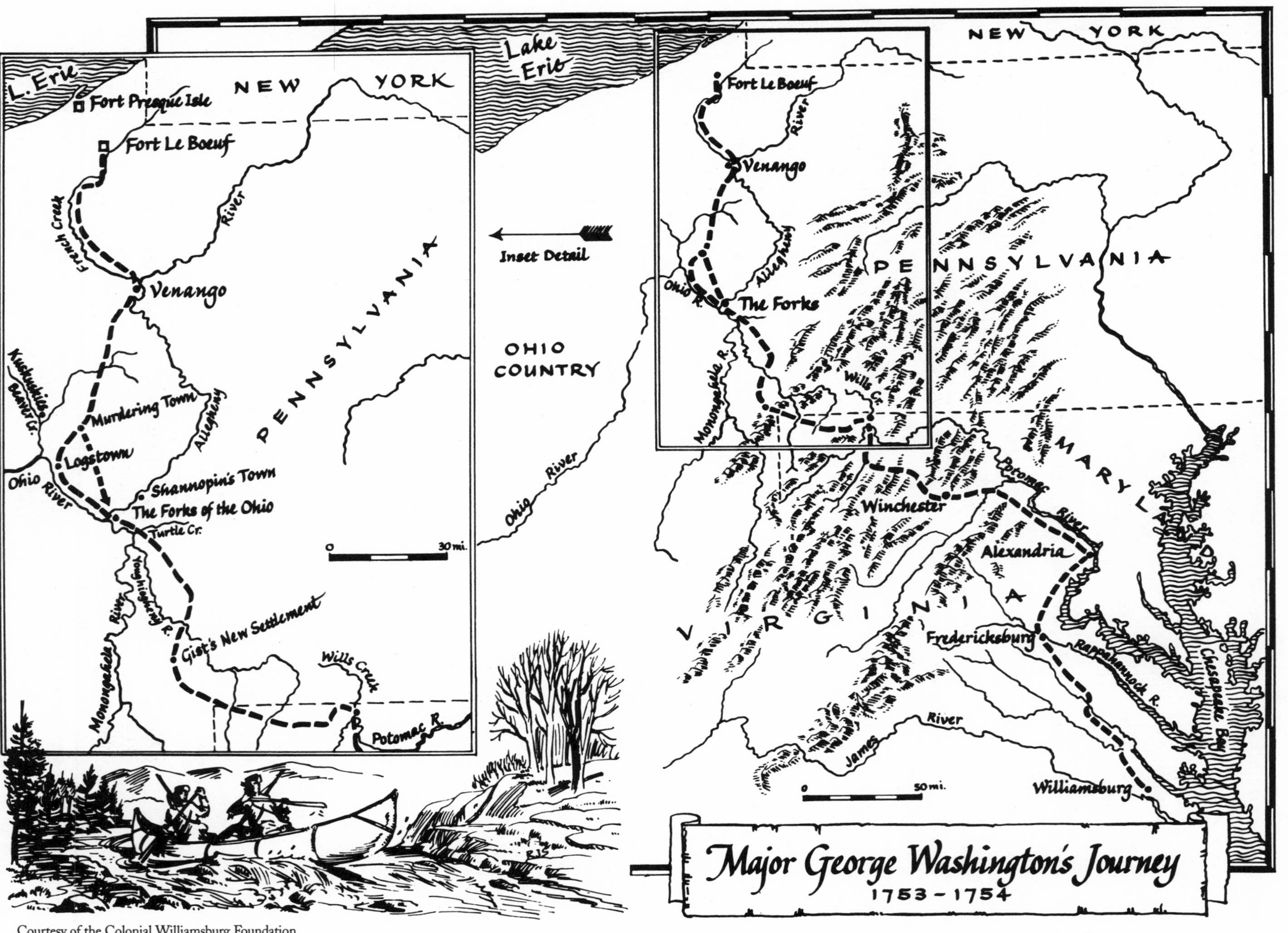

Courtesy of the Colonial Williamsburg Foundation

turns to watch over the guns. While he was thus occupied, Gist, a veteran woodsman, and accustomed to hold the life of an Indian rather cheap, was somewhat incommoded by the scruples of his youthful commander, which might enable the savage to carry out some scheme of treachery. He observed to Washington that, since he could not suffer the Indian to be killed, they must manage to get him out of the way, and then decamp with all speed, and travel all night to leave this perfidious neighborhood behind them; but first it was necessary to blind the guide as to their intentions. He accordingly addressed him in a friendly tone, and adverting to the late circumstances, pretended to suppose that he had lost his way, and fired his gun merely as a signal. The Indian, whether deceived or not, readily chimed in with the explanation. He said he now knew the way to his cabin, which was at no great distance. "Well then," replied Gist, "you can go home, and as we are tired we will remain here for the night, and follow your track at daylight. In the mean time here is a cake of bread for you, and you must give us some meat in the morning."

Whatever might have been the original designs of the savage, he was evidently glad to get off. Gist followed him cautiously for a distance, and listened until the sound of his footsteps died away; returning then to Washington, they proceeded about half a mile, made another fire, set their compass and fixed their course by the light of it, then leaving it burning, pushed forward, and travelled as fast as possible all night, so as to gain a fair start should any one pursue them at daylight. Continuing on the next day they never relaxed their speed until nightfall, when they arrived on the banks of the Allegany River, about two miles above Shannopins Town.

An Anxious Night

Washington had expected to find the river frozen completely over; it was so only for about fifty yards from either shore, while great quantities of broken ice were driving down the main channel. Trusting that he had out-travelled pursuit, he encamped on the border of the river; still it was an anxious night, and he was up at daybreak to devise some means of reaching the opposite bank. No other mode presented itself than by a raft, and to construct this they had but one poor hatchet. With this they set resolutely to work and labored all day, but the sun went down before their raft was finished. They launched it, however, and getting on board, endeavored to propel it across with setting poles. Before they were half way over the raft became jammed between cakes of ice, and they were in imminent peril. Washington planted his pole on the bottom of the stream, and leaned against it with all his might, to stay the raft until the ice should pass by. The rapid current forced the ice against the pole with such violence that he was jerked into the water, where it was at least ten feet deep, and only saved himself from being swept away and drowned by catching hold of one of the raft logs.

Saved from near drowning

It was now impossible with all their exertions to get to either shore; abandoning the raft therefore, they got upon an island, near which they were drifting. Here they passed the night exposed to intense cold, by which the hands and feet of Mr. Gist were frozen. In the morning they found the drift ice wedged so closely together, that they succeeded in getting from the island to the opposite side of the river; and before night were in comfortable quarters at the house of Frazier, the Indian trader, at the mouth of Turtle Creek on the Monongahela.

Here they learned from a war party of Indians that a band of Ottawas, a tribe in the interest of the French, had massacred a whole family of whites on the banks of the Great Kanawha River.

At Frazier's they were detained two or three days endeavoring to procure horses. In this interval Washington had again occasion to exercise Indian diplomacy. About three miles distant, at the mouth of the Youghiogeny River, dwelt a female sachem, Queen Aliquippa, as the English called her, whose sovereign dignity had been aggrieved that the party, on their way to Ohio, had passed near her royal wigwam without paying their respects to her.

Aware of the importance, at this critical juncture of securing the friendship of the Indians, Washington availed himself of the interruption of his journey, to pay a visit of ceremony to this native princess. Whatever anger she may have felt at past neglect, it was readily appeased by a present of his old watch-coat; and her good graces were completely secured by a bottle of rum, which, he intimates, appeared to be peculiarly acceptable to her majesty.

Leaving Frazier's on the 1st of January, they arrived on the 2d at the residence of Mr. Gist, on the Monongahela. Here they separated, and Washington having purchased a horse, continued his homeward course,

January 1–16, 1754

Benson J. Lossing, *Life of Washington,* Vol. I, 1856

WASHINGTON AND GIST VISIT QUEEN ALIQUIPPA

passing horses laden with materials and stores for the fort at the fork of the Ohio, and families going out to settle there.

Having crossed the Blue Ridge, and stopped one day at Belvoir to rest, he reached Williamsburg on the 16th of January, where he delivered to Governor Dinwiddie the letter of the French commandant, and made him a full report of the events of his mission.*

Test of Character

We have been minute in our account of this expedition, as it was an early test and development of the various talents and characteristics of Washington.

The prudence, sagacity, resolution, firmness, and self-devotion manifested by him throughout; his admirable tact and self-possession in treating with fickle savages and crafty white men; the soldier's eye with which he had noticed the commanding and defensible points of the country, and every thing that would bear upon military operations; and the hardihood with which he had acquitted himself during a wintry tramp through the wilderness, through constant storms of rain and snow; often sleeping on the ground without a tent in the open air, and in danger from treacherous foes,—all pointed him out, not merely to the governor, but to the public at large, as one eminently fitted, notwithstanding his youth, for important trusts involving civil as well as military duties.

Wilderness experience, foundation of future fortunes

It is an expedition that may be considered the foundation of his fortunes. From that moment he was the rising hope of Virginia.

*Facsimiles of four sample pages of the 1754 printed version of *George Washington's Journal to the Ohio,* and some of the related correspondence Verna Hall suggested for further study, are on Appendix pages A-10–12.

Trent's Mission to the Frontier

The reply of the Chevalier de St. Pierre [Piere] was such as might have been expected from that courteous, but wary commander. He should transmit, he said, the letter of Governor Dinwiddie to his general, the Marquis du Quesne, "to whom," observed he, "it better belongs than to me to set forth the evidence and reality of the rights of the king, my master, upon the land situated along the river Ohio, and to contest the pretensions of the king of Great Britain thereto. His answer shall be a law to me. . . . As to the summons you send me to retire, I do not think myself obliged to obey it. Whatever may be your instructions, I am here by virtue of the orders of my general; and I entreat you, sir, not to doubt one moment but that I am determined to conform myself to them with all the exactness and resolution which can be expected from the best officer, . . .

"I made it my particular care," adds he, "to receive Mr. Washington with a distinction suitable to your dignity, as well as his own quality and great merit. I flatter myself that he will do me this justice before you, sir, and that he will signify to you, in the manner I do myself, the profound respect with which I am, sir," &c. (*London Mag.* June, 1754.)

This soldierlike and punctilious letter of the chevalier was considered evasive, and only intended to gain time. The information given by Washington of what he had observed on the frontier, convinced Governor Dinwiddie and his council that the French were preparing to descend the Ohio in the spring, and take military possession of the country. Washington's journal was printed, and widely promulgated throughout the colonies and England, and awakened the nation to a sense of the impending danger, and the necessity of prompt measures to anticipate the French movements.

His journal alarms nation to imminent danger

Captain Trent was despatched to the frontier, commissioned to raise a company of one hundred men, march with all speed to the fork of the Ohio, and finish as soon as possible the fort commenced there by the Ohio Company. He was enjoined to act only on the defensive, but to capture or destroy whoever should oppose the construction of the works, or disturb their settlements. The choice of Captain Trent for this service, notwithstanding his late inefficient expedition, was probably owing to his being brother-in-law to George Croghan, who had grown to be quite a personage of consequence on the frontier, where he had an establishment or trading-house, and was supposed to have great influence among the western tribes, so as to be able at any time to persuade many of them to take up the hatchet.

Washington Recruits Troops

Washington was empowered to raise a company of like force at Alexandria; to procure and forward munitions and supplies for the projected fort at the fork, and ultimately to have command of both companies. When on the frontier he was to take counsel of George Croghan and Andrew Montour, the interpreter, in all matters relating to the Indians, they being esteemed perfect oracles in that department.

Governor Dinwiddie in the mean time called upon the governors of the provinces to make common cause against the foe; he endeavored, also, to effect alliances with the Indian tribes of the south, the Catawbas and Cherokees, by way of counter-balancing the Chippewas and Ottawas, who were devoted to the French.

Spirit of union among colonies wanting

The colonies, however, felt as yet too much like isolated territories; the spirit of union was wanting. Some pleaded a want of military funds; some questioned the justice of the cause; some declined taking any hostile step that might involve them in a war, unless they should have direct orders from the crown.

Doubts of the Burgesses

Dinwiddie convened the House of Burgesses to devise measures for the public security. Here his high idea of prerogative and gubernatorial dignity met with grievous countercheck from the dawning spirit of independence. High as were the powers vested in the colonial government of Virginia, of which, though but lieutenant-governor, he had the actual control; they were counterbalanced by the power inherent in the people, growing out of their situation and circumstances, and acting through their representatives.

There was no turbulent factious opposition to government in Virginia; no "fierce democracy," the rank growth of crowded cities, and a fermenting populace; but there was the independence of men, living apart in patriarchal style on their own rural domains; surrounded by their families, dependants and slaves, among whom their will was law,—and there was the individuality in character and action of men prone

A spirit of independence

to nurture peculiar notions and habits of thinking, in the thoughtful solitariness of country life.

When Dinwiddie propounded his scheme of operations on the Ohio, some of the burgesses had the hardihood to doubt the claims of the king to the disputed territory; a doubt which the governor reprobated as savoring strongly of a most disloyal French spirit; he fired, as he says, at the thought "that an English legislature should presume to doubt the right of his majesty to the interior parts of this continent, the back part of his dominions!"

Others demurred to any grant of means for military purposes which might be construed into an act of hostility. To meet this scruple, it was suggested that the grant might be made for the purpose of encouraging and protecting all settlers on the waters of the Mississippi. And under this specious plea, ten thousand pounds were grudgingly voted; but even this moderate sum was not put at the absolute disposition of the governor. A committee was appointed, with whom he was to confer as to its appropriation.

This precaution Dinwiddie considered an insulting invasion of the right he possessed as governor, to control the purse as well as the sword; and he complained bitterly of the Assembly, as deeply tinctured with a republican way of thinking, and disposed to encroach on the prerogative of the crown, "which he feared would render them more and more difficult to be *brought to order.*"

Ways and means being provided, Governor Dinwiddie augmented the number of troops to be enlisted to three hundred, divided into six companies. The command of the whole, as before, was offered to Washington; but he shrank from it, as a charge too great for his youth and inexperience. It was given, therefore, to Colonel Joshua Fry, an English gentleman of worth and education, and Washington was made second in command, with the rank of lieutenant-colonel.

Recruiting Expedients

The recruiting, at first, went on slowly. Those who offered to enlist, says Washington, were for the most part loose idle persons, without house or home, some without shoes or stockings, some shirtless, and many without coat or waistcoat.

He was young in the recruiting service, or he would have known that such is generally the stuff of which armies are made. . . .

Governor Dinwiddie became sensible of this, and resorted to an expedient rising out of the natural resource of the country, which has since been frequently adopted, and always with efficacy. He proclaimed a bounty of two hundred thousand acres of land on the Ohio River, to be divided among the officers and soldiers who should engage in this expedition; one thousand to be laid off contiguous to the fort at the fork, for the use of the garrison. This was a tempting bait to the sons of farmers, who readily enlisted in the hope of having, at the end of a short campaign, a snug farm of their own in this land of promise.

It was a more difficult matter to get officers than soldiers. Very few of those appointed made their appearance; one of the captains had been promoted; two declined; Washington found himself left, almost alone, to manage a number of self-willed, undisciplined recruits. Happily he had with him, in the rank of lieutenant, that soldier of fortune, Jacob Van Braam, his old "master of fence," and travelling interpreter.

Alone with unmanageable recruits

In his emergency he forthwith nominated him captain, and wrote to the governor to confirm the appointment, representing him as the oldest lieutenant, and an experienced officer.

On the 2d of April, Washington set off from Alexandria for the new fort, at the fork of the Ohio. He had but two companies with him, amounting to about one hundred and fifty men; the remainder of the regiment was to follow under Colonel Fry with the artillery, which was to be conveyed up the Potomac. While on the march he was joined by a detachment under Captain Adam Stephens [*sic*, Stephen], an officer destined to serve with him at distant periods of his military career.

April 2, 1754

At Winchester he found it impossible to obtain conveyances by gentle means, and was obliged reluctantly to avail himself of the militia law of Virginia, and impress horses and waggons for service; giving the owners orders on government for their appraised value. Even then, out of a great number impressed, he obtained but ten, after waiting a week; these, too, were grudgingly furnished by farmers with their worst horses, so that in steep and difficult passes they were incompetent to the draught, and the soldiers had continually to put their shoulders to the wheels.

Catastrophe at the Fort

Thus slenderly fitted out, Washington and his little force made their way toilfully across the mountains, having to prepare the roads as they went for the transportation of the cannon, which were to follow on with the other division under Colonel Fry. They cheered themselves with the thoughts that this hard work would cease when they should arrive at the company's trading-post and storehouse at Wills' Creek, where Captain Trent was to have packhorses in readiness, with which they might make the rest of the way by light stages. Before arriving there, they were startled by a rumor that Trent and all his men had been captured by the French. With regard to Trent, the news soon proved to be false, for they found him at Wills' Creek on the 20th of April. With regard to his men there was still an uncertainty. He had recently left them at the fork of the Ohio, busily at work on the fort, under the command of his lieutenant, Frazier, late Indian trader and gunsmith, but now a provincial officer. If the men had been captured, it must have been since the captain's departure. Washington was eager to press forward and ascertain the truth, but it was impossible. Trent, inefficient as usual, had failed to provide packhorses. It was necessary to send to Winchester, forty miles distant, for baggage waggons, and await their arrival. All uncertainty as to the fate of the men, however, was brought to a close by their arrival, on the 25th, conducted by an ensign, and bringing with them their working implements. The French might well boast that they had again been too quick for the English. Captain Contrecœur, an alert officer, had embarked about a thousand men with field-pieces, in a fleet of sixty batteaux and three hundred canoes, dropped down the river from Venango, and suddenly made his appearance before the fort, on which the men were working, and which was not half completed. Landing, drawing up his men, and planting his artillery, he summoned the fort to surrender, allowing one hour for a written reply.

April 20, 1754

What was to be done? The whole garrison did not exceed fifty men. Captain Trent was absent at Wills' Creek; Frazier, his lieutenant, was at his own residence at Turtle Creek, ten miles distant. There was no officer to reply but a young ensign of the name of Ward. In his perplexity, he turned for counsel to Tanacharisson, the half-king who was present in the fort. The chief advised the ensign to plead insufficiency of rank and powers, and crave delay until the arrival of his superior officer. The ensign repaired to the French camp to offer his excuse in person, and was accompanied by the half-king. They were courteously received, but Contrecœur was inflexible. There must be instant surrender, or he would take forcible possession. All that the ensign could obtain was permission to depart with his men, taking with them their working tools. The capitulation ended, Contrecœur, with true French gayety, invited the ensign to sup with him, treated him with the utmost politeness, and wished him a pleasant journey, as he set off the next morning with his men laden with their working tools.

Such was the ensign's story. He was accompanied by two Indian warriors, sent by the half-king to ascertain where the detachment was, what was its strength, and when it might be expected at the Ohio. They bore a speech from that sachem to Washington, and another, with a belt of wampum for the Governor of Virginia. In these he plighted his steadfast faith to the English, and claimed assistance from his brothers of Virginia and Pennsylvania.

One of these warriors Washington forwarded on with the speech and wampum to Governor Dinwiddie. The other he prevailed on to return to the half-king, bearing a speech from him addressed to the "sachems, warriors of the Six United Nations, Shannoahs and Delawares, our friends and brethren." In this he informed them that he was on the advance with a part of the army, to clear the road for a greater force coming with guns, ammunition, and provisions; and he invited the half-king and another sachem to meet him on the road as soon as possible to hold a council.

Increasing Dangers

In fact, his situation was arduous in the extreme. Regarding the conduct of the French in the recent occurrence an overt act of war, he found himself thrown with a handful of raw recruits far on a hostile frontier, in the midst of a wilderness, with an enemy at hand greatly superior in number and discipline; provided with artillery, and all the munitions of war, and within reach of constant supplies and reinforcements. Beside the French that had come from Venango, he had received credible accounts of another party ascending the Ohio; and of six hundred Chippewas and Ottawas marching down Scioto Creek to join the hostile camp. Still, notwithstanding the accumulating danger, it would not do to fall back, nor show signs of apprehension. His Indian allies in such case might desert him. The soldiery, too, might grow restless and dissatisfied. He was already annoyed by Captain Trent's men, who, having enlisted as volunteers, considered themselves exempt from the rigor of martial law; and by their example of loose and refractory conduct, threatened to destroy the subordination of his own troops.

In this dilemma he called a council of war, in which it was determined to proceed to the Ohio Company store-houses, at the mouth of Redstone Creek; fortify themselves there, and wait for reinforcements. Here they might keep up a vigilant watch upon the enemy, and get notice of any hostile movement in time for defence, or retreat; and should they be reinforced sufficiently to enable them to attack the fort, they could easily drop down the river with their artillery.

With these alternatives in view, Washington detached sixty men in advance to make a road; and at the same time wrote to Governor Dinwiddie for mortars and grenadoes, and cannon of heavy metal.

Aware that the Assembly of Pennsylvania was in session, and that the Maryland Assembly would also meet in the course of a few days, he wrote directly to the governors of those provinces, acquainting them with the hostile acts of the French, and with his perilous situation; and endeavoring to rouse them to co-operation in the common cause. We will here note in advance that his letter was laid before the Legislature of Pennsylvania, and a bill was about to be passed making appropriations for the service of the king; but it fell through, in consequence of a disagreement between the Assembly and the governor as to the mode in which the money should be raised; and so no assistance was furnished to Washington from that quarter. The youthful commander had here a foretaste, in these his incipient campaigns, of the perils and perplexities which awaited him from enemies in the field, and lax friends in legislative councils in the grander operations of his future years. Before setting off for Redstone Creek, he discharged Trent's refractory men from his detachment, ordering them to await Colonel Fry's commands; they, however, in the true spirit of volunteers from the backwoods, dispersed to their several homes. . . .

A foretaste of inaction by legislative councils

March to the Little Meadows

On the 29th of April, Washington set out for Wills' Creek, at the head of one hundred and sixty men. He soon overtook those sent in advance to work the road; they had made but little progress. It was a difficult task to break a road through the wilderness sufficient for the artillery coming on with Colonel Fry's division. All hands were now set to work, but with all their labor they could not accomplish more than four miles a day. They were toiling through Savage Mountain and that dreary forest region beyond it, since bearing the sinister name of "The Shades of Death." On the 9th of May they were not further than twenty miles from Wills' Creek, at a place called the Little Meadows.

April 29, 1754

Every day came gloomy accounts from the Ohio; brought chiefly by traders, who, with packhorses bearing their effects, were retreating to the more settled parts of the country. Some exaggerated the number of the French, as if strongly reinforced. All represented them as diligently at work constructing a fort. By their account, Washington perceived the French had chosen the very place which he had noted in his journal as best fitted for the purpose.

After infinite toil through swamps and forests, and over rugged mountains, the detachment arrived at the Youghiogeny River, where they were detained some days constructing a bridge to cross it.

This gave Washington leisure to correspond with Governor Dinwiddie, concerning matters which had deeply annoyed him. By an ill-judged economy of the Virginia government at this critical juncture, its provincial officers received less pay than that allowed in the regular army. It is true the regular officers were obliged to furnish their own table, but their superior pay enabled them to do it luxuriously; whereas the provincials were obliged to do hard duty on salt provisions and water. The provincial officers resented this inferiority of pay as an indignity, and declared that nothing prevented them from throwing up their commissions but unwillingness to recede before approaching danger.

Washington shared deeply this feeling. "Let him serve voluntarily, and he would with the greatest pleasure in life devote his services to the expedition—but to be slaving through woods, rocks, and mountains, for the shadow of pay—writes he, 'I would rather toil like a day laborer for a maintenance, if reduced to the necessity, than serve on such ignoble terms'." Parity of pay was indispensable to the dignity of the service.

Registers annoyance at the injustice of Virginian government

Other instances of false economy were pointed out by him, forming so many drags upon the expedition, that he quite despaired of success. "Be the consequence what it will, however," adds he, "I am determined not to leave the regiment, but to be among the last men that leave the Ohio; even if I serve as a private volunteer, which I greatly prefer to the establishment we are upon. . . . I have a constitution hardy enough to encounter and undergo the most severe trials, and I flatter myself resolution to face what any man dares, as shall be proved when it comes to the test."

Avows loyalty to cause and country

Washington's Motives of Action

And in a letter to his friend Colonel Fairfax—"For my own part," writes he, "it is a matter almost indifferent whether I serve for full pay or as a generous volunteer; indeed, did my circumstances correspond with my inclinations, I should not hesitate a moment to prefer the latter; *for the motives that have led me here are pure and noble. I had no view of acquisition but that of honor, by serving faithfully my king and country."*

Such were the noble impulses of Washington at the age of twenty-two, and such continued to actuate him throughout life. We have put the latter part of the quotation in italics, as applicable to the motives which in after life carried him into the Revolution.

Age twenty-two

While the bridge over the Youghiogeny was in the course of construction, the Indians assured Washington he would never be able to open a waggon-road across the mountains to Redstone Creek; he embarked therefore in a canoe with a lieutenant, three soldiers, and an Indian guide, to try whether it was possible to descend the river. They had not descended above ten miles before the Indian refused to go further. Washington soon ascertained the reason. "Indians," said he, "expect presents—nothing can be done without them. The French take this method. If you want one or more to conduct a party, to discover the country, to hunt, or for any particular purpose, they must be bought; their friendship is not so warm as to prompt them to these services gratis." The Indian guide, in the present instance, was propitiated by the promise of one of Washington's ruffled shirts and a watch-coat.

The river was bordered by mountains and obstructed by rocks and rapids. Indians might thread such a labyrinth in their light canoes, but it would never admit the transportation of troops and military stores. Washington kept on for thirty miles, until he came to a place where the river fell nearly forty feet in the space of fifty yards. There he ceased to explore, and returned to camp, resolving to continue forward by land.

Lurking Foes

On the 23d Indian scouts brought word that the French were not above eight hundred strong, and that about half their number had been detached at night on a secret expedition. Close upon this report came a message from the half-king, addressed "to the first of his majesty's officers whom it may concern."

May 23, 1754

"It is reported," said he, "that the French army is coming to meet Major Washington. Be on your guard against them, my brethren, for they intend to strike the first English they shall see. They have been on their march two days. I know not their number. The half-king and the rest of the chiefs will be with you in five days to hold a council."

In the evening Washington was told that the French were crossing the ford of the Youghiogeny about eighteen miles distant. He now hastened to take a position in a place called the Great Meadows, where he caused the bushes to be cleared away, made an intrenchment, and prepared what he termed "a charming field for an encounter." A party of scouts were mounted on waggon horses, and sent out to reconnoitre. They returned without having seen an enemy. A sensitiveness prevailed in the camp. They were surrounded by forests, threatened by unseen foes, and hourly in danger of surprise. There was an alarm about two o'clock in the night. The sentries fired upon what they took to be prowling foes. The troops sprang to arms, and remained on the alert until daybreak. Not an enemy to be seen. The roll was called. Six men were missing, who had deserted.

On the 25th Mr. Gist arrived from his place, about fifteen miles distant. La Force had been there at noon on the previous day, with a detachment of fifty men, and Gist had since come upon their track within five miles of the camp. Washington considered La Force a bold, enterprising man, subtle and dangerous; one to be particularly guarded against. He detached seventy-five men in pursuit of him and his prowling band.

About nine o'clock at night came an Indian messenger from the half-king, who was encamped with several of his people about six miles off. The chief had seen tracks of two Frenchmen, and was convinced their whole body must be in ambush near by.

Washington considered this the force which had been hovering about him for several days, and determined to forestall their hostile designs. Leaving a guard with the baggage and ammunition, he set out before ten o'clock, with forty men, to join his Indian ally. They groped their way in single file, by footpaths through the woods, in a heavy rain and murky darkness, tripping occasionally and stumbling over each other, sometimes losing the track for fifteen or twenty minutes, so that it was near sunrise when they reached the camp of the half-king.

That chieftain received the youthful commander with great demonstrations of friendship, and engaged to go hand in hand with him against the lurking enemy. He set out accordingly, accompanied by a few of his warriors and his associate sachem Scarooyadi, or Monacatoocha, and conducted Washington to the tracks which he had discovered. Upon these he put two of his Indians. They followed them up like hounds, and brought back word that they had traced them to a low bottom, surrounded by rocks and trees, where the French were encamped, having built a few cabins for shelter from the rain.

Skirmish with Jumonville

A plan was now concerted to come upon them by surprise: Washington with his men on the right; the half-king with his warriors on the left; all as silently as possible. Washington was the first upon the ground. As he advanced from among the rocks and trees at the head of his men, the French caught sight of him and ran to their arms. A sharp firing instantly took place, and was kept up on both sides for about fifteen minute. Washington and his party were most exposed, and received all the enemy's fire. The balls whistled around him; one man was killed close by him, and three others wounded. The French at length having lost several of their number, gave way and ran. They were soon overtaken; twenty-one were captured, and but one escaped, a Canadian, who carried the tidings of the affair to the fort on the Ohio. The Indians would have massacred the prisoners had not Washington prevented them. Ten of the French had fallen in the skirmish, and one been wounded. Washington's loss was the one killed and three wounded which we have mentioned. He had been in the hottest fire, and having for the first time heard balls whistle about him, considered his escape miraculous. Jumonville, the French leader, had been shot through the head at the first fire. He was a young officer of merit, and his fate was made the subject of lamentation in prose and verse—chiefly through political motives.

Intervenes in behalf of prisoners

Of the twenty-one prisoners, the two most important were an officer of some consequence named Drouillon, and the subtle and redoubtable La Force. As Washington considered the latter an arch mischief-maker, he was rejoiced to have him in his power. La Force and his companion would fain have assumed the sacred character of ambassadors, pretending they were coming with a summons to him to depart from the territories belonging to the crown of France.

Unluckily for their pretensions, a letter of instructions, found on Jumonville, betrayed their real errand, which was to inform themselves of the roads, rivers, and other features of the country as far as the Potomac; to send back from time to time, by fleet messengers, all the information they could collect, and to give word of the day on which they intended to serve the summons. Their conduct had been conformable. Instead of coming in a direct and open manner to his encampment, when they had ascertained where it was, and delivering their summons, as they would have done had their designs been frank and loyal, they had moved back two miles, to one of the most secret retirements, better for a deserter than an ambassador to encamp in, and staid there within five miles of his camp, sending spies to reconnoitre it, and despatching messengers to Contrecœur to inform him of its position and numerical strength, to the end, no doubt, that he might send a sufficient detachment to enforce the summons as soon as it should be given. In fact, the footprints which had first led to the discovery of the French lurking-place, were those of two "runners," or swift messengers, sent by Jumonville to the fort on the Ohio.

It would seem that La Force, after all, was but an instrument in the hands of his commanding officers, and not in their full confidence; for when the commission and instructions found on Jumonville were read before him, he professed not to have seen them before, and acknowledged, with somewhat of an air of ingenuousness, that he believed they had a hostile tendency.

Treatment of Prisoners

Upon the whole, it was the opinion of Washington and his officers that the summons, on which so much stress was laid, was a mere specious pretext to mask their real designs, and to be used as occasion might require. "That they were spies rather than any thing else," and were to be treated as prisoners of war.

The half-king joined heartily in this opinion; indeed had the fate of the prisoners been in his hands, neither diplomacy nor any thing else would have been of avail. "They came with hostile intentions," he said; "they had bad hearts, and if his English brothers were so foolish as to let them go, he would never aid in taking another Frenchman."

The prisoners were accordingly conducted to the camp at the Great Meadows, and sent on the following day (29th), under a strong escort, to Governor Dinwiddie, then at Winchester. Washington had treated them with great courtesy; had furnished Drouillon and La Force with clothing from his own scanty stock, and, at their request, given them letters to the governor, bespeaking for them "the respect and favor due to their character and personal merit."

May 29, 1754

A sense of duty, however, obliged him, in his general despatch, to put the governor on his guard against La Force. "I really think, if released, he would do more to our disservice than fifty other men, as he is a person whose active spirit leads him into all parties, and has brought him acquainted with all parts of the country. Add to this a perfect knowledge of the Indian tongue, and great influence with the Indians."

After the departure of the prisoners, he wrote again respecting them: "I have still stronger presumption, indeed almost confirmation, that they were sent as spies, and were ordered to wait near us till they were fully informed of our intentions, situation, and strength, and were to have acquainted their commander therewith, and to have been lurking here for reinforcements before they served the summons, if served at all.

"I doubt not but they will endeavor to amuse you with many smooth stories, as they did me; but they were confuted in them all, and, by circumstances too plain to be denied, almost made ashamed of their assertions.

Wisdom to confute enemy's smooth stories

"I have heard since they went away, they should say they called on us not to fire; but that I know to be false, for I was the first man that approached them, and the first whom they saw, and immediately they ran to their arms, and fired briskly till they were defeated. . . .

"I fancy they will have the assurance of asking the privileges due to an embassy, when in strict justice they ought to be hanged as spies of a the worst sort."

The situation of Washington was now extremely perilous. Contrecœur, it was said, had nearly a thousand men with him at the fort, beside Indian allies; and reinforcements were on the way to join him. The messengers sent by Jumonville, previous to the late affair, must have apprised him of the weakness of the encampment on the Great Meadows. Washington hastened to strengthen it. He wrote by express also to Colonel Fry, who lay ill at Wills' Creek, urging instant reinforcements; but declaring his resolution to "fight with very unequal numbers rather than give up one inch of what he had gained."

Fighting with unequal numbers

The half-king was full of fight. He sent the scalps of the Frenchmen slain in the late skirmish, accompanied by black wampum and hatchets, to all his allies, summoning them to take up arms and join him at Redstone Creek, "for their brothers the English had now begun in earnest." It is said he would even have sent the scalps of the prisoners had not Washington interfered. He went off for his home, promising to send down the river for all the Mingoes and Shawnees, and to be back at the camp on the 30th, with thirty or forty warriors, accompanied by their wives and children. To assist him in the transportation of his people and their effects thirty men were detached, and twenty horses.

Prevents the scalping of prisoners

Military Excitement

"I shall expect every hour to be attacked," writes Washington to Governor Dinwiddie, on the 29th, "and by unequal numbers, which I must withstand, if there are five to one, for I fear the consequence will be that we shall lose the Indians if we suffer ourselves to be driven back. Your honor may depend I will not be surprised, let them come at what hour they will, and this is as much as I can promise; but my best endeavors shall not be wanting to effect more. I doubt not if you hear I am beaten, but you will hear at the same time that we have done our duty in fighting as long as there is a shadow of hope."

Duty above all else

The fact is, that Washington was in a high state of military excitement. He was a young soldier; had been for the first time in action, and been successful. The letters we have already quoted show, in some degree, the fervor of his mind, and his readiness to brave the worst; but a short letter, written to one of his brothers, on the 31st, lays open the recesses of his heart.

"We expect every hour to be attacked by superior force; but if they forbear but one day longer we shall be prepared for them. . . . We have already got intrenchments, and are about a palisade, which, I hope, will be finished to-day. The Mingoes have struck the French, and, I hope, will give a good blow before they have done. I expect forty odd of them here to-night, which, with our fort, and some reinforcements from Colonel Fry, will enable us to exert our noble courage with spirit."

Alluding in a postscript to the late affair, he adds: "I fortunately escaped without any wound; for the right wing, where I stood, was exposed to, and received, all the enemy's fire: and it was the part where the man was killed and the rest wounded. *I heard the bullets whistle, and, believe me, there is something charming in the sound.*"

Escaped without any wound

Scarcity in the Camp

Scarcity began to prevail in the camp. Contracts had been made with George Croghan for flour, of which he had large quantities at his frontier establishment; for he was now trading with the army as well as with the Indians. None, however, made its appearance. There was mismanagement in the commissariat. At one time the troops were six days without flour; and even then had only a casual supply from an Ohio trader. In this time of scarcity the half-king, his fellow sachem, Scarooyadi, and thirty or forty warriors, arrived, bringing with them their wives and children—so many more hungry mouths to be supplied. Washington wrote urgently to Croghan to send forward all the flour he could furnish.

Death of Colonel Fry

News came of the death of Colonel Fry at Wills' Creek, and that he was to be succeeded in the command of the expedition by Colonel Innes of North Carolina, who was actually at Winchester with three hundred and fifty North Carolina troops. Washington, who felt the increasing responsibilities and difficulties of his situation, rejoiced at the prospect of being under the command of an experienced officer, who had served in company with his brother Lawrence at the siege of Carthagena. The colonel, however, never came to the camp, nor did the north Carolina troops render any service in the campaign—the fortunes of which might otherwise have been very different.

By the death of Fry, the command of a regiment devolved on Washington. Finding a blank major's commission among Fry's papers, he gave it to Captain Adam Stephens, who had conducted himself with spirit. As there would necessarily be other changes, he wrote to Governor Dinwiddie in behalf of Jacob Van Braam. "He has acted as captain ever since we left Alexandria. He is an experienced officer, and worthy of the command he has enjoyed."

The palisaded fort was now completed, and was named Fort Necessity, from the pinching famine that had prevailed during its construction. The scanty force in camp was augmented to three hundred, by the arrival from Wills' Creek of the men who had been under Colonel Fry. With them came the surgeon of the regiment, Dr. James Craik, a Scotchman by birth, and one destined to become a faithful and confidential friend of Washington for the remainder of his life.

A letter from Governor Dinwiddie announced, however, that Captain Mackay would soon arrive with an independent company, of one hundred men, from South Carolina.

The title of independent company had a sound ominous of trouble. Troops of the kind raised in the colonies, under direction of the governors, were paid by the crown, and the officers had king's commissions; such, doubtless, had Captian Mackay. "I should have been particularly obliged," writes Washington to Governor Dinwiddie, "if you had declared whether he was under my command, or independent of it. I hope he will have more sense than to insist upon any unreasonable distinction, because he and his officers have commissions from his majesty. Let him consider, though we are greatly inferior in respect to advantages of profit, yet we have the same spirit to serve our gracious king as they have, and are as ready and willing to sacrifice our lives for our country's good. And here, once more, and for the last time, I must say, that it will be a circumstance which will act upon some officers of this regiment, above all measure, to be obliged to serve upon such different terms, when their lives, their fortunes, and their operations are equally, and, I dare say, as effectually exposed as those of others, who are happy enough to have the king's commission."

Indian Ceremonials

On the 9th arrived Washington's early instructor in military tactics, Adjutant Muse, recently appointed a major in the regiment. He was accompanied by Mountour the Indian interpreter, now a provincial captain, and brought with him nine

Washington and the American Republic, Vol. I, by Benson J. Lossing, 1870

WASHINGTON READING PRAYERS IN HIS CAMP (age 22, 1754)

swivels, and a small supply of powder and ball. Fifty or sixty horses forthwith sent to Wills' Creek, to bring on further supplies, and Mr. Gist was urged to hasten forward the artillery.

Major Muse with likewise the bearer of a belt of wampun and a speech, from governor Dinwiddie, to the half-king; with medals for the chiefs, and good for presents among the friendly Indians, a measure which had been suggested by Washington. They were distributed with that grand ceremonial so dear to the red man. The chiefs assembled, painted and decorated in all their savage finery; Washington wore a medal sent to him by the governor for such occasions. The wampum and speech having been delivered, he advanced, and with all due solemnity, decorated the chiefs and warriors with the medals, which they were to wear in remembrance of their father the King of England.

Among the warriors thus decorated was a son of Queen Aliquippa, the savage princess whose good graces Washington had secured in the preceding year, by the present of an old watch-coat, and whose friendship was important, her town being at no great distance from the French fort. She had requested that her son might be admitted into the war councils of the camp, and receive an English name. The name of Fairfax was accordingly given to him, in the customary Indian form; the half-king being desirous of like distinction, received the name of Dinwiddie. The sachems returned the compliment in kind, by giving Washington the name of Connotaucarius; the meaning of which is not explained.

Public Prayers in Camp

June 10, 1754

William Fairfax, Washington's paternal adviser, had recently counselled him by letter, to have public prayers in his camp; especially when there were Indian families there; this was accordingly done at the encampment in the Great Meadows, and it certainly was not one of the least striking pictures presented in this wild campaign—the youthful commander, presiding with calm seriousness over a motley assemblage of half-equipped soldiery, leathern-clad hunters and woodsmen, and painted savages with their wives and children, and uniting them all in solemn devotion by his own example and demeanor.

On the 10th there was agitation in the camp. Scouts hurried in with word, as Washington understood them, that a party of ninety Frenchmen were approaching. He instantly ordered out a hundred and fifty of his best men; put himself at their head, and leaving Major Muse with the rest, to man the fort and mount the swivels, sallied forth "in the full hope," as he afterwards wrote to Governor Dinwiddie, "of procuring him another present of French prisoners."

Quick and bold in action

It was another effervescence of his youthful military ardor, and doomed to disappointment. The report of the scouts had been either exaggerated or misunderstood. The ninety Frenchmen in military array dwindled down into nine French deserters.

According to their account, the fort at the fork was completed, and named Duquesne, in honor of the Governor of Canada. It was proof against all attack, excepting with bombs on the land side. The garrison did not exceed five hundred; but two hundred more were hourly expected, and nine hundred in the course of a fortnight.

Washington's suspicions with respect to La Force's party were justified by the report of these deserters; they had been sent out as spies, and were to show the summons if discovered or overpowered. The French commander, they added, had been blamed for sending out so small a party.

On the same day Captain Mackay arrived, with his independent company of South Carolinians. The cross-purposes which Washington had apprehended, soon manifested themselves. The captain was civil and well disposed, but full of formalities and points of etiquette. Holding a commission direct from the king, he could not bring himself to acknowledge a provincial officer as his superior. He encamped separately, kept separate guards, would not agree that Washington should assign any rallying place for his men in case of alarm, and objected to receive from him the parole and countersign, though necessary for their common safety.

Washington conducted himself with circumspection, avoiding every thing that might call up a question of command, and reasoning calmly whenever such question occurred; but he urged the governor by letter, to prescribe their relative rank and authority. "He thinks you have not a power to give commissions that will command him. If so, I can very confidently say that his absence would tend to the public advantage."

On the 11th of June, Washington resumed the laborious march for Redstone Creek. As Captain Mackay could not oblige his men to work on the road, unless they were allowed a shilling sterling a day; and as Washington did not choose to pay this, nor to suffer them to march at their ease while his own faithful soldiers were laboriously employed; he left the captain and his independent company as a guard at Fort Necessity, and undertook to complete the military road with his own men.

June 11, 1754

Accordingly, he and his Virginia troops toiled forward through the narrow defiles of the mountains, working on the road as they went. Scouts were sent out in all directions, to prevent surprise. While on the march he was continually beset by sachems, with their tedious ceremonials and speeches, all to very little purpose. Some of these chiefs were secretly in the French interest; few rendered any real assistance, and all expected presents.

At Gist's establishment, about thirteen miles from Fort Necessity, Washington received certain intelligence that ample reinforcements had arrived at Fort Duquesne, and a large force would instantly be detached against him. Coming to a halt, he began to throw up intrenchments, calling in two foraging parties, and sending word to Captain Mackay to join him with all speed. The captain and his company arrived in the evening; the foraging parties the next morning. A council of war was held, in which the idea of awaiting the enemy at this place was unanimously abandoned.

A rapid and toilsome retreat ensued. There was a deficiency of horses. Washington gave up his own to aid in transporting the military munitions, leaving his baggage to be brought on by soldiers, whom he paid liberally. The other officers followed his example. The weather was sultry; the roads were rough; provisions were scanty, and the men dispirited by hunger. The Virginian soldiers took turns to drag the swivels, but felt almost insulted by the conduct of the South Carolinians, who, piquing themselves upon their assumed privileges as "king's soldiers," sauntered along at their ease; refusing to act as pioneers, or participate in the extra labors incident to a hurried retreat.

Other officers followed his example

On the 1st of July they reached the Great Meadows. Here the Virginians, exhausted by fatigue, hunger, and vexation, declared they would carry the baggage and drag the swivels no further. Contrary to his original intentions, therefore, Washington determined to halt here for the present, and fortify; sending off expresses, to hasten supplies and reinforcements from Wills' Creek, where he had reason to believe that two independent companies, from New York, were by this time arrived.

The retreat to the Great Meadows had not been in the least too precipitate. Captain de Villiers, a brother-in-law of Jumonville, had actually sallied forth from Fort Duquesne at the head of upwards of five hundred French, and several hundred Indians, eager to avenge the death of his relative. Arriving about dawn of day, at Gist's plantation, he surrounded the works which Washington had hastily thrown up there, and fired into them. Finding them deserted, he concluded that those of whom he came in search had made good their retreat to the settlements, and it was too late to pursue them. He was on the point of returning to Fort Duquesne, when a deserter arrived, who gave word that Washington had come to a halt in the Great Meadows, where his troops were in a starving condition; for his own part, he added, hearing that the French were coming, he had deserted to them to escape starvation.

Betrayal by a deserter

De Villiers ordered the fellow into confinement; to be rewarded if his words proved true, otherwise to be hanged. He then pushed forward for the Great Meadows.

In the mean time Washington had exerted himself to enlarge and strengthen Fort Necessity, nothing of which had been done by Captain Mackay and his men, while encamped there. The fort was about a hundred feet square, protected by trenches and palisades. It stood on the margin of a small stream, nearly in the centre of the Great Meadows, which is a grassy plain, perfectly level, surrounded by wooded hills of a moderate height, and at that place about two hundred and fifty yards wide. Washington asked no assistance from the South Carolina troops, but set to work with his Virginians, animating them by word and example; sharing in the labor of felling trees, hewing off the branches, and rolling up the trunks to form a breastwork.

Animated his men by word and example

Desertion of the Indian Allies

At this critical juncture he was deserted by his Indian allies. They were disheartened at the scanty preparations for defence against a superior force, and offended at being subjected to military command. The half-king thought he had not been sufficiently consulted, and that his advice had not been sufficiently followed; such, at least, were some of the reasons which he subsequently gave for abandoning the youthful commander on the approach of danger. The true reason was, a desire to put his wife and children in a place of safety. Most of the warriors followed his example; very few, and those probably who had no families at risk, remained in the camp.

Early in the morning of the 3rd, while Washington and his men were working on the fort, a sentinel came in wounded and bleeding, having been fired upon. Scouts brought word shortly afterwards that the French were in force, about four miles off. Washington drew up his men on level ground outside of the works to await their attack. About 11 o'clock, there was a firing of musketry from among trees on rising ground, but so distant as to do no harm; suspecting this to be a stratagem designed to draw his men into the woods, he ordered them to keep quiet, and refrain from firing until the foe should show themselves, and draw near.

July 3, 1754

The firing was kept up, but still under cover. He now fell back with his men into the trenches, ordering them to fire whenever they could get sight of an enemy. In this way there was skirmishing throughout the day; the French and Indians advancing as near as the covert of the woods would permit, which in the nearest place was sixty yards, but never into open sight. In the mean while the rain fell in torrents; the harassed and jaded troops were half drowned in their trenches, and many of their muskets were rendered unfit for use.

About eight at night the French requested a parley. Washington hesitated. It might be a stratagem to gain admittance for a spy into the fort. The request was repeated, with the addition that an officer might be sent to treat with them, under their parole for his safety. Unfortunately, the Chevalier de Peyrouney, engineer of the regiment, and the only one who could speak French correctly, was wounded and disabled. Washington had to send, therefore, his ancient swordsman and interpreter, Jacob Van Braam. The captain returned twice with separate terms, in which the garrison was required to surrender; both were rejected. He returned a third time, with written articles of capitulation. They were in French. As no implements of writing were at hand, Van Braam undertook to translate them by word of mouth. A candle was brought, and held close to the paper while he read. The rain fell in torrents; it was difficult to keep the light from being extinguished. The captain rendered the capitulation, article by article, in mongrel English, while Washington and his officers stood listening, endeavoring to disentangle the meaning. One article stipulated that on surrendering the fort they should leave all their military stores, munitions, and artillery in possession of the French. This was objected to, and was readily modified.

Terms of surrender modified

Capitulation at Fort Necessity

The main articles, as Washington and his officers understood them, were that they should be allowed to return to the settlements, without molestation from French or Indians. That they should march out of the fort with the honors of war, drums beating and colors flying, and with all their effects and military stores excepting the artillery, which should be destroyed. That they should be allowed to deposit their effects in some secret place, and leave a guard to protect them until they could send horses to bring them away; their horses having been nearly all killed or lost during the action. That they should give their word of honor not to attempt any buildings or improvements on the lands of his most Christian majesty, for the space of a year. That the prisoners taken in the skirmish of Jumonville should be restored, and until their delivery, Captain Van Braam and Captain Stobo should remain with the French as hostages.

The next morning accordingly, Washington and his men marched out of their forlorn fortress with the honors of war, bearing with them their regimental colors, but leaving behind a large flag, too cumbrous to be transported. Scarcely had they begun their march, however, when, in defiance of the terms of capitulation, they were beset by a large body of Indians, allies of the French, who began plundering the baggage, and committing other irregularities. Seeing that the French did not, or could not, prevent them, and that all the baggage which could not be transported on the shoulders of his troops would fall into the hands of these savages, Washington ordered it to be destroyed, as well as the artillery, gunpowder, and other military stores. All this detained him until ten o'clock, when he set out on his melancholy march. He had not proceeded above a mile when two or three of the wounded men were reported to be missing. He immediately detached a few men back in quest of them, and continued on until three miles from Fort Necessity, where he encamped for the night, and was rejoined by the stragglers.

July 4, 1754

In this affair, out of the Virginia regiment, consisting of three hundred and five men, officers included, twelve had been killed, and forty-three wounded. The number killed and wounded in Captain Mackay's company is not known. The loss of the French and Indians is supposed to have been much greater.

In the following days' march, the troops seemed jaded and disheartened; they were encumbered and delayed by the wounded; provisions were scanty, and they had seventy weary miles to accomplish before they could meet with supplies. Washington, however, encouraged them by his own steadfast and cheerful demeanor, and by sharing all their toils and privations; and at length conducted them in safety to Wills' Creek, where they found ample provisions in the military magazines. Leaving them here to recover their strength, he proceeded with Captain Mackay to Williamsburg, to make his military report to the governor.

Steadfast and cheerful demeanor

A copy of the capitulation was subsequently laid before the Virginia House of Burgesses, with explanations. Notwithstanding the unfortunate result of the campaign, the conduct of Washington and his officers was properly appreciated, and they received a vote of thanks for their bravery, and gallant defence of their country. Three hundred pistoles (nearly eleven hundred dollars) also were voted to be distributed among the privates who had been in action.

Properly appreciated

From the vote of thanks, two officers were excepted; Major Muse, who was charged with cowardice, and Washington's unfortunate master of fence and blundering interpreter, Jacob Van Braam, who was accused of treachery, in purposely misrepresenting the articles of capitulation. . . .

Washington Resigns Commission

In the month of October the House of Burgesses made a grant of twenty thousand pounds for the public service; and ten thousand more were sent out from England, beside a supply of fire-arms. The governor now applied himself to military matters with renewed spirit; increased the actual force to ten companies; and, as there had been difficulties among the different kinds of troops with regard to precedence, he reduced them all to independent companies; so that there would be no officer in a Virginia regiment above the rank of captain.

October, 1754

This shrewd measure, upon which Dinwiddie secretly prided himself as calculated to put an end to the difficulties in question, immediately drove

Washington out of the service; considering it derogatory to his character to accept a lower commission than that under which his conduct had gained him a vote of thanks from the Legislature.

Derogatory to his character

Governor Sharpe, of Maryland, appointed by the king commander-in-chief of all the forces engaged against the French, sought to secure his valuable services, and authorized Colonel Fitzhugh, whom he had placed in temporary command of the army, to write to him to that effect. The reply of Washington (15th Nov.) is full of dignity and spirit, and shows how deeply he felt his military degradation. . . .

Even had Washington hesitated to take this step, it would have been forced upon him by a further regulation of government, in the course of the ensuing winter, settling the rank of officers of his majesty's forces when joined or serving with the provincial forces in North America, "which directed that all such as were commissioned by the king, or by his general commander-in-chief in North America, should take rank of all officers commissioned by the governors of the respective provinces. And further, that the general and field officers of the provincial troops should have no rank when serving with the general and field officers commissioned by the crown; but that all captains and other inferior officers of the royal troops should take rank over provincial officers of the same grade, having older commissions."

These regulations, originating in that supercilious assumption of superiority which sometimes overruns and degrades true British pride, would have been spurned by Washington, as insulting to the character and conduct of his high-minded brethren of the colonies. How much did this open disparagement of colonial honor and understanding, contribute to wean from England the affection of her American subjects, and prepare the way for their ultimate assertion of independence. . . .

England assumes superiority over her American subjects

Return to Quiet Life

Having resigned his commission, and disengaged himself from public affairs, Washington's first care was to visit his mother, inquire into the state of domestic concerns, and attend to the welfare of his brothers and sisters. In these matters he was ever his mother's adjunct and counsellor, discharging faithfully the duties of an eldest son, who should consider himself a second father to the family.

1755

He now took up his abode at Mount Vernon, and prepared to engage in those agricultural pursuits, for which, even in his youthful days, he had as keen a relish as for the profession of arms. Scarcely had he entered upon his rural occupations, however, when the service of his country once more called him to the field. . . .

Military Preparations of British Government

The British government now prepared for military operations in America; none of them professedly aggressive, but rather to resist and counteract aggressions. A plan of campaign was devised for 1755, having four objects.

To eject the French from the lands which they held unjustly, in the province of Nova Scotia.

To dislodge them from a fortress which they had erected at Crown Point, on Lake Champlain, within what was claimed as British territory.

To dispossess them of the fort which they had constructed at Niagara, between Lake Ontario and Lake Erie.

To drive them from the frontiers of Pennsylvania and Virginia, and recover the valley of the Ohio.

The Duke of Cumberland, captain-general of the British army, had the organization of this campaign; and through his patronage, Major-general Edward Braddock was intrusted with the execution of it, being appointed generalissimo of all the forces in the colonies.

Major-General Edward Braddock

Braddock was a veteran in service, and had been upwards of forty years in the guards, that school of exact discipline and technical punctilio. Cumberland, who held a commission in the guards, and was bigoted to its routine, may have considered Braddock fitted, by his skill and preciseness as a tactician, for a command in a new country, inexperienced in military science, to bring its raw levies into order, and to settle those questions of rank and etiquette apt to arise where regular and provincial troops are to act together.

The result proved the error of such an opinion. Braddock was a brave and experienced officer; but his experience was that of routine, and rendered him pragmatical and obstinate; impatient of novel expedients "not laid down in the books," but dictated by emergen-

Braddock's character

cies in a "new country," and his military precision, which would have been brilliant on parade, was a constant obstacle to alert action in the wilderness.

Braddock was to lead in person the grand enterprise of the campaign, that destined for the frontiers of Virginia and Pennsylvania; it was the enterprise in which Washington became enlisted, and, therefore claims our especial attention.

Prior to the arrival of Braddock, came out from England Lieutenant-colonel Sir John St. Clair, deputy quartermaster-general, eager to make himself acquainted with the field of operations. He made a tour of inspection, in company with Governor Sharpe, of Maryland, and appears to have been dismayed at sight of the impracticable wilderness, the region of Washington's campaign. . . .

Impracticable wilderness

Indian Allies

When Sir John St. Clair had finished his tour of inspection, he descended Wills' Creek and the Potomac for two hundred miles in a canoe to Alexandria, and repaired to Virginia to meet General Braddock. The latter had landed on the 20th of February at Hampton, in Virginia, and proceeded to Williamsburg to consult with Governor Dinwiddie. Shortly afterwards he was joined there by Commodore Keppel, whose squadron of two ships of war, and several transports, had anchored in the Chesapeake. On board of these ships were two prime regiments of about five hundred men each; one commanded by Sir Peter Halket, the other by Colonel Dunbar; together with a train of artillery, and the necessary munitions of war. The regiments were to be augmented to seven hundred men each by men selected by Sir John St. Clair from Virginia companies recently raised.

February 20, 1755

Alexandria was fixed upon as the place where the troops should disembark, and encamp. The ships were accordingly ordered up to that place, and the levies directed to repair thither.

The plan of the campaign included the use of Indian allies. Governor Dinwiddie had already sent Mr. Gist, son of the pioneer, Washington's guide in 1753, to engage the Cherokees and Catawbas, the bravest of the Southern tribes, who he had no doubt would take up the hatchet for the English, peace being first concluded, through the mediation of his government, between them and the Six Nations; and he gave Braddock reason to expect at least four hundred Indians to join him at Fort Cumberland. He laid before him also contracts that he had made for cattle, and promises that the Assembly of Pennsylvania had made of flour; these, with other supplies, and a thousand barrels of beef on board of the transports, would furnish six months' provisions for four thousand men.

General Braddock apprehended difficulty in procuring waggons and horses sufficient to attend him in his march. Sir John St. Clair, in the course of his tour of inspection, had met with two Dutch settlers, at the foot of the Blue Ridge, who engaged to furnish two hundred waggons, and fifteen hundred carrying horses, to be at Fort Cumberland early in May.

Governor Sharp was to furnish above a hundred waggons for the transportation of stores, on the Maryland side of the Potomac.

Keppel furnished four cannons from his ships, for the attack on Fort Duquesne, and thirty picked seamen to assist in dragging them over the mountains; for "soldiers," said he, "cannot be as well acquainted with the nature of purchases, and making use of tackles as seamen." They were to aid also in passing the troops and artillery on floats or in boats, across the rivers, and were under the command of a midshipman and lieutenant.

"Every thing," writes Captain Robert Orme, one of the general's aides-de-camp, "seemed to promise so far the greatest success. The transport were all arrived safe, and the men in health. Provisions, Indians, carriages, and horses, were already provided; at least were to be esteemed so, considering the authorities on which they were promised to the general." Trusting to these arrangements, Braddock proceeded to Alexandria. . . .

Excitement of Washington

The din and stir of warlike preparation disturbed the quiet of Mount Vernon. Washington looked down from his rural retreat upon the ships of war and transports, as they passed up the Potomac, with the array of arms gleaming along their decks. The booming of cannon echoed among his groves. Alexandria was but a few miles distant. Occasionally he mounted his horse, and rode to that place; it was like a garrisoned town, teeming with troops, and resounding with the drum and fife. A brilliant campaign was about to open under the auspices of an experienced general, and with all the means and appurtenances of European warfare. How different from the starveling expeditions he had hitherto been doomed to conduct. What an opportunity to efface the memory of his recent disaster. All his thoughts of rural life were put to flight. The military part of his character was again in the ascendant; his great desire was to join the expedition as a volunteer.

Desire to enlist as a volunteer

It was reported to General Braddock. The latter was apprised by Governor Dinwiddie and others, of Washington's personal merits, his knowledge of the country, and his experience in frontier service. The consequence was, a letter from Captain Robert Orme, one of Braddock's aide-de-camp, written by the general's order, inviting Washington to join his staff; the letter concluded with frank and cordial expressions of esteem on the part of Orme, which were warmly reciprocated, and laid the foundation of a soldier-like friendship between them.

A volunteer situation on the staff of General Braddock offered no emolument nor command, and would be attended with considerable expense, beside a sacrifice of his private interests, having no person in whom he had confidence, to take charge of his affairs in his absence; still he did not hesitate a moment to accept the invitation. In the position offered to him, all the questions of military rank which had hitherto annoyed him, would be obviated. He could indulge his passion for arms without any sacrifice of dignity, and he looked forward with high anticipation to an opportunity of acquiring military experience in a corps well organized, and thoroughly disciplined, and in the family of a commander of acknowledged skill as a tactician. . . .

Military experience in a corps organized and disciplined

Washington at Alexandria

His arrival was hailed by his young associates, Captains Orme and Morris, the general's aides-de-camp, who at once received him into frank companionship, and a cordial intimacy commenced between them, that continued throughout the campaign.

He experienced a courteous reception from the general, who expressed in flattering terms the impression he had received of his merits. Washington soon appreciated the character of the general. He found him stately and somewhat haughty, exact in matters of military etiquette and discipline, positive in giving an opinion, and obstinate in maintaining it; but of an honorable and generous, though somewhat irritable nature.

There were at that time four governors, beside Dinwiddie, assembled at Alexandria, at Braddock's request, to concert a plan of military operations; Governor Shirley, of Massachusetts; Lieutenant-governor Delancey, of New York; Lieutenant-governor Sharpe, of Maryland; Lieutenant-governor Morris, of Pennsylvania. Washington was presented to them in a manner that showed how well his merits were already appreciated. Shirley seems particularly to have struck him as the model of a gentleman and statesman. He was originally a lawyer, and had risen not more by his talents, than by his implicit devotion to the crown. His son William was military secretary to Braddock.

A grand council was held on the 14th of April, composed of General Braddock, Commodore Keppel, and the governors, at which the general's commission was read, as were his instructions from the king, relating to a common fund, to be established by the several colonies, toward defraying the expenses of the campaign.

April 14, 1755

The governors were prepared to answer on this head, letters to the same purport having been addressed to them by Sir Thomas Robinson, one of the king's secretaries of state, in the preceding month of October. They informed Braddock that they had applied to their respective Assemblies for the establishment of such a fund, but in vain; and gave it as their unanimous opinion, that such a fund could never be established in the colonies without the aid of Parliament. They had found it impracticable, also, to obtain from their respective governments the proportions expected from them by the crown, toward military expenses in America; and suggested that ministers should find out some mode of compelling them to do it; and that, in the mean time, the general should make use of his credit upon government, for current expenses, lest the expedition should come to a stand.

Colonial assemblies refuse to establish a common war fund

In discussing the campaign, the governors were of opinion that New York should be made the centre of operations, as it afforded easy access by water to the heart of the French possessions in Canada. Braddock, however, did not feel at liberty to depart from his instructions, which specified the recent establishments of the French on the Ohio as the objects of his expedition.

Niagara and Crown Point were to be attacked about the same time with Fort Duquesne, the former by Governor Shirley, with his own and Sir William Pepperell's regiments, and some New York companies; the latter by Colonel William Johnson, sole manager and director of Indian affairs; a personage worthy of especial note. . . .

The business of the Congress being finished, General Braddock would have set out for Fredericktown, in Maryland, but few waggons or teams had yet come to remove the artillery. Washington had looked with wonder and dismay at the huge paraphernalia of war, and the world of superfluities to be transported across the mountains, recollecting the difficulties he had experienced in getting over them with his nine swivels and scanty supplies. "If our march is to be regulated by the slow movements of the train," said he, "it will be tedious, very tedious, indeed." His predictions excited a sarcastic smile in Braddock, as betraying the limited notions of a young provincial officer, little acquainted with the march of armies.

Huge paraphernalia of war

St. Clair's Explosions of Wrath

In the mean while, Sir John St. Clair, who had returned to the frontier, was storming at the camp at Fort Cumberland. The road required of the Pennsylvania government had not been commenced. George Croghan and the other commissioners were but just arrived in camp. . . .

The explosive wrath of Sir John, which was not to be appeased, shook the souls of the commissioners, and they wrote to Governor Morris, urging that people might be set at work upon the road, if the Assembly had made provision for opening it; and that flour might be sent without delay to the mouth of Canococheague River, "as being the only remedy left to prevent these threatened mischiefs."

In reply, Mr. Richard Peters, Governor Morris's secretary, wrote in his name: "Get a number of hands immediately, and further the work by all possible methods. Your expenses will be paid at the next sitting of Assembly. Do your duty, and oblige the general and quartermaster if possible. Finish the road that will be wanted first, and then proceed to any other that may be thought necessary."

An additional commission, of a different kind, was intrusted to George Croghan. Governor Morris by letter requested him to convene at Aughquick, in Pennsylvania, as many warriors as possible of the mixed tribes of the Ohio, distribute among them wampum belts sent for the purpose, and engage them to meet General Braddock when on the march, and render him all the assistance in their power.

Captain Jack and His Band

In reply, Croghan engaged to enlist a strong body of Indians, being sure of the influence of Scarooyadi, successor to the half-king, and of his adjunct, White Thunder, keeper of the speech-belts. At the instance of Governor Morris, Croghan secured the services of another kind of force. This was a band of hunters, resolute men, well acquainted with the country, and inured to hardships. They were under the command of Captain Jack, one of the most remarkable characters of Pennsylvania; a complete hero of the wilderness. He had been for many years a captive among the Indians; and, having learnt their ways, had formed this association for the protection of the settlements, receiving a commission of captain from the Governor of Pennsylvania. The band had become famous for its exploits, and was a terror to the Indians. Captain Jack was at present protecting the settlements on the Canococheague; but promised to march by a circuitous route and join Braddock with his hunters. "They require no shelter for the night," writes Croghan; "they ask no pay. If the whole army was composed of such men there would be no cause of apprehension. I shall be with them in time for duty."

"They ask no pay"

Washington Proclaimed Aide-de-Camp

General Braddock set out from Alexandria on the 20th of April. Washington remained behind a few days to arrange his affairs, and then rejoined him at Fredericktown, in Maryland, where, on the 10th of May, he was proclaimed one of the general's aides-de-camp.

The troubles of Braddock had already commenced. The Virginian contractors failed to fulfil their engagements; of all the immense means of transportation so confidently promised, but fifteen waggons and a hundred draft-horses had arrived, and there was no prospect of more. There was equal disappointment in provisions, both as to quantity and quality; and he had to send round the country to buy cattle for the subsistence of the troops.

May 10, 1755

Braddock and Franklin

Fortunately, while the general was venting his spleen in anathemas against army contractors, Benjamin Franklin arrived at Fredericktown. That eminent man, then about forty-nine years of age, had been for many years member of the Pennsylvania Assembly, and was now postmaster-general for America. The Assembly understood that Braddock was incensed against them, supposing them adverse to the service of the war. They had procured Franklin to wait upon him, not as if sent by them, but as if he came in his capacity of postmaster-general, to arrange for the sure and speedy transmission of despatches between the commander-in-chief and the governors of the provinces.

He was well received, and became a daily guest at the general's table. In his autobiography, he gives us an instance of the blind confidence and fatal prejudices by which Braddock was deluded throughout this expedition. "In conversation with him one day," writes Franklin, "he was giving me some account of his intended progress. 'After taking Fort Duquesne,' said he, 'I am to proceed to Niagara; and, having taken that, to Frontenac, if the season will allow time; and I suppose it will, for Duquesne can hardly detain me above three or four days: and then I can see nothing that can obstruct my march to Niagara.'

Blind confidence and fatal prejudice

"Having before revolved in my mind," continues Franklin, "the long line his army must make in their march by a very narrow road, to be cut for them through the woods and bushes, and also what I had heard of a former defeat of fifteen hundred French, who invaded the Illinois country, I had conceived some doubts and some fears for the event of the campaign; but I ventured only to say, 'To be sure, sir, if you arrive well before Duquesne with these fine troops, so well provided with artillery, the fort, though completely fortified, and assisted with a very strong garrison, can probably make but a short resistance. The only danger I apprehend of obstruction to your march, is from the ambuscades of the Indians, who, by constant practice, are dexterous in laying and executing them; and the slender line, nearly four miles long, which your army must make, may expose it to be attacked by surprise on its flanks, and to be cut like thread into several pieces, which, from their distance, cannot come up in time to support one another.'

Pennsylvanian diplomacy

"He smiled at my ignorance, and replied: 'These savages may indeed be a formidable enemy to raw American militia, but upon the king's regular and disciplined troops, sir, it is impossible they should make an impression.' I was conscious of an impropriety in my disputing with a military man in matters of his profession, and said no more."

As the whole delay of the army was caused by the want of conveyances, Franklin observed one day to the general, that it was a pity the troops had not been landed in Pennsylvania, where almost every farmer had his waggon. "Then, sir," replied Braddock, "you, who are a man of interest there, can probably procure them for me, and I beg you will." Franklin consented. An instrument in writing was drawn up, empowering him to contract for one hundred and fifty waggons, with four horses to each waggon, and fifteen hundred saddle or packhorses for the service of his majesty's forces, to be at Wills' Creek on or before the 20th of May, and he promptly departed for Lancaster to execute the commission.

After his departure, Braddock, attended by his staff, and his guard of light horse, set off for Wills' Creek by the way of Winchester, the road along the north side of the Potomac not being yet made. . . .

The discomforts of the rough road were increased with the general, by his travelling with some degree of state in a chariot which he had purchased of Governor Sharpe. In this he dashed by Dunbar's division of the troops, which he overtook near Wills' Creek; his body guard of light horse galloping on each side of his chariot, and his staff accompanying him; the drums beating the Grenadier's march as he passed. In this style, too, he arrived at Fort Cumberland, amid a thundering salute of seventeen guns.

By this time the general discovered that he was not in a region fitted for such display, and his travelling chariot was abandoned at Fort Cumberland; otherwise it would soon have become a wreck among the mountains beyond.

By the 19th of May, the forces were assembled at Fort Cumberland. The two royal regiments, originally one thousand strong, now increased to fourteen hundred, by men chosen from the Maryland and Virginia levies. Two provincial companies of carpenters, or pioneers, thirty men each, with subalterns and captains. A company of guides, composed of a captain, two aids, and ten men. The troop of Virginia light horse, commanded by Captain Stewart; the detachment of thirty sailors with their officers, and the remnants of two independent companies from New York, one of which was commanded by Captain Horatio Gates. . . .

May 19, 1755

Military Tactics

At Fort Cumberland, Washington had an opportunity of seeing a force encamped according to the plan approved of by the council of war; and military tactics, enforced with all the precision of a martinet.

The roll of each company was called over morning, noon, and night. There was strict examination of arms and accoutrements; the commanding officer of each company being answerable for their being kept in good order.

The general was very particular in regard to the appearance and drill of the Virginia recruits and companies, whom he had put under the rigorous discipline of Ensign Allen. . . .

The general held a levee in his tent every morning, from ten to eleven. He was strict as to the morals of the camp. Drunkenness was severely punished. A soldier convicted of theft was sentenced to receive one thousand lashes, and to be drummed out of his regiment. Part of the first part of the sentence was remitted. Divine service was performed every Sunday, at the head of the colors of each regiment, by the chaplain. . . .

Braddock's camp, in a word, was a complete study for Washington, during the halt at Fort Cumberland, where he had an opportunity of seeing military routine in its strictest forms. He had a specimen, too, of convivial life in the camp, which the general endeavored to maintain, even in the wilderness, keeping a hospitable table; for he is said to have been somewhat of a *bon vivant,* and to have had with him "two good cooks, who could make an excellent ragout out of a pair of boots, had they but materials to toss them up with. . . ."

A complete study for Washington

Indians in Camp

George Croghan reached the camp with but about fifty warriors, whom he had brought from Aughquick. At the general's request he sent a messenger to invite the Delawares and Shawnees from the Ohio, who returned with two chiefs of the former tribe. Among the sachems thus assembled were some of Washington's former allies; Scarooyadi, alias, Monacatoocha, successor to the half-king; White Thunder, the keeper of the speech-belts, and Silver Heels, so called, probably, from being swift of foot.

Notwithstanding his secret contempt for the Indians, Braddock, agreeably to his instructions, treated them with great ceremony. A grand council was held in his tent, where all his officers attended. The chiefs, and all the warriors, came painted and decorated for war. They were received with military honors, the guards resting on their fire-arms. The general made them a speech through his interpreter, expressing the grief of their father, the great king of England, at the death of the half-king, and made them presents to console them. They in return promised their aid as guides and scouts, and declared eternal enmity to the French, following the declaration with the war song, "making a terrible noise."

Braddock's secret contempt for the Indians

The general, to regale and astonish them, ordered all the artillery to be fired, "the drums and fifes playing and beating the point of war;" the fete ended by their feasting, in their own camp, on a bullock which the general had given them, following up their repast by dancing the war dance round a fire, to the sound of their uncouth drums and rattles, "making night hideous," by howls and yellings. . . .

Errand to Williamsburg

During the halt of the troops at Wills' Creek, Washington had been sent to Williamsburg to bring on four thousand pounds for the military chest. He returned after a fortnight's absence, escorted from Winchester by eight men, "which eight men," writes he, "were two days assembling, but I believe would not have been more than as many seconds dispersing if I had been attacked."

He found the general out of all patience and temper at the delays and disappointments in regard to horses, waggons, and forage, making no allowances for the difficulties incident to a new country, and to the novel and great demands upon its scanty and scattered resources. He accused the army contractors of want of faith, honor, and honesty; and in his moments of passion, which were many, extended the stigma to the whole country. This stung the patriotic sensibility of Washington, and overcame his usual self-command, and the proud and passionate commander was occasionally surprised by a well-merited rebuke from his aide-de-camp. "We have frequent disputes on this head," writes Washington, "which are maintained with warmth on both sides, especially on his; as he is incapable of arguing without it, or of giving up any point he asserts, be it ever so incompatible with reason or common sense."

The same pertinacity was maintained with respect to the Indians. George Croghan informed Washington that the sachems considered themselves treated with slight, in never being consulted in war matters. That he himself had repeatedly offered the services of the warriors under his command as scouts and outguards, but his offers had been rejected. Washington ventured to interfere, and to urge their importance for such purposes, especially now when they were approaching the stronghold of the enemy. As usual, the general remained bigoted in his belief of the all-sufficiency of well-disciplined troops.

Interference in behalf of Indians to no avail

Either from disgust thus caused, or from being actually dismissed, the warriors began to disappear from the camp. . . .

March from Fort Cumberland

On the 10th of June, Braddock set off from Fort Cumberland with his aides-de-camp, and others of his staff, and his body guard of light horse. Sir Peter Halket, with his brigade, had marched three days previously; and a detachment of six hundred men, under the command of Colonel Chapman, and the supervision of Sir John St. Clair, had been employed upwards of ten days in cutting down trees, removing rocks, and opening a road.

June 10, 1755

The march over the mountains proved, as Washington had foretold, a "tremendous undertaking." It was with difficulty the heavily laden waggons could be dragged up the steep and rugged roads, newly made, or imperfectly repaired. Often they extended for three or four miles in a straggling and broken line, with the soldiers so dispersed, in guarding them, that an attack on any side would have thrown the whole in confusion. It was the dreary region of the great Savage Mountain, and the "Shades of Death" that was again made to echo with the din of arms.

What outraged Washington's notions of the abstemious frugality suitable to campaigning in the "back-woods," was the great number of horses and waggons required by the officers for the transportation of their baggage, camp equipage, and a thousand articles of artificial necessity. Simple himself in his tastes and habits, and manfully indifferent to personal indulgences, he almost doubted whether such sybarites in the camp could be efficient in the field.

By the time the advanced corps had struggled over two mountains, and through the intervening forest, and reached (16th June) the Little Meadows, where Sir John St. Clair had made a temporary camp, General Braddock had become aware of the difference between campaigning in a new country, or on the old well beaten battle-grounds of Europe. He now, of his own accord, turned to Washington for advice, though it must have been a sore trial to his pride to seek it of so young a man; but he had by this time sufficient proof of his sagacity, and his knowledge of the frontier.

Division of Forces

Thus unexpectedly called on, Washington gave his counsel with becoming modesty, but with his accustomed clearness. There was just now an opportunity to strike an effective blow at Fort Duquesne, but it might be lost by delay. The garrison, according to credible reports, was weak; large reinforcements and supplies, which were on their way, would be detained by the drought, which rendered the river by which they must come low and unnavigable. The blow must be struck before they could arrive. He advised the general, therefore, to divide his forces; leave one part to come on with the stores and baggage, and all the cumbrous appurtenances of an army, and to throw himself in the advance with the other part, composed of his choicest troops, lightened of every thing superfluous that might impede a rapid march.

His advice was adopted. Twelve hundred men, selected out of all the companies, and furnished with ten field-pieces, were to form the first division, their provisions, and other necessaries, to be carried on pack-horses. The second division, with all the stores, munitions, and heavy baggage, was to brought on by Colonel Dunbar.

The least practicable part of the arrangement was with regard to the officers of the advance. Washington had urged a retrenchment of their baggage and camp equipage, that as many of their horses as possible might be used as packhorses. Here was the difficulty. Brought up, many of them, in fashionable and luxurious life, or the loitering indulgence of country quarters, they were so encumbered with what they considered indispensable necessaries, that out of two hundred and twelve horses generally appropriated to their use, not more than a dozen could be spared by them for the public service. Washington, in his own case, acted up to the advice he had given. He retained no more clothing and effects with him than would about half fill a portmanteau, and gave up his best steed as a packhorse,—which he never heard of afterwards.

Acted up to the advice he had given

Captain Jack and His Band of Forest Rangers

During the halt at the Little Meadows, Captain Jack and his band of forest rangers, whom Croghan had engaged at Governor Morris's suggestion, made their appearance in the camp; armed and equipped with rifle, knife, hunting-shirts, leggings and moccasins, and looking almost like a band of Indians as they issued from the woods.

The captain asked an interview with the general, by whom, it would seem, he was not expected. Braddock received him in his tent, in his usual stiff and stately manner. The "Black Rifle" spoke of himself and his followers as men inured to hardships, and accustomed to deal with Indians who preferred stealth and stratagem to open warfare. He requested his company should be employed as a reconnoitering party, to beat up the Indians in their lurking-places and ambuscades.

Men inured to hardship

Braddock, who had a sovereign contempt for the chivalry of the woods, and despised their boasted strategy, replied to the hero of the Pennsylvania settlements in a manner to which he had not been accustomed. "There was time enough," he said, "for making arrangements; and he had experienced troops, on whom he could completely rely for all purposes."

Captain Jack withdrew, indignant at so haughty a reception, and informed his leathern-clad followers of his rebuff. They forthwith shouldered their rifles, turned their backs upon the camp, and, headed by the captain, departed in Indian file through the woods, for the usual scenes of their exploits, where men knew their value, the banks of the Juniata or the Conococheague.

A Scientific March

On the 19th of June Braddock's first division set out, with less than thirty carriages, including those that transported ammunition for the artillery, all strongly horsed. The Indians marched with the advanced party. In the course of the day, Scarooyadi and his son being at a small distance from the line of march, were surrounded and taken by some French and Indians. His son escaped, and brought intelligence to his warriors; they hastened to rescue or revenge him, but found him tied to a tree. The French had been disposed to shoot him, but their savage allies declared they would abandon them should they do so; having some tie of friendship or kindred with the chieftain, who thus rejoined the troops unharmed.

June 19, 1755

Washington was disappointed in his anticipations of a rapid march. The general, though he had adopted his advice in the main, could not carry it out in detail. His military education was in the way: bigoted to the regular and elaborate tactics of Europe, he could not stoop to the make-shift expedients of a new country, where every difficulty is encountered and mastered in a rough-and-ready style. "I found," said Washington, "that instead of pushing on with vigor, without regarding a little rough road, they were halting to level every mole hill, and to erect bridges over every brook, by which means we were four days in getting twelve miles."

Illness of Washington

For several days Washington had suffered from fever, accompanied by intense headache, and his illness increased in violence to such a degree that he was unable to ride, and had to be conveyed for a part of the time in a covered waggon. His illness continued without intermission until the 23d, "when I was relieved," says he, "by the general's absolutely ordering the physician to give me Dr. James's powders; one of the most excellent medicines in the world. It gave me immediate relief, and removed my fever and other complaints in four days' time."

He was still unable to bear the jolting of the waggon, but it needed another interposition of the kindly intended authority of General Braddock, to bring him to a halt at the great crossings of the Youghiogeny. Here the general assigned him a guard, provided him with necessaries, and requested him to remain, under care of his physician, Dr. Craik, until the arrival of Colonel Dunbar's detachment, which was two days' march in the rear; giving him his word of honor that he should, at all events, be enabled to rejoin the main division before it reached the French fort.

This kind solicitude on the part of Braddock, shows the real estimation in which he was held by that officer. Doctor Craik backed the general's orders, by declaring that should Washington persevere in his attempts to go on in the condition he then was, his life would be in danger. Orme also joined his entreaties, and promised, if he would remain, he would keep him informed by letter of every occurrence of moment. . . .

Dangerous to his life

Camp of the Monongahela

Orme, . . . according to promise, kept him informed of the incidents of the march; the frequent night alarms, and occasional scalping parties. The night alarms Washington considered mere feints, designed to harass the men and retard the march; the enemy, he was sure, had not sufficient force for a serious attack; and he was glad to learn from Orme that the men were in high spirits and confident of success.

He now considered himself sufficiently recovered to join the troops, and his only anxiety was, that he should not be able to do it in time for the great blow. He was rejoiced, therefore, on the 3d of July, by the arrival of an advanced party of one hundred men convoying provisions. Being still too weak to mount his horse, he set off with the escort in a covered waggon; and after a most fatiguing journey, over mountain and through forest, reached Braddock's camp on the 8th of July. It was on the east side of the Monongahela, about two miles from the river, in the neighborhood of the town of Queen Aliquippa, and about fifteen miles from Fort Duquesne.

In consequence of adhering to technical rules and military forms, General Braddock had consumed a month in marching little more than a hundred miles. . . .

Washington was warmly received on his arrival, especially by his fellow aides-de-camp, Morris and Orme. He was just in time, for the attack upon Fort Duquesne was to be made on the following day. The neighboring country had been reconnoitred to determine upon a plan of attack. The fort stood on the same side of the Monongahela with the camp; but there was a narrow pass between them of about two miles, with the river on the left and a very high mountain on the right, and in its present state quite impassable for carriages. The route determined on was to cross the Monongahela by a ford immediately opposite to the camp; proceed along the west bank of the river, for about five miles, then recross by another ford to the eastern side, and push on to the fort. The river at these fords was shallow, and the banks were not steep.

According to the plan of arrangement, Lieutenant-colonel Gage, with the advance, was to cross the river before daybreak, march to the second ford, and recrossing there, take post to secure the passage of the main force. The advance was to be composed of two companies of grenadiers, one hundred and sixty infantry, the independent company of Captain Horatio Gates, and two six-pounders.

Washington, who had already seen enough of regular troops to doubt their infallibility in wild bush-fighting, and who knew the dangerous nature of the ground they were to traverse, ventured to suggest, that on the following day the Virginia rangers, being accustomed to the country and to Indian warfare, might be thrown in the advance. The proposition drew an angry reply from the general, indignant, very probably, that a young provincial officer should presume to school a veteran like himself.

Knew dangers of the ground they were to traverse

Fording of the Monongahela

Early next morning (July 9th), before daylight, Colonel Gage crossed with the advance. He was followed, at some distance, by Sir John St. Clair, quartermaster-general, with a working party of two hundred and fifty men, to make roads for the artillery and baggage. They had with them their waggons of tools, and two six-pounders. A party of about thirty savages rushed out of the woods as Colonel Gage advanced, but were put to flight before they had done any harm.

July 9, 1755

By sunrise the main body turned out in full uniform. At the beating of the general, their arms, which had been cleaned the night before, were charged with fresh cartridges. The officers were perfectly equipped. All looked as if arrayed for a fête, rather than a battle. Washington, who was still weak and unwell, mounted his horse, and joined the staff of the general, who was scrutinizing every thing with the eye of a martinet. As it was supposed the enemy would be on the watch for the crossing of the troops, it had been agreed that they should do it in the greatest order, with bayonets fixed, colors flying, and drums and fifes beating and playing. They accordingly made a gallant appearance as they forded the Monongahela, and wound along its banks, and through the open forests, gleaming and glittering in morning sunshine, and stepping buoyantly to the Grenadier's march.

Washington, with his keen and youthful relish for military affairs, was delighted with their perfect order and equipment, so different from the rough bush-fighters, to which he had been accustomed. Roused to new life, he forgot his recent ailments, and broke forth in expressions of enjoyment and admiration, as he rode in company with his fellow aides-de camp, Orme and Morris. Often, in after life, he used to speak of the effect upon him

First sight of a well-disciplined army

of the first sight of a well-disciplined European army, marching in high confidence and bright array, on the eve of a battle.

About noon they reached the second ford. Gage with the advance, was on the opposite side of the Monongahela, posted according to orders; but the river bank had not been sufficiently sloped. The artillery and baggage drew up along the beach and halted until one, when the second crossing took place, drums beating, fifes playing, and colors flying, as before. When all had passed, there was again a halt close by a small stream called Frazier's Run, until the general arranged the order of march.

First went the advance, under Gage, preceded by the engineers and guides, and six light horsemen.

Then, Sir John St. Clair and the working party, with their waggons and the two six-pounders. On each side were thrown out four flanking parties.

Then, at some distance, the general was to follow with the main body, the artillery and baggage preceded and flanked by light horse and squads of infantry; while the Virginian, and other provincial troops, were to form the rear guard.

The ground before them was level until about half a mile from the river, where a rising ground, covered with long grass, low bushes, and scattered trees, sloped gently up to a range of hills. The whole country, generally speaking, was a forest, with no clear opening but the road, which was about twelve feet wide, and flanked by two ravines, concealed by trees and thickets.

Had Braddock been schooled in the warfare of the woods, or had he adopted the suggestions of Washington, which he rejected so impatiently, he would have thrown out Indian scouts or Virginia rangers in the advance, and on the flanks, to beat up the woods and ravines; but, as has been sarcastically observed, he suffered his troops to march forward through the centre of the plain, with merely their usual guides and flanking parties, "as if in a review in St. James's Park."

Suggestion overridden by Braddock

The Battle

It was now near two o'clock. The advanced party and the working party had crossed the plain and were ascending the rising ground. Braddock was about to follow with the main body, and had given the word to march, when he heard an excessively quick and heavy firing in front. Washington, who was with the general, surmised that the evil he had apprehended had come to pass. For want of scouting parties ahead the advance parties were suddenly and warmly attacked. Braddock ordered Lieutenant-colonel Burton to hasten to their assistance with the vanguard of the main body, eight hundred strong. The residue, four hundred, were halted, and posted to protect the artillery and baggage.

The firing continued, with fearful yelling. There was a terrible uproar. By the general's orders an aide-de-camp spurred forward to bring him an account of the nature of the attack. Without waiting for his return the general himself, finding the turmoil increase, moved forward, leaving Sir Peter Halket with the command of the baggage.

The van of the advance had indeed been taken by surprise. It was composed of two companies of carpenters or pioneers to cut the road, and two flank companies of grenadiers to protect them. Suddenly the engineer who preceded them to mark out the road gave the alarm, "French and Indians!" A body of them was approaching rapidly, cheered on by a Frenchman in gaily fringed hunting-shirt, whose gorget showed him to be an officer.

There was sharp firing on both sides at first. Several of the enemy fell; among them their leader; but a murderous fire broke out from among trees and a ravine on the right, and the woods resounded with unearthly whoops and yellings. The Indian rifle was at work, levelled by unseen hands. Most of the grenadiers and many of the pioneers were shot down. The survivors were driven in on the advance.

Gage ordered his men to fix bayonets and form in order of battle. They did so in hurry and trepidation. He would have scaled a hill on the right whence there was the severest firing. Not a platoon would quit the line of march. They were more dismayed by the yells than by the rifles of the unseen savages. The latter extended themselves along the hill and in the ravines; but their whereabouts was only known by their demoniac cries and the puffs of smoke from their rifles. The soldiers fired wherever they saw the smoke. Their officers tried in vain to restrain them until they should see their foe. All orders were unheeded; in their fright they shot at random, killing some of their own flanking parties, and of the vanguard, as they came running in. The covert fire grew more intense. In a short time most of the officers and many of the men of the advance were killed or wounded. Colonel Gage himself received a wound. The advance fell back in dismay upon Sir John St. Clair's corps, which was equally dis-

Invisible foe

mayed. The cannon belonging to it were deserted.

Colonel Burton had come up with the reinforcement, and was forming his men to face the rising ground on the right, when both of the advanced detachments fell back upon him, and all now was confusion.

By this time the general was upon the ground. He tried to rally the men. "They would fight," they said, "if they could see their enemy; but it was useless to fire at trees and bushes, and they could not stand to be shot down by an invisible foe."

The colors were advanced in different places to separate the men of the two regiments. The general ordered the officers to form the men, tell them off into small divisions, and advance with them; but the soldiers could not be prevailed upon either by threats or entreaties. The Virginia troops, accustomed to the Indian mode of fighting, scattered themselves, and took post behind trees, where they could pick off the lurking foe. In this way they, in some degree, protected the regulars. Washington advised General Braddock to adopt the same plan with the regulars; but he persisted in forming them into platoons; consequently they were cut down from behind logs and trees as fast as they could advance. Several attempted to take to the trees without orders, but the general stormed at them, called them cowards, and even struck them with the flat of his sword. Several of the Virginians, who had taken post and were doing good service in this manner, were slain by the fire of the regulars, directed wherever a smoke appeared among the trees.

Washington's advice rebuffed at great cost

The officers behaved with consummate bravery; and Washington beheld with admiration those who, in camp or on the march, had appeared to him to have an almost effeminate regard for personal ease and convenience, now exposing themselves to imminent death, with a courage that kindled with the thickening horrors. In the vain hope of inspiriting the men to drive off the enemy from the flanks and regain the cannon, they would dash forward singly or in groups. They were invariably shot down; for the Indians aimed from their coverts at every one on horseback, or who appeared to have command. . . .

Washington in the Action

Throughout this disastrous day, Washington distinguished himself by his courage and presence of mind. His brother aids, Orme and Morris, were wounded and disabled early in the action, and the whole duty of carrying the orders of the general devolved on him. His danger was imminent and incessant. He was in every part of the field, a conspicuous mark for the murderous rifle. Two horses were shot under him. Four bullets passed through his coat. His escape without a wound was almost miraculous. Dr. Craik, who was on the field attending to the wounded, watched him with anxiety as he rode about in the most exposed manner, and used to say that he expected every moment to see him fall. At one time he was sent to the main body to bring the artillery into action. All there was likewise in confusion; for the Indians had extended themselves along the ravine so as to flank the reserve and carry slaughter into the ranks. Sir Peter Halket had been shot down at the head of his regiment. The men who should have served the guns were paralyzed. Had they raked the ravines with grape-shot the day might have been saved. In his ardor, Washington sprang from his horse; wheeled and pointed a brass field-piece with his own hand, and directed an effective discharge into the woods; but neither his efforts nor example were of avail. The men could not be kept to the guns.

His escape almost miraculous

Braddock still remained in the centre of the field, in the desperate hope of retrieving the fortunes of the day. The Virginia rangers, who had been most efficient in covering his position, were nearly all killed or wounded. His secretary, Shirley, had fallen by his side. Many of his officers had been slain within his sight, and many of his guard of Virginia light horse. Five horses had been killed under him; still he kept his ground, vainly endeavoring to check the flight of his men, or at least to effect their retreat in good order. At length a bullet passed through his right arm, and lodged itself in his lungs. He fell from his horse, but was caught by Captain Stewart of the Virginia guards, who, with the assistance of another American, and a servant, placed him in a tumbril. It was with much difficulty they got him out of the field—in his despair he desired to be left there.

Braddock fallen in battle

The rout now became complete. Baggage, stores, artillery, every thing was abandoned. The waggoners took each a horse out of his team, and fled. The officers were swept off with the men in this headlong flight. It was rendered more precipitate by the shouts and yells of the savages, numbers of whom rushed forth from their coverts, and pursued the fugitives to the river side, killing several as they dashed across in tumultuous confusion. Fortunately for the latter, the victors gave up the pursuit in their eagerness to collect the spoil.

The Retreat

The shattered army continued its flight after it had crossed the Monongahela, a wretched wreck of the brilliant little force that had recently gleamed along its banks, confident of victory. Out of eighty-six officers, twenty-six had been killed, and thirty-six wounded. The number of rank and file killed and wounded was upwards of seven hundred. The Virginia corps had suffered the most; one company had been almost annihilated, another, beside those killed and wounded in the ranks, had lost all its officers, even to the corporal.

About a hundred men were brought to a halt about a quarter of a mile from the ford of the river. Here was Braddock, with his wounded aides-de-camp and some of his officers; Dr. Craik dressing his wounds, and Washington attending him with faithful assiduity. Braddock was still able to give orders, and had a faint hope of being able to keep possession of the ground until reinforced. . . .

Washington, in the mean time, notwithstanding his weak state, being found most efficient in frontier service, was sent to Colonel Dunbar's camp, forty miles distant, with orders for him to hurry forward provisions, hospital stores, and waggons for the wounded, under the escort of two grenadier companies. It was a hard and a melancholy ride throughout the night and the following day. The tidings of the defeat preceded him, borne by the waggoners, who had mounted their horses, on Braddock's fall, and fled from the field of battle. They had arrived, haggard, at Dunbar's camp at mid-day; the Indian yells still ringing in their ears, "All was lost!" they cried. "Braddock was killed!" They had seen wounded officers borne off from the field in bloody sheets! The troops were all cut to pieces! A panic fell upon the camp. The drums beat to arms. Many of the soldiers, waggoners and attendants, took to flight; but most of them were forced back by the sentinels.

Found most efficient in frontier service

Washington arrived at the camp in the evening, and found the agitation still prevailing. The orders which he brought were executed during the night, and he was in the saddle early in the morning accompanying the convoy of supplies. . . .

Death of Braddock

The proud spirit of Braddock was broken by his defeat. He remained silent the first evening after the battle, only ejaculating at night, "Who would have thought it!" He was equally silent the following day; yet hope still seemed to linger in his breast, from another ejaculation: "We shall better know how to deal with them another time!"

He was grateful for the attentions paid to him by Captain Stewart and Washington, and more than once, it is said, expressed his admiration of the gallantry displayed by the Virginians in the action. It is said, moreover, that in his last moments, he apologized to Washington for the petulance with which he had rejected his advice, and bequeathed to him his favorite charger and his faithful servant, Bishop, who had helped to convey him from the field.

Some of these facts, it is true, rest on tradition, yet we are willing to believe them, as they impart a gleam of just and generous feeling to his closing scene. He died on the night of the 13th, at the Great Meadows, the place of Washington's discomfiture in the previous year. His obsequies were performed before break of day. The chaplain having been wounded, Washington read the funeral service. All was done in sadness, and without parade, so as not to attract the attention of lurking savages, who might discover, and outrage his grave. It is doubtful even whether a volley was fired over it, that last military honor which he had recently paid to the remains of an Indian warrior. The place of his sepulture, however, is still known, and pointed out.

July 13, 1755

Reproach spared him not, even when in his grave. The failure of the expedition was attributed both in England and America to his obstinacy, his technical pedantry, and his military conceit. He had been continually warned to be on his guard against ambush and surprise, but without avail. Had he taken the advice urged on him by Washington and others, to employ scouting parties of Indians and rangers, he would never have been so signally surprised and defeated.

Still his dauntless conduct on the field of battle shows him to have been a man of fearless spirit; and he was universally allowed to be an accomplished disciplinarian. His melancholy end, too, disarms censure of its asperity. Whatever may have been his faults and errors, he, in a manner, expiated them by the hardest lot that befall a brave soldier, ambitious of renown—an unhonored grave in a strange land; a memory clouded by misfortune, and a name forever coupled with defeat.

Arrival at Fort Cumberland

The obsequies of the unfortunate Braddock being finished, the escort continued its retreat with the sick and wounded. Washington, assisted by Dr. Craik, watched with assiduity over his comrades, Orme and Morris. As the horses which bore their litters were nearly knocked up, he despatched messengers to the commander of Fort Cumberland, requesting that others might be sent on, and that comfortable quarters might be prepared for the reception of those officers.

On the 17th, the sad cavalcade reached the fort, and were relieved from the incessant apprehension of pursuit. Here, too, flying reports had preceded them, brought by fugitives from the battle; who, with the disposition usual in such cases to exaggerate, had represented the whole army as massacred. Fearing these reports might reach home, and affect his family, Washington wrote to his mother, and his brother, John Augustine, apprising them of his safety. . . .

The true reason why the enemy did not pursue the retreating army was not known until some time afterwards, and added to the disgrace of the defeat. They were not the main force of the French, but a mere detachment of 72 regulars, 146 Canadians, and 637 Indians, 855 in all, led by Captain de Beaujeu. de Contrecœur, the commander of Fort Duquesne, had received information, through his scouts, that the English, three thousand strong, were within six leages of his fort. Despairing of making an effectual defence against such a superior force, he was balancing in his mind whether to abandon his fort without awaiting their arrival, or to capitulate on honorable terms. In this dilemma Beaujeu prevailed on him to let him sally forth with a detachment to form an ambush, and give check to the enemy. De Beaujeu was to have taken post at the river, and disputed the passage at the ford. For that purpose he was hurrying forward when discovered by the pioneers of Gage's advance party. He was a gallant officer, and fell at the beginning of the fight. The whole number of killed and wounded of French and Indians, did not exceed seventy.

Such was the scanty force which the imagination of the panic-stricken army had magnified into a great host, and from which they had fled in breathless terror, abandoning the whole frontier. No one could be more surprised than the French commander himself, when the ambuscading party returned in triumph with a long train of packhorses laden with booty, the savages uncouthly clad in the garments of the slain, grenadier caps, officer's gold-laced coats, and glittering epaulettes; flourishing swords and sabres, or firing off muskets, and uttering fiendlike yells of victory. But when de Contrecœur was informed of the utter rout and destruction of the much dreaded British army, his joy was complete. He ordered the guns of the fort to be fired in triumph, and sent out troops in pursuit of the fugitives.

The affair of Braddock remains a memorable event in American history, and has been characterized as "the most extraordinary victory ever obtained, and the farthest flight ever made." It struck a fatal blow to the deference for British prowess, which once amounted almost to bigotry, throughout the provinces.

A fatal blow to deference for British prowess

"This whole transaction," observes Franklin, in his autobiography, "gave us the first suspicion that our exalted ideas of the prowess of British regular troops had not been well founded."

Costs of Campaigning

Washington arrived at Mount Vernon on the 26th of July, still in feeble condition from his long illness. His campaigning, thus far, had trenched upon his private fortune, and impaired one of the best of constitutions.

In a letter to his brother Augustine, then a member of Assembly at Williamsburg, he casts up the result of his frontier experience. "I was employed," writes he, "to go a journey in the winter, when I believe few or none would have undertaken it, and what did I get by it?—my expenses borne! I was then appointed, with trifling pay, to conduct a handful of men to the Ohio. What did I get by that? Why, after putting myself to a considerable expense in equipping and providing necessaries for the campaign, I went out, was soundly beaten, and lost all! Came in, and had my commission taken from me; or, in other words, my command reduced, under pretence of an order from home (England). I then went out a volunteer with General Braddock, and lost all my horses, and many other things. But this being a voluntary act, I ought not to have mentioned it; nor should I have done it, were it not to show that I have been on the losing order ever since I entered

August 2, 1755

the service, which is now nearly two years."

What a striking lesson is furnished by this brief summary! How little was he aware of the vast advantages he was acquiring in this school of bitter experience! "In the hand of heaven he stood," to be shaped and trained for its great purpose; and every trial and vicissitude of his early life, but fitted him to cope with one or other of the varied and multifarious duties of his future destiny.

"In the hand of heaven he stood"

But though, under the saddening influence of debility and defeat, he might count the cost of his campaigning, the martial spirit still burned within him. His connection with the army, it is true, had ceased at the death of Braddock, but his military duties continued as adjutant-general of the northern division of the province, and he immediately issued orders for the county lieutenants to hold the militia in readiness for parade and exercise, foreseeing that in the present defenceless state of the frontier, there would be need of their services.

Adjutant-general of northern Virginia

Tidings of the rout and retreat of the army had circulated far and near, and spread consternation throughout the country. Immediate incursions both of French and Indians were apprehended; and volunteer companies began to form, for the purpose of marching across the mountains to the scene of danger. It was intimated to Washington that his services would again be wanted on the frontier. He declared instantly that he was ready to serve his country to the extent of his powers; but never on the same terms as heretofore.

On the 4th of August, Governor Dinwiddie convened the Assembly to devise measures for the public safety. The sense of danger had quickened the slow patriotism of the burgesses; they no longer held back supplies; forty thousand pounds were promptly voted, and orders issued for the raising of a regiment of one thousand men. Washington's friends urged him to present himself at Williamsburg as a candidate for the command; they were confident of his success, notwithstanding that strong interest was making for the governor's favorite, Colonel Innes. With mingled modesty and pride, Washington declined to be a solicitor. The only terms, he said, on which he would accept a command, were a certainty as to rank and emoluments, a right to appoint his field officers, and the supply of a sufficient military chest; but to solicit the command, and, at the same time, to make stipulations, would be a little incongruous, and carry with it the face of self-sufficiency. "If," added he, "the command should be offered to me, the case will then be altered, as I should be at liberty to make such objections as reason, and my small experience, have pointed out."

August 4, 1755

Washington in Command

While this was in agitation, he received letters from his mother, again imploring him not to risk himself in these frontier wars. His answer was characteristic, blending the filial deference with which he was accustomed from childhood to treat her, with a calm patriotism of the Roman stamp.

"Honored Madam: If it is in my power to avoid going to the Ohio again, I shall; but if the command is pressed upon me by the general voice of the country, and offered upon such terms as cannot be objected against, it would reflect dishonor on me to refuse it; and that, I am sure, must, and ought, to give you greater uneasiness, than my going in an honorable command. Upon no other terms will I accept it. At present I have no proposals made to me, nor have I any advice of such an intention, except from private hands."

Command on his terms

On the very day that this letter was despatched (Aug. 14), he received intelligence of his appointment to the command on the terms specified in his letters to his friends. His commission nominated him commander-in-chief of all the forces raised, or to be raised, in the colony. The Assembly also voted three hundred pounds to him, and proportionate sums to the other officers, and to the privates of the Virginia companies, in consideration of their gallant conduct, and their losses in the late battle.

August 14, 1755

The officers next in command under him were Lieutenant-colonel Adam Stephens [*sic*, Stephen], and Major Andrew Lewis. The former, it will be recollected, had been with him in the unfortunate affair at the Great Meadows; his advance in rank shows that his conduct had been meritorious.

The appointment of Washington to his present station was the more gratifying and honorable from being a popular one, made in deference to public sentiment; to which Governor Dinwiddie was obliged to sacrifice his strong inclination in favor of Colonel Innes. It is thought that the governor never afterwards regarded Washington with a friendly eye.

His conduct towards him subsequently, was on various occasions cold and ungracious.

It is worthy of note, that the early popularity of Washington was not the result of brilliant achievements nor signal success; on the contrary, it rose among trials and reverses, and may almost be said to have been the fruit of defeats. It remains an honorable testimony of Virginian intelligence, that the sterling, enduring, but undazzling qualities of Washington were thus early discerned and appreciated, though only heralded by misfortunes. The admirable manner in which he had conducted himself under these misfortunes, and the sagacity and practical wisdom he had displayed on all occasions, were universally acknowledged; and it was observed that, had his modest counsels been adopted by the unfortunate Braddock, a totally different result might have attended the late campaign.

An instance of this high appreciation of his merits occurs in a sermon preached on the 17th of August, by the Rev. Samuel Davies, wherein he cites him as "that heroic youth, Colonel Washington, *whom I cannot but hope Providence has hitherto preserved in so signal a manner for some important service to his country.*" The expressions of the worthy clergyman may have been deemed enthusiastic at the time; viewed in connection with subsequent events they appear almost prophetic.

Having held a conference with Governor Dinwiddie at Williamsburg, and received his instructions, Washington repaired, on the 14th of September, to Winchester, where he fixed his head-quarters. It was a place as yet of trifling magnitude, but important from its position; being a central point where the main roads meet, leading from north to south, and east to west, and commanding the channels of traffic and communication between some of the most important colonies and a great extent of frontier.

Here he was brought into frequent and cordial communication with his old friend Lord Fairfax....

Washington, having visited the frontier posts, established recruiting places, and taken other measures of security, had set off for Williamsburg on military business, when an express arrived at Winchester from Colonel Stephens [*sic*, Stephen], who commanded at Fort Cumberland, giving the alarm that a body of Indians were ravaging the country, burning the houses, and slaughtering the inhabitants. The express was instantly forwarded after Washington; in the mean time, Lord Fairfax sent out orders for the militia of Fairfax and Prince William counties to arm and hasten to the defence of Winchester, where all was confusion and affright....

In the height of the confusion, Washington rode into the town. He had been overtaken by Colonel Stephen's express. His presence inspired some degree of confidence, and he succeeded in stopping most of the fugitives. He would have taken the field at once against the savages, believing their numbers to be few; but not more than twenty-five of the militia could be mustered for the service. The rest refused to stir—they would rather die with their wives and children.

Expresses were sent off to hurry up the militia ordered out by Lord Fairfax. Scouts were ordered out to discover the number of the foe, and convey assurances of succor to the rangers said to be blocked up in the fortresses, though Washington suspected the latter to be "more encompassed by fear than by the enemy." Smiths were set to work to furbish up and repair such fire-arms as were in the place, and waggons were sent off for musketballs, flints, and provisions.

Instead, however, of animated co-operation, Washington was encountered by difficulties at every step. . . . At length the band of Indians, whose ravages had produced this consternation throughout the land, and whose numbers did not exceed one hundred and fifty, being satiated with carnage, conflagration, and plunder, retreated, bearing off spoils and captives. Intelligent scouts sent out by Washington, followed their traces, and brought back certain intelligence that they had recrossed the Allegany Mountains and returned to their homes on the Ohio. This report allayed the public panic, and restored temporary quiet to the harassed frontier.

Most of the Indians engaged in these ravages were Delawares and Shawnees, who, since Braddock's defeat, had been gained over by the French. A principal instigator was said to be Washington's old acquaintance, Shengis[*sic*], and a reward was offered for his head.

Scarooyadi, successor to the half-king, remained true to the English, and vindicated his people to the Governor and Council of Pennsylvania from the charge of having had any share in the late massacres. As to the defeat at the Monongahela, "it was owing," he said, "to the pride and ignorance of that great general (Braddock) that came from England. . . ."

Scarooyadi was ready with his warriors to take up the hatchet again with their English brothers against the French. "Let us unite our strength," said he; "you are numerous, and all the English governors along your sea-shore can raise men enough; but don't let those that come from over the great seas be concerned any more. *They are unfit to fight in the woods. Let us go ourselves—we that came out of this ground.*"

No one felt more strongly than Washington the importance, at this trying juncture, of securing the assistance of these forest warriors. "It is in their power," said he, "to be of infinite use to us; and without Indians, we shall never be able to cope with these cruel foes to our country."

Felt importance of securing assist of forest warriors

Washington had now time to inform himself of the fate of the other enterprises included in this year's plan of military operations. . . .

Reform in the Militia Laws—Discipline of the Troops

Mortifying experience had convinced Washington of the inefficiency of the milita laws, and he now set about effecting a reformation. Through his great and persevering efforts, an act was passed in the Viriginia Legislature giving prompt operation to courts-martial; punishing insubordination, mutiny and desertion with adequate severity; strengthening the authority of a commander, so as to enable him to enforce order and discipline among officers as well as privates; and to avail himself, in time of emergency, and for the common safety, of the means and services of individuals.

This being effected, he proceeded to fill up his companies, and to enforce this newly-defined authority within his camp. All gaming, drinking, quarelling, swearing, and similar excesses, were prohibited under severe penalties.

Moral vices prohibited

In disciplining his men, they were instructed not merely in ordinary and regular tactics, but in all the strategy of Indian warfare, and what is called "bush-fighting,"—a knowledge indispensable in the wild wars of the wilderness. Stockaded forts, too, were constructed at various points, as places of refuge and defence, in exposed neighborhoods. Under shelter of these, the inhabitants began to return to their deserted homes. A shorter and better road, also, was opened by him between Winchester and Cumberland, for the transmission of reinforcements and supplies.

Bush-fighting

His exertions, however, were impeded by one of those questions of precedence, which had so often annoyed him, arising from the difference between crown and provincial commissions. Maryland having by a scanty appropriation raised a small militia force, stationed Captain Dagworthy, with a company of thirty men, at Fort Cumberland, which stood within the boundaries of that province. Dagworthy had served in Canada in the preceding war, and had received a king's commission. This he had since commuted for half-pay, and, of course, had virtually parted with its privileges. He was nothing more, therefore, than a Maryland provincial captain, at the head of thirty men. He now, however, assumed to act under his royal commission, and refused to obey the orders of any officer, however high his rank, who merely held his commission from a governor. . . .

So difficult was it, however, to settle these disputes of precedence, especially where the claims of two governors came in collision, that it was determined to refer the matter to Major-general Shirley, who had succeeded Braddock in the general command of the colonies. For this purpose Washington was to go to Boston, obtain a decision from Shirley of the point in dispute, and a general regulation, by which these difficulties could be prevented in future. It was thought, also, that in a conference with the commander-in-chief he might inform himself of the military measures in contemplation.

Journey to Boston

Accordingly, on the 4th of February (1756), leaving Colonel Adam Stephens in command of the troops, Washington set out on his mission, accompanied by his aide-de-camp, Captain George Mercer of Virginia, and Captain Stewart of the Virginia light horse; the officer who had taken care of General Braddock in his last moments. In those days, the conveniences of travelling, even between our main cities, were few, and the roads execrable. The party, therefore, travelled in Virginia style, on horseback, attended by their black servants in livery. In this way they accomplished a journey of five hundred miles in the depth of winter; stopping for some days at Philadelphia and New York. Those cities were then comparatively small, and the arrival of a party of young Southern officers attracted attention. The late disastrous battle was still the theme of every tongue, and the honorable way in which these young officers had acquitted themselves in it, made them objects of universal interest. Wash-

February 4, 1756

ington's fame, especially, had gone before him; having been spread by the officers who had served with him, and by the public honors decreed him by the Virginia Legislature. . . .

His fame preceded him

With these prepossessions in his favor, when we consider Washington's noble person and demeanor, his consummate horsemanship, the admirable horses he was accustomed to ride, and the aristocratical style of his equipments, we may imagine the effect produced by himself and his little cavalcade, as they clattered through the streets of Philadelphia, and New York, and Boston. It is needless to say, their sojourn in each city was a continual fête. . . . *

The Earl of Loudoun

The general command in America, however, was to be held by the Earl of Loudoun, who was invested with powers almost equal to those of a viceroy, being placed above all the colonial governors. These might claim to be civil and military representatives of their sovereign within their respective colonies; but, even there, were bound to defer and yield precedence to this their official superior. This was part of a plan devised long since, but now first brought into operation, by which the ministry hoped to unite the colonies under military rule, and oblige the Assemblies, magistrates, and people to furnish quarters and provide a general fund subject to the control of this military dictator. . . .

Military dictator

* Elevated Notions as to Style in Dress

We have hitherto treated of Washington in his campaigns in the wilderness, frugal and scanty in his equipments, often, very probably, in little better than hunter's garb. His present excursion through some of the Atlantic cities presents him in a different aspect. His recent intercourse with young British officers, had probably elevated his notions as to style in dress and appearance; at least we are inclined to suspect so from the following aristocratical order for clothes, sent shortly before the time in question, to his correspondent in London.

"2 complete livery suits for servants; with a spare cloak, and all other necessary trimmings for two suits more. I would have you choose the livery by our arms, only as the field of the arms is white, I think the clothes had better not be quite so, but nearly like the inclosed. The trimmings and facings of scarlet, and a scarlet waist-coat. If livery lace is not quite disused, I should be glad to have the cloaks laced. I like that fashion best, and two silver-laced hats for the above servants.

"1 set of horse furniture, with livery lace, with the Washington crest on the housings, &c. The cloak to be of the same piece and color of the clothes.

"3 gold and scarlet sword-knots. 3 silver and blue do. 1 fashionable gold-laced hat."

Washington remained ten days in Boston, attending, with great interest, the meetings of the Massachusetts Legislature, in which the plan of military operations was ably discussed; and receiving the most hospitable attentions from the polite and intelligent society of the place, after which he returned to New York. . . .

In the latter part of March we find him at Williamsburg, attending the opening of the Legislature of Virginia, eager to promote measures for the protection of the frontier and the capture of Fort Duquesne, the leading object of his ambition. Maryland and Pennsylvania were erecting forts for the defence of their own borders, but showed no disposition to co-operate with Virginia in the field; and artillery, artillerymen, and engineers were wanting for an attack on fortified places. Washington urged, therefore, an augmentation of the provincial forces, and various improvements in the militia laws. . . .

March, 1756

Expresses from Winchester brought word that the French had made another sortie from Fort Duquesne, accompanied by a band of savages, and were spreading terror and desolation through the country. . . .

Troubles in the Shenandoah Valley

Report had not exaggerated the troubles of the frontier. It was marauded by merciless bands of savages, led, in some instances, by Frenchmen. Travellers were murdered, farm-houses burnt down, families butchered, and even stockaded forts, or houses of refuge, attacked in open day. The marauders had crossed the mountains and penetrated the valley of the Shenandoah; and several persons had fallen beneath the tomahawk in the neighborhood of Winchester.

Washington's old friend, Lord Fairfax, found himself no longer safe in his rural abode. Greenway Court was in the midst of a woodland region, affording a covert approach for the stealthy savage. His lordship was considered a great chief, whose scalp would be an inestimable trophy for an Indian warrior. . . .

Washington, on his arrival at Winchester, found the inhabitants in great dismay. He resolved immediately to organize a force, composed partly of troops from Fort Cumberland, partly of militia from Winchester and its vicinity; to put himself at its head, and "scour the woods and suspected places in all the mountains and valleys of this part of the frontier, in quest of the Indians and their more cruel associates."

He accordingly despatched an express to Fort Cumberland with orders for a detachment from the garrison; "but how," said he, "are men to be raised at Winchester, since orders are no longer regarded in the county?"

Lord Fairfax, and other militia officers with whom he consulted, advised that each captain should call a private muster of his men, and read before them an address, or "exhortation" as it was called, being an appeal to their patriotism and fears, and a summons to assemble on the 15th of April to enroll themselves for the projected mountain foray.

This measure was adopted; the private musterings occurred; the exhortation was read; the time and place of assemblage appointed; but, when the day of enrolment arrived, not more than fifteen men appeared upon the ground. In the mean time the express returned with sad accounts from Fort Cumberland. No troops could be furnished from that quarter. The garrison was scarcely strong enough for self-defence, having sent out detachments in different directions. The express had narrowly escaped with his life, having been fired upon repeatedly, his horse shot under him, and his clothes riddled with bullets. The roads, he said, were infested by savages; none but hunters, who knew how to thread the forests at night, could travel with safety.

Horrors accumulated at Winchester. Every hour brought its tale of terror, true or false, of houses burnt, families massacred, or beleaguered and famishing in stockaded forts. The danger approached. . . .

Terror of the People of Winchester

An attack on Winchester was apprehended, and the terrors of the people rose to agony. They now turned to Washington as their main hope. The women surrounded him, holding up their children, and imploring him with tears and cries to save them from the savages. The youthful commander looked round on the suppliant crowd with a countenance beaming with pity, and a heart wrung with anguish. A letter to Governor Dinwiddie shows the conflict of his feelings. "I am too little acquainted with pathetic language to attempt a description of these people's distresses. But what can I do? I see their situation; I know their danger, and participate their sufferings, without having it in my power to give them further relief than uncertain promises.— The supplicating tears of the women, and moving petitions of the men, melt me into such deadly sorrow, that I solemnly declare, if I know my own mind, I could offer myself a willing sacrifice to the butchering enemy, provided that would contribute to the people's ease."

The unstudied eloquence of this letter drew from the governor an instant order for a militia force from the upper counties to his assistance; but the Virginia newspapers, in descanting on the frontier troubles, threw discredit on the army and its officers, and attached blame to its commander. Stung to the quick by this injustice, Washington publicly declared, that nothing but the imminent danger of the times prevented him from instantly resigning a command from which he could never reap either honor or benefit. His sensitiveness called forth strong letters from his friends, assuring him of the high sense entertained at the seat of government, and elsewhere, of his merits and services. . . .

Sting of unjust blame

"Our hopes, dear George," wrote Mr. Robinson, the Speaker of the House of Burgesses, "are all fixed on you for bringing our affairs to a happy issue. Consider what fatal consequences to your country your resigning the command at this time may be, especially as there is no doubt most of the officers will follow your example."

In fact, the situation and services of the youthful commander, shut up in a frontier town, destitute of forces, surrounded by savage foes, gallantly, though despairingly, devoting himself to the safety of a suffering people, were properly understood throughout the country, and excited a glow of enthusiasm in his favor. The Legislature, too, began at length to act, but timidly and inefficiently. "The country knows her danger," writes one of the members, "but such is her parsimony, that she is willing to wait for the rains to wet the powder, and the rats to eat the bowstrings of the enemy, rather than attempt to drive them from her frontiers."

The measure of relief voted by the Assembly, was an additional appropriation of twenty thousand pounds, and an increase of the provincial force to fifteen hundred men. With this, it was proposed to erect and garrison a chain of frontier forts, extending through the ranges of the Allegany Mountains, from the Potomac to the borders of North Carolina, a distance of between three and four hundred miles. This was one of the inconsiderate projects devised by Governor Dinwiddie.

Suggestions of Washington

Washington, in letters to the governor and to the speaker of the House of Burgesses, urged the impolicy of such a plan, with their actual force and means. The forts, he observed, ought to be within fifteen or eighteen miles of each other, that their spies might be able to keep watch over the intervening country; otherwise the Indians would pass between them unperceived, effect their ravages, and escape to the mountains, swamps, and ravines, before the troops from the forts could be assembled to pursue them. They ought each to be garrisoned with eighty or a hundred men, so as to afford detachments of sufficient strength, without leaving the garrison too weak; for the Indians are the most stealthy and patient of spies and lurkers; will lie in wait for days together about small forts of the kind, and, if they find, by some chance prisoner, that the garrison is actually weak, will first surprise and cut off its scouting parties, and then attack the fort itself. It was evident, therefore, observed he, that to garrison properly such a line of forts, would require, at least, two thousand men. And even then, a line of such extent might be broken through at one end before the other end could yield assistance. Feint attacks, also, might be made at one point, while the real attack was made at another, quite distant, and the country be overrun before its widely-posted defenders could be alarmed and concentrated. Then must be taken into consideration the immense cost of building so many forts, and the constant and consuming expense of supplies and transportation.

Indians—stealthy and patient spies

His idea of a defensive plan was to build a strong fort at Winchester, the central point, where all the main roads met of a wide range of scattered settlements, where tidings could soonest be collected from every quarter, and whence reinforcements and supplies could most readily be forwarded. It was to be a grand deposit of military stores, a residence for commanding officers, a place of refuge for the women and children in time of alarm, when the men had suddenly to take the field; in a word, it was to be the citadel of the frontier.

Beside this, he would have three or four large fortresses erected at convenient distances upon the frontier, with powerful garrisons, so as to be able to throw out, in constant succession, strong scouting parties, to range the country. Fort Cumberland he condemned as being out of the province, and out of the track of Indian incursions; insomuch that it seldom received an alarm until all the mischief had been effected.

His representations with respect to military laws and regulations were equally cogent. . . .

All these suggestions, showing at this youthful age that forethought and circumspection which distinguished him throughout life, were repeatedly and eloquently urged upon Governor Dinwiddie, with very little effect. The plan of a frontier line of twenty-three forts was persisted in. Fort Cumberland was pertinaciously kept up at a great and useless expense of men and money, and the militia laws remained lax and inefficient. It was decreed, however, that the great central fort at Winchester, recommended by Washington, should be erected. . . .

Forethought and circumspection distinguished his life

Founding of Fort Loudoun—Washington's Tour of Inspection

Throughout the summer of 1756, Washington exerted himself diligently carrying out measures determined upon for frontier security. The great fortress at Winchester was commenced, and the work urged forward as expeditiously as the delays and perplexities incident to a badly organized service would permit. It received the name of Fort Loudoun, in honor of the commander-in-chief, whose arrival in Virginia was hopefully anticipated.

As to the sites of the frontier posts, they were decided upon by Washington and his officers, after frequent and long consultations; parties were sent out to work on them, and men recruited, and militia drafted, to garrison them. Washington visited occasionally such as were in progress and near at hand. It was a service of some peril, for the mountains and forests were still infested by prowling savages, especially in the neighborhood of these new forts. . . .

In the autumn, he made a tour of inspection along the whole line, accompanied by his friend, Captain Hugh Mercer, who had recovered from his recent wounds. This tour furnished repeated proofs of the inefficiency of the militia system. In one place he attempted to raise a force with which to scour a region infested by roving bands of savages. After waiting several days, but five men answered to his summons. . . .

Autumn, 1756

When the militia were drafted, and appeared under arms, the case was not much better. It was now late in the autumn; their term of service, by the act of the Legislature, expired in December,—half of the time, therefore, was lost in marching out and home. Their waste of provisions was enormous. To be put on allowance, like other soldiers, they considered an indignity. They would sooner starve than carry a few days' provisions on their backs. On the march, when breakfast was wanted, they would knock down the first beeve they met with, and, after regaling themselves, march on till dinner, when they would take the same method; and so for supper, to the great oppression of the people. For the want of proper military laws, they were obstinate, self-willed, and perverse. Every individual had his own crude notion of things, and would undertake to direct. If his advice were neglected, he would think himself slighted, abused, and injured, and, to redress himself, would depart for his home.

Want of proper military laws

The garrisons were weak for want of men, but more so from indolence and irregularity. None were in a posture of defence; few but might be surprised with the greatest ease.... [T]he inhabitants of the country were in a wretched situation, feeling the little dependence to be put on militia, who were slow in coming to their assistance, indifferent about their preservation, unwilling to continue, and regardless of every thing but of their own ease. In short, they were so apprehensive of approaching ruin, that the whole back country was in a general motion towards the southern colonies....

Cross-Purposes with Dinwiddie

What rendered this year's service peculiarly irksome and embarrassing to Washington, was the nature of his correspondence with Governor Dinwiddie. That gentleman, either from the natural hurry and confusion of his mind, or from a real disposition to perplex, was extremely ambiguous and unsatisfactory in most of his orders and replies. "So much am I kept in the dark," says Washington, in one of his letters, "that I do not know whether to prepare for the offensive or defensive. What would be absolutely necessary for the one, would be quite useless for the other." And again: "The orders I receive are full of ambiguity. I am left like a wanderer in the wilderness, to proceed at hazard. I am answerable for consequences, and blamed, without the privilege of defence."...

Whence all this contradiction and embarrassment arose has since been explained, and with apparent reason. Governor Dinwiddie had never recovered from the pique caused by the popular elevation of Washington to the command in preference to his favorite, Colonel Innes. His irritation was kept alive by a little Scottish faction, who were desirous of disgusting Washington with the service, so as to induce him to resign, and make way for his rival. They might have carried their point during the panic at Winchester, had not his patriotism and his sympathy with the public distress been more powerful than his self-love. He determined, he said, to bear up under these embarrassments, in the hope of better regulations when Lord Loudoun should arrive; to whom he looked for the future fate of Virginia....

Patriotism more powerful than self-love

Washington Vindicates His Conduct to Lord Loudoun

Circumstances had led Washington to think that Lord Loudoun "had received impressions to his prejudice by false representations of facts," and that a wrong idea prevailed at head-quarters respecting the state of military affairs in Virginia. He was anxious, therefore, for an opportunity of placing all these matters in a proper light; and, understanding that there was to be a meeting in Philadelphia in the month of March, between Lord Loudoun and the southern governors, to consult about measures of defence for their respective provinces, he wrote to Governor Dinwiddie for permission to attend it. "I cannot conceive," writes Dinwiddie in reply, "what service you can be of in going there, as the plan concerted will, in course, be communicated to you and the other officers. However, as you seem so earnest to go, I now give you leave."

March, 1757

This ungracious reply seemed to warrant the suspicions entertained by some of Washington's friends, that it was the busy pen of Governor Dinwiddie which had given the "false representation of facts," to Lord Loudoun. About a month, therefore, before the time of the meeting, Washington addressed a long letter to his lordship, explanatory of military affairs in the quarter where he had commanded. In this he set forth the various defects in the militia laws of Virginia; the errors in its system of defence, and the inevitable confusion which had thence resulted....

The manner in which Washington was received by Lord Loudoun on arriving in Philadelphia, showed him at once, that his long, explanatory letter, had produced the desired effect, and that his character and conduct were justly appreciated. During his sojourn in Philadelphia he was frequently consulted in points of frontier service, and his advice was generally adopted. On one point it failed. He advised that an attack should be made on Fort Duquesne, simultaneous with the attempts on Canada. At such time a great part of the garrison would be drawn away to aid in the defence of that province, and a blow might be struck more likely to insure the peace and safety of the southern frontier, than all its forts and defences.

Lord Loudoun, however, was not to be convinced, or at least persuaded. According to his plan the middle and southern provinces were to maintain a merely defensive warfare; and as Virginia would be required to send four hundred of her troops to the aid of South Carolina, she would, in fact, be left weaker than before.

Disappointment

Washington was also disappointed a second time, in the hope of having his regiment placed on the same footing as the regular army, and of obtaining a king's commission;—the latter he was destined never to hold.

His representations with respect to Fort Cumberland had the desired effect, in counteracting the mischievous intermeddling of Dinwiddie. The Virginia troops and stores were ordered to be again removed to Fort Loudoun, at Winchester, which once more became head-quarters, while Fort Cumberland was left to be occupied by a Maryland garrison. Washington was instructed, likewise, to correspond and co-operate, in military affairs, with Colonel Stanwix, who was stationed on the Pennsylvania frontier, with five hundred men from the Royal American regiment, and to whom he would be, in some measure, subordinate. This proved a correspondence of friendship, as well as duty; Colonel Stanwix being a gentleman of high moral worth, as well as great ability in military affairs.

Louisburg

The great plan of operations at the north was again doomed to failure. The reduction of Crown Point, on Lake Champlain, which had long been meditated, was laid aside, and the capture of Louisburg substituted, as an acquisition of far greater importance. . . .

Lord Loudoun Sails for Halifax

In the course of July, Lord Loudoun set sail for Halifax with all the troops he could collect, amounting to about six thousand men, to join with Admiral Holbourne, who had just arrived at that port with eleven ships of the line, a fire-ship, bomb-ketch, and fleet of transports, having on board six thousand men. With this united force Lord Loudoun anticipated the certain capture of Louisburg.

Montcalm

Scarce had the tidings of his lordship's departure reached Canada, when the active Montcalm again took the field, to follow up the successes of the preceding year. Fort William Henry, which Sir Wm. Johnson had erected on the southern shore of Lake George, was now his object; it commanded the lake, and was an important protection to the British frontier. A brave old officer, Colonel Monro, with about five hundred men, formed the garrison; more than three times that number of militia were intrenched near by. . . . Montcalm invested the fort, made his approaches, and battered it with his artillery. For five days its veteran commander kept up a vigorous defence, trusting to receive assistance from General Webb who had failed to relieve Fort Oswego in the preceding year, and who was now at Fort Edward, about fifteen miles distant, with upwards of five thousand men. Instead of this, Webb, who overrated the French forces, sent him a letter, advising him to capitulate. . . . At length, in the month of August, he hung out a flag of truce, and obtained honorable terms from an enemy who knew how to appreciate his valor. Montcalm demolished the fort, carried off all the artillery and munitions of war, with vessels employed in the navigation of the lake; and having thus completed his destruction of the British defences on this frontier, returned once more in triumph with the spoils of victory, to hang up fresh trophies in the churches of Canada.

Fresh trophies in Canadian churches

Lord Loudoun, in the mean time, formed his junction with Admiral Holbourne at Halifax, and the troops were embarked with all diligence on board of the transports. Unfortunately, the French were again too quick for them. . . . Thus ended the northern campaign by land and sea; a subject of great mortification to the nation, and ridicule and triumph to the enemy.

During these unfortunate operations to the north, Washington was stationed at Winchester, shorn of part of his force by the detachment to South Carolina, and left with seven hundred men to defend a frontier of more than three hundred and fifty miles in extent. The capture and demolition of Oswego by Montcalm had produced a disastrous effect. The whole country of the five nations was abandoned to the French. The frontiers of Pennsylvania, Maryland, and Virginia were harassed by repeated inroads of French and Indians, and Washington had the mortification to see the noble valley of the Shenandoah almost deserted by its inhabitants, and fast relapsing into a wilderness.

The year wore away on his part in the harassing service of defending a wide frontier with an insufficient and badly organized force, and the vexations he experienced were heightened by continual misunderstandings with Governor Dinwiddie. . . .

Continual misunderstandings with Dinwiddie

The multiplied vexations which Washington had latterly experienced from this man, had preyed upon his spirits, and contributed, with his incessant toils and anxieties, to undermine his health. For some time he struggled with repeated attacks of dysentery and fever, and continued in the exercise of his duties; but the increased violence of his malady, and the urgent advice of his friend Dr. Craik, the army surgeon, induced him to relinquish his post towards the end of the year, and retire to Mount Vernon.

The administration of Dinwiddie, however, was now at an end. He set sail for England in January, 1758, very little regretted, excepting by his immediate hangers-on; and leaving a character overshadowed by the imputation of avarice and extortion in the exaction of illegal fees, and of downright delinquency in regard to large sums transmitted to him by government, to be paid over to the province in indemnification of its extra expenses; for the disposition of which sums he failed to render an account. . . .

January, 1758

Washington Recovers His Health

For several months, Washington was afflicted by returns of his malady, accompanied by symptoms indicative, as he thought, of a decline. "My constitution," writes he to his friend Colonel Stanwix, "is much impaired, and nothing can retrieve it but the greatest care and the most circumspect course of life. This being the case, as I have now no prospect left of preferment in the military way, and despair of rendering that immediate service which my country may require from the person commanding its troops, I have thoughts of quitting my command and retiring from all public business, leaving my post to be filled by some other person more capable of the task, and who may, perhaps, have his endeavors crowned with better success than mine have been."

NATIONAL PORTRAIT GALLERY, LONDON — Artist unknown, approx. 1760–1765

GOVERNOR ROBERT DINWIDDIE
COLONIAL GOVERNOR OF VIRGINIA

A gradual improvement in his health, and a change in his prospects, encouraged him to continue in what really was his favorite career, and at the beginning of April he was again in command at Fort Loudoun. Mr. Francis Fauquier had been appointed successor to Dinwiddie, and, until he should arrive, Mr. John Blair, president of the council, had, from his office, charge of the government. In the latter, Washington had a friend who appreciated his character and services, and was disposed to carry out his plans.

April, 1758

The general aspect of affairs, also, was more animating. Under the able and intrepid administration of William Pitt, who had control of the British cabinet, an effort was made to retrieve the disgraces of the late American campaign, and to carry on the war with greater vigor. . . .

Able administration of William Pitt

It was with the greatest satisfaction Washington saw his favorite measure at last adopted, the reduction of Fort Duquesne; and he resolved to continue in the service until that object was accomplished.

In a letter to Stanwix, who was now a brigadier-general, he modestly requested to be mentioned in favorable terms to General Forbes; "not," said he, "as a person who would depend upon him for further recommendation to military preferment (for I have long conquered all such inclinations, and shall serve this campaign merely for the purpose of affording my best endeavors to bring matters to a conclusion), but as a person who would gladly be distinguished in some measure from the *common run* of provincial officers, as I understand there will be a motley herd of us." He had the satisfaction subsequently of enjoying the fullest confidence of General Forbes, who knew too well the sound judgment and practical ability evinced by him in the unfortunate campaign of Braddock, not to be desirous of availing himself of his counsels.

Washington Commander-in-Chief of the Virginia Troops

Washington still was commander-in-chief of the Virginia troops, now augmented, by an act of the Assembly, to two regiments of one thousand men each; one led by himself, the other by Colonel Byrd; the whole destined to make a part of the army of General Forbes in the expedition against Fort Duquesne.

Fort Duquesne—long-desired campaign

Of the animation which he felt at the prospect of serving in this long-desired campaign, and revisiting with an effective force the scene of past disasters, we have a proof in a short letter, written during the excitement of the moment, to Major Francis Halket, his former companion in arms.

"My dear Halket:—Are we to have you once more among us? And shall we revisit together a hapless spot, that proved so fatal to many of our former brave companions? Yes; and I rejoice at it, hoping it will now be in our power to testify a just abhorrence of the cruel butcheries exercised on our friends in the unfortunate day of General Braddock's defeat; and, moreover, to show our enemies, that we can practise all that lenity of which they only boast, without affording any adequate proof." . . .

Washington Orders Out the Militia

Operations went on slowly in that part of the year's campaign in which Washington was immediately engaged—the expedition against Fort Duquesne. Brigadier-general Forbes, who was commander-in-chief, was detained at Philadelphia by those delays and cross-purposes incident to military affairs in a new country. Colonel Bouquet, who was to command the advanced division, took his station, with a corps of regulars, at Raystown in the centre of Pennsylvania. There slowly assembled troops from various parts. Three thousand Pennsylvanians, twelve hundred and fifty South Carolinians, and a few hundred men from elsewhere.

Washington, in the mean time, gathered together his scattered regiment at Winchester, some from a distance of two hundred miles, and diligently disciplined his recruits. He had two Virginia regiments under him, amounting, when complete, to about nineteen hundred men. Seven hundred Indian warriors, also, came lagging into his camp, lured by the prospect of a successful campaign.

The president of the council had given Washington a discretionary power in the present juncture, to order out militia for the purpose of garrisoning the fort in the absence of the regular troops. Washington exercised the power with extreme reluctance. He considered it, he said, an affair of too important and delicate a nature for him to manage, and apprehended the discontent it might occasion. In fact, his sympathies were always with the husbandmen and the laborers of the soil, and he deplored the evils imposed upon them by arbitrary drafts for militia service; a scruple not often indulged by youthful commanders.

The force thus assembling was in want of arms, tents, field-equipage, and almost every requisite. Washington had made repeated representations, by letter, of the destitute state of the Virginia troops, but without avail; he was now ordered by Sir John St. Clair, the quartermaster-general of the forces under General Forbes, to repair to Williamsburg, and lay the state of the case before the council. He set off promptly on horseback, attended by Bishop, the well-trained military servant, who had served the late General Braddock. It proved an eventful journey, though not in a military point of view. In crossing a ferry of the Pamunkey, a branch of York River, he fell in company with a Mr. Chamberlayne, who lived in the neighborhood, and who, in the spirit of Virginian hospitality, claimed him as a guest. It was with difficulty Washington could be prevailed on to halt for dinner, so impatient was he to arrive at Williamsburg, and accomplish his mission.

Diverted from Williamsburg as Chamberlayne's dinner guest

GEORGE WASHINGTON AT AGE TWENTY-FIVE
Miniature on ivory by J. De Mare
from a painting by Charles Willson Peale

MARTHA DANDRIDGE CUSTIS AT AGE TWENTY-SIX
Engraved by J. Rogers from the painting
by John Wollaston, 1757

Mrs. Martha Custis

Among the guests at Mr. Chamberlayne's was a young and blooming widow, Mrs. Martha Custis, daughter of Mr. John Dandridge, both patrician names in the province. Her husband, John [*sic*, Daniel] Parke Custis, had been dead about three years, leaving her with two young children, and a large fortune. She is represented as being rather below the middle size, but extremely well shaped, with an agreeable countenance, dark hazel eyes and hair, and those frank, engaging manners, so captivating in Southern women. We are not informed whether Washington had met with her before; probably not during her widowhood, as during that time he had been almost continually on the frontier. We have shown that, with all his gravity and reserve, he was quickly susceptible to female charms; and they may have had a greater effect upon him when thus casually encountered, in fleeting moments snatched from the cares and perplexities and rude scenes of frontier warfare. At any rate, his heart appears to have been taken by surprise.

His heart taken by surprise

The dinner, which in those days was an earlier meal than at present, seemed all too short. The afternoon passed away like a dream. Bishop was punctual to the orders he had received on halting; the horses pawed at the door; but for once Washington loitered in the path of duty. The horses were countermanded, and it was not until the next morning that he was again in the saddle, spurring for Williamsburg. Happily, the White House, the residence of Mrs. Custis, was in New Kent County, at no great distance from that city, so that he had opportunities of visiting her in the intervals of business. His time for courtship, however, was brief. Military duties called him back almost immediately to Winchester; but he feared, should he leave the matter in suspense, some more enterprising rival might supplant him during his absence, as in the case of Miss Philipse, at New York. He improved, therefore, his brief opportunity to the utmost. The blooming widow had many suitors, but Washington was graced with that renown so ennobling in the eyes of woman. In a word, before they separated, they had mutually plighted their faith, and the marriage was to take place as soon as the campaign against Fort Duquesne was at an end.

Marriage at the end of his campaign

Before returning to Winchester, Washington was obliged to hold conferences with Sir John St. Clair and Colonel Bouquet, at an intermediate rendezvous, to give them information respecting the frontiers, and arrange about the marching of his troops. His constant word to them was forward! forward! For the precious time for action was slipping away, and he feared their Indian allies, so important to

Alonzo Chappel, 1856

WASHINGTON'S FIRST INVERVIEW WITH MRS. CUSTIS, AFTERWARDS MRS. WASHINGTON

their security while on the march, might, with their usual fickleness, lose patience, and return home.

On arriving at Winchester, he found his troops restless and discontented, from prolonged inaction; the inhabitants impatient of the burdens imposed on them, and of the disturbances of an idle camp; while the Indians, as he apprehended, had deserted outright. It was a great relief, therefore, when he received orders from the commander-in-chief to repair to Fort Cumberland. He arrived there on the 2d of July, and proceeded to open a road between that post and head-quarters, at Raystown, thirty miles distant, where Colonel Bouquet was stationed.

July 2, 1758

The Rifle Dress

His troops were scantily supplied with regimental clothing. The weather was oppressively warm. He now conceived the idea of equipping them in the light Indian hunting garb, and even of adopting it himself. Two companies were accordingly equipped in this style, and sent under the command of Major Lewis to head-quarters. "It is an unbecoming dress, I own, for an officer," writes Washington, "but convenience rather than show, I think, should be consulted. The reduction of bat-horses alone would be sufficient to recommend it; for nothing is more certain than that less baggage would be required."

The experiment was successful. "The dress takes very well here," writes Colonel Bouquet; "and, thank God, we see nothing but shirts and blankets. . . . Their dress should be one pattern for this expedition." Such was probably the origin of the American rifle dress, afterwards so much worn in warfare, and modelled on the Indian costume.

The army was now annoyed by scouting parties of Indians hovering about the neighborhood. Expresses passing between the posts were fired upon; a waggoner was shot down. Washington sent out counter-parties of Cherokees. Colonel Bouquet required that each party should be accompanied by an officer and a number of white men. Washington complied with the order, though he considered them an encumbrance rather than an advantage. "Small parties of Indians," said he, "will more effectually harass the enemy, by keeping them under continual alarms, than any parties of white men can do. For small parties of the latter are not equal to the task, not being so dexterous at skulking as Indians; and large parties will be discovered by their spies early enough to have a superior force opposed to them." With all his efforts, however, he was never able fully to make the officers of the regular army appreciate the importance of Indian allies in these campaigns in the wilderness.

Efforts to make officers appreciate Indian allies

On the other hand, he earnestly discountenanced a proposition of Colonel Bouquet, to make an irruption into the enemy's country with a strong party of regulars. Such a detachment, he observed, could not be sent without a cumbersome train of supplies, which would discover it to the enemy, who must at that time be collecting his whole force at Fort Duquesne; the enterprise, therefore, would be likely to terminate in a miscarriage, if not in the destruction of the party. We shall see that his opinion was oracular.

Washington Elected to the House of Burgesses

As Washington intended to retire from military life at the close of this campaign, he had proposed himself to the electors of Frederick County as their representative in the House of Burgesses. The election was coming on at Winchester; his friends pressed him to attend it, and Colonel Bouquet gave him leave of absence; but he declined to absent himself from his post for the promotion of his political interests. There were three competitors in the field, yet so high was the public opinion of his merit, that, though Winchester had been his headquarters for two or three years past, and he had occasionally enforced martial law with a rigorous hand, he was elected by a large majority. The election was carried on somewhat in the English style. There was much eating and drinking at the expense of the candidate. Washington appeared on the hustings by proxy, and his representative was chaired by about the town with enthusiastic applause and huzzaing for Colonel Washington.

High public opinion of his merit

Tidings of Amherst's Success

On the 21st of July arrived tidings of the brilliant success of that part of the scheme of the year's campaign, conducted by General Amherst and Admiral Boscawen, who had reduced the strong town of Louisburg, and gained possession of the Island of Cape Breton. This intelligence increased Washington's impatience at the delays of the expedition with which he was connected. He wished to rival these successes by a brilliant blow in the south. Perhaps a desire for personal distinction in the eyes of the lady of his choice may have been at the bottom of this impatience; for we are told that he kept up a constant correspondence with her throughout the campaign.

July 21, 1758

Understanding that the commander-in-chief had some thoughts of throwing a body of light troops in the advance, he wrote to Colonel Bouquet, earnestly soliciting his influence to have himself and his Virginia regiment included in the detachment. "If any argument is needed to obtain this favor," said he, "I hope, without vanity, I may be allowed to say, that from long intimacy with these woods, and frequent scoutings in them, my men are at least as well acquainted with all the passes and difficulties as any troops that will be employed."

A New Road to Fort Duquesne

He soon learned to his surprise, however, that the road to which his men were accustomed, and which had been worked by Braddock's troops in his campaign, was not to be taken in the present expedition, but a new one opened through the heart of Pennsylvania, from Raystown to Fort Duquesne, on the track generally taken by the northern traders. He instantly commenced long and repeated remonstrances on the subject; representing that Braddock's road, from recent examination, only needed partial repairs, and showing by clear calculation that an army could reach Fort Duquesne by that route in thirty-four days, so that the whole campaign might be effected by the middle of October; whereas the extreme labor of opening a new road across mountains, swamps, and through a densely wooded country, would detain them so late, that the season would be over before they could reach the scene of action. His representations were of no avail. The officers of the regular service had received a fearful idea of Braddock's road from his own despatches, wherein he had described it as lying "across mountains and rocks of an excessive height, vastly steep, and divided by torrents and rivers." Whereas the Pennsylvania traders, who were anxious for the opening of the new road through their province, described the country through which it would pass as less difficult, and its streams less subject to inundation; above all, it was a direct line, and fifty miles nearer. This route, therefore, to the great regret of Washington, and the indignation of the Virginia Assembly, was definitely adopted, and sixteen hundred men were immediately thrown in the advance from Raystown to work upon it.

The first of September found Washington still encamped at Fort Cumberland; his troops sickly and dispirited, and the brilliant expedition which he had anticipated, dwindling down into a tedious operation of road-making. In the mean time, his scouts brought him word that the whole force at Fort Duquesne on the 13th of August, Indians included, did not exceed eight hundred men: had an early campaign been pressed forward, as he recommended, the place by this time would have been captured. At length, in the month of September, he received orders from General Forbes to join him with his troops at Raystown, where he had just arrived, having been detained by severe illness. He was received by the general with the highest marks of respect. On all occasions, both in private and at councils of war, that commander treated his opinions with the greatest deference. He, moreover, adopted a plan drawn out by Washington for the march of the army, and an order of battle which still exists, furnishing a proof of his skill in frontier warfare.

September 1, 1758

Proof of his skill in frontier warfare

It was now the middle of September; yet the great body of men engaged in opening the new military road, after incredible toil, had not advanced above forty-five miles, to a place called Loyal Hannan, a little beyond Laurel Hill. Colonel Bouquet, who commanded the division of nearly two thousand men sent forward to open this road, had halted at Loyal Hannan to establish a military post and deposit.

Disastrous Consequences

He was upwards of fifty miles from Fort Duquesne, and was tempted to adopt the measure, so strongly discountenanced by Washington, of sending a party on a foray into the enemy's country. He accordingly detached Major Grant with eight hundred picked men, some of them Highlanders, others, in Indian garb, the part of Washington's Virginian regiment sent forward by him from Cumberland under command of Major Lewis.

The instructions given to Major Grant were merely to reconnoitre the country in the neighborhood of Fort Duquesne, and ascertain the strength and position of the enemy. He conducted the enterprise with the foolhardiness of a man eager for personal notoriety. His whole object seems to have been by open bravado to provoke an action. The enemy were apprised, through their scouts, of his approach, but suffered him to advance unmolested. Arriving at night in the neighborhood of the fort, he posted his men on a hill, and sent out a party of observation, who set fire to a log house near the walls and returned to the encampment. As if this were not sufficient to put the enemy on the alert, he ordered the reveille to be beaten in the morning in several places; then, posting Major Lewis with his provincial troops at a distance in the rear, to protect the baggage, he marshalled his regulars in battle array, and sent an engineer, with a covering party, to take a plan of the works in full view of the garrison.... A scene now occurred similar to that at the defeat of Braddock. The British officers marshalled their men according to European tactics, and the Highlanders for some time stood their ground bravely; but the destructive fire and horrid yells of the Indians soon produced panic and confusion.

Major Grant eager for personal notoriety

Major Lewis, at the first noise of the attack, left Captain Bullitt, with fifty Virginians, to guard the baggage, and hastened with the main part of his men to the scene of action. The contest was kept up for some time, but the confusion was irretrievable. The Indians sallied from their concealment, and attacked with the tomahawk and scalping-knife. Lewis fought hand to hand with an Indian brave, whom he laid dead at his feet; but was surrounded by others, and only saved his life by surrendering himself to a French officer. Major Grant surrendered himself in like manner. The whole detachment was put to the rout with dreadful carnage....

The routed detachment came back in fragments to Colonel Bouquet's camp at Loyal Hannan, with the loss of twenty-one officers, and two hundred and seventy-three privates, killed and taken. The Highlanders and the Virginians were those that fought the best, and suffered the most in this bloody battle. Washington's regiment lost six officers and sixty-two privates. . . .Washington, who was at Raystown when the disastrous news arrived, was publicly complimented by General Forbes, on the gallant conduct of his Virginian troops, and Bullitt's behaviour was "a matter of great admiration." The latter was soon after rewarded with a major's commission.

As a further mark of the high opinion now entertained of provincial troops for frontier service, Washington was given the command of a division, partly composed of his own men, to keep in the

Benson J. Lossing, *Life of Washington*, Vol. I, 1856

RAISING THE BRITISH FLAG AT FORT DUQUESNE, NOVEMBER 25, 1758

advance of the main body, clear the roads, throw out scouting parties, and repel Indian attacks.

Fort Duquesne Taken

It was the 5th of November before the whole army assembled at Loyal Hannan. Winter was now at hand, and upwards of fifty miles of wilderness were yet to be traversed, by a road not yet formed, before they could reach Fort Duquesne. . . .

November 5, 1758

At length the army arrived in sight of Fort Duquesne, advancing with great precaution, and expecting a vigorous defence; but that formidable fortress, the terror and scourge of the frontier, and the object of such warlike enterprise, fell without a blow. The recent successes of the English forces in Canada, particularly the capture and destruction of Fort Frontenac, had left the garrison without hope of reinforcements and supplies. The whole force, at the time, did not exceed five hundred men, and the provisions were nearly exhausted. The commander, therefore, waited only until the English army was within one day's march, when he embarked his troops at night in batteaux, blew up his magazines, set fire to the fort, and retreated down the Ohio, by the light of the flames.

On the 25th of November, Washington, with the advanced guard, marched in, and planted the British flag on the yet smoking ruins. . . .

November 25, 1758

The ruins of the fortress were now put in a defensible state, and garrisoned by two hundred men from Washington's regiment; the name was changed to that of Fort Pitt, in honor of the illustrious British minister, whose measures had given vigor and effect to this year's campaign; it has since been modified into Pittsburg, and designates one of the most busy and populous cities of the interior.

The reduction of Fort Duquesne terminated, as Washington had foreseen, the troubles and dangers of the southern frontier. The French domination of the Ohio was at an end; the Indians, as usual, paid homage to the conquering power, and a treaty of peace was concluded with all the tribes between the Ohio and the lakes.

French domination at an end

Virginia Museum of Fine Arts, Richmond
Gift of Colonel and Mrs. Edgar Garbish

by Junius Brutus Stearns, 1849
Photo: Ron Jennings © Virginia Museum of Fine Arts

THE WEDDING OF GEORGE WASHINGTON AND MARTHA CUSTIS

"Domestic Concerns and Public Duties"

Conflict with England

Marriage with Mrs. Custis

The Life of George Washington, Vol. I, by Washington Irving, 1856

With this campaign ended, for the present, the military career of Washington. His great object was attained, the restoration of quiet and security to his native province; and, having abandoned all hope of attaining rank in the regular army, and his health being much impaired, he gave up his commission at the close of the year, and retired from the service, followed by the applause of his fellow-soldiers, and the gratitude and admiration of all his countrymen.

His marriage with Mrs. Custis took place shortly after his return. It was celebrated on the 6th of January, 1759, at the White House, the residence of the bride, in the good old hospitable style of Virginia, amid a joyous assemblage of relatives and friends. . . .

January 6, 1759

George Washington's Installation in the House of Burgesses

For three months after his marriage, Washington resided with his bride at the "White House." During his sojourn there, he repaired to Williamsburg, to take his seat in the House of Burgesses. By a vote of the House, it had been determined to greet his instalment by a signal testimonial of respect. Accordingly, as soon as he took his seat, Mr. Robinson, the speaker, in eloquent language, dictated by the warmth of private friendship, returned thanks, on behalf of the colony, for the distinguished military services he had rendered to his country.

Testimonial of respect

Washington rose to reply; blushed—stammered—trembled, and could not utter a word. "Sit down, Mr. Washington," said the speaker, with a smile; "your modesty equals your valor, and that surpasses the power of any language I possess."

Such was Washington's first launch into civil life, in which he was to be distinguished by the same judgment, devotion, courage, and magnanimity exhibited in his military career. He attended the House frequently during the remainder of the session, after which he conducted his bride to his favorite abode of Mount Vernon.

Mr. Custis, the first husband of Mrs. Washington, had left large landed property, and forty-five thousand pounds sterling in money. One third fell to his widow in her own right; two thirds were inherited equally by her two children—a boy of six, and a girl of four years of age. By a decree of the General Court, Washington was intrusted with the care of the property inherited by the

Miss Custis — to — George Washington — Dr.

1769.	To the Expences of a Journey to the Fredk. Springs in Aug.t 1769 — Undertaken solely on her Acct. to try (by the advice of her Physician) the effect of the Waters on her Complaint — Viz. —		
July.	To a Cot		15 —
From 1st. to 2d. &c. of Aug.	To Travelling Expen.s up — to wit		
	At Wm. Carr Lanes	£0. 7. 9	
	Lodging &ca. at Chs. Wests	14. 4½	
	Dinner &ca. at Snicker's	7 —	
	Ditto &ca. on Opeckon	6. 9	
	Lodging &ca. at Hedges	11 —	
	Dinner &ca. at Herrefords	8 —	2 — 14. 10½
From the 6th. of Aug.t to 9th. Sepr.	To Cash pd. for Sundries while there viz		
	For Repairg. Houses & Buildg. an Arbr.	15 —	
	Butcher's Meat	4. 15. 11	
	Poultry Eggs & Milk	1. 0. 9	
	Butter 34½ lbs	1. 6. 5½	
	Roots Green's & Fruit	1. 18. 7½	
	Baker for Bread & Flour	4. 4. 8	
	Wood	6. 8	
	Washing	1. 18. 1½	
	Smith	3. 1½	
	Paid the Bath keeper	1. 10 —	
	Oats & Pasturage for my Horses	8. 4. 1	
		26 — 3 — 5.	
	Deduct 25 pr. Ct. to reduce it to Virga. Currency	5. 4. 8	20 — 18. 9
From 9th. to 12th. Septr.	To Exp.s in Travellg. down — viz. —		
	Dinner, Oats, &ca. at Morgans	8. 6	
	Logings &ca. at Hedges	12 —	
	Feeding &ca. on the Road	8. 6	
	Oats &ca. under the Ridge	8. 9	
	Lodging &ca. at Chas. Wests	14. 6	
	Dinner &ca. at Wm. Carr Lanes	6. 7½	2. 18. 10½
	To Waggonage of our Necesy. up & down		9 —
	Exp.s of the Servants with the Waggon		6. 9
			£36 — 14. 3

Errs. excepted pr.

Sepr. 13th. 1769.

Go. Washington

FACSIMILE OF WASHINGTON'S ACCOUNT RECORDS FOR MARTHA CUSTIS, 1769

children; a sacred and delicate trust, which he discharged in the most faithful and judicious manner; becoming more like a parent, than a mere guardian to them. . . .

A faithful and judicious parent

Mount Vernon and Its Vicinity

Mount Vernon was his harbor of repose, where he repeatedly furled his sail, and fancied himself anchored for life. No impulse of ambition tempted him thence; nothing but the call of his country, and his devotion to the public good. The place was endeared to him by the remembrance of his brother Lawrence, and of the happy days he had passed here with that brother in the days of boyhood; but it was a delightful place in itself, and well calculated to inspire the rural feeling. . . .

"No estate in United America," observes he, in one of his letters, "is more pleasantly situated. In a high and healthy country; in a latitude between the extremes of heat and cold; on one of the finest rivers in the world; a river well stocked with various kinds of fish at all seasons of the year, and in the spring with shad, herrings, bass, carp, sturgeon, &c., in great abundance. The borders of the estate are washed by more than ten miles of tide water; several valuable fisheries appertain to it: the whole shore, in fact, is one entire fishery."

These were, as yet, the aristocratical days of Virginia. The estates were large, and continued in the same families by entails. Many of the wealthy planters were connected with old families in England. The young men, especially the elder sons, were often sent to finish their education there, and on their return brought out the tastes and habits of the mother country. The governors of Virginia were from the higher ranks of society, and maintained a corresponding state. The "established," or Episcopal Church, predominated throughout the "ancient dominion," as it was termed; each county was divided into parishes, as in England,—each with its parochial church, its parsonage, and glebe. Washington was vestryman of two parishes, Fairfax and Truro; the parochial church of the former was at Alexandria, ten miles from Mount Vernon; of the latter, at Pohick, about seven miles. The church at Pohick was rebuilt on a plan of his own, and in a great measure at his expense. At one or other of these churches he attended every Sunday, when the weather and the roads permitted. His demeanor was reverential and devout. Mrs. Washington knelt during the prayers; he always stood, as was the custom at that time. Both were communicants. . . .

Vestryman of two parishes

Domestic Habits

Washington, by his marriage, had added above one hundred thousand dollars to his already considerable fortune, and was enabled to live in ample and dignified style. His intimacy with the Fairfaxes, and his intercourse with British officers of rank, had perhaps had their influence on his mode of living. He had his chariot and four, with black postilions in livery, for the use of Mrs. Washington and her lady visitors. As for himself, he always appeared on horseback. His stable was well filled, and admirably regulated. His stud was thorough-bred and in excellent order. His household books contain registers of the names, ages, and marks of his favorite horses; such as Ajax, Blueskin, Valiant, Magnolia (an Arab), &c. Also his dogs, chiefly foxhounds, Vulcan, Singer, Ringwood, Sweetlips, Forrester, Music, Rockwood, Truelove, &c.

Mode of living 1759–1763

A large Virginia estate, in those days, was a little empire. The mansion-house was the seat of government, with its numerous dependencies, such as kitchens, smoke-house, workshops and stables. In this mansion the planter ruled supreme; his steward or overseer was his prime minister and executive officer; he had his legion of house negroes for domestic service, and his host of field negroes for the culture of tobacco, Indian corn, and other crops, and for other out of door labor. Their quarter formed a kind of hamlet apart, composed of various huts, with little gardens and poultry yards, all well stocked, and swarms of little negroes gambolling in the sunshine. Then there were large wooden edifices for curing tobacco, the staple and most profitable production, and mills for grinding wheat and Indian corn, of which large fields were cultivated for the supply of the family and the maintenance of the negroes.

Among the slaves were artificers of all kinds, tailors, shoemakers, carpenters, smiths, wheel-wrights, and so forth; so that a plantation produced every thing within itself for ordinary use: as to articles of fashion and elegance, luxuries, and expensive clothing, they were imported from London; for the planters on the main rivers, especially the Potomac, carried on an immediate trade with England. Their tobacco was put up by their own negroes, bore their own marks, was shipped on board of vessels which came

"A large Virginia estate, in those days, was a little empire."

MOUNT VERNON by Benson J. Lossing

up the rivers for the purpose, and consigned to some agent in Liverpool or Bristol with whom the planter kept an account.

The Virginia planters were prone to leave the care of their estates too much to their overseers, and to think personal labor a degradation. Washington carried into his rural affairs the same method, activity, and circumspection that had distinguished him in military life. He kept his own accounts, posted up his books, and balanced them with mercantile exactness. We have examined them as well, as his diaries recording his daily occupations, and his letter-books, containing entries of shipments of tobacco, and correspondence with his London agents. They are monuments of his business habits.

The products of his estate also became so noted for the faithfulness, as to quality and quantity, with which they were put up, that it is said any barrel of flour that bore the brand of George Washington, Mount Vernon, was exempted from the customary inspection in the West India ports.

Daily Habits

He was an early riser, often before daybreak in the winter when the nights were long. On such occasions he lit his own fire, and wrote or read by candle-light. He breakfasted at seven in summer, at eight in winter. Two small cups of tea and three or four cakes of Indian meal (called hoe-cakes), formed his frugal repast. Immediately after breakfast, he mounted his horse and visited those parts of the estate where any work was going on, seeing to every thing with his own eyes, and often aiding with his own hand.

Dinner was served at two o'clock. He ate heartily, but was no epicure, nor critical about his food. His beverage was small beer or cider, and two glasses of old Madeira. He took tea, of which he was very fond, early in the evening, and retired for the night about nine o'clock.

If confined to the house by bad weather, he took that occasion to arrange his papers, post up his accounts, or write letters; passing part of the time in reading, and occasionally reading aloud to the family.

Read aloud to his family

He treated his negroes with kindness; attended to their comforts; was particularly careful of them in sickness; but never tolerated idleness, and exacted a faithful performance of all their allotted tasks. He had a quick eye at calculating each man's capabilities. An entry in his diary gives a curious instance of this. Four of his negroes, employed as carpenters, were hewing and shaping timber. It appeared to him, in noticing the amount of work accomplished between two succeeding mornings, that they loitered at their labor. Sitting down quietly he timed their operations; how long it took them to get their cross-cut saw and other implements ready; how long to clear away the branches from the trunk of a fallen tree; how long to hew and saw it; what time was expended in considering and consulting, and after all, how much work was effected during the time he looked on. From this he made his computation how much they could execute in the course of a day, working entirely at their ease.

At another time we find him working for a part of two days with Peter, his smith, to make a plough on a new invention of his own. This, after two or three failures, he accomplished. Then, with less than his usual judgment, he put his two chariot horses to the plough, and ran a great risk of spoiling them, in giving his new invention a trial over ground thickly swarded. . . .

A new invention of his own

Washington delighted in the chase. In the hunting season, when he rode out early in the morning to visit distant parts of the estate, where work was going on, he often took some of the dogs with him for the chance of starting a fox, which he occasionally did, though he was not always successful in killing him. He was a bold rider and an admirable horseman, though he never claimed the merit of being an accomplished fox-hunter. . . .

A bold rider and an excellent horseman

Occasionally he and Mrs. Washington would pay a visit to Annapolis, at that time the seat of government of Maryland, and partake of the gayeties which prevailed during the session of the legislature. The society of these seats of provincial governments was always polite and fashionable, and more exclusive than in these republican days, being, in a manner, the outposts of the English aristocracy, where all places of dignity or profit were secured for younger sons, and poor, but proud relatives. During the session of the Legislature, dinners and balls abounded, and there were occasional attempts at theatricals. The latter was an amusement for which Washington always had a relish, though he never had an opportunity of gratifying it effectually. Neither was he disinclined to mingle in the dance, and we remember to have heard venerable ladies, who had been belles in his day, pride themselves on having had him for a partner, though, they added, he was apt to be a ceremonious and grave one.

In this round of rural occupation, rural amusements, and social intercourse, Washington passed several tranquil years, the halcyon season of his life. His already established reputation drew many visitors to Mount Vernon; some of his early companions in arms were his occasional guests, and his friendships and connections linked him with some of the most prominent and worthy people of the country, who were sure to be received with cordial, but simple and unpretending hospitality. His marriage was unblessed with children; but those of Mrs. Washington experienced from him parental care and affection, and the formation of their minds and manners was one of the dearest objects of his attention. His domestic concerns and social enjoyments, however, were not permitted to interfere with his public duties. He was active by nature, and eminently a man of business by habit. As judge of the county court, and member of the House of Burgesses, he had numerous calls upon his time and thoughts, and was often drawn from home; for whatever trust he undertook, he was sure to fulfil with scrupulous exactness.

The halcyon season of his life

Dismal Swamp

About this time we find him engaged, with other men of enterprise, in a project to drain the great Dismal Swamp, and render it capable of cultivation. This vast morass was about thirty miles long, and ten miles wide, and its interior but little known. With his usual zeal and hardihood he explored it on horseback and on foot. In many parts it was covered with dark and gloomy woods of cedar, cypress, and hemlock, or deciduous trees, the branches of which were hung with long drooping moss. Other parts were almost inaccessible, from the density of brakes and thickets, entangled with vines, briers and creeping plants, and intersected by creeks and standing pools. Occasionally the soil, composed of dead vegetable fibre, was over his horse's fetlocks, and sometimes he had to dismount and make his way on foot over a quaking bog that shook beneath his tread.

In the centre of the morass he came to a great piece of water, six miles long, and three broad, called Drummond's Pond, but more poetically celebrated as the Lake of the Dismal Swamp. It was more elevated than any other part of the swamp, and capable of feeding canals, by which the whole might be traversed. Having made the circuit of it, and noted all its characteristics, he encamped for the night upon the firm land which bordered it, and finished his explorations on the following day.

In the ensuing session of the Virginia Legislature, the association in behalf of which he had acted, was chartered under the name of the Dismal Swamp

Company; and to his observations and forecast may be traced the subsequent improvement and prosperity of that once desolate region.

Treaty of Peace—Pontiac's War

Tidings of peace gladdened the colonies in the spring of 1763. The definitive treaty between England and France had been signed at Fontainebleau. Now, it was trusted, there would be an end to those horrid ravages that had desolated the interior of the country. "The desert and the silent place would rejoice, and the wilderness would blossom like the rose."

The month of May proved the fallacy of such hopes. In that month the famous insurrection of the Indian tribes broke out, which, from the name of the chief who was its prime mover and master spirit, is commonly called Pontiac's war. . . .

Fortunately, Washington's retirement from the army prevented his being entangled in this savage war, which raged throughout the regions he had repeatedly visited; or rather his active spirit had been diverted into a more peaceful channel, for he was at this time occupied in the enterprise just noticed, for draining the great Dismal Swamp.

Public events were now taking a tendency which, without any political aspiration or forethought of his own, was destined gradually to bear him away from his quiet home and individual pursuits, and launch him upon a grander and wider sphere of action than any in which he had hitherto been engaged. . . .

Preserved for a grander and wider sphere of action

Washington occupied his seat in the House of Burgesses, when, on the 29th of May, the stamp act became a subject of discussion. We have seen no previous opinions of his on the subject. His correspondence hitherto had not turned on political or speculative themes; being engrossed by either military or agricultural matters, and evincing little anticipation of the vortex of public duties into which he was about to be drawn. All his previous conduct and writings show a loyal devotion to the crown, with a patriotic attachment to his country. It is probable that on the present occasion that latent patriotism received its first electric shock.

May 29, 1765

Among the Burgesses sat Patrick Henry, a young lawyer, who had recently distinguished himself by pleading against the exercise of the royal prerogative in church matters, and who was now for the first time a member of the House. Rising in his place, he introduced his celebrated resolutions, declaring that the General Assembly of Virginia had the exclusive right and power to lay taxes and impositions upon the inhabitants, and that whoever maintained the contrary should be deemed an enemy to the colony. . . .

Virginia Resolutions

Washington's Ideas Concerning the Stamp Act

Washington returned to Mount Vernon full of anxious thoughts inspired by the political events of the day, and the legislative scene which he witnessed. His recent letters had spoken of the state of peaceful tranquillity in which he was living; those now written from his rural home show that he fully participated in the popular feeling, and that while he had a presentiment of an arduous struggle, his patriotic mind was revolving means of coping with it. Such is the tenor of a letter written to his wife's uncle Francis Dandridge, then in London. "The stamp act," said he, "engrosses the conversation of the speculative part of the colonists, who look upon this unconstitutional method of taxation as a direful attack upon their liberties, and loudly exclaim against the violation. What may be the result of this, and of some other (I think I may add ill-judged) measures, I will not undertake to determine; but this I may venture to affirm, that the advantage accruing to the mother country, will fall greatly short of the expectation of the ministry; for certain it is, that our whole substance already in a manner flows to Great Britain, and that whatsoever contributes to lessen our importations must be hurtful to her manufactures. The eyes of our people already begin to be opened; and they will perceive that many luxuries, for which we lavish our substance in Great Britain, can well be dispensed with. This, consequently, will introduce frugality, and be a necessary incitement to industry. . . . As to the stamp act, regarded in a single view, one of the first bad consequences attending it, is, that our courts of judicature must inevitably be shut up; for it is impossible, or next to impossible, under our present circumstances, that the act of Parliament can be complied with, were we ever so willing to enforce its execution. And not to say (which alone would be sufficient) that we have not money enough to pay for the stamps, there are many other cogent reasons which prove that it would be ineffectual." . . .

"Unconstitutional method of taxation"

In the mean time, from his quiet abode at Mount Vernon, he seemed to hear the patriotic voice of

Patrick Henry, which had startled the House of Burgesses, echoing throughout the land, and rousing one legislative body after another to follow the example of that of Virginia. . . . Union was becoming the watch-word. The merchants of New York, Philadelphia, Boston, and such other colonies as had ventured publicly to oppose the stamp act, agreed to import no more British manufactures after the 1st of January unless it should be repealed. So passed away the year 1765.

Union becoming the watch-word

As yet Washington took no prominent part in the public agitation. Indeed he was never disposed to put himself forward on popular occasions, his innate modesty forbade it; it was others who knew his worth that called him forth; but when once he engaged in any public measure, he devoted himself to it with conscientiousness and persevering zeal. At present he remained a quiet but vigilant observer of events from his eagle nest at Mount Vernon. He had some few intimates in his neighborhood who accorded with him in sentiment. One of the ablest and most efficient of these was Mr. George Mason, with whom he had occasional conversations on the state of affairs. His friends, the Fairfaxes, though liberal in feelings and opinions, were too strong in their devotion to the crown not to regard with an uneasy eye the tendency of the popular bias. From one motive or other, the earnest attention of all the inmates and visitors at Mount Vernon was turned to England, watching the movements of the ministry. . . .

The act was repealed on the 18th of March, 1766, to the great joy of the sincere friends of both countries, and to no one more than to Washington. In one of his letters he observes: "Had the Parliament of Great Britain resolved upon enforcing it, the consequences, I conceive, would have been more direful than is generally apprehended, both to the mother country and her colonies. All, therefore, who were instrumental in procuring the repeal, are entitled to the thanks of every British subject, and have mine cordially.". . .

Washington and George Mason—Correspondence Concerning the Non-Importation Agreement

. . . . A letter written on the 5th of April, 1769, to his friend, George Mason, shows the important stand he was disposed to take. In the previous year, the merchants and traders of Boston, Salem, Connecticut, and New York, had agreed to suspend for a time the importation of all articles subject to taxation. Similar resolutions had recently been adopted by the merchants of Philadelphia. Washington's letter is emphatic in support of the measure. "At a time," writes he, "when our lordly masters in Great Britain will be satisfied with nothing less than the deprivation of American freedom, it seems highly necessary that something should be done to avert the stroke, and maintain the liberty which we have derived from our ancestors. But the manner of doing it, to answer the purpose effectually, is the point in question. That no man should scruple, or hesitate a moment in defence of so valuable a blessing, is clearly my opinion; yet arms should be the last resource—the *dernier ressort*. We have already, it is said, proved the inefficacy of addresses to the throne, and remonstrances to Parliament. How far their attention to our rights and interests is to be awakened, or alarmed, by starving their trade and manufactures, remains to be tried.

April 5, 1769

"Maintain the liberty . . . derived from our ancestors"

"Arms . . . the last resource"

"The northern colonies, it appears, are endeavoring to adopt this scheme. In my opinion, it is a good one, and must be attended with salutary effects, provided it can be carried pretty generally into execution. . . . That there will be a difficulty attending it every where from clashing interests, and selfish, designing men, ever attentive to their own gain, and watchful of every turn that can assist their lucrative views, cannot be denied; and in the tobacco colonies where the trade is so diffused, and in a manner wholly conducted by factors for their principals at home, these difficulties are certainly enhanced, but I think not insurmountably increased, if the gentlemen in their several counties will be at some pains to explain matters to the people, and stimulate them to cordial agreements to purchase none but certain enumerated articles out of any of the stores, after a definite period, and neither import, nor purchase any themselves. . . . I can see but one class of people, the merchants excepted, who will not, or ought not, to wish well to the scheme,—namely, they who live genteelly and hospitably on clear estates. Such as these, were they not to consider the valuable object in view, and the good of others, might think it hard to be curtailed in their living and enjoyments."

This was precisely the class to which Washington belonged; but he was ready and willing to make the sacrifices required. "I think the scheme a good one," added he, "and that it ought to be tried here, with such alterations as our circumstances render absolutely necessary."

Mason, in his reply, concurred with him in opinion. "Our all is at stake," said he, "and the little conveniences and comforts of life, when set in competition with our liberty, ought to be rejected, not with reluctance, but with pleasure. Yet it is plain that, in the tobacco colonies, we cannot at present confine our importations within such narrow bounds as the northern colonies. A plan of this kind, to be practicable, must be adapted to our circumstances; for, if not steadily executed, it had better have remained unattempted. We may retrench all manner of superfluities, finery of all descriptions, and confine ourselves to linens, woolens, &c., not exceeding a certain price. It is amazing how much this practice, if adopted in all the colonies, would lessen the American imports, and distress the various trades and manufactures of Great Britain. This would awaken their attention. They would see, they would feel, the oppressions we groan under, and exert themselves to procure us redress. This once obtained, we should no longer discontinue our importations, confining ourselves still not to import any article that should hereafter be taxed by act of Parliament for raising a revenue in America; for, however, singular I may be in the opinion, *I am thoroughly convinced, that, justice and harmony happily restored, it is not the interest of these colonies to refuse British manufactures. Our supplying our mother country with gross materials, and taking her manufactures in return, is the true chain of connection between us. These are the bands which, if not broken by oppressions, must long hold us together, by maintaining a constant reciprocation of interests.*". . .

Plan of Association

The result of the correspondence between Washington and Mason was the draft by the latter of a plan of association, the members of which were to pledge themselves not to import or use any articles of British merchandise or manufacture subject to duty. This paper Washington was to submit to the consideration of the House of Burgesses, at the approaching session in the month of May.

The Legislature of Virginia opened on this occasion with a brilliant pageant. While military force was arrayed to overawe the republican Puritans of the east, it was thought to dazzle the aristocratical descendants of the Cavaliers by the reflex of regal splendor. Lord Botetourt, one of the king's lords of the bed-chamber, had recently come out as governor of the province. Junius described him as "a cringing, bowing, fawning, sword-bearing courtier." Horace Walpole predicted that he would turn the heads of the Virginians in one way or other. . . .

His opening of the session was in the style of the royal opening of Parliament. He proceeded in due parade from his dwelling to the capitol, in his state coach, drawn by six milk-white horses. Having delivered his speech according to royal form, he returned home with the same pomp and circumstance.

The time had gone by, however, for such display to have the anticipated effect. The Virginian legislators penetrated the intention of this pompous ceremonial, and regarded it with a depreciating smile. Sterner matters occupied their thoughts; they had come prepared to battle for their rights, and their proceedings soon showed Lord Botetourt how much he had mistaken them. Spirited resolutions were passed, denouncing the recent act of Parliament imposing taxes; the power to do which, on the inhabitants of this colony, "was legally and constitutionally vested in the House of Burgesses, with consent of the council and of the king or of his governor, for the time being." Copies of these resolutions were ordered to be forwarded by the speaker to the Legislatures of the other colonies, with a request for their concurrence. . . .

As Massachusetts had no General Assembly at this time, having been dissolved by government, the Legislature of Virginia generously took up the cause. An address to the king was resolved on, stating, that all trials for treason, or misprision of treason, or for any crime whatever, committed by any person residing in a colony, ought to be in and before his majesty's courts within said colony; and beseeching the king to avert from his loyal subjects those dangers and miseries which would ensue from seizing and carrying beyond sea any person residing in America suspected of any crime whatever, thereby depriving them of the inestimable privilege of being tried by a jury from the vicinage, as well as the liberty of producing witnesses on such trial.

Deprived of ancient rights

Disdaining any further application to Parliament, the House ordered the speaker to transmit this address to the colonies' agent in England, with directions to cause it to be presented to the king, and afterwards to be printed and published in the English papers.

Lord Botetourt was astonished and dismayed when he heard of these high-toned proceedings. Repairing to the capitol on the following day at noon, he summoned the speaker and members to the council chamber, and addressed them in the following words: "Mr. Speaker, and gentlemen of the House of Burgesses, I have heard of your resolves, and augur ill of their effects. You have made it my duty to dissolve you, and you are dissolved accordingly."

House of Burgesses dissolved

The spirit conjured up by the late decrees of Parliament was not so easily allayed. The Burgesses adjourned to a private house. Peyton Randolph, their late speaker, was elected moderator. Washington now brought forward a draft of the articles of association, concerted between him and George Mason. They formed the groundwork of an instrument signed by all present, pledging themselves neither to import, nor use any goods, merchandise, or manufactures taxed by Parliament to raise a revenue in America. This instrument was sent throughout the country for signature, and the scheme of nonimportation, hitherto confined to a few northern colonies, was soon universally adopted. For his own part, Washington adhered to it rigorously throughout the year. The articles proscribed by it were never to be seen in his house, and his agent in London was enjoined to ship nothing for him while subject to taxation. . . .

Washington's articles universally adopted

Expedition of Washington to the Ohio, in Behalf of Soldiers' Claims

In the midst of these popular turmoils, Washington was induced, by public as well as private considerations, to make another expedition to the Ohio. He was one of the Virginia Board of Commissioners, appointed, at the close of the late war, to settle the military accounts of the colony. Among the claims which came before the board, were those of the officers and soldiers who had engaged to serve until peace, under the proclamation of Governor Dinwiddie, holding forth a bounty of two hundred thousand acres of land, to be apportioned among them according to rank. Those claims were yet unsatisfied, for governments, like individuals, are slow to pay off in peaceful times the debts incurred while in the fighting mood. Washington became the champion of those claims, and an opportunity now presented itself for their liquidation. The Six Nations, by a treaty in 1768, had ceded to the British crown, in consideration of a sum of money, all the lands possessed by them south of the Ohio. Land offices would soon be opened for the sale of them. Squatters and speculators were already preparing to swarm in, set up their marks on the choicest spots, and establish what were called pre-emption rights. Washington determined at once to visit the lands thus ceded; affix his mark on such tracts as he should select, and apply for a grant from government in behalf of the "soldiers' claim.". . .

Washington had for a companion in this expedition his friend and neighbor, Dr. Craik, and it was with strong community of feeling they looked forward peaceably to revisit the scenes of their military experience. They set out on the 5th of October with three negro attendants, two belonging to Washington, and one to the doctor. The whole party was mounted, and there was a led horse for the baggage.

October 5, 1770

After twelve days' travelling they arrived at Fort Pitt (late Fort Duquesne). It was garrisoned by two companies of royal Irish, commanded by a Captain Edmonson. A hamlet of about twenty log-houses, inhabited by Indian traders, had sprung up within three hundred yards of the fort, and was called "the town.". . .

Here at dinner Washington met his old acquaintance, George Croghan, who had figured in so many capacities and experienced so many vicissitudes on the frontier. He was now Colonel Croghan, deputy-agent to Sir William Johnson, and had his residence—or seat, as Washington terms it—on the banks of the Allegany River, about four miles from the fort. . . .

At Pittsburg the travellers left their horses, and embarked in a large canoe, to make a voyage down the Ohio as far as the Great Kanawha. Colonel Croghan engaged two Indians for their service, and an interpreter named John Nicholson. . . .

About seventy-five miles below Pittsburg the voyagers landed at a Mingo town, which they found in a stir of warlike preparation—sixty of the warriors being about to set off on a foray into the Cherokee country against the Catawbas. . . .

Two days more of voyaging brought them to an Indian hunting camp, near the mouth of the Muskingum. Here it was necessary to land and make a ceremonious visit, for the chief of the hunting party was Kiashuta, a Seneca sachem, the head of the river tribes. . . .

At the mouth of the Great Kanawha, the voyagers encamped for a day or two to examine the lands in the neighborhood, and Washington set up his mark upon such as he intended to claim on behalf of the soldiers' grant. It was a fine sporting country, having small lakes or grassy ponds abounding with water-fowl, such as ducks, geese, and swans. Flocks of turkeys, as usual; and, for larger game, deer and buffalo; so that their camp abounded with provisions.

Here Washington was visited by an old sachem, who approached him with great reverence, at the head of several of his tribe, and addressed him through Nicholson, the interpreter. He had heard, he said, of his being in that part of the country, and had come from a great distance to see him. On further discourse, the sachem made known that he was one of the warriors in the service of the French, who lay in ambush on the banks of the Monongahela, and wrought such havoc in Braddock's army. He declared that he and his young men had singled out Washington, as he made himself conspicuous riding about the field of battle with the general's orders, and had fired at him repeatedly, but without success; whence they had concluded that he was under the protection of the Great Spirit, had a charmed life, and could not be slain in battle.

Washington under the protection of the Great Spirit

At the Great Kanawha Washington's expedition down the Ohio terminated; having visited all the points he wished to examine. His return to Fort Pitt, and thence homeward, affords no incident worthy of note. . . .

Lord Dunmore, Governor of Virginia

The discontents of Virginia, which had been partially soothed by the amiable administration of Lord Botetourt, were irritated anew under his successor, the Earl of Dunmore. This nobleman had for a short time held the government of New York. When appointed to that of Virginia, he lingered for several months at his former post. In the mean time, he sent his military secretary, Captain Foy, to attend to the despatch of business until his arrival; awarding to him a salary and fees to be paid by the colony.

1773

The pride of the Virginians was piqued at his lingering at New York, as if he preferred its gayety and luxury to the comparative quiet and simplicity of Williamsburg. Their pride was still more piqued on his arrival, by what they considered haughtiness on his part. The spirit of the "Ancient Dominion" was roused, and his lordship experienced opposition at his very outset.

The first measure of the Assembly, at its opening, was to demand by what right he had awarded a salary and fees to his secretary without consulting it; and to question whether it was authorized by the crown.

His lordship had the good policy to rescind the unauthorized act, and in so doing mitigated the ire of the Assembly; but he lost no time in proroguing a body, which, from various symptoms, appeared to be too independent, and disposed to be untractable. He continued to prorogue it from time to time, seeking in the interim to conciliate the Virginians, and soothe their irritated pride. At length, after repeated prorogations, he was compelled by circumstances to convene it on the 1st of March, 1773.

Washington was prompt in his attendance on the occasion; and foremost among the patriotic members, who eagerly availed themselves of this long wished for opportunity to legislate upon the general affairs of the colonies. . . .

Notwithstanding the decided part taken by Washington in the popular movement, very friendly relations existed betweeen him and Lord Dunmore. The latter appreciated his character, and sought to avail himself of his experience in the affairs of the province. It was even concerted that Washington should accompany his lordship on an extensive tour, which the latter intended to make in the course of the summer along the western frontier. A melancholy circumstance occurred to defeat this arrangement.

Death of Miss Custis

We have spoken of Washington's paternal conduct towards the two children of Mrs. Washington. The daughter, Miss Custis, had long been an object of extreme solicitude. She was of a fragile constitution, and for some time past had been in very declining health. Early in the present summer, symptoms indicated a rapid change for the worse. Washington was absent from home at the time. On his return to Mount Vernon, he found her in the last stage of consumption.

Though not a man given to bursts of sensibility, he is said on the present occasion to have evinced the deepest affliction; kneeling by her bedside, and pouring out earnest prayers for her recovery. She expired on the 19th of June, in the seventeenth year of her age. This, of course, put an end to Washington's intention of accompanying Lord Dunmore to the frontier; he remained at home to console Mrs. Wash-

June 19, 1773

ington in her affliction,—furnishing his lordship, however, with travelling hints and directions, and recommending proper guides. . . .

Virginia's Indignation at Boston Port Bill

The social position of Lord Dunmore had been strengthened in the province by the arrival of his lady, and a numerous family of sons and daughters. The old Virginia aristocracy had vied with each other in hospitable attention to the family. A court circle had sprung up.

Regulations had been drawn up by a herald, and published officially, determining the rank and precedence of civil and military officers, and their wives. The aristocracy of the "Ancient Dominion" was furbishing up its former splendor. Carriages and four rolled into the streets of Williamsburg, with horses handsomely caparisoned, bringing the wealthy planters and their families to the seat of government.

Washington arrived in Williamsburg on the 16th, and dined with the governor on the day of his arrival, having a distinguished position in the court circle, and being still on terms of intimacy with his lordship. The House of Burgesses was opened in form, and one of its first measures was an address of congratulation to the governor, on the arrival of his lady. It was followed up by an agreement among the members to give her ladyship a splendid ball, on the 27th of the month. All things were going on smoothly and smilingly, when a letter, received through the corresponding committee, brought intelligence of the vindictive measure of Parliament, by which the port of Boston was to be closed on the approaching 1st of June.

The letter was read in the House of Burgesses, and produced a general burst of indignation. All other business was thrown aside, and this became the sole subject of discussion. A protest against this and other recent acts of Parliament was entered upon the journal of the House, and a resolution was adopted, on the 24th of May, setting apart the 1st of June as a day of fasting, prayer, and humiliation; in which the divine interposition was to be implored, to avert the heavy calamity threatening destruction to their rights, and all the evils of civil war; and to give the people one heart and one mind in firmly opposing every injury to American liberties.

On the following morning while the Burgesses were engaged in animated debate, they were summoned to attend Lord Dunmore in the council chamber, where he made them the following laconic speech: "Mr. Speaker, and Gentlemen of the House of Burgesses: I have in my hand a paper, published by order of your House, conceived in such terms, as reflect highly upon his majesty; and the Parliament of Great Britain, which makes it necessary for me to dissolve you, and you are dissolved accordingly."

Lord Dunmore dissolves the House of Burgesses

As on a former occasion, the Assembly, though dissolved, was not dispersed. The members adjourned to the long room of the old Raleigh tavern, and passed resolutions, denouncing the Boston port bill as a most dangerous attempt to destroy the constitutional liberty and rights of all North America; recommending their countrymen to desist from the use, not merely of tea, but of all kinds of East Indian commodities; pronouncing an attack on one of the colonies, to enforce arbitrary taxes, an attack on all; and ordering the committee of correspondence to communicate with the other corresponding committees, on the expediency of appointing deputies from the several colonies of British America, to meet annually in General Congress, at such place as might be deemed expedient, to deliberate on such measures as the united interests of the colonies might require. . . .

As to Washington, widely as he differed from Lord Dunmore on important points of policy, his intimacy with him remained uninterrupted. By memorandums in his diary, it appears that he dined and passed the evening at his lordship's on the 25th, the very day of the meeting at the Raleigh tavern. That he rode out with him to his farm, and breakfasted there with him on the 26th, and on the evening of the 27th attended the ball given to her ladyship. Such was the well-bred decorum that seemed to quiet the turbulence of popular excitement, without checking the full and firm expression of popular opinion.

On the 29th, two days after the ball, letters arrived from Boston giving the proceedings of a town meeting, recommending that a general league should be formed throughout the colonies suspending all trade with Great Britain. But twenty-five members of the late House of Burgesses, including Washington, were at that time remaining in Williamsburg. They held a meeting on the following day, at which Peyton Randolph presided as moderator. After some discussion, it was determined to issue a printed circular, bearing their signatures, and calling a meeting of all the members of the late House of Burgesses, on the 1st of August, to take into consideration this measure of

May 29, 1774

a general league. The circular recommended them, also, to collect, in the mean time, the sense of their respective counties.

Washington was still at Williamsburg on the 1st of June, the day when the port bill was to be enforced at Boston. It was ushered in by the tolling of bells, and observed by all true patriots as a day of fasting and humiliation. Washington notes in his diary that he fasted rigidly, and attended the services appointed in the church. Still his friendly intercourse with the Dunmore family was continued during the remainder of his sojourn in Williamsburg, where he was detained by business until the 20th, when he set out on his return to Mount Vernon. . . .

Washington Chairman of a Political Meeting

Shortly after Washington's return to Mount Vernon, in the latter part of June, he presided as moderator at a meeting of the inhabitants of Fairfax County, wherein, after the recent acts of Parliament had been discussed, a committee was appointed, with himself as chairman, to draw up resolutions expressive of the sentiments of the present meeting, and to report the same at a general meeting of the county, to be held in the court-house on the 18th of July.

The course that public measures were taking, shocked the loyal feelings of Washington's valued friend, Bryan Fairfax, of Tarlston Hall, a younger brother of George William, who was absent in England. He was a man of liberal sentiments, but attached to the ancient rule; and, in a letter to Washington, advised a petition to the throne, which would give Parliament an opportunity to repeal the offensive acts.

"I would heartily join you in your political sentiments," writes Washington in reply, "as far as relates to a humble and dutiful petition to the throne, provided there was the most distant hope of success. But have we not tried this already? Have we not addressed the Lords, and remonstrated to the Commons? And to what end? Does it not appear as clear as the sun in its meridian brightness, that there is a regular, systematic plan to fix the right and practice of taxation upon us? . . .

"Systematic plan to fix the right . . . of taxation"

Is not the attack upon the liberty and property of the people of Boston, before restitution of the loss to the India Company was demanded, a plain and self-evident proof of what they are aiming at? Do not the subsequent bills for depriving the Massachusetts bay of its charter, and for transporting offenders to other colonies or to Great Britain for trial, where it is impossible, from the nature of things, that justice can be obtained, convince us that the administration is determined to stick at nothing to carry its point? Ought we not, then, to put our virtue and fortitude to the severest tests?"

Resolutions of the Committee

The committee met according to appointment, with Washington as chairman. . . .

Opinions and feelings of Washington

These resolutions are the more worthy of note, as expressive of the opinions and feelings of Washington at this eventful time, if not being entirely dictated by him. The last sentence is of awful import, suggesting the possibility of being driven to appeal to arms. . . .

★ ★ ★ ★ ★

Fairfax County (Virginia) Resolutions

American Archives, Fouth Series, Vol. I, Peter Force, 1837

At a General Meeting of the Freeholders and other Inhabitants of the County of *Fairfax,* at the Court House in the town of *Alexandria,* on *Monday,* the 18th day of July, 1774:

July 18, 1774

George Washington, Esquire, *Chairman,* and Robert Harrison, Gentleman, *Clerk.*

Resolved, That this Colony and Dominion of *Virginia* cannot be considered as a conquered country, and, if it was, that the present inhabitants are the descendants, not of the conquered, but of the conquerors. That the same was not settled at the national expense of *England,* but at the private expense of the adventurers, our ancestors, by solemn compact with, and under the auspices and protection of, the *British* Crown, upon which we are, in every respect, as dependent as the people of *Great Britain,* and in the same manner subject to all his Majesty's just, legal, and constitutional prerogatives; that our ancestors, when they left their native land, and settled in *America,* brought with them, even if the same had not been confirmed by Charters, the civil Constitution and form of Government of the country they came from, and were by the laws of nature and Nations entitled to all its privileges, immunities, and advantages, which have descended to us, their posterity, and ought of right to be as fully enjoyed as if we had still continued within the Realm of *England.*

Resolved, That the most important and valuable part of the *British* Constitution, upon which its very existence depends, is the fundamental principle of the people's being governed by no laws to which they have not given their consent by Representatives freely chosen by themselves, who are affected by the laws they enact equally with their constituents, to whom they are accountable, and whose burthens they share, in which consists the safety and happiness of the community; for if this part of the Constitution was taken away, or materially altered, the Government must degenerate either into an absolute and despotick monarchy, or a tyrannical aristocracy, and the freedom of the people be annihilated.

Consent, fundamental principle of civil government

Resolved, Therefore, as the inhabitants of the *American* Colonies are not, and from their situation, cannot be represented in the *British* Parliament, that the Legislative power here can, of right, be exercised only by our Provincial Assemblies, or Parliaments, subject to the assent or negative of the *British* Crown, to be declared within some proper limited time; but as it was thought just and reasonable that the people of *Great Britain* should reap advantages from the Colonies adequate to the protection they afforded them, the *British* Parliament have claimed and exercised the power of regulating our trade and commerce, so as to restrain our importing from foreign countries such articles as they could furnish us with, of their own growth and manufacture, or exporting to foreign countries such articles and portions of our produce as *Great Britain* stood in need of, for her own consumption or manufacture. Such a power directed with wisdom and moderation, seems necessary for the general good of that great body politick of which we are a part, although in some degree repugnant to the principles of the Constitution. Under this idea, our ancestors submitted to it, the experience of more than a century, during the government of his Majesty's royal predecessors, have proved its utility, and the reciprocal benefits flowing from it produced mutual uninterrupted harmony and good will between the inhabitants of *Great Britain* and her Colonies, who during that long period always considered themselves as one and the same people; and though such a power is capable of abuse, and in some instances hath been stretched beyond the original design and institution, yet to avoid strife and contention with our fellow-subjects, and strongly impressed with the experience of mutual benefits, we always cheerfully acquiesced in it while the entire regulation of our internal policy, and giving and granting our own money, were preserved to our own Provincial Legislatures.

American legislative power exercised only in the provincial assemblies

Suffered abuses as long as taxation was preserved to Provincial Legislatures

Resolved, That it is the duty of these Colonies, on all emergencies, to contribute in proportion to their abilities, situation, and circumstances, to the necessary charge of supporting and defending the *British* Empire, of which they are a part; that while we are treated upon an equal footing with our fellow-subjects, the motives of self-interest and preservation will be a sufficient obligation, as was evident through the course of the last war; and that no argument can be fairly applied to the *British* Parliament's taxing us, upon a presumption that we should refuse a just and reasonable contribution, but will equally operate in justification of the Executive power taxing the people of *England,* upon a supposition of their Representatives refusing to grant the necessary supplies.

Based upon an unfair presumption

Resolved, That the claim lately assumed and exercised by the *British* Parliament for making all such laws as they think fit to govern the people of these Colonies, and to extort from us our money without our consent, is not only diametrically contrary to the first principles of the Constitution and the original compacts by which we are dependent upon the *British* Crown and Government, but is totally incompatible with the privileges of a free people and the natural rights of mankind, will render our own Legislatures merely nominal and nugatory, and is calculated to reduce us from a state of freedom and happiness to slavery and misery.

Calculated to reduce us from a state of freedom . . . to slavery

Resolved, That taxation and representation are in their nature inseparable; that the right of withholding, or of giving and granting their own money, is the only effectual security to a free people against the encroachments of despotism and tyranny; and that whenever they yield the one, they must quickly fall a prey to the other.

Taxation and representation inseparable

Resolved, That the powers over the people of *America,* now claimed by the *British* House of Commons, in whose election we have no share; in whose determinations we have no influence; whose information must be always defective, and often false;

who in many instances may have a separate, and in some an opposite interest to ours; and who are removed from those impressions of tenderness and compassion, arising from personal intercourse and connection, which soften the rigours of the most despotick Governments, must, if continued, establish the most grievous and intolerable species of tyranny and oppression that ever was inflicted upon mankind.

Despotick Governments

Resolved, That it is our greatest wish and inclination, as well as interest, to continue our connection with, and dependence upon, the *British* Government; but though we are its subjects, we will use every means which Heaven hath given us to prevent our becoming its slaves.

Every means to prevent our becoming slaves

Resolved, That there is a premeditated design and system formed and pursued by the *British* Ministry to introduce an arbitrary Government into his Majesty's *American* Dominions, to which end they are artfully prejudicing our Sovereign and inflaming the minds of our fellow-subjects in *Great Britain,* by propagating the most malevolent falsehoods, particularly that there is an intention in the *American* Colonies to set up for independent states, endeavouring at the same time, by various acts of violence and oppression, by sudden and repeated dissolutions of our Assemblies, whenever they presume to examine the illegality of Ministerial mandates, or deliberate on the violated rights of their constituents, and by breaking in upon the *American* Charters, to reduce us to a state of desperation, and dissolve the original compact, by which our ancestors bound themselves and their posterity to remain dependent upon the *British* Crown; which measures, unless effectually counteracted, will end in the ruin, both of *Great Britain* and her Colonies.

Premeditated design to introduce arbitrary government

Resolved, That the several Acts of Parliament for raising a revenue upon the people of *America,* without their consent; the erecting new and dangerous jurisdictions here; the taking away our trials by jury; the ordering persons, upon criminal accusations, to be tried in another country than that in which the fact is charged to have been committed; the Act inflicting Ministerial vengeance upon the town of *Boston*; and the two Bills lately brought into Parliament for abrogating the Charter of the Province of *Massachusetts Bay*, and for the protection and encouragement of murderers in the said Province, are part of the abovementioned iniquitous system; that the inhabitants of the town of *Boston* are now suffering in the common cause of all *British America,* and are justly entitled to its support and assistance; and, therefore, that a subscription ought immediately to be opened, and proper persons appointed, in every county in this Colony, to purchase provisions and consign them to some gentlemen of character in *Boston,* to be distributed among the poorer sort of the people there.

Boston suffering in the common cause of all British America

Resolved, That we will cordially join with our friends and brethren of this and the other Colonies, in such measures as shall be judged most effectual, for procuring a redress of our grievances; and that, upon obtaining such redress, if the destruction of the tea at *Boston* be regarded as an invasion of private property, we shall be willing to contribute towards paying the *East India* Company the value; but, as we consider the said Company as the tools and instruments of oppression in the hands of Government, and the cause of the present distress, it is the opinion of this meeting, that the people of these Colonies should forebear all further dealings with them, by refusing to purchase their merchandise, until that peace, safety, and good order, which they have disturbed, be perfectly restored; and that all tea now in this Colony, or which shall be imported into it, shipped before the first day of *September* next, should be deposited in some store-house, to be appointed by the respective Committees of each county, until a sufficient sum of money be raised, by subscription, to reimburse the owners the value, and then to be publickly burnt and destroyed; and if the same is not paid for and destroyed as aforesaid, that it remain in the custody of the said Committees, at the risk of the owners, until the Act of Parliament imposing a duty upon tea for raising a revenue in *America,* be repealed; and immediately afterwards be delivered unto the several proprietors thereof, their agents or attornies.

United in measures to redress grievances

Resolved, That nothing will so much contribute to defeat the pernicious designs of the common enemies of Great Britain and her Colonies, as a firm union of the latter, who ought to regard every act of violence or oppression inflicted upon any one of them, as aimed at all; and to effect this desirable purpose, that a Congress should be appointed, to consist of Deputies from all the Colonies, to concert a general and uniform plan for the defence and preservation of our common rights, and continuing the connection and dependence

Union, a Congress of deputies from all colonies to concert a uniform plan

of the said Colonies upon *Great Britain,* under a just, lenient, permanent, and constitutional form of Government.

RESOLVED, That our most sincere and cordial thanks be given to the patrons and friends of liberty in *Great Britain,* for their spirited and patriotick conduct in support of our constitutional rights and privileges, and their generous efforts to prevent the present distress and calamity of *America.*

RESOLVED, That every little jarring interest and dispute which hath ever happened between these Colonies, should be buried in eternal oblivion; that all manner of luxury and extravagance ought immediately to be laid aside, as totally inconsistent with the threatening and gloomy prospect before us; that it is the indispensable duty of all the gentlemen and men of fortunes to set examples of temperance, fortitude, frugality, and industry, and give every encouragement in their power, particularly by subscriptions and premiums, to the improvement of arts and manufactures in *America;* that great care and attention should be had to the cultivation of flax, cotton, and other materials for manufactures; and we recommend it to such of the inhabitants as have large stocks of sheep, to sell to their neighbors at a moderate price, as the most certain means of speedily increasing our breed of sheep and quantity of wool.

American Christian principle of political union

RESOLVED, That until *American* grievances be redressed, by restoration of our just rights and privileges, no goods or merchandise whatsoever ought to be imported into this Colony, which shall be shipped from *Great Britain,* or *Ireland,* after the first day of *September* next, except linens not exceeding fifteen pence per yard, coarse woolen cloth, not exceeding two shillings sterling per yard; nails, wire, and wire cards, needles and pins, paper, saltpetre, and medicines, which may be imported until the first day of *September,* 1776; and if any goods or merchandise, other than those hereby excepted, should be shipped from *Great Britain* after the time aforesaid, to this Colony, that the same, immediately upon their arrival, should either be sent back again by the owners, their agents or attornies, or stored and deposited in some warehouse, to be appointed by the Committee for each respective county, and there kept at the risk and charge of the owners, to be delivered to them when a free importation of goods hither shall again take place; and that the merchants and venders of goods and merchandise within this Colony ought not to take advantage of our present distress, but continue to sell the goods and merchandise which they now have, or which may be shipped to them before the first day of *September* next, at the same rates and prices they have been accustomed to do within one year last past; and if any person shall sell such goods on any other terms than above expressed, that no inhabitant of this Colony should, at any time forever thereafter, deal with him, his agent, factor, or storekeeper, for any commodity whatsoever.

A non-importation policy until grievances can be addressed

RESOLVED, That it is the opinion of this meeting, that the merchants and venders of goods and merchandise within this Colony should take an oath not to sell or dispose of any goods or merchandise whatsoever which may be shipped from *Great Britain* after the first day of *September* next, as aforesaid, except the articles before excepted; and that they will, upon the receipt of such prohibited goods, either send the same back again by the first opportunity, or deliver them to the Committees of the respective counties, to be deposited in some warehouse, at the risk and charge of the owners, until they, their agents, or factors, shall be permitted to take them away by the said Committees; and that the names of those who refuse to take such oath, be advertised by the respective Committees, in the counties where-in they reside; and to the end, that the inhabitants of this Colony may know what merchants and venders of goods and merchandise have taken such oath, that the respective Committees should grant a certificate thereof to every such person who shall take the same.

Joint action by oath

RESOLVED, That it is the opinion of this meeting, that during our present difficulties and distress, no slaves ought to be imported into any of the *British* Colonies on this Continent; and we take this opportunity of declaring our most earnest wishes to see an entire stop forever put to such a wicked, cruel, and unnatural trade.

A wicked, cruel and unnatural trade ended

RESOLVED, That no kind of lumber should be exported from this Colony to the *West Indies,* until *America* be restored to her constitutional rights and liberties, if the other Colonies will accede to a like resolution; and that it be recommended to the general Congress to appoint as early a day as possible for stopping such exports.

Restored to constitutional rights and privileges

RESOLVED, That it is the opinion of this meeting, if *American* grievances be not redressed before the first day of *November,* 1775, that all exports of produce from the several Colonies to *Great Britain,* should cease; and to carry the said resolution more effectually into execution, that we will not plant or cultivate any tobacco after the crop now growing, provided the same measure shall be adopted by the other Colonies on this Continent, as well as those who have heretofore made tobacco, as those who have not. And it is our opinion, also, if the Congress of Deputies form the several Colonies shall adopt the measure of non-exportation to *Great Britain,* as the people will be thereby disabled from paying their debts, that no judgments should be rendered by the Courts in the said Colonies, for any debt, after information of the said measures being determined upon.

Resolved, That it is the opinion of this meeting, that a Solemn Covenant and Association should be entered into by the inhabitants of all the Colonies, upon oath, that they will not, after the time which shall be respectively agreed on at the general Congress, export any manner of lumber to the *West Indies;* nor any of their produce to *Great Britain;* or sell or dispose of the same to any person who shall not have entered into the said Covenant and Association; and also, that they will not import or receive any goods or merchandise which shall be shipped from *Great Britain,* after the first day of *September* next, other than the before enumerated articles; nor buy or purchase any goods, except as before excepted, of any person whatsoever, who shall not have taken the oath herein before recommended to be taken by the merchants and venders of goods; nor buy or purchase any slaves hereafter imported into any part of this Continent, until a free exportation and importation be again resolved on by a majority of the Representatives or Deputies of the Colonies; and that the respective Committees of the counties in each Colony, so soon as the Covenant and Association becomes general, publish by advertisements in their several counties, a list of the names of those, (if any such there be) who will not accede thereto, that such traitors to their country may be publickly known and detested.

Solemn covenant and association

Resolved, That it is the opinion of this meeting, that this and the other associating Colonies should break off all trade, intercourse, and dealings, with that Colony, Province, or town, which shall decline or refuse to agree to the plan which shall be adopted by the general Congress.

Resolved, That should the town of *Boston* be forced to submit to the late cruel and oppressive measures of Government, that we shall not hold the same to be binding upon us, but will, notwithstanding, religiously maintain, and inviolably adhere to, such measures as shall be concerted by the general Congress, for the preservation of our lives, liberties, and fortunes.

Shall adhere to measures by the general Congress

Resolved, That it be recommended to the Deputies of the general Congress, to draw up and transmit an humble and dutiful Petition and Remonstrance to his Majesty, asserting in decent firmness our just and constitutional rights and privileges, lamenting the fatal necessity of being compelled to enter into measures disgusting to his Majesty and his Parliament, or injurious to our fellow-subjects in *Great Britain;* declaring, in the strongest terms, our duty and affection to his Majesty's person, family, and Government, and our desire forever to continue our dependence upon *Great Britain;* and most humbly conjuring and beseeching his Majesty not to reduce his faithful subjects of *America* to a state of desperation, and to reflect, that from our Sovereign there can be but one appeal. And it is the opinion of this meeting, that after such Petition and Remonstrance shall have been presented to his Majesty, the same shall be printed in the public papers in all the principal towns in *Great Britain.*

Answering in decent firmness

Resolved, That *George Washington,* Esquire, and *Charles Broadwater,* Gentleman, lately elected our Representatives to serve in the General Assembly, attend the Convention at *Williamsburg,* on the first day of *August* next, and present these Resolves as the sense of the people of this county upon the measures proper to be taken in the present alarming and dangerous situation of *America.*

Resolved, That *George Washington,* Esquire, *John West, George Mason, William Rumney, William Ramsay, George Gilpton, Robert Hanson Harrison, John Carlyle, Robert Adam, John Dalton, Philip Alexander, James Kirk, William Brown, Charles Broadwater, William Payne, Martin Cockburne, Lee Massey, William Harts-horne, Thomas Triplett, Charles Alexander, Thomas Pollard, Townsend Dade, Junior, Edward Payne, Henry Gunnell,* and *Thomas Lewis,* be a Committee for this county; that they, or a majority of them, on any emergency, have power to call a general meeting, and to concert and adopt such measures as may be thought most expedient and necessary.

Commitee formed with power to call meetings and adopt measures

Resolved, That a copy of these Proceedings be transmitted to the Printer at *Williamsburg,* to be published.

★

First Virginia Convention

. . . .The resolutions reported by the committee were adopted, and Washington was chosen a delegate to represent the county at the General Convention of the province, to be held at Williamsburg on the 1st of August. . . .

On the 1st of August, the Convention of representatives from all parts of Virginia assembled at Williamsburg. Washington appeared on behalf of Fairfax County, and presented the resolutions, already cited, as the sense of his constituents. He is said, by one who was present, to have spoken in support of them in a strain of uncommon eloquence, which shows how his latent ardor had been excited on the occasion, as eloquence was not in general among his attributes. It is evident, however, that he was roused to an unusual pitch of enthusiasm, for he is said to have declared that he was ready to raise one thousand men, subsist them at his own expense, and march at their head to the relief of Boston.

The Convention was six days in session. Resolutions, in the same spirit with those passed in Fairfax County, were adopted, and Peyton Randolph, Richard Henry Lee, George Washington, Patrick Henry, Richard Bland, Benjamin Harrison, and Edmund Pendleton, were appointed delegates, to represent the people of Virginia in the General Congress. . . .

Meeting of the First Congress

When the time approached for the meeting of the General Congress at Philadelphia, Washington was joined at Mount Vernon by Patrick Henry and Edmund Pendleton, and they performed the journey together on horseback. It was a noble companionship. Henry was then in the youthful vigor and elasticity of his bounding genius; ardent, acute, fanciful, eloquent. Pendleton, schooled in public life, a veteran in council, with native force of intellect, and habits of deep reflection. Washington, in the meridian of his days, mature in wisdom, comprehensive in mind, sagacious in foresight. Such were the apostles of liberty, repairing on their august pilgrimage to Philadelphia from all parts of the land, to lay the foundations of a mighty empire. Well may we say of that eventful period, "There were giants in those days."

Apostles of liberty

Congress assembled on Monday, the 5th of September, in a large room in Carpenter's Hall. There were fifty-one delegates, representing all the colonies excepting Georgia. The meeting has been described as "awfully solemn." The most eminent men of the various colonies were now for the first time brought together; they were known to each other by fame, but were, personally, strangers. The object which had called them together, was of incalculable magnitude. The liberties of no less than three millions of people, with that of all their posterity, were staked on the wisdom and energy of their councils.

September 5, 1774

The Life of George Washington, Vol. I, by Washington Irving, 1856

"It is such an assembly," writes John Adams, who was present, "as never before came together on a sudden, in any part of the world. Here are fortunes, abilities, learning, eloquence, acuteness, equal to any I ever met with in my life. Here is a diversity of religions, educations, manners, interests, such as it would seem impossible to unite in one plan of conduct."

There being an inequality in the number of delegates from the different colonies, a question arose as to the mode of voting; whether by colonies, or by the poll, or by interests. . . .

After some debate, it was determined that each colony should have but one vote, whatever might be the number of delegates. The deliberations of the House were to be with closed doors, and nothing but the resolves promulgated, unless by order of the majority.

To give proper dignity and solemnity to the proceedings of the House, it was moved on the following day, that each morning the session should be opened by prayer. To this it was demurred, that as the delegates were of different religious sects, they might not consent to join in the same form of worship.

Each morning opened by prayer

Upon this, Mr. Samuel Adams arose, and said: "He would willingly join in prayer with any gentleman of piety, and virtue, whatever might be his cloth, provided he was a friend of his country;" and he moved that the reverend Mr. Duché, of Philadelphia, who answered to that description, might be invited to officiate as chaplain. This was one step towards unanimity of feeling, Mr. Adams being a strong Congregationalist, and Mr. Duché an eminent Episcopalian clergyman. The motion was carried into effect; the invitation was given and accepted.

Samuel Adams makes first step towards unanimity

In the course of the day, a rumor reached Philadelphia that Boston had been cannonaded by the British. It produced a strong sensation; and when Congress met on the following morning (7th), the

Library of Congress

by T. H. Matteson, 1849

THE FIRST PRAYER IN CONGRESS, 1774

effect was visible in every countenance. The delegates from the East were greeted with a warmer grasp of the hand by their associates from the South.

The reverend Mr. Duché, according to invitation, appeared in his canonicals, attended by his clerk. The morning service of the Episcopal church was read with great solemnity; the clerk making the responses. The Psalter for the 7th day of the month includes the 35th Psalm, wherein David prays for protection against his enemies. . . .

The imploring words of this psalm, spoke the feelings of all hearts present; but especially of those from New England. John Adams writes in a letter to his wife: . . .

★ ★ ★ ★ ★

John Adams to Mrs. Adams
Philadelphia, 16th September, 1774

Letters of the Members of the Continental Congress, Vol. I, Edited by Edmund C. Burnett, 1921

Having a leisure moment, while the Congress is assembling, I gladly embrace it to write you a line.

When the Congress first met, Mr. Cushing made a motion that it should be opened with prayer. It was opposed by Mr. Jay, of New York, and Mr. Rutledge, of South Carolina, because we were so divided in religious sentiments, some Episcopalians, some Quakers, some Anabaptists, some Presbyterians, and some Congregationalists, that we could not join in the same act of worship. Mr. Samuel Adams arose and said, he was no bigot, and could hear a prayer from a gentleman of piety and virtue, who was at the same time a friend to his country. He was a stranger in Philadelphia, but had heard that Mr. Duché (Dushay they pronounce it) deserved that character, and therefore he moved that Mr. Duché, an Episcopal clergyman, might be desired to read prayers to the Congress to-morrow morning. The motion was seconded and passed in the affirmative. Mr. Randolph, our president, waited on Mr. Duché, and received for answer that if his health would permit he certainly would. Accordingly, next morning he appeared with his clerk and in his pontificals, and read several prayers in the established form; and then read the collect for the seventh day of September, which was the thirty-fifth Psalm. You must remember, this was the next morning after we heard the horrible rumor of the cannonade of Boston. I never saw a greater effect upon an audience. It seemed as if Heaven had ordained that Psalm to be read on that morning.

After this, Mr. Duché, unexpectedly to every body, struck out into an extemporary prayer, which filled the bosom of every man present. I must confess I never heard a better prayer, or one so well pronounced. Episcopalian as he is, Dr. Cooper himself never prayed with such fervor, such ardor, such earnestness and pathos, and in language so elegant and sublime—for America, for the Congress, for the Province of Massachusetts Bay, and especially the town of Boston. It has had an excellent effect upon every body here. I must beg you to read that Psalm. If there was any faith in the sortes Virgilianae, or sortes Homericae, or especially the sortes Biblicae, it would be thought providential.

It will amuse your friends to read this letter and the thirty-fifth Psalm to them. Read it to your father and Mr. Wibird. I wonder what our Braintree Churchmen would think of this! Mr. Duché is one of the most ingenious men, and best characters, and greatest orators in the Episcopal order, upon this continent; yet a zealous friend of liberty and his country.

★ ★ ★ ★ ★

The Life of George Washington, Vol. I, by Washington Irving, 1856

It has been remarked that Washington was especially devout on this occasion—kneeling, while others stood up. In this, however, each no doubt observed the attitude in prayer to which he was accustomed. Washington knelt, being an Episcopalian.

The rumored attack upon Boston, rendered the service of the day deeply affecting to all present. They were one political family, actuated by one feeling, and sympathizing with the weal and woe of each individual member. The rumor proved to be erroneous; but it had produced a most beneficial effect, in calling forth and quickening the spirit of union, so vitally important in that assemblage.

Owing to closed doors, and the want of reporters, no record exists of the discussions and speeches made in the first Congresses. Mr. Wirt, speaking from tradition, informs us that a long and deep silence followed the organization of that august body; the members looking round upon each other, individually reluctant to open a business so fearfully momentous. This "deep and deathlike silence" was beginning to become painfully embarrassing, when Patrick Henry arose. He faltered at first, as was his habit; but his exordium was impressive; and as he launched forth into a recital of colonial wrongs, he kindled with his subject, until he poured forth one of those eloquent appeals which had so often shaken the House of Burgesses, and gained him the fame of being the greatest orator of Virginia. He sat down, according to Mr. Wirt, amidst murmurs of astonishment and applause, and was now admitted, on every hand, to be the first orator of America. He was followed by Richard Henry Lee, who, according to the same writer, charmed the House with a different kind of eloquence, chaste and classical; contrasting, in its cultivated graces, with the wild and grand effusions of Henry. "The superior powers of these great men, however," adds he, "were manifested only in debate, and while general grievances were the topic; when called down from the heights of declamation to that severer test of intellectual excellence, the details of business, they found themselves in a body of cool-headed, reflecting, and most able men, by whom they were, in their turn, completely thrown into the shade."

A body of cool-headed, reflecting and most able men

Declaration of Colonial Rights

The first public measure of Congress was a resolution, declaratory of their feelings with regard to the recent acts of Parliament, violating the rights of the people of Massachusetts, and of their determination to combine in resisting any force that might attempt to carry those acts into execution. . . .

From the secrecy that enveloped its discussions, we are ignorant of the part taken by Washington in the debates; the similarity of the resolutions, however, in spirit and substance, to those of the Fairfax County meeting, in which he presided, and the coincidence of the measures adopted with those therein recommended, show that he had a powerful agency in the whole proceedings of this eventful assembly. Patrick Henry, being asked, on his return home, whom he considered the greatest man in Congress, replied: "If you speak of eloquence, Mr. Rutledge, of South Carolina, is by far the greatest orator; but if you speak of solid information and sound judgment, Colonel Washington is unquestionably the greatest man on that floor."

How thoroughly and zealously he participated in the feelings which actuated Congress in this memorable session, may be gathered from his correspondence with a friend enlisted in the royal cause. This was Captain Robert Mackenzie, who had formerly served under him in his Virginia regiment during the French war, but now held a commission in the regular army, and was stationed among the British troops at Boston.

His feelings gathered in correspondence with Capt. Mackenzie

Mackenzie, in a letter, had spoken with loyal abhorrence of the state of affairs in the "unhappy province" of Massachusetts, and the fixed aim of its inhabitants at "total independence." "The rebellious and numerous meetings of men in arms," said he, "their scandalous and ungenerous attacks upon the best characters in the province, obliging them to save themselves by flight, and their repeated, but feeble threats, to dispossess the troops, have furnished sufficient reasons to General Gage to put the town in a formidable state of defence, about which we are now fully employed, and which will be shortly accomplished to their great mortification."...

★

George Washington
To Captain Robert Mackenzie
Philadelphia, October 9, 1774

The Writings of George Washington Vol. 3, Edited by John C. Fitzpatrick, 1931

Dear Sir:

Your letter of the 13th, ultimo from Boston gave me pleasure, as I learnt thereby, that you were well, and might be expected at Mount Vernon on your way to or from James River, in the course of the winter.

When I have said this, permit me with the freedom of a friend (for you know I always esteemed you) to express my sorrow, that fortune should place you in a service, that must fix curses to the latest posterity upon the diabolical contrivers, and if success (which, by the by, is impossible) accompanies it, execrations upon all those, who have been instrumental in the execution.

I do not mean by this to insinuate, that an officer is not to discharge his duty, even when chance, not choice, has placed him in a disagreeable situation; but I conceive, when you condemn the conduct of the Massachusetts people, you reason from effects, not causes; otherwise you would not wonder at a people, who are every day receiving fresh proofs of a systematic assertion of an arbitrary power, deeply planned to overturn the laws and constitution of their country, and to violate the most essential and valuable rights of mankind, being irritated, and with difficulty restrained from acts of the greatest violence and intemperance. For my own part, I confess to you candidly, that I view things in a very different point of light to the one in which you seem to consider them; and though you are led to believe by venal men, for such I must take the liberty of calling those new-fangled counsellors, which fly to and surround you, and all others, who, for honorary or pecuniary gratifications, will lend their aid to overturn the constitution, and introduce a system of arbitrary government, although you are taught, I say, by discoursing with such men, to believe, that the people of Massachusetts are rebellious, setting up for independency, and what not, give me leave, my good friend, to tell you, that you are abused, grossly abused, and this I advance with a degree of confidence and boldness, which may claim your belief, having better opportunities of knowing the real sentiments of the people you are among, from the leaders of them, in opposition to the present measures of the administration, than you have from those whose business it is, not to disclose truths, but to misrepresent facts in order to justify as much as possible to the world their own conduct; for give me leave to add, and I think I can announce it as a fact, that it is not the wish or interest of that government, or any other upon this continent, separately or collectively, to set up for independency; but this you may at the same time rely on, that none of them will ever submit to the loss of those valuable rights and privileges, which are essential to the happiness of every free state, and without which, life, liberty, and property are rendered totally insecure.

Securing life, liberty, and property

These, Sir, being certain consequences, which must naturally result from the late acts of Parliament relative to America in general, and the government of Massachusetts Bay in particular, is it to be wondered at, I repeat, that men, who wish to avert the impending blow, should attempt to oppose it in its progress, or prepare for their defence, if it cannot be diverted? Surely I may be allowed to answer in the negative; and again give me leave to add as my opinion, that more blood will be spilt on this occasion, if the ministry are determined to push matters to extremity, than history has ever yet furnished instances of in the annals of North America, and such a vital wound given to the peace of this great country, as time itself cannot cure, or eradicate the remembrance of.

But I have done. I was involuntarily led into a short discussion of this subject by your remarks on the conduct of the Boston people, and your opinion of their wishes to set up for independency. I am as well satisfied as I can be of my existence that no such thing is desired by any thinking man in all North America; on the contrary, that it is the ardent wish of the warmest advocates for liberty, that peace and tranquility, upon constitutional grounds, may be restored, and the horrors of civil discord prevented. . . .

Restore peace on constitutional grounds

★ ★ ★ ★ ★

The Life of George Washington, Vol. I, by Washington Irving, 1856

On the breaking up of Congress, Washington hastened back to Mount Vernon, where his presence was more than usually important to the happiness of Mrs. Washington, from the loneliness caused by the recent death of her daughter, and the absence of her son. . . .

INDEPENDENT COMPANIES IN VIRGINIA

Virginia was among the first to buckle on its armor. It had long been a custom among its inhabitants to form themselves into independent companies, equipped at their own expense, having their own peculiar uniform, and electing their own officers, though holding themselves subject to militia law. They had hitherto been self-disciplined; but now they continually resorted to Washington for instruction and advice; considering him the highest authority on military affairs. He was frequently called from home, therefore, in the course of the winter and spring, to different parts of the country to review independent companies; all of which were anxious to put themselves under his command as field-officer.

Mount Vernon, therefore, again assumed a military tone as in former days, when he took his first lessons there in the art of war. He had his old campaigning associates with him occasionally, Dr. Craik and Captain Hugh Mercer, to talk of past scenes and discuss the possibility of future service. Mercer was already bestirring himself in disciplining the militia about Fredericksburg, where he resided.

Two occasional and important guests at Mount Vernon, in this momentous crisis, were General Charles Lee, . . . and Major Horatio Gates. . . .

To Washington the visits of these gentlemen were extremely welcome at this juncture, from their military knowledge and experience, especially as much of it had been acquired in America, in the same kind of warfare, if not the very same campaigns in which he himself had mingled. Both were interested in the popular cause. Lee was full of plans for the organization and disciplining of the militia, and occasionally accompanied Washington in his attendance on provincial reviews. He was subsequently very efficient at Annapolis in promoting and superintending the organization of the Maryland militia.

It is doubtful whether the visits of Lee were as interesting to Mrs. Washington as to the general. He was whimsical, eccentric, and at times almost rude; negligent also, and slovenly in person and attire; for though he had occasionally associated with kings and princes, he had also campaigned with Mohawks and Cossacks, and seems to have relished their "good breeding." What was still more annoying in a well-regulated mansion, he was always followed by a legion of dogs, which shared his affections with his horses, and took their seats by him at table. "I must have some object to embrace," said he misanthropically. "When I can be convinced that men are as worthy objects as dogs, I shall transfer my benevolence, and become as stanch a philanthropist as the canting Addison affected to be.". . .

SECOND VIRGINIA CONVENTION

In the month of March the second Virginia Convention was held at Richmond. Washington attended as delegate from Fairfax County. In this assembly, Patrick Henry, with his usual ardor and eloquence, advocated measures for embodying, arming and disciplining a militia force, and providing for the defence of the colony. "It is useless," said he, "to address further petitions to government, or to await the effect of those already addressed to the throne. The time for supplication is past; the time for action is at hand. We must fight, Mr. Speaker," exclaimed he emphatically; "I repeat it, sir, we must fight! An appeal to arms, and to the God of Hosts, is all that is left us!"

March, 1775

Washington joined him in the conviction, and was one of a committee that reported a plan for carrying those measures into effect. He was not an impulsive man to raise the battle cry, but the executive man to marshal the troops into the field, and carry on the war.

His brother, John Augustine, was raising and disciplining an independent company; Washington offered to accept the command of it, *should occasion require it to be drawn out.* He did the same with respect to an independent company at Richmond. "It is my full intention, if needful," writes he to his brother, *"to devote my life and fortune to the cause."*. . .

The Cry of Blood through the Land

The cry of blood from the field of Lexington, went through the land. None felt the appeal more than the old soldiers of the French war. It roused John Stark, of New Hampshire—a trapper and hunter in his youth, a veteran in Indian warfare, a campaigner under Abercrombie and Amherst, now the military oracle of a rustic neighborhood. Within ten minutes after receiving the alarm, he was spurring towards the sea-coast, and on the way stirring up the volunteers of the Massachusetts borders, to assemble forthwith at Medford, in the vicinity of Boston.

Equally alert was his old comrade in frontier exploits, Colonel Israel Putnam. A man on horseback, with a drum, passed through his neighborhood in Connecticut, proclaiming British violence at Lexington. Putnam was in the field ploughing, assisted by his son. In an instant the team was unyoked; the plough left in the furrow; the lad sent home to give word of his father's departure; and Putnam, on horseback, in his working garb, urging with all speed to the camp. Such was the spirit aroused throughout the country. The sturdy yeomanry, from all parts, were hastening toward Boston with such weapons as were at hand; and happy was he who could command a rusty fowling-piece and a powder-horn.

The news reached Virginia at a critical moment. Lord Dunmore, obeying a general order issued by the ministry to all the provincial governors, had seized upon the military munitions of the province. Here was a similar measure to that of Gage. The cry went forth that the subjugation of the colonies was to be attempted. All Virginia was in combustion. The standard of liberty was reared in every county; there was a general cry to arms. Washington was looked to, from various quarters, to take

by Allan Ramsay

King George III

command. His old comrade in arms, Hugh Mercer, was about marching down to Williamsburg at the head of a body of resolute men, seven hundred strong, entitled, "The friends of constitutional liberty in America," whom he had organized and drilled in Fredericksburg, and nothing but a timely concession of Lord Dunmore, with respect to some powder which he had seized, prevented his being beset in his palace.

Washington was looked to to take command

Before Hugh Mercer and the Friends of Liberty disbanded themselves they exchanged a mutual pledge to reassemble at a moment's warning, whenever called on to defend the liberty and rights of this or any other sister colony.

Different Effects of the Tidings

Washington was at Mount Vernon, preparing to set out for Philadelphia as a delegate to the second Congress, when he received tidings of the affair at Lexington. Bryan Fairfax and Major Horatio Gates, were his guests at the time. They all regarded the event as decisive in its consequences; but they regarded it with different feelings. The worthy and gentle-spirited Fairfax deplored it deeply. He foresaw that it must break up all his pleasant relations in life; arraying his dearest friends against the government to which, notwithstanding the errors of its policy, he was loyally attached and resolved to adhere.

Gates, on the contrary, viewed it with the eye of a soldier and a place-hunter—hitherto disappointed in both capacities. This event promised to open a new avenue to importance and command, and he determined to enter upon it.

Washington's feelings were of a mingled nature. They may be gathered from a letter to his friend and neighbor, George William Fairfax, then in England, in which he lays the blame of this "deplorable affair" on the ministry and their military agents. . . .

★ ★ ★ ★ ★

The Writings of George Washington Vol. 3, Edited by John C. Fitzpatrick, 1931

George Washington
To George William Fairfax
Philadelphia, May 31, 1775

. . . Before this Letter can reach you, you must, undoubtedly, have received an Account of the engagement in the Massachusetts Bay between the Ministerial Troops (for we do not, nor cannot yet prevail upon ourselves to call them the King's Troops), and the Provincials of that Government: But as you may not have heard how that affair began, I inclose you the several Affidavits that were taken after the Action.

General Gage acknowledges, that the detachment under Lieutenant Colonel Smith was sent out to destroy private property; or, in other Words, to destroy a Magazine which self preservation obliged the Inhabitants to establish. And he also confesses, in effect at least, that his Men made a very precipitate retreat from Concord, notwithstanding the reinforcement under Lord Piercy, the last of which may serve to convince Lord Sandwich (and others of the same sentiment) that the Americans will fight for their Liberties and property, however pusilanimous, in his Lordship's Eye, they may appear in other respects.

From the best Accounts I have been able to collect of that affair; indeed from every one, I believe the fact, stripped of all colouring, to be plainly this, that if the retreat had not been as precipitate as it was (and God knows it could not well have been more so) the Ministerial Troops must have surrendered, or been totally cut off; For they had not arrived in Charlestown (under cover of their Ships) half an hour, before a powerful body of Men from Marblehead and Salem were at their heels, and must, if they had happened to have been up one hour sooner, inevitably intercepted their retreat to Charlestown. Unhappy it is though to reflect, that a Brother's Sword has been sheathed in a Brother's breast, and that, the once happy and peaceful plains of America are either to be drenched with Blood, or Inhabited by Slaves. Sad alternative! But can a virtuous Man hesitate in his choice?

A Brother's Sword sheathed in a Brother's breast

I am, With sincere Regard and Affectionate compliments to Mrs. Fairfax, Dear Sir, etc.

★ ★ ★ ★ ★

The Life of George Washington, Vol. I, by Washington Irving, 1856

Second Session of Congress

The second General Congress assembled at Philadelphia on the 10th of May. Peyton Randolph was again elected as president; but being obliged to return, and occupy his place as speaker of the Virginia Assembly, John Hancock, of Massachusetts, was elevated to the chair. . . .

May 10, 1775

The public sense of Washington's military talents and experience, was evinced in his being chairman of all the committees appointed for military affairs. Most of the rules and regulations for the army, and the measures for defence, were devised by him. The situation of the New England army, actually besieging Boston, became an early and absorbing consideration. It was without munitions of war, without arms, clothing, or pay; in fact, without legislative countenance or encouragement. Unless sanctioned and assisted by Congress, there was danger of its dissolution. If dissolved, how could another be collected? If dissolved, what would there be to prevent the British from sallying out of Boston, and spreading desolation throughout the country?

Public sense of his military talents

All this was the subject of much discussion out of doors. The disposition to uphold the army was general; but the difficult question was, who should be commander-in-chief? Adams, in his diary, gives us glimpses of the conflict of opinions and interests within doors. There was a southern party, he said, which could not brook the idea of a New England army, commanded by a New England gen-

Engraving: J. Rogers

From *Washington and the Republic,* Vol. I,
by Benson J. Lossing

WASHINGTON TAKING COMMAND OF THE ARMY AT CAMBRIDGE, 1775

eral. "Whether this jealousy was sincere," writes he, "or whether it was mere pride, and a haughty ambition of furnishing a southern general to command the northern army, I cannot say; but the intention was very visible to me, that Colonel Washington was their object; and so many of our stanchest men were in the plan, that we could carry nothing without conceding to it. There was another embarrassment, which was never publicly known, and which was carefully concealed by those who knew it: the Massachusetts and other New England delegates were divided. Mr. Hancock and Mr. Cushing hung back; Mr. Paine did not come forward, and even Mr. Samuel Adams was irresolute. Mr. Hancock himself had an ambition to be appointed commander-in-chief. Whether he thought an election a compliment due to him, and intended to have the honor of declining it, or whether he would have accepted it, I know not. To the compliment, he had some pretentions; for, at that time, his exertions, sacrifices, and general merits in the cause of his country, had been incomparably greater than those of Colonel Washington. But the delicacy of his health, and his entire want of experience in actual service, though an excellent militia officer, were decisive objections to him in my mind."

John Hancock

General Charles Lee was at that time in Philadelphia. His former visit had made him well acquainted with the leading members of Congress. The active interest he had manifested in the cause was well known, and the public had an almost extravagant idea of his military qualifications. He was of foreign birth, however, and it was deemed improper to confide the supreme command to any but a native-born American.

General Charles Lee

The opinion evidently inclined in favor of Washington; yet it was promoted by no clique of partisans or admirers. More than one of the Virginia delegates, says Adams, were cool on the subject of his appointment; and particularly Mr. Pendleton, was clear and full against it. It is scarcely necessary to add, that Washington in this, as in every other situation in life, made no step in advance to clutch the impending honor.

Adams, in his diary, claims the credit of bringing the members of Congress to a decision. Rising in his place, one day, and stating briefly, but earnestly, the exigencies of the case, he moved that Congress should adopt the army at Cambridge, and appoint a general. Though this was not the time to nominate the person, "yet," adds he, "as I had reason to believe this was a point of some difficulty, I had no hesitation to declare, that I had but one gentleman in my mind for that important command, and that was a gentleman from Virginia, who was among us, and very well known to all of us; a gentleman, whose skill and experience as an officer, whose independent fortune, great talents, and excellent universal character, would command the approbation of all America, and unite the cordial exertions of all the colonies better than any other person in the Union. Mr. Washington, who happened to sit near the door, as soon as he heard me allude to him, from his usual modesty, darted into the library-room. Mr. Hancock, who was our president, which gave me an opportunity to observe his countenance, while I was speaking on the state of the colonies, the army at Cambridge, and the enemy, heard me with visible pleasure; but when I came to describe Washington for the commander, I never remarked a more sudden and striking change of countenance. Mortification and resentment were expressed as forcibly as his face could exhibit them."

"When the subject came under debate, several delegates opposed the appointment of Washington; not from personal objections, but because the army were all from New England, and had a general of their own, General Artemas Ward, with whom they appeared well satisfied; and under whose command they had proved themselves able to imprison the British army in Boston; which was all that was to be expected or desired."

The subject was postponed to a future day. In the interim, pains were taken out of doors to obtain a unanimity; and the voices were in general so clearly in favor of Washington, that the dissentient members were persuaded to withdraw their opposition.

Washington Commander-in-Chief

On the 15th of June, the army was regularly adopted by Congress, and the pay of the commander-in-chief fixed at five hundred dollars a month. Many still clung to the idea, that in all these proceedings they were merely opposing the measures of the ministry, and not the authority of the crown; and thus the army before Boston was designated as the Continental Army, in contradistinction to that under General Gage, which was called the Ministerial Army.

June 15, 1775

In this stage of the business, Mr. Johnson, of

Maryland, rose, and nominated Washington for the station of commander-in-chief. The election was by ballot, and was unanimous. It was formally announced to him by the president, on the following day, when he had taken his seat in Congress. Rising in his place, he briefly expressed his high and grateful sense of the honor conferred on him, and his sincere devotion to the cause. . . .

Election was by ballot and unanimous

At Washington's express request, his old friend, Major Horatio Gates, then absent at his estate in Virginia, was appointed adjutant-general, with the rank of brigadier.

Adams, according to his own account, was extremely loth to admit either Lee or Gates into the American service, although he considered them officers of great experience and confessed abilities. He apprehended difficulties, he said, from the "natural prejudices and virtuous attachment of our countrymen to their own officers." "But," adds he, "considering the earnest desire of General Washington to have the assistance of those officers, the extreme attachment of many of our best friends in the southern colonies to them, the reputation they would give to our arms in Europe, and especially with the ministerial generals and army in Boston, as well as the real American merit of both, I could not withhold my vote from either."

The reader will possibly call these circumstances to mind when, on a future page, he finds how Lee and Gates requited the friendship to which chiefly they owed their appointments.

In this momentous change in his condition, which suddenly altered all his course of life, and called him immediately to the camp, Washington's thoughts recurred to Mount Vernon, and its rural delights, so dear to his heart, whence he was to be again exiled. His chief concern, however, was on account of the distress it might cause to his wife. His letter to her on the subject is written in a tone of manly tenderness. . . .

Suddenly altered the course of his life

On the 20th of June, he received his commission from the president of Congress. The following day was fixed upon for his departure for the army. He reviewed previously, at the request of their officers, several militia companies of horse and foot. Every one was anxious to see the new commander, and rarely has the public *beau ideal* of a commander been so fully answered. He was now in the vigor of his days, forty-three years of age, stately in person, noble in his demeanor, calm and dignified in his deportment; as he sat his horse, with manly grace, his military presence delighted every eye, and wherever he went the air rang with acclamations. . . .

June 20, 1775

Providential Preparation

Religious Training and School Subjects

George Washington's Religious Training at Home

. . . [T]ill March 1748, when he engaged as a surveyor with Lord Fairfax, being just sixteen years of age, George, it is believed, resided at Mount Vernon, and with his mother at her abode opposite to Fredericksburg. In that town he went to school, and as Mrs. Washington was connected with the church there, her son no doubt shared, under her own eye, the benefits of divine worship, and such religious instruction as mothers in that day were eminently accustomed to give their children. It was the habit to teach the young the first principles of religion according to the formularies of the church, to inculcate the fear of God, and the strict observance of the moral virtues, such as truth, justice, charity, humility, modesty, temperance, chastity, and industry. That such instruction was not withheld in the case under consideration, we have good reason to believe, and think a confirmation thereof may be found, not only in the known spirit of the age, but in the subsequent life of him who thus shared the advantages of so excellent a means of grace.

—E. C. McGuire
The Religious Opinions and Character of Washington, 1836

Mary Washington

The Women of the American Revolution, by Elizabeth F. Ellet, 1849

The Mother of Washington! There needs no eulogy to awaken the associations which cling around that sacred name. Our hearts do willing homage to the venerated parent of the chief—

> Who 'mid his elements of being wrought
> With no uncertain aim—nursing the germs
> Of godlike virtue in his infant mind.

The contemplation of Washington's character naturally directs attention to her whose maternal care guided and guarded his early years. What she did, and the blessing of a world that follows her—teach impressively—while showing the power—the duty of those who mould the characters of the age to come. The principles and conduct of this illustrious matron were closely interwoven with the destinies of her son. Washington ever acknowledged that he owed everything to his mother—in the education and habits of his early life. His high moral principle, his perfect self-possession, his clear and sound judgment, his inflexible resolution and untiring application—were developed by her training and example. A believer in the truths of religion, she inculcated a strict obedience to its injunctions. She planted the seed, and cherished the growth, which bore such rich and glorious fruit. . . .

The course of Mrs. Washington's life, exhibiting her qualities of mind and heart, proved her fitness for the high trust committed to her hands. She was remarkable for vigor of intellect, strength of resolution, and inflexible firmness wherever principle was concerned. Devoted to the education of her children, her parental government and guidance have been described by those who knew her as admirably adapted to train the youthful mind to wisdom and virtue. With her, affection was regulated by a calm and just judgment. . . .

The life of Mrs. Washington, so useful in the domestic sphere, did not abound in incident. She passed through the trials common to those who lived amid the scenes of the Revolutionary era. She saw the son whom she had taught to be *good*—whom she had reared in the principles of true honor, walking the perilous path of duty with firm step, leading his country to independence, and crowned with his reward—a nation's gratitude; yet in all these changes, her simple, earnest nature remained the same. She loved to speak, in her latter days, of her boy's merits in his early life, and of his filial affection and duty; but never dwelt on the glory he had won as the deliverer of his country, the chief magistrate of a great republic. This was because her ambition was too high for the pride that inspires and rewards common souls. The greatness she discerned and acknowledged in the object of her solicitous tenderness was beyond that which this world most esteems.

. . . . In the old days of Virginia, women were taught habits of industry and self-reliance, and in these Mrs. Washington was nurtured. The early death of her husband involved her in the cares of a young family with limited resources, which rendered prudence and economy necessary to provide for and educate her children. Thus circumstanced, it was left to her unassisted efforts to form in her son's mind, those essential qualities which gave tone and character to his subsequent life. George was only twelve years old at his father's death, and retained merely the remembrance of his person, and his parental fondness. Two years after this event, he obtained a midshipman's warrant; but his mother opposed the plan, and the idea of entering the naval service was relinquished.

The home in which Mrs. Washington presided, was a sanctuary of the domestic virtues. The levity of youth was there tempered by a well regulated restraint, and the enjoyments rational and proper for that age were indulged in with moderation. The future chief was taught the duty of obedience, and was thus prepared to command. The mother's authority never departed from her, even when her son had attained the height of his renown; for she ruled by the affection which had controlled his spirit when he needed a guardian; and she claimed a reverence next to that due to his Creator. This claim he admitted, mingling the deepest respect with enthusiastic attachment, and yielding to her will the most implicit obedience, even to the latest hours of her life. One of the associates of his juvenile years, Lawrence Washington, of Chotank, thus speaks of his home:

"I was often there with George, his playmate, schoolmate, and young man's companion. Of the mother I was ten times more afraid than I ever was of my own parents; she awed me in the midst of her kindness, for she was indeed truly kind. And even now, when time has whitened my locks, and I am the grandparent of a second generation, I could not behold that majestic woman without feelings it is impossible to describe. Whoever has seen that awe-inspiring air and manner, so characteristic of the Father of his country, will remember the matron as she appeared, the presiding genius of her well-ordered household, commanding and being obeyed." Educated under such influences, it is not to be wondered at that Washington's deportment toward his mother at all times, testified his appreciation of her elevated character, and the excellence of her lessons."

"On his appointment to the command-in-chief of the American armies," says Mr. Custis, "previously to his joining the forces at Cambridge, he removed his mother from her country residence, to the village of Fredericksburg, a situation remote from danger and contiguous to her friends and relatives. There she remained, during nearly the whole of the trying period of the Revolution. Directly in the way of the news, as it passed from north to south; one courier would bring intelligence of success to our arms; another, "swiftly coursing at his heels," the saddening reverse of disaster and defeat. While thus ebbed and flowed the fortunes of our cause, the mother, trusting to the wisdom and protection of Divine Providence, preserved the even tenor of her life; affording an example to those matrons whose sons were alike engaged in the arduous contest; and showing that unavailing anxieties, however belonging to nature, were unworthy of mothers whose sons were combating for the inestimable rights of man, and the freedom and happiness of the world."

When news arrived of the passage of the Delaware in December, 1776, the mother received calmly the patriots who came with congratulations; and while expressing pleasure at the intelligence, disclaimed for her son the praises in the letters from which extracts were read. When informed by express of the surrender of Cornwallis, she lifted her hands in gratitude towards heaven, and exclaimed, "Thank God! war will now be ended, and peace, independence and happiness bless our country!"

Her housewifery, industry, and care in the management of her domestic concerns, were not intermitted during the war. "She looketh well to the ways of her household," and "worketh willingly with her hands," said the wise man, in describing a virtuous woman; and it was the pride of the exemplary women of that day, to fill the station of mistress with usefulness as well as dignity. Mrs. Washington was remarkable for a simplicity which modern refinement might call severe, but which became her not less when her fortunes were clouded, than when the sun of glory arose upon her house. Some of the aged inhabitants of Fredericksburg long remembered the matron, "as seated in an old-fashioned open chaise she was in the habit of visiting, almost daily, her little farm in the vicinity of the town. When there, she would ride about her fields giving her orders and seeing that they were obeyed." When on one occasion an agent departed from his instructions—she reproved him for exercising his own judgment in the matter; "I command you," she said; there is nothing left for you but to obey."

Her charity to the poor was well known; and having not wealth to distribute, it was necessary that what her benevolence dispensed should be supplied by domestic economy and industry. How peculiar a grace does this impart to the benefits flowing from a sympathizing heart! . . .

Her meeting with Washington, after the victory which decided the fortune of America, illustrates her character too strikingly to be omitted. "After an absence of nearly seven years, it was, at length, on the return of the combined armies from Yorktown, permitted to the mother again to see and embrace her illustrious son. So soon as he had dismounted, in the midst of a numerous and brilliant suite, he sent to apprize her of his arrival and to know when it would be her pleasure to receive him. And now, mark the force of early education and habits, and the superiority of the Spartan over the Persian schools, in this interview of the great Washington with his admirable parent and instructor. No pageantry of war proclaimed his coming—no trumpets sounded—no banners waved. Alone, and on foot, the marshal of France, the general-in-chief of the combined armies of France and America, the deliverer of his country, the hero of the age, repaired to pay his humble duty to her whom he venerated as the author of his being, the founder of his fortune and his fame. For full well he knew that the matron was made of sterner stuff than to be moved by all the pride that glory ever gave, or by all the 'pomp and circumstance' of power.

"The lady was alone—her aged hands employed in the works of domestic industry, when the good news was announced; and it was further told, that the victor-chief was in waiting at the threshold. She welcomed him with a warm embrace, and by the well-remembered and endearing names of his childhood. Inquiring as to his health, she remarked the lines which mighty cares, and many trials, had made on his manly countenance—spoke much of old times, and old friends; but of his glory, *not one word!*

"Meantime, in the village of Fredericksburg, all was joy and revelry. The town was crowded with the officers of the French and American armies, and with gentlemen from all the country around, who hastened to welcome the conquerors of Cornwallis. The citizens made arrangements for a splendid ball, to which the mother of Washington was specially invited. She observed, that although her dancing days were *pretty well over*, she should feel happy in contributing to the general festivity, and consented to attend.

"The foreign officers were anxious to see the mother of their chief. They had heard indistinct rumor respecting her remarkable life and character; but forming their judgment from European examples, they were prepared to expect in the mother, that glare and show which would have been attached to the parents of the great in the old world. How were they surprized when the matron, leaning on the arm of her son, entered the room! She was arrayed in the very plain, yet becoming garb worn by the Virginia lady of the olden time. Her address, always dignified and imposing, was courteous, though reserved. She received the complimentary attentions which were profusely paid her, without evincing the slightest elevation; and at an early hour, wishing the company much enjoyment of their pleasures, and observing that it was time for old people to be at home, retired, leaning as before, on the arm of her son."

To this picture may be added another:

"The Marquis de La Fayette repaired to Fredericksburg, previous to his departure for Europe, in the fall of 1784, to pay his parting respects to the mother, and to ask her blessing. Conducted by one of her grandsons, he approached the house, when the young gentleman observed: 'There, sir, is my grandmother,' La Fayette beheld—working in the garden, clad in domestic-made clothes, her gray head covered with a plain straw hat—the mother of 'his hero, his friend and a country's preserver!' The lady saluted him kindly, observing, 'Ah, marquis! you see an old woman; but come, I can make you welcome to my poor dwelling, without the parade of changing my dress.'"

To the encomiums lavished by the marquis on his chief, the mother replied: "I am not surprised at what George has done, for he was always a very good boy." So simple in her true greatness of soul, was this remarkable woman.

Her piety was ardent; and she associated devotion with the grand and beautiful in nature. She was in the habit of repairing every day for prayer to a secluded spot, formed by rocks and trees, near her dwelling.

After the organization of the government, Washington repaired to Fredericksburg, to announce to his mother his election to the chief magistracy, and bid her farewell, before assuming the duties of his office. Her aged frame was bowed down by disease; and she felt that they were parting to meet no more in this world. But she bade him go, with heaven's blessing and her own, to fulfil the high destinies to which he had been called. Washington was deeply affected, and wept at the parting. . . .

Religious Training

Matthew Hale

Train up a child in the way he should go:
and when he is old, he will not depart from it.

Proverbs 22:6

Immediately following this statement, will be found "The Great Audit" by Sir Matthew Hale, Knight; late Chief Justice of the Kings-Bench, from his work Contemplations, Moral and Divine *published in London in 1679. To describe the importance of this in the life of George Washington, I quote from an early biographer of him, James K. Paulding, who records having seen the original volume at Mount Vernon. Unfortunately, the original volume mentioned by Mr. Paulding is no longer at Mount Vernon, having disappeared during those difficult years around 1859 when it was questionable whether or not Mount Vernon itself would be preserved by the American people. The 1679 edition from which 'The Great Audit' appearing here is taken, is the same text as that of 1685.*

Mr. Paulding says: "I have now before me a venerable volume, printed in the year 1685, entitled, Contemplations, Moral and Divine, *by Sir Matthew Hale, late Chief-justice of the Court of King's-Bench, in which is written, with her own hand, the name of 'Mary Washington.' It bears the appearance of frequent use, and particular chapters are designated by marks of reference. It is the volume from which the mother of Washington was accustomed to read daily lessons of piety, morality, and wisdom to her children. The value of such a relic cannot be better set forth than in the language which accompanies its transmission; and I can only devoutly hope that the hallowed sanctuary of Mount Vernon may ever continue to be possessed by such kindred spirits as the writer of that letter.*

"I beg it may be carefully preserved and returned, as one of the family heirlooms which better feelings than pride would retain for future generations to look on, even should they not study it. There is something in a reverence for religion favourable to a virtuous character; and that reverence is in some measure kept alive by looking on a family Bible, and solid works of divinity, which have descended from past generations. We associate with them recollections of ancestral virtues, and when family tradition assures us they were the counsellors of past days, there is a feeling of the heart which turns to them in time of trial, and makes it good, I think, to leave them an honourable station, as friends to those that have gone before, and those who shall come after us, to speak in the cause of truth when we shall sleep in the grave.

"One of the chapters which appears to have been selected as an ordinary lesson, and marked for that purpose in the table of contents, is denominated 'The Great Audit,' and seems to me to contain as much true wisdom as was ever imbodied in the same compass. I shall extract those parts which most singularly assimilate with the character of Washington, in order that my youthful readers may see whence it was that, in all probability, the Father of his Country derived his principles of action, and, if possible, imitate his virtues." (Paulding, James K. *A Life of Washington*, 1782. Vol. I, pp. 24–26)

I find it of particular interest, and one of the many indications of George Washington's Providential preparation, that he, a Virginian and a member of the Episcopal church, should have received this early home training from one of England's finest Puritan divines. This early appreciation of Puritan theology would be a great help to him in later years when called to begin his military career for the United Colonies, in New England.

—Verna M. Hall, Compiler.

CONTEMPLATIONS MORAL AND DIVINE:

In two Parts.

By Sir Matthew Hale *Knight, late Chief Justice of the* Kings-Bench.

Imprimatur.

Ex Edibus *Lambethanis* Martij 13. 167⁵⁄₆.

Antonius Saunders, Reverendissimo D^no^, Domino *Gilberto* Archi-Episc. Cant. a Sacris Domesticis.

LONDON,
Printed for *William Shrowsbury* at the Bible in *Duke-lane*, and *John Leigh* at the Blew Bell in *Fleetstreet* near *Chancery-lane*
M. DC. LXXIX.

Contemplations Moral and Divine

The Great Audit
with
The Account of the Good Steward

Matthew Hale, 1679

The Great Audit

The Great Lord of the World hath placed the Children of Men in this Earth as his Stewards; and according to the Parable in *Matthew 25*. He delivers to every person his *Talents*, a Stock of advantages or opportunities: to some he commits more, to some less, to all some.

This Stock is committed to every person under *a Trust*, or Charge, to imploy the same in ways, and to ends and in proportion suitable to the Talents thus committed to them, and to the measure and quality of them.

The *Ends* of this deputing of the Children of men to this kind of imployment of their Talents, are divers. 1. That they may be kept in continual action and motion suitable to the condition of reasonable Creatures, as almost every thing else in the World is continued in motion suitable to its own nature, which is the subject of the wiseman's discourse, *Eccles.* 1.8. *All things are full of labour.* 2. That in that regular motion they may attain ends of Advantage to themselves; for all things are so ordered by the most Wise God, that every Being hath its own proportionable Perfection and Happiness inseparably annexed to that way and work which his Providence hath destined it unto. 3. That in that due and regular imployment, each man might be in some measure serviceable and advantagious to another. 4. That although the great Lord of this Family, can receive no Advantage by the Service of his Creature, because he is Perfect and All-sufficient in himself; yet he receives Glory and Praise by it, and a Complacency in the beholding a Conformity in the Creature, to his own most Perfect Will.

To the due Execution of this trust committed to the Children of Men, and for their incouragement in it, he hath annexed *a Reward* by his Promise and the free appointment of his own good pleasure: This reward therefore is not meritoriously due to the imployment of the Talent; for as the Talent is the Lords, so is the strength and ability whereby it is imployed; but by his own good pleasure and free promise, the reward is knit to the work. In this case therefore, the reward is not demandable, so much upon the account of the Divine Justice, as upon the account of the Divine Truth and Fidelity. On the other side, to the male administration of this trust, there is annexed a retribution of Punishment, and this most naturally and meritoriously; for the Law of common Justice and Reason doth most justly subject the Creature, that depends in his Being upon his Creator, to the Law and Will of that Creator; and therefore, having received a Talent from his

Lord, and together with his Being, an ability to imploy it according to the Will of his Lord, a non-imployment, or mis-imployment thereof doth most justly oblige him to Guilt and Punishment, as the natural and just consequent of his demerit.

Of *the Persons* that do receive these Talents, *some do imploy them well*, though in various degrees; some to more advantage, some to less; and although the best Husbands come short of what they should do, and at best are in this respect unprofitable Servants, yet if there be a Faithful, Conscientious, and Sincere Indeavour to imploy that Talent to their Masters honour, they are accounted *Good Stewards*, and the Merits of Christ supply by Faith, that wherein they come short.

On the other side, some persons are *Unfaithful Stewards* of their Talents, and these are *of three kinds*: 1. Such as wholly misimploy their Talents, turning them to the Dishonour and Disservice of their Lord, which they should have imployed to his Service; and these have a double account to make, *viz.* of their Talents, and of their misimployment. 2. Such as do not at all imploy their *Talent*, but as they do no harm, so they do no good with it; these are *Negligent Servants*, and have the single, but full account of their *Talents* to make. 3. Such as do make some use of their *Talents*, but do not produce an increase proportionable to their Stock; and so, though they are not debtors for their whole *Talents*, yet are in arrear and grown behind hand; & so upon the foot of their account are found Debtors to their Lord, which without Faith in Christ, and his Merits coming in to make up the Sum, will be enough to cast them in Prison, and there keep them to Eternity.

And according to these varieties of degrees, of good or bad administration, are the *degrees of Reward or Punishment*. He that hath administered his Trust well, so that there is a great access of his improvement, hath the greater access of Glory; & he that hath less surplussage upon his account, shall have the less degree of Glory; and on the other side, he that hath many Talents, and made no improvement, his Debt and Punishment shall be the greater: He that hath fewer Talents, his Non-improvement leaves him a debtor in a less sum, and consequently subject to less punishment.

The Great Day of Account will be the great Day of Judgment, when the Lord of the Families of the whole Earth, will call every man to his account of his Stewardship here on Earth. Wherein we may with reverence, and for the better fastening it upon our affections, suppose the Lord thus to be speaking all, and every particular persons of the World.

The Charge.

'Come ye Children of men, as I have formerly made you Stewards, of my Blessings upon Earth, and committed to every one of you that come to the use of your understanding, several Talents to imploy and improve to the honour and service of me your Lord and Master; so now I come to call you to render an Account of your Stewardship: and because you shall see the particular *Charge* of your several Receipts, whereunto you may give your Answers, behold, here is a Schedule of the Particulars with which I will charge you. Give in your particular Answer how you have imployed and improved them, and see you do it truly; for know I have a controle and check upon you; a controle within you, your own Consciences, and a controle without you, my Book of Remembrance, wherein all your Receipts, Disbursments, and Imployments are Registered.

1. 'I have given unto you all your *Senses*, and principally those two great Senses of discipline, your *Sight* and your *Hearing*.

'*Item*. I have given unto you all, *Understanding* and *Reason* to be a guide of your actions, and to some of you more eminent degrees thereof.

'*Item*. I have given you all, *Memory*, a treasury of things past heard and observed.

'*Item*. I have given you a *Conscience* to direct you, and to check you in your mis-carriages, and to encourage you in well-doing; and I have furnished that Conscience of yours with light, and principles of truth and practice, conformable to my Will.

'*Item*. I have laid open to all your view, *the Works of my Power and Providence*, the Heavens and the Earth, the conspicuous administration of my Wisdom and Power in them.

'*Item*. I have delivered over to your view, my more *Special Providences* over the Children of men, the Dispensation of Rewards and Punishments, according to eminent deserts or demerits.

'*Item*. I have given you the advantage of *Speech*, whereby to communicate your minds to one another, and to instruct and advantage one another by the help thereof.

'*Item*. I have given you *Time* of life in this World, to some longer, to some shorter, to all a time of life, a season wherein you might exercise those other Talents I have entrusted you withal.

'*Item.* I have delivered over unto you the rule and *Dominion over my Creatures*, allowing you the use of them for your Food, Raiment, and other Conveniences.

'*Item.* Besides these common Talents, I have intrusted you withal, I have delivered over to you, and to you, &c. divers *special and eminent Talents* above others, *viz*, *of the Mind*, or such as concern you as intellectual Creatures.

1. 'Great *Learning and Knowledge* in the Works of Nature, *Arts and Sciences*; great *Prudence and Wisdom* in the conduct of Affairs, [*Elocution*] excellent *Education*.

2. '*Of the Body*, a firm and *Healthy* Constitution, *Strength*, *Beauty*, and *Comeliness*.

3. 'Of *Externals*. Great Affluence of *Wealth and Riches*, *Eminence of Place*, and *Power and Honour*; great *Reputation* and Esteem in the World; great *Success* in enterprizes and undertakings, publick and private; Relations œconomical.

4. 'Of things *of a mixt Nature*. Christian and liberal *Education*; Counsel and advice of faithful and judicious *Friends*, good *Laws* in the place and Country where you live; the written *Word of God*, acquainting you with my Will, and the way to Eternal Life; the Word preached by able and powerful *Ministers* thereof; the *Sacraments*, both for your *initiation* and *confirmation*; special and powerful *Motions and Impulses of my Spirit* upon your Consciences, dissuading from sin, and encouraging in, and to holiness: Special Providence: abstracting and diverting you from the commission of things contrary to my Will, dishonourable to my Name, and hurtful to your selves: *Chastisements and Corrections* eminently and plainly inflicted for sin committed by your selves and others, so that the guilt was legible in the punishment; *Eminent Blessings* upon the ways of holiness and virtue, even to the view of the World: Eminent Restitution and *Deliverances*: upon Repentance and amendment of life; most clear and sensible *Experiences* of my Love, Favour, and Listening to your Prayers, to encourage you to a Dependance upon me; singular *Opportunities* put into your hands, of instructing the Ignorant, delivering the Oppressed, promoting my Honour.

'These are some of the many Talents which I have committed to you, though in differing degrees: Give up your accounts, you Children of men, how you have employed them.

Lord before I enter into Account with thy Majesty, I must confess, that if thou shoudst enter into Judgment with me, and demand that Account which in Justice thou mayest require of me, I should be found thy Debtor: I confess I have not improved my Talents according to that measure of ability that thou hast lent me: I therefore most humbly offer unto thee the redundant Merit of thy own Son to supply my defects, and to make good what is wanting in my accompt; yet according to thy command, I do humbly render *my Discharge* of the Truth thou hast committed to me, as followeth:

1. *In General.*

As to *all the Blessings and Talents* wherewith thou hast intrusted me:

I have looked up to thee with a thankful heart, as the only Author and Giver of them.

I have looked upon my self as Unworthy of them.

I have looked upon them as committed to my Trust and Stewardship, to manage them for the ends that they were given, the honour of my Lord and Master.

I have therefore been Watchful and Sober in the use and exercise of them, lest I should be unfaithful in them.

If I have at any time, through weakness, or inadvertence, or temptation, mis-imployed any of them, I have been restless till I have in some measure rectified my miscarriage by Repentance and Amendment.

2. *In Particular.*

Concerning *my Senses*, and the use of them:

I have made a covenant with my *Eyes*, that they should not rove after Vanity, or forbidden Objects: I have imployed them in beholding thy works of wonder and wisdom.

I have busied them in reading those Books and Writings, that may instruct me in the great concernments of Eternal Life.

I have stopt my *Ears* against sinful and unprofitable discourse, and against slandering, and lying, and flattering tongues.

I have exercised them in listening to those things that might increase my Faith, Knowledge, and Piety.

I have kept them open to the cry of the Poor and Oppressed, to relieve them; the rest of the imployments of these and my *other Senses*, have been for my necessary preservation, and the honest exercise of an honest Calling and Conversation.

3. *As to the* Reason and Understanding *thou hast given me*:

I have been careful to govern my Senses and sensual Appetite by my Reason, and to govern my Reason by thy Word.

I have endeavoured to use and imploy it, but not lean or depend upon it; I make it my Assistant, but not my Idol.

I have been careful to wind up my Reason and Understanding to the highest key in the searching out of Truths, but especially those that are of the greatest concernment in matters of Faith. I have made my Understanding to be laborious and industrious, but still kept under Yoke and Rule of thy Word, lest it should grow extravagant and petulant.

I have looked upon my Understanding and Reason, as a Ray of thy Divine Light; and therefore I have used it for thee, and have counted it a most high Sacrilege, Ingratitude and Rebellion, to imploy it against thee, thy Honour or Service.

I have endeavoured principally to furnish it with that knowledge, which will be of use in the other World: this hath been my business, other studies or acquests of other knowledge, have been either for the necessary use of this life, or harmless divertisements, or recreations. In the exercise of my Reason, as on the one side, I have avoided Idleness, Supineness, or Neglect, so on the other side, I have not imployed it in Vain, Curious, Unprofitable, Forbidden Inquiries; I have studied to use it with Sobriety, Moderation, Humility, and Thankfulness; and as I have been careful to imploy it, so I have been as careful not to mis-imploy it. I looked upon it as thy Talent; and therefore gave unto thee the Glory, the use and service of it.

4. *As to the* Memory *thou hast lent me.*

On the Contemplation of that strange and wonderful faculty, that distinctly, and notwithstanding the intervention of thousands of objects, retains their Images and Representations, with all their Circumstances and Consequents, I have admired the wonderful Wisdom, Power, and Perfection of the Lord.

I have endeavoured principally to treasure up in it those things that may be most of use for the life to come, and most conducible to the attaining of it; thy Mercies, Commands, Directions, Promises; my own Vows, Resolutions, Experiences, Failings; to keep me Constant in my Duty, Dependant upon thy Goodness, Humble and Penitent.

Some things I have studied to forget; injuries, vain and hurtful discourses, and such things as either would make me the worse by remembring them, or take up too much room in my memory, which might be imployed and stored with better furniture.

The rest of the imployment of my Memory hath been to assist me in the ordinary and necessary conversation with others, the ways of my Calling, the performing of my Promises and Undertakings, the preservation of good and lawful Learning, that thereby I might do service to thy Name, serve my Generation, and improve my self in Knowledge, Wisdom and Understanding.

5. *As touching my* Conscience, *and the light thou hast given me in it.*

1. It hath been my care to improve that Natural Light, and to furnish it with the best principles I could: Before I had the knowledge of thy Word, I got as much furniture as I could from the Writings of the best Moralists, and the Examples of the best Men; after I had the light of thy Word, I furnished it with those most pure and unerring Principles that I found in it.

2. I have been very diligent to keep my Conscience clean, to incourage it in the Vicegerency that thou hast given it over my Soul and Actings. I have kept it in the throne and greatest reverence and authority in my heart.

3. In actions to be done or omitted. I have always advised with it, and taken its advice, I have neither stifled, nor forced, nor bribed it; but gave it a free liberty to advise and speak out, and free subjection of my Will, Purposes, add Actions to it.

4. If through inadvertency of mind, or importunity of temptations, or precipitancy of occasion, or necessity of the times, I have at any time done amiss, I have not taken her up short, or stopped her mouth, or my own attention to her chiding and reproof; but I have, with much submission of mind, born her Chastisement, and improved it to a humbling of my self before thee for my failings; for I looked upon her as acting by thy Authority, for thy Service, and to thy Glory; and I durst not discourage, discountenance, or disobey her.

5. When she was pleased, and gave me good words, I was glad; for I esteemed her as a glass that represented to my Soul the favour or displeasure of God himself, and how he stood affected towards me.

6. I have more trembled under the fear of a seared or discouraged Conscience, than under the fear of a sharp or scrupulous Conscience; because I always counted the latter, though more troublesome, yet more safe.

7. I have been very jealous either of wounding, or grieving, or discouraging, or deading my Conscience. I have therefore chosen rather to forbear that which seemed but indifferent, lest there should be somewhat in it that might be unlawful; and would rather gratifie my Conscience, with being too scrupulous, than displease, disquiet, or flat it, by being too venturous: I have still chosen rather to forbear what might be probably lawful, than to do that which might be possibly unlawful; because I could not err in the former, I might in the latter. If things were disputable whether they might be done; I rather chose to forbear, because the lawfulness of my forbearance was unquestionable.

8. As I have been careful to advise impartially with my Conscience before my Actions, so left either through inadvertence, precipitancy, incogitancy or sudden emergencies, I had committed any thing amiss, either in the nature or manner of the Action, I commonly, Every Night, brought my actions of the day past, before the Judicatory of my Conscience, and left her to a free and impartial censure of them; and what she sentenced well done, I with humility returned the praise thereof to thy Name; what she sentenced done amiss, I did humbly sue unto thee for Pardon, and for Grace to prevent me from the like miscarriages. By this means I kept my Conscience active, renewed, and preserved my peace with thee, and leaned Vigilance, and Caution for the time to come.

6. *As touching thy great* Works of Creation and Providence.

1. I have not looked upon thy works inconsiderately and commonly, passed them over as common and ordinary things, as men usually do upon things of common and ordinary occurrence; but I have searched into them as things of great Eminence and Wonder, and have esteemed it a great part of my duty, that the wise God of Nature requires of the Children of men, who therefore exposed these his Great Works to our view, and gave us Eyes to behold, and Reason in some measure to observe and understand them; and therefore I have strictly observed the Frame of the World, the Motion, Order, and Divine Œconomy of them; I have searched into their Qualities, Causes, and Operations, and have discovered as great, if not greater, matter of admiration therein, than in the external beauty and prospect, that at the first view they presented to my sense.

2. And this disquisition and observation did not rest only in the bare perusal of the works themselves, or their immediate natural Causes, upon which they depended: but I traced their Being, Dependance, and Government unto thee, the First Cause, and by this prosecution and tracing of things to their Original, I was led up to a most demonstrative conviction, That there is a God that is the First cause of their Being, and Motion: and in the contemplation of the admirable Vastness of the works, mine eyes behold, their singular Beauty and Order, the admirable Usefulness, Convenience, and Adaptation of one thing to another; the Constancy, Regularity, and Order of the Motion of the Heavens and Heavenly Bodies; the Mutual Subservency of one thing to another, the Order and Useful Position of the Elements, the Fertility of the Earth, the Variety of Beauty, and Usefulness of the Creatures, their admirable Instincts, the wonderful Fabrick of the Body of Man, the Admirableness and Usefulness of his Faculties animal, and the singular Adaptation of the Organs to those faculties, the strong Powers of the Reasonable Soul. In the contemplation of these, and such as these Varieties, I did to the everlasting silencing of the Atheism, that my own Corruptions were apt to nourish, conclude, That there is but One God, that he is most Powerful, most Wise, Knowing all things, Governing all things, Supporting all things. Upon these convictions, I was strengthened in the Belief of thy Holy Word, which had so great a congruity with these Truths, that the strict and due contemplation of thy Creatures did so demonstratively evince.

3. And upon these Convictions, I did learn the more to Honour, Reverence, and Admire Thee, and to Worship, Serve, and Obey Thee, to depend and Rest upon Thee, to walk Humbly, and Sincerely, and Awefully before Thee, as being present with me, and beholding me; to Love and Adore Thee as the Fountain of all Being and Good. When I looked upon the Glory and Usefulness of the Sun, I admired the God that made it, chalked out its motions for it, placed it in that due distance from the

Earth, for its use and conveniency. When I looked upon the Stars, those huge and wonderful balls of light, placed in that immense distance from the Inferior Bodies, and one from another, their Multitude and Motion; I admired the Wisdom and Power of that God, whose Hand spans the Heavens, and hath fixed every thing in its place. Nay, when I looked upon the poor little Herbs that arise out of the Earth, the lowest of Vegetables, and considered the secret spark of life that is in it, that Attracts, Increaseth, Groweth, Seminateth, Preserves it self and its kinds; the various virtues that are in them for the Food, Medicine, and delight of more perfect Creatures, my Mind was carried up to the Admiration, and Adoration, and Praise of that God, whose Wisdom, Power and Influence, and Government is seen in these little, small Footsteps, of his Goodness; so that take all the wisest, ablest, most powerful and knowing men under Heaven, they cannot equal that Power and Wisdom of thine, that is seen in a blade of grass; nor so much as trace out, or clearly, or distinctly decipher the great Varieties in the production, growth, and process of its short, yet wonderful continuance; in so much that there is scarce any thing that we converse withal, but yielded me Inscriptions of the Power and Wisdom of their Maker written upon them.

4. In the contemplation of thy great works of the Heavens, those goodly, beautiful, and numerous Bodies, so full of Glory and Light, I ever reflected upon my self with *David's* meditation; *Lord, what is man that thou art mindful of him, or the Son of Man that thou regardest him!* It is true, Man in himself considered, is a Creature full of wonder, but compared with these goodly Creatures, he is but an inconsiderable thing. I learnt by thy Creatures to be humble, and adore thy condescention, that art pleased from Heaven, the dwelling place of thy Majesty and Glory, to take care of such a worm as Man, Sinful man.

5. In the contemplation of thy Power and Wisdom in Creating and Governing the World, I have learned Submission to thy Will, as being the Will of the same most Wise God, that by his Wisdom hath Created and Governs all things, and therefore his Will, a most Wise perfect Will. I have learned to depend upon thy Providence, who though I am but a Worm, in comparison of thy Heavenly works, yet I am an Excellent and eminent Creature, in comparison of the Ravens and the Grass of the Fields; yet those he feeds, and these he cloaths, and shall he not much more cloath and feed me? Thus I have in some measure improved the Talents of thy works, thereby to find and trace out thy Majesty, thy Power, Wisdom, and Greatness, and my own Duty.

7. *Touching thy more* Special Providences toward the Children of Men.

1. As by the Works of Nature, I have learned what thou art, and something of my Duty thereupon to thee; so by thy Providence towards the Children of Men I have in some measure learned the same, and a farther lesson, *viz.* What thy Will is; for thou hast not left thy self without a witness thereof to a mere natural man, observing thy Providence towards the Children of men. I have observed some men of eminent Justice and Uprightness of Life, Purity and Sanctimony, Temperance and Sobriety, Mercy and Gentleness, Patience and Forbearance, Bounty and Liberality; and I have observed them to be very Happy men and blessed in what was most desired by them. It may be they were Rich and Great; but if they were not, it was because Riches and Greatness was not the thing they most valued, perchance it might have been a burden to them to be such; but I have always observed them to be Happy in what they most desired and valued; they had Serenity and Quietness of Mind: If they were not Rich, yet they were visibly Happy in their Contentedness; and if they were not Great, yet they were apparently Honourable in the esteem and value of others; nay, if they were under external Losses, Crosses, Reproaches, yet in the midst thereof, it was most apparent to all men, they enjoyed that which they more valued, a most composed, chearful patient, contented Soul; and this hath been apparently as visible to all spectators, as if they had enjoyed a full Confluence of external happiness, and very many times, unless upon eminent and visible reasons, before the end of their days, they had signal returns of Eternal Enjoyments. I have observed men of notorious and wicked lives, Traytors, Murderers, Oppressors, Adulterers, Covenant-breakers, and other Villanies, secured by eminent power, policy, or secrecy; yet by wonderful Providence that Power broken, that policy disappointed, that secrecy discovered, and Eminent Judgments answerable to their eminent demerits, have overtaken them. I have seen and observed both in my self and others, our Sins and Offences so suitably and proportionably answered with punishments, that though they seem to be produced by strange and most casual conjunc-

tures, yet so exactly conformable to the nature, quality, and degree of the offence, that they carried in them the very effigies of the sins, and made it legible in the punishment, *sic ille manus, sic ora gerebat.* And from these observations I found that those sins were displeasing to thee; that thou were most Wise to discover, and most Just and Powerful to punish them; and did thereupon conclude, *Verily there is a Reward for the Righteous; verily he is a God that Judgeth in the Earth.*

8. *Concerning my Speech.*

I have always been careful that I offend not with my tongue; my Words have been Few, unless necessity or thy Honour required more speech than ordinary; my words have been True, representing things as they were; and Sincere, bearing conformity to my heart and mind; my words have been Seasonable, suitable to the occasion, and seasoned with grace and usefulness.

I have esteemed my Words, though transient and passing away, yet treasured up in thy remembrance; for by my words I shall be justified, by my words condemned; and therefore I have reflected often upon my words; and when I have found any thing, through inadvertency, or passion hath passed from me, I have endeavoured to reform it, and humbled my self before thee for it.

I have esteemed it the most natural and excellent Use of my Tongue, to set forth thy Glory, Goodness, Power, Wisdom and Truth; to instruct others as I had opportunity, in the knowledge of thee, in their duty to thee, to themselves, and others; to reprove Vice and Sin; to encourage Virtue and good living; to convince Errors; to maintain the Truth; to call upon thy Name, and by vocal Prayers to sanctifie my tongue, and to fix my thoughts to the duty about which I was; to persuade to Peace, and Charity, and Good works; and in these Imployments I endeavoured to wind up my tongue to the highest degree of Elocution, that I was capable of.

I have often contemplated thy wonderful Wisdom and Goodness to the Children of men, in giving them not only Reason and Understanding, but that admirable faculty of Speech, whereby one man might communicate his mind, and thoughts, and wants, and desires, and counsels, and assistance to others, the great engine of upholding of mutual Society, and without which our Reason and Understanding were imprisoned within our selves, and confusion would ensue, as once it did at the confusion of tongues, by the most Wise Providence for most excellent Ends.

In sum, I have looked upon this amongst the many other conveniencies I enjoy, as a treasure committed to my trust for my Master's use. I have accordingly imployed it conscionably, seemly, and humbly, as thy gift, not my own acquest.

9. *Touching* my Time *of Life.*

First, I have duely considered what it is, and for what end thou gavest it me; that it is but a short time, and the minutes that are passed, and the opportunities in them, are irrevocably and irrecoverably lost, that all the wealth of the World cannot redeem it; that the time that is before me, is uncertain: when I look upon an Hour-glass, or the shadow of a Dyal, I can guess that here is half an hour, or a quarter, or more or less to come, but I cannot guess what proportion of time remains in the Hour-glass of my life; only I know it is short, but I know not how short it is, whether a year, or a week, or a day, or an hour, and yet upon this little uncertain portion of time, and the due use of it, depend my Everlasting Happiness or Misery. It is my Seeds-time, and if I sow not my Seed here, it is too late to think of that Husbandry after death; and if I sow, and sow not good Seed, my crop will be thereafter in that other World that immediately expects upon the issue of this; and I have a thousand diversions that rob me of much of this little portion of time, and yields me no accompt in order to my great Concernment, when I cast out from the accompt of my time the unprofitableness of my Childhood and Youth, the hours spent in sleeping, eating, and drinking, recreations, travels, and other things that carry no sin in them, there remains but a small portion of short life for concernments of Everlasting Importance; a great business to be done, great difficulties and impediments in the doing of it, and but a little portion of time of a short and uncertain life to do it in; and yet this life of mine was by thee given, not to be trifled and squandred away, either in Sin or Idleness; not to gain Riches, Honour, or Reputation; for when Sickness comes, these will appear insipid and vain things; and when death comes, they will be merely useless: but it was for a hither end, *viz.* A time to trade for the most valuable Jewel of Eternal Happiness; a time to sow such Seed as might yield a Crop of Blessedness in the next World; a time to secure a title to an Everlasting Inheritance; such a time, as if once lost, the opportunity is lost for ever, lost irrecoverably; for the Night cometh wherein no man can work, *for there is no work, no devise, nor knowledge, nor wisdom in the Grave whither thou goest,* Eccles. 9.10.

And upon this consideration of the great end of my life, the great importance of the business that is to be done in it; the brevity, and great uncertainty of this life, and the utter impossibility after death, to redeem the neglect of the proper and important Business of my life, I have endeavoured to husband this short, uncertain, important Talent as well as I can:

1. By a careful *Avoiding of Sinful Imployments,* which at once do wast this precious Talent, and contract a farther debt upon me, renders me in arrears for the time mispent, and the guilt contracted.

2. By avoiding *Idleness,* burning out my Candle to no purpose.

3. By avoiding *Unnecessary Consumption of Time,* by long Feastings, Excessive Sleep, impertinent Visits, seeing of Interludes, unnecessary Recreations, Curious and Impertinent Studies and Inquiries, that when attained, serve to no purpose.

4. By applying, directing, and *ordering* even *my studies of Humane Learning*, Histories, Natural or Moral Philosophy, Mathematicks, Languages, Laws to an end beyond themselves, *viz.* thereby to enable me to understand, and observe thy excellent Wisdom and Power, to maintain and uphold thy cause against Atheism, Idolatry, and Errors; to fit me for serving of thee and my Country, in the station wherein I live.

5. By exercising my self in the very business of *my Calling* as an Act of Duty and Obedience to thee, acting in it those Virtues of Christianity that might be honourable to thy Name, of good example to others, of improvement of Grace unto my self; using in it Diligence without Anxiety; Dependence upon thee without Presumption; Contentedness, Patience, Thankfulness, Honesty, Justice, Uprightness, Plain dealing, Liberality; and by this means translated my Secular imployment into an exercise of Christian Duty, serving thee while I served myself, and converting that very imployment and the time spent therein, to the Use, Honour and Advantage of my Lord and Master, the good example of others, and the increase of my Spiritual advantage, as well as my Temporal.

6. By religiously observing those *Times* that have been *set apart to Religious Duties,* especially *the Lord's Day,* not mingling with it secular thoughts or imployments, but with much attention, strictness, and care, laying hold upon those times and opportunities, and carefully applying them singly to the proper business of the times.

7. By dedicating and setting apart some portion of my time to *Prayer and Reading* of thy Word, which I have constantly and peremptorily observed, whatever occasions interposed, or importunity persuaded the contrary.

8. By making the *magnum oportet,* the Great and One thing necessary, the choice *and principal business of my life,* and the great design of it; and esteeming that time spent most naturally, profitably, and suitably, that was spent in order to it; observing thy great Works of wisdom and Power; contemplating upon thy Goodness and Excellency; hearing and reading thy Word; calling upon thy Name; Crucifying my Corruptions; exercising thy Graces; humbling my self for my Sins; returning thanks for thy Mercies; studying the mystery of God manifest in the flesh; striving to bring my self conformable to my Pattern, and to have him formed in my heart, and his life in mine; Crucifying my self to the World, and the World to me; fitting my self for Death, Judgment and Eternity. These, and the like imployments I esteemed the flower, the glory, the best of my spent time, because they will be carried over with advantage into the life to come; and therefore this I reckoned my business, and accordingly I made it: other matters, that only served for the Meridian of this life, I used either barely for necessity of my present subsistence, or as a divertisement, and sparingly, or in order to those great Ends. Those were the business, these only the *parerga* of my life.

10. *Touching* thy Creatures, *and the Use of them, and the Dominion over them.*

I have esteemed them as thine in Propriety: thou hast committed unto me the use, and a subordinate Dominion over them; yet I ever esteemed my self an Accountant to Thee for them, and therefore I have received them with Thankfulness unto Thee, the great Lord both of them and me; When the Earth yielded me a good Crop of Corn, or other Fruits; when Flocks increased; when my honest labours brought me in a plentiful or convenient supply, I looked up to Thee as the Giver, to thy Providence and Blessings, as the Original of all my increase; I did not sacrifice to my own Net, or Industry, or Prudence, but I received all, as the gracious and bountiful returns of thy liberal hand: I looked upon every grain of Corn that I sowed as buried and lost, unless thy power quickened and revived it; I esteemed the best production would have been but stalk and straw, unless thou hadst increased it; I esteemed my own hand and industry but impotent, unless thou hadst blessed it; for it is thy blessing that maketh Rich, and it is Thou that givest power to get wealth, *Prov.* 10.22. *Deut.* 8.18.

2. I esteemed it my duty to make a Return of this my acknowledgment, by giving the tribute of my increase in the maintenance of thy Ministers, and the relief of the Poor; and I esteemed the Practice enjoined to thy ancient People of giving the Tenth of their Increase, a sufficient not only Warrant, but Instruction to me under the Gospel, to do the like.

3. I have not only looked upon thy Blessings and Bounty, in lending me thy own Creatures for my use, but I have sought unto Thee for a Blessing upon them in my use of them. I did very well observe, that there is by my sin a Curse in the very Creatures that I receive, unless thy blessing fetch it out; an emptiness in them, unless thy Goodness fill them: though thou shouldest give me Quailes and Manna from Heaven; yet without thy blessing upon them, they would become rottenness, and putrefaction to me; and therefore I ever beg'd thy blessing upon thy Blessings, as well as the Blessings themselves, and attribute the good I found or was to expect in them, to the same hand that gave them.

4. I received and used thy Creatures as committed to me under a Trust, and as a Steward and Accomptant for them; and therefore I was always careful to use them according to those limits, and in order for those ends, for which thou didst commit them to me: 1. With Temperance and Moderation; I did not use thy Creatures to Luxury and Excess, to make provision for my Lusts, with vain Glory or Ostentation, but for the convenient support of the Exigencies of my nature and condition; and if at any time thy Goodness did indulge me an use of them for Delight, as well as necessity, I did it but rarely and watchfully. I looked not upon the Wine when it gave its colour in the Cup, nor gave my self over either to excess or curiosity in meats or drinks; I checked my self therein, as being in thy presence, and still remembred I had thy Creatures under an accompt; and was ever careful to avoid excess or intemperance, because every excessive Cup or Meal was in danger to leave me somewhat in *super* and arrear to my Lord. 2. With Mercy and Compassion to the Creatures themselves, which thou hast put under my power and disposal. When I considered the admirable powers of life and sense, which I saw in the Birds and Beasts, and that all the men in the World could not give the like being to any thing, nor restore that life and sense, which is once taken from them; when I considered how innocently and harmlesly the Fowls and the Fish, and the Sheep and Oxen take their Food, that thou the Lord of all hast given them, I have been apt to think that surely thou didst intend a more innocent kind of food to man, than such as must be taken with such detriment to those living part of thy Creation; and although thy wonderful Goodness hath so much indulged to Man-kind, as to give up the lives of these Creatures for the Food of man by thy express Commission, yet I still do, and ever did think that there was *a Justice due* from man, even *to these sensible Creatures,* that he should take them sparingly, for Necessity, and not for Delight; or if for Delight, yet not for Luxury. I have been apt to think, that if there were any more liberal use of Creatures for Delight or Variety, it should be of Fruits or such other delicacies as might be had without the loss of life, but however it be, this very consideration hath made me very sparing and careful, not vainly or superfluously, or unnecessarily, or prodigally, to take away the life of thy Creatures for feasting and excess. And the very same Consideration hath always gone along with me, *In reference to the labours of thy Creatures.* I have ever thought that there was a certain degree of Justice due from Man to the Creatures, as from man to man, and that an excessive, immoderate, unseasonable use of the Creatures labour, is an Injustice for which he must accompt; to deny domestical Creatures their convenient Food; to exact that labour from them, that they are not able to perform; to use extremity or cruelty towards them is a breach of that Trust, under which the Dominion of the Creatures was committed to us, and a breach of that Justice that is due from men to them: and therefore I have always esteemed it as part of my Duty, and it hath been always my practice to be merciful to Beasts; and upon the same account I have ever esteemed it a breach of Trust, and have accordingly declined any cruelty to any of thy Creatures, and as much as I might, prevented it in others, as a tyranny inconsistent with the Trust and Stewardship that thou hast committed to me. I have abhorred those sports that consist in the torturing of the Creatures: and if either noxious Creatures must be destroyed, or Creatures for Food must be taken, it hath been my practice to do it in that manner, that may be with the least torture or cruelty to the Creature; and I have still thought it an unlawful thing to destroy those Creatures for

Recreation-sake, that either were not hurtful when they lived, or are not profitable when they are killed; ever remembering, that thou hast given us a dominion over thy Creatures; yet it is under a Law of Justice, Prudence, and Moderation, otherwise we should become Tyrants, not Lords over thy Creatures: and therefore those things of this nature, that others have practised as Recreations, I have avoided as Sins. (Prov. 12.10)

As to those Habits of Mind *and Knowledge that I have had or acquired; and namely,*
11. *My* Learning *of Natural Causes and Effects, and of* Arts and Sciences.

I have not esteemed them the chiefest or best furniture of my mind, but have accompted them but dross in comparison of the knowledge of thee and thy Christ, and him crucified. In the acquiring of them, I have always observed this care: 1. That I might not too prodigally bestow my time upon them, to the prejudice of that time and pains for the acquiring of more excellent knowledge, and the greater concernments of thy Everlasting Happiness.

2. I carried along with me in all my studies of this nature, this great design of improving them, and the knowledge acquired by them, to the Honour of thy Name, and the greater discovery of thy Wisdom, Power, and Truth, and so translated my secular learning into an improvement of divine knowledge; and had I not had, and practised that design in my acquests of Humane Learning, I had concluded my time mis-pent; because I ever thought it unworthy of a man, that had an Everlasting Soul, to furnish it only with such Learning as either would dye with his Body, and so became unuseful for his everlasting state; or that in the next moment after death, would be attained without labour or toil in this life; yet this advantage I made and found in my Application to secular studies.

1. It inlarged and habituated my mind for more useful inquiries.

2. It carried me up in a great measure to the sound and grounded knowledge of thee, the First Cause of all things.

3. It kept me from idleness and rust.

4. It kept my thoughts, and life oftentimes, from temptations to worse imployments.

My learning and Knowledge did not heighten my opinion of my self, parts, or abilities; but the more I knew, the more Humble I was:

1. I found it was thy Strength and Blessing that enabled me to it; that gave me understanding and enlarged it. I did look upon it as a Talent lent me, not truly acquired by me.

2. The more I knew, the more I knew my own Ignorance. I found my self convinced, that there was an Ignorance in what I thought I knew; my knowledge was but imperfect, and defective; and I found an infinite latitude of things which I knew not; the farther I waded into knowledge, the deeper still I found it, and it was with me, just as it is with a Child that thinks, that if he could but come to such a field, he should be able to touch the Hemisphere of the Heavens; but when he comes thither, he finds it as far off as it was before. Thus while my mind pursued knowledge, I found the object still as far before me as it was, if not much farther, and could no more attain the full and exact knowledge of any one subject, than the hinder Wheel of a Chariot can over-take the former; though I knew much of what others were ignorant, yet still I found there was much more, whereof I was ignorant, than what I knew, even in the compass of a most confined and inconsiderable subject. And as my very knowledge taught me Humility in the sense of my own Ignorance, so it taught me that my Understanding was of finite and limited power, that takes in things by little and little, and gradually. 2. That thy Wisdom is unsearchable and past finding out. 3. That thy Works, which are but finite in themselves, and necessarily short of that infinite Wisdom by which they are contrived, are yet so wonderful, that as the Wiseman saith, *No man can find out the work, that thou makest from the Beginning to the end,* Eccles. 3.11. If a man would spend his whole life in the study of a poor Fly, there would be such a confluence of so many wonderful and difficult Exhibits in it, that it would still leave much more undiscovered than the most singular wit ever yet attained.

3. It taught me also with the Wise-man, to write Vanity and Vexation upon all my secular Knowledge and Learning, *Eccles.* 1.14. That little that I know, was not attained without much Labour, nor yet free from much Uncertainty; and the great *residuum* which I knew not, rendred that I knew poor and inconsiderable; and therefore,

4. I did most evidently conclude, that the Happiness and Perfection of my Intellectual Power, was not to be found in this kind of Knowledge; in a Knowledge thus sensibly mingled with Ignorance in the things it seems to know; mingled with a Dissatisfaction in respect of the things I know not; mingled with a difficulty in attaining, and restless-

ness when attained: the more I knew, the more I knew that I knew not; and the more I knew, the more impatient my mind was to know what it knew not; my Knowledge did rather inlarge my desire of knowing, then satisfie it; and the most intemperate Sensual Appetite under Heaven was more capable of satisfaction by what it enjoyed, than my Intellectual Appetite or desire was, or could be satisfied with the things I knew; but the inlarging of my Understanding with Knowledge, did but inlarge and amplifie the desire and appetite I had to know; so that what *Job's* return was upon his inquisition after Wisdom, *Job* 28.14. *The depth saith, It is not in me, and the Sea saith, It is not in me;* the same account all my several Boxes or kinds of knowledge gave me, when I enquired for satisfaction in them: My abstract and choice speculations in the *Metaphysicks* were of that abstract and comprehensive nature, that when I had perused great Volumes of it, and intended my mind close to it, yet it was so Mercurial, that I could hardly hold it; and yet so extensive and endless, that the more I read or thought of it, the more I might. *Natural Philosophy* (though it were more tractable, because holding a greater vicinity to Sense and Experiment, yet) I found full of uncertainty, much of it grounded upon Imaginary Suppositions, impossible to be experimented, the latter Philosophers censuring the former, and departing from them, and the latter despising and rejecting both; the Subject as vast as the visible or tangible Universe, and yet every individual so complicated that if all the rest were omitted, any one had more lines concentred in it, than were possible for any one Age to sift to the bottom; yet any one lost, or not exactly scanned, leaves all the rest uncertain and conjectural: the very disquisition concerning any one part of the Brain, the Eye, the Nerves, the Blood hath perplexed the most exact Scrutators. Those more dry, yet more demonstrable conclusions in the *Mathematicks*, yet they are endless and perplexed; The Proportion of Lines to Lines, of Superficies to Superficies, Bodies to Bodies, Numbers to Numbers; nay, to leave the whole latitude of the subjects, see what long and intricate, and unsatisfactory pains men have taken about some one particular subject, the Quadrature of the Circle, Conical, Oval, and Spiral Lines; and yet if it could be attained in the perfection of it, yet these three unhappiness attend it.

1. That it is but of little Use; it is only known that it may be known: That which is of ordinary use either in Architecture, Measuring of Bodies, and Superficies, Mechanicks, business of Accounts, and the like, is soon attained, and by ordinary capacities; the rest are but curious impertinents, in respect of use and application.

2. That they serve only for the Meridian of this life, and of corporal converse; a separated Soul, or a spiritualized Body will not be concerned in the use and employment of them.

3. But admit they should, yet doubtless a greater measure of such knowledge will be attained in one hour after our dissolution, than the toilsom expense of an Age in this life would produce. And the like may be said for *Astronomical disquisitions.* What a deal of doe there is touching the motion or consistency of the Sun or Earth; the quality and habitableness of the Moon; the matter, quantity, and distance of the Stars; the several positions, continuity, contiguity, and motions of the Heavens; the various Influences of the heavenly Bodies in their Oppositions, Conjunctions, Aspects? When once the Immortal Soul hath flown through the stories of the Heavens, in one moment all these will be known distinctly, clearly, and evidently, which here are nothing but conjectures and opinions, gained by long reading or observation.

Upon all these considerations, I concluded that my Intellectual Power, and the exercise of it in this life, was given me for a more sure and certain, useful, advantagious, suitable and becoming object, even *to know thee, the only true God, and Jesus Christ, whom thou hast sent.* Jo. 17.3. A knowledge that is useful for the acquiring of Happiness here and hereafter; a knowledge of a subject, though infinitely comprehensive, yet but one; a knowledge, that though it still move farther, yet it satisfies in what is acquired, and doth not disquiet in attaining more; a knowledge that is of such Use in the World that is to come, as it is here; a knowledge that the more it is improved in this life, the more it is improved in that which is to come, every grain of it here, is inlarged to a vast proportion hereafter; a knowledge that is acquired even with a consent, a desire to know, because thy Goodness pleaseth to fill such a desire, to instruct from thy self, and there is none teacheth like Thee.

12. *Concerning* Humane Prudence, *and Understanding in Affairs, and Dexterity in the managing of them.*

I have been always careful to mingle Justice and Honesty with my Prudence; and have always esteemed Prudence, acted by Injustice and Falsity, the arrantest and most devilish practice in the World; because it prostitutes thy gift to the service of Hell, and mingles a Beam of thy Divine Excellence with an extraction of the Devil's furnishing, making a man so much the worse by how much he is wiser than others. I always thought that Wisdom, which in a Tradesman, and in a Politician, was mingled with Deceit, Falsity, and Injustice, deserved the same name: only the latter is so much the worse, because it was of the more publick and general concernment; yet because I have often observed great Employments, especially in publique Affairs, are sometimes under great temptations of mingling too much craft with prudence, and then to miscal it Policy, I have, as much as may be, avoided such temptations, and if I have met with them, I have resolvedly rejected them.

I have always observed, that Honesty and Plain-dealing in transactions, as well publique as private, is the best and soundest Prudence and Policy, and commonly at the long-run over-matcheth Craft and Subtilty for the Deceived and Deceiver are thine, and thou art privy to the Subtilty of the one, and the Simplicity of the other; and as thou, the great Moderator and Observer of men, dost dispense success and disappointments accordingly. *Job.* 12.16.

As Humane Prudence is abused, if mingled with Falsity and Deceit, though the End be never so good; so it is much more imbased, if directed to a bad End, to the dishonour of thy Name, the oppression of thy People, the corrupting of thy Worship or Truth, or to execute any injustice towards any person. It hath been my care, as not to err in the manner, so neither in the End of the exercising of thy Providence. I have ever esteemed thy Prudence then best employed, when it was exercised in the preservation and support of thy Truth, in the upholding of thy faithful Ministers, in countermining, discovering, and disappointing the designs of evil and treacherous men, in delivering the Oppressed, in righting the Injured, in prevention of Wars and Discords, in preserving the Publique Peace, and Tranquillity of the people where I live, in faithful advising of my Prince, and in all those Offices incumbent upon me by thy Providence, under every relation.

When my End was most unquestionably good, I ever then took most heed that the Means were suitable and justifiable. 1. Because the better the End was, the more easily we are cousened into the use of ill Means to effect it; we are too apt to dispense with our selves in the practice of what is amiss, in order to the accomplishing of an End that is good; we are apt, while with great intention of mind we gaze upon the End, not to care what course we take, so as we attain it, and are apt to think that God will dispense with, or at least over-look the miscarriage in our attempts, if the End be good. 2. Because many times, if not most times, thy Name and Honour do more suffer attempting a good End by bad Means, than by attempting both a bad End, and also by bad Means; for bad Ends are suitable to bad Means; they are alike; and it doth not immediately, as such, concern thy Honour; but every thing that is Good, hath somewhat of thee in it, thy Name and thy Nature, and thy Honour is written upon it; and the blemish that is cast upon it, is in some measure cast upon thee; and the Evil and Scandal, and Infamy and Ugliness that is in the Means, is cast upon the End, and doth disparage and blemish it, and consequently it dishonours thee. To Rob for Burnt-offerings and to Lye for God, is a greater disservice to thy Majesty, than Rob for Rapin, or to Lye for advantage.

Whensoever my Prudence was Successful, duely to attain a good End, I ever gave thy Name the Glory, and that in Sincerity. I have known some men, (and if a man will observe his own heart, he will find it there also, unless it be strictly denied,) that will give God the Glory of the success of a good enterprize, but yet with a kind of a secret invitation of somewhat of praise for themselves, their prudence, conduct, and wisdom; and will be glad to hear of it, and secretly angry and discontented if they miss it; and many times give God the Glory, with a kind of ostentation and vain Glory in doing so: but I have given thee the Glory of it upon the account of my very Judgment, that it is due, and due only to thee. I do know that that Prudence that I have, comes from Thee; and I do know that it is Thy Providential ordering of occurrences that makes prudential deliberations successful; and more is due unto thy ordering, disposing, sitting, timing, directing of all in seeming casualties, than there is to that humane Counsel by which it is acted, or seems to be acted; the least whereof, if not marshalled by thy hand, would have shattered and broken the Counsel to a thousand pieces: Thou givest the advice by thy Wisdom, and secondest it by thy Providence; thou dealest by us as we do by our Children when we set them to lift a heavy staff, or a weight, and we lift with them; and we again are too like those Children that think we move the weight, when we move not a grain of it.

13. *Concerning the gift of* Elocution.

I have ever used that gift *with Humility,* not thereby seeking applause to my self, or owning it; because Pride and Ostentation in this gift would be secret Idolatry to my self, and sacriledge to thee, robbing thee of thy Glory, and therefore signally vindicated in the example of *Herod,* Act. 12.

2. *With Truth;* I never used the advantage of my Elocution, either to maintain a falshood, or to abuse credulity into a foolish opinion or persuasion.

3. With Integrity; I never used the advantage of *Eloquence* or *Rhetorick* to deceive people, or to cousen them into any thing. My heart always went along with my tongue; and if I used intention of speech upon any occasion, it was upon an intention of conviction in my self, of the truth, necessity, usefulness, and fitness of what I so persuaded: If my Judgment was doubtful or uncertain, so was my Speech. I never used Elocution or specious Arguments to invite any to that, which in my own judgment I doubted, or doubted whether it were fit or seasonable, all circumstances considered. I never used my Elocution to give credit to an ill cause; to justifie that which deserved blame; to justifie the Wicked, or to condemn the Righteous; to make any thing appear more specious or enormous than it deserves. I never thought my Profession should either necessitate a man to use his Eloquence by extenuations, or aggravations to make any thing worse or better than it deserves, or could justifie a man in it: to prostitute my Elocution or Rhetorick in such a way, I ever held to be most basely mercenary, and that it was below the worth of a man, much more of a Christian, so to do. When the case was good, and fully so appeared to me, I thought then was that season, that the use of that ability was my duty, and that it was given me for such a time as that, and I spared not the best of my ability in such a season: and indeed Elocution or Rhetorick is a dead and insipid peice, unless it come from, and with a heart full of the sense and conviction of what the tongue expresseth, and then, and not till then, Elocution hath its life and energy. I esteemed these cases best deserving my Elocution; and in these I was warm and earnest; the setting forth of thy Glory; the asserting of thy Truth; the detection and conviction of Errors; the clearing of the Innocent; the aggravating of Sins, Oppressions, and Deceits: and though I was careful that I did not exceed the bounds of truth, or due moderation, yet I ever thought that these were the seasons for which that Talent was given me, and accordingly I imployed it.

14. *Touching my Body and* Bodily Endowments *of Health, Strength, and Beauty.*

1. In general: I looked upon my Body but as the Instrument, the *Vehiculum Animæ,* and not so much given for its own sake, as to be an Engine for the exercise of my Soul, and a Cottage, wherein it might inhabit and perfect it self; and upon that reason I was very careful to keep it useful for that end; and that as on the one side, by over-much Severity or Tyranny over it, I might not tire it; so on the other side, by over-much Pampering or pleasing it might not make it unruly or masterless, though I held the latter far more dangerous: for,

2. I considered and found that my Body was the harbour of the most dangerous temptations, and the receptacle of the most dangerous Enemies to my Soul. The greatest, and most intimate, and most assiduous temptations for the most part made their applications to my Body, and held correspondence with the Lusts and Inclinations of my Flesh and Blood; the Wine, when it gave its colour in the Cup, and the pleasantness of it, Variety and Curiosity of Meats, beautiful and fleshly Allurements, costly and excessive Apparel, Precedence and Honour, Wealth and Power, the Purveyor of all Provisions convenient for the sufficing of fleshly desires, opportunities of Revenging sense of Injuries, Ease, Idleness and Delicacy; these, and a thousand more made their applications and addresses to my sensual and corporal Appetite; the motions of my Blood, the Constitution or Complexion of my Body, the Lust and desires of my Flesh; or rather this Lust reached and hunted after them, whereby my Body, which was given to be instrumental and subservient unto my Soul, was ready still to cast off the yoak, and set up for it self, and prostitute that noble part to be a Servant, a Baud unto it, and bring her to that Servitude and Vassalage, that all her Wit, Skill, Activity, and Power, was wholly taken up in contriving and making provisions for the Flesh. I found that the Sensual and the Beastly part was ready still to thrust the Heavenly and Intellectual part out of her Throne, and to usurp it, and to invert the very order of Nature it self; so that both the parts of my Composition were disordered, and out of their place, and lost their use. My Body, which was given to serve and obey, became the Empress, and commanded and corrupted my Soul, embased and en-

slaved it to Lust and disorder; and my Soul, which was given to rule, became but the minister and slave of my Body, and was tainted and emasculated by the Empire and Dominion of my Body, and the Lusts and steams of Concupiscence that did arise from it; and I considered that if the business was thus carried, my happiness was only in this life. When Sickness, or Diseases, or Death should seize upon my Body, I had an immortal Soul, that had lost her time wholly in this World; and not only so, but was imbased and putrified by these noisom Lusts; and that the very contagion of my Body was incorporated and diffused through my Soul, and could carry nothing with her but Immortality and Disappointment, and Defilement; and consequently could expect, to all Eternity, nothing but Vexation and Dissatisfaction, and everlasting Confusion. Upon all these considerations, I resolved and practised Severity over this unruly Beast, brought my Body into subjection, refused to gratify her intemperate desires, denied them, kept them in awe and under discipline; and because I found that my fleshly Lusts grew petulant, imperious, and unruly by Variety, Curiosity, and plenty of Meats, Drinks, and by Ease and Idleness, I subdued them by moderate Diet and Temperance, by hard Labour and Diligence, till I had reduced my Body to that state and order that became it, that it might be in subjection, and not in dominion, might serve and not rule. I denied satisfaction to an intemperate Appetite, a wanton Eye, a vain wish, a worldly desire. My Table was sparing to my self, my Cloaths plain, my Retinue and Attendance but necessary. I chased away my Lust, with the Contemplations of the Presence of God, the end of Christ's Sufferings, the certainty, yet uncertainty of Death, the State after Death: and mingled all my Enjoyments and Desires with these serious and cleansing considerations: and I peremptorily refused to gratify the cravings of an importunate, inordinate, sensual Appetite; and did resolutely let them know, they should not, might not expect any better dealing from me, and my practice was accordingly.

3. I found by evident Experience, that it is the greatest difficulty that can be, for a man in a good condition to give himself leave to think it may be otherwise. There is a vanity that accompanies *Health,* that we can scarce persuade our selves that we shall ever be Sick or Dye: we cannot put on another estimate of our condition than we do at present injoy, especially if it be pleasing and delightful. To wean my self from this impotency of mind, although it hath pleased thee to give me a strong and healthy constitution, yet I often put my self into the imagination and supposition of Sickness, thoughts of my Mortality, abstracted my self from my present condition of Life and Health, and preapprehended Sickness, Diseases, old Age, Infirmity and Death; and by this means broke and scattered my confidence of long Life, continued Health, and took up thoughts becoming a Sick, Infirm, or Dying man; considered how my Accounts stood, if God should please to call me away, how I could alienate my mind from the World; what Patience I had to bear Pain, and Weakness, and Sickness. In my most intire and firmest Health, it was my care so to order my Life and Actions, as if the next hour might dispoil me of my Life and Health too; I did not, durst not allow my self in any considerate practice of any known sin, in procrastination of my Repentance, in a Toleration of Passions, upon a supposition of a continuance of Life, or of an unshaken Health; but still cast with my self, Would I do thus, were the firmness of my Health, or the thred of my Life to be broken off the next hour? My firm and strong constitution made me neither Proud nor Presumptuous, but the frequent interpositions of the thoughts of my change kept me Humble and Watchful.

4. In reference to my *Health,* I alwaies avoided these two extreams: 1. I never made it my Idol, I declined not the due imployment of my Body in the works of Charity or Necessity, or my ordinary Calling, out of a vain fear of injuring my Health; for I reckoned my Health given me in order to these imployments; and as he is over-curious that will not put on his Cloaths for fear of wearing them out, or use his Ax in his proper employment, for fear of hurting it; so he gives but an ill account of a healthy body, that durst not employ it in an imployment proper for him, for fear of hurting his health. 2. I never was vainly prodigal of it, but careful in a due manner to preserve it; I would decline places of infection, if I had no necessary Calling that brought me to them; unnecessary Journeys, exposing my body *gratis* to unnecessary dangers, especially Intemperance in Eating and Drinking.

5. I esteemed *Strength,* and *Beauty,* and Comliness of Body thy Blessing, and invitation to Thankfulness; I esteemed it to carry with it a secret admonition to bear a proportionable Mind and Life to a comely or beautiful body; and I look't upon a beautiful countenance, as a just reprehension of a deformed or ugly Life or disposition, but I never found in it matter of Pride or Vain Glory. 1. Because it is

thy Gift, and not my own Acquisition. 2. Because a small matter quite spoils it; a fall, or a disease spoils the greatest strength; a Humor in the Face, a Rheume in the eye, a Palsie, or the Small Pox, ruines the greatest Beauty; or if none of these happen, yet either old Age, or Death, turns all into Weakness, Deformity or Rottenness. I learn therefore in the Enjoyments of these Blessings to enjoy them with Humility and Thankfulness; in the loss of them, to lose them with Patience and Contentedness; for I acknowledge thy hand both in the Gift, and in the Loss. I looked upon them as Flowers of the Spring, pleasing to the eye, but of short continuance; the casuality of an unruly wind, an unseasonable frost, a Worm or Fly might intercept their natural course of continuance; but they that escaped best an Autumn or Winter, will infallibly over-take and destroy them.

15. *Concerning my* Wealth, *and temporal subsistence.*

1. I esteemed these acquisitions rather the effects of thy Providence and Blessing, than of my Power or Industry; for if instrumentally my Industry acquired them, yet that very industry is thy gift; it is thou that givest me power to get wealth Again, 2. Though my Industry and Dexterity to get wealth were never so great, yet a small interposition either of thy Providence or Permission might soon disappoint and frustrate all that Dexterity or Industry: a Thief, or a Storm, or a Fire, or a Leak, or the discomposure of the Times, or a prodigal Wife or Son, or an unfaithful Servant, or a long Sickness, or a Misfortune in others whom I trust, or a flaw in a Title, or a word mis-interpreted, or a thousand other emergencies may in a little space ruine the product of many years labour and care. When I have looked upon a Spider framing his Web with a great deal of curiosity and care, and after his industry of many days, the Maid with the Broom, at one brush, spoils all; or when I have seen a Republick of Pismires with great circumspection choosing the seat of their Residence, and every one carrying his Egg and Provisions to their common Store-house, and the Boy with a stick stirring it all abroad, or a Hen or Partridge scattering it all a sunder, so that in a little moment, all the labour of those poor innocent Creatures is disappointed; it hath often put me in mind, how easily and suddenly the collection of many years may be dissipated; and the Experience of these latter times give sad and plentiful instances of it. 3. But if none of all these visible emergencies happen, yet it is most plain, that without thy secret Blessing upon honest and commendable industry it proves unsuccessful to that end. I have known in my own observations oftentimes two men equally Industrious, Sober, Watchful of opportunities, Sparing, yet one gets up in the World, the other goes backwards; and neither they, nor I could possibly attribute it to any other cause but this thou didst bless the labour of the one, and blow upon the labour of the other. And upon all these considerations I learned in the midst of all my affluence, not to sacrifice to my own Net, nor to say in my Heart, My Might, and the power of my hands have gotten me this wealth; but I did remember the Lord my God, for it is he that gave me Power to get Wealth, *Deut.* 8.17.

2. I did not measure thy Favour to me, or the Goodness or Safety of my own condition by my Wealth and Plenty; for I found that those Externals were either indifferently dispensed to the Good and Bad, or if there were any odds, the advantage of Externals seemed to be to those, whose portion we might probably conjecture was only in this life. My Wealth and Plenty therefore rather made me the more jealous of my condition, than secure in it: It made me search and examine my condition the more strictly and carefully, and when upon the result, I found my Sincerity and Uprightness of Heart, though I with all thankfulness acknowledge thy Goodness in giving me Externals, yet I often begg'd of thee that my portion might not be in this life only; that as thou gavest me Wealth, so thou wouldest give and increase thy Grace in my Heart; that though I could wish the continuance of any External advantages as an opportunity to do the more good, yet if it were inconsistent with my everlasting interest, my great expectation in the life to come, I should chuse to be without the former rather than lose the latter; and I made it my choice rather to be poor here, and rich in the life to come, than to be rich here, and lost in the life to come.

3. And upon the same consideration, I judged my self never the better Man nor the better Christian, for having much of these Worldly advantages. I looked upon them as External and adventitious advantages, that had no ingredience at all into my Soul, unless possibly for the worse. I found a man might be Rich or Honourable, in respect of his Birth or Place, and yet a Fool, a Glutton, Luxurious, Vain, Imperious, Covetous, Proud, and in all probability the more obnoxious to these distempers by his wealth or greatness: on the other side a man

might be Poor and Wise, and Learned, Sober, Humble, and possibly his poverty might in reference to these Virtuous Habits be an advantage. My Riches and Honour therefore never made me set one grain of value the more upon my self, than if I had been without them. I esteemed it as an Instrument, that being put into a Wise, Prudent, Faithful, and Liberal hand, might be of use; but gave no more value to that inherent worth of the man, than the Ax or the Saw gives skill to the Carpenter.

4. I esteemed all the Wealth and Honour that I had, but intrusted to me by the Great Master of the World; a Talent which thou committest to me as thy Steward, and upon account; and this consideration caused me to judge and esteem of my Wealth, and dispense the same quite in another way, than is ordinarily done.

1. I did not esteem my self the Richer at all for my multitude of Riches; I esteemed no more given me than what was in a reasonable manner proportionable to my Necessities, to my Charge and Dependance, and to the Station I had in the World; all the rest I looked upon as none of mine, but my Masters; it was rather my burthen than my possession; the more I had, the more was my Care, and the greater the Charge that I had under my hands, and the more was my Solicitude to be a Faithful Steward of it, to the Honour and Use of my Master; but my part was the least that was in it: Indeed I rejoyced in this, that my Master esteemed me Wise and Faithful, committing the Dispensation thereof to my Trust; but I thought it no more mine, than the Lord's Baily, or the Merchant's Cashkeeper thinks his Master's Rents or Money his.

2. And therefore thought it would be a breach of my Trust to consume or imbezil that wealth in Excessive Superfluities of Meat, Drink, or Apparel, or in advancing my self, or my posterity to a massy or huge Acquest.

3. But I imployed that over-plus in support of the Ministry, in Relief of the Poor, in Redemption of Captives, in placing Children to School and Apprentice, in setting the Poor on work; and with submission to thy Wisdom, I thought that this latter was an equal, if not a greater Charity than the incouragement of idle or dissolute persons by liberal supplies: because it kept them in their way that Wisdom and Providence hath designed for the Children of Men.

4. And in those Imployments of Men in their Labours I still held this course: 1. To allow them competent Wages. 2. That the greatest expence should be rather in the Labour, than in the Materials. 3. That the nature of the work should be such as might bring me in a return of Profit, rather than of Curiosity: because the Proceed might be a Stock for farther Charity, or Publique Advantage. 4. But rather than the Poor should want imployment and subsistence, I thought it allowable to imploy them in such Labours as might yield them a lawful profit, though it yielded Me only a lawful Contentment; as in Building, Planting, and the like honest, though not altogether profitable, imployments; in all which, my principal Design was the support of others, and my own contentation was only a concomitant of it; and I thought such an unprofitable Contentment lawfully acquired, when it was attained by the honest Labour and convenient profit of those that I imployed. 5. And by this consideration, I kept my heart from making my Wealth, either my Confidence or my Treasures; I kept a loose affection towards it; If I had it, I esteemed it as thy *depositum*, an increase of my account and care; if I lost it without my own folly or fault, I looked upon that loss as a discharge of so much of my accounts and charge; I had the less to answer for.

5. I esteemed my wealth, 1. As uncertain to continue with me, for it hath its wings, and might take its flight, when I little thought of it. 2. As that which I must leave when I dye. 3. As not useful after death for any purpose whatsoever unto me. 4. As that which makes me obnoxious to Envy and Rapine, while I live. 5. As Unuseful at all, but when it is going away, *viz.* in the Expence of it. 6. As a great temptation to Pride, Vanity, Insolence and Luxury. And upon all these and many more considerations, I ever thought it too low to set my Heart upon it, and too weak to place any Confidence in it. When I had it therefore, I received it Thankfully, used it Soberly and Faithfully; when I lost it, I lost it Patiently and Contentedly.

2. In as much as my Wealth *in specie,* must be left when I dye, and I could not possibly carry that luggage into the other World; and if could, it would not be of use there, I endeavoured so to order and husband it, that I might receive it, though not in kind, yet by way of exchange after death; and because I found in thy Word, that *he that giveth to the Poor, lendeth to the Lord,* Pro. 19.17. and *he that giveth to a Prophet but a cup of cold water, in the name of a Prophet, should receive a Prophet's Reward,* Mat. 10.41. I have taken that course so to dispose this unrighteous Mammon here, that I might make the God of Heaven my Debtor, not by Merit, but by Prom-

ise; and so I have made over that great wealth, that thou didst send me, unto the other World; and blessed be thy condescention to thy Creatures, that when thou makest us thy Debtors and Accountants in this World, by thy Talent of all kinds that thou deliverest us, thou art pleased upon the Performance of our Duty in that Trust, to make thy self a Debtor to thy Creature by a Promise of an Everlasting Reward.

16. *Touching my* Eminence of Place or Power *in this World, this is my Accompt.*

1. I never sought or desired it, and that upon these reasons: 1. Because I easily saw that it was rather a Burthen than a Priviledge; it made my Charge and my Accompts the greater, my Contentment and Rest the less; I found enough in it to make me decline it in respect of my self, but not any thing that could invite me to seek or desire it. 2. That external Glory and Splendor that attended it, I esteemed as Vain and Frivolous in it self, a bait to allure Vain and Inconsiderate persons to affect and delight, not valuable enough to invite a Considerate Judgment to desire or undertake it. I esteemed them as the Gilt that covers a bitter Pill, and I looked through this dress and outside, and easily saw that it covered a State obnoxious to Danger, Solicitude, Care, Trouble, Envy, Discontent, Unquietness, Temptation, and Vexation. I esteemed (it) a condition, which if there were any distemper abroad, they would infallibly be hunting and pushing at it; and if it found any corruptions within, either of Pride, Vain Glory, Insolence, Vindictiveness, or the like, it would be sure to draw them out, and set them to work, which if they prevailed, it made my Power and Greatness not only my Burthen, but my Sin; if they prevailed not, yet it required a most Watchful, Assiduous, and Severe Vigilant Labour and Industry to suppress them.

2. When I *Undertook* any Place of Power or Eminence, first I looked to my Call thereunto, to be such as I might discern to be thy Call, not my own Ambition. 2. That the Place were such as might be answered by suitable Abilities in some measure to perform. 3. That my End in it might not be the satisfaction of any Pride, Ambition, or Vanity in my self, but to serve thy Providence and my Generation honestly and faithfully. In all which, my undertaking was not an act of my Choice, but of my Duty.

3. In the *Holding or Exercising* of these Places, 1. I kept my heart humble, I valued not my self one rush the more for it. 1. Because I easily found that that base affection of Pride, which commonly is the Fly that haunts such imployments, would render me dishonourable to thy Majesty, and disserviceable in the imployment. 2. Because I easily saw Great Places were Slippery Places, the mark of Envy. It was therefore always my care so to behave my self in it, as I might be in a capacity to leave it; and so to leave it, as that when I had left it, I might have no scars or blemishes stick upon me. I carried therefore the same evenness of temper in holding it, as might become me if I were without it. 3. I found enough in Great imployments, to make me sensible of the Danger, Troubles, and Cares of it; enough to make me Humble, but not enough to make me Proud and Haughty.

4. I never made use of my Power or Greatness to serve my own Turns, either to heap up Riches, or to oppress my Neighbour, or to Revenge Injuries, or to Uphold or bolster out Injustice; for though others thought me Great, I knew my self to be still the same, and in all things, besides the due execution of my place, my deportment was just the same, as if I had been no such man: for first, I knew that I was but thy Steward and Minister, and placed there to serve thee and those Ends which thou proposedst in my preferment, and not to serve my self, much less my Passions or Corruptions. And further, I very well and practically knew, that Place, and Honour, and Preferment, are things Extrinsecal, and have no ingredience into the Man: his value and estimate before, and under, and after his Greatness, is still the same in it self, as the Counter that now stands for a penny, anon for six pence, anon for twelve pence, is still the same Counter, though its place and extrinsecal denomination be changed.

5. I improved the opportunity of my Place, Eminence, and Greatness, to serve Thee and my Country in it, with all Vigilance, Diligence and Fidelity. I protected, countenanced, and encouraged thy Worship, Name, Day, People. I did faithfully Execute Justice according to that Station I had; I rescued the Oppressed from the Cruelty, Malice, and Insolence of their Oppressors; I cleared the Innocent from unjust Calumnies and Reproaches; I was instrumental to place those in Offices, Places, and Imployments of trust and consequence, that were Honest and Faithful; I removed those that were Dishonest, Irreligious, False or Unjust; I did discountenance, and as they justly fell under the Verge of the Law, I punished Prophane, Turbulent, Athe-

istical, Licentious persons. My Greatness was a shelter to Virtue and Goodness, and a terror to Vice and Irreligion; I interposed to cool the ferocity and violence of others against good men, upon mistake or slight, and inconsiderable differences: In sum, I so used my Place and Greatness, and so carried my self in all things, as if all the while I had seen thee, the great Master of all the Families in Heaven and Earth standing by me. I often consulted my Instructions, by written Word, and the impartial Answers of my Conscience; and I strictly pursued it; and when I found my self at any time at a loss, by reason of the difficulty and perplexity of emergencies, I did in an especial manner apply my self unto Thee for Advice and Direction.

17. *Touching my* Reputation and Credit.

1. I never affected the Reputation of being Rich, Great, Crafty, Politick; but I esteemed much a deserved reputation of Justice, Honesty, Integrity, Virtue, and Piety.

2. I never thought that Reputation was the thing primarily to be looked after in the exercise of Virtue; for that were to affect the substance for the sake of the shadow, which had been a kind of levity and impotence of mind; but I looked at Virtue, and the worth of it, as that which was the first desirable, and Reputation as a handsome and useful accession to it.

3. The Reputation of Justice and Honesty I was always careful to keep untainted, upon these grounds: 1. Because a Blemish in my Reputation would be dishonourable to thee. 2. It would be an abuse of a Talent which thou hadst committed to me. 3. It would be a weakning of an instrument which thou hadst put into my hands, upon the strength whereof, much good might be done by me.

4. I found both in my self and others a Good Reputation had these two great *Advantages* in it: 1. In respect of the party that had it, it was a handsome Incentive to Virtue, and did strengthen the Vigilance and Care of them that had it, to preserve it. There is a certain honest worth and delight in it, that adds somewhat to the care and jealousie of good minds not rashly to lose it. The value and worth of Virtue, though it far exceeds the value of that Reputation that ariseth from it, yet it is more Platonick and Spiritual, and hath not alwaies that impression upon us, as the sense of our Reputation hath; and I alwaies looked upon it as no small evidence of thy Wisdom in Governing Men, in adding a kind of external Splendor and Glory to Goodness and Virtue, which might be, and is a means to preserve the other, as the Shell or Husk to preserve a Kernal. 2. In respect of others, because it is both an allurement to the practice of that Virtue which attends, and also gives a man a fairer opportunity and Strength to exercise any worthy and Good actions for the Good of others. A man of a deserved Reputation hath often-times an opportunity to do that good which another wants, and may practice it with more security and success.

5. These *Temptations* I alwaies found *attending* a *fair Reputation,* and I still watched and declined them as Pests and Cankers. 1. Pride and Vain-glory; I esteemed this as that which would spoil and deface not only my Soul, but even that very Reputation which I had acquired. There is nothing sooner undoes Reputation, than the Pride and Vain-glory that a man takes in it. 2. Idleness and Remisness, when a man begins to think that he hath such a stock thereof, that he may now sit still, and with the Rich man in the Gospel, please himself that he hath enough laid up for many years, and therefore he at once starves both his Goodness and Reputation. 3. A daring to adventure upon some very ill action, upon a secret and deceitful confidence in his Reputation, thinking now he hath acquired such a stock of Reputation, that he may with secrecy and safety, and success, adventure upon any thing in confidence that his Reputation will bear him out. 4. A man of great Reputation shall be sure by those in Power, to be put upon actions that may serve a Turn; this is the Devil's Skill; for if he carry it out upon the strength of his Reputation, the Devil makes the very result of Virtue and Worth the instrument of Injustice and Villany; but if he miscarry, the Devil hath got his end upon him, in that he hath blasted him, and wounded thy Honour which suffers in his dis-reputation. 5. A great Reputation, and the sense of it, and delight in it, it is apt to put a man upon any Shifts, though never so unhandsome to support it. 6. It makes a man often-times over-timerous in doing that which is Good and Just, lest he should suffer in his Reputation with some party, whose concernment may lye in it. 7. It is apt to make a man impatient of any the least blemish that may be causelesly cast upon him, and to sink under it. A man of a great Reputation, and (who) sets his heart upon it, is desperately sensible of any thing that may wound it. Therefore,

6. Though I have loved my Reputation, and have been vigilant not to lose or impair it by my own

default or neglect, yet I have looked upon it as a brittle thing, a thing that the Devil aims to hit in a special manner, a thing that is much in the power of a false report, a mistake, a mis-apprehension to wound and hurt; notwithstanding all my care, I am at the mercy of others, without God's wonderful over-ruling Providence. And as my Reputation is the esteem that others have of me, so that Esteem may be blemished without my default. I have therefore always taken this Care, not to set my Heart upon my Reputation. I will use all Fidelity and Honesty, and take care it shall not be lost by any default of mine; and if notwithstanding all this, my Reputation be soiled by evil, or envious Men or Angels, I will patiently bear it, and content my self with the Serenity of my own Conscience, *Hic murus ahenius esto.*

7. When thy Honour, or the good of my Country was concerned, I then thought it was a seasonable time to lay out my Reputation for the advantage of either, and to act it, and by, and upon it, to the highest, in the use of all lawful Means; and upon such an occasion the Councel of *Mordecai* to *Hesther* was my incouragement, *Hesther* 5. Who knoweth whether God hath given thee this Reputation and Esteem for such a time as this?

Rules of Civility

Labour to keep alive in your Breast that Little Spark of Ce[les]tial fire Called Conscience.

Among the extant school books and papers of George Washington is his Rules of Civility & Decent Behaviour in Company and Conversation. *Most biographers refer to these maxims and quote a few, but it is felt that the entire number should be reproduced here in a typed version, and samples of the pages in George Washington's handwriting* (Appendix A 2–3), *inasmuch as the original is not in all cases clearly legible due to the age of the paper and the hard treatment it has had during the intervening years before it was finally lodged in the Library of Congress. The copy which follows is from the study of the rules made by Charles Moore in 1926.*

Over the years a number of studies have been made to ascertain the history of these rules which young George Washington copied so carefully. Perhaps the best description is given in the little book by General William H. Wilbur, entitled The Making of George Washington, *first edition, pp. 109–110).*

"Biographers who wrote about Washington during the first fifty years after his death, make no mention of the rules. The existence of the notebooks was unknown during that period. Later writers did mention the rules, but made the incorrect assumption that young George was the author. This false conclusion went unchallenged for almost fifty years until Moncure D. Conway gave the code serious study.

"Conway traced the rules to England. He showed that there was identity of words and ideas which proved conclusively that the precepts came from some French document which had been translated into English by Francis Hawkins.

"Conway then undertook the arduous task of finding the French book which Hawkins had translated. He finally found it, a small volume titled, Bienseance de la Conversation entree less Hommes, *produced at the College of La Fleche in France. Conway was so certain that he had found the original source of the Rules that he published a book in 1890, which he titled, 'George Washington's Rules of Civility Traced to Their Source.'*

"Since 1890 Conway's conclusion that the original source of the rules was the Jesuit College of La Fleche in France, has been generally accepted as the final word in this matter. However in making a study of the educational philosophy which prevailed in European Schools during the 1600s your author first suspected, then became convinced that the rules went back to an earlier period. As a result your author undertook what was both a difficult and challenging search. This was so because although the subject matter and content of the item sought was known, there was no clue as to its title or authorship. This interesting search even went as far afield as the Great Manuscript Library in Prague, Czechoslovakia.

"Extensive research finally produced gratifying success. It can now be stated with complete assurance that the original author of the rules was Giovanni Della Casa, Archbishop of Benevenuto, one time Secretary of State under Pope Paul IV.

"Fully half a century before the Fathers at La Fleche published their rules, Della Casa wrote a book titled, Calateo, A treatise on Politeness and Delicacy of Manners. *The date of its completion as a manuscript in Latin, appears to have been about 1551. One source states that the book had been in preparation over a period of 40 years. The first printed edition, in Latin, was issued in 1558. What appears to have been the earliest Italian printed edition was produced in Milan in 1559. A French translation appeared in 1562. An English version was printed in 1576 by Robert Peterson for Raufe Newberry, London.*

"As the La Fleche version of the rules was not written until about 1600 and first appeared in print in 1617, there can be no question of the primacy of the Della Casa authorship."

★

"Good manners" *or* "Rules of Civility" *belong to the benevolent influence of Christianity in the life of the individual; contrariwise, when the influence is allowed to fade, the good manners begin to fade. It is hoped that as these "rules" are studied and applied by each rising generation of Americans, that their manners will return to the standard set by George Washington.*

— Verna Hall, Compiler.

Rules of Civility & Decent Behaviour in Company and Conversation

Rules of Civility as copied by George Washington

Facsimile first and last pages, Appendix A 2–3

1st Every Action done in Company, ought to be with Some Sign of Respect, to those that are Present.

2d When in Company, put not your Hands to any Part of the Body, not usualy Discovered.

3d Shew Nothing to your Freind that may affright him.

4 In the Presence of Others Sing not to yourself with a humming Noise, nor Drum with your Fingers or Feet.

5th If You Cough, Sneeze, Sigh, or Yawn, do it not Loud, but Privately; and Speak not in your Yawning, but put Your handkercheif or Hand before your face and turn aside.

6th Sleep not when others Speak, Sit not when others stand, Speak not when you Should hold your Peace, walk not on when others Stop.

7th Put not off your Cloths in the presence of Others, nor go out your Chamber half Drest

8th At Play and at Fire its Good manners to Give Place to the last Commer, and affect not to Speak Louder than Ordinary

9th Spit not in the Fire, nor Stoop low before it neither Put your Hands into the Flames to warm them, nor Set your Feet upon the Fire especially if there be meat before it

10th When you Sit down, Keep your Feet firm and Even, without putting one on the other or Crossing them

11th Shift not yourself in the Sight of others nor Gnaw your nails

12th Shake not the head, Feet, or Legs rowl not the Eys lift not one eyebrow higher than the other wry not the mouth, and bedew no mans face with your Spittle, by appr[oaching too nea]r him [when] you Speak

13th Kill no Vermin as Fleas, lice ticks &c in the Sight of Others, if you See any filth or thick Spittle put your foot Dexteriously upon it if it be upon the Cloths of your Companions, Put it off privately, and if it be upon your own Cloths return Thanks to him who puts it off

14th Turn not your Back to others especially in Speaking, Jog not the Table or Desk on which Another reads or writes, lean not upon any one

15th Keep your Nails clean and Short, also your Hands and Teeth Clean yet without Shewing any great Concern for them

16th Do not Puff up the Cheeks, Loll not out the tongue rub the Hands, or beard, thrust out the lips, or bite them or keep the Lips too open or too Close

17th Be no Flatterer, neither Play with any that delights not to be Play'd Withal.

18th Read no letters, Books, or Papers in Company but when there is a Necessity for the doing of it you must ask leave: come not near the Books or Writings of Another so as to read them unless desired or give your opinion of them unask'd also look not nigh when another is writing a Letter.

19th Let your Countenance be pleasant but in Serious Matters Somewhat grave.

20th The Gestures of the Body must be Suited to the discourse you are upon.

21st Reproach none for the Infirmaties of Nature, nor Delight to Put them that have in mind thereof.

22d Shew not yourself glad at the Misfortune of another though he were your enemy.

23d When you see a Crime punished, you may be inwardly Pleased; but always shew Pity to the Suffering Offender

[24th Do not laugh too loud or] too much at any Publick [Spectacle].

25th Superfluous Complements and all Affectation of Ceremonie are to be avoided, yet where due they are not to be Neglected

26th In Pulling off your Hat to Persons of Distinction, as Noblemen, Justices, Churchmen &c. make a Reverence, bowing more or less according to the Custom of the Better Bred, and Quality of the Person. Amongst your equals expect not always that they Should begin with you first, but to Pull off the Hat when there is no need is Affectation, in the Manner of Saluting and resaluting in words keep to the most usual Custom

27th Tis ill manners to bid one more eminent than yourself be covered as well as not to do it to whom it's due Likewise he that makes too much haste to Put on his hat does not well, yet he ought to Put it on at the first, or at most the Second time of being ask'd; now what is herein Spoken, of Qualification in behaviour in Saluting, ought also to be observed in taking of Place, and Sitting down for ceremonies without Bounds is troublesome

28th If any one come to Speak to you while you are Sitting Stand up tho he be your Inferiour, and when you Present Seats let it be to every one according to his Degree

29th When you meet with one of Greater Quality than yourself, Stop, and retire especially if it be at a Door or any Straight place to give way for him to Pass

30th In walking the highest Place in most Countrys Seems to be on the right hand therefore Place yourself on the left of him whom you desire to Honour: but if three walk together the mid[dest] Place is the most Honourable the wall is usually given to the most worthy if two walk together

31st If any one far Surpasses others, either in age, Estate, or Merit [yet] would give Place to a meaner than hims[elf in his own lodging or elsewhere] the one ought not to except it, S[o he on the other part should not use much earnestness nor offer] it above once or twice.

32d To one that is your equal, or not much inferior you are to give the cheif Place in your Lodging and he to who 'tis offered ought at the first to refuse it but at the Second to accept though not without acknowledging his own unworthiness.

33d They that are in Dignity or in office have in all places Preceedency but whilst they are Young they ought to respect those that are their equals in Birth or other Qualitys, though they have no Publick charge.

34th It is good Manners to prefer them to whom we Speak befo[re] ourselves especially if they be above us with whom in no Sort we ought to begin.

35th Let your Discourse with Men of Business be Short and Comprehensive.

36th Artificers & Persons of low Degree ought not to use many ceremonies to Lords, or Others of high Degree but Respect and highly Honour them, and those of high Degree ought to treat them with affibility & Courtesie, without Arrogancy

37th In Speaking to men of Quality do not lean nor Look them full in the Face, nor approach too near them at lest Keep a full Pace from them

38th In visiting the Sick, do not Presently play the Physicion if you be not Knowing therein

39th In writing or Speaking, give to every Person his due Title According to his Degree & the Custom of the Place.

40th Strive not with your Superiers in argument, but always Submit your Judgment to others with Modesty

41st Undertake not to Teach your equal in the art himself Professes; it Savours of arrogancy

[42d Let thy ceremonies in] Courtesie be proper to the Dignity of his place [with whom thou conversest for it is absurd to ac]t ye same with a Clown and a Prince

43d Do not express Joy before one sick or in pain for that contrary Passion will aggravate his Misery.

44th When a man does all he can though it Succeeds not well blame not him that did it.

45th Being to advise or reprehend any one, consider whether it ought to be in publick or in Private; presently, or at Some other time in what terms to do it & in reproving Shew no Sign of Cholar but do it with all Sweetness and Mildness

46th Take all Admonitions thankfully in what Time or Place Soever given but afterwards not being culpable take a Time [&] Place convenient to let him know it that gave them.

[4]7th Mock not nor Jest at any thing of Importance break [n]o Jest that are Sharp Biting and if you Deliver any thing witty and Pleasent abtain from Laughing thereat yourself.

48th Wherein you reprove Another be unblameable yourself; for example is more prevalent than Precepts

[4]9 Use no Reproachfull Language against any one neither Curse nor Revile

[5]0th Be not hasty to beleive flying Reports to the Disparag[e]ment of any

51st Wear not your Cloths, foul, unript or Dusty but See they be Brush'd once every day at least and take heed tha[t] you approach not to any uncleaness

52d In your Apparel be Modest and endeavour to accomodate Nature, rather than to procure Admiration keep to the Fashio[n] of your equals Such as are Civil and orderly with respect to Times and Places

53d Run not in the Streets, neither go t[oo s]lowly nor wit[h] Mouth open go not Shaking yr Arms [kick not the earth with yr feet, go] not upon the Toes, nor in a Dancing [fashion].

54th Play not the Peacock, looking every where about you, to See if you be well Deck't, if your Shoes fit well if your Stokings Sit neatly, and Cloths handsomely.

55th Eat not in the Streets, nor in ye House, out of Season

56th Associate yourself with Men of good Quality if you Esteem your own Reputation; for 'tis better to be alone than in bad Company

57th In walking up and Down in a House, only with One in Compan[y] if he be Greater than yourself, at the first give him the Right hand and Stop not till he does and be not the first that turns, and when you do turn let it be with your face towards him, if he be a Man of Great Quality, walk not with him Cheek by Joul but Somewhat behind him; but yet in Such a Manner that he may easily Speak to you

58th Let your Conversation be without Malice or Envy, for 'tis a Sig[n o]f a Tractable and Commendable Nature: And in all Causes of Passion [ad]mit Reason to Govern

59th Never express anything unbecoming; nor Act agst ye Rules Mora[l] before your inferiours

60th Be not immodest in urging your Freinds to Discover a Secret

61st Utter not base and frivilous things amongst grave and Learn'd Men nor very Difficult Questians or Subjects, among the Ignorant or things hard to be believed, Stuff not your Discourse with Sentences amongst your Betters nor Equals

62d Speak not of doleful Things in a Time of Mirth or at the Table; Speak not of Melancholy Things as Death and Wounds, and if others Mention them Change if you can the Discourse tell not your Dreams, but to your intimate Friend

63d A Man ought not to value himself of his Atchievements, or rare Qua[lities of wit; much less of his rich]es Virtue or Kindred

64th Break not a Jest where none take pleasure in mirth Laugh not aloud nor at all without Occasion, deride no mans Misfortune, tho' there seem to be Some cause

65th Speak not injurious Words neither in Jest nor Earnest Scoff at none although they give Occasion

66th Be not froward but friendly and Courteous; the first to Salute hear and answer & be not Pensive when it's a time to Converse

67th Detract not from others neither be excessive in Commanding

68th Go not thither, where you know not, whether you Shall be Welcome or not. Give not Advice whth being Ask'd & when desired [d]o it briefly

[6]9 If two contend together take not the part of either unconstrain[ed]; and be not obstinate in your own Opinion, in Things indifferent be of the Major Side

70th Reprehend not the imperfections of others for that belong[s] to Parents Masters and Superiours

71st Gaze not on the marks or blemishes of Others and ask not how they came. What you may Speak in Secret to your Friend deliver not before others

72d Speak not in an unknown Tongue in Company but in your own Language and that as those of Quality do and not as ye Vulgar; Sublime matters treat Seriously

73d Think before you Speak pronounce not imperfectly nor bring ou[t] your Words too hastily but orderly & distinctly

74th When Another Speaks be attentive your Self and disturb not the Audience if any hesitate in his Words help him not nor Prompt him without desired, Interrupt him not, nor Answer him till his Speec[h] be ended

75th In the midst of Discourse ask [not of what one treateth] but if you Perceive any Stop because of [your coming you may well intreat him gently]

76th While you are talking, Point not with your

Finger at him of Whom you Discourse nor Approach too near him to whom you talk especially to his face

77th Treat with men at fit Times about Business & Whisper not in the Company of Others

78th Make no Comparisons and if any of the Company be Commended for any brave act of Vertue, commend not another for the Same

79th Be not apt to relate News if you know not the truth thereof. In Discoursing of things you Have heard Name not your Author always A [Se]cret Discover not

80th Be not Tedious in Discourse or in reading unless you find the Company pleased therewith

81st Be not Curious to Know the Affairs of Others neither approach those that Speak in Private

82d Undertake not what you cannot Perform but be Carefull to keep your Promise

83th When you deliver a matter do it without Passion & with Discretion, howev[er] mean ye Person be you do it too

84th When your Superiours talk to any Body hearken not neither Speak nor Laugh

85th In Company of these of Higher Quality than yourself Speak not ti[ll] you are ask'd a Question then Stand upright put of your Hat & Answer in few words

86th In Disputes, be not So Desireous to Overcome as not to give Liberty to each one to deliver his Opinion and Submit to ye Judgment of ye Major Part especially if they are Judges of the Dispute

[87th Let thy carriage be such] as becomes a Man Grave Settled and attentive [to that which is spoken. Contra]dict not at every turn what others Say

88th Be not tedious in Discourse, make not many Digressions, nor rep[eat] often the Same manner of Discourse

89th Speak not Evil of the absent for it is unjust

90 Being Set at meat Scratch not neither Spit Cough or blow your Nose except there's a Necessity for it

91st Make no Shew of taking great Delight in your Victuals, Feed no[t] with Greediness; cut your Bread with a Knife, lean not on the Table neither find fault with what you Eat

92 Take no Salt or cut Bread with your Knife Greasy

93 Entertaining any one at table it is decent to present him wt meat, Undertake not to help others undesired by ye Master

[9]4th If you Soak bread in the Sauce let it be no more than what you [pu]t in your Mouth at a time and blow not your broth at Table [bu]t Stay till Cools of it Self

[95]th Put not your meat to your Mouth with your Knife in your ha[nd ne]ither Spit forth the Stones of any fruit Pye upon a Dish or Cast [an]ything under the table

[9]6 It's unbecoming to Stoop much to ones Meat Keep your Fingers clean [&] when foul wipe them on a Corner of your Table Napkin

[97]th Put not another bit into your Mouth til the former be Swallowed [l]et not your Morsels be too big for the Gowls.

98th Drink not nor talk with your mouth full neither Gaze about you while you are a Drinking

99th Drink not too leisurely nor yet too hastily. Before and after Drinking wipe your Lips breath not then or Ever with too Great a Noise, for its uncivil

100 Cleanse not your teeth with the Table Cloth Napkin Fork or Knife but if Others do it let it be done wt a Pick Tooth

101st Rince not your Mouth in the Presence of Others

102d It is out of use to call upon the Company often to Eat nor need you Drink to others every Time you Drink

103d In Company of your Betters be no[t longer in eating] than they are lay not your Arm but o[nly your hand upon the table]

104th It belongs to ye Chiefest in Company to unfold his Napkin and fall to Meat first, But he ought then to Begin in time & to Dispatch [w]ith Dexterity that ye Slowest may have time allowed him

[1]05th Be not Angry at Table whatever happens & if you have reason to be so, Shew it not but on a Chearfull Countenace especially if there be Strangers for Good Humour makes one Dish of Meat a Feas[t]

[1]06th Set not yourself at ye upper of ye Table but if it be your Due or that ye Master of ye house will have it So, Contend not, least you Should Trouble ye Company

107th If others talk at Table be attentive but talk not with Meat in your Mouth

108th When you Speak of God or his Atributes, let it be Seriously & [with] Reverence. Honour & Obey your Natural Parents altho they be Poor

109th Let your Recreations be Manfull not Sinfull

110th Labour to keep alive in your Breast that Little Spark of Ce[les]tial fire Called Conscience.

Finis

George Washington's School Subjects

The illustrations found in the Appendix on pp. A 4–9 are from one of George Washington's surviving school notebooks or "Copy-Books." It is significant to see what a young man of fourteen or fifteen in our southern states, in the years around 1745, was taught. Only seven pages of 178 have been included, but it is hoped these will give some indication of the variety and practicality of the subjects taught and mastered. Facsimiles included show subjects related to geometry, plane trigonometry, simple interest, and surveying. Additional subjects in his copy-book not represented here include compound interest, logarithms, square root, surface and solid measure, triangles, gauging, calendar and leap year calculations, geographical definitions, multiplication of feet and inches, parallelograms, decimals, case, and so on.

General William H. Wilbur, in the book The Making of George Washington, *first edition, pp. 104–105, has this to say about these pages:*

"Young George's handwriting in these notebooks is the first thing that arrests our attention. It flows smoothly, is easy to read, has commendable uniformity, and a maturity that one does not expect. It gives unquestionable proof that the boy had been given high-grade instruction in penmanship over a period of many years. It also shows that during that period he was constantly held to a standard of nothing less than perfection.

Facsimile pages, Appendix A 4–9

"The arithmetic books could well be used as texts on basic arithmetic, so remarkable is their standard of excellence. The Geometry notebook has a title page with George's signature written large; some decorative swirls are included. This notebook would make an excellent treatise on geometry. First we find a general statement, then definitions, followed by many references to Euclid, and 29 problems. Each page of problems is headed by a large title, "Geometrical Problems"; each problem has its own bold heading, usually with some scrolls beside it. The problems are worked out carefully; the geometrical figures are very close to perfection.

"Finally the Geometry notebook runs naturally into practical problems in surveying.

"Geography and what might be termed practical astronomy are also covered. One of the notebooks contains copies of many useful legal and business forms. Taken as a whole they are the cumulative total of the years of instruction which George received from age six to age twelve."

—Verna Hall, Compiler.

Christianity, the Key to Washington's Character

"... [T]hat he would most graciously be pleased to dispose us all, to do Justice, to love mercy, and to demean ourselves with that Charity, humility, and pacific temper of mind, which were the Characteristicks of the *Divine Author of our blessed Religion*, without an humble imitation of whose example in these things, we can never hope to be a happy Nation." —George Washington

(Circular Letter to the States, June 8, 1783, *italics added*)

GEORGE WASHINGTON AS PATRIAE PATER
"Father of His Country"

BY REMBRANDT PEALE, 1824

(DETAIL)

COURTESY OF THE MOUNT VERNON LADIES' ASSOCIATION

Christianity, The Key to the Character of Washington

If one is not himself knowledgeable of the admonitions in the Bible, the fruits of the Spirit and the fruits of the flesh, he cannot fully comprehend the Christian life of George Washington. Additionally, even a Christian must not judge George Washington from a doctrinal or sectarian prejudice, otherwise the full wonder of this Bible-Christian life cannot be recognized.

George Washington is unique, but not unique from his times. He is the natural product of a Bible-believing people. If one would truly know George Washington, one must be a Bible-believing scholar such as he.

—Verna M. Hall

Christianity, the Key to the Character and Career of Washington by Philip Slaughter, D.D., 1886

Daniel Webster said: "America furnished the character of Washington, and if she had done nothing more, she would deserve the respect of mankind."

James Russell Lowell said:

> "Virginia gave us this imperial man—
> —This unblemished gentleman:—
> What can we give her back but love and praise?"

I trust that I shall not be deemed presumptuous if I add: the Colonial Church gave Washington to Virginia, to America, and to the world; and if she had done nothing else she would deserve well of the country and of mankind. He was born in her bosom, baptized at her altar, trained in her catechism, worshipped in her courts, and was buried with her offices. She signed him with the sign of the cross, in token that he should not be ashamed of the faith of Christ crucified, but manfully fight under His banner against sin, the world, and the devil, and continue Christ's faithful soldier and servant unto his life's end. By this sign he conquered—not only the independence of his country—but he conquered himself, thus realizing the proverb of Solomon, "He who ruleth his own spirit, is better than he who taketh a city." Such a man's character is worthy of study. The theme is a trite one, in the sense of being well-worn. All the Muses have tried their hands upon it. The historian and the orator have represented him on their pictured pages; artists have painted his portrait in every form and phase; sculptors have carved his image in marble and cast it in bronze, and poets have sung *arma virumque* in all their metres. Many persons will think that there is nothing more to be said. The whole field has been reaped, every bough beaten, and not a sheaf nor an olive is left for the poor who come after the great reapers. This would be true if I proposed to tread in the beaten track. But it is not my intention to recount Washington's weary wanderings in the wilderness, nor to rehearse the

Christian principle of self-government

Pohick Church
Truro Parish, Fairfax County, Virginia

Pohick, a brick church on the creek, after which it was named, succeeded the old church of wood which was on the opposite side of the creek. All the details of choosing the site, of the contract for building it, the materials of which it was made, its furniture, the sale of the pews, the names of the purchasers, etc., are given in full in the Vestry Book, so long lost, and which I have been so fortunate as to find. . . .

The Vestry who chose the site of the present Pohick Church, and who signed the contract with Daniel French for building it, were—

Daniel McCarty (Ch. Warden).
Edward Payne. George Washington.
G. Wm. Fairfax. George Mason.
John Posey. Wm. Gardner.
Thomazin Ellzey.

The Building Committee who superintended it, were G. W. Fairfax, G. Washington, George Mason, Capt. Daniel McCarty, and Edward Payne. On 20th Nov., 1772, twelve pews were sold at auction. George Mason bought Nos. 3 and 4, next to the south wall, for £14 11s. 6d. each. No. 5, on south wall, near front door, to Thos. Withers Coffer, for £14 13s. No. 13, north wall, Martin Cockburn, £15 10s. No. 14, north wall, next above rector's pew, Daniel McCarty, £15 10s. No. 21, centre pew on south aisle, next to communion table, G. W. Fairfax, £16. Nos. 22 and 23, centre pews, south aisle, Alexander Henderson, £13 10s. each. No. 28, centre pew on north aisle, next to the communion table, George Washington, £16. No. 29, Lund Washington, afterwards bought from him by George Washington, £13 10s. No. 31, Harrison Manley, £15. No. 15, north wall, next above pulpit, was vested in the Rector of the Parish and his successors forever. The two corner pews between two west doors, being where the font ought to be, were ordered to be taken down. It was agreed to pay Wm. Capon £6 for making a stone font, according to 150th plate in Langley's Designs. On inquiring for that font, we learned that there was a stone vessel in the vicinity supposed to be it, and now used for watering horses. It is a coarse structure. I bought it from its owner, and it will be preserved in the church as a relic of the olden times.

dramas of the French war and the American Revolution, "the battles, sieges, fortunes that he passed, and his hair-breadth 'scapes in the imminent deadly breach." It is enough to say, in the words of Chief Justice Marshall, that he did more than any other man, and as much as any one man could do, to achieve our independence. Nor shall I attempt to expound the Constitution, over whose making he presided as master-workman—a Constitution so contrived as to crown the pillars of the States like a great dome, binding them in a compact union, and yet, according to the true theory of it, resting upon them so gracefully and so lightly that, as Michael Angelo said of the dome of St. Peter's, it seems to "hang in the air." According to Bancroft, "Without him the Union would never have been formed," and the grand discovery of '89, a machine of self-government, would never have been put in motion. Nor will I speak of his election to the Presidency, except to say that he did not climb into the presidential chair by crooked ways; nor did he, like a supple serpent, insinuate himself into it from below; but he descended into it from above, like an eagle to his eyrie, as if sent from Heaven in answer to the unanimous prayers of the people. Rather will I describe how gladly and how gracefully he came down from the mount, turning his sword into a plough-share, and returning to the shade of his old oaks; not blinded by gifts, not retiring on a pension, for Washington had thanks and nought beside, save the "all-cloudless glory to free his country." Such a character is worthy of thoughtful study. No amount of treatment can exhaust its interest. . . .

Chief Justice John Marshall

A machine of self-government

Character worthy of thoughtful study

. . . . That all Americans should have given their votes for him is not surprising. When he died, at the call of President Adams, all the people of the United States went into mourning. The voice of lamentation was heard in the land like that in Israel when their great leader and law-giver was gathered to his fathers. From New England to Charleston, halls of legislation, academies of science, churches and theatres, resounded with funeral sermons, orations, dirges and dead marches. Civic, Military, Masonic, and other associations marched in processions, and white-robed vestal virgins chanted elegies and strewed flowers upon memorials draped in mourning. Statues and monuments were decreed, and to the latter, not only the old thirteen States, but the younger

The Moses of America

sisters who came later into the constellation, brought their blocks of marble or granite to swell their pile, as the twelve tribes of Israel brought each its stone to commemorate the miracle of the passage of the ark over Jordan. This was all natural. These were the voices of children honoring their father. For it has been said with Attic aptness—Providence denied Washington children of his own that he might be the Father of his Country. . . .

WASHINGTON'S FAITH

When it was determined to run up the Washington Monument to a height overtopping all other monuments, as Washington surpasses other men, it became necessary to deepen and widen the foundation to enable it to bear the superadded weight. So it seems to me that we must seek a broader and firmer foundation for his colossal character than the shifting sands of earth. After the best study of which I am capable, I am convinced that the bed-rock upon which it rests is Faith. Not faith like that of Timoleon in the fickle Goddess, Fortune, nor like that of Mohammed in a fixed fate, nor like that of Napoleon in his star. Not faith like that of some modern scientists in an unreasoning, unmoral force at the back of, or inhering in, physical phenomena, and evolving out of them, by mechanical motion and chemical affinities, all moral phenomena—but faith in a personal God who created the heavens and the earth, and who made man after His own image, who upholds all things by the word of His power, watches over them with His parental providence, and blesses them with His super-abounding bounty. But he was not a mere natural religionist, believing that God had only written his name and attributes in an alphabet of stars upon the blue pages of heaven, and in picturesque illustrations upon the green pages of earth, and in mysterious characters upon the table of the human heart. He believed that God no longer dwelt in a light inaccessible which no man can approach unto and survive the vision, but that He had manifested Himself in the person of Jesus Christ, and that, instead of being blinded and blasted by the vision, we can look with delight upon the light of the knowledge of the glory of God in the face of Jesus Christ. In fine, he believed in the Bible and in the Apostles' Creed as the best summary of the faith, and in the Catechism as one of the best expositions of those duties to God and to our neighbor, which he exemplified in his daily life. All which propositions will be proved and illustrated in the progress of this discourse. . . .

Faith in God and in His Son Jesus Christ

BIBLE AND PRAYER BOOK

The Bible and the Prayer-book were text-books in those primitive times. I remember in my childhood to have heard a very old gentleman, who was a contemporary of Washington, say that in the last century proficiency in the Bible was a test of scholarship; that a man who had only read half the Bible was only half educated; but that Washington was well educated, he having read and studied both the Old and the New Testaments.

Proficiency in the Bible a test of scholarship

It was while under the influence of his mother and pastor at Pope's Creek Church, and afterwards at the Washington farm, opposite Fredericksburg, that he formed those habits of daily reading the Bible, of habitual attendance at public worship, of keeping holy the Sabbath day, which characterized his whole life, as is attested by his wife, by Mr. and Miss Custis, inmates of his house, and by his brother officers in the army. It was then, too, that he was indoctrinated in those duties towards his neighbor so clearly set forth in the Catechism—such as honoring his father and mother; obeying the civil authority; bearing no malice in his heart; hurting no one by word or deed; being true and just in all his dealings; keeping his hands from picking and stealing; his tongue from evil speaking, lying and slandering; his body in temperance, soberness, and chastity; not coveting other men's goods; learning and laboring truly to get his own living, and to do his duty in that state of life unto which it should please God to call him. . . .

Love of God and love of neighbor

CHURCH ACTIVITIES

. . . . While Washington was in public life, it was easy to feel his spiritual pulse; its beatings were indicated in all the public documents he issued. But after his marriage, except when the General Assembly was in session, he was enjoying *otium cum dignitate* at Mt. Vernon, until the independence bell began to ring. This is just the interval during which links are wanting in the chain of evidence. But luckily, I have lately found them in the old vestry book of Truro, which has been lost to public view from time immemorial, and which enables us to supply the missing links. This precious record discloses the fact that,

Record preserved

during this interval, he and George Mason, and the Fairfaxes, Alexander Henderson, and the McCartys, and others, were active official Church workers, busily engaged in building those historic edifices known as Payne's and Pohick churches, in sending their friend and neighbor, Lee Massey, to England for orders, and in buying a glebe, or fitting up a rectory with all comfortable appurtenances for their pastor. It is pleasing to see how punctual he was at the vestry meetings, having been first made a vestryman in October, 1762. In 1763, with George W. Fairfax as his associate, he was church warden. In November, 1764, he was present and participating at meetings held for three days in succession. On February 3d, 1766, he and G. W. Fairfax, Daniel McCarty, and Alexander Henderson were chosen as a building committee. On the 4th of February, 1766, they signed testimonials commending their friend, Lee Massey, to Governour Fauquier for orders, and pledging themselves to wait for him until he returned from England. On the 23d of February, 1767, he took part in deliberations about a glebe. On 22d March he prepared a bond for the glebe land. On 25th July he exhibited an account of sales of the parish tobacco. He was again present on the 20th of September and on the 25th of November. On the 9th of September, 1768, he took part in considering proposals from the undertaker for building a church, and surveyed the parish to fix upon the most eligible site, to settle a difference of opinion in the vestry. On the 3d of March and 25th of September, 1769, he assisted in making a contract for building Pohick Church, and signed the articles of agreement with Daniel French, the undertaker. In 1771 he was suggesting improvements in the finish of the church. In 1772 George Washington and G. W. Fairfax presented to the parish gold-leaf for gilding the ornaments within the tabernacle frames, the palm branches and drapery in front of the pulpit, and the eggs on the cornice. In November, 1772, the vestry requested Colonel Washington to import cushions for the pulpit and cloth for the desk and communion table of crimson velvet and with gold fringe, and two folio Prayer books covered with blue Turkey leather, with the name of the parish thereon in gold letters.

A vestryman; church warden

Church building committee

But now men began to scent the smoke of battle from afar, and conventions and congresses were the order of the day. In 1774 the House of Burgesses, of which he was a member, appointed a day of fasting and prayer, and we find at that date this entry in his private diary: "Went to church and fasted all day." In September of the same year he was in Philadelphia, a member of the First Congress, and he says in his journal of the first three Sundays that he went three times to Episcopal churches and once to the Presbyterian, Quaker, and Roman Catholic churches, that being the first opportunity he had of observing some of these modes of worship. On taking command of the army in 1775 he issued an order requiring of "all officers and soldiers punctual attendance on divine service, to implore the blessing of Heaven on the means used for our safety and defence." In 1776, Congress having set apart a day of humiliation, he commanded a strict obedience to the order of Congress that "by unfeigned and pure observance of their religious duties they might incline the Lord and giver of victory to prosper our arms." He sternly forbade, on pain of the lash, gambling, drunkenness, and profane swearing—"wicked practices," he said, "hitherto but little known in the American army"—and he adds: "We can have but little hope of the blessing of God if we insult Him by our blasphemies, vices so low and without temptation that every man of sense and character detests them."

Punctual attendance at Divine Service

Forbade profane swearing

War Years and Presidency

He describes the bloodless evacuation of Boston and the surrender of Burgoyne as signal strokes of "that divine providence which has manifestly appeared in our behalf during our whole struggle." In 1778, after the battle of Monmouth, he tells his mother "all would have been lost but for that bountiful providence which has never failed us in the hour of distress." To General Nelson he says: "The hand of providence has been so conspicuous that he must be worse than an infidel that lacks faith, and more than wicked that has not gratitude enough to acknowledge his obligations."

In 1781 he wrote to General Armstrong: "The many remarkable interpositions of the divine government in our deepest distress and darkness have been too luminous to suffer me to doubt the issue of the present contest."

When peace was proclaimed in April, 1783, he issued an order from Newburgh commanding the chaplains with the army, "to render thanks to God for His overruling the wrath of man to His own glory and causing the rage of war to cease." He calls it a "morn-

Gives God the glory

ing star heralding in a brighter day than has hitherto illumined this Western hemisphere." "Thrice happy are they who have done the meanest office in creating this stupendous fabric of freedom and empire, and establishing an asylum for the poor and oppressed of all nations and religions." On June 18th he issued a letter to the Governors of the States, which concludes with the "earnest prayer that God may have you and the States over which you preside in His Holy protection; that He would incline the citizens to obedience to government, to entertain a brotherly love for one another, for their fellow-citizens of the United States in general, and particularly for those who have served in the field; that He would be pleased to dispose them to do justice, to love mercy, and to demean ourselves with that charity, humility, and pacific temper which were the characteristics of the Divine Author of our blessed religion, without an humble imitation of whose example in these things we can never hope to be a happy nation."

Christian character requisite to maintaining a republic

In his Farewell Address to the army, November 2d, 1783, he gives them his benediction and invokes for them "Heaven's choicest favours both here and hereafter." In resigning his military commission to Congress, he says: "In this last act of my official life I consider it my indispensable duty to commend the interests of our dear country to the protection of Almighty God and those who have the superintendence of them to His holy keeping."

In his Farewell Address to the people of the United States, which the British historian Alison pronounced "unequalled by any composition of uninspired wisdom," he said words which have been quoted all around the globe: "Of all the dispositions and habits which lead to political prosperity, religion and morality are indispensable supports. In vain would that man claim the tribute of patriotism who shall labor to subvert these great pillars of human happiness—these firmest props of the duties of men and citizens. The mere politician, equally with the pious man, ought to respect and cherish them. A volume would not trace all their connections with private and public felicity. Where is the security for property, for reputation, for life, if the sense of religious obligation desert the oaths which are the instruments of investigation in courts of justice? And let us with caution indulge the supposition that morality can be maintained without religion. Whatever may be conceded to the influence of refined education on minds of a peculiar structure, reason and experience both forbid us to expect that national morality can prevail in exclusion of religious principle."

Farewell Address

In a letter to Mr. Smith, of Connecticut, who had applauded his services, he replied: "To the Great Ruler of Events, and not to any services of mine, I ascribe the termination of our contest for liberty. I never considered the fortunate issue of any measure adopted by me in the progress of the Revolution in any other light than as the ordering of Divine Providence."

To these might be added many like confessions of faith from his private letters and from nearly every public document issued by him from the beginning to the close of his career, as soldier and statesman; there is nothing like it in the history of Christendom.

Nothing like it in the history of Christendom

Impressions of Daily Life

Now let us look for a moment at the impressions made by his daily life on those who were nearest to him, in his home, in his parish, in the field, and in the councils of the country. I hold in my hand a catalogue of nearly two hundred funeral sermons and orations, etc., delivered on the occasion of his death. Many of them I have read, and from them a volume of testimonials could be collected illustrating his Christian creed and character. A few citations from this cloud of witnesses must suffice.

Testimonies of his Christian Creed and character

General Harry Lee said: "First in war, first in peace, first in the hearts of his countrymen—sincere, humane, pious. The finger of an overruling Providence, pointing at Washington as the man designed by Heaven to lead us in war and in peace, was not mistaken. He laid the foundations of our policy in the unerring principles of morality based on religion."

General Harry Lee

Major Jackson, his aid, speaks of the radiance of religion shining in his character and of his being beloved by the ministers of religion. The Honorable Mr. Sewall, of New Hampshire, said: "To crown all his virtues, he had the deepest sense of religion. He was a constant attendant on public worship and a communicant at the Lord's table. I shall never forget the impression made by seeing this leader of our hosts bending in this house of prayer in humble adoration of the God of Armies and the author of our salvation."

Religious character

The Rev. Mr. Kirkland, of Boston, said: "He was known to be habitually devout." His pastor, Rev. Lee Massey, trusted and beloved by George Mason and George Washington, testifies: "He was the most punctual attendant at church I have ever known. No company ever prevented his coming, and his behavior was so reverential as to greatly aid me in my labors." Bishop Meade, who was intimate at Mt. Vernon and with Mr. Massey's family, says they affirmed that "Washington was a communicant." We have seen that he chose a pew next to the communion table; and Miss Custis, a member of the family, attests that "her grandmother, Mrs. Washington, told her often that General Washington always communed with her before the Revolution." G. W. P. Custis, Washington's ward and a member of the family, says, in his printed reminiscences: "Washington was a strict and decorous observer of the Sabbath. He always attended Divine service in the morning, and read a sermon or some portion of the Bible to Mrs. Washington in the afternoon. "On Sunday," Mr. Custis says, "there were no visitors to the President's house except relations, and Mr. Speaker Trumbull in the evening; so that if the bell rang the porter knew it to be the 'Speaker's bell,' as it was called." To this statement of Mr. Custis, his editor, Lossing, thoroughly versed in the family history, appends this note: "Washington was a member in full communion with the Protestant Episcopal Church." The doubt which has been expressed by some persons on this point has arisen, I think, from the conceded fact that he did not always commune, as attested by Bishop White, while Congress sat in Philadelphia, and by Miss Custis as to Alexandria, after services ceased at Pohick Church. In explanation of this fact I would suggest that it was the custom of the Colonial Church only to administer the communion at Christmas, Easter, and Whitsuntide, and the people fell into the habit of limiting their communion to these occasions. The canons of the English Church only required the communion to be administered three times a year. This is made probable by the express declaration of the General Porterfield to General Samuel Lewis, both of whom were known by many persons now living to have been men of spotless truth: "General Washington was a pious man, a member of the Episcopal Church. I saw him myself on his knees receive the Lord's Supper at Philadelphia." Porterfield, being brigade inspector, often waited on Washington in the army, and going once without warning to Washington's headquarters, he says: "I found him on his knees at his morning devotions." He added: "I was often in Washington's company under very exciting circumstances and never heard him swear or profane the name of God in any way."

Observer of the Sabbath

Morning devotions

And now as to his habits in New York. Major Popham, a Revolutionary officer much with Washington, and whose high character is attested by Bishop Meade and Dr. Berrien, of Trinity Church, New York, in a letter to Mrs. John A. Washington, of Mt. Vernon, affirms that he attended the same church with Washington during his Presidency. "I sat in Judge Morris' pew, and I am as confident as a memory now laboring under the pressure of 87 years will serve, that the President often communed, and I had the privilege of kneeling with him. My elder daughter distinctly remembers hearing her grandmamma, Mrs. Morris, mention the fact with pleasure."

Dr. Berrien says Major Popham was erect and but little broken in his age, and his mind and memory unimpaired. . . .

A Mason

Washington was a Mason, and if we apply to his character in a moral sense, the rules applied by that order to his monument, we shall find it square, level, and plumb. Its distinguishing features were a sense of duty and self-control. His passions were by nature strong, and yet, in general, he had complete mastery of them. He ruled his own spirit as men harness electricity and steam, and make them do their work. He struck the golden mean between extremes. He was a Virginian, but not a sectionalist. He was an American, and yet, like Socrates, a citizen of the world. He was an Episcopalian, and yet, to use his own words, he always "strove to prove a faithful and impartial patron of *genuine vital* religion" wherever found; and he so demeaned himself that all Christians honored and revered him. The Presbyterians, Lutherans, Episcopalians, and Methodists sent him addresses of confidence and admiration, and the Baptist University at Providence, Rhode Island conferred upon him the degree of Doctor of Laws. Bishops Coke and Asbury (Methodist) visited him at Mt. Vernon, 1785, and Dr. Coke records in his diary: "He is a plain country gentleman, polite and easy of access, and a friend of mankind. I was loath to leave him, for I greatly

Struck a golden mean between extremes

Honored and revered by all Christians

love and esteem him, and if there was no pride in it I would say, we are surely kindred spirits, formed in the same mould." Socially he was intimate with P. E. Bishop White, and the R. C. Bishop Carroll, and his pastors, Drs. Griffith and Massey, and the Rev. Bryan Fairfax. He seems to have lived in a serene atmosphere above the clouds of sectarian jealousy, sectional hate, and national pride, which so obscure our vision, and hide from us the boundless landscape of truth.

Friend of pastors of all denominations

Lived above sectarian jealousy

In considering Christian character it is not fair to make the prevailing type of religion in one generation a Procrustean bed, to which men of past generations must be fitted, before they are recognized as Christians. Time and place weigh heavily upon all men. To be born in a particular degree of latitude is to be an American or a Chinaman. To be born in a particular epoch is to have the dominant opinions and manners of that epoch. If Washington had been born in Paris, or Napoleon in America, the outcome of each might have been very different from their history as it is written. So the type of religion varies with time and place. Between St. Augustine at one end of the scale and John Bunyan at the other, there are many degrees, and all within the limits of saving faith. The inward spiritual grace was the same, but the outward expression of it in the life varied with time and circumstance. In Washington's mature life the favorite divines were Barrow, Secker, Sherlock, Tillotson, and Blair. These authors had place in the libraries of clergymen of the latter part of the last century. These authors made the fruits of Christianity more prominent than its root, and yet the root of the matter was in them in all.

Here again, I think our Hero struck the golden mean. For in commending to his countrymen morality he warned them against the error of supposing that morality could live long unless it was rooted in religious principle. He was not a metaphysician, but a man of action all his life. So he added to his faith virtue, knowledge, temperance, godliness, brotherly kindness, charity. His first wish, he said, "is to see the whole world at peace, and its inhabitants one band of brothers, striving who should contribute most to the happiness of mankind."

Morality rooted in religious principle

During the Revolution, he directed one of his agents (Peake) to keep one corn-house for the use of the poor, and instructed his steward (Lund Washington) never to allow the poor to go from his house hungry, and directed him to spend $250 of his money *per annum* in charity. He gave the use of several farms to the homeless; established a charity school at Alexandria; gave $10,000 to what is now Washington and Lee University; educated young men at college; made provision for orphans, and for aged and infirm servants.

Charitable gifts

Let no one suppose that I am trying to paint a perfect portrait. *Humanum est errare.* The sun has its spots. And those whose taste leads them to look at these through magnifying glasses, must allow us the liberty of rather rejoicing in the light and warmth and bliss in which he bathes all nature. There is but one spotless page in history; it is that which records the life and death of the spotless Lamb of God.

Neither let it be suspected that we deem the authority of Washington needed to buttress Christianity. As well might it be said that the satellites which the sun attracts around him, and which reflect his light, uphold that great luminary. The sun is self-poised, and shines by his own light, and so does Christianity. They both uphold their satellites instead of being supported by them. If Washington, and Henry, and Marshall, and Mason, and the Lees and Randolphs, and George Nicholas and Archy Cary, and Pendleton and Nelson, and Page and other stars in the Colonial Church constellation, bring the laurels they reaped in the fields of their fame and lay them as humble offerings upon the altar of Christ, we gratefully accept the offerings, but give the glory where it is due. . . .

Give Christ the glory for Washington's Christian character

Philip Slaughter, D.D

★

The Character and Reputation of Washington

The Religious Opinions and Character of Washington by E. C. McGuire, 1836

The character of Washington, on which time has fixed its authentic and unequivocal seal, is justly considered the property of his country, and, in a measure, of the civilized world. They may fairly claim him as their own, for whom, when living, he hazarded his all—his honour, fortune, and life! for whom he ever cherished anxious cares—for whom he toiled and suffered. Nor are *they* without a title, who, partaking of our common nature, shared his philanthropic sympathies, and earnest prayers.

Such a reputation is a treasure to mankind which

never can be told. Blessings innumerable descend upon the favoured people who rest under its shadow. It sheds upon them peace, security, and credit. They shine in its light, and derive from it, directly and indirectly, many eminent advantages.

But some of the choicest benefits of so rare a character, are found in its influence upon the principles and conduct of those, who are taught to regard the same with attention and reverence. A virtuous example is very powerful to persuade and control the human mind. Abundant evidence have we of this, in the happy fruits of that ascendancy which has marked the honoured name before us. The good effects which have flowed to our land from the moral weight of his excellent life, cannot be justly estimated. These effects have been increasing with the rapid growth of our country, and must continue to multiply as she advances in numbers and intelligence. Nor will the limits of his own country confine the virtue of his high example. It has already extended in its salutary efficacy to other climes, and no doubt will prevail wherever goodness is revered, or greatness respected.

Good effects of his excellent life inestimable

High example extends to the world

As few men have acted a more important or spirit-stirring part in the drama of human life, so few have awakened a deeper interest, or a more rigid scrutiny of their principles, motives, and actions. The inquiry, prompted by an ardent sympathy, has been attended by much diligent research, severe analysis, and patient reflection. Whatever he thought, or said, or did, has been examined, considered, and weighed, with a solicitude and caution, prompted by the wish to understand aright, and fitly appreciate, the character of one so eminently useful to his kind, and signally owned of Heaven. The fruit of this investigation is so well known, that it is scarcely necessary to add, that the trial to which his fame has been subjected, has issued in the universal admission, that *greatness* and *goodness* attach to his character, in a degree, seldom found to exist in the same human being.

Character has withstood every trial and scrutiny

It appears, however, to the writer, that among the various traits distinguishing so rare a personage, the attention of the public has been rather partially distributed. The qualities of the hero and statesman, universally attractive as they are, have been those on which the most have chiefly delighted to dwell. Here they have lingered, with fixed and unwearied admiration. In the mean time other important peculiarities of disposition and habit, have been suffered to pass unnoticed, or with only a reluctant and impatient glance. Among these may be especially numbered the religious views and character of this illustrious man. These, indeed, have not been entirely unobserved by the public, and no doubt have much engaged the attention of some. But they have not shared a due proportion of interest, or their merited pre-eminence in the constellation of his virtues.

Early Attacks on Washington

It is well known, that distinguished persons in our land, have evinced a strange anxiety to impress the world with a belief that the Father of his Country was sceptical at heart, in regard to the Divine Authority of the Bible. . . . Instances of this singular zeal could readily be specified, if it was expedient to do so. The remarkable fact, however, is within the recollection of many, that a public discussion took place some few years ago, in one of our principal cities, in reference to this very question—Washington's faith in Christianity being boldly denied by one individual, and as positively affirmed by another.*

Washington's faith in Christianity debated

Without attaching any undue importance to the judgment of any mere man, in reference to the Holy Scriptures, or indeed on any other subject, the writer is yet impressed with the belief that a useful service may be rendered the cause of religion and morality, by placing the question of Washington's religious opinions and conduct, in a satisfactory point of view. The solicitude which others have manifested to perplex and mislead inquirers, may be considered a justification of any effort, fairly made, to disabuse the public mind of false impressions. The truth being once established, it may then pass for what it is worth, and every man be left to draw his own conclusions, and place upon the result such an estimate as he may think fit.

This humble performance is presented by the author to his fellow-citizens, without any of the pomp of literary pretence, or the hope of literary reward. He has but one design in contemplation, as the fruit of his labour, and that is, the advancement of true religion and virtue in his native land; and with this cherished view, does he lay upon the altar of his

* This public debate was held in the City of New-York, and conducted by Mr. Owen, of radical memory, and Mr. Bachelor. (*E. C. McGuire.*)

country, this offering of a single heart, if not of an accomplished pen.

Religious Education of Washington

The advantages of early religious instruction, imparted with due affection and skill, have long since been decided by the testimony of human experience, as well as by the voice of divine revelation. So well established is the principle, that the character of the man may in general be safely inferred from the moral discipline of the youth. The consent and approval of mankind, has in one sense consecrated the familiar adage:—

"Just as the twig is bent, the tree's inclined;"

And the Wise Man declares the same in substance, when he says, "Train up a child in the way he should go, and when he is old, he will not depart from it."

Early religious education evidenced

"It is true, indeed," says Rev. J. W. Cunningham, A.M., "that our first years seldom supply that sober ear, which the lessons of religion demand; but then every avenue of heart is open; and whatever spirit is introduced into the system, often lives, though latent, and animates the frame forever. Early piety may sometimes languish, but then it is often but for a season, as rivers sometimes suddenly disappear, but as often rise again in a distant spot, with brighter waves and increased rapidity.—Early scholars in religion are the best, for they have less to unlearn. Indeed, it is rare to see the gray hairs of Devotion silver the head which was not *early* taught of Heaven."

A striking confirmation of the doctrine in question appears to be furnished by the life and character of Washington. Of this, however, we must leave our readers to form their own judgment, when the evidences of his religious education shall have been laid before them. There is reason, indeed, to regret that the amount of positive knowledge on this subject is not so ample as could have been desired. And yet there are some things known to us, which afford very strong presumptive testimony, while a few scattered examples of parental care have been given, which enable us to conclude, with considerable certainty, in regard to the general course of moral and spiritual instruction pursued in his case.

The record of his early reception into the Christian church, by the sacred rite of baptism, has been copied from the family Bible. It is here submitted, not only as an article of some interest in itself, but as serving to introduce reflections which may shed a little light upon our subject.

"George Washington, Son to Augustine and Mary his Wife, was born the 11th day of February, 1731–2 about 10 in the morning, and was baptized the 5th of April following—Mr. Beverly Whiting and Captain Christopher Brooks, Godfathers, and Mrs. Mildred Gregory, Godmother."

The parents of Washington, as the reader will no doubt understand, were members of the Church of England; which was almost the only denomination of Christians then known in the colony of Virginia. And in the matter before us, the baptism of their child, and the accompanying sponsorial provision, they acted, it would seem, in precise and scrupulous conformity with the rules of that ancient Church.

In the absence of accurate information, as before intimated, there is very good ground of belief that the course subsequently pursued by the parents, was according to the good beginning here made. The vows of those who devoted their offspring to God in holy baptism, as administered by the Church of England, were very solemn, and the *age* distinguished by a rigid punctuality respecting the duties enjoined by those vows. The solemnity of the engagements incurred, may be more clearly perceived, and fully understood from the emphatic terms of the following exhortation, always delivered in the conclusion of the service, by the officiating minister:—

Parents devoted him to God through baptism

"Forasmuch as this child hath promised, by you, his Sureties, to renounce the devil and all his works, to believe in God, and to serve him; ye must remember, that it is your parts and duties to see that this infant be taught, so soon as he shall be able to learn, what a solemn vow, promise and profession, he hath here made by you. And that he may know these things the better, ye shall call upon him to hear Sermons; and chiefly ye shall provide, that he may learn the Creed, the Lord's Prayer, and the Ten Commandments, and all other things which a Christian ought to know, and believe to his soul's health; and that this Child may be virtuously brought up, to lead a godly and a Christian life—remembering always that Baptism doth represent unto us our profession; which is; to follow the example of our Saviour Christ, and to be made like unto him, that as he died and rose again for us, so should we, who are baptized, die from sin, and rise again unto righteousness; continually mortifying all our evil, and corrupt affections, and daily proceeding in all virtue and godliness of living."

These peculiarities are referred to, solely for the purpose of exhibiting the nature of the obligations incurred, equally by the sponsors and parents of Washington, in the religious observance under consideration—obligations which we have good reason to believe they conscientiously fulfilled. Their exact conformity with the regulation of the church in the original instance, seems to authorize the conclusion, that they subsequently acted with the same scrupulous regard to engagements, bound upon them by the solemn sanctions of religion, and enforced by motives drawn from the hopes and fears of another world. . . .

Religious obligations to young George fulfilled

ATHEISTIC FRENCH REVOLUTION RESPONSIBLE FOR ATTACKS UPON WASHINGTON'S CHRISTIAN CONVICTION

Impressed, as we have seen, at an early age, with reverence for the Divine Being, and educated in the principles of Christianity, the next subject of inquiry claiming attention, involves the question of Washington's matured opinions, in regard to the truth of those things, which had been received by him, in the less competent season of youth. It has been affirmed by some, that whatever may have been imagined on the subject, he never did in fact fully embrace the Christian system, or admit its divine authority. To establish this point, has been a favourite design with individuals of a certain class, ever since his eminence has imparted peculiar weight to his opinions. With the motives, which have induced these statements, we have not so much to do, as with their want of claim to public confidence.

The following incident, taken from a northern journal, will at once explain the allusions just indulged, and introduce the written testimony of Washington, in favour of a sincere belief, on his part, in the truth and divinity of the Holy Scriptures.

Washington's views on the Bible

"MESSRS EDITORS.—The publication in your last paper on the subject of the religious sentiments of General Washington, and other distinguished men of the revolution, reminds me of a conversation I heard some years ago on the same subject, at the residence of the late Judge Boudinot, at Newark, N. J. It was asserted by some one, that although General Washington had, in his public documents, acknowledged the existence and sovereignty of a Supreme Being, who governed and ruled the affairs of this world, yet there was no proof that he was a *Christian*, or acknowledged a divine revelation or belief in a Saviour. This, Judge Boudinot remarked, was a mistake. 'The General,' he observed, 'was a Christian,' and cited the address or circular letter* to the several governours of the different states, as a proof. This address he produced, and from it I extracted the part bearing on this subject, a copy of which I now enclose for publication, if you think proper."

Proof of his Christianity in a circular letter, 1783

"The citizens of America, placed in the most enviable condition, as the sole lords and proprietors of a vast tract of continent, comprehending all the various soils and climates of the world, and abounding with all the necessaries and conveniences of life, are now, by the late satisfactory pacification, acknowledged to be possessed of absolute freedom and independency. They are, from this period, to be considered as the actors on a most conspicuous theatre, which seems to be peculiarly designated by Providence, for the display of human greatness and felicity. Here, they are not only surrounded with every thing, which can contribute to the completion of private and domestic enjoyment, but heaven has crowned all its other blessings, by giving a fairer opportunity for political happiness, than any other nation has ever been favoured with. Nothing can illustrate these observations more forcibly, than a recollection of the happy conjuncture of times and circumstances, under which, our republic assumed its rank among the nations. The foundation of our empire, was not laid in the gloomy age of ignorance and superstition; but at an epocha, when the rights of mankind were better understood, and more clearly defined, than at any former period. The researches of the human mind after social happiness, have been carried to a great extent: the treasures of knowledge, acquired by the labours of philosophers, sages and legislators, through a long succession of years, are laid open for our use, and their collected wisdom may be happily applied in the establishment of our forms of government. The free cultivation of letters, the unbounded extension of commerce, the progressive refinement of manners, the growing liberality of sentiment, and *above all, the pure and benign light of Revelation*, have had a meliorating influence on mankind, and increased the blessings of society. At this auspicious period, the United States came into existence as a nation, and if their citizens should not be completely free and happy, the fault will be entirely their own."

* George Washington, *Circular Letter,* 8 June, 1783. (See p. 208.)

Having thus supplied us, especially in the words which we have italicized, with a conclusive proof of his belief in revealed religion, we have from his pen, in the conclusion of the "Letter," if possible, a still stronger expression of his faith in the fundamental verities of the Gospel. His words are:

"It remains then to be my final and only request, that your Excellency will communicate these sentiments to your legislature at their next meeting, and that they may be considered as the legacy of one, who has ardently wished, on all occasions, to be useful to his country, and who, even in the shade of retirement, will not fail to implore the Divine benediction upon it.

"I now make it my earnest prayer, that God would have you, and the State over which you preside, in his holy protection; that he would incline the hearts of the citizens to cultivate a spirit of subordination and obedience to government; to entertain a brotherly affection and love for one another, for their fellow-citizens of the United States at large, and particularly for their brethren who served in the field; and finally, that he would most graciously be pleased, to dispose us all to do justice, to love mercy, and to demean ourselves with that humility and pacific temper of mind, which were the characteristics of the Divine Author of our blessed religion, and without an humble imitation of whose example in these things, we can never hope to be a happy nation."

Does the language here quoted require any comment? What more satisfactory evidence could be asked or given, of unqualified faith in Revelation as a fact, or in the doctrines announced thereby. The illustrious author dwells, delighted, on the sources of national good, distinguishing the age. He refers to education, commerce, refinement of manners, and liberality of sentiment, as promising a favourable influence; and then adds—"But, *above all, the pure and benign light of Revelation* has had a meliorating influence on mankind and increased the blessings of society." Revelation in his view, has not only shed "light" upon the world, but that light is "pure and benign." By it the condition of mankind has been improved, and the "blessings of society increased." Nor does his testimony end with this strong expression of his belief. He proceeds, in the closing paragraph of this memorable letter, to give utterance to opinions, which must be regarded as still stronger than those before recorded, as more decisive of his evangelical convictions. In urging upon his fellow-citizens the amiable virtues of social life, such as justice, mercy, humility, and charity; their observance is enforced by no less a motive, than the example of Jesus Christ, as the "Divine Author of our blessed religion." Let the reader mark the force of the language. It is not Jesus Christ "the Author," but the "Divine Author." Nor is it the "Divine Author of our religion," but of our "blessed religion."

Evangelical convictions

With so good a confession before them, subject to their investigation and scrutiny, how is it, that men have professed doubt and ignorance, in relation to the religious belief of Washington. Could terms more explicit, or language more transparent, be employed to announce the honest convictions of the mind? Or was there ever an individual, on whose formal declarations of opinion, more entire reliance might be placed?

There is yet another public official expression of his religious sentiments, to which we are concerned in giving special attention. In his "Farewell Address to the People of the United States," when retiring from the Presidential Chair, we have a forcible and unequivocal declaration of his confirmed opinions, in relation to the doctrines of Revelation. Having devoted the greater part of his days to the service of his country—to the good of his fellow-citizens—he takes his final leave of them, and of all the employments of public life, in this Address, celebrated by a judicious writer, as "an enduring monument of the goodness of his heart, the wisdom of his head, and the eloquence of his pen." Among many other truths of the highest political value and practical excellence, his parting advice on the subject of religion, was conveyed in the following accents of unfaltering conviction, and emphatic warning.

Farewell Address

"Of all the dispositions and habits which lead to political prosperity, religion and morality are indispensable supports. In vain would that man claim the tribute of patriotism, who should labour to subvert these great pillars of human happiness; these firmest props of the duties of men and citizens. The mere politician, equally with the pious man, ought to respect and cherish them. A volume could not trace all their connexions with private and public felicity. Let it simply be asked, where is the security for property, for reputation, for life, if the sense of religious obligation desert the oaths, which are the instruments of investigation in courts of justice? And let us with caution indulge the supposition, that morality can be maintained without religion. Whatever may be conceded to the influence of refined education, on minds of peculiar structure, reason and experience both forbid us to expect, that national morality can prevail in exclusion of religious principles.

"It is substantially true, that virtue or morality, is a necessary spring of popular government. The rule, indeed, extends with more or less force, to every species of government. Who that is a sincere friend to it, can look with indifference upon attempts to shake the *foundation* of the fabric?"

In the well-weighed instruction of this valuable extract, we have a vindication of evangelical doctrine, which cannot, we think, be too highly estimated. A full development of the pregnant meaning of its statements, cannot fail to give entire assurance, not only of the faith of the writer in the truth of Christianity, but also to impress us with the most gratifying views of the accuracy and soundness of his theological tenets.

Vindication of evangelical doctrine

French Revolution, 1789–1801

That his testimony, however, may be duly appreciated, it will be necessary to consider the circumstances which induced this manly and seasonable confession, as well as the intrinsic value and orthodoxy of the truths embraced in its unequivocal terms.

Prevailing spirit of infidelity

The period at which the views before us were expressed, was distinguished by the alarming prevalence, in another hemisphere, of a reckless and heaven-daring spirit of infidelity. The principles of its system, industriously circulated, greedily received, and widely pervading the mass of mind in the land—if not of their first germination, yet of their rank and luxuriant growth—had already produced their own bitter fruit, in the unparalleled succession of civil commotions, tumults, conspiracies and murders, by which, the recent revolution in that afflicted country, had been signalized. Had the evil been restricted to its native clime, there had not been so much reason to assail it, or warn of its danger. Unhappily it was not so confined. Unpropitious winds had wafted the foul contagion to our distant shores, and its fatal breath was fast infecting our hitherto untainted population. The profane dogmas of the Gallic philosophers, had been imbibed by some of our eminent countrymen, and diffused through their agency, were eagerly fostered by the people, in their sympathy with a nation, to whom we were under real obligations for the essential aid they had rendered us, in our recent arduous struggle for independence. But he, whom Providence had raised up, to guard the interests of America, was on his watchtower, in the exercise of a vigilance that never slumbered. The portentous mischief did not long escape his penetrating eye. He saw it in the principles of some, secretly debauched by a foreign residence, but near his person for a time, and otherwise in his confidence. The influence of great abilities on humbler minds was not unknown to him. He could not, therefore, hesitate about his course. Impelled by his ardent love of country and honest regard for truth, he resolved to throw his weight into the scale of revealed religion, and essay to neutralize the deadly poison of infidelity, before the foundations of public and private felicity should be totally corrupted and irretrievably undermined.

Infidelity produces civil and political revolt

Save his nation from corruption by deadly poison of infidelity

In putting forth his magnanimous efforts for this end, he has not only furnished a conclusive proof of his own individual belief in Divine Revelation, as refused and denied by the new philosophy; but has left on record an imperishable memorial of the substantial agreement of his religious views, with those of the great body of orthodox believers, in every age and country. The existence of this pleasing harmony may be clearly traced, in the just and scriptural ideas advanced in the Address, as cited, respecting the intimate connexion, subsisting in the economy of Heaven, betwixt *religion and morality.* We quote his words again.—*"Let us with caution indulge the supposition, that morality can be maintained without religion. Whatever may be conceded to the influence of refined education, on minds of peculiar structure, reason and experience both forbid us to expect, that national morality can prevail in exclusion of religious principle."* The position here presented, briefly, but explicitly, appears plainly to be this.—"There is not in man, unassisted by religion, strength enough to ensue a moral life; nor motives accessible to him, sufficient to dissuade from vice, or persuade to virtue; or in other words,—the corruption of human nature is such, that immorality of life will certainly ensue, if the depraved principle is not subdued, and the heart purified by a divine influence; religion being the consecrated channel of that influence, operating on the soul directly by grace applied, or indirectly by motives competent to sway the reason and control the affections." It may be said, that there is in the text, *a concession*, admitting an exception to the

Unpopular principle laid down—the depravity of man

main position of the writer. That a moral life may sometimes exist without religious principle, through "the influence of refined education, on minds of peculiar structure," is the exception alluded to. This, however, is not positively asserted by the author, but as it would seem, reluctantly "conceded." Nor does this admission on his part, involve any surrender of the principle laid down, nothing being therein allowed, but what the scriptures admit, and experience attests, with certain limitations.

That the principal doctrine here maintained is, by no means, a favourite one with the world, is well known; nor is it always admitted in so unqualified a sense, by some, who profess acquiescence in the truth of Christianity. It is, in fact, a view held only with decision, by the most evangelical religious communions. *The natural man* does not readily discern, nor his heart admit, that all human goodness—that every social and domestic virtue, to be perfect, must have its source in the principles of religion, implanted in the soul by a divine power. Human pride, disdaining reliance on supernatural aid, for those moral accomplishments which sustain its loudest boast, repels with scorn, a doctrine, which aims its blows unsparingly, at the foundation of its fondly-cherished and vaunted self-sufficiency.

But is not the truth in question, however refused and contradicted, susceptible of an ample and satisfactory vindication? Does it assert that, ordinarily, the life will be bad, where the restraints of religion do not exist? And may not this proposition be easily sustained? If man is a depraved creature, as all experience shows him to be, what will probably be his life, if left to the unrestrained impulse of his own wayward inclinations? Is it as true in the moral, as in the physical world, that nothing can rise above its level? Can a "clean thing be brought out of an unclean?" Will not the stream partake of the nature of the fountain?—the fruit of the quality of the tree? "Does the same fountain send forth sweet waters and bitter?" "Do men gather grapes of thorns, or figs of thistles?" Is there any result more certain, as a consequence of man's moral constitution, than a life of unlimited indulgence, where the lusts and desires of the mind are inordinate, and the means of gratification within his reach? This effect must follow the violence of passion, operating on a mind destitute of moral ability, or of inclination to resist the seducing charms of sensual and worldly good.

Is it, however, denied that Passion is irresistible, and a sufficiency of moral strength claimed for man, to authorize a belief in the theory of Human Virtue. Where, then, apart from religion, do you find motives, by which the love of pleasure may be dethroned, and that of moral excellence made supreme. What inducements can be held out, which shall operate effectually upon the understanding, as well as upon the affections? If the understanding does give its cold approbation, will your boasted motives be able to curb the fury of the passions when roused into a tempest? Whence, then, are they derived? From a philosophic love of goodness for its own sake, or an estimate of the delights arising from its practice, or from calculations, as to the comparative advantages of Vice and Virtue? And what are these to a man in the hour of temptation? When passion stimulates, and appetite goads him, of what avail to restrain and allay the tumult of the soul, will fine spun moral theories be? Or of what avail, the intimation of future inconveniences, which may never arrive, or if they do, may not be serious or difficult to bear?

In excluding religion, then, there is no other influence left, by which the conduct of mankind can be controlled. No agency exists for rectifying the disorders of the soul, nor does any motive remain, of sufficient power, to operate on the judgment, or affect the heart. Such a system, therefore, of necessity, is destructive of all genuine morality, and giving up mankind at large, to the blind and lawless impulses of sinful passions, turns the world into a dreary scene of confusion, tumult, and crime.

Nothing outside of religion can rectify disorders of the soul

In regard to the *concession*, implying the efficacy of causes, other than those of religion, in producing the fruits of morality—there is no ground for serious doubt as to the fact. Many there are in society, who have been rendered useful members thereof, by influences, far less sacred than those, which come down from above. Refined education, good examples, respectable associations, a high standard of morals in the community, a regard to secular interest—all these have great power over the minds of men, inspiring them with just and liberal sentiments, and gradually new-modeling the character, making them upright, honest, truthful, humane, gentle, courteous.—And yet, so far do these things fall short of the fruits of true religion, in respect to uniformity of result, number, and quality of the virtues produced—that the principle of the "Address," remains unshaken, by all that

The fruits of morality produced by true religion are superior

has been conceded. Of how much greater worth, then, will that principle appear, when it is remembered, that besides the morality arising from other causes, being of meagre and stunted growth—it is but a very small proportion of mankind, that share even this equivocal and unequal agency. This one consideration, of itself, furnishes a conclusive answer to every vain objection, and gives irresistible energy to the argument in favour of that divine system, which, all-powerful to bless, alone can become universal, and influential alike with high and low, rich and poor, bond and free.

French Revolution: Décadis and Republican Festivals, 1797–1799

The Cambridge Modern History, Lord Acton, 1904, p. 514

It was not by persecution alone that the Directory attempted to destroy Christianity. At a time when the country was in imminent danger of invasion, when every industry required support, when financial disaster threatened to overwhelm the State, when the chaos of conflicting laws rendered the administration of justice almost impossible, the Directors and their Ministers made it the main object of their domestic policy to suppress the Christian Sundays and festivals and to substitute for them the observance of the *décadis* and republican *fêtes*. Their object is expressed clearly in these terms: "to destroy the influence of the Roman religion by substituting for worn-out impressions new ones more conformable to reason." To achieve this they issued laws, orders and circulars sufficient to fill volumes—the purport of all being to erect the *décadi* into a sort of Jewish Sabbath on which no Court, public office, shop, or factory, should be open, and no work publicly performed in town or country. All officials and school-children were ordered to attend on each *décadi* at the appointed meeting-place of the Commune, usually the parish church, where a function took place consisting of the recitation of the official "*Bulletin décadaire*" containing laws and judiciously selected news of the day, followed by tales of civic virtue and moral instructions often of inconceivable banality, and ending with the celebration of marriages, which could be legally performed only on that day. In Paris fifteen churches were appropriated to these services, all of which were renamed; Notre Dame becoming the Temple of the Supreme Being, Saint Eustache the Temple of Agriculture, and so forth.

Attempt to destroy Christianity

Forced attendance at the décadis

On the other hand everything possible was done to suppress the observance of Sunday; schools were ordered to be kept open. No official or person over whom the government could exercise an influence was allowed to absent himself from work or to show any sign of holiday-making. In communes, where the administration was in the hands of the Directors' nominees, the churches were locked up as Sunday came round. The same regulations were applied to all fasts and festivals; even the markets were ordered to be so arranged that fish should not be sold on Fridays or fast days. For the old festivals were substituted a series of *fêtes*: some moral, such as the *fête* of Youth in March, of Marriage in April, of Old Age in July; others political, as the Execution of the last tyrant (January 21), Capture of the Bastille (July 14), Foundation of the Republic (September 22), Eighteenth Fructidor (September 4). But it was beyond the power of the Directors to force the whole nation to attend the *décadis* and *fêtes* or to forget the old Sunday holiday. Spectators came to see the marriages on the *décadis*; when there were none they stayed away. The peasants danced and drank on Sunday and refused to do either on the *décadi*. As for the *fêtes* so eagerly celebrated in the early days of enthusiasm, they became a weariness to the flesh in these times of apathy, contempt, and disgust.

Christian holidays and Sabbaths profaned

Christian year abolished

French Republican Calendar

Encyclopædia Britannica, 11th Edition, Vol. 11–12, pp. 170–171

Among the changes made during the Revolution was the substitution of a new calendar, usually called the revolutionary or republican calendar, for the prevailing Gregorian system. . . . The objects which the advocates of a new calendar had in view were to strike a blow at the clergy and to divorce all calculations of time from the Christian associations with which they were loaded, in short, to abolish the Christian year. . . . The new order was soon in force in France and the new method was employed in all public documents, but it did not last many years. In September 1805 it was decided to restore the Gregorian calendar, and the republican one was officially discontinued on the 1st of January 1806.

The Accuser of Washington, Robert Owen, English Socialist

Encyclopædia Britannica, 11th Edition, Vol. 19–20, pp. 394–396

Robert Owen, (1771–1858), English social reformer, was born at Newton, Montgomeryshire, in North Wales, on the 14th of May, 1771. His father had a small business in Newtown as saddler and ironmonger, and there young Owen received all his school education, which terminated at the age of nine. After serving in a draper's shop for some years he settled in Manchester. His success was very rapid. When only nineteen years of age he became manager of a cotton mill in which five hundred people were employed, and by his administrative intelligence and energy soon made it one of the best establishments of the kind in Great Britain. In this factory Owen used the first bags of American sea-island cotton ever imported into the country; it was the first sea-island cotton from the Southern States. Owen also made remarkable improvement in the quality of the cotton spun; and indeed there is no reason to doubt that at this early age he was the first cotton-spinner in England, a position entirely due to his own capacity and knowledge of the trade.

In 1794 or 1795 he became manager and one of the partners of the Chorlton Twist Company at Manchester. During a visit to Glasgow he had fallen in love with the daughter of the proprietor of the New Lanark mills, David Dale. Owen induced his partners to purchase New Lanark; and after his marriage with Miss Dale he settled there, as manager and part owner of the mills (1800). Encouraged by his great success in the management of cotton factories in Manchester, he had already formed the intention of conducting New Lanark on higher principles than the current commercial ones.

Social reform through philanthropy

The factory of New Lanark had been started in 1784 by Dale and Arkwright, the water-power afforded by the falls of the Clyde being the great attraction. Connected with the mills were about two thousand people, five hundred of whom were children, brought, most of them, at the age of five or six from the poorhouses and charities of Edinburgh and Glasgow. The children especially had been well treated by Dale, but the general condition of the people was very unsatisfactory. Many of them were the lowest of the population, the respectable country people refusing to submit to the long hours and demoralizing drudgery of the factories; theft, drunkenness, and other vices were common; education and sanitation were alike neglected; most families lived only in one room. It was this population, thus committed to his care, which Owen now set himself to elevate and ameliorate. He greatly improved their houses, and by the unsparing and benevolent exertion of his personal influence trained them to habits of order, cleanliness and thrift. He opened a store, where the people could buy goods of the soundest quality at little more than cost price; and the sale of drink was placed under the strictest supervision.

Education of Young

His greatest success, however, was in the education of the young, to which he devoted special attention. He was the founder of infant schools in Great Britain; and, though he was anticipated by reformers on the continent of Europe, he seems to have been led to institute them by his own views of what education ought to be, and without hint from abroad. In all these plans Owen obtained the most gratifying success. Though at first regarded with suspicion as a stranger, he soon won the confidence of his people. The mills continued to be a great commercial success, but it is needless to say, that some of Owen's schemes involved considerable expense, which was displeasing to his partners. Tired at last of the restrictions imposed on him by men who wished to conduct the business on the ordinary principles, Owen formed a new firm, who, content with 5% of return for their capital, were ready to give freer scope to his philanthropy (1813). In this firm Jeremy Bentham and the well-known Quaker, William Allen, were partners.

Essays on Formation of Human Character

In the same year Owen first appeared as an author of essays, in which he expounded the principles on which his system of educational philanthropy was based. From an early age he had lost all belief in the prevailing forms of religion, and had thought out a creed for himself, which he considered an entirely new and original discovery. The chief points in this philosophy were that man's character is made not by him but for him; that it has been formed by circumstances over which he had

Infidel and philanthropist

no control; that he is not a proper subject either of praise or blame,—these principles leading up to the practical conclusion that the great secret in the right formation of man's character is to place him under the proper influences—physical, moral and social—from his earliest years. These principles—of the irresponsibility of man and of the effect of early influences—are the keynote of Owen's whole system of education and social amelioration. As we have said, they are embodied in his first work, *A New View of Society, or Essays on the Principle of the Formation of the Human Character,* the first of these essays (there are four in all) being published in 1813. It is needless to say that Owen's new views theoretically belong to a very old system of philosophy, and that his originality is to be found only in his benevolent application of them.

Principles of educational philanthropy

For the next few years Owen's work at New Lanark continued to have a national and even a European significance. His schemes for the education of his workpeople attained to something like completion on the opening of the institution at New Lanark in 1816. He was a zealous supporter of the factory legislation resulting in the act of 1819, which, however, greatly disappointed him. He had interviews and communications with the leading members of government, including the premier, Lord Liverpool, and with many of the rulers and leading statesmen of Europe. New Lanark itself became a much-frequented place of pilgrimage for social reformers, statesmen, and royal personages, including Nicholas, afterwards emperor of Russia. According to the unanimous testimony of all who visited it, the results achieved by Owen were singularly good. The manners of the children, brought up under his system, were beautifully graceful, genial and unconstrained; health, plenty, and contentment prevailed; drunkenness was almost unknown, and illegitimacy was extremely rare. The most perfect good feeling subsisted between Owen and his work-people, and all the operations of the mill proceeded with the utmost smoothness and regularity; and the business was a great commercial success.

From Philanthropist to Socialist

Hitherto Owen's work had been that of a philanthropist, whose great distinction was the originality and unwearying unselfishness of his methods. His first departure in socialism took place in 1817, and was embodied in a report communicated to the committee of the House of Commons on the poor law. The general misery and stagnation of trade consequent on the termination of the great war was engrossing the attention of the country. After clearly tracing the special causes connected with the war which had led to such a deplorable state of things, Owen pointed out that the permanent cause of distress was to be found in the competition of human labour with machinery, and that the only effective remedy was the united action of men, and the subordination of machinery. His proposals for the treatment of pauperism were based on these principles. He recommended that communities of about twelve hundred persons each should be settled on quantities of land from 1000 to 1500 acres, all living in one large building in the form of a square, with public kitchen and mess-rooms. Each family should have its own private apartments, and the entire care of the children till the age of three, after which they should be brought up by the community, their parents having access to them at meals and all other proper times. These communities might be established by individuals, by parishes, by counties, or by the state; in every case there should be effective supervision by duly qualified persons. Work, and the enjoyment of its results, should be in common. The size of his community was no doubt partly suggested by his village of New Lanark; and he soon proceeded to advocate such a scheme as the best form for the reorganization of society in general. In its fully developed form—and it cannot be said to have changed much during Owen's lifetime—it was as follows. He considered an association of from 500 to 3000 as the fit number for a good working community. While mainly agricultural, it should possess all the best machinery, should offer every variety of employment, and should, as far as possible, be self-contained. "As these townships," as he also called them, "should increase in number, unions of them federatively united shall be formed in circles of tens, hundreds and thousands," till they should embrace the whole world in a common interest.

Departure from philanthropy

Experiment in America

His plans for the cure of pauperism were received with great favour. *The Times* and the *Morning Post* and many of the leading men of the country countenanced them; one of his most steadfast friends was the duke of Kent, father of Queen Victoria. He had indeed gained the ear of the country, and had the prospect before him of a great career as a social reformer, when he went out of his way at a large meeting in London to declare his hostility to all the received forms of religion. After this defiance to the religious sentiment of the country, Owen's theories were in the popular mind associated with infidelity, and were henceforward suspected and discredited. Owen's own confidence, however, remained unshaken; and he was anxious that his scheme for establishing a community should be tested. At last, in 1825, such an experiment was attempted under the direction of his disciple, Abram Combe, at Orbiston near Glasgow; and in the next year Owen himself commenced another at New Harmony, Indiana, U.S.A. After a trial of about two years both failed completely. Neither of them was a pauper experiment; but it must be said that the members were of the most motley description, many worthy people of the highest aims being mixed with vagrants, adventurers, and crotchety, wrong-headed enthusiasts. After a long period of friction with William Allen, and some of his other partners, Owen resigned all connexion with New Lanark in 1828. On his return from America he made London the centre of his activity. Most of his means having been sunk in the New Harmony experiment, he was no longer a flourishing capitalist, but the head of a vigorous propaganda, in which socialism and secularism were combined. One of the most interesting features of the movement at this period was the establishment in 1832 of an equitable labour exchange system, in which exchange was effected by means of labour notes, the usual means of exchange and the usual middlemen being alike superseded.

Father of Socialism

The word "socialism" first became current in the discussions of the Association of all Classes of all Nations, formed by Owen in 1835. During these years also his secularistic teaching gained such influence among the working classes as to give occasion for the statement in the *Westminster Review* (1839) that his principles were the actual creed of a great portion of them.

His views on marriage, which were certainly lax, gave just ground for offence. At this period some more communistic experiments were made, of which the most important were that at Ralahine, in the county of Clare, Ireland, and that at Tytherly in Hampshire. It is admitted that the former (1831) was a remarkable success for three and a half years, till the proprietor, having ruined himself by gambling, was obliged to sell out. Tytherly, begun in 1839, was an absolute failure. By 1846 the only permanent result of Owen's agitation, so zealously carried on by public meetings, pamphlets, periodicals, and occasional treatises, was the co-operative movement, and for the time even that seemed to have utterly collapsed. In his later years Owen became a firm believer in spiritualism.

★ ★ ★ ★ ★

George Washington's View of Divine Providence

The Religious Opinions and Character of Washington, by E. C. McGuire, 1836

There are few doctrines of religion about which men are more divided, than that of the Providence of God. They are indeed generally united as to the *fact* of a providence exercised over the world, but are very widely separated in opinion as to its nature. According to the system of some, there is a *general*, but not a *particular*, Providence, displayed in the affairs of men. The Deity is regarded as having originally impressed upon the machinery of the universe those great laws which he intended should govern it, and having done so, leaves it to roll on with a process so uniform and settled, that no departure from its great leading operations may ever be expected.

Nature of Providence

Deists hold only to a general Providence

That this is a cold and comfortless speculation, must be admitted by all. But it is as irrational, as it is gloomy. It certainly is entirely at variance with the animating disclosures of Revelation. Indeed the whole theory is based upon a gratuitous assumption, unsupported, save by the fancy of its framers. For how is it known that the Author of all things has so settled and fixed the laws of his kingdom that the possibility of departure has been excluded. How do we know, in fact, what is uniformity, and what irregularity? That which we may call a *detour*, in the march of his laws, may be only the result of a primeval impulse given them. It is impossible for us to know what principles the Almighty has thought proper to adopt for the government of his universe. We talk of the order of Nature, and of the great principles which prevail therein, and of the straightforward course, and the overwhelming energy of its powers; and having settled it, in our minds, that such is the system adopted by the Creator, we forthwith apply this ideal standard to every thing *extraordinary* in the occurrences of earth. Thus a miracle, no matter how unexceptionable in regard to the *design* of its performance, or how well attested by credible witnesses—is at once cried down as a fraud upon the senses, because, forsooth, it is in opposition to a theory having for its basis our *experience* of the uniformity of Nature. It is, in the mean time, forgotten by the objector, that his experience is very limited, and that the experience of another man may be the very reverse of his. He rejects what is credibly reported to him as extraordinary, because he has never seen, or heard, or felt, any thing of the kind, yet is strangely offended because his informer believes what *he* has seen, heard, and felt. The same inconsistency marks the decision to which some men come, in regard to events, involving merely a digression, as it were, and not a suspension, of the laws of the universe. Every thing of this kind, in the course of events, is held to be strange and unaccountable, and rather to be ascribed to chance, or accident, than to any direct agency of God.

The Providence of God—both general and particular

Whilst we, by no means, call in question the systematic action of Deity, in carrying on the affairs of his universal kingdom, yet we do object to a rigid adjustment of the principles of his system by the mere dictum of human authority. We do not doubt that there is a beautiful order in the Divine operations, and that they all tend, with infinite harmony, to some great and good result. And yet we are assured that the Almighty is as methodical, in deviating from his ordinary course, as he is in the most regular and uniform of his processes.

It is not, then, in disparagement of a *general*, that we contend for a *particular* Providence. The terms, in truth, should not be set in opposition to each other. The Providence of God is both general and particular. He acts by general laws in the government of his universe, physical and moral; and yet can bend them, at any moment, to the production of any given result, as he may, in his sovereign pleasure, see fit; whether at the beseeching voice of his humble and dependant creatures, or from other motives which may arise to sway his Divine agency. Nor is there, in all this, any want of foresight, or any thing like variableness, or mutability implied. It is Deity in motion, for the accomplishment of the greatest amount of good, in the way which seems best in his sight. "Many persons," says a judicious writer, "when they hear any event spoken of as providential, seem to understand it as signifying, that all the circumstances which have conduced to bring it about, have been arranged for that particular purpose, and if left to their natural course, they would have produced different results. But I consider this to be a complete misapprehension. The doctrine of an over-ruling Providence does not imply the interruption of the regular operations of cause and effect in nature, any more than our seeing these operations proceed regularly, proves that there is no such thing as an over-ruling Providence." Here we have the sublimity of the general, with the comfort of the particular Providence of God. He now wheels the planets in their courses, and preserves the host of heaven, in unfading splendour, and yet guards the feeble sparrow, so that it cannot fall to the ground without Him. He preserves the seasons, in their unwearied rounds, causing summer and winter, night and day, seed-time and harvest, to follow each other in regular and constant successions—and yet he controls the elements at his pleasure. When he would punish, he "makes the heavens above, brass, and the earth beneath, iron." He "commands the clouds that they rain no rain." He "sends the palmer-worm, the caterpillar, and the locust." Sometimes he "causes it to rain upon one city, and not upon another—to rain upon one piece, and not upon another." Or, would he reward and bless, he then reverses these dispensations, and causes those who obey Him to rejoice in all "good things."

Comfort in the particular Providence of God

Such we conceive to be the testimony of the Holy Scriptures, on the subject before us, and, in accordance with these views, have been the sentiments of the majority of believers in Christianity.

That such were the views of the distinguished subject of our present work, admits of evidence as satisfactory as the reflection is gratifying. The abundant proof is furnished by his writings of every date. It was one of the earliest and the latest of those convictions, by which his life was materially governed.

★ ★ ★ ★ ★

Doctrine of Providence

George Washington

The Writings of George Washington
Edited by John C. Fitzpatrick, 1931

Letter,
George Washington to Brigadier General Thomas Nelson,
Camp at the White Plains, August 20, 1778

It is not a little pleasing, nor less wonderful to contemplate, that after two years Manœuvring and undergoing the strangest vicissitudes that perhaps ever attended any one contest since the creation both Armies are brought back to the very point they set out from and, that that, which was the offending party in the beginning is now reduced to the use of the spade and pick axe for defence. The hand of Providence has been so conspicuous in all this, that he must be worse than an infidel that lacks faith, and more than wicked, that has not gratitude enough to acknowledge his obligations, but, it will be time enough for me to turn preacher, when my present appointment ceases; and therfore, I shall add no more on the Doctrine of Providence; but make a tender of my best respects to your good Lady; the Secretary and other friends assure you that with the most perfect regard I am etc.

CHRISTIAN CONVICTION STATEMENTS

EXCERPTS FROM GEORGE WASHINGTON'S WRITINGS, 1755–1789

The Writings of George Washington Vols. 1–30, & 37 Edited by John C. Fitzpatrick, 1931

[Except where another source is noted]

Only a Christian can really appreciate George Washington, for only if one knows the language of the Bible, can one value the words and phrases chosen by George Washington for his correspondence.

Only as a Christian can one appreicate his consistency in the use of his language and his giving credit always to God in his life for whatever is accomplished.

—Verna M. Hall

TO JOHN AUGUSTINE WASHINGTON

Dear Jack:

As I have heard since my arriv'l at this place, a circumstantial acct. of my death and dying speech, I take this early oppertunity of contradicting both, and of assuring you that I now exist and appear in the land of the living by the miraculous care of Providence, that protected me beyond all human expectation; I had 4 Bullets through my Coat, and two Horses shot under me, and yet escaped unhurt. . . .

Miraculous care of Providence

(Fort Cumberland, July 18, 1755)

TO ROBERT JACKSON

. . . . Its true, we have been beaten, most shamefully beaten, by a handful of Men! who only intended to molest and disturb our March; Victory was their smallest expectation, but see the wondrous works of Providence! the uncertainty of Human things! . . .

(Mount Vernon, August 2, 1755)

MORNING ORDERS

The men are to parade at beating the long roll to-morrow morning at 10 o'clock; and be marched as usual to the Fort, to attend Divine Service. The Officers to be present at calling the roll, and see that the men do appear in the most decent manner they can.

(Winchester, September 25, 1756)

TO RICHARD WASHINGTON

. . . and I have order'd my present Crop (which at this time wears a very favourable Aspect, and without some Signal Stroke of Providence will equal my most Sanguine expectations) to be got ready for the first Ships. . . .

(Fort Loudoun, September 10, 1757)

PRAYER BOOK ORDERED

. . . .Prayr. Book with the new Version of Psalms and good plain type, covd. with red Moroco., to be 7 Inchs. long 4½ wide, and as thin as possible for the greatr. ease of caryg. in the Pocket. . . .

(Invoice of Goods to be Shipd, July 18, 1771)

To Burwell Bassett

I was favoured with your Epistle wrote on a certain 25th of July when you ought to have been at Church, praying as becomes every good Christian Man who has as much to answer for as you have; strange it is that you will be so blind to truth that the enlightning sounds of the Gospel cannot reach your Ear, nor no Examples awaken you to a sense of Goodness; could you but behold with what religious zeal I hye me to Church on every Lords day, it would do your heart good, and fill it I hope with equal fervency; but heark'ee; I am told you have lately introduced into your Family, a certain production which you are lost in admiration of, and spend so much time in contemplating the just proportion of its parts, the ease, and conveniences with which it abounds, that it is thought you will have little time to animadvert upon the prospect of your crops &c; pray how will this be reconciled to that anxious care and vigilance, which is so escencially necessary at a time when our growing Property, meaning the Tobacco, is assailed by every villainous worm that has had an existence since the days of Noah (how unkind it was of Noah now I have mentioned his name to suffer such a brood of vermin to get a birth in the Ark) but perhaps you may be as well of as we are; that is, have no Tobacco for them to eat and there I think we nicked the Dogs, as I think to do you if you expect any more; but not without a full assurance of being with a very sincere regard etc. . . .

At church praying as becomes every good Christian man

(Mount Vernon, August 28, 1762)

Established Church

. . . . The expediency of an American Episcopate was long and warmly debated, and at length rejected. As a substitute, the House attempted to frame an Ecclesiastical Jurisdiction, to be composed of a President and four other clergymen, who were to have full power and authority to hear and determine all matters and causes relative to the clergy, and to be vested with the (power) of Suspension, deprivation, and visitation. From this Jurisdiction an Appeal was to be had to a Court of Delegates, to consist of an equal number of Clergymen and Laymen; but this Bill, after much canvassing, was put to Sleep, from an opinion that the subject was of too much Importance to be hastily entered into at the end of a Session. . . . —and a Bill went through the House, but rejected in the Council, for having Septenniel Vestrys, and a general dissolution of all those now in existence. . . .

Church episcopacy inconsistent with practice of local self-government

(To Reverend Jonathan Boucher,
Mount Vernon, May 4, 1772)

Christ Church Pews

I am obliged to you for the notice you have given me of an intended meeting of your Vestry* on Tuesday next. I do not know however that it will be in my power to attend, nor do I conceive it at all necessary that I should, as I am an avowed Enemy to the Scheme I have heard (but never till of late believed) that some Members of your Vestry are Inclined to adopt.

If the Subscription to which among others I put my name was set on foot under Sanction of an Order of Vestry as I always understood it to be, I own myself at a loss to conceive, upon what principle it is, that there should be an attempt to destroy it; repugnant it is to every Idea I entertain of justice to do so; and the right of reclaiming the Pews by the Vestry in behalf of the Parish (which have been Built by Private contribution granting the Subscription Money to be refunded with Interest), I most clearly deny; therefore, as a parishioner who is to be saddled with the extra charge of the Subscription Money I protest against the Measure. As a Subscriber who meant to lay the foundation of a Family Pew in the New Church, I shall think myself Injured; For give me leave to ask, can the raising of that £150 under the present Scheme be considered in any other light than that of a deception? Is it presumable that this money would have been advanced if the Subscribers could possibly have conceived, that after a Solemn Act of Vestry under faith of which the Money was Subscribed the Pews would be reclaimed? Surely not! the thought is absurd! and can be stated in no better point of view than this: Here is a Parish wanting a large Church but considering the Circumstances of its Constituents is content with a Small one, till an offer is made to enlarge it by Subscription (under certain Privileges), which is acceded by the Vestry;

Unprincipled scheme

* Of Christ Church, Alexandria, Virginia Washington was elected a vestryman of Fairfax Parish March 28, 1765, and his name had not been submitted at the Truro election on March 25. July 22, 1765, he was chosen a vestryman for Truro and his name omitted in the Fairfax election of July 25. (*Fitzpatrick.*)

and when Effected and the Parish better able to bear a fresh Tax what does it want? Why to destroy a solemn Compact and reclaim the Priviledges they had granted. For I look upon the refunding of Money as totally beside the question. And for what purpose, I beg leave to ask, is this to be done? I own to you I am at a loss to discover; for as every Subscriber has an undoubted right to a Seat in the Church what matters it whether he Assembles his whole Family into one Pew, or, as the Custom is have them dispers'd into two or three; and probably it is these families will increase in a proportionate degree with the rest of the Parish, so that if the Vestry had a right to annul the agreement, no disadvantage would probably happen on that account.

Upon the whole, Sir, as I observed to you before, considering myself as a Subscriber, I enter my Protest against the measure in Agitation. As a Parishioner, I am equally averse to a Tax which is intended to replace the Subscription Money. These will be my declared Sentiments if present at the Vestry; if I am not I shall be obliged to you for Communicating them, I am, etc.

(To John Dalton, Mt. Vernon, February 15, 1773)

Divine Service

. . . . The General most earnestly requires, and expects, a due observance of those articles of war, established for the Government of the army, which forbid profane cursing, swearing and drunkenness; And in like manner requires and expects, of all Officers, and Soldiers, not engaged on actual duty, a punctual attendance on divine Service, to implore the blessings of heaven upon the means used for our safety and defence.

Blessings of heaven to be implored

(General Orders, Head Quarters, Cambridge, July 4, 1775)

Fast Day

The Continental Congress having earnestly recommended, that "Thursday next the 20th. Instant, be observed by the Inhabitants of all the english colonies upon this Continent, as a Day of public Humiliation, Fasting and Prayer; that they may with united Hearts and Voice unfeignedly confess their Sins before God, and supplicate the all wise and merciful disposer of events, to avert the Desolation and Calamities of an unnatural war." The General orders, that Day to be religiously observed by the Forces under his Command, exactly in manner directed by the proclamation of the Continental Congress: It is therefore strictly enjoin'd on all Officers and Soldiers, (not upon duty) to attend Divine Service, at the accustomed places of worship, as well in the Lines, as the Encampments and Quarters; and it is expected, that all those who go to worship, do take their Arms, Ammunitions and Accoutrements and are prepared for immediate Action if called upon. If in the judgment of the Officers, the Works should appear to be in such forwardness as the utmost security of the Camp requires, they will command their men to abstain from all Labour upon that solemn day. . . .

Only Divine Providence could avert an unnatural war

(General Orders, Head Quarters, Cambridge, July 16, 1775)

General Orders

. . . . The Church to be cleared to morrow, and the Rev'd Mr. Doyles will perform Divine Service therein at ten OClock.

(Head Quarters, Cambridge, August 5, 1775)

To the Major and Brigadier Generals

. . . . It is to know whether, in your judgment, we cannot make a successful attack upon the Troops in Boston, by means of Boats, coöperated by an attempt upon their Lines at Roxbury. The success of such an Enterprize depends, I well know, upon the all wise disposer of Events, and is not within the reach of human wisdom to foretell the Issue; but, if the prospect is fair, the undertaking is justifiable under the following, among other reasons which might be assigned. . . .

(Camp at Cambridge, September 8, 1775)

Canadian Expedition

. . . . That you check by every Motive of Duty and Fear of Punishment, every Attempt to plunder or insult any of the Inhabitants of Canada. Should any American Soldier be so base and infamous as to injure any Canadian or Indian, in his Person or Property, I do most earnestly enjoin you to bring him to such severe and exemplary Punishment as the Enormity of the Crime may require. Should it extend to

Death itself it will not be disproportional to its Guilt at such a Time and in such a Cause: But I hope and trust, that the brave Men who have voluntarily engaged in this Expedition, will be governed by far different Views, that Order, Discipline and Regularity of Behaviour will be as conspicuous, as their Courage and Valour. I also give it in Charge to you to avoid all Disrespect to or Contempt of the Religion of the Country and its Ceremonies. Prudence, Policy, and a true Christian Spirit, will lead us to look with Compassion upon their Errors without insulting them. While we are contending for our own Liberty, we should be very cautious of violating the Rights of Conscience in others, ever considering that God alone is the Judge of the Hearts of Men, and to him only in this Case, they are answerable. . . .

God alone is the Judge of the Hearts of Men

(To Colonel Benedict Arnold, Camp at Cambridge, September 14, 1775)

Instructions to Colonel Benedict Arnold

1st. You are immediately on their March from Cambridge to take the Command of the Detachment from the Continental Army again[st] Quebec, and use all possible Expedition, as the Winter Season is now advancing and the Success of this Enterprize, (under God) depends wholly upon the Spirit with which it is pushed, and the favorable Disposition of the Canadians and Indians. . . .

Act as under God

14th. As the Contempt of the Religion of a Country by ridiculing any of its Ceremonies or affronting its Ministers or Votaries has ever been deeply resented, you are to be particularly careful to restrain every Officer and Soldier from such Imprudence and Folly and to punish every Instance of it. On the other Hand, as far as lays in your power, you are to protect and support the free Exercise of the Religion of the Country and the undisturbed Enjoyment of the rights of Conscience in religious Matters, with your utmost Influence and Authority.

Free exercise of religion and enjoyment of the rights of conscience

Given under my Hand, at Head Quarters, Cambridge, this 14th Day of September one Thousand seven Hundred and seventy-five.

Mission to the Indians

The Revd Mr. Kirkland the Bearer of this, having been introduced to the Honorable Congress, can need no particular Recommendation from me: But as he now wishes to have the Affairs of his Mission and public Employ, put upon some suitable Footing, I cannot but intimate my Sense of the Importance of his Station, and the great Advantages which have and may result to the United Colonies from his Situation being made respectable.

All Accounts agree that much of the favorable Disposition shewn by the Indians may be ascribed to his Labour and Influence. He has accompanied a Chief of the Oneidas to this Camp, which I have endeavored to make agreeable to him both by Civility and some small Presents. . . .

Christian influence upon the disposition of Indians

(To the President of Congress, Camp Cambridge, September 30, 1775)

Capture of St. Johns

This moment a confirmation is arrived of the glorious Success of the Continental Arms, in the Reduction, and Surrender, of the Fortress of St. Johns; the Garrisons of that place and Chamblee being made Prisoners of war. The Commander in Chief is confident, the Army under his immediate direction, will shew their Gratitude to providence, for thus favouring the Cause of Freedom and America; and by their thankfulness to God, their zeal and perseverance in this righteous Cause, continue to deserve his future blessings. . . .

Favor of Providence in the cause of freedom

(General Orders, Head Quarters, Cambridge, November 14, 1775)

Public Thanksgiving

. . . . The Honorable the Legislature of this Colony having thought fit to set apart Thursday the 23d of November Instant, as a day of public thanksgiving "to offer up our praises, and prayers to Almighty God, the Source and Benevolent Bestower of all good; That he would be pleased graciously to continue, to smile upon our Endeavours, to restore peace, preserve our Rights, and Privileges, to the latest posterity; prosper the American Arms, preserve and strengthen the Harmony of the United Colonies, and avert the Calamities of a civil war." The General therefore commands that day to be observed with all the Solemnity directed by the Legislative Proclamation, and all Officers, Soldiers and others, are hereby di-

God, the Source and Benevolent Bestower of all good

rected, with the most unfeigned Devotion, to obey the same. . . .

(General Orders, Head Quarters, Cambridge, November 18, 1775)

Charity at Mount Vernon

. . . . Let the Hospitality of the House, with respect to the poor, be kept up; Let no one go hungry away. If any of these kind of People should be in want of Corn, supply their necessities, provided it does not encourage them in idleness; and I have no objection to your giving my Money in Charity, to the Amount of forty or fifty Pounds a Year, when you think it well bestowed. What I mean, by having no objection, is, that it is my desire that it should be done. You are to consider that neither myself or Wife are now in the way to do these good Offices. In all other respects, I recommend it to you, and have no doubts, of your observing the greatest Œconomy and frugality; as I suppose you know that I do not get a farthing for my services here more than my Expenses; It becomes necessary, therefore, for me to be saving at home. . . .

Provided it does not encourage them in idleness

(To Lund Washington, November 26, 1775)

To Governor Jonathan Trumbull

. . . . Having heard that It's doubtful, whether the Reverend Mr. Leonard from your Colony, will have it in his power to Continue here as a Chaplain, I cannot but express some Concern, as I think his departure will be a loss. His General Conduct has been exemplary and praiseworthy: In discharging the duties of his Office, active and industrious; he has discovered himself warm and steady friend to his Country, and taken great pains to animate the Soldiery and Impress them with a knowledge of the important rights we are contending for. Upon the late desertion of the Troops, he gave a Sensible and judicious discourse, holding forth the Necessity of courage and bravery and at the same time of Obedience and Subordination to those in Command.

Clergy able to instruct in civil government

In justice to the merits of this Gentleman, I thought it only right to give you this Testimonial of my Opinion of him and to mention him to you, as a person worthy of your esteem and that of the Public.

(Cambridge, December 15, 1775)

Pay of Chaplains

I have long had it on my mind to mention to Congress, that frequent applications had been made to me respecting the Chaplain's pay, which is too small to encourage men of Abilities. Some of them who have left their Flocks, are Obliged to pay the parson acting for them more than they receive. I need not point out the great utility of Gentlemen whose lives and conversation are unexceptionable, being employed for that service in this Army. There are two ways of making it worth the Attention of such; one is, an advancement of their pay, the other, that one Chaplain be appointed to two regiments; this last I think may be done without Inconvenience, I beg leave to recommend this matter to Congress whose sentiments thereon I shall impatiently expect.

Great utility of clergy of unexceptionable character to the Army

(To the President of Congress, Cambridge, December 31, 1775)

Difficulties

. . . . It is easier to conceive than to describe the situation of my mind for some time past, and my feelings under our present circumstances. Search the vast volumes of history through, and I much question whether a case similar to ours is to be found; to wit, to maintain a post against the flower of the British troops for six months together, without (*powder*), and at the end of them to have one army disbanded and another to raise within the same distance of a reinforced enemy. It is too much to attempt. What may be the final issue of the last manœuvre, time only can tell. I with this month was well over our heads. The same desire of retiring into a chimney-corner seized the troops of New Hampshire, Rhode Island, and Massachusetts, (so soon as their time expired,) as had worked upon those of Connecticut, notwithstanding many of them made a tender of their services to continue, till the lines could be sufficiently strengthened. We are now left with a good deal less than half raised regiments, and about five thousand militia, who only stand ingaged to the middle of this month; when, according to custom, they will depart, let the necessity of their stay be never so urgent. Thus it is, that for more than two months past, I have scarcely immerged from one difficulty before I have (been) plunged into another. How will it end, God in his great goodness will direct. I am thankful for his protection to this time. We are told that we shall soon get the army completed, but I have been told so many things which have never come to pass, that I distrust every thing. . . .

God in his great goodness will direct the end

(To Joseph Reed, Cambridge, January 4, 1776)

"The Finger of Providence Is in It"

How to get furnished I know not. I have applied to this and the neighbouring colonies, but with what success time only can tell. The reflection on my situation, and that of this army, produces many an uneasy hour when all around me are wrapped in sleep. Few people know the predicament we are in, on a thousand accounts; fewer still will believe, if any disaster happens to these lines, from what cause it flows. I have often thought how much happier I should have been, if, instead of accepting a command under such circumstances, I had taken my musket on my shoulder and entered the ranks, or, if I could have justified the measure to posterity and my own conscience, had retired to the back country, and lived in a wigwam. If I shall be able to rise superior to these and many other difficulties, which might be enumerated, I shall most religiously believe, that the finger of Providence is in it, to blind the eyes of our enemies; for surely if we get well through this month, it must be for want of their knowing the disadvantages we labour under. . . .

Eyes of the enemies blinded

(To Joseph Reed, Cambridge, January 14, 1776)

To Major General Philip Schuyler

. . . . It is high Time to begin with our internal foes when we are threatened with such Severity of Chastisement from our kind Parent without. That the supreme Dispenser of every Good, may bestow Health, Strength and Spirit to you and your Army, is the fervent Wish of, Dear Sir, etc.

(Cambridge, January 27, 1776)

Chaplains

The Continental Congress having been pleased to order, and direct, that there shall be one Chaplain to two Regiments, and that the pay of each Chaplain shall be *Thirty-three* dollars and *one third*, pr Kalendar Month—The Revd. Abiel Leonard is appointed Chaplain to the Regiment Artillery, under the command of Col Knox, and to the 20th. Regiment, at present commanded by Lt. Col. Durkee.

As there can be but fourteen Chaplains under this establishment, to the 28 Regiments (including the Artillery, and Riffle Regiments) and as preference will be given to those Chaplains who served last Year, provided their conduct, and attendance, have been unexceptionable: The Brigadiers are to enquire into this matter and with the Colonels, and commanding Officers of the several Regiments, arrange them agreeable to the above direction, and make report thereof that orders, may issue accordingly. . . .

(General Orders, Head Quarters, Cambridge, February 7, 1776)

General Orders

As the Season is now fast approaching, when every man must expect to be drawn into the Field of action, it is highly necessary that he should prepare his mind, as well as every thing necessary for it. It is a noble Cause we are engaged in, it is the Cause of virtue, and mankind, every temporal advantage and comfort to us, and our posterity, depends upon the Vigour of our Exertions; in short, Freedom, or Slavery must be the result of our conduct, there can therefore be no greater Inducement to men to behave well: —But it may not be amiss for the Troops to know, that if any Man in action shall presume to skulk, hide himself, or retreat from the enemy, without the orders of his commanding Officer; he will be instantly shot down, as an example of cowardice; —Cowards having too frequently disconcerted the best form'd Troops, by their dastardly behaviour.

Next to the favour of divine providence, nothing is more essentially necessary to give this Army the victory over all its enemies, than Exactness of discipline, Alertness when on duty, and Cleanliness in their arms and persons; unless the Arms are kept clean, and in good firing Order, it is impossible to vanquish the enemy; and Cleanliness of the person gives health, and soldier-like appearance. . . .

Favor of Providence most essential

(Head Quarters, Cambridge, February 27, 1776)

Fast Day Ordered

. . . . Thursday the seventh Instant, being set apart by the Honourable the Legislature of this province, as a day of fasting, prayer, and humiliation, "to implore the Lord, and Giver of all victory, to pardon our manifold sins and wickedness's, and that it would please him to bless the Continental Arms, with his divine favour and protection" —All Officers, and Soldiers, are strictly enjoined to pay all due reverance, and attention on that day, to the sacred duties due to the Lord of hosts, for his mercies already received, and for those blessings, which our Holiness and Uprightness of life can alone encourage us to hope through his mercy to obtain. . . .

Seek the favor and protection of Providence

(Head Quarters, Cambridge, March 6, 1776)

VICTORY AT DORCHESTER

. . . . We had prepared boats, a detachment of 4000 men, &c., &c., for pushing to the west part of Boston, if they had made any formidable attack upon Dorchester. I will not lament or repine at any act of Providence because I am in a great measure a convert to Mr. Pope's opinion, that whatever is, is right, but I think everything had the appearance of a successful issue, if we had come to an engagement on that day. It was the 5th of March, which I recalled to their remembrance as a day never to be forgotten; an engagement was fully expected, and I never saw spirits higher, or more prevailing. . . .

An act of Providence

(To Joseph Reed, Cambridge, March 7, 1776)

TO JOHN AUGUSTINE WASHINGTON

. . . . Upon their discovery of the Works next Morning, great preparations were made for attacking them, but not being ready before the Afternoon and the Weather getting very tempestuous, much blood was Saved, and a very important blow (to one side or the other) prevented. That this remarkable Interposition of Providence is for some wise purpose, I have not a doubt; but as the principal design of the Manouvre was to draw the Enemy to an Ingagement under disadvantages, as a premeditated Plan was laid for this purpose, and seemed to be succeeding to my utmost wish, and as no Men seem'd better disposed to make the appeal than ours did upon that occasion, I can scarce forbear lamenting the disappointment, unless the dispute is drawing to an accommodation, and the Sword going to be Sheathed. . . .

Remarkable Interposition of Providence for some wise purpose

(Cambridge, March 31, 1776)

TO REVEREND WILLIAM GORDON

. . . . The fortunate discovery, of the Intentions of Ministry, in Lord George Germains Letter to Govr. Eden is to be Rank'd among many other signal Interpositions of Providence, and must serve to inspire every reflecting Mind with Confidence. No Man has a more perfect Reliance on the alwise, and powerful dispensations of the Supreme Being than I have nor thinks his aid more necessary. . . .

(New York, May 13, 1776)

FAST DAY

The Continental Congress having ordered, Friday the 17th. Instant to be observed as a day of "fasting, humiliation and prayer, humbly to supplicate the mercy of Almighty God, that it would please him to pardon all our manifold sins and transgressions, and to prosper the Arms of the United Colonies, and finally, establish the peace and freedom of America, upon a solid and lasting foundation"— The General commands all officers, and soldiers, to pay strict obedience to the Orders of the Continental Congress, and by their unfeigned, and pious observance of their religious duties, incline the Lord, and Giver of Victory, to prosper our arms. . . .

Incline the Lord, the Giver of Victory

(General Orders, Head Quarters, New York, May 15, 1776)

GENERAL ORDERS

. . . . As the Troops are to be exempt from all duties of fatigue to morrow, the regiments are to parade on their regimental parades, and to be marched from thence a little before Ten, to hear divine service from their respective chaplains. . . .

(Head Quarters, New York, May 16, 1776)

FORMING A NEW GOVERNMENT

. . . . To form a new Government, requires infinite care, and unbounded attention; for if the foundation is badly laid the superstructure must be bad, too much time therefore, cannot be bestowed in weighing and digesting matters well. We have, no doubt, some good parts in our present constitution; many bad ones we know we have, wherefore no time can be mispent that is imployed in seperating the Wheat from the Tares. My fear is, that you will all get tired and homesick, the consequence of which will be, that you will patch up some kind of Constitution as defective as the present; this should be avoided, every Man should consider, that he is lending his aid to frame a Constitution which is to render Million's happy, or Miserable, and that a matter of such moment cannot be the Work of a day. . . .

The necessity of Providential care in laying a good foundation

We expect a very bloody Summer of it at New York and Canada, as it is there I expect the grand efforts of the Enemy will be aim'd; and I am sorry to say that we are not, either in Men, or Arms, prepared for it; however, it is to be hoped, that if our cause is just, as I do most religiously believe it to be, the same Providence which has in many Instances appear'd for us, will still go on to afford its aid. . . .

If our cause is just, Providence will afford its aid

(To John Augustine Washington, Philadelphia, May 31, 1776)

TO MAJOR GENERAL HORATIO GATES

. . . . The distance of the Scene, and the frequent Changes which have happened in the State of our Affairs in Canada, do not allow me to be more particular in my Instructions. The Command is important, the Service difficult, but honourable; and I most devoutly pray that Providence may crown your Arms with abundant Success.

(New York, June 24, 1776)

ENCOURAGEMENT OF TROOPS

. . . . The time is now near at hand which must probably determine, whether Americans are to be, Freemen, or Slaves; whether they are to have any property they can call their own; whether their Houses, and Farms, are to be pillaged and destroyed, and they consigned to a State of Wretchedness from which no human efforts will probably deliver them. The fate of unborn Millions will now depend, under God, on the Courage and Conduct of this army— Our cruel and unrelenting Enemy leaves us no choice but a brave resistance, or the most abject submission; this is all we can expect— We have therefore to resolve to conquer or die: Our own Country's Honor, all call upon us for a vigorous and manly exertion, and if we now shamefully fail, we shall become infamous to the whole world. Let us therefore rely upon the goodness of the Cause, and the aid of the supreme Being, in whose hands Victory is, to animate and encourage us to great and noble Actions— The Eyes of all our Countrymen are now upon us, and we shall have their blessings, and praises, if happily we are the instruments of saving them from the Tyranny meditated against them. Let us therefore animate and encourage each other, and shew the whole world, that a Freeman contending for LIBERTY on his own ground is superior to any slavish mercenary on earth.

Rely on the aid of the Supreme Being in whose hands the Victory is

The General recommends to the officers great coolness in time of action, and to the soldiers a strict attention and obedience with a becoming firmness and spirit. . . .

(General Orders, Head Quarters, New York, July 2, 1776)

"TO LIVE AND ACT AS BECOMES A CHRISTIAN SOLDIER"

. . . . The Hon. Continental Congress having been pleased to allow a Chaplain to each Regiment, with the pay of Thirty-three Dollars and one third pr month—The Colonels or commanding officers of each regiment are directed to procure Chaplains accordingly; persons of good Characters and exemplary lives— To see that all inferior officers and soldiers pay them a suitable respect and attend carefully upon religious exercises. The blessing and protection of Heaven are at all times necessary but especially so in times of public distress and danger—The General hopes and trusts, that every officer and man, will endeavour so to live, and act, as becomes a Christian Soldier defending the dearest Rights and Liberties of his country.

Blessings and protection of Heaven are at all times necessary

THE DECLARATION READ

The Hon. The Continental Congress, impelled by the dictates of duty, policy and necessity, having been pleased to dissolve the Connection which subsisted between this Country, and Great Britain, and to declare the United Colonies of North America, free and independent STATES: The several brigades are to be drawn up this evening on their respective Parades, at Six OClock, when the declaration of Congress, shewing the grounds and reasons of this measure, is to be read with an audible voice.

The General hopes this important Event will serve as a fresh incentive to every officer, and soldier, to act with Fidelity and Courage, as knowing that now the peace and safety of his Country depends (under God) solely on the success of our arms: And that he is now in the service of a State, possessed of sufficient power to reward his merit, and advance him to the highest Honors of a free Country. . . .

Country depends (under God) solely on the success of our arms

(General Orders, Head Quarters, New York, July 9, 1776)

To the President of Congress

I perceive that Congress have been employed in deliberating on measures of the most interesting Nature. It is certain that it is not with us to determine in many instances what consequences will flow from our Counsels, but yet it behoves us to adopt such, as under the smiles of a Gracious and all kind Providence will be most likely to promote our happiness; I trust the late decisive part they have taken, is calculated for that end, and will secure us that freedom and those priviledges, which have been, and are refused us, contrary to the voice of Nature and the British Constitution. Agreeable to the request of Congress I caused the Declaration to be proclaimed before all the Army under my immediate Command, and have the pleasure to inform them, that the measure seemed to have their most hearty assent; the Expressions and behaviour both of Officers and Men testifying their warmest approbation of it. . . .

Gracious and all kind Providence

The Intelligence we have from a few Deserters that have come over to us, and from others, is, that General Howe has between 9. and 10.000 Men, who are chiefly landed on the Island, posted in different parts, and securing the several communications from the Jerseys with small Works and Intrenchments, to prevent our people paying them a visit; that the Islanders have all joined them, seem well disposed to favor their Cause and have agreed to take up Arms in their behalf. They look for Admiral Howe's arrival every day, with his Fleet and a large Reinforcement, are in high Spirits, and talk confidently of Success and carrying all before them when he comes. I trust through Divine Favor and our own Exertions they will be disappointed in their Views, and at all Events, any advantages they may gain will cost them very dear. If our Troops will behave well, which I hope will be the case, having every thing to contend for that Freemen hold dear, they will have to wade thro' much Blood and Slaughter before they can carry any part of our Works, if they carry them at all; and at best be in possession of a Melancholly and Mournful Victory. May the Sacredness of our cause inspire our Soldiery with Sentiments of Heroism, and lead them to the performance of the noblest Exploits.

The Sacredness of our cause

(New York, July 10, 1776)

Anniversary of an Escape

. . . . I did not let the Anniversary of the 3d. or 9th. of this Instt. pass of with out a grateful remembrance of the escape we had at the Meadows and on the Banks of Monongahela,* the same Providence that protected us upon those occasions will, I hope, continue his Mercies, and make us happy Instruments in restoring Peace and liberty to this once favour'd, but now distressed Country.

Providence . . . make us Instruments

(To Colonel Adam Stephen, New York, July 20, 1776)

Defense of Charleston

. . . . The General has great pleasure in communicating to the officers, and soldiers of this Army, the signal success of the American Arms under General Lee at South Carolina. The Enemy having attempted to land at the same time that a most furious Cannonade for *twelve* hours was made upon the Fortifications near Charlestown; Both Fleet and Army have been repulsed with great loss by a small number of gallant troops just raised. The Enemy have had one hundred and seventy two men, killed and wounded, among whom were several officers; Two capital Ships much damaged; one Frigate of Twenty-eight Guns entirely lost being abandoned and blown up by the Crew and others so hurt that they will want great repair before they can be fit for service; And all with a loss on our Part of ten killed and twenty-two wounded. The Firmness,

* Stephen had been with Washington at Fort Necessity and at Braddock's defeat. (*Fitzpatrick.*)

Courage and Bravery of our Troops, has crowned them with immediate Honor. The dying Heroes conjured their Brethren never to abandon the Standard of Liberty, and even those who had lost their Limbs, continued at their posts: Their Gallantry and Spirit extorted applause from their enemies, who dejected and defeated, have retired to their former station, out of the reach of our troops.

This glorious Example of our Troops, under the like Circumstances with us, The General hopes will animate every officer, and soldier, to imitate, and even out do them, when the enemy shall make the same attempt on us: With such a bright example before us, of what can be done by brave and spirited men, fighting in defence of their Country, we shall be loaded with a double share of Shame and Infamy, if we do not acquit ourselves with Courage, or a determined Resolution to conquer or die: With this hope and confidence, and that this Army will have its equal share of Honour, and Success; the General most earnestly exhorts every officer, and soldier, to pay the utmost attention to his Arms, and Health; to have the former in the best order for Action, and by Cleanliness and Care, to preserve the latter; to be exact in their discipline, obedient to their Superiors and vigilant on duty: With such preparation, and a suitable Spirit there can be no doubt, but by the blessing of Heaven, we shall repel our cruel Invaders; preserve our Country, and gain the greatest Honor. . . .

By the blessing of Heaven

(General Orders, Head Quarters,
New York, July 21, 1776)

Provincial Prejudices

It is with great concern, the General understands, that Jealousies &c. are arisen among the troops from the different Provinces, of reflections frequently thrown out, which can only tend to irritate each other, and injure the noble cause in which we are engaged, and which we ought to support with one hand and one heart. The General most earnestly entreats the officers, and soldiers, to consider the consequences; that they can no way assist our cruel enemies more effectually, than making division among ourselves; That the Honor and Success of the army, and the safety of our bleeding Country, depends upon harmony and good agreement with each other; That the Provinces are all United to oppose the common enemy, and all distinctions sunk in the name of an American; to make this honorable, and preserve the Liberty of our Country, ought to be our only emulation, and he will be the best Soldier, and the best Patriot, who contributes most to this glorious work, whatever his Station, or from whatever part of the Continent, he may come: Let all distinctions of Nations, Countries, and Provinces, therefore be lost in the generous contest, who shall behave with the most Courage against the enemy, and the most kindness and good humour to each other—If there are any officers, or soldiers, so lost to virtue and a love of their Country as to continue in such practices after this order; The General assures them, and is directed by Congress to declare, to the whole Army, that such persons shall be severely punished and dismissed the service with disgrace.

American Christian unity

(General Orders, Head Quarters,
New York, August 1, 1776)

Vice of Swearing

That the Troops may have an opportunity of attending public worship, as well as take some rest after the great fatigue they have gone through; The General in future excuses them from fatigue duty on Sundays (except at the Ship Yards, or special occasions) until further orders. The General is sorry to be informed that the foolish, and wicked practice, of profane cursing and swearing (a Vice heretofore little known in an American Army) is growing into fashion; he hopes the officers will, by example, as well as influence, endeavour to check it, and that both they, and the men will reflect, that we can have little hopes of the blessing of Heaven on our Arms, if we insult it by our impiety, and folly; added to this, it is a vice so mean and low, without any temptation, that every man of sense, and character, detests and despises it.

Little hope of the blessings of Heaven

(General Orders, Head Quarters,
New York, August 3, 1776)

"Liberty, Property, Life and Honor, Are All at Stake"

. . . . The Enemy's whole reinforcement is now arrived, so that an Attack must, and will soon be made; The General therefore again repeats his earnest request, that every officer, and soldier, will have his Arms and Ammunition in good Order, keep within their quarters and encampment, as much as possible; be ready for action at a moments call; and when called to it, remember that Liberty, Property, Life and Honor, are all at stake; that upon their Courage and Conduct, rest the hopes of their bleeding and insulted Country; that their Wives, Children and Parents, expect Safety from them only, and that we have every reason to expect Heaven will crown with Success, so just a cause. The enemy will endeavour to intimidate by shew and appearance, but remember how they have been repulsed, on various occasions, by a few brave Americans; Their Cause is bad; their men are conscious of it, and if opposed with firmness, and coolness, at their first onsett, with our advantage of Works, and Knowledge of the Ground; Victory is most assuredly ours. Every good Soldier will be silent and attentive, wait for Orders and reserve his fire, 'till he is sure of doing execution. The Officers to be particularly careful of this. The Colonels, or commanding Officers of Regiments, are to see their supernumerary officers so posted, as to keep the men to their duty; and it may not be amiss for the troops to know, that if any infamous Rascal, in time of action, shall attempt to skulk, hide himself or retreat from the enemy without orders of his commanding Officer; he will instantly be shot down as an example of Cowardice: On the other hand, the General solemnly promises, that he will reward those who shall distinguish themselves, by brave and noble actions; and he desires every officer to be attentive to this particular, that such men may be afterwards suitably noticed. . . .

Heaven will crown with success so just a cause

(General Orders, Head Quarters,
New York, August 13, 1776)

General Orders

. . . . The General flatters himself, that every man's mind and arms are now prepared for the glorious Contest, upon which so much depends. The time is too precious, nor does the General think it necessary to spend it in exhorting his brave Countrymen and fellow Soldiers to behave like men, fighting for every thing that can be dear to Freemen— We must resolve to conquer, or die; with this resolution and the blessing of Heaven, Victory and Success certainly will attend us. There will then be a glorious Issue to this Campaign, and the General will reward, his brave Fellow Soldiers! with every Indulgence in his power. . . .

(Head Quarters, New York,
August 14, 1776)

Removal of Civilians

Whereas a bombardment and attack upon the city of New York, by our cruel and inveterate enemy, may be hourly expected; and as there are great numbers of women, children, and infirm persons, yet remaining in the city, whose continuance will rather be prejudicial than advantageous to the army, and their persons exposed to great danger and hazard; I Do, therefore recommend it to all such persons, as they value their own safety and preservation, to remove with all expedition out of the said town, at this critical period,—trusting that, with the blessing of Heaven upon the American arms, they may soon return to it in perfect security. And I do enjoin and require all the officers and soldiers in the army under my command to forward and assist such persons in their compliance with this recommendation. Given under my hand, etc.

Trusting the blessing of Heaven

(Proclamation, Head Quarters,
August 17, 1776)

Connecticut Reinforcements

Sir: I have been duly honored with your favor of the 13th. Instant; and, at the same time, that I think you and your honorable Council of Safety highly deserving of the thanks of the States, for the Measures you have adopted, in order to give the most early and Speedy Succour to this Army; give me leave to return you mine in a particular Manner. When the whole of the Reinforcements do arrive, I flatter my self we shall be competent to every exigency; and, with the Smiles of Providence upon our Arms and Vigorous Exertions, we shall baffle the designs of our Inveterate Foes, formidable as they are. Our Situation was truly Alarming, a little while Since; but, by the kind Interpositions and Aid of our Friends, is much bettered. . . .

With the Smiles of Providence

(To Governor Jonathan Trumbull,
New York, August 18, 1776)

How Our Country Can Be Saved

. . . . The General hopes the justice of the great cause in which they are engaged, the necessity and importance of defending this Country, preserving its Liberties, and warding off the destruction meditated against it, will inspire every man with Firmness and Resolution, in time of action, which is now approaching— Ever remembring that upon the blessing of Heaven, and the bravery of the men, our Country only can be saved. . . .

Saved by the blessing of Providence

(General Orders, Head Quarters, New York, September 3, 1776)

To Colonel Fisher Gay
Connecticut State Regiment

. . . . Your own Reputation, the safety of the Army, and the good of the cause depends, under God, upon our vigilance and readiness to oppose a Crafty and enterprising enemy, who are always upon the watch to take advantages. . . .

(New York, September 4, 1776)

To Major General Horatio Gates

. . . I expect Genl. Lee will be there this Evening or to morrow, who will be followed by Genl. Heath and his division. If we can draw our forces together, I trust, under the smiles of providence, we may yet effect an important stroke, or at least prevent Genl. Howe from executing his plans. Philadelphia is now the object of our care, you know the importance of it, and the fatal consequences that must attend its loss. . . .

Overseeing Providence

(Head Quarters at Keiths, December 14, 1776)

To the Massachusetts Legislature

. . . . Convinced that Philadelphia was the object of Mr. Howe's movements and of the fatal Consequences that would attend the loss of it, I wrote for Genl. [Charles] Lee to reinforce me, with the Troops under his immediate Command. By some means or other, their Arrival has been retarded and unhappily on friday last, the Genl., having left his Division and proceeded three or four Miles nearer the Enemy, then 18. Miles from him; of which they were informed by some Tories, was surprised and carried off about 11 O'Clock, by a party of 70 Light Horse; I will not comment upon this unhappy accident; I feel much for his Misfortune and am sensible that in his Captivity, our Country has lost a Warm friend and an able officer. Upon the whole our affairs are in a Much less promising condition than could be wished; Yet I trust, under the Smiles of Providence and by our own exertions, we shall be happy. Our cause is righteous, and must be Supported. Every nerve should be strained, to Levy the New Army. If we can but procure a respectable one in Season, All may be well, and to this end no pains can be too great. The next Campaign will be of importance and the Issue may lead to happiness or the most melancholly of all events.

By Divine favor and human exertions

(Head Quarters at Keith's, December 18, 1776)

Difficulties

. . . . The misfortune of short enlistments, and an unhappy dependance upon militia, have shown their baneful influence at every period, and almost upon every occasion, throughout the whole course of this war. At no time, nor upon no occasion, were they ever more exemplified than since Christmas; for if we could but have got in the militia in time, or prevailed upon those troops whose times expired (as they generally did) on the first of this instant, to have continued (not more than a thousand or twelve hundred agreeing to stay) we might, I am persuaded, have cleared the Jerseys entirely of the enemy. Instead of this, all our movements have been made with inferior numbers, and with a mixed, motley crew, who were here to-day, gone to-morrow, without assigning a reason, or even apprizing you of it. In a word, I believe I may with truth add, that I do not think that any officer since the creation ever had such a variety of difficulties and perplexities to encounter as I have. How we shall be able to rub along till the new army is raised, I know not. Providence has heretofore saved us in a remarkable manner, and on this we must principally rely. . . .

Reliance upon Providence under profound difficulties

(To John Parke Custis, Morris Town, January 22, 1777)

Fast Day

The Hon'ble The Governor and Assembly of New Jersey, having directed Thursday the 6th. day of this Month, to be observed as a Day of Fasting, Humiliation and Prayer, by the Inhabitants of the State— The General desires the same may be observed by the Army. . . .

Invoking Providence

(General Orders, Head-Quarters, Morristown, February 4, 1777)

FAST DAY

The Fast day directed in Yesterday's General Orders was a mistake, it being ordered by the Governor and Assembly of this State, to be kept the 6th. of March, not the 6th. of this Month; which the Army is to take notice of.

(General Orders, Head-Quarters, Morristown, February 5, 1777)

SIZE OF ARMY

. . . .Your remark "that you cannot depend upon the Reports of our strength" is most litterally true. It is morally impossible that any body at a distance, should know it with precision and certainty; because, while it depends upon Militia, who are here to-day, and gone tomorrow; *whose ways, like the ways of Providence are, almost, inscrutable;* and when it is our Interest, however much our characters may suffer by it, to make small numbers appear large, it is impossible you should; for in order to deceive the Enemy effectually, we must not communicate our weakness to anybody. . . .

Ways of Providence inscrutable

(To John Augustine Washington, Morristown, February 24, 1777)

CRITICISM OF CONGRESS

. . . . Congress, therefore, should be cautious how they adopt measures, which cannot be carried into execution without involving a train of evils that may be fatal in their consequences. In a Word, common prudence dictates the necessity of duly attending to the circumstances of both Armies, before the style of Conquerors is assumed by either; and sorry, I am to add, that this does not appear to be the case with us; Nor is it in my power to make Congress fully sensible of the real situation of our Affairs, and that it is with difficulty (if I may use the expression) that I can, by every means in my power, keep the Life and Soul of this army together. In a word, when they are at a distance, they think it is but to say Presto begone, and everything is done. They seem not to have any conception of the difficulty and perplexity attending those who are to execute. Indeed, Sir, your observations on the want of many capital Characters in that Senate, are but too just. However, our cause is good and I hope Providence will support it. . . .

Support of Providence hoped for

(To Robert Morris, Morristown, March 2, 1777)

TO EDMUND PENDLETON

. . . . Your friendly, and affectionate wishes for my health and success, has a claim to my thankful acknowledgements; and, that the God of Armies may enable me to bring the present contest to a speedy and happy conclusion, thereby gratifying me in a retirement to the calm and sweet enjoyment of domestick happiness, is the fervent prayer, and most ardent wish of my Soul. My best respects attend Mrs. Pendleton, and with every Sentiment of regard and Affection, I am, etc.

The God of Armies

(Morris Town, April 12, 1777)

DIVINE WORSHIP

All the troops in Morristown, except the Guards, are to attend divine worship to morrow morning at the second Bell; the officers commanding Corps, are to take especial care, that their men appear clean, and decent, and that they are to march in proper order to the place of worship.

Decently and in order

(General Orders Head-Quarters, Morristown, April 12, 1777)

TO LANDON CARTER

. . . .Your friendly and affectionate wishes for my health and success has a claim to my most grateful acknowledgements. That the God of Armies may Incline the Hearts of my American Brethren to support, and bestow sufficient abilities on me to bring the present contest to a speedy and happy conclusion, thereby enabling me to sink into sweet retirement, and the full enjoyment of that Peace and happiness which will accompany a domestick Life, is the first wish, and most fervent prayer of my Soul. . . .

Incline hearts of American brethren to support him

(Morristown in New Jersey, April 15, 1777)

PAY OF CHAPLAINS

. . . . By some late Regulations, the Pay of Majors of Brigade is augmented to 50 Dollars pr. Month, Chaplains to 40 Dollars pr. Month, and Regimental Surgeons to two dollars pr. Day. I hope this will influence Gentlemen of Merit, Abilities and Skill

Chaplains of merit

(especially in Physic) to Step forth.
(To Brigadier General Samuel Holden Parsons, Head Quarters, Morris Town, April 19, 1777)

Languor and Supineness

. . . . You will not remit your exertions, in forwarding the men, as fast as Circumstances will admit. No time is to be lost; the exigency of our Affairs having been never more pressing, nor requiring more strenuous efforts than at present. The Languor and Supineness that have taken place, but too generally, of late, are truly mortifying, and are difficult to be accounted for. All agree our claims are righteous and must be supported; Yet all, or at least, too great a part among us, withhold the means, as if Providence, who has already done much for us, would continue his gracious interposition and work miracles for our deliverance, without troubling ourselves about the matter. . . .

Providence interposes man's efforts

(To Brigadier General Samuel Holden Parsons Morris Town, April 23, 1777)

Divine Service

All the troops in, and about Morristown, (those on duty excepted) are to attend divine service, to morrow morning.
(General Orders, Head-Quarters, Morristown, May 17, 1777)

Chaplain

. . . . A Chaplain is part of the Establishment of a Corps of Cavalry, and I see no Objection to your having One, Unless you suppose yours will be too virtuous and Moral to require instruction. Let him be a Man of Character and good conversation, and who will influence the manners of the Corps both by precept and example. . . .
(To Colonel George Baylor, Morristown, May 23, 1777)

Divine Service

. . . . All the troops in, and near Morristown, (except on duty) to attend divine service, to morrow morning.
(General Orders Head-Quarters, Morristown, May 24, 1777)

Vice Discouraged

. . . . Let Vice, and Immorality of every kind, be discouraged, as much as possible, in your Brigade; and as a Chaplain is allowed to each Regiment, see that the Men regularly attend divine Worship. Gaming of every kind is expressly forbid, as the foundation of evil and the cause of many Gallant and Brave Officer's Ruin. Games of exercise, for amusement, may not only be permitted but encouraged. . . .
(To Brigadier General William Smallwood, Head Quarters, Morris Town, May 26, 1777)

Profane Swearing

. . . . It is much to be lamented, that the foolish and scandalous practice of *profane Swearing* is exceedingly prevalent in the American Army—Officers of every rank are bound to discourage it, first by their example, and then by punishing offenders— As a mean to abolish this, and every other species of immorality—Brigadiers are enjoined, to take effectual care, to have divine service duly performed in their respective brigades. . . .
(General Orders, Head-Quarters, Middle-Brook, May 31, 1777)

Chaplains

. . . . I shall order a return to be made of the Chaplains in Service, which shall be transmitted, as soon as it is obtained. At present, as the Regiments are greatly dispersed, part in one place and part in another, and accurate States of them have not been made, it will not be in my power to forward it immediately. I shall here take occasion to mention, that I communicated the Resolution, appointing a Brigade Chaplain in the place of all others, to the several Brigadiers; they are all of opinion, that it will be impossible for them to discharge the duty; that many inconveniences and much dissatisfaction will be the result, and that no Establishment appears so good in this instance as the Old One. Among many other weighty objections to the Measure, It has been suggested, that it has a tendency to introduce religious disputes into the Army, which above all things should be avoided, and in many instances would compel men to a mode of Worship which they do not profess. The old Establishment gives every Regiment an Opportunity of having a Chaplain of their own religious Sentiments, it is founded on a plan of a more generous toleration, and

A Chaplain of their own religious sentiments

the choice of the Chaplains to officiate, has been generally in the Regiments. Supposing one Chaplain could do the duties of a Brigade, (which supposition However is inadmissible, when we view things in practice) that being composed of four or five, perhaps in some instances, Six Regiments, there might be so many different modes of Worship. I have mentioned the Opinion of the Officers and these hints to Congress upon this Subject; from a principle of duty and because I am well assured, it is most foreign to their wishes or intention to excite by any act, the smallest uneasiness and jealousy among the Troops. . . .

(To the President of Congress, Head Quarters, Middle Brook, June 8, 1777)

Divine Service

. . . . All Chaplains are to perform divine service to morrow, and on every succeeding Sunday, with their respective brigades and regiments, where the situation will possibly admit of it. And the commanding officers of corps are to see that they attend; themselves, with officers of all ranks, setting the example. The Commander in Chief expects an exact compliance with this order, and that it be observed in future as an invariable rule of practice—And every neglect will be considered not only a breach of orders, but a disregard to decency, virtue and religion.

Officers setting the example

(General Orders, Head-Quarters, Middle Brook, June 28, 1777)

. . . . Divine Service to be performed to-morrow, in all the regiments which have chaplains.

(General Orders, Head Quarters, Morristown, July 5, 1777)

Reduction in Chaplains

. . . . Since the Congress passed the Resolve that there should be but one Chaplain to three Regiments, nothing has been done towards reducing them, and I have my doubts whether the Resolve will ever be carried into execution. The appointment you mention had therefore better be suspended for a while. . . .

(To Major General William Heath, Head Quarters at the Clove, July 19, 1777)

Condolence

. . . . I most sincerely condole with you on your late loss [of his wife]; and doubt not your feeling it in the most sensible manner; nor do I expect that human Fortitude, and reason, can so far overcome natural affection, as to enable us to look with calmness upon losses wh. distress us altho they are acts of Providence, and in themselves unavoidable, yet acquiescence to the divine will is not only a duty, but is to be aided by every manly exertion to forget the causes of such uneasiness. . . .

An act of Providence

(To Samuel Washington, Germantown near Philadelphia, August 10, 1777)

Thanks to Troops

The General, with peculiar satisfaction, thanks those gallant officers and soldiers, who, on the 11th. instant, bravely fought in their country and its cause. If there are any whose conduct reflects dishonour upon soldiership, and their names are not pointed out to him, he must, for the present, leave them to reflect, how much they have injured their country, how unfaithful they have proved to their fellow-soldiers; but with this exhortation, that they embrace the first opportunity which may offer to do justice to both, and to the profession of a soldier. Altho' the event of that day, from some unfortunate circumstances, was not so favorable as could be wished, the General has the satisfaction of assuring the troops, that from every account he has been able to obtain, the enemy's loss greatly exceeded ours; and he has full confidence that in another Appeal to Heaven (with the blessing of providence, which it becomes every officer and soldier humbly to supplicate), we shall prove successful.

Supplicate the blessing of Providence

(General Orders, Head Quarters, near Germantown, September 13, 1777)

Divine Service

. . . . As the troops will rest to day, divine service is to be performed in all the corps which have chaplains. . . .

(General Orders, Head Quarters, at Pennybecker's Mills, September 27, 1777)

[Saturday]

. . . . The situation of the army, frequently not admitting, of the regular performance of divine service, on Sundays, the Chaplains of the army are forthwith to meet together, and agree on some method of performing it, at other times, which method they will make known to the Commander in Chief. . . .

(General Orders, Head Quarters, Perkiomy, October 7, 1777)

Burgoyne's Surrender

The General has his happiness completed relative to the success of our northern Army. On the 14th. instant, General Burgoyne, and his whole Army, surrendered themselves prisoners of war. Let every face brighten, and every heart expand with grateful Joy and praise to the supreme disposer of all events, who has granted us this signal success. The Chaplains of the army are to prepare short discourses, suited to the joyful occasion to deliver to their several corps and brigades at 5 O'clock this afternoon—immediately after which, *Thirteen* pieces of cannon are to be discharged at the park of artillery, to be followed by a *feu-de-joy* with blank cartridges, or powder, by every brigade and corps of the army, beginning on the right of the front line, and running on to the left of it, and then instantly beginning on the left of the 2nd. line, and running to the right of it where it is to end. The Major General of the day will superintend and regulate the *feu-de-joy*. . . .

The Supreme Disposer of events

(General Orders, Head Quarters, at Wentz's, Worcester Township, October 18, 1777)

To Brigadier General James Potter

Dear Sir: I congratulate you upon the glorious Success of our Arms in the North an account of which is enclosed. This singular favor of Providence is to be received with thankfulness and the happy moment which Heaven has pointed out for the firm establishment of American Liberty ought to be embraced with becoming spirit; it is incumbent upon every man of influence in his country to prevail upon the militia to take the field with that energy which the present crisis evidently demands. . . .

American Liberty owed to the favor of Providence

(Head Quarters, Peter Wentz's, October 18, 1777)

To Baron D'Arendt

. . . . I shall not prescribe any particular line for your conduct, because I repose the utmost confidence in your bravery, knowledge and judgment; and because the mode of defence must depend on a variety of circumstances, which will be best known to those, who are on the spot. I will add, that the maintenance of this post is of the last importance to the States of America, and that preventing the enemy from obtaining possession of it, under the smiles of Heaven, will be the means of our defeating the Army to which we are opposed, or of obliging them disgracefully to abandon the City of Philadelphia, which is now in their hands.

(Head Quarters, October 18, 1777)

Battle of Germantown

. . . . The anxiety you have been under, on Acct. of this Army, I can easily conceive; would to God there had been less Cause for it; or, that our Situation at present, was such, as to promise much from it. The Enemy crossed the Schuylkill, which, by the by, above the Falls (and the Falls you know is only five Miles from the City) is as easily crossed in any place as Potomack Run, Aquia, or any other broad and Shallow Water, rather by stratagem; tho' I do not know that it was in our power to prevent it, as their Manœuvres made it necessary for us to attend to our Stores which lay at Reading, towards which they seemed bending their course, and the loss of which must have proved our Ruin. After they had crossed, we took the first favourable oppertunity of attacking them; this was attempted by a Nights March of fourteen Miles to Surprize them (which we effectually did) so far as reaching their Guards before they had notice of our coming, and but for a thick Fog rendered so infinitely dark at times, as not to distinguish friend from Foe at the distance of 30 Yards, we should, I believe, have made a decisive and glorious day of it. But Providence or some unaccountable something, designd it otherwise; for after we had driven the Enemy a Mile or two, after they were in the utmost confusion, and flying before us in most places, after we were upon the point, (as it appeard to every body) of grasping a compleat Victory, our own Troops took fright and fled with precipitation and disorder. How to acct. for this I know not, unless, as I before observed, the Fog represented their own Friends to them for a Reinforcement of the Enemy as we attacked in different Quarters at the same time, and were about closing the Wings of our Army when this happened. One thing indeed contributed not a little to our Misfortune, and that was want of Ammunition

Providence designed defeat

on the right wing, which began the Ingagement, and in the course of two hours and 40 Minutes which it lasted, had (many of them) expended the 40 Rounds which they took into the Field. . . .

The Enemy are making vigorous efforts to remove the obstructions in the Delaware, and to possess themselves of the Works which have been constructed for the Defence of them. I am doing all I can in my present situation to save them, God only, knows which will succeed. . . .

P.S. I had scarce finish'd this Letter when by express from the State of New York, I received the Important and glorious News which follows . . . . (Burgoyne's surrender)

I most devoutly congratulate you, my Country, and every well wisher to the Cause on this Signal Stroke of Providence.

Stroke of Providence

(To John Augustine Washington, Philadelphia County, October 18, 1777)

To Major General Israel Putman

. . . . The defeat of Genl. Burgoyne is a most important event, and such as must afford the highest satisfaction to every well affected American breast. Should providence be pleased to crown our Arms in the course of the Campaign, with one more fortunate stroke, I think we shall have no great cause for anxiety respecting the future designs of Britain. I have trust all will be well in his good time. . . .

Providence pleased to crown our Arms

I am extremely sorry for the death of Mrs. Putnam and Sympathise with you upon the occasion. Remembring that all must die, and that she had lived to an honourable age, I hope you will bear the misfortune with that fortitude and complacency of mind, that becomes a Man and a Christian.

(Camp, 20 Miles from Philada., October 19, 1777)

To Landon Carter

. . . . I have this Instant received an acct. of the Prisoners taken by the Northern Army (Including Tories in arms agt. us) in the course of the Campaign. This singular Instance of Providence, and our good fortune under it exhibits a striking proof of the advantages which result from unanimity and a spirited conduct in the Militia. The Northern army, before the surrender, of Genl. Gates was reenforced by upwards of 12000 Militia who shut the only door by which Burgoyne could Retreat, and cut of all his supplies. How different our case! the disaffection of great part of the Inhabitants of this State, the languor of others and internal distraction of the whole, have been among the great and insuperable difficulties I have met with, and have contributed not a little to my embarassrassment this Campaign; but enough! I do not mean to complain, I flatter myself that a Superintending Providence is ordering every thing for the best and that, in due time, all will end well. That it may do so, and soon, is the most fervent wish of &c. . . .

A Superintending Providence is ordering every thing for the best

(Philadelphia County, October 27, 1777)

To Brigadier General Thomas Nelson

. . . . It is in vain to look back to our disappointment on the 4th. Instant at Germantown. We must endeavour to deserve better of Providence, and, I am persuaded, she will smile upon us. The rebuff which the Enemy met with at Red Bank (in which Count Donop and about four or 500 Hessians were killed and wounded) and the loss of the Augusta of 64 and Merlin of 18 Guns, have, I dare say, been fully related to you, which renders it unnecessary for me to dwell on it. They are using every effort for the reduction of Fort Mifflin and we, under our present circumstances, to save it. The event is left to Heaven.

We must endeavour to deserve better of Providence

(Camp at White Marsh, 12 Miles from Philadelphia, November 8, 1777)

Thanksgiving Day

On the 25th of November instant, the Honorable Continental Congress passed the following resolve, vizt:

"Resolved. That General Washington be directed to publish in General orders, that Congress will speedily take into consideration the merits of such officers as have distinguished themselves by their intrepidity and their attention to the health and discipline of their men; and adopt such regulations as shall tend to introduce order and good discipline into the army, and to render the situation of the officers and soldiery, with respect to cloathing and other necessaries, more eligible than it has hitherto been.

"Forasmuch as it is the indispensable duty of all men, to adore the superintending providence of Almighty God; to acknowledge with gratitude their obligations to him for benefits received, and to implore such further blessings as they stand in need of; and it having pleased him, in his abundant mercy, not only to continue to us the innumerable bounties of his common providence, but also, to smile upon us in the prosecution of a just and necessary war, for the defence of our unalienable rights and liberties."

Providence of Almighty God to be adored

It is therefore recommended by Congress, that Thursday the 18th Day of December next be set apart for Solemn Thanksgiving and Praise; that at one time, and with one voice, the good people may express the grateful feelings of their hearts, and consecrate themselves to the service of their divine benefactor; and that, together with their sincere acknowledgements and offerings, they may join the penitent confession of their sins; and supplications for such further blessings as they stand in need of. The Chaplains will properly notice this recommendation, that the day of thanksgiving may be duly observed in the army, agreeably to the intentions of Congress.

(General Orders, Head Quarters,
White Marsh, November 30, 1777)

Power of America—Preparing for Valley Forge

The Commander in Chief with the highest satisfaction expresses his thanks to the officers and soldiers for the fortitude and patience with which they have sustained the fatigues of the Campaign. Altho' in some instances we unfortunately failed, yet upon the whole Heaven hath smiled on our Arms and crowned them with signal success; and we may upon the best grounds conclude, that by a spirited continuance of the measures necessary for our defence we shall finally obtain the end of our Warfare, Independence, Liberty and Peace. These are blessings worth contending for at every hazard. But we hazard nothing. The power of America alone, duly exerted, would have nothing to dread from the force of Britain. Yet we stand not wholly upon our ground. France yields us every aid we ask, and there are reasons to believe the period is not very distant, when she will take a more active part, by declaring war against the British Crown. Every motive therefore, irresistibly urges us, nay commands us, to a firm and manly perseverance in our opposition to our cruel oppressors, to slight difficulties, endure hardships, and contemn every danger. The General ardently wishes it were now in his power, to conduct the troops into the best winter quarters. But where are these to be found? Should we retire to the interior parts of the State, we should find them crowded with virtuous citizens, who, sacrificing their all, have left Philadelphia, and fled thither for protection. To their distresses humanity forbids us to add. This is not all, we should leave a vast extent of fertile country to be despoiled and ravaged by the enemy, from which they would draw vast supplies, and where many of our firm friends would be exposed to all the miseries of the most insulting and wanton depredation. A train of evils might be enumerated, but these will suffice. These considerations make it indispensibly necessary for the army to take such a position, as will enable it most effectually to prevent distress and to give the most extensive security; and in that position we must make ourselves the best shelter in our power. With activity and diligence Huts may be erected that will be warm and dry. In these the troops will be compact, more secure against surprises than if in a divided state and at hand to protect the country. These cogent reasons have determined the General to take post in the neighbourhood of this camp; and influenced by them, he persuades himself, that the officers and soldiers, with one heart, and one mind, will resolve to surmount every difficulty, with a fortitude and patience, becoming their profession, and the sacred cause in which they are engaged. He himself will share in the hardship, and partake of every inconvenience.

Heaven hath smiled on our Arms

To morrow being the day set apart by the Honorable Congress for public Thanksgiving and Praise; and duty calling us devoutly to express our grateful acknowledgements to God for the manifold blessings he has granted us. The General directs that the army remain in it's present quarters, and that the Chaplains perform divine service with their several Corps and brigades. And earnestly exhorts, all officers and soldiers, whose absence is not indispensibly necessary, to attend with reverence the solemnities of the day.

A divine service for grateful acknowledgments to God for manifold blessings

(General Orders, Head Quarters,
at the Gulph, December 17, 1777)

To Reverend Nathaniel Whitaker

Revd. Sir: Your favour of the 24th. of September inclosing a discourse against Toryism, came safe to my hands. For the honour of the dedication, I return you my sincere thanks, and wish most devoutly that your labour may be crowned with the success it deserves.*

(Valley Forge, December 20, 1777)

General Instructions for the Colonels and Commanding Officers of Regiments in the Continental Service

.... Let Vice and immorality of every kind be discouraged as much as possible in your Regiment; and see, as a Chaplain is allowed to it, that the Men regularly attend divine Worship. Gaming of every kind is expressly forbid as the foundation of evil, and the ruin of many a brave, and good Officer. Games of exercise, for amusement, may be not only allowed of, but Incouraged. . . .

(Valley Forge, 1777)

The Conway Cabal

I have attended to your information and remark, on the supposed intention of placing General L__,** at the head of the army: whether a serious design of that kind had ever entered into the head of a member of C__*** or not, I never was at the trouble of enquiring. I am told a scheme of that kind is now on foot by some, in behalf of another gentleman, but whether true or false, whether serious, or merely to try the pulse, I neither know nor care; neither interested nor ambitious views led me into the service, I did not solicit the command, but accepted it after much entreaty, with all that diffidence which a conscious want of ability and experience equal to the discharge of so important a trust, must naturally create in a mind not quite devoid of thought; and after I did engage, pursued the great line of my duty, and the object in view (as far as my judgement could direct) as pointedly as the needle to the pole. So soon then as the public gets dissatisfied with my services, or a person is found better qualified to answer her expectation, I shall quit the helm with as much satisfaction, and retire to a private station with as much content, as ever the wearied pilgrim felt upon his safe arrival in the Holy-land, or haven of hope; and shall wish most devoutly, that those who come after may meet with more prosperous gales than I have done, and less difficulty. If the expectation of the public has not been answered by my endeavours, I have more reasons than one to regret it; but at present shall only add, that a day may come when the public cause is no longer to be benefited by a concealment of our circumstances; and till that period arrives, I shall not be among the first to disclose such truths as may injure it.

(To Reverend William Gordon,
Head Quarters, Valley Forge, January 23, 1778)

* A Presbyterian minister of Salem, Mass. Whitaker had delivered a discourse on Judges 5:23, and afterwards published it (34 pp., Newbury Port, 1777) under the title, "An Antidote of Toryism," and dedicated it to Washington. (*Fitzpatrick*)

**Gen. Charles Lee. (*Fitzpatrick.*)

***Congress. (*Fitzpatrick.*)

Kindness to a Friend of Differing Opinions: Bryan Fairfax

Dear Sir: Your favor of the 8th. of Decr. came safe to my hands after a considerable delay in its passage.* The sentiments you have expressed of me in this Letter are highly flattering, meriting my warmest acknowledgements, as I have too good an Opinion of your sincerity and candour to believe that you are capable of unmeaning professions and speaking a language foreign from your Heart. The friendship I ever professed, and felt for you, met with no diminution from the difference in our political Sentiments. I know the rectitude of my own intentions, and believing in the sincerity of yours, lamented, though I did not condemn, your renunciation of the creed I had adopted. Nor do I think any a person, or power, ought to do it, whilst your conduct is not opposed to the general Interest of the people and the measures they are pursuing; the latter, that is our actions, depending upon ourselves, may be controuled, while the powers of thinking originating in higher

* Bryan Fairfax had returned to Virginia after attempting to go to England to live because his political views were so far out of accord with his Virginia friends and neighbors. He had repaired to Continental Army headquarters and obtained from Washington a passport to go to New York. Arrived there, he found that the British required him to take certain oaths before allowing him to go to England. Fairfax's conscience would not permit him to subscribe to such restrictions, and he returned to Virginia, where he remained throughout the war, unmolested and respected. After his return home he wrote to Washington (Dec. 8, 1777), to which the above letter is a reply: "There are times when Favours conferred make a greater Impression than at others, for, tho' I have received many, and hope I have not been unmindful of them, yet that, at a Time your Popularity was at highest and mine at the lowest, and when it is so common for Men's Resentments to run high agst those that differ from them in Opinion You should act with your wonted Kindness towards me, hath affected me more than any Favour I have received; and could not be believed by some in N: York, it being above the Run of common Minds." (*Fitzpatrick*)

causes, cannot always be moulded to our wishes.

The determinations of Providence are all ways wise; often inscrutable, and though its decrees appear to bear hard upon us at times is nevertheless meant for gracious purposes; in this light I cannot help viewing your late disappointment; for if you had been permitted to have gone to england, unrestrained even by the rigid oaths which are administred on those occns. your feelings as a husband, Parent, &ca. must have been considerably wounded in the prospect of a long, perhaps lasting seperation from your nearest relatives. What then must they have been if the obligation of an oath had left you without a Will? Your hope of being instrumental in restoring Peace would prove as unsubstantial as mist before the Noon days Sun and would as soon dispel: for believe me Sir great Britain understood herself perfectly well in this dispute but did not comprehend America. She meant as Lord Campden in his late speech in Parlt. clearly, and explicitly declared, to drive America into rebellion that her own purposes might be more fully answered by it but take this along with it, that this Plan originating in a firm belief, founded on misinformation, that no effectual opposition would or could be made, they little dreamt of what has happened and are disappd. in their views; does not every act of administration from the Tea Act to the present Session of Parliament declare this in plain and self evidt. Characters? Had the Comrs. any powers to treat with America? If they meant Peace, would Lord Howe have been detaind in England 5 Months after passing the Act? Would the powers of these Comrs. have been confined to mere acts of grace, upon condition of absolute submission? No, surely, No! they meant to drive us into what they termed rebellion, that they might be furnished with a pretext to disarm and then strip us of the rights and privileges of Englishmen and Citizens. If they were actuated by principles of justice, why did they refuse indignantly to accede to the terms which were humbly supplicated before the hostilities commenced and this Country deluged in Blood; and now make their principal Officers and even the Comrs. themselves say, that these terms are just and reasonable; Nay that more will be granted than we have yet asked, if we will relinquish our Claim to Independency. What Name does such conduct as this deserve? and what punishment is there in store for the Men who have distressed Millions, involved thousands in ruin, and plunged numberless families in inextricable woe? Could that wch is just and reasonable now, have been unjust four Years ago? If not upon what principles, I say does Administration act? they must either be wantonly wicked and cruel, or (which is only anr. mode of describing the same thing) under false colours are now endeavouring to deceive the great body of the people, by industriously propagating a belief that G. B. is willing to offer any, and that we will accept of no terms; thereby hoping to poison and disaffect the Minds of those who wish for peace, and create feuds and dissentions among ourselves. In a word, having less dependance now, in their Arms than their Arts, they are practising such low and dirty tricks, that Men of Sentiment and honr. must blush at their Villainy, among other manoeuvres, in this way they are counterfeiting Letters, and publishing them, as intercepted ones of mine to prove that I am an enemy to the present measures, and have been led into them step by step still hoping that Congress would recede from their present claims.

Determinations of Providence are always wise

Wantonly wicked and cruel

(To Bryan Fairfax, Valley Forge, March 1, 1778)

Praise of Troops

The Commander in Chief again takes occasion to return his warmest thanks to the virtuous officers and soldiery of this Army for that persevering fidelity and Zeal which they have uniformly manifested in all their conduct. Their fortitude not only under the common hardships incident to a military life, but also under the additional sufferings to which the peculiar situation of these States have exposed them, clearly proves them worthy the enviable privelege of contending for the rights of human nature, the *Freedom and Independence* of their Country. The recent Instance of uncomplaining Patience during the scarcity of provisions in Camp is a fresh proof that they possess in an eminent degree the spirit of soldiers and the magninimity of Patriots. The few refractory individuals who disgrace themselves by murmurs it is to be hoped have repented such unmanly behaviour, and resolved to emulate the noble example of their associates upon every trial which the customary casualties of war may hereafter throw in their way. Occasional distress for want of provisions and other necessaries is a spectacle that frequently occurs in every army and perhaps there never was one which has been in general so plentifully supplied in respect

Magninimity of Patriots

ADORNS THE HOUSE OF REPRESENTATIVES AT HARRISBURG. REPRODUCED BY PERMISSION. PHOTOGRAPHED BY BRIAN HUNT.

THE CAMP OF THE AMERICAN ARMY AT VALLEY FORGE, FEBRUARY, 1778
Baron von Steuben Drilling the Army
by E. A. Abbey

to the former as ours. Surely we who are free Citizens in arms engaged in a struggle for every thing valuable in society and partaking in the glorious task of laying the foundation of an *Empire*, should scorn effeminately to shrink under those accidents and rigours of War which mercenary hirelings fighting in the cause of lawless ambition, rapine and devastation, encounter with cheerfulness and alacrity, we should not be merely equal, we should be superior to them in every qualification that dignifies the man or the soldier in proportion as the motive from which we act and the final hopes of our Toils, are superior to theirs. Thank Heaven! our Country abounds with provision and with prudent management we need not apprehend want for any length of time. Defects in the Commissaries department, Contingencies of weather and other temporary impediments have subjected and may again subject us to a deficiency for a few days, but soldiers! American soldiers! will despise the meanness of repining at such trifling strokes of Adversity, trifling indeed when compared to the transcendent *Prize* which will undoubtedly crown their Patience and Perseverence, Glory and Freedom, Peace and Plenty to themselves and their Community; The admiration of the World, the Love of their Country and the Gratitude of Posterity!

American soldiers—free Citizens in arms

Your General unceasingly employs his thoughts on the means of relieving your distresses, supplying your wants and bringing your labours to a speedy and prosperous issue. Our Parent Country he hopes will second his endeavours by the most vigorous exertions and he is convinced the faithful officers and soldiers associated with him in the great work of rescuing our Country from Bondage and Misery will continue in the display of that patriotic zeal which is capable of smoothing every difficulty and vanquishing every Obstacle. . . .

(General Orders Head-Quarters,
V. Forge, Sunday, March 1, 1778)

To Reverend Israel Evans

Revd. Sir: Your favor of the 17th. Ulto., inclosing the discourse which you delivered on the 18th. of December; the day set a part for a general thanksgiving; to Genl. Poors Brigade, never came to my hands till yesterday.

I have read this performance with equal attention and pleasure, and at the same time that I admire, and feel the force of the reasoning which you have displayed through the whole, it is more especially incumbent upon me to thank you for the honorable, but partial mention you have made of my character; and to assure you, that it will ever be the first wish of my heart to aid your pious endeavours to inculcate a due sense of the dependance we ought to place in that all wise and powerful Being on whom alone our success depends; and moreover, to assure you, that

Inculcate a due sense of dependence we ought to place in Providence with respect and regard, I am, etc.

(Head Qrs. Valley-Forge, March 13, 1778)

Fast Day

. . . . The Honorable Congress having thought proper to recommend to the United States of America to set apart Wednesday the 22nd. instant to be observed as a day of Fasting, Humiliation and Prayer, that at one time and with one voice the righteous dispensations of Providence may be acknowledged and His Goodness and Mercy toward us and our Arms supplicated and implored; the General directs that this day *also* shall be religiously observed in the Army, that no work be done thereon and that the Chaplains prepare discourses suitable to the Occasion. . . .

Reasons for prayer and fast days

(General Orders, Head Quarters, V. Forge, Sunday, April 12, 1778)

Divine Service

The Commander in Chief directs that divine Service be performed every Sunday at 11 oClock in those Brigades to which there are Chaplains; those which have none to attend the places of worship nearest to them. It is expected that Officers of all Ranks will by their attendence set an Example to their men.

While we are zealously performing the duties of good Citizens and soldiers we certainly ought not to be inattentive to the higher duties of Religion. To the distinguished Character of Patriot, it should be our highest Glory to add the more distinguished Character of Christian. The signal Instances of providential Goodness which we have experienced and which have now almost crowned our labours with complete Success, demand from us in a peculiar manner the warmest returns of Gratitude and Piety to the Supreme Author of all Good. . . .

Highest glory to add Christian Character to Character of the Patriot

Providential goodness demands return of gratitude and piety

(General Orders, Head Quarters, V. Forge, Saturday, May 2, 1778)

The French Alliance

It having pleased the Almighty ruler of the Universe propitiously to defend the Cause of the United American-States and finally by raising us up a powerful Friend among the Princes of the Earth to establish our liberty and Independence up lasting foundations, it becomes us to set apart a day for gratefully acknowledging the divine Goodness and celebrating the important Event which we owe to his benign Interposition.

Providence raised up a Friend of American liberty

Benign Interposition

The several Brigades are to be assembled for this Purpose at nine o'Clock tomorrow morning when their Chaplains will communicate the Intelligence contain'd in the Postscript to the Pennsylvania Gazette of the 2nd. instant and offer up a thanksgiving and deliver a discourse suitable to the Occasion. At half after ten o'Clock a Cannon will be fired, which is to be a signal for the men to be under Arms. The Brigade Inspectors will then inspect their Dress and Arms, form the Battalions according to instructions given them and announce to the Commanding Officers of Brigades that the Battalions are formed. The Brigadiers or Commandants will then appoint the Field Officers to command the Battalions, after which each Battalion will be ordered to load and ground their Arms.

At half after eleven a second Cannon be fired as a signal for the march upon which the several Brigades will begin their march by wheeling to the right by Platoons and proceed by the nearest way to the left of their ground in the new Position; this will be pointed out by the Brigade Inspectors. A third signal will be given upon which there will be a discharge of thirteen Cannon; When the thirteen has fired a runing fire of the Infantry will begin on the right of Woodford's and continue throughout the whole front line, it will then be taken on the left of the second line and continue to the right. Upon a signal given, the whole Army will Huzza! "Long live the King of France." The Artillery then begins again and fires thirteen rounds, this will be succeeded by a second general discharge of the Musquetry in a runing fire. Huzza! "And long live the friendly European Powers." Then the last discharge of thirteen Pieces of Artillery will be given, followed by a General runing fire and Huzza! "To the American States."

There will be no Exercise in the morning and the guards of the day will not parade 'till after the feu de joie is finished, when the Brigade Major will march them out to the Grand Parade. The Adjutants then will tell off their Battalions into eight Platoons and the commanding officer will reconduct them to their Camps marching by the Left. . . .

(General Orders, Head Quarters, V. Forge, Tuesday, May 5, 1778)

COURTESY OF UNIVERSITY OF CALIFORNIA, BERKELEY, ART MUSEUM

GIFT OF MRS. MARK HOPKINS, SAN FRANCISCO

WASHINGTON RALLYING THE TROOPS AT MONMOUTH
by Emanuel Leutze, 1854
General George Washington, closely followed by Alexander Hamilton and the Marquis de Lafayette (hatless), intercepts General Charles Lee and his forces in retreat at the Battle of Monmouth, June 28, 1778.

To Landon Carter

I thank you much for your kind and affectionate remembrance and mention of me, and for that solicitude for my welfare, which breathes through the whole of your letters. Were I not warm in my acknowledgments for your distinguished regard, I should feel that sense of ingratitude, which I hope will never constitute a part of my character, nor find a place in my bosom. My friends therefore may believe me sincere in my professions of attachment to them, whilst Providence has a joint claim to my humble and grateful thanks, for its protection and direction of me, through the many difficult and intricate scenes, which this contest hath produced; and for the constant interposition in our behalf, when the clouds were heaviest and seemed ready to burst upon us.

Protection and direction of Providence and its constant interposition

To paint the distresses and perilous situation of this army in the course of last winter, for want of cloaths, provisions, and almost every other necessary, essential to the well-being, (I may say existence,) of an army, would require more time and an abler pen than mine; nor, since our prospects have so miraculously brightened, shall I attempt it, or even bear it in remembrance, further than as a memento of what is due to the great Author of all the care and good, that have been extended in relieving us in difficulties and distress. . . .

Author of all the care and good extended

. . . . This last trite performance of Master North's is neither more nor less than an insult to common sense, and shows to what extremity of folly wicked men in a bad cause are sometimes driven; for this rude Boreas, who was to bring America to his feet, knew at the time of draughting these bills, or had good reason to believe, that a treaty had actually been signed between the court of France and the United States. By what rule of common sense, then, he could expect that such an undisguised artifice would go down in America I cannot conceive. But, thanks to Heaven, the tables are turned; and we, I hope, shall have our independence secured, in its fullest extent, without cringing to this Son of Thunder, who I am persuaded will find abundant work for his troops elsewhere; on which happy prospect I sincerely congratulate you and every friend to American liberty. . . .

Extreme folly of wicked men, but Heaven turns the tables

(Valley Forge, May 30, 1778)

BY ALONZO CHAPPEL

The Marquis de Lafayette (1757–1834)

He arrived from France in 1777 and immediately developed a father-son relationship with George Washington. He fought in many battles and was wounded at Brandywine. His affection and respect for Washington led him to name his son George Washington Lafayette.

Victory at Monmouth

The Commander in Chief congratulates the Army on the Victory obtained over the Arms of his Britanick Majesty yesterday and thanks most sincerely the gallant officers and men who distinguished themselves upon the occasion and such others as by their good order and coolness gave the happiest presages of what might have been expected had they come to Action. . . .

(General Orders, Head Quarters, Freehold,
Monmouth County, June 29, 1778)

The Men are to wash themselves this afternoon and appear as clean and decent as possible.

Seven o'Clock this evening is appointed that We may publickly unite in thanksgiving to the supreme Disposer of human Events for the Victory which was obtained on Sunday over the Flower of the British Troops. . . .

Supreme Disposer of human Events

(General Orders Head Quarters,
Englishtown, June 30, 1778)

To John Augustine Washington

Dear Brother: Your Letter of the 20th. Ulto. came to my hands last Night; before this will have reached you, the Acct. of the Battle of Monmouth probably will get to Virginia; which, from an unfortunate, and bad beginning, turned out a glorious and happy day. . . .

General [Charles] Lee having the command of the Van of the Army, consisting of fully 5000 chosen Men, was ordered to begin the Attack next Morning so soon as the enemy began their March, to be supported by me. But, strange to tell! when he came up with the enemy, a retreat commenced; whether by his order, or from other causes, is now the subject of inquiry, and consequently improper to be descanted on, as he is in arrest, and a Court Martial sitting for tryal of him. A Retreat however was the fact, be the causes as they may; and the disorder arising from it would have proved fatal to the Army had not that bountiful Providence which has never failed us in the hour of distress, enabled me to form a Regiment or two (of those that were retreating) in the face of the Enemy, and under their fire, by which means a stand was made long enough (the place through which the enemy were pursuing being narrow) to form the Troops that were advancing, upon an advantageous piece of Ground in the rear; hence our affairs took a favourable turn, and from being pursued, we drove the Enemy back, over the ground they had followed us, recovered the field of Battle, and possessed ourselves of their dead. But, as they retreated behind a Morass very difficult to pass, and had both Flanks secured with thick Woods, it was found impracticable with our Men fainting with fatigue, heat, and want of Water, to do anything more that Night. In the Morning we expected to renew the Action, when behold the enemy had stole of as Silent as the Grave in the Night after having sent away their wounded. Getting a Nights March of us, and having but ten Miles to a strong post, it was judged inexpedient to follow them any further, but move towards the North River least they should have any design upon our posts there. . . .

Lee's retreat reversed by Providence which has never failed

(Brunswick in New Jersey, July 4, 1778)

Doctrine of Providence

. . . . It is not a little pleasing, nor less wonderful to contemplate, that after two years Manœuvring and undergoing the strangest vicissitudes that perhaps ever attended any one contest since the creation both Armies are brought back to the very point they set out from and, that that, which was the offending party in the beginning is now reduced to the use of the spade and pick axe for defence. The hand of Providence has been so conspicuous in all this, that he must be worse than an infidel that lacks faith, and more than wicked, that has not gratitude enough to acknowledge his obligations, but, it will be time enough for me to turn preacher, when my present appointment ceases; and therefore, I shall add no more on the Doctrine of Providence; but make a tender of my best respects to your good Lady; the Secretary and other friends assure you that with the most perfect regard I am etc. . . .

The hand of God so conspicuous

(To Brigadier General Thomas Nelson
Camp at the White-plains,
August 20, 1778)

To Governor Jonathan Trumbull

. . . . The violent gale which dissipated the two fleets when on the point of engaging, and the withdrawing of the Count D'Estaing to Boston may appear to us as real misfortunes; but with you I consider storms and victory under the direction of a wise providence who no doubt directs them for the best of purposes, and to bring round the greatest degree of happiness to the greatest number of his people. . . .

Directs storms and victory for the best of purposes

(Head Quarters, September 6, 1778)

Laxness of Public Virtue

. . . . I can assign but two causes for the enemys continuance among us, and these balance so equally in my Mind, that I scarce know which of the two preponderates. The one is, that they are waiting the ultimate determination of Parliament; the other, that of our distresses; by which I know the Commissioners went home not a little buoyed up; and sorry I am to add, not without cause. What may be the effect of such large and frequent emissions, of the dissentions, Parties, extravagance, and a general lax of public virtue Heaven alone can tell! I am affraid even to think of It; but it appears as clear to me as ever the Sun did in its meredian brightness, that America never stood in more eminent need of the wise, patriotic, and Spirited exertions of her Sons than at this period and if it is not a sufficient cause for genl. lamentation, my misconception of the matter impresses it too strongly upon me, that the States seperately are too much engaged in their local concerns, and have too many of their ablest men withdrawn from the general Council for the good of the common weal; in a word, I think our political system may, be compared to the mechanism of a Clock; and that our conduct should derive a lesson from it for it answers no good purpose to keep the smaller Wheels in order if the greater one which is the support and prime mover of the whole is neglected. How far the latter is the case does not become me to pronounce but as there can be no harm in a pious wish for the good of ones Country I shall offer it as mine that each State wd. not only choose, but absolutely compel their ablest Men to attend Congress; that they would instruct them to go into a thorough investigation of the causes that have produced so many disagreeable effects in the Army and Country; in a word that public abuses should be corrected, and an entire reformation worked; without these it does not, in my judgment, require the spirit of divination to foretell the consequences of the present Administration, nor to how little purpose the States, individually, are framing constitutions, providing laws, and filling Offices with the abilities of their ablest Men. These, if the great whole is mismanaged must sink in the general wreck and will carry with it the remorse of thinking that we are lost by our own folly and negligence, or the desire perhaps of living in ease and tranquility during the expected accomplishment of so great a revolution in the effecting of which the greatest abilities and the honestest Men our (i.e. the American) world affords ought to be employed. It is much to be feared my dear Sir that the States in their seperate capacities have very inadequate ideas of the present danger. Removed (some of them) far distant from the scene of action and seeing, and hearing such publications only as flatter their wishes they conceive that the contest is at an end, and that to regulate the government and police of their own State is all that remains to be done; but it is devoutly to be wished that a sad reverse of this may not fall upon them like a thunder clap that is little expected. . . .

America's political system compared to the mechanism of a clock

The general government—the support and prime mover of the whole

(To Benjamin Harrison, Head Qrs., Middle Brook, December 18, 1778)

Day of Thanksgiving

. . . .The 30th. of this Month being prescribed by the honorable Congress as a day of thanksgiving, you will be pleased to have the same observed in the army under your command.
(To Major General John Sullivan, Head Quarters, Middle Brook, December 20, 1778)

General Orders

. . . . The Honorable The Congress having been pleased by their Proclamation of the 21st. of November last to appoint Wednesday the 30th. instant as a day of Thanksgiving and Praise for the great and numerous Providential Mercies experienced by the People of These States in the course of the present War, the same is to be religiously observed throughout the Army in the manner therein directed, and the different Chaplains will prepare discourses suited to the Occasion. . . .

Great Providential Mercies

(Head Quarters, Middle Brook, Tuesday, December 22, 1778)

Dangerous Situation

. . . . Though it is not in my power to devote much time to private corrispondences, owing to the multiplicity of public letters (and other business) I have to read, write, and transact; yet I can with great truth assure you, that it would afford me very singular pleasure to be favoured at all times with your sentiments in a leizure hour, upon public matters of general concernment as well as those which more immediately respect your own State (if proper conveyances would render prudent a free communication). I am particularly desirous of it at this time, because I view things very differently, I fear, from what people in general do who seem to think the contest is at an end; and to make money, and get places, the only things now remaining to do. I have seen without dispondency (even for a moment) the hours which America have stiled her gloomy ones, but I have beheld no day since the commencement of hostilities that I have thought her liberties in such eminent danger as at present. Friends and foes seem now to combine to pull down the goodly fabric we have hitherto been raising at the expence of so much time, blood, and treasure; and unless the bodies politick will exert themselves to bring things back to first principles, correct abuses, and punish our internal foes, inevitable ruin must follow. Indeed we seem to be verging so fast to destruction, that I am filled with sensations to which I have been a stranger till within these three Months. Our Enemy behold with exultation and joy how effectually we labour for their benefit; and from being in a state of absolute despair, and on the point of evacuating America, are now on tiptoe; nothing therefore in my judgment can save us but a total reformation in our own conduct, or some decisive turn to affairs in Europe. The former alas! to our shame be it spoken! is less likely to happen than the latter, as it is now consistent with the views of the Speculators, various tribes of money makers, and stock jobbers of all denominations to continue the War for their own private emolument, without considering that their avarice, and thirst for gain must plunge every thing (including themselves) in one common Ruin. . . .

Total reformation in our own conduct to save us from ruin and self-destruction

(To George Mason, Camp at Middlebrook, March 27, 1779)

Day of Fasting

. . . . The Act recommending a day of fasting, humiliation and prayer shall be duly attended to. . . .

(To The President of Congress, Head Quarters, Middle Brook, April 2, 1779)

. . . . The Honorable the Congress having recommended it to the United States to set apart Thursday the 6th day of May next to be observed as a day of fasting, humiliation and prayer, to acknowledge the gracious interpositions of *Providence*; to deprecate deserved punishment for our Sins and Ingratitude, to unitedly implore the Protection of Heaven; Success to our Arms and the Arms of our Ally: The Commander in Chief enjoins a religious observance of said day and directs the Chaplains to prepare discourses proper for the occasion; strictly forbiding all recreations and unnecessary labor.

Acknowledging gracious interpositions of Providence

(General Orders, Head Quarters, Middle Brook, Monday, April 12, 1779)

The General reminds the Army that tomorrow is the General Fast; He expects it will be observed according to the order of the 12th. of April last. No exercising or fatigue to be permitted thereon.

(General Orders, Head Quarters, Middle Brook, Wednesday, May 5, 1779)

Religion of Jesus Christ

. . . . Brothers: I am glad you have brought three of the Children of your principal Chiefs to be educated with us. I am sure Congress will open the Arms of love to them, and will look upon them as their own Children, and will have them educated accordingly. This is a great mark of your confidence and of your desire to preserve the friendship between the Two Nations to the end of time, and to become One people with your Breth[r]en of the United States. My ears hear with pleasure the other matters you mention. Congress will be glad to hear them too. You do well to wish to learn our arts and ways of life, and above all, the religion of Jesus Christ. These will make you a greater and happier people than you are. Congress will do every thing they can to assist you in this wise intention; and to tie the knot of friendship and union so fast, that nothing shall ever be able to loose it. . . .

Indian American Christian Education

(Speech to the Delaware Chiefs, Head Quarters, Middle Brook, May 12, 1779)

Critical Situation

. . . . I never was, much less reason have I now, to be affraid of the enemys Arms; but I have no scruple in declaring to you, that I have never yet seen the time in which our affars in my opinion were at so low an ebb as the present and witht. a speedy and capital change we shall not be able in a very short time to call out the strength and resources of the Country. The hour therefore is certainly come when party differences and disputes should subside; when every Man (especially those in Office) should with one hand and one heart pull the same way and with their whole strength. Providence has done, and I am perswaded is disposed to do, a great deal for us, but we are not to forget the fable of Jupiter and the Countryman.

Party disputes should subside

(To John Armstrong, Delegate to Congress from Pennsylvania, Head Qrs., Middle brook, May 18, 1779)

To Lund Washington

Dear Lund: Your letter of the 19th, which came to hand by the last post, gives a melancholy account of your prospects for a crop, and a still more melancholy one of the decay of public virtue. The first I submit to with the most perfect resignation and cheerfulness. I look upon every dispensation of Providence as designed to answer some valuable purpose, and hope I shall always possess a sufficient degree of fortitude to bear without murmuring any stroke which may happen, either to my person or estate, from that quarter. But I cannot, with any degree of patience, behold the infamous practices of speculators, monopolizers, and all that class of gentry which are preying upon our very vitals, and, for the sake of a little dirty pelf, are putting the rights and liberties of the country into the most imminent danger, and continuing a war destructive to the lives and property of the valuable part of this community, which would have ceased last fall as certain as we now exist but for the encouragements the enemy derived from this source, the depreciation of the money (which in a great measure is the consequence of it) and our own internal divisions.

Every dispensation of Providence designed to answer some valuable purpose

No patience with war-mongers

(Headquarters, Middlebrook, May 29, 1779)

The Dutch Reformed Church at Raritan

Gentlemen: To meet the approbation of good men cannot but be agreeable. Your affectionate expressions make it still more so.

In quartering an army, and in supplying its wants, distress and inconvenience will often occur to the citizen. I feel myself happy in a consciousness that these have been strictly limited by necessity, and in your opinion of my attention to the rights of my fellow citizens.

I thank you gentlemen sincerely for the sense you entertain of the conduct of the army; and for the interest you take in my welfare. I trust the goodness of the cause and the exertions of the people under divine protection will give us that honourable peace for which we are contending. Suffer me Gentlemen to wish the reformed church at Raritan a long continuance of its present Minister and consistory and all the blessings which flow from piety and religion.

Trust in divine protection

(Middle brook Camp, June 2, 1779)

An Abominable Habit

. . . . Many and pointed orders have been issued against that unmeaning and abominable custom of *Swearing*, not withstanding which, with much regret the General observes that it prevails, *if possible,* more than ever; His feelings are continually wounded by the Oaths and Imprecations of the soldiers whenever he is in hearing of them.

The Name of That Being, from whose bountiful goodness we are permitted to exist and enjoy the comforts of life is incessantly imprecated and prophaned in a manner as wanton as it is shocking. For the sake therefore of religion, decency and order the General hopes and trusts that officers of every rank will use their influence and authority to check a vice, which is as unprofitable as it is wicked and shameful.

If officers would make it an invariable rule to reprimand, and if that does not do punish soldiers for offences of this kind it could not fail of having the desired effect.

Profanity to be checked by officers

(General Orders, Head Quarters, Moores House, Thursday, July 29, 1779)

A Sermon

Revd. Sir: I have received, and with pleasure read, the Sermon you were so obliging as to send me. I thank you for this proof of your attention. I thank you also for the favourable sentiments you have been pleased to express of me. But in a more especial mannr. I thank you for the good wishes and prayers you offer in my behalf. These have a just claim to the gratitude of Revd. Sir, Yr., etc.

(To the Reverend Uzal Ogden, of Newton, Sussex County, N.J., West-point, August 5, 1779)

Importance of Public Virtue

. . . . A New scene, though rather long delayed, is opening to our view and of sufficient importance to interest the hopes and fears of every well wisher to his Country and will engage the attention of all America. This I say on a supposition that the delays to the Southward and advanced season does not prevent a full and perfect co-operation with the French fleet in this quarter. Be this as it may; every thing in the preparatory way that depends upon me is done, and doing. To Count D'Estaing then, and that good Providence wch. has so remarkably aided us in all our difficulties, the rest is committed. . . .

Having done all, committing the rest to Providence

. . . I am under no apprehension of a capital injury from any other source than that of the continual depreciation of our Money. This indeed is truly alarming, and of so serious a nature that every other effort is in vain unless something can be done to restore its credit. Congress, the States individually, and individuals of each state, should exert themselves to effect this great end. It is the only hope; the last resource of the enemy; and nothing but our want of public virtue can induce a continuance of the War. Let them once see, that as it is in our power, so it is our inclination and intention to overcome this difficulty, and the idea of conquest, or hope of bringing us back to a state of dependance, will vanish like the morning dew; they can no more encounter this kind of opposition than the hoar frost can withstand the rays of an all chearing Sun. The liberties and safety of this Country depend upon it. The way is plain, the means are in our power, but it is virtue alone that can effect it, for without this, heavy taxes, frequently collected, (the only radical cure) and loans, are not to be obtained. Where this has been the policy (in Connecticut for instance) the prices of every article have fallen and the money consequently is in demand; but in the other States you can scarce get a single thing for it, and yet it is with-held from the public by speculators, while every thing that can be useful to the public is engrossed by this tribe of black gentry, who work more effectually against us than the enemys Arms; and are a hundd. times more dangerous to our liberties and the great cause we are engaged in.

(To Edmund Pendleton, West-point,
November 1, 1779)

THANKSGIVING

The Honorable the Congress has been pleased to pass the following proclamation.

"Whereas it becomes us humbly to approach the throne of Almighty God, with gratitude and praise for the wonders which his goodness has wrought in conducting our forefathers to this western world; for his protection to them and to their posterity amid difficulties and dangers; for raising us, their children, from deep distress to be numbered among the nations of the earth; and for arming the hands of just and mighty princes in our deliverance; and especially for that he hath been pleased to grant us the enjoyment of health, and so to order the revolving seasons, that the earth hath produced her increase in abundance, blessing the labors of the husbandmen, and spreading plenty through the land; that he hath prospered our arms and those of our ally; been a shield to our troops in the hour of danger, pointed their swords to victory and led them in triumph over the bulwarks of the foe; that he hath gone with those who went out into the wilderness against the savage tribes; that he hath stayed the hand of the spoiler, and turned back his meditated destruction; that he hath prospered our commerce, and given success to those who sought the enemy on the face of the deep; and above all, that he hath diffused the glorious light of the gospel, whereby, through the merits of our gracious Redeemer, we may become the heirs of his eternal glory; therefore,

The wonderful works of God remembered

Heirs of eternal glory through Christ

"RESOLVED, That it be recommended to the several states, to appoint Thursday, the 9th of December next, to be a day of public and solemn thanksgiving to Almighty God for his mercies, and of prayer for the continuance of his favor and protection to these United States; to beseech him that he would be graciously pleased to influence our public councils, and bless them with wisdom from on high, with unanimity, firmness, and success; that he would go forth with our hosts and crown our arms with victory; that he would grant to his church the plentiful effusions of divine grace, and pour out his holy spirit on all ministers of the gospel; that he would bless and prosper the means of education, and spread the light of christian knowledge through the remotest corners of the earth; that he would smile upon the labours of his people and cause the earth to bring forth her fruits in abundance; that we may with gratitude and gladness enjoy them; that he would take into his holy protection our illustrious ally, give him victory over his enemies, and render him signally great, as the father of his people and the protector of the rights of mankind; that he would graciously be pleased to turn the hearts of our enemies, and to dispense the blessings of peace to contending nations; that he would in mercy look down upon us, pardon our sins and receive us into his favor, and finally, that he would establish the independence of these United States upon the basis of religion and virtue, and support and protect them in the enjoyment of peace, liberty and safety."

Subjects of national prayer

Divine influence in public councils

Turn the hearts of our enemies

Establish independence

A strict observance to be paid by the Army to this proclamation and the Chaplains are to prepare and deliver discourses suitable to it.

(General Orders, Head Quarters, Moore's
House, Saturday, November 27, 1779)

Arnold's Treason

. . . . Treason of the blackest dye was yesterday discovered! General Arnold who commanded at West-point, lost to every sentiment of honor, of public and private obligation, was about to deliver up that important Post into the hands of the enemy. Such an event must have given the American cause a deadly wound if not a fatal stab. Happily the treason has been timely discovered to prevent the fatal misfortune. The providential train of circumstances which led to it affords the most convincing proof that the Liberties of America are the object of divine Protection.

At the same time that the Treason is to be regretted the General cannot help congratulating the Army on the happy discovery. Our Enemies despairing of carrying their point of force are practising every base art to effect by bribery and Corruption what they cannot accomplish in a manly way.

The happy discovery

Great honor is due to the American Army that this is the first instance of Treason of the kind where many were to be expected from the nature of the dispute, and nothing is so bright an ornament in the Character of the American soldiers as their having been proof against all the arts and seduction of an insidious enemy.

Arnold has made his escape to the Enemy but Mr. André the Adjutant General to the British Army who came out as a spy to negotiate the Business is our Prisoner.

(General Orders, Head Quarters, Orangetown, Tuesday, September 26, 1780)

To Lund Washington

. . . . You ask how I am to be rewarded for all this? There is one reward that nothing can deprive me of, and that is, the consciousness of having done my duty with the strictest rectitude, and most scrupulous exactness, and the certain knowledge, that if we should, ultimately, fail in the present contest, it is not owing to the want of exertion in me, or the application of every means that Congress and the United States, or the States individually, have put into my hands.

Consciousness of having done my duty —a reward

[multilated] dence, to whom we are infinitely more indebted than we are to our own wisdom, or our own exertions, has always displayed its power and goodness, when clouds and thick darkness seemed ready to overwhelm us. The hour is now come when we stand much in need of another manifestation of its bounty however little we deserve it. . . .

(Morris-Town, May 19, 1780)

Condolence to Governor Trumbull

. . . . I most sincerely condole with your Excellency on the late severe stroke which you have met with in your family. Although calamities of this kind are what we should all be prepared to expect, yet few, upon their arrival, are able to bear them with a becoming fortitude. Your determination however to seek assistance from the great disposer of all human events is highly laudable, and is the source from whence the truest consolation is to be drawn.

Assistance from the great disposer of all human events

(Head Quarters, near Springfield, June 11, 1780)

To James Duane

. . . . The satisfaction I have in any successes that attend us or even in the alleviation of misfortunes is always allayed by a fear that it will lull us into security. Supineness and a disposition to flatter ourselves seem to make parts of our national character; when we receive a check and are not quite undone, we are apt to fancy we have gained a victory; and when we do gain any little advantage, we imagine it decisive and expect the war is immediately to end. The history of the war is a history of false hopes and temporary expedients. Would to God they were to end here! This winter, if I am not mistaken, will open a still more embarrassing scene than we have yet experienced to the Southward. . . .

Supineness and a disposition to flatter

(Hd. Qrs., Tappan, October 4, 1780)

Arnold's Character

. . . . In no instance since the commencement of the War has the interposition of Providence appeared more conspicuous than in the rescue of the Post and Garrison of West point from Arnolds villainous perfidy. How far he meant to involve me in the catastrophe of this place does not appear by any indubitable evidence, and I am rather inclined to think he did not wish to hazard the more important object of his treachery by attempting to combine two events the lesser of which might have marred the greater. A combination of

Most conspicuous Providence in rescue of West point

extraordinary circumstances. An unaccountable deprivation of presence of Mind in a man of the first abilities, and the virtuous conduct of three Militia men, threw the Adjutant General of the British forces in America (with full proofs of Arnolds treachery) into our hands; and but for the egregious folly, or the bewildered conception of Lieutt. Colo. Jameson who seemed lost in astonishment and not to have known what he was doing I should as certainly have got Arnold. André has met his fate, and with that fortitude which was to be expected from an accomplished man, and gallant Officer. But I am mistaken if at *this time*, Arnold is undergoing the torments of a mental Hell. He wants feeling! From some traits of his character which have lately come to my knowledge, he seems to have been so hackneyed in villainy, and so lost to all sense of honor and shame that while his faculties will enable him to continue his sordid pursuits there will be no time for remorse. . . .

(To Lieutenant Colonel John Laurens,
Hd. Qrs., Passaic Falls, October 13, 1780)

To President Joseph Reed

. . . . Arnold's conduct is so villainously perfidious, that there are no terms that can describe the baseness of his heart. That over-ruling Providence which has so often, and so remarkably interposed in our favor, never manifested itself more conspicuously than in the timely discovery of his horrid design of surrendering the Post and Garrison of West point into the hands of the enemy. I confine my remark to this single Act of perfidy for I am far from thinking he intended to hazard a defeat of this important object by combining another with it, altho' there were circumstances which led to a contrary belief. The confidence, and folly which has marked the subsequent conduct of this man, are of a piece with his villainy; and all three are perfect in their kind. . . .

Over-ruling Providence remarkably interposed in our favor

(Hd. Qrs., Passaic Falls, October 18, 1780)

New York Complaints

. . . . To learn from so good authority as your information, that the distresses of the Citizens of this State are maturing into complaints which are likely to produce serious consequences is a circumstance as necessary to be known as it is unpleasing to hear, and I thank you for the communication. The Committees now forming, are at this crisis, disagreeable things; and if they cannot be counteracted or diverted from their original purposes may outgo the views of the well meaning members of them and plunge this Country into deeper distress and confusion than it has hitherto experienced, though I have no doubt but that the same bountiful Providence which has relieved us in a variety of difficulties heretofore will enable us to emerge from them ultimately, and crown our struggles with success.

Bountiful Providence received in a variety of difficulties

To trace these evils to their sources is by no means difficult; and errors once discovered are more than half corrected. . . .

(To Robert R. Livingston,
New Windsor, January 31, 1781)

To Reverend William Gordon

. . . . I came here the 6th on business and as soon as that business is finished I shall return to my dreary quarters at New Windsor. We have, as you very justly observe, abundant reason to thank providence for its many favourable interpositions in our behalf. It has, at time been my only dependence for all other resources seemed to have fail'd us.

Many favorable interpositions

(Newport, March 9, 1781)

To the Inhabitants of Providence

. . . . The determination you are pleased to express of making every effort for giving vigour to our military operations is consonant with the Spirit that has uniformly actuated this State. It is by this disposition alone we can hope, under the protection of Heaven, to secure the important blessings for which we contend.

Heaven's protection

(Providence, R.I., March 14, 1781)

To Reverend Jacob Johnson

In answer to your request to be appointed Chaplain of the Garrison at Wyoming I have to observe; that there is no provision made by Congress for such an establishment; without which, I should not be at liberty to make any appointment of the kind, however necessary or expedient (in my opinion) or however I might be disposed to give every species of countenance and encouragement to the

Cultivation of Virtue, Morality, and Religion

cultivation of Virtue, Morality and Religion.
(Head Quarters, New Windsor, March 23, 1781)

INTERPOSITIONS OF DIVINE GOVERNMENT

.... We ought not to look back, unless it is to derive useful lessons from past errors, and for the purpose of profiting by dear bought experience. To enveigh against things that are past and irremediable, is unpleasing; but to steer clear of the shelves and rocks we have struck upon, is the part of wisdom, equally incumbent on political, as other men, who have their own little bark, or that of others to navigate through the intricate paths of life, or the trackless Ocean to the haven of secury and rest.

Made more conspicuous

Our affairs are brought to an awful crisis, that the hand of Providence, I trust, may be more conspicuous in our deliverance. The many remarkable interpositions of the divine governmt. in the hours of our deepest distress and darkness, have been too luminous to suffer me to doubt the happy issue of the present contest; but the period for its accomplishmt. may be too far distant for a person of my years, whose Morning and Evening hours, and every moment (unoccupied by business), pants for retirement; and for those domestic and rural enjoyments which in my estimation far surpasses the highest pageantry of this world. . . .

(To Major General John Armstrong, New Windsor, March 26, 1781)

FAST DAY

Strict obedience demanded

Congress having been pleased to set apart and appoint Thursday the 3d. of May next for fasting humiliation and prayer, the General enjoins a strict obedience to it in the Army and calls upon the Chaplains thereof to prepare discourses suitable to the occasion.

All duties of Fatigue are to cease on that day.

(General Orders, Head Quarters, New Windsor, Friday, April 27, 1781)

TO THE CITIZENS AND INHABITANTS OF THE TOWN OF BALTIMORE

Providence aid our united Exertions

.... I most sincerely thank you for your Prayers and good Wishes. May the Author of all Blessing aid our united Exertions in the Cause of Liberty. And may the particular Favor of Heaven rest on you Gentlemen, and the worthy Citizens of this flourishing Town of Baltimore.

(Baltimore, September 8, 1781)

VICTORY AT YORKTOWN

.... Divine Service is to be performed tomorrow in the several Brigades or Divisions.

Astonishing interposition of Providence

The Commander in Chief earnestly recommends that the troops not on duty should universally attend with that seriousness of Deportment and gratitude of Heart which the recognition of such reiterated and astonishing interposition of Providence demand of us.

(General Orders, Head Quarters Before York, Saturday, October 20, 1781)

PROCLAMATION FOR DAY OF FASTING

Interposing Hand of Heaven

I have the Honor to acknowledge the Receipt of your Favor. of the 31st. ulto. covering the Resolutions of Congress of 29th. and a Proclamation for a Day of public Prayer and Thanksgiving; And have to thank you Sir! most sincerely for the very polite and affectionate Manner in which these Inclosures have been conveyed. The Success of the Combined Arms against our Enemies at York and Gloucester, as it affects the Welfare and Independence of the United States, I viewed as a most fortunate Event. In performing my Part towards its Accomplishment, I consider myself to have done only my Duty and in the Execution of that I ever feel myself happy. And at the same time, as it agurs [*sic*] well to our Cause, I take a particular Pleasure in acknowledging, that the interposing Hand of Heaven in the various Instances of our extensive Preparations for this Operation, has been most conspicuous and remarkable. . . .

(To Thomas McKean, Mount Vernon, November 15, 1781)

INHABITANTS OF ALEXANDRIA

Great Director of events

.... The great Director of events has carried us thro' a variety of Scenes during this long and bloody contest in which we have been for Seven Campaigns, most nobly struggling. The present prospect is pleasing, the late success at York Town is very promising, but on our own Improvement depend its future good consequences, a vigorous prosecution of this Success, will in all probability, procure us what we have so long wished to secure, an establishment of Peace, liberty and Independence. A Relaxation of our Exertions at this moment may cost us many more toilsome Campaigns, and be attended with the most unhappy consequences. . . .

(November 19, 1781)

Delusion That War Is Ended

. . . . While I agree in Sentiment with the Honorable Body over whom you preside that we may entertain a rational ground of belief, that under the favor of divine providence the Freedom, Independence and happiness of America will shortly be established upon the surest foundation; I think it a duty incumbent upon me to observe, that those most desirable objects are not to be fully attained but by a continuance of those exertions which have already so greatly humbled the power of our inveterate enemies. Relaxation upon our parts will give them time to recollect and recover themselves, whereas a vigorous prosecution of the War, must inevitably crush their remaining force in these States or put them to the shameful necessity of intirely withdrawing themselves. . . .

Freedom, Independence, and happiness established under favor of divine Providence

(To George Plater and Thomas Cockey Dey, Maryland, Annapolis, November 23, 1781)

To Governor Jonathan Trumbull

. . . . I most earnestly hope that this Event may be productive of the happy Consequences your Excellency mentions, and I think that its good Effects cannot fail to be very extensive, unless from a mistaken Idea of the Magnitude of this Success, unhappily a Spirit of Remissness should seize the Minds of the States, and they should sitt themselves down in quiet, with a Delusive Hope of the Contest being bro't to its Close. I hope this may not be the Case; to prevent so great an Evil, shall be the Study of my Winters Endeavour, and I cannot but flatter myself that the States, rather than relax in their Exertions, will be stimulated to the most vigorous preparations, for another Active, glorious and Decisive Campaign, which if properly prosecuted, will I trust under the Smiles of Heaven, lead us to the End of this long and tedious War, and sitt us Down in the full Security of the great Object of our Toils, the Establishment of Peace, Liberty and Independence.

Properly prosecuted campaign under the Smiles of Heaven will end the war

Whatever may be the Policy of European Courts during this Winter, their Negociations will prove too precarious a Dependence for us to trust to. Our Wisdom should dictate a serious Preparation for War, and in that State we shall find ourselves in a Situation secure against every Event. . . .

(Philadelphia, November 28, 1781)

Circular to the States

. . . . However, at this advanced stage of the War, it might seem to be an insult upon the understanding to suppose a long train of reasoning necessary to prove that a respectable force in the field is essential to the establishment of our liberties and independence; yet as I am apprehensive the prosperous issue of the combined operation in Virginia, may have (as too common in such cases) the pernicious tendency of lulling the Country into a lethargy of inactivity and security; and as I feel my own reputation, as well as the interest, the honor, the glory, and the happiness of my Country intimately concerned in the event, I will ask the indulgence to speak more freely on those accounts, and to make some of those observations, which the present moment seems to suggest; that the broken and perplexed state of the Enemy's affairs, and the successes of the last Campaign on our part, ought to be a powerful incitement to vigorous preparations for the next; that, unless we strenuously exert ourselves to profit by these successes, we shall not only lose all the solid advantages that might be derived from them, but we shall become contemptible in our own eyes, in the eyes of our Enemy, in the opinion of Posterity, and even in the estimation of the whole World; which will consider us as a nation unworthy of Prosperity, because we know not how to make a right use of it; that, altho' we cannot, by the best concerted plans, absolutely command success, altho', the race is not always to the swift, or the Battle to the strong, yet without presumptuously waiting for Miracles to be wrought in our favour, it is our *indispensible Duty*, with the deepest gratitude to Heaven for the past, and humble confidence in its smiles on our future operations, to make use of all the Means in our power for our defence and secu-

Humble confidence in smiles of Heaven on future operations

rity; that this period is particularly important, because no circumstances since the commencement of the War have been so favourable to the recruiting service; and because it is to be presumed from the encrease of population and the brilliant prospects before us, it is actually in our power to complete the Army before the opening of the Campaign; that, however flattering these prospects may be, much still remains to be done, which cannot probably be effected unless the Army is recruited to its establishment; and consequently the continuance or termination of the War seem principally to rest on the vigor and decision of the States in this interesting point. . . .

And soon might that day arrive, soon might we hope to enjoy all the blessings of peace, if we could see again the same animation in the cause of our Country inspire every breast, the same passion for freedom and military glory impel our Youths to the field, and the same disinterested patriotism pervade every rank of Men, as was conspicuous at the commencement of this glorious revolution; and I am persuaded only some great occasion was wanting, such as the present moment exhibits, to rekindle the latent sparks of that patriotic fire into a generous flame, to rouse again the unconquerable Spirit of Liberty, which has sometimes seemed to slumber for a while, into the full vigor of action. . . .

Spirit of Liberty sometimes slumbers

(Head Quarters, Philadelphia, January 31, 1782)

A FAST DAY

The United States in Congress Assembled having been pleased by their Proclamation, dated the 19th March last, to appoint Thursday next the 25th. Instant to be set apart as a day of Fasting, humiliation and Prayr for certain special purposes therein Mentioned: the same is to be Observed accordingly throughout the Army, and the different Chaplains will prepare Discourses Suited to the Several Objects enjoin'd by the said Proclamation.

For certain special purposes

(General Orders, Head Quarters, Newburgh, Monday, April 22, 1782)

TO THE MINISTERS, ELDERS, AND DEACONS OF THE REFORMED DUTCH CHURCH AT ALBANY

Gentlemen: I am extremely happy in this opportunity of blending my public duty with my private satisfaction, by paying a due attention to the Frontiers and advanced Posts of this State, and at the same time visiting this antient and respectable City of Albany.

While I consider the approbation of the Wise and the Virtuous as the highest possible reward for my services, I beg you will be assured, Gentlemen, that I now experience the most sensible pleasure from the favorable sentiments you are pleased to express of my Conduct.

Your benevolent wishes and fervent prayers for my personal wellfare and felicity, demand all my gratitude. May the preservation of your civil and religious Liberties still be the care of an indulgent Providence; and may the rapid increase and universal extension of knowledge virtue and true Religion be the consequence of a speedy and honorable Peace.

Liberties preserved by an indulgent Providence

(Albany, June 28, 1782)

TO THE MAGISTRATES AND MILITARY OFFICERS OF SCHENECTADY

Gentlemen: I request you to accept my warmest thanks for your affectionate address.

In a cause so just and righteous as ours, we have every reason to hope the divine Providence will still continue to crown our Arms with success, and finally compel our Enemies to grant us that Peace upon equitable terms, which we so ardently desire.

Hope in divine Providence to crown Arms with success

May you, and the good People of this Town, in the mean time be protected from every insiduous or open foe, and may the complicated blessings of Peace soon reward your arduous Struggles for the establishment of the freedom and Independence of our common Country.

(Schenectady, June 30, 1782)

TO THE MINISTERS, ELDERS, AND DEACONS OF THE REFORMED DUTCH CHURCH OF SCHENECTADY

Gentlemen: I sincerely thank you for your Congratulations on my arrival in this place.

Whilst I join in adoring that Supreme being to whom alone can be attrebuted the signal successes of our Arms I can not but express gratitude to you, for so distinguished a testemony of your regard.

May the same providence that has hitherto in so

remarkable a manner Evinced the Justice of our Cause, lead us to a speedy and honorable peace; and may its attendant Blessings soon restore this once flourishing Town to its former Prosperity.

May Providence lead to speedy and honorable peace

(Schenectady, June 30, 1782)

To James McHenry

.... At present, we are inveloped in darkness; and no Man, I believe, can foretell all the consequences which will result from the Naval action in the West Indies, to say no worse of it, it is an unfortunate affair, and if the States cannot, or will not rouse to more vigorous exertions, they must submit to the consequences. Providence has done much for us in this contest, but we must do something for ourselves, if we expect to go triumphantly through with it. . . .

God works that we may work

(Philadelphia, July 18, 1782)

To Reverend Samuel Cooper

.... In one Opinion however I am most firmly fixed; that in the present Situation it is our Duty to be preparing in the best manner possible for a Continuance of the War, and to exert our utmost powers to bring to a happy Conclusion, in the Way we have hitherto pursuied it, a Contest in which we have so long been engaged, and in which we have so often, and conspicuously experienced, the Smiles of Heaven, and in this Circumstance, to wait the Issue of Events.

America has so often experienced the favor of Heaven

(Head Quarters, Verplanks Point, September 24, 1782)

Thanksgiving

.... Congress having been pleased to set a part Thursday the 28th, instant as a day of Solemn thanksgiving to god for all his Mercies, The General desires it may be most religiously observed by the army; and that the Chaplains will prepare discourses suitable to the occasion.

Thankful for all His mercies

(General Orders, Head Quarters, Newburgh, Thursday, November 14, 1782)

To the Minister, Elders, and Deacons of the Reformed Protestant Dutch Church of Kingston

Gentlemen: I am happy in receiving this public mark of the esteem of the Minister, Elders and Deacons of the Reformed Protestant Dutch church in Kingston.

Convinced that our Religious Liberties were as essential as our Civil, my endeavours have never been wanting to encourage and promote the one, while I have been contending for the other; and I am highly flattered by finding that my efforts have met the approbation of so respectable a body.

Religious liberties as essential as our civil liberties

In return for your kind concern for my temporal and eternal happiness, permit me to assure you that my wishes are reciprocal; and that you may be enabled to hand down your Religion pure and undefiled to a Posterity worthy of their Ancestors is the fervent prayer of Gentn.

Liberty to hand down to posterity religion pure and undefiled

(Kingston, November 16, 1782)

Divine Service

The New building being so far finished as to admit the troops to attend public worship therein after tomorrow, it is directed that divine Service should be performed there every Sunday by the several Chaplains of the New Windsor Cantonment, in rotation and in order that the different brigades may have an oppertunity of attending at different hours in the same day (when ever the weather and other circumstances will permit which the Brigadiers and Commandants of brigades must determine) the General recommends that the Chaplains should in the first place consult the Commanding officers of their Brigades to know what hour will be most convenient and agreeable for attendance that they will then settle the duty among themselves and report the result to the Brigadiers and Commandants of Brigades who are desired to give notice in their orders and to afford every aid and assistance in their power for the promotion of that public Homage and adoration which are due to the supreme being, who had through his infinite goodness brought our public Calamities and dangers (in all humane probability) very near to a happy conclusion.

God has brought calamities and dangers to a happy conclusion

The General has been surprised to find in Winter

Qrs. that the Chaplains have frequently been almost all absent, at the same time, under an idea their presence could not be of any utility at that season; he thinks it is proper, he should be allowed to judge of that matter himself, and therefore in future no furloughs will be granted to Chaplains except in consequence of permission from Head quarters, and any who may be now absent without such permission are to be ordered by the Commanding officers of their Brigades to join immediately, after which not more than one third of the whole number will be indulged with leave of absence at a time. They are requested to agree among themselves upon the time and length of their furloughs before any application shall be made to Head quarters on the subject.

The Commander in Chief also desires and expects the Chaplains in addition to their public functions will in turn constantly attend the Hospitals and visit the sick, and while they are thus publickly and privately engaged in performing the sacred duties of their office they may depend upon his utmost encouragement and support on all occasions, and that they will be considered in a very respectable point of light by the whole Army.

(General Orders, Head Quarters,
Newburgh, Saturday, February 15, 1783)

Divine Service

In justice to the zeal and ability of the Chaplains, as well as to his own feelings, the Commander in chief thinks it a duty to declare the regularity and decorum with which divine service is now performed every Sunday, will reflect great credit on the army in general, tend to improve the morals, and at the same time, to increase the happiness of the soldiery, and must afford the most pure and rational entertainment for every serious and well disposed mind. . . .

(General Orders, Head Quarters, Newburgh,
Saturday, March 22, 1783)

Peace Rejoicing

The Commander in Chief orders the Cessation of Hostilities between the United States of America and the King of Great Britain to be publickly proclaimed tomorrow at 12 o'clock at the Newbuilding, and that the Proclamation which will be communicated herewith, be read tomorrow evening at the head of every regiment and corps of the army. After which the Chaplains with the several Brigades will render thanks to almighty God for all his mercies, particularly for his over ruling the wrath of man to his own glory, and causing the rage of war to cease amongst the nations.

Over ruling the wrath of man to His own glory

Although the proclamation before alluded to, extends only to the prohibition of hostilities and not to the annunciation of a general peace, yet it must afford the most rational and sincere satisfaction to every benevolent mind, as it puts a period to a long and doubtful contest, stops the effusion of human blood, opens the prospect to a more splendid scene, and like another morning star, promises the approach of a brighter day than hath hitherto illuminated the Western Hemisphere; on such a happy day, a day which is the harbinger of Peace, a day which compleats the eighth year of the war, it would be ingratitude not to rejoice! It would be insensibility not to participate in the general felicity.

The Commander in Chief far from endeavouring to stifle the feelings of Joy in his own bosom, offers his most cordial Congratulations on the occasion to all the Officers of every denomination, to all the Troops of the United States in General, and in particular to those gallant and persevering men who had resolved to defend the rights of their invaded country so long as the war should continue. For these are the men who ought to be considered as the pride and boast of the American Army; And, who crowned with well earned laurels, may soon withdraw from the field of Glory, to the more tranquil walks of civil life.

While the General recollects the almost infinite variety of Scenes thro which we have passed, with a mixture of pleasure, astonishment, and gratitude; While he contemplates the prospects before us with rapture; he can not help wishing that all the brave men (of whatever condition they may be) who have shared in the toils and dangers of effecting this glorious revolution, of rescuing Millions from the hand of oppression, and of laying the foundation of a great Empire, might be impressed with a proper idea of the dignifyed part they have been called to act (under the Smiles of providence) on the stage of human affairs: for, happy, thrice happy shall they be pronounced hereafter, who have contributed any thing, who have performed the meanest office in erecting this steubendous *fabrick of Freedom* and *Empire* on the broad basis of Indipendency; who have assisted in protecting the rights of humane nature and establishing an Asylum for the poor and oppressed of all nations and religions. The glorious task for which we first fleu to Arms being thus accomplished, the liberties of our Country being fully acknowledged, and firmly secured by the smiles of heaven, on the purity of our cause, and the honest exertions of a feeble people (determined to be free) against a powerful Nation (disposed to oppress them) and the Character of those who have persevered, through every extremity of hardship; suffering and danger being immortalized by the illustrious appellation of the *patriot Army*: Nothing now remains but for the actors of this mighty Scene to preserve a perfect, unvarying, consistency of character through the very last act; to close the Drama with applause; and to retire from the Military Theatre with the same approbation of Angells and men which have crowned all their former vertuous Actions. For this purpose no disorder or licentiousness must be tolerated, every considerate and well disposed soldier must remember it will be absolutely necessary to wait with patience untill peace shall be declared or Congress shall be enabled to take proper measures for the security of the public stores &ca.; as soon as these Arrangements shall be made the General is confident there will be no delay in discharging with every mark of distinction and honor all the men enlisted for the war who will then have faithfully performed their engagements with the public. . . .

Purity of cause secures Heaven's favor

(General Orders, Headquarters,
Newburgh, April 18, 1783)

"Foundation of Our Empire"
Washington's Legacy*

Sir: The great object for which I had the honor to hold an appointment in the Service of my Country, being accomplished, I am now preparing to resign it into the hands of Congress, and to return to that domestic retirement, which, it is well known, I left with the greatest reluctance, a Retirement, for which I have never ceased to sigh through a long and painful absence, and in which (remote from the noise and trouble of the World) I meditate to pass the remainder of life in a state of undisturbed repose; But before I carry this resolution into effect, I think it a duty incumbent on me, to make this my last official communication, to congratulate you on the glorious events which Heaven has been pleased to produce in our favor, to offer my sentiments respecting some important subjects which appear to me, to be intimately connected with the tranquility of the United States, to take my leave of your Excellency as a public Character, and to give my final blessing to that Country, in whose service I have spent the prime of my life, for whose sake I have consumed so many anxious days and watchfull nights, and whose happiness being extremely dear to me, will always constitute no inconsiderable part of my own.

Washington's greatness, faith in God's Providence, love of America, and Christianity shown.

Providence produces events in our favor

Impressed with the liveliest sensibility on this pleasing occasion, I will claim the indulgence of dilating the more copiously on the subjects of our mutual felicitation. When we consider the magnitude of the prize we contended for, the doubtful nature of the contest, and the favorable manner in which it has terminated, we shall find the greatest possible reason for gratitude and rejoicing; this is a theme that will afford infinite delight to every benevolent and liberal mind, whether the event in contemplation, be considered as the source of present enjoyment or the parent of future happiness; and we shall have equal occasion to felicitate ourselves on the lot which Providence has assigned us, whether we view it in a natural, a political or moral point of light.

Providence has assigned our lot

The Citizens of America, placed in the most enviable condition, as the sole Lords and Proprietors of a vast Tract of Continent, comprehending all the various soils and climates of the World, and abounding with all the necessaries and conveniencies of life, are now by the late satisfactory pacification, acknowledged to be possessed of absolute freedom and Independency; They are, from this period, to be considered as the Actors on a most conspicuous Theatre, which seems to be peculiarly designated by Providence for the display of human greatness and felicity; Here, they are not only surrounded with every thing which can contribute to the completion of private and domestic enjoyment, but Heaven has crowned all its other blessings, by giving a fairer oppertunity for political happiness, than any other Nation has ever been favored with. Nothing can illustrate these observations more forcibly, than a recollection of the happy conjuncture of times and circumstances under which our Republic assumed its rank among the Nations; The foundation of our Empire was not laid in the

Favored with more political happiness than any other nation

* Verna M. Hall, Compiler

gloomy age of Ignorance and Superstition, but at an Epocha when the rights of mankind were better understood and more clearly defined, than at any former period, the researches of the human mind, after social happiness, have been carried to a great extent, the Treasures of knowledge, acquired by the labours of Philosophers, Sages and Legislatures, through a long succession of years, are laid open for our use, and their collected wisdom may be happily applied in the Establishment of our forms of Government; the free cultivation of Letters, the unbounded extension of Commerce, the progressive refinement of Manners, the growing liberality of sentiment, and above all, the pure and benign light of Revelation, have had a meliorating influence on mankind and increased the blessings of Society. At this auspicious period, the United States came into existence as a Nation, and if their Citizens should not be completely free and happy, the fault will be intirely their own.

Greatest influence—light of Revelation

Such is our situation, and such are our prospects: but notwithstanding the cup of blessing is thus reached out to us, notwithstanding happiness is ours, if we have a disposition to seize the occasion and make it our own; yet, it appears to me there is an option still left to the United States of America, that it is in their choice, and depends upon their conduct, whether they will be respectable and prosperous, or contemptable and miserable as a Nation; This is the time of their political probation, this is the moment when the eyes of the whole World are turned upon them, this is the moment to establish or ruin their national Character forever, this is the favorable moment to give such a tone to our Federal Government, as will enable it to answer the ends of its institution, or this may be the ill-fated moment for relaxing the powers of the Union, annihilating the cement of the Confederation, and exposing us to become the sport of European politics, which may play one State against another to prevent their growing importance, and to serve their own interested purposes. For, according to the system of Policy the States shall adopt at this moment, they will stand or fall, and by their confirmation or lapse, it is yet to be decided, whether the Revolution must ultimately be considered as a blessing or a curse: a blessing or a curse, not to the present age alone, for with our fate will the destiny of unborn Millions be involved.

With this conviction of the importance of the present Crisis, silence in me would be a crime; I will therefore speak to your Excellency, the language of freedom and of sincerity, without disguise; I am aware, however, that those who differ from me in political sentiment, may perhaps remark, I am stepping out of the proper line of my duty, and they may possibly ascribe to arrogance or ostentation, what I know is alone the result of the purest intention, but the rectitude of my own heart, which disdains such unworthy motive, the part I have hitherto acted in life, the determination I have formed, of not taking any share in public business hereafter, the ardent desire I feel, and shall continue to manifest, of quietly enjoying in private life, after all the toils of War, the benefits of a wise and liberal Government, will, I flatter myself, sooner or later convince my Countrymen, that I could have no sinister views in delivering with so little reserve, the opinions contained in this Address.

There are four things, which I humbly conceive, are essential to the well being, I may even venture to say, to the existence of the United States as an Independent Power:

1st. An indissoluble union of the States under one Federal Head.

2dly. A Sacred regard to Public Justice.

3dly. The adoption of a proper Peace Establishment, and

4thly. The prevalence of that pacific and friendly Disposition, among the People of the United States, which will induce them to forget their local prejudices and policies, to make those mutual concessions which are requisite to the general prosperity, and in some instances, to sacrifice their individual advantages to the interest of the Community.

These are the Pillars on which the glorious Fabrick of our Independency and National Character must be supported; Liberty is the Basis, and whoever would dare to sap the foundation, or overturn the Structure, under whatever specious pretexts he may attempt it, will merit the bitterest execration, and the severest punishment which can be inflicted by his injured Country. . . .

It remains then to be my final and only request, that your Excellency will communicate these sentiments to your Legislature at their next meeting, and that they may be considered as the Legacy of One, who has ardently wished, on all occasions, to be useful to his Country, and who, even in the shade of Retirement, will not fail to implore the divine benediction upon it.

I now make it my earnest prayer, that God would have you, and the State over which you preside, in his holy protection, that he would incline the hearts of the Citizens to cultivate a spirit of subordination and obedience to Government, to entertain a brotherly affection and love for one another, for their fellow Citizens of the United States at large, and particularly for their brethren who have served in the Field, and finally, that he would most graciously be pleased to dispose us all, to do Justice, to love mercy, and to demean ourselves with that Charity, humility and pacific temper of mind, which were the Characteristicks of the Divine Author of our blessed Religion, and without an humble imitation of whose example in these things, we can never hope to be a happy Nation.

Character for a Christian Republic

(Circular to the States, Head Quarters, Newburgh, June 8, 1783)

Presenting Soldiers the Aitken Bible

Dear Sir: I accept, with much pleasure your kind Congratulations on the happy Event of Peace, with the Establishment of our Liberties and Independence.

Glorious indeed has been our Contest: glorious, if we consider the Prize for which we have contended, and glorious in its Issue; but in the midst of our Joys, I hope we shall not forget that, to divine Providence is to be ascribed the Glory and Praise.

Glory of America's peace, liberties and independence ascribed to Providence

Your proposition respecting Mr. Aikins Bibles would have been particularly noticed by me, had it been suggested in Season; but the late Resolution of Congress for discharging Part of the Army, takg off near two thirds of our Numbers, it is now too late to make the Attempt. It would have pleased me, if Congress should have made such an important present, to the brave fellows, who have done so much for the Security of their Country's Rights and Establishment.

I hope it will not be long before you will be able to go peaceably to N York; some patience however will yet be necessary; but Patience is a noble Virtue, and when rightly exercised, does not fail of its Reward.

(To Reverend John Rodgers, Head Quarters, June 11, 1783)

To George William Fairfax

. . . . I unite my prayers most fervently with yours, for Wisdom to these U States and have no doubt, after a little while all errors in the present form of their Government will be corrected and a happy temper be diffused through the whole; but like young heirs come a little prematurely perhaps to a large Inheritance it is more than probable they will riot for a while; but, in this, if it should happen tho' it is a circumste wch is to be lamented (as I would have the National character of America be pure and immaculate) will work its own cure, as there is virtue at the bottom. . . .

National character of America

(State of New York, July 10, 1783)

To the Magistrates and Supervisors of Tryon County

. . . . In the course of my tour thro a small part of this County I have had an opportunity of observing more particularly the severe distress that has fallen on the Inhabitants by the cruel devastations of the Enemy; the patience and fortitude with which they have borne these distresses, and their very spirited conduct throughout the whole of the War have done them the highest honor, and will give the Inhabitants of Tryon Co. a distinguished place in the History of this revolution.

Accept Gentlemen my thanks for your kind wishes for my welfare be assured it will be my earnest prayer that by the blessing of Providence on the fine Country you possess you may soon be enabled to recover your former ease, and to enjoy that happiness you have so well deserved.

Blessings of Providence enable recovery from war

(August 1, 1783)

To the Massachusetts Senate and House of Representatives

Gentlemen: The Address of so respectable a Body as the Senate and House of Representatives of the Commonwealth of Massachusetts, congratulating me on so auspicious an Event as the Return of Peace, cannot fail to affect me with the highest pleasure and gratification.

Be assured Gentlemen, that, through the many and complicated vicissitudes of an arduous Conflict, I have ever turned my Eye, with a fixed Confidence on that superintendg. Providence which governs all Events; and the lively Gratitude I now feel, at the happy termination of our Contest, is beyond my Expression.

Superintending Providence governs all events

If, dependg on the Guidance of the same Allwise Providence, I have performed my part in this great Revolution, to the acceptance of my fellow Citizens, It is a source of high satisfaction to me; and forms an additional Motive of Praise to that Infinite Wisdom, which directs the Minds of Men. This Consideration will attend me in the Shades of retirement, and furnish one of the most pleasing Themes of my Meditation.

All-wise Providence directs the minds of men

So great a revolution as this Country now experiences, doubtless ranks high in the Scale of human Events, and in the Eye of Omnipotence is introductive to some noble Scenes of future Grandeur to this happy fated Continent. May the States have Wisdom to discern their true Interests at this important period!

Impressed with sentiments of Gratitude for your benevolent Expressions for my personal Happiness and prosperity, I can make you no better return, than to pray, that Heaven, from the Stores of its Munificence, may shower its choisest blessings on you Gentlemen, and the People of the Commonwealth of Massachusetts, and to entreat that Our Liberties, now so happily established, may be continued in perfect Security, to the latest posterity.

(Head Quarters, August 10, 1783)

To the Inhabitants of Princeton and Neighborhood, Together with the President and Faculty of the College

Gentlemen: I receive with the utmost satisfaction and acknowledge with great sensibility your kind congratulations.

The prosperous situation of our public affairs, the flourishing state of this place and the revival of the Seat of Literature from the ravages of War, encrease to the highest degree, the pleasure I feel *in visiting* (at the return of Peace) the scene of our important military transactions, and *in recollecting* the period when the tide of adversity began to turn, and better fortune to smile upon us.

If in the execution of an arduous Office I have been so happy as to discharge my duty to the Public with fidelity and success, and to obtain the good opinion of my fellow Soldiers and fellow Citizens; I attribute all the glory to that Supreme Being, who hath caused the several parts, which have been employed in the production of the wonderful Events we now contemplate, to harmonize in the most perfect manner, and who was able by the humblest instruments as well as by the most powerful means to establish and secure the liberty and happiness of these United States.

All glory to that Supreme Being

By humblest instruments to establish and secure liberty

I now return you Gentlemen my thanks for your benevolent wishes, and make it my earnest prayer to Heaven, that every temporal and divine blessing may be bestowed on the Inhabitants of Princeton, on the neighbourhood, and on the President and Faculty of the College of New Jersey, and that the usefulness of this Institution in promoting the interests of Religion and Learning may be universally extended.

Promote interests of religion and learning

(Rocky Hill, August 25, 1783)

President of Continental Congress to General George Washington

Sir, Congress feel a particular pleasure in seeing your Excellency, and in congratulating you on the success of a war, in which you have acted so conspicuous a part.

It has been the singular happiness of the United States, that, during a war so long, so dangerous, and so important, Providence has been graciously pleased to preserve the life of a general, who has merited and possessed the uninterrupted confidence and affection of his fellow-citizens. In other nations many have performed services, for which they have deserved and received the thanks of the public. But to you, sir, peculiar praise is due. Your services have been essential in acquiring and establishing the freedom and independence of your country. They deserve the grateful acknowledgments of a free and independent nation. Those acknowledgments, Congress have the satisfaction of expressing to your Excellency.

Washington providentially preserved for America's independence

Hostilities have now ceased, but your country still needs your services. She wishes to avail herself of your talents in forming the arrangements that will be necessary for her in the time of peace. For this reason your attendance at Congress has been requested. A committee is appointed to confer with your Excellency, and to receive your assistance in preparing and digesting plans relative to those important objects.

(Princeton, August 26, 1783)

COURTESY OF YALE UNIVERSITY ART GALLERY

RESIGNATION OF GENERAL WASHINGTON, December 23, 1783
by John Trumbull

Answer to Congress

Mr. President: I am too sensible of the honorable reception I have now experienced not to be penetrated with the deepest feelings of gratitude.

Notwithstanding Congress appear to estimate the value of my life beyond any Services I have been able to render the U States, yet I must be permitted to consider the Wisdom and Unanimity of our National Councils, the firmness of our Citizens, and the patience and Bravery of our Troops, which have produced so happy a termination of the War, as the most conspicuous effect of the divine interposition, and the surest presage of our future happiness.

Most conspicuous effect of divine interposition

Highly gratified by the favorable sentiments which Congress are pleased to express of my past conduct, and amply rewarded by the confidence and affection of my fellow Citizens, I cannot hesitate to contribute my best endeavours, towards the establishment of the National security, in whatever manner the Sovereign Power may think proper to direct, until the ratification of the Definitive Treaty of Peace, or the final evacuation of our Country by the British Forces; after either of which events, I shall ask permission to retire to the peaceful shade of private life.

Whatever manner the Sovereign Power may think proper to direct

Perhaps, Sir, No occasion may offer more suitable than the present, to express my humble thanks to God, and my grateful acknowledgements to my Country, for the great and uniform support I have received in every vicissitude of Fortune, and for the many distinguished honors which Congress have been pleased to confer upon me in the course of the War.

Humble thanks to God for support and honors

(Princeton, August 26, 1783)

Workings of Providence

. . . . New York is not evacuated, nor is the Definitive Treaty arrived. Upon the happening of either of these events, I shall bid a final adieu to a military life, and in the shade of retirement ruminate on the marvellous scenes that are passed; and in contemplating the wonderful workings of that Providence which has raised up so many instruments, and such powerful Engines (among which your nation stands first) to over throw the British pride and power, by so great a revolution. . . .

(To Duc de Lauzun, Princeton, October 15, 1783)

Farewell Orders to the Armies of the United States

The United States in Congress assembled after giving the most honorable testimony to the merits of the fœderal Armies, and presenting them with the thanks of their Country for their long, eminent, and faithful services, having thought proper by their proclamation bearing date the 18th. day of October last, to discharge such part of the Troops as were engaged for the war, and to permit the Officers on furlough to retire from service from and after tomorrow; which proclamation having been communicated in the publick papers for the information and government of all concerned; it only remains for the Comdr in Chief to address himself once more, and that for the last time, to the Armies of the U States (however widely dispersed the individuals who compose them may be) and to bid them an affectionate, a long farewell. . . .

A contemplation of the compleat attainment (at a period earlier than could have been expected) of the object for which we contended against so formidable a power cannot but inspire us with astonishment and gratitude. The disadvantageous circumstances on our part, under which the war was undertaken, can never be forgotten. The singular interpositions of Providence in our feeble condition were such, as could scarcely escape the attention of the most unobserving; while the un-paralleled perseverence of the Armies of the U States, through almost every possible suffering and discouragement for the space of eight long years, was little short of a standing miracle.

Perseverence of the armies . . . little short of a standing miracle

It is not the meaning nor within the compass of this address to detail the hardships peculiarly incident to our service, or to describe the distresses, which in several instances have resulted from the extremes of hunger and nakedness, combined with the rigours of an inclement season; nor is it necessary to dwell on the dark side of our past affairs. Every American Officer and Soldier must now console himself for any unpleasant circumstances which may have occurred by a recollection of the uncommon scenes in which he has been called to Act no inglorious part, and the astonishing events of which he

Astonishing events

has been a witness, events which have seldom if ever before taken place on the stage of human action, nor can they probably ever happen again. For who has before seen a disciplined Army form'd at once from such raw materials? Who, that was not a witness, could imagine that the most violent local prejudices would cease so soon, and that Men who came from the different parts of the Continent, strongly disposed, by the habits of education, to despise and quarrel with each other, would instantly become but one patriotic band of Brothers, or who, that was not on the spot, can trace the steps by which such a wonderful revolution has been effected, and such a glorious period put to all our warlike toils?...

Disciplined army

Patriotic unity and union

...To the various branches of the Army the General takes this last and solemn opportunity of professing his inviolable attachment and friendship. He wishes more than bare professions were in his power, that he were really able to be useful to them all in future life. He flatters himself however, they will do him the justice to believe, that whatever could with propriety be attempted by him has been done, and being now to conclude these his last public Orders, to take his ultimate leave in a short time of the military character, and to bid a final adieu to the Armies he has so long had the honor to Command, he can only again offer in their behalf his recommendations to their grateful country, and his prayers to the God of Armies. May ample justice be done them here, and may the choicest of heaven's favours, both here and hereafter, attend those who, under the devine auspices, have secured innumerable blessings for others; with these wishes, and this benediction, the Commander in Chief is about to retire from Service. The Curtain of seperation will soon be drawn, and the military scene to him will be closed for ever.

Under divine auspices secured innumerable blessings for others

(Rock Hill, near Princeton, November 2, 1783)

To the Officers of the Somerset County Militia

.... I now bid you Gentlemen a long farewell in the fullest confidence that Men who have so bravely defended their Country, will likewise in their peaceable retirements contribute their best endeavours to confirm and perpetuate that happy Union of the States and its Citizens which under Providence has so visibly been the means of our deliverance and Independance.

Providence effected Union, the means of deliverance and Independence

(Somerset, November 7, 1783)

To the Minister, Elders, and Deacons of the Two United Dutch Reformed Churches of Hackensack and Schalenburgh and the Inhabitants of Hackensack

.... Having shared in common, the hardships and dangers of the War with my virtuous fellow Citizens in the field, as well as with those who on the Lines have been immediately exposed to the Arts and Arms of the Enemy, I feel the most lively sentiments of gratitude to that divine Providence which has graciously interposed for the protection of our Civil and Religious Liberties.

Interposed for protection of liberties

In retireing from the field of Contest to the sweets of private life, I claim no merit, but if in that retirement my most earnest wishes and prayers can be of any avail, nothing will exceed the prosperity of our common Country, and the temporal and spiritual felicity of those who are represented in your Address.

(November 10, 1783)

To the Ministers, Elders, Deacons, and Members of the Reformed German Congregation of New York

.... Disposed, at every suitable opportunity to acknowledge publicly our infinite obligations to the Supreme Ruler of the Universe for rescuing our Country from the brink of destruction; I cannot fail at this time to ascribe all the honor of our late successes to the same glorious Being. And if my humble exertions have been made in any degree subservient to the execution of the divine purposes, a contemplation of the benediction of Heaven on our righteous Cause, the approbation of my virtuous Countrymen, and the testimony of my own Conscience, will be a sufficient reward and augment my felicity beyond anything which the world can bestow.

All honor to God for rescuing country from destruction

Exertions made subservient to execution of the divine purposes

The establishment of Civil and Religious Liberty was the Motive which induced me to the Field; the object is attained, and it now remains to be my earnest wish and prayer, that the Citizens of the United States would make a wise and virtu-

Motive which induced Washington to the field of arms

ous use of the blessings, placed before them; and that the reformed german Congregation in New York; may not only be conspicuous for their religious character, but as examplary, in support of our inestimable acquisitions, as their reverend Minister has been in the attainment of them.

(New York, November 27, 1783)

To the Freeholders and Inhabitants of Kings County

Gentlemen: While you speak the language of my heart, in acknowledging the magnitude of our obligations to the Supreme Director of all human events; suffer me to join you in celebration of the present glorious and ever memorable Æra, and to return my best thanks for your kind expressions in my favour.

Supreme Director of all human events

I cannot but rejoice sincerely that the national dignity and glory will be greatly encreased, in consequence of the good order and regularity which have prevailed universally since the City of New York has been repossessed by us; this conduct exhibits to the world a noble instance of magnanimity and will doubtless convince any who from ignorance or prejudice may have been of a different sentiment; that the Laws do govern, and that the Civil Magistrates are worthy of the highest respect and confidence.

For my own part, Gentlemen, in whatever situation I shall be hereafter, my supplications, will ever ascend to Heaven, for the prosperity of my Country in general; and for the individual happiness of those who are attached to the Freedom, and Independence of America.

(New York, December 1, 1783)

To the Legislature of New Jersey

Gentlemen: I want Words to express the heartfelt pleasure I experience on receiving the congratulation and plaudit of so respectable a Body, as the Legislature of the State of New Jersey. I cannot however suppress the effusions of my gratitude for their flattering allusion to an event which hath signalized the name of Trenton; for the delicate manner of their recalling to mind none but grateful ideas; as well as for all their former assistance at the period of our deepest distress.

I am heartily disposed to join with you, Gentlemen, in adoration to that all-wise and most gracious Providence which hath so conspicuously interposed in the direction of our public affairs and the establishment of our national Independence.

Interposition in direction of public affairs and establishment of national Independence

The faithful page of History, will I doubt not, record all the patriotic sufferings and meritorious Services of the gallant little Army I have had the honor to command; nor, (if my testimony and the voice of truth can avail anything), shall the efficacious exertions of the State of New Jersey, or the almost unrivalled bravery of its Militia ever be forgotten. Let the fact be made known to the whole world, let it be remembered forever as an example to succeeding Ages, that, after a large extent of Country had been overrun by a formidable Enemy, and thousands of Citizens driven from their possessions; the virtuous freedom of New Jersey, recovering from the temporary shock, stung by the remembrance of what their wives, their children and Friends had already suffered, by the thought of losing all they yet held dear and sacred, animated by an enthusiastic hope of success, and buoyed, by a reliance on the aid of Heaven, above the fear of danger and death itself then began to stem the tide of adversity; and, in concert with our other force, recoiling like an impetuous torrent on our lately victorious foes, confined them within narrow limits 'till compelled to take their final departure from the State. For me, it is enough to have seen the divine Arm visibly outstretched for our deliverance, and to have recd the approbation of my Country, and my Conscience on account of my humble instrumentality in carrying the designs of Providence into effect; but for my gallant Associates in the Field, who have so essentially contributed to the establishment of our Independence and national glory, no rewards can be too great.

Buoyed by a reliance on the aid of Heaven

Divine Arm visibly outstretched for our deliverance

Carrying the designs of Providence into effect

I am now to bid you a long farewell, and to recommend, you Gentlemen, and the State whose wellfare you are appointed to superintend, to the indulgent care of Heaven. May unanimity and wisdom ever prevail in your public Councils! May Justice and liberality distinguish the Administration of your Government! and may the Citizens of New Jersey be completely happy in the practice of Industry œconomy and every private Virtue.

([Trenton], December 6, 1783)

To the General Assembly of Pennsylvania

. . . . A sense of duty impelled me to contribute, whatever my Sword or my Pen could effect, towards the establishment of our Freedom and Independence. The smiles of Providence on the United exertions of my fellow Citizens have compleated our successes, and it remains to be my first and most earnest desire that the United States may profit by the happy occasion and preserve by wisdom and justice that liberty and honor they have so nobly maintained by Arms. . . .

Smiles of Providence upon United exertions

(December 9, 1783)

To the Militia Officers of the City and Liberties of Philadelphia

. . . . It would have been a proof of the want of Patriotism and every social Virtue not to have assumed the character of a Soldier when the exigency of the Public demanded, or not to have returned to the Class of Citizens when the necessity of farther Service ceased to exist. I can therefore claim no merit beyond that of having done my duty with fidelity.

While the various Scenes of the War, in which I have experienced the timely aid of the Militia of Philadelphia, recur to my mind, my ardent prayer ascends to Heaven that they may long enjoy the blessings of that Peace which has been obtained by the divine benediction on our common exertions.

Peace: divine benediction on our common exertions

(Philadelphia,
December 12, 1783)

To the Magistrates of the City and County of Philadelphia

. . . . Nothing could have been more proper on this occasion than to attribute our glorious successes in the manner you have done, to the bravery of our Troops, the assistance of our Ally and the interposition of Providence. Having by such means acquired the inestimable blessings of Peace Liberty and Independence; the preservation of these important acquisitions must now, in a great measure, be committed to an able and faithful Magistracy. . . .

(Philadelphia,
December 13, 1783)

To the Trustees and Faculty of the University of the State of Pennsylvania

. . . . Desirous of being considered the friend, and (as far as consists with my abilities), The Patron of the Arts and Sciences; I must take the liberty of expressing my sense of the obligations I am under to the Trustees and Faculty of the University of Pennsylvania for paying me so flattering a Compliment, and on so pleasing a subject.*

I accept, Gentlemen, the honors you have had the goodness to confer upon me, with the greatest deference and respect.

May the Revolution prove extensively propitious to the cause of Literature; may the tender plants of Science which are cultivated by your assiduous care under the fostering influence of Heaven, soon arrive at an uncommon point of maturity and perfection, and may this University long continue to diffuse throughout an enlightened Empire, all the blessing of virtue, learning and urbanity.

Cultivate Science under the fostering influence of Heaven

(Philadelphia, December 13, 1783)

To the Learned Professions of Philadelphia

. . . . Conscious of no impropriety in wishing to merit the esteem of my fellow Citizens in general; I cannot hesitate to acknowledge that I feel a certain pleasing sensation in obtaining the good opinion of men eminent for their virtue, knowledge and humanity; but I am sensible at the same time, it becomes me to receive with humility the warm commendations you are pleased to bestow on my conduct: for if I have been led to detest the folly and madness of unbounded ambition, if I have been induced from other motives to draw my sword and regulate my public behaviour, or if the management of the War has been conducted upon purer principles: let me not arrogate the merit to human imbecility, but rather ascribe whatever glory may result from our successful struggle to a higher and more efficient Cause. For the re-establishment of our once violated rights; for the confirmation of our Independence; for the protection of Virtue, Philosophy and Literature: for the present flourishing state of the Sciences, and for the en-

Glory to a higher and more efficient Cause

* The degree of doctor of laws from the University of Pennsylvania. (*Fitzpatrick*)

larged prospect of human happiness, it is our common duty to pay the tribute of gratitude to the greatest and best of Beings. . . .

(Philadelphia, December 13, 1783)

To the American Philosophical Society

Gentlemen: While you recall to my mind the honor formerly done me by enrolling my name in the List of the Members of your Society, you greatly heighten the pleasure of your present congratulations.

For if I know my own inclination, it is to be the friend and associate to men of Virtue and philosophical knowledge; or if I have a wish ungratified, it is that the Arts and Sciences may continue to flourish with encreasing lustre.

In the philosophic retreat to which I am retiring, I shall often contemplate with pleasure the extensive utility of your Institution. The field of investigation is ample, the benefits which will result to Human Society from discoveries yet to be made, are indubitable, and the task of studying the works of the great Creator, inexpressibly delightful.

Studying the works of the great Creator inexpressibly delightful

(Philadelphia, December 13, 1783)

To the Burgesses and Common Council of the Borough of Wilmington

. . . . Altho' the prospect of our public affairs has been sometimes gloomy indeed; yet the well-known firmness of my Countrymen, and the expected aid of Heaven, supported me in the trying hour, and have finally reallised our most sanguine wishes. . . .

Expected aid of Heaven

(Wilmington, December 16, 1783)

To the Mayor, Recorder, Aldermen, and Common Council of Annapolis

. . . . If my Conduct throughout the War has merited the confidence of my fellow Citizens, and has been instrumental in obtaining for my Country the blessings of Peace and Freedom, I owe it to that Supreme being who guides the hearts of all; who has so signally interposed his aid in every Stage of the Contest and who has graciously been pleased to bestow on me the greatest of Earthly rewards: *the approbation and affections of a free people.*

Guides the hearts of all and interposes his aid

Tho' I retire from the employments of public life I shall never cease to entertain the most anxious care for the welfare of my Country. May the Almighty dispose the heart of every Citizen of the United States to improve the great prospect of happiness before us, and may you Gentlemen, and the Inhabitants of this City long enjoy every felicity, this World can Afford.

Disposes the heart

(December 22, 1783)

Address to Congress on Resigning His Commission

Mr. President: The great events on which my resignation depended having at length taken place; I have now the honor of offering my sincere Congratulations to Congress and of presenting myself before them to surrender into their hands the trust committed to me, and to claim the indulgence of retiring from the Service of my Country.

Happy in the confirmation of our Independence and Sovereignty, and pleased with the oppertunity afforded the United States of becoming a respectable Nation, I resign with satisfaction the Appointment I accepted with diffidence. A diffidence in my abilities to accomplish so arduous a task, which however was superseded by a confidence in the rectitude of our Cause, the support of the Supreme Power of the Union, and the patronage of Heaven.

Patronage of Heaven

The Successful termination of the War has verified the most sanguine expectations, and my gratitude for the interposition of Providence, and the assistance I have received from my Countrymen, encreases with every review of the momentous Contest.

Gratitude for the interposition of Providence

While I repeat my obligations to the Army in general, I should do injustice to my own feelings not to acknowledge in this place the peculiar Services and distinguished merits of the Gentlemen who have been attached to my person during the War. It was impossible the choice of confidential Officers to compose my family should have been more fortunate. Permit me Sir, to recommend in particular those, who have continued in Service to the present moment, as worthy of the favorable notice and patronage of Congress.

I consider it an indispensable duty to close this last solemn act of my Official life, by commending the Interests of our dearest Country to the protection of Almighty God, and those who have the superintendence of them, to his holy keeping.

Commends nation to protection and keeping of Almighty God

Having now finished the work assigned me, I retire from the great theatre of Action; and bidding an Affectionate farewell to this August body under whose orders I have so long acted, I here offer my Commission, and take my leave of all the employments of public life.

(Annapolis, December 23, 1783)

The President of Congress Answers General George Washington

Journals of the Continental Congress, Vol. xxv, 1783, p. 838

Sir, The United States in Congress assembled receive with emotions, too affecting for utterance, the solemn resignation of the authorities under which you have led their troops with success through a perilous and a doubtful war. Called upon by your country to defend its invaded rights, you accepted the sacred charge, before it had formed alliances, and whilst it was without funds or a government to support you. You have conducted the great military contest with wisdom and fortitude, invariably regarding the rights of the civil power through all disasters and changes. You have, by the love and confidence of your fellow-citizens, enabled them to display their martial genius, and transmit their fame to posterity. You have persevered, till these United States, aided by a magnanimous king and nation, have been enabled, under a just Providence, to close the war in freedom, safety and independence; on which happy event we sincerely join you in congratulations.

Defense of invaded rights a sacred charge

Enabled under a just Providence to close war in freedom, safety and independence

Having defended the standard of liberty in this new world: having taught a lesson useful to those who inflict and to those who feel oppression, you retire from the great theatre of action, with the blessings of your fellow-citizens, but the glory of your virtues will not terminate with your military command, it will continue to animate remotest ages.

We feel with you our obligations to the army in general; and will particularly charge ourselves with the interests of those confidential officers, who have attended your person to this affecting moment.

We join you in commending the interests of our dearest country to the protection of Almighty God, beseeching him to dispose the hearts and minds of its citizens, to improve the opportunity afforded them, of becoming a happy and respectable nation. And for you we address to him our earnest prayers, that a life so beloved may be fostered with all his care; that your days may be happy as they have been illustrious; and that he will finally give you that reward which this world cannot give.

(Annapolis, December 23, 1783)

To the Mayor and Commonalty of Fredericksburg

. . . . To a beneficent Providence, and to the fortitude of a brave and virtuous Army, supported by the general exertion of our common Country I stand indebted for the plaudits you now bestow; The reflection however, of having met the congratulating smiles and approbation of my fellow-Citizens for the part I have acted in the cause of liberty and Independence cannot fail of adding pleasure to the sweets of domestic life; and my sensibility of them is heightened by their coming from the respectable Inhabitants of the place of my growing Infancy and the honorable mention wch. is made of my revered Mother; by whose Maternal hand (early deprived of a Father) I was led from Childhood.

Indebted to a beneficent Providence

For the expressions of personal Affection and attachment, and for your kind wishes for my future welfare, I offer grateful thanks and my sincere prayers for the happiness and prosperity of the Corporate Town of Fredericksburgh.

(Fredericksburg, February 14, 1784)

To Major General Henry Knox

. . . . I am just beginning to experience that ease, and freedom from public cares which, however desirable, takes some time to realize; for strange as it may tell, it is nevertheless true, that it was not 'till lately I could get the better of my usual custom of ruminating as soon as I waked in the Morning, on the business of the ensuing day; and of my surprize, after having revolved many things in my mind, to find that I was no longer a public Man, or had any thing to do with public transactions.

I feel now, however, as I conceive a wearied Traveller must do, who, after treading many a painful step, with a heavy burden on his shoulders, is eased of the latter, having reached the Goal to which all the former were directed; and from his House top is looking back, and tracing with a grateful eye the

Meanders by which he escaped the quicksands and Mires which lay in his way; and into which none but the All-powerful guide, and great disposer of human Events could have prevented his falling. . . .

The all-powerful guide and great disposer of human events prevented his falling

(Mount Vernon, February 20, 1784)

VESTRYMAN

Dr. Sir: It is not convenient for me to be at Colchester tomorrow, and as I shall no longer act as a vestryman [of Truro Parish, Va.], the sooner my place is filled with another the better. This letter, or something more formal if required, may evidence my resignation, and authorize a new choice.

I shall be very sorry if your apprehensions on account of the poor should be realized, but have not the Church-Wardens power to provide for their relief? And may not those Vestrymen who do meet, supposing the number insufficient to constitute a *legal* Vestry, express their sentiments on this head to the Wardens? Nay go further, and from the exigency of the case, give directions for the temporary relief of the needy and distressed. As a Vestryman or as a private parishioner, I should have no scruple to do either under such circumstances as you have described.

Relief of needy and distressed

(To Daniel McCarty, Mount Vernon, February 22, 1784)

LAND FOR LEASE

. . . . It has been my intention in every thing I have said, and will be so in every thing I shall say on this subject, to be perfectly candid; for my feelings would be as much hurt, if I shou'd deceive others by a too favourable description, as theirs would be who might suffer by the deception.

I will only add, that it would give me pleasure to see these Lands seated by particular Societies, or religious Sectaries with their Pastors. It would be a means of connecting friends in a small circle, and making life, in a new and rising Empire (to the Inhabitants of which, and their habits new comers would be strangers) pass much more agreeably, than in a mixed, or dispersed situation. . . .

Lands seated by particular Societies or religious Sectaries with their Pastors

(To John Witherspoon, Mount Vernon, March 10, 1784)

INDENTURED SERVANTS

Dear Sir: I am informed that a Ship with Palatines is gone up to Baltimore, among whom are a number of Trademen. I am a good deal in want of a House Joiner and Bricklayer, (who really understand their profession) and you would do me a favor by purchasing one of each, for me. I would not confine you to Palatines. If they are good workmen, they may be of Asia, Africa, or Europe. They may be Mahometans, Jews or Christian of an Sect, or they may be Atheists. I would however prefer middle aged, to young men. and those who have good countenances and good characters on ship board, to others who have neither of these to recommend them, altho, after all, the proof of the pudding must be in the eating. . . .

Workmen of good character preferred over other considerations

(To Tench Tilghman, Mount Vernon, March 24, 1784)

OBJECTIONS TO MEMOIRS

. . . . I will frankly declare to you, My Dr. Doctor that any memoirs of my life, distinct and unconnected with the general history of the war, would rather hurt my feelings than tickle my pride whilst I lived. I had rather glide gently down the stream of life, leaving it to posterity to think and say what they please of me, than by any act of mine to have vanity or ostentation imputed to me. And I will further more confess that I was rather surprised into a consent, when Doctr. Witherspoon (very unexpectedly) made the application, than considered the tendency of that consent. It did not occur to me at that moment, from the manner in which the question was propounded, that no history of my life, without a very great deal of trouble indeed, could be written with the least degree of accuracy, unless recourse was had to me, or to my papers for information; that it would not derive sufficient authenticity without a promulgation of this fact; and that such a promulgation would subject me to the imputation I have just mentioned, which would hurt me the more, as I do not think vanity is a trait of my character.

Vanity is not a trait of his character

It is for this reason, and candour obliges me to be explicit, that I shall stipulate against the publication of the memoirs Mr. Bowie has in contemplation to give the world, 'till I shou'd see more probability of avoiding the darts which *I think* would be pointed at me on such an occasion; and how far, under these

Mellon Collection, National Gallery of Art, Washington
Photo © Board of Trustees

by Edward Savage, 1796

The Washington Family

circumstances, it wou'd be worth Mr. Bowie's while to spend time which might be more usefully employed in other matters, is with him to consider; as the practicability of doing it efficiently, without having free access to the documents of this War, which must fill the most important pages of the Memoir, and which for the reasons already assigned cannot be admitted at present, also is. If nothing happens more than I at present foresee, I shall be in Philadelphia on or before the first of May; where 'tis probable I may see Mr. Bowie and converse further with him on this subject; in the mean while I will thank you for communicating these Sentiments.

(To Doctor James Craik, Mount Vernon, March 25, 1784)

Legislative Sessions

.... Annual Sessions would always produce a full representation, and alertness at business. The Delegates, after a recess of 8 or 10 Months would meet each other with glad Countenances; they would be complaisant; they would yield to each other as much as the duty they owed their constituents would permit; and they would have oppertunities of becoming better acquainted with the Sentiments of them and removing their prejudices, during the recess. Men who are always together get tired of each others Company; they throw off the proper restraint; they say and do things which are personally disgusting; this begets opposition; opposition begets faction; and so it goes on till business is impeded, often at a stand. I am sure (having the business prepared by proper Boards or a Committee) an Annual Session of two Months would dispatch more business than is now done in twelve; and this by a full representation of the Union. . . .

Annual Sessions of two months

(To Thomas Jefferson, Mount Vernon, March 29, 1784)

To Marchioness de Lafayette

.... From the clangor of arms and the bustle of a camp, freed from the cares of public employment, and the responsibility of office, I am now enjoying domestic ease under the shadow of my own Vine, and my own Fig tree; and in a small Villa, with the implements of Husbandry, and Lambkins

Enjoying domestic ease

around me, I expect to glide gently down the stream of life, 'till I am entombed in the dreary mansions of my Fathers.

(Mount Vernon, April 4, 1784)

HISTORY OF REVOLUTION

. . . . It ever has been my opinion however, that no Historian can be possessed of sufficient materials to compile a *perfect* history of the revolution, who has not free access to the archives of Congress, to those of the respective States; to the papers of the Commander in chief, and to those of the officers who have been employed in separate Departments. Combining and properly arranging the information which is to be obtained from these sources must bring to view all the material occurrences of the War. Some things probably, will never be known.

Added to this, I have always thought that it would be respectful to the Sovereign power of these United States, to *follow*, rather than to take the lead of them in disclosures of this kind: but if there should be political restraints under which Congress are not inclined at this time to lay open their papers; and these restraints do not in their opinion extend to mine, the same being signified by that honorable Body to me, my objections to your request will cease. I shall be happy then, as at all times to see you at Mount Vernon, and will lay before you with chearfulness, my *public* papers for your information.

Respectful to the sovereign power of the U.S.

(To Reverend William Gordon, Philadelphia, May 8, 1784)

RETROSPECTION

It is indeed a pleasure, from the walks of private life to view in retrospect, all the meanderings of our past labors, the difficulties through which we have waded, and the fortunate Haven to which the Ship has been brought! Is it possible after this that it should founder? Will not the All Wise, and all powerful director of human events, preserve it? I think he will, he may however (for wise purposes not discoverable by finite minds) suffer our indiscretions and folly to place our national character low in the political Scale; and this, unless more wisdom and less prejudice take the lead in our governments, will most assuredly be the case.

For wise purposes Providence will suffer indiscretions and folly

Believe me, my dear Sir, there is no disparity in our ways of thinking and acting, tho there may happen to be a little in the years we have lived; which places the advantages of the corrispondence between us to my Acct., as I shall benefit more by your experience and observations than you can by mine. No corrispondence can be more pleasing than one which originates from similar sentiments, and similar Conduct through (tho' not a long War, the importance of it, and attainments considered) a painful contest. I pray you therefore to continue me among the number of your friends, and to favor me with such observations as shall occur.

(To Governor Jonathan Trumbull, Philadelphia, May 15, 1784)

TO THE SOUTH CAROLINA SENATE AND HOUSE OF REPRESENTATIVES

. . . . Permit me, Gentlemen, on this occasion of general joy, to congratulate you and your State in a particular manner upon its present repose, and recovery from those scenes of accumulated distresses for which it has been remarkable. and whilst we have abundt. cause to rejoice at the fair prospect which a beneficient Provide. has ld. before us to assure you of my entire belief that the wisdom and liberallity of the People of So. Carolina will leave nothing unessayed to make the revolution as beneficial to mankind as it hath been glorious in the Accomplishmnt.

Beneficent Providence

For the favorable wishes you have kindly bestowed on me you have all my gratitude; and my prayers for the welfare of your State, shall never cease.

(May 28, 1784)

TO THE MAYOR, RECORDER, ALDERMEN AND COMMON COUNCIL OF THE CITY OF RICHMOND

. . . . To the Smiles of Heaven, to a virtuous and gallant Army, and to the exertions of my fellow Citizens of the Union, (not to superior talents of mine) are to be ascribed the blessings of that liberty, Independence and peace, of wch. we are now in the enjoyment. Whilst these are afforded us, and while the advantages of commerce are not only offered but are solliciting our acceptance, it must be our own fault indeed if we do not make them productive of a rich and plenteous harvest, and of that National honor and glory, which should be

Enjoyment of liberty, independence and peace ascribed to Smiles of Heaven

characteristic of a young, and rising Empire. . . .
(November 15, 1784)

Education of Youth

My sentiments are perfectly in unison with yours sir, that the best means of forming a manly, virtuous and happy people, will be found in the right education of youth. Without *this* foundation, every other means, in my opinion, must fail; and it gives me pleasure to find that Gentlemen of your abilities are devoting their time and attention in pointing out the way. . . .

Character for a republic founded in the right education of youth

(To George Chapman, Mount Vernon, December 15, 1784)

War in Europe

. . . . If we are to credit newspaper accounts, the flames of war in Europe are again kindling: how far they may spread, neither the Statesman or soldier can determine; as the great governor of the Universe causes contingencies which baffle the wisdom of the first, and the foresight and valor of the Second.

Great governor of the Universe causes contingencies which baffle

All I pray for, is, that you may keep them among yourselves. If a single spark should light among the inflameable matter in these States, it may set them in a combustion, altho' they may not be able to assign a good reason for it. . . .

(To David Humphreys, Mount Vernon, February 7, 1785)

Instrument in the Hands of Providence

. . . . At best I have only been an instrument in the hands of Providence, to effect, with the aid of France and many virtuous fellow Citizens of America, a revolution which is interesting to the general liberties of mankind, and to the emancipation of a country which may afford an Asylum, if we are wise enough to pursue the paths wch. lead to virtue and happiness, to the oppressed and needy of the Earth. Our region is extensive, our plains are productive, and if they are cultivated with liberallity and good sense, we may be happy ourselves, and diffuse happiness to all who wish to participate. . . .

In the interest of the general liberties of mankind

(To Lucretia Wilhemina Van Winter, Mount Vernon, March 30, 1785)

Effect of Divine Wisdom

. . . . To have had the good fortune amidst the viscissitudes of a long and arduous contest "never to have known a moment when I did not possess the confidence and esteem of my Country." And that my conduct should have met the approbation, and obtained the affectionate regard of the State of New York (where difficulties were numerous and complicated) may be ascribed more to the effect of divine wisdom, which has disposed the minds of the people, harassed on all sides, to make allowances for the embarrassments of my situation, whilst with fortitude and patience they sustained the loss of their Capitol, and a valuable part of their territory, and to the liberal sentiments, and great exertion of her virtuous Citizens, than to any merit of mine. . . .

Confidence and esteem of my Country

I pray that Heaven may bestow its choicest blessings on your City. That the devastations of War, in which you found it, may soon be without a trace. That a well regulated and benificial Commerce may enrichen your Citizens. And that, your State (at present the Seat of the Empire) may set such examples of wisdom and liberality, as shall have a tendency to strengthen and give permanency to the Union at home, and credit and respectability to it abroad.

(To the Mayor, Recorder, Aldermen, and Commonalty of the City of New York, April 10, 1785)

To Marquis de Chastellux

. . . . It gives me great pleasure to find by my letters from France, that the dark clouds which hung over your hemisphere, are vanishing before the all-chearing Sunshine of peace. My first wish is to see the blessings of it diffused through all Countries, and among *all* ranks in every Country; and that we should consider ourselves as the children of a common parent, and be disposed to acts of brotherly kindness towards one another. In that case all restrictions of trade would vanish; we should take your Wines, your fruits and surplusage of other articles: and give you in return our oils, our Fish, Tobacco, naval stores &ca., and in like manner we should exchange produce with other Countries, to our reciprocal advantage: the Globe is large enough, why then need we wrangle for a small spot of it? If one Country cannot contain us another should open

As children of a common parent

its arms to us. But these halcyon days (if they ever did exist) are now no more; a wise providence, I presume, has ordered it otherwise, and we must go on in the old way disputing, and now and then fighting, until the Globe itself is dissolved. . . .

Wise Providence ordains the times

(Mount Vernon, September 5, 1785)

RELIGIOUS TAX

. . . . Altho, no man's sentiments are more opposed to *any kind* of restraint upon religious principles than mine are; yet I must confess, that I am not amongst the number of those who are so much alarmed at the thoughts of making people pay towards the support of that which they profess, if of the denomination of Christians; or declare themselves Jews, Mahomitans or otherwise, and thereby obtain proper relief. As the matter now stands, I wish an assessment had never been agitated, and as it has gone so far, that the Bill could die an easy death; because I think it will be productive of more quiet to the State, than by enacting it into a Law; which, in my opinion, would be impolitic, admitting there is a decided majority for it, to the disquiet of a respectable minority. In the first case the matter will soon subside; in the latter, it will rankle and perhaps convulse the State.*

Oppressive restraint upon religious principles

(To George Mason, Mount Vernon, October 3, 1785)

A TUTOR NEEDED

. . . . Having already informed you what my wants are, it is needless to add what those of the children must be; your own judgement, when I inform you that I mean to fit the boy, in my own family, for a University, will point these out. The greater the knowledge of his preceptor is, the better he would suit. To teach French grammatically is essential, as it is now becoming a part of the education of youth in this Country.

I could not afford to give more than £50 Sterlg. pr.ann: but this sum, except in the article of cloathing, wou'd be clear, as the Gentleman would eat at my table; and have his lodging and washing found him; and his Linen and stockings mended by the Servants of my Family. It may happen that an Episcopal clergyman with a small living, and unencumbered by a family may be had to answer this description, such an one would be preferred; but I except none who is competent to my purposes, if his character is unimpeached. . . .

Competent and Christian in character

(To George Chapman, Mount Vernon, November 10, 1785)

TO MARQUIS DE LAFAYETTE

. . . . The account given of your tour thro' Prussia and other States of Germany, to Vienna and back; and of the Troops which you saw reviewed in the pay of those Monarchs, at different places, is not less pleasing than it is interesting; and must have been as instructive as entertaining to yourself. . . . To have viewed the several fields of Battle over which you passed, could not, among other sensations, have failed to excite this thought, here have fallen thousands of gallant spirits to satisfy the ambition of, or to support their sovereigns perhaps in acts of oppression or injustice! melancholy reflection! For what wise purposes does Providence permit this? Is it as a scourge for mankind, or is it to prevent them from becoming too populous? If the latter, would not the fertile plains of the Western world receive the redundancy of the old. . . .

Providence permits oppression and injustice for wise purposes

The benevolence of your heart my Dr. Marqs. is so conspicuous upon all occasions, that I never wonder at any fresh proofs of it; but your late purchase of an estate in the colony of Cayenne, with a view of emancipating the slaves on it, is a generous and noble proof of your humanity. Would to God a like spirit would diffuse itself generally into the minds of the people of this country; but I despair of seeing it. Some petitions were presented to the Assembly, at its last Session, for the abolition of slavery, but they could scarcely obtain a reading. To set them afloat at once would, I really believe, be productive of much inconvenience and mischief; but by degrees it certainly might, and assuredly ought to be effected; and that too by Legislative authority. . . .

Abolition of slavery effected by degrees and by legislative authority

(Mount Vernon, May 10, 1786)

* The bill in question was to provide for teachers of the Christian religion in Virginia by means of a specified tax, the money to be paid out on order of the vestries, elders, etc., of each religious society to a teacher or minister of its denomination. It could also be used to provide places of worship. Mason had printed the remonstrance against the bill and sent it to Washington, asking him to sign it. (*Fitzpatrick*)

To Chevalier de La Luzerne

. . . . In other respects our internal Governments are daily acquiring strength. The laws have their fullest energy; justice is well administered; robbery, violence or murder is not heard of from Nw. Hampshire to Georgia. The people at large (as far as I can learn) are more industrious than they were before the war. Œconomy begins, partly from necessity and partly from choice and habit, to prevail. The seeds of population are scattered over an immense tract of western country. In the old States, wch. were the theatres of hostility, it is wonderful to see how soon the ravages of war are repaired. Houses are rebuilt, fields enclosed, stocks of cattle which were destroyed are replaced, and many a desolated territory assumes again the cheerful appearance of cultivation. In many places the vestiges of conflagration and ruin are hardly to be traced. The arts of peace, such as clearing rivers, building bridges, and establishing conveniences for travelling &c. are assiduously promoted. In short, the foundation of a great Empire is laid, and I please myself with a persuasion, that Providence will not leave its work imperfect. . . .

Providence will not leave His work imperfect

(Mount Vernon, August 1, 1786)

Political Conditions

. . . . Your sentiments, that our affairs are drawing rapidly to a crisis, accord with my own. What the event will be, is also beyond the reach of my foresight. We have errors to correct; we have probably had too good an opinion of human nature in forming our confederation. Experience has taught us, that men will not adopt and carry into execution measures the best calculated for their own good, without the intervention of a coercive power. I do not conceive we can exist long as a nation without having lodged some where a power, which will pervade the whole Union in as energetic a manner, as the authority of the State Governments extends over the several States.

We have errors to correct

To be fearful of investing Congress, constituted as that body is, with ample authorities for national purposes, appears to me the very climax of popular absurdity and madness. Could Congress exert them for the detriment of the public, without injuring themselves in an equal or greater proportion? Are not their interests inseparably connected with those of their constituents? By the rotation of appointment, must they not mingle frequently with the mass of Citizens? Is it not rather to be apprehended, if they were possessed of the powers before described, that the individual members would be induced to use them, on many occasions, very timidly and inefficaciously for fear of losing their popularity and future election? We must take human nature as we find it: perfection falls not to the share of mortals. . . .

Republic rests upon capacity for self-government

What astonishing changes a few years are capable of producing. I am told that even respectable characters speak of a monarchical form of Government without horror. From thinking proceeds speaking, thence to acting is often but a single step. But how irrevocable and tremendous! what a triumph for our enemies to verify their predictions! what a triumph for the advocates of despotism to find that we are incapable of governing ourselves, and that systems founded on the basis of equal liberty are merely ideal and fallacious! Would to God that wise measures may be taken in time to avert the consequences we have but too much reason to apprehend. . . .

Popular absurdity and madness

(To the Secretary for Foreign Affairs,
Mount Vernon, August 1, 1786)

To Marquis de Chastellux

I cannot omit to seize the earliest occasion, to acknowledge the receipt of the very affectionate letter you did me the honor of writing to me on the 22d. of May; as well as to thank you for the present of your Travels in America and the translation of Colo. Humphrey's Poem, all of which came safe to hand by the same conveyance. . . .

Colo. Humphreys (who has been some weeks at Mount Vernon) confirm'd me in the sentiment by giving a most flattering account of the whole performance: he has also put into my hands the translation of that part in which you say such, and so many handsome things of me; that (altho' no sceptic on ordinary occasions) I may perhaps be allowed to doubt whether your friendship and partiality have not, in this one instance, acquired an ascendency over your cooler judgment.

Having been thus unwarily, and I may be permitted to add, almost unavoidably betrayed into a kind of necessity to speak of myself, and not wishing to resume that subject, I choose to close it forever by observing, that as, on the one hand, I consider it an indubitable mark of mean-spiritedness and pitiful vanity to court applause from the pen or tongue of man; so on the other, I believe it to be a proof of false modesty or an unworthy affectation of humility to appear altogether insensible to the *commendations* of the virtuous and enlightened part of our species. Perhaps nothing can excite more perfect harmony in the soul than to have this string vibrate in unison with the internal consciousness of rectitude in our intentions and an humble hope of approbation from the supreme disposer of all things. . . .

Supreme disposer of all things

Some objects in our federal system might probably be altered for the better. I rely much on the good sense of my countrymen, and trust that a superintending Providence will disappoint the hopes of our Enemies.

A superintending Providence

(Mount Vernon, August 18, 1786)

Owning of Slaves

. . . . With respect to the first, I never mean (unless some particular circumstance should compel me to it) to possess another slave by purchase; it being among my first wishes to see some plan adopted by which slavery in this country may be abolished by slow, sure and imperceptible degrees.

Abolished at Mt. Vernon

(To John Francis Mercer,
Mount Vernon,
September 9, 1786)

The Convention

. . . . You will I dare say, be surprized my dear Marquis to receive a letter from me at this place, you will probably, be more so, when you hear that I am again brought, contrary to my public declaration, and intention, on a public theatre, such is the vicissitude of human affairs, and such the frailty of human nature that no man I conceive can well answer for the resolutions he enters into.

The pressure of the public voice was so loud, I could not resist the call to a convention of the States which is to determine whether we are to have a Government of respectability under which life, liberty, and property will be secured to us, or are to submit to one which may be the result of chance or the moment, springing perhaps from anarchy and Confusion, and dictated perhaps by some aspiring demagogue who will not consult the interest of his Country so much as his own ambitious views. What may be the result of the present deliberation is more than I am able, at present, if I was at liberty, to inform you, and therefore I will make this letter short, with the assurance of being more particular when I can be more satisfactory. . . .

Two forms of government

(To Marquis de LaFayette,
Philadelphia, June 6, 1787)

Quality of Government

. . . . Persuaded I am, that the primary cause of all our disorders lies in the different State governments, and in the tenacity of that power, which pervades the whole of their systems. Whilst independent sovereignty is so ardently contended for, whilst the local views of each State, and separate interests, by which they are too much governed, will not yield to a more enlarged scale of politics, incompatibility in the laws of different States, and disrespect to those of the general government, must render the situation of this great country weak, inefficient, and disgraceful. It has already done so, almost to the final dissolution of it. Weak at home and disregarded abroad is our present condition, and contemptible enough it is.

Primary cause of disorders—demogoguery of state governments

Entirely unnecessary was it to offer any apology for the sentiments you were so obliging as to offer me. I have had no wish more ardent, through the whole progress of this business, than that of knowing what kind of government is best calculated for us to live under. No doubt there will be a diversity of sentiments on this important subject; and to inform the judgment, it is necessary to hear all arguments that can be advanced. To please all is impossible, and to attempt it would be vain. The only way, therefore, is, under all the views in which it can be placed, and with a due consideration to circumstances, habits, &c., &c., to form such a government as will bear the scrutinizing eye of criticism, and trust it to the good sense and patriotism of the people to carry it into effect. Demagogues, men who are unwilling to lose any of their State consequence, and interested characters in each, will oppose any general government. But let these be regarded rightly, and justice, it is to be hoped, will at length prevail.

(To David Stuart, Philadelphia. July 1, 1787)

To Marquis de LaFayette

. . . . Newspaper accts. inform us that the Session of the Assembly of Notables is ended. and you have had the goodness (in your letter of the 5th of May) to communicate some of the proceedings to me, among which is that of the interesting motion made by yourself respecting the expenditure of public money by Monsr. de Callonne, and the consequence thereof.

The patriotism, by which this motion was dictated throws a lustre on the action, which cannot fail to dignify the Author, and I sincerely hope with you, that much good will result from the deliberations of so respectable a Council, I am not less ardent in my wish that you may succeed in your plan of toleration in religious matters. Being no bigot myself to any mode of worship, I am disposed to indulge the professors of Christianity in the church, that road to Heaven, which to them shall seem the most direct, plainest easiest and least liable to exception. . . .

No bigot to any mode of worship

(Philadelphia, August 15, 1787)

Constitution

In the first moment after my return I take the liberty of sending you a copy of the Constitution which the Fœderal Convention has submitted to the People of these States. I accompany it with no observations; your own Judgment will at once discover the good, and the exceptionable parts of it. And your experience of the difficulties, which have ever arisen when attempts have been made to reconcile such variety of interests and local prejudices as pervade the several States will render explanation unnecessary. I wish the Constitution which is offered had been made more perfect, but I sincerely believe it is the best that could be obtained at this time; and, as a constitutional door is opened for amendment hereafter, the adoption of it under the present circumstances of the Union, is in my opinion desirable.

Constitutional door opened for amendment hereafter

From a variety of concurring accounts it appears to me that the political concerns of this Country are, in a manner, suspended by a thread. That the Convention has been looked up to by the reflecting part of the community with a solicitude which is hardly to be conceived, and that if nothing had been agreed on by that body, anarchy would soon have ensued, the seeds being richly [*sic*] sown in every soil.

(To Patrick Henry, Mount Vernon, September 24, 1787)

European Wars

. . . . For our situation is such as makes it not only unnecessary, but extremely imprudent for us to take a part in their quarrels; and whenever a contest happens among them, if we wisely and properly improve the advantages which nature has given us, we may be benifitted by their folly, provided we conduct ourselves with circumspection and under proper restrictions, for I perfectly agree with you, that an extensive speculation, a spirit of gambling, or the introduction of any thing which will divert our attention from Agriculture, must be extremely prejudicial, if not ruinous to us. but I conceive under an energetic general Government such regulations might be made, and such measures taken, as would render this Country the asylum of pacific and industrious characters from all parts of Europe, would encourage the cultivation of the Earth by the high price which its products would command, and would draw the wealth, and wealthy men of other Nations, into our bosom, by giving security to property, and liberty to its holders.

A general government to secure property and liberty

(To Thomas Jefferson, Mount Vernon, January 1, 1788)

Constitution

. . . . With regard to the two great points (the pivots upon which the whole machine must move,) my Creed is simply,

1st. That the general Government is not invested with more Powers than are indispensably necessary to perform the functions of a good Government; and, consequently, that no objection ought to be made against the quantity of Power delegated to it.

Delegated authority limited

2ly. That these Powers (as the appointment of all Rulers will for ever arise from, and, at short stated intervals, recur to the free suffrage of the People) are so distributed among the Legislative, Executive, and Judicial Branches, into which the general Government is arranged, that it can never be in danger of degenerating into a monarchy, an Oligarchy, an Aristocracy, or any other despotic or oppressive form, so long as there shall remain any virtue in the body of the People.

Success of republic dependent upon virtue in the people

I would not be understood my dear Marquis to speak of consequences which may be produced, in the revolution of ages, by corruption of morals, profligacy of manners, and listlessness for the preservation of the natural and unalienable rights of mankind; nor of the successful usurpations that may be established at such an unpropitious juncture, upon the ruins of liberty, however providently guarded and secured, as these are contingencies against which no human prudence can effectually provide. It will at least be a recommendation to the proposed Constitution that it is provided with more checks and barriers against the introduction of Tyranny, and those of a nature less liable to be surmounted, than any Government hitherto instituted among mortals, hath possessed. We are not to expect perfection in this world; but mankind, in modern times, have apparently made some progress in the science of government. Should that which is now offered to the People of America, be found on experiment less perfect than it can be made, a Constitutional door is left open for its amelioration . . . .

More checks and balances against tyranny than any hitherto instituted

(To Marquis de Lafayette,
Mount Vernon, February 7, 1788)

CONDOLENCE

. . . . Yes, my dear Sir, I sincerely condole with you the loss of a worthy, amiable, and valuable Son! Altho' I had not the happiness of a personal acquaintance with him, yet the character which he sustained, and his near connexion with you, are, to me, sufficient reasons, to lament his death. It is unnecessary for me to offer any consolation on the present occasion; for to a mind like yours it can only be drawn from that source which never fails to give a bountiful supply to those who reflect justly. Time *alone* can blunt the keen edge of afflictions; Philosophy and our Religion holds out to us such hopes as will, upon proper reflection, enable us to bear with fortitude the most calamitous incidents of life and these are all that can be expected from the feelings of humanity; is all which they will yield. . . .

Christianity enables us to bear with fortitude the most calamitous incidents

(To Benjamin Lincoln,
Mount Vernon, February 11, 1788)

. . . . While I sincerely condole with you on the loss of your good father; you will permit me to remind you, as an inexhaustible subject of consolation, that there is a good Providence which will never fail to take care of his Children: . . .

Providence will never fail

(To Pierre Charles L'Enfant,
Mount Vernon, April 28, 1788)

CHANCELLOR OF THE COLLEGE OF WILLIAM AND MARY

. . . . Influenced by a heart-felt desire to promote the cause of Science in general, and the prosperity of the College of William and Mary in particular, I accept the office of Chancellor in the same; and request you will be pleased to give official notice thereof to the learned Body, who have thought proper to honor me with the appointment. I confide fully in their strenuous endeavours for placing the system of Education on such a basis, as will render it most beneficial to the State and the Republic of letters, as well as to the more extensive interests of humanity and religion. . . .

System of education for the Republic

(To Samuel Griffin,
Mount Vernon, April 30, 1788)

TO MARQUIS DE CHASTELLUX

. . . . While you have been making love, under the banner of Hymen, the great Personages in the North have been making war, under the inspiration, or rather under the infatuation of Mars. Now, for my part, I humbly conceive, you have had much the best and wisest of the bargain. For certainly it is more consonant to all the principles of reason and religion (natural and revealed) to replenish the earth with inhabitants, rather than to depopulate it by killing those already in existence, besides it is time for the age of Knight-Errantry and mad-heroism to be at an end. Your young military men, who want to reap the harvest of laurels, don't care (I suppose) how many seeds of war are sown; but for the sake of humanity it is devoutly to be wished, that the manly employment of agriculture and the humanizing benefits of commerce, would supersede the waste of war and the rage of conquest; that the swords might be turned into plough-shares, the spears into pruning hooks, and, as the Scripture expresses it, "the nations learn war no more."...

It is flattering and consolatory reflection, that our rising Republics have the good wishes of all the Philosophers, Patriots, and virtuous men in all nations: and that they look upon them as a kind of Asylum for mankind. God grant that we may not disappoint their honest expectations, by our folly or perverseness. . . .

Republics, a kind of asylum for mankind

(Mount Vernon, April 25, 1788)

Converting Indians to Christianity

Reverend Sir: I have received your obliging letter of the 28th of March, enclosing a copy of some remarks on the Customs, Languages &c. of the Indians, and a printed pamphlet containing the stated rules of a Society for propagating the Gospel among the Heathen, for which tokens of polite attention and kind remembrance I must beg you to accept my best thanks.

So far as I am capable of judging, the principles upon which the society is founded and the rules laid down for its government, appear to be well calculated to promote so laudable and arduous an undertaking, and you will permit me to add that if an event so long and so earnestly desired as that of converting the Indians to Christianity and consequently to civilization, can be effected, the Society of Bethlehem bids fair to bear a very considerable part in it.

Long and earnestly desired event

(To Reverend John Ettwein, a Moravian bishop, Mount Vernon, May 2, 1788)

Nephew's Conduct

. . . . One strong motive for my placing you in your present lodgings was that you might, in your conduct out of school, be guided by Mr. Hanson's advice and directions, as I confide very much in his discretion and think that he would require nothing of you but what will conduce to your advantage; and at the age to which you have now arrived you must be capable of distinguishing between a proper and improper line of conduct, and be sensible of the advantages or disadvantages which will result to you through life from the one or the other.

Capable of distinguishing between proper and improper conduct

Your future character and reputation will depend very much,if not entirely, upon the habits and manners, which you contract in the present period of your life; they will make an impression upon you which can never be effaced. You should therefore be extremely cautious how you put yourself into the way of imbibing those customs which may tend to corrupt your manners or vitiate your heart. I do not write to you in this style from knowing or suspecting that you are addicted to any vice, but only to guard you against pursuing a line of conduct which may imperceptibly lead on to vicious courses. . . .

(To George Steptoe Washington, Mount Vernon, May 5, 1788)

Holland Refugees

I had always hoped that this land might become a safe and agreeable Asylum to the virtuous and persecuted part of mankind, to whatever nation they might belong; but I shall be the more particularly happy, if this Country can be, by any means, useful to the Patriots of Holland, with whose situation I am peculiarly touched, and of whose public virtue I entertain a great opinion.

You may rest assured, Sir of my best and most friendly sentiments of your suffering compatriots, and that, while I deplore the calamities to which many of the most worthy members of your Community have been reduced by the late foreign interposition in the interior affairs of the United Netherlands; I shall flatter myself that many of them will be able with the wrecks of their fortunes which may have escaped the extensive devastation, to settle themselves in comfort, freedom and ease in some corner of the vast regions of America. The spirit of the Religions and the genius of the political Institutions of this Country must be an inducement. Under a good government (which I have no doubt we shall establish) this Country certainly promises greater advantages, than almost any other, to persons of moderate property, who are determined to be sober, industrious and virtuous members of Society. And it must not be concealed, that a knowledge that these are the general characteristics of your compatriots would be a principal reason to consider their advent as a valuable acquisition to our infant settlements. If you should meet with as favorable circumstances, as I hope will attend your first operations; I think it probable that your coming will

America, of greatest advantage to the sober, industrious, and virtuous be the harbinger for many more to adventure across the Atlantic. . . .

(To Reverend Francis Adrian Vanderkemp, a Menonite minister from Holland, Mount Vernon, May 28, 1788)

To Marquis de LaFayette

. . . . Since I had the pleasure of writing to you by the last Packet, the Convention of Maryland has ratified the federal Constitution by a majority of 63 to 11 voices. That makes the seventh State which has adopted it, next Monday the Convention in Virginia will assemble; we have still good hopes of its adoption here: though by no great plurality of votes. South Carolina has probably decided favourably before this time. The plot thickens fast. A few short weeks will determine the political fate of America for the present generation and probably produce no small influence on the happiness of society through a long succession of ages to come. Should every thing proceed with harmony and consent according to our actual wishes and expectations; I will confess to you sincerely, my dear Marquis; it will be so much beyond any thing we had a right to imagine or expect eighteen months ago, that it will demonstrate as visibly the finger of Providence, as any possible event in the course of human affairs can ever designate it. It is impracticable for you or any one who has not been on the spot, to realise the change in men's minds and the progress towards rectitude in thinking and acting which will then have been made. . . .

The finger of Providence

(Mount Vernon, May 28, 1788)

Constitution Struggle

. . . . The Conventions of New York and New Hampshire assemble both this week; a large proportion of members, with the Governor at their head, in the former, are said to be opposed to the government in contemplation: New Hampshire it is thought will adopt it without much hesitation or delay. It is a little strange that the men of large property in the South, should be more afraid that the Constitution will produce an Aristocracy or a Monarchy, than the genuine democratical people of the East. Such are our actual prospects. The accession of one State more will complete the number, which by the Constitutional provision, will be sufficient in the first instance to carry the Government into effect.

And then, I expect, that many blessings will be attributed to our new government, which are now taking their rise from that industry and frugality into the practice of which the people have been forced from necessity. I really believe, that there never was so much labour and economy to be found before in the country as at the present moment. If they persist in the habits they are acquiring, the good effects will soon be distinguishable. When the people shall find themselves secure under an energetic government, when foreign nations shall be disposed to give us equal advantages in commerce from dread of retaliation, when the burdens of war shall be in a manner done away by the sale of western lands, when the seeds of happiness which are sown here shall begin to expand themselves, and when every one (under his own vine and fig-tree) shall begin to taste the fruits of freedom, then all these blessings (for all these blessings will come) will be referred to the fostering influence of the new government. Whereas many causes will have conspired to produce them. You see I am not less enthusiastic than ever I have been, if a belief that peculiar scenes of felicity are reserved for this country, is to be denominated enthusiasm. Indeed, I do not believe, that Providence has done so much for nothing. It has always been my creed that we should not be left as an awful monument to prove, "that Mankind, under the most favourable circumstances for civil liberty and happiness, are unequal to the task of Governing themselves, and therefore made for a Master.". . .

Washington's creed

(To Marquis de LaFayette, Mount Vernon, June 19, 1788)

America's Blessings

. . . . No one *can* rejoice more than I do at every step the people of this great Country take to preserve the Union, establish good order and government, and to render the Nation happy at home and respectable abroad. No Country upon Earth ever had it more in its power to attain these blessings than United America. Wondrously strange then, and much to be regretted indeed would it be, were we to neglect the means, and to depart from the road which Providence has pointed us to, so plainly; I cannot believe it will ever come to pass. The great Governor of the Universe has led us too long and too far on the road to happiness and glory, to forsake us in the midst of it. By

The Governor of the Universe does not forsake

folly and improper conduct, proceeding from a variety of causes, we may now and then get bewildered; but I hope and trust that there is good sense and virtue enough left to recover the right path before we shall be entirely lost. . . .

(To Benjamin Lincoln, Mount Vernon, June 29, 1788)

Trust in Providence

. . . . I wish I may be mistaken in imagining, that there are persons, who, upon finding they could not carry their point by an open attack against the Constitution, have some sinister designs to be silently effected, if possible. But I trust in that Providence, which has saved us in six troubles yea in seven, to rescue us again from any imminent, though unseen, dangers. Nothing, however, on our part ought to be left undone. I conceive it to be of unspeakable importance, that whatever there be of wisdom, and prudence, and patriotism on the Continent, should be concentred in the public Councils, at the first outset. Our habits of intimacy will render an apology unnecessary. Heaven is my witness, that an inextinguishable desire (that) the felicity of my country may be promoted is my only motive in making these observations.

To rescue from unseen dangers

(To Benjamin Lincoln, Mount Vernon, August 28, 1788)

The New Government

. . . . It is true, that, for the want of a proper Confœderation, we have not yet been in a situation fully to enjoy those blessings which God and Nature seemed to have intended for us. But I begin to look forward, with a kind of political faith, to scenes of National happiness, which have not heretofore been offered for the fruition of the most favoured Nations. The natural political, and moral circumstances of our Nascent empire justify the anticipation. We have an almost unbounded territory whose natural advantages for agriculture and Commerce equal those of any on the globe. In a civil point of view we have unequalled previledge of choosing our own political Institutions and of improving upon the experience of Mankind in the formation of a confœderated government, where due energy will not be incompatible with unalienable rights of freemen. To complete the picture, I may observe, that the information and morals of our Citizens appear to be peculiarly favourable for the introduction of such a plan of government as I have just now described.

Although there were some few things in the Constitution recommended by the Fœderal Convention to the determination of the People, which did not full accord with my wishes; yet, having taken every circumstance seriously into consideration, I was convinced it approached nearer to perfection than any government hitherto instituted among Men. I was also convinced, that nothing but a genuine spirit of amity and accommodation could have induced the members to make those mutual concessions and to sacrafice (at the shrine of enlightened liberty) those local prejudices, which seemed to oppose an insurmountable barrier, to prevent them from harmonising in any system whatsoever.

Nearer to perfection than any government instituted

But so it has happened by the good pleasure of Providence, and the same happy disposition has been diffused and fostered among the people at large. You will permit me to say, that a greater Drama is now acting on this Theatre than has heretofore been brought on the American Stage, or any other in the World. We exhibit at present the Novel and astonishing Spectacle of a whole People deliberating calmly on what form of government will be most conducive to their happiness; and deciding with an unexpected degree of unanimity in favour of a System which they conceive calculated to answer the purpose. . . .

Providence diffused spirit of amity at large

(To Sir Edward Newenham, Mount Vernon, August 29, 1788)

The Presidency

. . . . I would willingly pass over in silence that part of your letter, in which you mention the persons who are Candidates for the two first Offices in the Executive, if I did not fear the omission might seem to betray a want of confidence. Motives of delicacy have prevented me hitherto from conversing or writing on this subject, whenever I could avoid it with decency. I may, however, with great sincerity and I believe without offending against modesty or propriety say to *you*, that I most heartily wish the choice to which you allude may not fall upon me: and that, if it should, I must reserve to myself the right of making up my final decision, at the last moment when it can be brought into one view, and when the expediency or inexpediency of a *refusal* can be more judiciously determined than at present. But be assured, my dear Sir, if from any inducement I shall be persuaded ultimately to accept, it will not be (so far as I know my own heart) from any of a private or personal nature. Every personal consideration conspires to rivet me (if I may use the expression) to retirement. At my time of life, and under my circumstances, nothing in this world can ever draw me from it, unless it be a *conviction* that the partiality of my Countrymen had made my services absolutely necessary, joined to a *fear* that my refusal might induce a belief that I preferred the conversation of my own reputation and private ease, to the good of my Country. After all, if I should conceive myself in a manner constrained to accept, I call Heaven to witness, that this very act would be the greatest sacrifice of my personal feelings and wishes that ever I have been called upon to make. It would be to forego repose and domestic enjoyment, for trouble, perhaps for public obloquy: for I should consider myself as entering upon an unexplored field, enveloped on every side with clouds and darkness. . . .

Conviction that the partiality of his countrymen make his services absolutely necessary

(To Benjamin Lincoln, Mount Vernon, October 26, 1788)

HIS PERPLEXITY

. . . . I believe you know me sufficiently well, my dear Trumbull, to conceive that I am very much perplexed and distressed in my own mind, respecting the subject to which you allude. If I should (unluckily for me) be reduced to the necessity of giving an answer to the question, which you suppose will certainly be put to me, I would fain do what is in all respects best. But how can I know what is best, or on what I shall determine? May Heaven assist me in forming a judgment: for at present I see nothing but clouds and darkness before me. Thus much I may safely say to you in confidence; if ever I should, from any apparent necessity, be induced to go from home in a public character again, it will certainly be the greatest sacrifice of feeling and happiness that ever was or ever can be made by him, who will have, in all situations, the pleasure to profess himself yours, &c.

Greatest sacrifice of personal feeling

(To Jonathan Trumbull, Mount Vernon, December 4, 1788)

TO REVEREND WILLIAM GORDON

. . . . I flatter myself my countrymen are so fully persuaded of my desire to remain in private life; that I am not without hopes and expectations of being left quietly to enjoy the repose, in which I am at present. Or, in all events, should it be their wish (as you suppose it will be) for me to come again on the Stage of public affairs, I certainly will decline it, if the refusal can be made consistently with what I conceive to be the dictates of propriety and duty. For the great Searcher of human hearts knows there is no wish in mine, beyond that of living and dying an honest man, on my own farm. . . .

Desires to be consistent with dictates of propriety and duty

(Mount Vernon, December 23, 1788)

A VIEW OF THE WORK AT THE SEVERAL PLANTATIONS IN THE YEAR 1789, AND GENERAL DIRECTIONS FOR THE EXECUTION OF IT

. . . . To request that my people may be at their work as soon as it is light, work till it is dark, and be diligent while they are at it, can hardly be necessary; because the propriety of it must strike every Manager who attends to my interest, or regards his own character; and who, on reflecting, must be convinced that lost labour is never to be regained; the presumption being that every labourer (male or female) does as much in the 24 hours as their strength without endangering the health, or constitution will allow of; but there is much more in what is called head work, that is in the manner of conducting business, than is generally imagined. For take two Managers and give to each the same number of labourers, and let these labourers be equal in all respects. Let both these Managers rise equally early, go equally late to rest, be equally active, sober and industrious, and yet, in the course of the year, one of them, without pushing the hands that are under him more than the other, shall have performed infinitely more work. To what is this owing? Why, simply to contrivance resulting from that forethought and arrangement which will guard against the misapplication of labour, and doing it unseasonably: For in the affairs of farming or Planting, more perhaps than in any other, it may justly be said there is a time for all things. Because if a man will do that kind of work in clear and mild weather which can as well be done in frost, Snow and rain, when these come, he has nothing to do; consequently, during that period there is a total loss of labour. In plowing too, though the field first intended for it, or in which the plows may actually have been at work, should, from its situation, be rendered unfit (by rain or other causes) to be worked; and other spots even though the call for them may not be so urgent can be plowed, this business ought to go on; because the general operation is promoted by it. So with respect to other things, and particularly Carting; where nothing is more common than, when loads are to go to a place, and others to be brought from it, though not equally necessary at the same moment, to make two trips when one would serve. These things are only enumerated to shew that the Manager who takes a comprehensive view of his business, will throw no labour away.

Management and forethought

For this reason it is, I have here endeavoured to give a general view of my plans, with the business of the year, that the concerns of the several plantations may go on without application daily, for orders unless it be in particular cases, or where these directions are not clearly understood.

(To John Fairfax, January, 1789)

The Presidency

. . . . I can say little or nothing new, in consequence of the repetition of your opinion, on the expediency there will be, for my accepting the office to which you refer. Your sentiments, indeed, coincide much more nearly with those of my other friends, than with my own feelings. In truth my difficulties encrease and magnify as I draw towards the period, when, according to the common belief, it will be necessary for me to give a definitive answer, in one way or another. Should the circumstances render it, in a manner inevitably necessary, to be in the affirmative: be assured, my dear Sir, I shall assume the task with the most unfeigned reluctance, and with a real diffidence for which I shall probably receive no credit from the world. If I know my own heart, nothing short of a conviction of duty will induce me again to take an active part in public affairs; and, in that case, if I can form a plan for my own conduct, my endeavours shall be unremittingly exerted (even at the hazard of former fame or present popularity) to extricate my country from the embarrassments in which it is entangled, through want of credit; and to establish a general system of policy, which if pursued will ensure permanent felicity to the Commonwealth. I think I see a *path*, as clear and as direct as a ray of light, which leads to the attainment of that object. Nothing but harmony, honesty, industry and frugality are necessary to make us a great and happy people. Happily the present posture of affairs and the prevailing disposition of my countrymen promise to co-operate in establishing those four great and essential pillars of public felicity. . . .

Conviction of duty

Four pillars of public felicity

(To Marquis de Lafayette, Mount Vernon, January 29, 1789)

The New Government

. . . . Notwithstanding it might probably, in a commercial view, be greatly for the advantage of America that a war should rage on the other side of the Atlantic; yet I shall never so far divest myself of the feelings of a man, interested in the happiness of his fellow-men, as to wish my country's prosperity might be built on the ruins of that of other nations. On the contrary, I cannot but hope, that the Independence of America, to which you have so gloriously contributed, will prove a blessing to mankind. It is thus you see, My dear Count, in retirement, upon my farm, I speculate upon the fate of nations; amusing myself with innocent Reveries, that mankind will, one day, grow happier and better. . . .

Independence of America will bless mankind

(To Comte de Rochambeau, Mount Vernon, January 29, 1789)

Friendship and Applications for Office

My friendship is not in the least lessened by the difference, which has taken place in our political sentiments; nor is my regard for you diminished by the part you have acted. Men's minds are as varient as their faces, and, where the motives to their actions are pure, the operation of the former is no more to be imputed to them as a crime, than the appearance of the latter; for both, being the work of nature, are equally unavoidable. Liberality and charity, instead of clamor and misrepresentation (which latter only serve to foment the passions, without enlightening the understanding) ought to govern in all disputes about matters of importance: whether the former have appeared in some of the leaders of opposition, the impartial world will decide.

Govern disputes with liberality and charity

by Alonzo Chappel

The First Cabinet:
Knox, Jefferson, Randolph, Hamilton, Washington

According to report, your individual endeavors to prevent inflammatory measures from being adopted, redounds greatly to your credit. The reasons, my dear Sir, why I have not written to you for a long time are two; first, because I found it an insupportable task to answer the letters, which were written to me, and at the same time, to pay that attention to my private concerns which they required; and there being lately little besides politics worthy of notice; secondly, because I did not incline to appear as a partisan in the interesting subject, that has agitated the public mind since the date of my last letter to you. For it was my sincere wish that the Constitution, which had been submitted to the People, might, after a fair and dispassionate investigation, stand or fall according to its merits or demerits. Besides I found from disagreeable experience, that almost all the sentiments extracted from me in answer to private letters or communicated orally, by some means or another found their way into the public Gazettes; as well as some other sentiments ascribed to me, which never had an existence in my imagination.

In touching upon the more delicate part of your letter (the communication of which fills me with real concern) I will deal by you, with all that frankness, which is due to friendship, and which I wish should be a characteristic feature in my conduct through life. I will therefore declare to you, that, if it should be my inevitable fate to administer the government (for Heaven knows, that no event can be less desired by me; and that no earthly consideration short of so general a call, together with a desire to reconcile contending parties as far as in me lays, could again bring me into public life) I will go to the chair under no pre-engagement of any kind or nature whatsoever. But, when in it, I will, to the best of my Judgment, discharge the duties of the office with that impartiality and zeal for the public good, which ought never to suffer connections of blood or friendship to intermingle, so as to have the least sway on decisions of a public nature. I may err, notwithstanding my most strenuous efforts to execute the difficult trust with fidelity and unexceptionably; but my errors shall be of the head, not of the heart. For all recommendations for appointments, so far as they may depend upon or come from me, a due regard shall be had to the fitness of characters, the pretensions of different candidates, and, so far as is proper, to political considerations. These shall be invariably my governing motives. . . .

Frankness

Impartiality and zeal for the public good

(To Benjamin Harrison, Mount Vernon, March 9, 1789)

Advice to a Nephew

As it is probable I shall soon be under the necessity of quitting this place, and entering once more into the bustle of public life, in conformity to the voice of my Country, and the earnest entreaties of my friends, however contrary it is to my own desires or inclinations, I think it incumbent on me as your uncle and friend, to give you some advisory hints, which, if properly attended to, will, I conceive, be found very useful to you in regulating your conduct and giving you respectability, not only at present, but thro' every period of life. You have now arrived to that age when you must quit the trifling amusements of a boy, and assume the more dignified manners of a man.

At this crisis your conduct will attract the notice of those who are about you, and as the first impressions are generally the most lasting, your doings now may mark the leading traits of your character through life. It is therefore absolutely necessary if you mean to make any figure upon the stage, that you should take the first steps right. What these steps are, and what general line is to be pursued to lay the foundation of an honourable and happy progress, is the part of age and experience to point out. This I shall do, as far as in my power with the utmost chearfulness; and, I trust, that your own good sense will shew you the necessity of following it. The first and great object with you at present is to acquire, by industry, and application, such knowledge as your situation enables you to obtain as will be useful to you in life. In doing this two other important advantages will be gained besides the acquisition of knowledge: namely, a habit of industry, and a disrelish of that profusion of money and dissipation of time which are ever attendant upon idleness. I do not mean by a close application to your studies that you should never enter into those amusements which are suited to your age and station: they can be made to go hand in hand with each other, and, used in their proper seasons, will ever be found to be a mutual assistance to one another. But what amusements, and when they are to be taken, is the great matter to be attended to. Your own judgment, with the advice of your *real* friends who may have an opportunity of a personal intercourse with you, can point out the particular manner in which you may best spend your moments of relaxation, better than I can at a distance. One thing, however, I would strongly impress upon you, vizt. that when you have leisure to go into company that it should always be of the best kind that the place you are in will afford; by this means you will be constantly improving your manners and cultivating your mind while you are relaxing from your books; and good company will always be found much less expensive than bad. You cannot offer, as an excuse for not using it, that you cannot gain admission there, or that you have not a proper attention paid you in it: this is an apology made only those whose manners are disgusting, or whose character is exceptionable; neither of which I hope will ever be said of you. I cannot enjoin too strongly upon you a due observance of œconomy and frugality, as you well know yourself, the present state of your property and finances will not admit of any unnecessary expense. The article of clothing is now one of the chief expences, you will incur, and in this, I fear, you are not so œconomical as you should be. Decency and cleanliness will always be the first object in the dress of a judicious and sensible man; a conformity to the prevailing fashion in a certain degree is necessary; but it does not from thence follow that a man should always get a new Coat, or other clothes, upon every trifling change in the mode, when perhaps he has two or three very good ones by him. A person who is anxious to be a leader of the fashion, or one of the first to follow it will certainly appear in the eyes of judicious men, to have nothing better than a frequent change of dress to recommend him to notice. I would always wish you to appear sufficiently decent to entitle you to admission into any company where you may be; but I cannot too strongly enjoin it upon you, and your own knowledge must convince you of the truth of it, that you should be as little expensive in this respect as you properly can. You should always keep some clothes to wear to Church, or on particular occasions, which should not be worn everyday; this can be done without any additional expence; for whenever it is necessary to get new clothes, those which have been kept for particular occasions will then come in as every-day ones, unless they should be of a superior quality to the new. What I have said with respect to clothes will apply perhaps more pointedly to Lawrence than to you; and as you are much older than he is, and more capable of judging of the propriety of what I have here observed, you must pay attention to him in this respect, and see that he does not wear his Clothes improperly or extravagantly. Much more might be said to you, as a young man, upon the necessity of paying due attention to the moral virtues; but this may, perhaps, more properly be the subject of a future letter when you may be about to enter into the world. If you comply with the advice herein given to pay a diligent attention to your studies, and employ your time of relaxation in proper company, you will find but few opportunities and little inclination, while you continue at an Acadimy, to enter into those scenes of vice and dissipation which too often present themselves to youth in every place, and particularly in towns. If you are determined to neglect your books, and plunge into extravagance and dissipation, nothing I could say now would prevent it; for you must be employed, and if it is not in pursuit of those things which are profitable, it must be in pursuit of those which are destructive. . . .

Knowledge, industry, and good company

Economy and frugality

Decency and cleanliness

Attention to moral virtues

Pursuit of things profitable

(To George Steptoe Washington,
Mount Vernon, March 23, 1789)

An Official Dwelling

With very great sensibility I have received the honor of your letter dated the 10th instant, and consider the kind and obliging invitation to your house, until suitable accommodations can be provided for the President, as a testimony of your friendship and politeness, of which I shall ever retain a grateful sense. But if it should be my lot (for Heaven knows it is not my wish) to appear again in a public *Station*, I shall make it a point to take hired lodgings, or Rooms in a Tavern until some House can be provided. Because it would be wrong, in my real Judgment, to impose such a burden on any private family, as must unavoidably be occasioned by my company: and because I think it would be generally expected, that, being supported by the public at large, I should not be burdensome to Individuals. . . .

Wrong to impose and be burdensome

(To Governor George Clinton,
Mount Vernon, March 25, 1789)

To Hector St. John de Crevecœur

. . . . A Combination of circumstances and events seems to have rendered my embarking again on the Ocean of public affairs inevitable. How opposite this is to my own desires and inclinations I need not say. Those who know me are, I trust, convinced of it. For the rectitude of my intentions I appeal to the great Searcher of Hearts; and if I have any knowledge of myself I can declare that no prospects however flattering, no personal advantage however great, no desire of fame however easily it might be acquired, could induce me to quit the private walks of life at my age and in my situation. But if by any exertion or services of mine my Country can be benefitted I shall feel more amply compensated for the sacrifices which I make than I possibly can be by any other means. . . .

Benefits to country ample compensation

(Mount Vernon, April 10, 1789)

Farewell to Alexandrians

Although I ought not to conceal, yet I cannot describe, the painful emotions which I felt in being called upon to determine whether I would accept or refuse the Presidency of the United States.

The unanimity of the choice, the opinion of my friends, communicated from different parts of Europe, as well as of America, the apparent wish of those, who were not altogether satisfied with the Constitution in its present form, and an ardent desire on my own part, to be instrumental in conciliating the good will of my countrymen towards each other have induced an acceptance.

Those, who have known me best (and you, my fellow citizens, are from your situation, in that number) know better than any others that my love of retirement is so great, that no earthly consideration, short of a conviction of duty, could have prevailed upon me to depart from my resolution, *"never more to take any share in transactions of a public nature."* For, at my age, and in my circumstances, what possible advantages could I propose to myself, from embarking again on the tempestuous and uncertain ocean of public-life?

Prevailed upon by a conviction of duty

I do not feel myself under the necessity of making public declarations, in order to convince you, Gentlemen, of my attachment to yourselves, and regard for your interests. The whole tenor of my life has been open to your inspection; and my past actions, rather than my present declarations, must be the pledge of my future conduct.

In the mean time I thank you most sincerely for the expressions of kindness contained in your valedictory address. It is true, just after having bade adieu to my domestic connexions, this tender proof of your friendship is but too well calculated still farther to awaken my sensibility, and encrease my regret at parting from the enjoyments of private life.

All that now remains for me is to commit myself and you to the protection of that beneficent Being, who, on a former occasion has happily brought us together, after a long and distressing separation. Perhaps the same gracious Providence will again indulge us with the same heartfelt felicity. But words, my fellow-citizens, fail me: *Unutterable sensations must then be left to more expressive silence: while, from an aching heart, I bid you all, my affectionate friends and kind neighbours, farewell!*

Protection committed to gracious Providence

(To the Mayor, Corporation, and
Citizens of Alexandria, April 16, 1789)

To the Citizens of Baltimore

. . . . I cannot now, Gentlemen, resist my feelings so much, as to withhold the communication of my ideas, respecting the actual situation and prospect of our national affairs. It appears to me, that little more than common sense and common honesty, in the transactions of the community at large, would be necessary to make us a great and happy Nation. For if the general Government, lately adopted, shall be arranged and administered in such a manner as to acquire the full confidence of the American People, I sincerely believe, they will have greater advantages, from their Natural, moral and political circumstances, for public felicity, than any other People ever possessed.

In the contemplation of those advantages, now soon to be realized, I have reconciled myself to the sacrifice of my fondest wishes, so far as to enter again upon the stage of Public life. I know the delicate nature of the duties incident to the part which I am called to perform; and I feel my incompetence, without the singular assistance of Providence to discharge them in a satisfactory manner. But having undertaken the task, from a sense of duty, no fear of encountering difficulties and no dread of losing popularity, shall ever deter me from pursuing what I conceive to be the true interests of my Country.

Assistance of Providence

Nothing shall deter from pursuing interests of his Country

(April 17, 1789)

The First Inaugural Address

Fellow Citizens of the Senate and the House of Representatives.

Among the vicissitudes incident to life, no event could have filled me with greater anxieties than that of which the notification was transmitted by your order, and received on the fourteenth day of the present month. On the one hand, I was summoned by my Country, whose voice I can never hear but with veneration and love, from a retreat which I had chosen with the fondest predilection, and, in my flattering hopes, with an immutable decision, as the asylum of my declining years: a retreat which was rendered every day more necessary as well as more dear to me, by the addition of habit to inclination, and of frequent interruptions in my health to the gradual waste committed on it by time. On the other hand, the magnitude and difficulty of the trust to which the voice of my Country called me, being sufficient to awaken in the wisest and most experienced of her citizens, a distrustful scrutiny into his qualifications, could not but overwhelm with dispondence, one, who, inheriting inferior endowments from nature and unpractised in the duties of civil administration, ought to be peculiarly conscious of his own deficencies. In this conflict of emotions, all I dare aver, is, that it has been my faithful study to collect my duty from a just appreciation of every circumstance, by which it might be affected. All I dare hope, is, that, if in executing this task I have been too much swayed by a grateful remembrance of former instances, or by an affectionate sensibility to this transcendent proof, of the confidence of my fellow-citizens; and have thence too little consulted my incapacity as well as disinclination for the weighty and untried cares before me; my *error* will be palliated by the motives which misled me, and its consequences be judged by my Country, with some share of the partiality in which they originated.

Such being the impressions under which I have, in obedience to the public summons, repaired to the present station; it would be peculiarly improper to omit in this first official Act, my fervent supplications to that Almighty Being who rules over the Universe, who presides in the Councils of Nations, and whose providential aids can supply every human defect, that his benediction may consecrate to the liberties and happiness of the People of the United States, a Government instituted by themselves for these essential purposes: and may enable every instrument employed in its administration to execute with success, the functions allotted to his charge. In tendering this homage to the Great Author of every public and private good, I assure myself that it expresses your sentiments not less than my own; nor those of my fellow-citizens at large, less than either. No People can be bound to acknowledge and adore the invisible hand, which conducts the Affairs of men more than the People of the United States. Every step, by which they have advanced to the character of an independent nation, seems to have been distinguished by some token of providential agency. And in the important revolution just accomplished in the system of their United Government, the tranquil deliberations and voluntary consent of so many distinct communities, from which the event has resulted, cannot be compared with the means by which most Governments have been established, without some return of pious gratitude along with an humble anticipation of the future blessings which the past seem to presage. These reflections, arising out of the present crisis, have forced themselves too strongly on my mind to be suppressed. You will join

The invisible hand which conducts the affairs of men

with me I trust in thinking, that there are none under the influence of which, the proceedings of a new and free Government can more auspiciously commence.

By the article establishing the Executive Department, it is made the duty of the President "to recommend to your consideration, such measures as he shall judge necessary and expedient." The circumstances under which I now meet you, will acquit me from entering into that subject, farther than to refer to the Great Constitutional Charter under which you are assembled; and which, in defining your powers, designates the objects to which your attention is to be given. It will be more consistent with those circumstances, and far more congenial with the feelings which actuate me, to substitute, in place of a recommendation of particular measures, the tribute that is due to the talents, the rectitude, and the patriotism which adorn the characters selected to devise and adopt them. In these honorable qualifications, I behold the surest pledges, that as on one side, no local prejudices, or attachments; no seperate views, nor party animosities, will misdirect the comprehensive and equal eye which ought to watch over this great assemblage of communities and interests: so, on another, that the foundations of our National policy will be laid in the pure and immutable principles of private morality; and the pre-eminence of a free Government, be exemplfied by all the attributes which can win the affections of its Citizens, and command the respect of the world.

National policy laid in principles of private morality

I dwell on this prospect with every satisfaction which an ardent love for my Country can inspire: since there is no truth more thoroughly established, than that there exists in the œconomy and course of nature, an indissoluble union between virtue and happiness, between duty and advantage, between the genuine maxims of an honest and magnanimous policy, and the solid rewards of public prosperity and felicity: Since we ought to be no less persuaded that the propitious smiles of Heaven, can never be expected on a nation that disregards the eternal rules of order and right, which Heaven itself has ordained: And since the preservation of the sacred fire of liberty, and the destiny of the Republican model of Government, are justly considered as *deeply*, perhaps as *finally* staked, on the experiment entrusted to the hands of the American people.

Ardent love of Country

Heaven's favor upon nations that regard rules which Heaven has ordained

Besides the ordinary objects submitted to your care, it will remain with your judgment to decide how far an exercise of the occasional power delegated by the Fifth article of the Constitution is rendered expedient at the present juncture by the nature of objections which have been urged against the System, or by the degree of inquietude which has given birth to them. Instead of undertaking particular recommendations on this subject, in which I could be guided by no lights derived from official opportunities, I shall again give way to my entire confidence in your discernment and pursuit of the public good: For I assure myself that whilst you carefully avoid every alteration which might endanger the benefits of an United and effective Government, or which ought to await the future lessons of experience; a reverence for the characteristic rights of freemen, and a regard for the public harmony, will sufficiently influence your deliberations on the question how far the former can be more impregnably fortified, or the latter be safely and advantageously promoted.

Balance to maintain self-government with union

To the preceeding observations I have one to add, which will be most properly addressed to the House of Representatives. It concerns myself, and will therefore be as brief as possible When I was first honoured with a call into the Service of my Country, then on the eve of an arduous struggle for its liberties, the light in which I contemplated my duty required that I should renounce every pecuniary compensation. From this resolution I have in no instance departed. And being still under the impressions which produced it, I must decline as inapplicable to myself, any share in the personal emoluments, which may be indispensably included in a permanent provision for the Executive Department; and must accordingly pray that the pecuniary estimates for the Station in which I am placed, may, during my continuance in it, be limited to such actual expenditures as the public good may be thought to require.*

Having thus imparted to you my sentiments, as they have been awakened by the occasion which brings us together, I shall take my present leave; but not without resorting once more to the benign parent of the human race, in humble supplication that

* This request was, after consideration, seen to establish an awkward precedent, and Congress fixed the compensation of the President at $25,000 a year. (*Fitzpatrick*)

GEORGE WASHINGTON

since he has been pleased to favour the American people, with opportunities for deliberating in perfect tranquility, and dispositions for deciding with unparallelled unanimity on a form of Government, for the security of their Union, and the advancement of their happiness; so his divine blessing may be equally *conspicuous* in the enlarged views, the temperate consultations, and the wise measures on which the success of this Government must depend.

(April 30, 1789)

HUMAN PERVERSENESS*

. . . . I pretend to no unusual foresight into futurity, and therefore cannot undertake to decide, with certainty, what may be its ultimate fate. If a promised good should terminate in an unexpected evil, it would not be a solitary example of disappointment in this mutable state of existence. If the blessings of Heaven showered thick around us should be spilled on the ground or converted to curses, through the fault of those for whom they were intended, it would not be the first instance of folly (34) or perverseness in short-sighted mortals. The blessed Religion revealed in the word of God will remain an eternal and awful monument to prove that the best Institutions may be abused by human depravity; and that they may even, in some instances be made subservient to the vilest of purposes. Should, hereafter, those who are intrusted with the management of this government, incited by the lust of power and prompted by the Supineness or venality of their Constituents, overleap the known barriers of this Constitution and violate the unalienable rights of humanity: it will only serve to shew, that no compact among men (however provident in its construction and sacred in its ratification) can be pronounced everlasting and inviolable, and if I may so express myself, that no Wall of words, that no mound of parchmt. can be so formed as to stand against the sweeping torrent of boundless ambition on the one side, aided by the sapping current of corrupted morals on the other. . . .

The Scriptures teach human depravity

No compact among men everlasting and inviolable

(April (?) 1789)

* PROPOSED ADDRESS TO CONGRESS:
This document now exists in fragmentary form only. The first pages are missing. Apparently intended as Washington's inaugural address, or as his first annual message to Congress, it was discarded and not used. Jared Sparks, finding that the document had no official existence, did as he had done in other instances (specifically the Washington "Diaries"), split up the document and presented pages and cuttings of pages to his friends. The complete manuscript was more than 62 pages in length, Washington having numbered each page himself. It was most carefully written and evidently was considered of importance at the time it was inscribed. (*Fitzpatrick.*)

★ ★ ★ ★ ★

The Writings of Washington, Edited by Jared Sparks, 1837

TO THE MINISTERS, CHURCH WARDENS, AND VESTRY-MEN OF THE GERMAN LUTHERAN CONGREGATION IN AND NEAR PHILADELPHIA

While I request you to accept my thanks for your kind address, I must profess myself highly gratified by the sentiments of esteem and consideration contained in it. The approbation my past conduct has received from so worthy a body of citizens, as that whose joy for my appointment you announce, is a proof of the indulgence with which my future transactions will be judged by them.

I could not, however, avoid apprehending that the partiality of my countrymen in favor of the measures now pursued has led them to expect too much from the present government; did not the same providence which has been visible in every stage of our progress to this interesting crisis, from a combination of circumstances, give us cause to hope for the accomplishment of all our reasonable desires.

Providential combination of circumstances

Thus partaking with you in the pleasing anticipation of the blessings of a wise and efficient government; I flatter myself opportunities will not be wanting for me to shew my disposition to encourage the domestic and public virtues of industry, œconomy, patriotism, philanthropy, and that righteousness which exalteth a nation.

Disposed to encourage public virtues

I rejoice in having so suitable an occasion to testify the reciprocity of my esteem for the numerous people whom you represent. From the excellent character for diligence, sobriety, and virtue, which the Germans in general, who are settled in America, have ever maintained; I cannot forbear felicitating myself on receiving from so respectable a number of them such strong assurances of their affection for my person, confidence in my integrity, and zeal to support me in my endeavors for promoting the welfare of our common country.

So long as my conduct shall merit the approbation of the *wise and the good*, I hope to hold the same place in your affections, which your friendly declarations induce me to believe I possess at present; and amidst all the vicissitudes that may await me in this mutable state of existence, I shall earnestly desire the continuation of an interest in your intercessions at the Throne of Grace.

Intercessions at the Throne of Grace desired

(April 20, 1789)

TO THE GENERAL COMMITTEE, REPRESENTING THE UNITED BAPTIST CHURCHES IN VIRGINIA

I request that you will accept my best acknowledgments for your congratulation on my appointment to the first office in the nation. The kind manner in which you mention my past conduct equally claims the expression of my gratitude.

After we had, by the smiles of Heaven on our exertions, obtained the object for which we contended, I retired at the conclusion of the war, with an idea that my country could have no farther occasion for my services, and with the intention of never entering again into public life: But when the exigence of my country seemed to require me once more to engage in public affairs, an honest conviction of duty superseded my former resolution, and became my apology for deviating from the happy plan which I had adopted.

Honest conviction of duty

If I could have entertained the slightest apprehension that the Constitution framed in the Convention, where I had the honor to preside, might possibly endanger the religious rights of any ecclesiastical Society, certainly I would never have placed my signature to it; and if I could now conceive that the general Government might ever be so administered as to render the liberty of conscience insecure, I beg you will be persuaded that no one would be more zealous than myself to establish effectual barriers against the horrors of spiritual tyranny, and every species of religious persecution—For you, doubtless, remember that I have often expressed my sentiments, that every man, conducting himself as a good citizen, and being accountable to God alone for his religious opinions, ought to be protected in worshipping the Deity according to the dictates of his own conscience.

Keep the liberty of conscience secure

Individual accountable to God for his religious opinions

While I recollect with satisfaction that the religious Society of which you are Members, have been, throughout America, uniformly, and almost unanimously, the firm friends to civil liberty, and the persevering Promoters of our glorious revolution; I cannot hesitate to believe that they will be the faithful Supporters of a free, yet efficient general Government. Under this pleasing expectation I rejoice to assure them that they may rely on my best wishes and endeavors to advance their prosperity.

Faithful supporters of the Constitution

In the meantime be assured, Gentlemen, that I entertain a proper sense of your fervent supplications to God for my temporal and eternal happiness.

(May, 1789)

TO THE GENERAL ASSEMBLY OF THE PRESBYTERIAN CHURCH IN THE UNITED STATES OF AMERICA

I receive with great sensibility the testimonial, given by the General Assembly of the Presbyterian Church in the United States of America, of the lively and unfeigned pleasure experienced by them on my appointment to the first office in the nation.

Although it will be my endeavor to avoid being elated by the too favorable opinion which your kindness for me may have induced you to express of the importance of my former conduct, and the effect of my future services: yet, conscious of the disinterestedness of my motives, it is not necessary for me to conceal the satisfaction I have felt upon finding, that my compliance with the call of my country, and my dependence on the assistance of Heaven to support me in my arduous undertakings, have, so far as I can learn, met the universal approbation of my countrymen.

Dependence upon the assistance of Heaven

While I reiterate the profession of my dependence upon Heaven as the source of all public and private blessings; I shall observe that the general prevalence of piety, philanthropy, honesty, industry and œconomy seems, in the ordinary course of human affairs, particularly necessary for advancing and confirming the happiness of our country. While all men within our

The source of all public and private blessings

territories are protected in worshipping the Deity according to the dictates of their consciences; it is rationally to be expected from them in return, that they will all be emulous of evincing the sincerity of their professions by the innocence of their lives, and the beneficence of their actions: For no man, who is profligate in his morals, or a bad member of the civil community, can possibly be a true Christian, or a credit to his own religious society.

Liberty of conscience protected

A true Christian

I desire you to accept my acknowledgements for your laudable endeavors to render men sober, honest, and good citizens, and the obedient subjects of a lawful government; as well as for your prayers to Almighty God for his blessing on our common country and the humble instrument, which he has been pleased to make use of in the administration of it's government.

Humble instrument

(May 1789)

To William Heath

The Writings of George Washington Vol. 30 Edited by John C. Fitzpatrick, 1931

The numerous congratulations which I have received from Public Bodies and respectable individuals since my appointment to my present station, are truly grateful, as they hold forth the strongest assurances of support to the Government as well as a warm attachment to myself. It is from the good dispositions of the people at large, from the influence of respectable Characters, and from the patriotic cooperation of a wise and virtuous legislature, more than from any abilities of mine that I can promise success to my administration. The kind interposition of Providence which has been so often manifested in the affairs of this country, must naturally lead us to look up to that divine source for light and direction in this new and untried Scene. . . .

Must look up to that divine source

(United States, May 9, 1789)

To the Bishops of the Methodist Episcopal Church in the United States of America

The Writings of Washington, Edited by Jared Sparks, 1837

I return to you individually, and (through you) to your Society collectively in the United States my thanks for the demonstrations of affection, and the expressions of joy, offered in their behalf, on my late appointment. It shall still be my endeavor to manifest, by overt acts, the purity of my inclinations for promoting the happiness of mankind, as well as the sincerity of my desires to contribute whatever may be in my power towards the preservation of the civil and religious liberties of the American People. In pursuing this line of conduct, I hope, by the assistance of divine providence, not altogether to disappoint the confidence which you have been pleased to repose in me.

Dependence upon the assistance of divine providence

It always affords me satisfaction, when I find a concurrence in sentiment and practice between all conscientious men in acknowledgments of homage to the great Governor of the Universe, and in professions of support to a just, civil government. After mentioning that I trust the people of every denomination, who demean themselves as good citizens, will have occasion to be convinced that I shall always strive to prove a faithful and impartial Patron of genuine, vital religion: I must assure you in particular that I take in the kindest part the promise you make of presenting your prayers at the Throne of Grace for me, and that I likewise implore the divine benedictions on yourselves and your religious community.

Faithful and impartial patron of genuine and vital religion

(May 29, 1789)

To the Ministers and Elders of the German Reformed Congregations in the United States

I am happy in concurring with you in the sentiments of gratitude and piety towards Almighty-God, which are expressed with such fervency of devotion in your address; and in believing, that I shall always find in you, and the German Reformed Congregations in the United States a conduct correspondent to such worthy and pious expressions.

At the same time, I return you my thanks for the manifestation of your firm purpose to support in your persons a government founded in justice and equity, and for the promise that it will be your constant study to impress the minds of the People entrusted to your care with a due sense of the necessity of uniting reverence to such a government and obedience to its laws with the duties and exercises of religion.

Government founded in justice and equity

Christianity and the constitution

Be assured, Gentlemen, it is, by such conduct,

very much in the power of the virtuous Members of the community to alleviate the burden of the important office which I have accepted; and to give me Occasion to rejoice, in this world, for having followed therein the dictates of my conscience.

Be pleased also to accept my acknowledgements for the interest you so kindly take in the prosperity of my person, family, and administration. May your devotions before the Throne of Grace be prevalent in calling down the blessings of Heaven upon yourselves and your country.

(June 11, 1789)

To the Directors of the Society of the United Brethren [Moravian] for Propagating the Gospel among the Heathen

I receive with satisfaction the congratulations of your Society and of the Brethren's Congregations in the United States of America—For you may be persuaded that the approbation and good wishes of such a peaceable and virtuous Community cannot be indifferent to me.

You will also be pleased to accept my thanks for the Treatise which you present; and be assured of my patronage in your laudable undertakings.

In proportion as the general Government of the United States shall acquire strength by duration, it is probable they may have it in their power to extend a salutary influence to the aborigines in the extremities of their territory. In the meantime, it will be a desirable thing for the protection of the Union to co-operate, as far as the circumstances may conveniently admit, with the disinterested endeavors of your Society to civilize and christianize the Savages of the Wilderness.

In support of Christianizing Indians by the church

Under these impressions I pray Almighty God to have you always in his holy keeping.

(July 10, 1789)

To the Bishops, Clergy, and Laity of the Protestant Episcopal Church in the States of New York, New Jersey, Pennsylvania, Delaware, Maryland, Virginia, and South Carolina, in General Convention Assembled

I sincerely thank you for your affectionate congratulations on my election to the chief Magistracy of the United States.

After having received from my fellow-citizens in general the most liberal treatment—after having found them disposed to contemplate in the most flattering point of view, the performance of my military services, and the manner of my retirement at the close of the war—I feel that I have a right to console myself in my present arduous undertakings, with a hope that they will still be inclined to put the most favorable construction on the motives which may influence me in my future public transactions. The satisfaction arising from the indulgent opinion entertained by the American People of my conduct, will, I trust, be some security for preventing me from doing anything, which might justly incur the forfeiture of that opinion—and the consideration that human happiness and moral duty are inseparably connected, will always continue to prompt me to promote the progress of the former, by inculcating the practice of the latter.

On this occasion it would ill become me to conceal the joy I have felt in perceiving the fraternal affection which appears to encrease every day among the friends of genuine religion— It affords edifying prospects indeed to see Christians of different denominations dwell together in more charity, and conduct themselves in respect to each other with a more christian-like spirit than ever they have done in any former age, or in any other Nation.

Biblical Christianity, the basis of constitutional union

I receive with the greater satisfaction your congratulations, on the establishment of the new constitution of government; because I believe it's mild, yet efficient, operations will tend to remove every remaining apprehension of those with whose opinions it may not entirely coincide, as well as to confirm the hopes of it's numerous friends; and because the moderation, patriotism, and wisdom of the present federal Legislature, seem to promise the restoration of Order, and our ancient virtues; the extension of genuine religion, and the consequent advancement of our respectability abroad, and of our substantial happiness at home.

Form of government, mild and efficient

I request most reverend and respected Gentlemen that you will accept my cordial thanks for your devout supplications to the Supreme Ruler of the Universe in behalf of me—May you, and the People whom you represent be the happy subjects of the divine benedictions both here and hereafter.

Supreme Ruler of the Universe supplicated

(August 19, 1789)

Washington's Attendance at Various Churches

As a devout Christian, George Washington recorded in his Diary the occasions he attended Church Services. He was an active member of the Episcopal Church, but attended church services of any denomination, wherever he happened to be.
—Editor

The Diaries of George Washington Vols. 1–5 Edited by John C. Fitzpatrick, 1931

Added text is in Brackets. Editorial notes by Fitzpatrick from the Diaries *are not italicized. Italics indicate editorial notation from Compiler Verna M. Hall*

1748, March 11 – April 13
'A Journal of my Journey over the Mountains began Fryday the 11th of March 1747/8'
[*No references to church attendance.*]

1748, April 14 – December 31
1749–1750
1751, January 1 – October 3
[Diaries not kept, or missing]

1751–1752, October 4 – March 4
[The Journey to Barbadoes]
November 11th. Dressed in order for Church but got to town two Late dined at Majr. Clarkes with ye S:G: went to Evening Service and return'd to our Lodgings.

1753–1754, October 31 – January 16
[The Journey to the French Commandant]
[*No references to church attendance*]

1754, January 17 – March 30
[Diary missing, or not kept]

1754, March 31 – June 27
[Journal of the march toward the Ohio]
June 2nd. Two or three families of the Shawanese and Loups arrived: we had prayers at the Fort.

1754, June 28 – December 31
1755–1759
[Diaries missing, or not kept]

1760, January 1 – May 22
February 3. . . . Mrs. Possey went home and we to Church at Alexandria: dind at Colo. Carlyle's and returnd in the Evening.
February 17th. The Wind blew cold and fresh from the No. West. Went to Church and Dind at Belvoir.
April 27th. Went to Church. In the afternoon some Rain and a great deal of severe lightning but not much Thunder. [*Williamsburg*]
May 4. Warm and fine. Set out for Frederick to see my Negroes that lay ill of the Small Pox. Took Church in my way to Coleman's, where I arrivd about Sun setting.

1760, May 23 – December 31
1761, January 1 – May 23
[Diaries missing, or not kept]

GENERAL GEORGE WASHINGTON IN PRAYER AT VALLEY FORGE
by James Edward Kelly

General George Washington in Prayer at Valley Forge
by James Edward Kelly (American, 1855–1933)
bronze bas-relief, 48 x 36 in. 1904.
united states sub-treasury building, new york, new york
courtesy of library of congress, washington. d.c.

"... Washington himself, ... stands peerless among the great and good of all ages. In a most emphatic sense, Washington was a man prepared by Providence for a special end. In the long and dreary war, commencing in the spring of 1775, and which was not closed for seven years, what was wanting was a permanent military chieftain, who should be possessed of the rare qualities of patience, perseverance and endurance; and all these qualities Washington had in so very high a degree, that it may be said with entire truth, that there never was his superior in such endowments. Calm, wise, incorruptible, he was pre-eminently the man for the times.

"I see, further, the Hand of God in his unmistakable help in the hour of Conflict. We attained our national independence against all probabilities. Often, in the dark hours of the struggle, nothing saved the American cause from entire destruction but the divine interposition. It had its days of darkness, suffering, and reverses, when it seemed as if success were impossible. A country without resources, an army gathered on short enlistments, and without discipline, a Congress sometimes tardy in supplying the means of carrying on the war, were not the most encouraging conditions of success. It is a matter of astonishment, that the spirit of the great leader did not break down, and that the internal supports of his hope and courage did not give way. But for the firm hope he had upon first and highest principles, and the confidence that he felt in God as their defender, his spirit must have sunk within him long before the close of the war. Whether he himself recognized a Divine Providence as working in the American cause; whether he regarded his country's success as dependent upon that Providence, he would have told you, had you asked him, as he came from his knees in the forest seclusion, where he was accustomed to bow in prayer, while passing that dark winter at Valley Forge. God was as certainly in the lives of Washington, and Lafayette, and Marion, as he was in the lives of Moses, and Joshua, and Daniel; he was no more present at Megiddo and Jericho, than at White Plains and Valley Forge. The battle was the Lord's and it could not be lost."

(Rev. S. W. Foljambe, Annual Election Sermon: The Hand of God in American History, Boston, Mass., January 5, 1876. Reprinted in *The Christian History of the American Revolution: Consider and Ponder,* compiled by Verna M. Hall, 1975, p. 52b-c.)

1761, May 24 – October 22
[*No references to church attendance*]

1761, October 23 – December 31
1762
1763, January 1 – March 1
[Diaries missing, or not kept]

1763, March 2 – November 18
[*No references to church attendance*]

1763, November 19 – December 31
1764, January 1 – March 28
[Diaries missing, or not kept]

1764, March 29 – October 18
[*No references to church attendance*]

1764, October 19 – December 31
[Diary missing, or not kept]

1765, January 1 – November 13
[*No references to church attendance; no listing of visiting any place; just agriculture planting*]

1765, November 14 – December 31
1766, January 1 – January 13
[Diaries missing, or not kept]

1766, January 14 – October 29
[*No reference to church attendance. No listing or travelling; just agriculture*]

1766, October 30 – December 31
[In November 1766, Washington attended the sessions of the Burgesses from November 6th to December 16th, with ten days of travelling.]

1767, January 1 – January 31
[Diaries missing, or not kept]

1767, February 1 – November 20
February 13th. Vestry to meet by Qr. appoinmt.
February 16th. Vestry to meet at Pohick.
November 20. Vestry in Truro Parish.*
[*Washington was chosen a vestryman for Truro Parish, October 25, 1762. October 3, 1763, he and George William Fairfax were chosen as church wardens for Pohick. According to the original Vestry Book of Pohick, Washington attended vestry meetings as follows:

1763, March 28
1764, October 9
1766, February 3–4
July 10
1767, February 23
May 27
July 25
September 28
November 20
1768, September 9
1769, March 3,
September 21
1771, July 6
November 29
1772, June 5
1774, February 15
February 24].

1767, November 21 – December 31
[Diary missing, or not kept]

1768, January 1 – December 31
April 3. Went to Pohick Church and returnd to Dinner. Mr. Crawford returnd in the Afternoon.*
[*Pohick Church, on Pohick Creek, about seven miles from Mount Vernon. The Church now standing is the third Pohick Church to be built. It was finished in 1772. Washington's pew therein is No. 28. —Toner]
April 17. Went to Church and returnd to Dinner.
May 8. Went to Church and returnd to Dinner. [*Williamsburg*]
May 22. Went to Church at (Nomony) and returnd to Mr. Booth's to Dinner, who was also from home in Gloucester. Mr. Smith,* the Parson, dind with us.
[*Augustine? Smith. —Toner]
May 23. At Mr. Booth's all day with Revd. Mr. Smith.
May 29. Went to St. Paul's Church and Dined at my Brother's.
June 5. Went to Church at Alexandria and dined at Colo. Carlyle's.
June 12. Went to Pohick Church and returned to Dinner.
July 10. Went to Church and returnd to Dinner.
July 16. Went by Muddy hole and Doeg Run to the vestry at Pohick Church. Stayd there till half after 3 oclock and only 4 members coming, returned by Captn. McCarty's and dind there.
July 24. Went to Pohick Church.

July 31. Went to Alexa. Church. Dind. at Colo. Carlyle's and returnd in the afternoon.

August 28. Went to Nomony Church and returnd to my Brother's to Dinner.

August 29. Went into Machodack Ck. fishing, and dined with the Revd. Mr. Smith.

September 4. Went to Church, dind at Colo. Harrison's and returned to my Brs. in the afternoon. [*Probably in Stafford*]

September 9. Proceeded to the Meeting of our vestry at the New Church and lodgd at Captn. Edwd. Payne's.*

[*The 'New Church' here mentioned was that chapel of ease of Truro Parish which was built on the Ox Road above the springs of Pohick Run, near the present-day Fairfax Court-House. It was usually called 'Payne's Church,' as Edward Payne, a Truro vestryman, whom Washington visited on this occasion, built the church under contract with the Truro Vestry, in 1766, at a contract price of £579. The interesting history of this church is told by Dr. E. L. Goodwin in his edition of Philip Slaughter's *History of Truro Parish* (Philadelphia, 1908).]

October 16. Went to Pohick Church. Dind at Captn. McCarty's and came home at Night. Doctr. Rumney who came here last Night went away this Morning and Mr. Ramsay and Mr. Adams came here at Night.

November 13. Went to Pohick Church and dined at Home with Mr. Ths. Triplet H. Manley and Mr. Peake.

November 27. Went to Church.

November 28. Went to the Vestry at Pohick Church.

1769, January 1 – December 31

January 22. Went to Pohick Church. Doctr. Rumney stayd all day and Night.

February 19. Went to Pohick Church, and returnd to Dinner.

March 3. Went to the Vestry at Pohick Church and returnd abt. 11 Oclock at Night; found Mr. Tibbles here.

April 7. Went a fox hunting in the Morning and catchd a dog fox after running him an hour and treeing twice. After this went to an intended meeting of ye Vestry, but there was none. When I came home found Mr. Buchanon and Captn. McGachin here, also Captn. Weeden and my Br. Charles.

April 16. Went to Pohick Church and returnd home to Dinner.

May 28. Returnd home early in the Morning and went to Pohick Church, returning to Dinner. [*from Alexandria*]

June 11. Went to Pohick Church—dined at Captn McCartys. Stood for Mr. Chichester's Child and came home in ye Aftern.

July 23. Went to Pohick Church and returnd to Dinner. Mr. Magowan w[ith] us.

July 24. Went to an intended vestry at ye cross Roads—but disappointed of one by Mr. Henderson's refusg. to act.

August 20. Went to Church in the fore and afternoon. Mr. Jno. Lewis dind here. Lord Fairfax, ye two Colo. Fairfax's and others drank Tea here.

September 3. Went to Church in the fore and afternoon, and dined with Lord Fairfax.

September 21. Captn. Posey calld here in the Morng. and we went to a Vestry. Upon my return found Mr. B. Fairfax and Mr. P. Wagener here.

November 19. [*Williamsburg*] Went to Church and Returnd to Eltham to Dinner, wt Mr. Dangerfd. and the Parson.

December 24. Went to Prayers, and dined afterw[ar]ds at Colo. Lewis. Spent the Evening with Mr. Jones, at Julian's.

1770, January 1 – December 31

February 18. Went to Pohick Church and returnd to Dinner.

March 18. Went to Pohick Church and returnd to Dinner. Colo. Lewis, &ca. went away this Morning and Jno. Ball the Millwright came in the afternoon.

April 1. Went to Pohick Church and returnd home to Dinner.

May 13. Went to Church with all the Compy. here. Dind at Belvoir and returnd in the afternoon.

June 17. [*Williamsburg*] Went to Church in the Forenoon, and from thence to Colo. Burwell's where I dind and lodgd.

July 8. Went to Pohick Church and returnd to Dinner. Mr. Smith went to Colo. Fairfax's and returnd to Dinner, and Mr. Stedlar went away after Breakft.

August 5. Went to Church (in Fredg.) and dind with Colo. Lewis.

August 19. Went to Pohick Church. Calld in our

POHICK CHURCH
Sketch by Benson J. Lossing

way at Belvoir to take leave of Sir Thos. Returnd to Dinner.

October 5. Began a journey to Ohio. . . . [*Gone nine weeks, one day*]

December 9. Went to Pohick Church and returnd to Dinner.

December 25. Went to Pohick Church and returnd to Dinner.

1771, January 1 – December 31

January 20. Went to Pohick Church with Mrs. Washington and returnd to Dinr. Mr. Ball dined here.

April 14. Went to Pohick church and came home to Dinner, Mr. Magowan with us. Found Mr. Adam, Mr. Matthew Campbell and Captns. Conway and Adam, who Dined and went away afterwds.

May 19. Went to Church [Saint Peter's Episcopal Church, New Kent County] and returnd to Colo. Bassett's to Dinner with other Compy., among whom were the two Mr. Dandridge's.

June 23. Went to Pohick Church and returnd home to Dinner.

July 8. Went to a Vestry held at the New Church at Pohick. Doctr. Rumney and Mr. Robt. Harrison came home with me.

August 4. Went to Pohick Church, and came home to Dinner.

August 29. Went to the Vestry at Pohick Church and reachd home in the Evening. Found Mr. Johnson here.

December 25. Went to Pohick Church with Mrs. Washington and returnd to Dinner.

1772, January 1 – December 31

April 26. Colo. Bassett and Mrs. Bassett, Mrs. Washington and Self, went to Pohick Church and returnd to Dinr.

May 10. Went to Pohick Church and returnd home to Dinner. Mr. Campbell Dined here.

June 5. Met the Vestry at our New Church and came home in the afternoon where I found Capt. Posey, who had been here since I w[en]t.

June 7. Went to Pohick Church and Return'd to Dinner J. P. C. came.

June 21. Mr. Andrews and Mr Wagener went away. Mr. Byrd and I went to Pohick Church and returnd to Dinner.

July 12. Mr. B. Dulany, &ca. went up to Church in Alexa. and returnd again in the afternoon.

July 19. Went with Mr. Byrd and J. P. Custis to Pohick Church and Dined at Belvoir. Returnd in the Evening.

August 2. Went to Pohick Church and Dined with Mrs. Washington and Patcy Custis at Captn. McCarty's. Came home in ye afternn.

September 6. Went to Church with Govr. Eden in his Phaeton. [*Saint Anne's Parish, Annapolis, Md.*]

September 27. Set of for Pohick Church and got almost there, when word was brought that Mr. Massey was sick. Returnd and found Nanny Peake and Biddy Fleming here, who went away after Dinner.

December 25. Went to Pohick Church and returnd to Dinner. Found Mr. Tilghman here.

1773, January 1 – December 3

[Written on the second fly-leaf of the 1773 diary.]

. . . . Sales of the Pews in Alexandria Church—to whom—&ca.

Nos.	Purchasers	Price
4	Mr. Townsd. Dade	£28.
5	Colo. G. Washington	36.10
13	Mr. Robt. Adam	30.
14	Mr. Robt. Alexander	30.10
15	Mr. Dalton	20.
18	Mr. Thos. Fleming	21.5
19	Colo. Carlyle	30.
20	Mr. Wm. Ramsay	33.
28	Messrs. Jno. Muir &ca	36.5
29	Mr. Jno. West Junr	33.
		£298.10
	Average price	£ 29.17

April 11. Went to Pohick Church with Mrs. Washington and Mr. Custis, and returnd to Dinner.

June 13. Went up with Miss Reed, etca., to Alexa. Church. Returnd to Dinner with Mr. Willis. Doctr. Rumney w[en]t away.

July 18. Mr. Tilghman returnd to Alexa. Miss Calvert and Mrs. Washington and self went to Pohick Church. In the Afternoon Mr. B. Fairfax came.

July 25. Went up to Alexandria Church and returnd to Dinner.

August 8. Went up to Alexa. Church and returnd to Dinner. Captn. Posey and Son Price here, the last of whom went away after Dinner.

August 14. Very warm. Rid to an intended meeting of Vestry at the New Church.

August 22. Went up to Church at Alexandria and returnd to Dinner. Found Doctr. Craik here, who stayd all Night.

September 5. Went up with him [*Mr. Magowan*] and Miss Nelly Calvert to Alexa. Church. Returnd. Dinner.

October 10. Mr. Herbert went away before Breakfast. Mr. Tilghman went with Mrs. Washington and I to Pohick Church and returnd with us.

1774, January 1 – December 31

March 27. Went to Pohick Church and returnd to Dinner.

April 10. Went with Colo. Bassett, etca. to Pohick Church. Returnd to Dinner. Doctr. Brown dined here.

April 17. Attempted to go to Alex. Church, but broke the Pole of the Chariot and returnd. Colo. Lee went away after Breakfast.

May 8. Mr. Tilghman and Mr. Milner went away after Breakfast. We (that is the rest) went to Pohick Church.

May 29. Went to Church [*Williamsburg*] in the fore and afternoon. Dined at Mrs. Dawson's and spent the Eveng. at my Lodgings.

June 1. Went to Church and fasted all day.*
[*In conformity with the vote of the Burgesses to fast in sympathy with Massachusetts on the day the Boston Port Bill went into operation.]

June 26. Went up to Church at Alexr. Returnd to Dinner.

July 3. Went to Pohick Church and returnd home to Dinner.

July 17. Went to Pohick Church and returnd to Dinner. Colo. Mason came in the afternoon and stayed all Night.

July 24. Went up to Church at Alexandria. Returnd to Dinner.

August 14. Went to Pohick Church with Mr. Custis. Found Messrs. Carlyle, Dalton, Ramsay, Adam, and Doctr. Rumney here upon my return. Doctr. Craik also came in the afternoon.*
[*. . . . Washington's accounts at this point give us a rare glimpse of the sincere sentiment that was so much a part of him. He paid William Copan for putting his (Washington's) 'cypher' on his pew at Pohick Church, and, although he knew Colonel George William Fairfax would probably never return to America, he paid Copan to put the Fairfax cipher on the Fairfax pew.]

August 28. Went to Pohick Church. Mess. Stuart, Herbert, Mease, Doctr. Jenifer,* Mr. Stone** and Mr. Digges, dind here. The first three stayed all Night.
[Notes: *Dr. Daniel Jenifer (1756–1809), of Kent County, Maryland. Surgeon in the Continental Hospital during the Revolution. **Thomas Stone (1743–87), of Maryland. Signer of the Declaration of Independence.]

September 25. [*Philadelphia.*] Went to the Quaker Meeting in the Forenoon and St. Peter's in the afternoon. Din'd at my Lodgings.

October 2. Went to Christ Church* and dined at the New Tavern. [*Episcopal; on Second Street betwen Market and Arch.]

October 9. Went to the Presbeterian Meeting in the forenoon and Romish Church in the afternoon. Dind at Bevan's.

October 16. Went to Christ Church in the forenoon. After which rid to, and dind in the Provence Island. Suppd at Byrns's.

November 5. Mr. Piercy, a Presbeterian Minister, dined here.

November 6. Went to Pohick Church. Mr. Triplet, and Mr. Peake and Daughter dined here.

November 13. Went up to Alexandria Church in the Evening. Colo. Blackburn, Mr. Lee, and Mr. Richd. Graham came here as a Committee from the Prince Wm. Independent Compy.

December 4. At home all day. Mr. Willis and a Mr. Harrison dind here, and Parson Morton lodged here.

1775, January 1 – June 19

January 15. Went to Pohick Church and Returnd to dinner. Colo. Mason and son, Mr. Dulany and Mr. Cockburn, came home with me and stayed all Night.

February 26. Mrs. Washington and self went to Pohick Church. Dind at Captn. McCarty's. Mrs. Craik came home with us.

CHRIST CHURCH
Sketch by Benson J. Lossing

March 12. Went to Pohick Church and returnd to Dinner. Found Mr. Jno. Stone here, who went away afterwards. Jas. Cleveland came in the afternoon.

April 9. Went to Pohick Church and returnd to Dinner. Doctr. Craik and Mr. Danl Jenifer came in the afternoon and stayed all Night.

June 11. [*Philadelphia*] Went to Church in the forenoon and then went out and Dined at Mr. H. Hill's. Returnd in the afternoon.

[Note: From this point until May, 1781, Washington did not keep a diary. He set out for the Army at Cambridge, Massachusetts, June 23d. Although elected by unanimous vote in Congress, June 15th, to be Commander-in-Chief of all forces raised, or to be raised by the United Colonies, Washington's commission was not engrossed and signed until four days later. It is dated June 19, 1775.]

1781, May 1 – November 5.

May.

To have the clearer understanding of the entries which may follow, it would be proper to recite, in detail, our wants and our prospects—but this alone, would be a work of much time, and great magnitude. It may suffice to give the sum of them wch. I shall do in a few words—*viz.*

Instead of having Magazines filled with provisions, we have a scanty pittance scattered here and there in the different States. Instead of having our Arsenals well supplied with Military Stores, they are poorly provided, and the Workmen all leaving them. Instead of having the various articles of Field equipage in readiness to deliver, the Quarter Master General (as the denier resort, according to his acct.) is but now applying to the several States to provide these things for the Troops respectively. Instead of having a regular System of transportation established upon credit—or funds in the Qr. Masters hands to defray the contingent expences of it we have neither the one nor the other and all that business, or a great part of it, being done by Military Impress, we are daily and hourly oppressing the people—souring their tempers—and alienating the affections. Instead of having the Regiments compleated to the new establishment and which ought to have been so by the ____ of ____ agreeably to the requisitions of Congress, scarce any State in the Union has, at this hour, an eighth part of its quota in the field and little prospect, that I can see, of ever getting more than half. In a word—instead of having everything in readiness to take the Field, we have nothing and instead of having the prospect of a glorious offensive campaign before us, we have a bewildered and gloomy defensive one—unless we should receive a powerful aid of Ships—Land Troops—and Money from our generous allies and these, at present, are too contingent to build upon.

1781, November 6 – December 31
1782–1783
1784, January 1 – August 31
[Diaries not kept]

1784, September 1 – October 4
[*Journey over Mountains*]

1784, October 5 – December 31
[Diary missing, or not kept]

1785, January 1 – December 31
[*Most Sundays omitted. Those included show visitors staying or arriving at Mount Vernon.*]

October Sunday, 2d. Went with Fanny Bassett, Burwell Bassett, Doctr. Stuart, G. A. Washington, Mr. Shaw and Nelly Custis to Pohick Church; to hear a Mr. Thomspon preach, who returned home with us to Dinner, where I found the Revd. Mr. Jones, formerly a Chaplin in one of the Pennsylvania Regiments.

After we were in Bed (about eleven Oclock in the Evening) Mr. Houdon, sent from Paris by Doctr. Franklin and Mr. Jefferson to take my Bust, in behalf of the State of Virginia, with three young men assistants, introduced by a Mr. Perin a French Gentlemen of Alexandria, arrived here by Water from the latter place.

1786, January 1 – December 31

October Sunday, 15th. Accompanied by Majr. Washington his wife, Mr. Lear and the two Childn., Nelly and Washington Custis, went to Pohick Church and returned to Dinner. Fell in with on the Road, Colo. Jno Mercer, his Lady and Child, coming here, and their Nurse. [*Most Sundays omitted. Those included show visitors staying or arriving at Mount Vernon.*]

1787, January 1 – December 31
[*Same situation as above, until May.*]

May [*Entry written after entry May 8th*]
A concise Acct. of my journey to Philadelphia, and the manner of spending my time there, and places where, will now follow.* After wch. I shall return to the detail of Plantation occurrances as they respect my Crops and intended experiments agreeably to the Reports which have been made to me by my Nephew, Geo. Auge. Washington in my absence.
[*For the period of Washington's attendance in the Constitutional Convention. . . .]

May Sunday, 27th. Went to the Romish Church,* to high mass. Dined, drank Tea, and spent the evening at my lodgings. [*St. Mary's, Fourth Street above Spruce. (Baker)]

June Sunday, 17th. Went to Church. Heard Bishop White* preach, and see him ordain two Gentlemen [into the order of] Deacons. After wch. rid 8 miles into the Country and dined with Mr. Jno. Ross in Chester County. Returned [to town again about dusk] in the afternoon.
[*Bishop William White, chaplain of the Continental Congress, 1787–1801, and the first Protestant Episcopal Bishop of Pennsylvania.]

October Sunday, 28th. Went to Pohick Church. Mr. Lear and Washington Custis in the Carriage with me.

Mr. Willm. Stuart came from Church with me and Mr. Geo. Mason Junr. came in soon after [both stayed all Night].

1788, January 1 – December 31

February Sunday, 24th. In the Evening the Revd. Mr. Fairfax came in.

April Sunday, 13th. Went to Church at Alexandria accompanied by Colo. Humphreys, Mr. Lear, and Washington Custis. Brought Hariot Washington home with us who had been left at Abingdon and came to Church with Mrs. Stuart.

June Tuesday, 10th. (*Fredericksburgh*)....On Sunday we went to Church, the Congregation being alarmed (without cause) and supposg. the Gallery at the No. End was about to fall, were thrown into the utmost confusion; and in the precipitate retreat to the doors many got hurt. . . .

October Sunday, 26th. Went to Pohick Church and returned home to dinner. Found Dr. Stuart at Mt. Vernon who dined there and returned home afterwards.

1789, January 1 – February 2

January Sunday, 4th. The Revd. Mr. Fairfax came here in the evening and stayed all Night.

February 3 – September 30
[Diary missing.]
[*During this period Washington was elected our First President.*]

October 1 – December 31

October Sunday, 4th. [*New York*] Went to St. Paul's Chappel in the forenoon. Spent the remainder of the day in writing private letters for to-morrow's Post.

October Sunday, 18th. [*On Tour*] Went in the forenoon to the Episcopal Church, and in the afternoon to one of the Congregational Meeting Houses. Attended to the first by the Speaker of the Assembly, Mr. Edwards, and a Mr. Ingersoll, and to the latter by the Governor, the Lieut. Governor, the Mayor, and Speaker. . . . [*New Haven, Conn.*]

October Sunday, 25th. [*Boston*] Attended Divine Service at the Episcopal Church, whereof Doctor Parker* is the Incumbent, in the forenoon, and the Congregational Church of Mr. Thatcher** in the afternoon. Dined at my lodgings with the Vice-President. Mr. Bowdoin accompanied me to both Churches. . . .

[*Dr. Samuel Parker. The church was old Trinity. **The Reverend Peter Thacher, of the Brattle Street Congregational Church.]

November Sunday, 1st. [*Portsmouth*] Attended by the President of the State (Genl. Sullivan), Mr. Langdon, and the Marshall, I went in the forenoon to the Episcopal Church, under the incumbency of a Mr. Ogden*; and in the afternoon to one of the Presbyterian or Congregational Churches, in which a Mr Buckminster** Preached. Dined at home with the Marshall, and spent the afternoon in my own room writing letters.

[*The Reverend John Cosens Ogden. **The Reverend Joseph Buckminster, North Church.]

November Sunday, 8th. It being contrary to law and disagreeble to the People of this State (Connecticut) to travel on the Sabbath day—and my horses, after passing through such intolerable roads, wanting rest, I stayed at Perkins' tavern (which, by the bye, is not a good one,) all day—and a meeting-house being within few rods of the door, I attended morning and evening service, and heard very lame discourses from a Mr. Pond.*

[*The Reverend Enoch Pond.]

November Sunday, 15th. [*New York*] Went to St. Paul's Chapel in the forenoon—and after returning from thence was visited by Majr. Butler, Majr. Meredith and Mr. Smith, So. Car'a . . . .

TRINITY CHURCH
Sketch by Benson J. Lossing

November Sunday, 22d. Went to St. Paul's Chapel in the forenoon—heard a charity sermon for the benefit of the Orphan's School of this city. . . .

November Sunday, 29th. Went to St. Paul's Chapel in the forenoon.

December Sunday, 6th. Went to St. Paul's Chapel in the forenoon.

December Sunday, 13th. Went to St. Paul's Chapel in the forenoon.

December Sunday, 20th. Went to St. Paul's Chapel in the forenoon.

December Friday, 25th, Christmas Day. Went to St. Paul's Chapel in the forenoon. . . .

1790, January 1 – March 10

January Sunday, 3d. Went to St. Paul's Chapel.

January Sunday, 10th. Went to St. Paul's Chapel in the forenoon—wrote private letters in the afternoon for the Southern mail.

January Sunday, 17th. At home all day—not well.

January Sunday, 24th. Went to St. Paul's Chapel in the forenoon. Writing private letters in the afternoon.

January Sunday, 31. Went to St. Paul's Chapel in the forenoon. . . .

February Sunday, 7th. Went to St. Paul's Chapel in the forenoon.

February Sunday, 21st. Went to St. Paul's Chapel in the forenoon—wrote letters respecting my domestic concerns afterwards.

February Sunday, 28th. Went to St. Paul's Chapel in the forenoon. Wrote letters on private business afterwards.

March 11 – July 14

March Sunday, 14th. Went to St. Paul's Chapel in the forenoon—wrote letters on private business afterwards.

March Sunday, 21st. Went to St. Paul's Chappel in the forenoon—wrote private letters in the afternoon. Received Mr. Jefferson, Minister of State about one o'clock.

March Sunday, 28th. Went to St. Paul's Chapel in the forenoon.

April Sunday, 11th. Went to Trinity Church* in the forenoon—and [wrote] several private letters in the afternoon.

[**Bishop Samuel Provoost, first Protestant Episcopal Bishop of New York State, and Rector of Trinity Church, New York City.*]

April Sunday, 25th. Went to Trinity Church, and wrote letters home after dinner.

May Sunday, 2d. Went to Trinity Church in the forenoon—writing letters on private business in the afternoon—among other letters one by my order to Genl. Moylan, to know if he would accept the Consulate at Lisbon, as it was not proposed to give Salaries therewith.

May Sunday, 9th. Indisposed with a bad cold, and at home all day writing letters on private business.

A severe illness with which I was siezed the 10th of this month and which left me in a convalescent state for several weeks after the violence of it had passed; and little inclination to do more than what duty to the public required at my hands occasioned the suspension of this Diary.

June Sunday, 27th. Went to Trinity Church in the forenoon—employed myself in writing business in the afternoon.

July Sunday, 4th. Went to Trinity Church in the forenoon. This day being the Anniversary of the declaration of Independency the celebration of it was put of until tomorrow.

July Monday, 5th. The members of the Senate, House of Representatives, Public Officers, Foreign Characters, etc., The Members of the Cincinnati, Officers of the Militia, etc., came with the compliments of the day to me—about one o'clock a sensible Oration was delivered in St. Pauls Chapel by Mr. Brockholst Livingston, on the occasion of the day—the tendency of which was to show the different situation we are now in, under an excellent government of our own choice, to what it would have been if we had not succeeded in our opposition to the attempts of Great Britain to enslave us; and how much we ought to cherish the blessings which are within our reach, and to cultivate the seeds of harmony and unanimity in all our public Councils. There were several other points touched upon in sensible manner. . . .

1790, July 15 – December 31
1791, January 1 – March 20
[Diaries missing]

1791, March 21 – June 1

March Monday, 21st. [*began tour of Southern States, from Philadelphia*]

April Thursday, 7th. . . . In attempting to cross the ferry at Colchester with the four horses hitched to the Chariot by the neglect of the person who stood before them, one of the leaders got overboard when the boat was in swimming water and 50 yards from the shore—with much difficulty he escaped drowning before he could be disengaged. His struggling frightened the others in such a manner that one after another and in quick succession they all got overboard harnessed and fastened as they were and with the utmost difficulty they were saved and the Carriage escaped been dragged after them, as the whole of it happened in swimming water and at a distance from the shore. Providentially—indeed miraculously—by the exertions of people who went off in Boats and jumped into the River as soon as the Batteau was forced into wading water—no damage was sustained by the horses, Carriage or harness. . . .

May Sunday, 8th. [*Charlestown, S. Car.*] Went to Crowded Churches in the morning and afternoon. To [Saint Philip's Church] in the morning and [Saint Michael's] in the afternoon. Dined with General Moultree.

May Sunday, 15th. [*Savannah, Ga.*] After morning Service, and receiving a number of visits from the most respectable ladies of the place (as was the case yesterday) I set out for Augusta, Escorted beyd. the limits of the City by most of the Gentlemen in it, and dining at Mulberry Grove the Seat of Mrs. Green, lodged at one Spencers—distant 15 miles. . . .

June Wednesday, 1st. [*Salem, North Car.*]. . . . Spent the forenoon in visiting the Shops of the different Tradesmen, The houses of accommodation for the single men and Sisters of the Fraternity, and their place of worship. Invited six of their principal people to dine with me, and in the evening went to hear them sing, and perform on a variety of instruments Church music. . . .

July Sunday, 3d. [*Yorktown, Pa.*] Received, and answered an address from the Inhabitants of York town and there being no Episcopal Minister present in the place, I went to hear morning Service performed in the Dutch reformed Church—which, being in that language not a word of which I understood I was in no danger of becoming a proselyte to its religion by the eloquence of the Preacher. . . .

July Monday 4th. This being the Anniversary of American Independence and being kindly requested to do it, I agreed to halt here this day and partake of the entertainment which was preparing for the celebration of it. In the forenoon I walked about the town—at half passed 2 oclock I received, and answered an address from the Corporation and the complimts of the Clergy of different denominations. . . .

1791, July 5 – December 31
1792 – 1793
1794, January 1 – September 29
[Diaries missing]

1794, September 30 – October 20
[*The Whiskey Insurrection*]
October Sunday, 5th. Went to the Presbiterian meeting and heard Doctr. Davidson Preach a political Sermon, recommendations of order and good government; and the excellence of that of the United States. [*Carlisle, Pa.*]

1794, October 21 – December 31
1795, January 1 – April 13
[Diaries missing]

1795, April 14 – December 21
[*Weather reports and travel.*]

1795, December 22 – December 31
1796 [Diaries missing]

1797, January 1 – December 31
January 1. Clear, wind westerly, went to church. [*Philadelphia*]
January 8. Clear and cold, wind at No. Wt. Went to a charity Sermon in Christ Church. Alarmed by a cry of fire while there.
February 19. Clear, Wind Westerly in the Morning but cloudly afterwards. Mer:30. Went to church.
[*Returns to Private Life.*]
[*Diary mostly weather and record of visitors.*]
September 24. Went to Church in Alexa.

1798, January 1 – December 31
May 9. Mr. Lewis went away after breakfast. I went to the Proclamn. Sermon* in Alexandria. [*In expectation of a war with France, President John Adams (March 23d) had proclaimed May 9th a day of fasting and prayer. The Reverend William Linn preached the sermon, and, later, sent Washington a printed copy of it from New York.]
Sept. 30. Went to Church in Alexa.
November 19. [*Philadelphia*] Do. at Doctr. White's —Bishop.

1799, January 1 – 21
[Pages containing these entries were torn from the original.]

1799, January 22 – December 13
[Several pages are missing from original.]
June 2. Returned home to dinner, takg. Church at Alexa. in my way. Found Doctr. Stuart here.
November 17. Went to Church in Alexandria and dined with Mr. Fitzhugh. On my return fd. young Mr. McCarty here on his way back from the Federal City. Young McCarty came to Dinr.

General George Washington passed away,
December 14, 1799.

George Washington's Religious Library

Excerpts from a Catalogue of the Washington Collection in The Boston Athenæum,
Compiled and Annotated by Appleton P. C. Griffin, 1897
University Press: John Wilson and Son, Cambridge, U.S.A.

It was the intention of Miss Verna Hall, Compiler, to record for the Reader the extent of the religious books George Washington chose for his Library. This gives us an insight into the kind of literature appealing to him.—Editor

The Boston Athenæum by Appleton P. C. Griffin, 1897

The inventory of Washington's books made at the time of his death by the appraisers of his estate shows that his library then numbered about nine hundred volumes. These under his will became the property of his nephew Judge Bushrod Washington, who also inherited his papers and the Mansion House of Mount Vernon. Here Judge Washington lived and added to General Washington's library a part at least of his own books. In his will in 1826, he provided as follows: "All the papers and letter books devised to me by my uncle, Gen'l Washington, as well as the books in my study, other than law books, I give to my nephew Geo. C. Washington; the books in the cases in the dining-room, I give to my nephew John A. Washington."...

Mount Vernon was next occupied by John A. Washington. The books left to George C. Washington remained there for many years, but in 1847 or 1848, a considerable portion of them, perhaps all that remained, were sold to Henry Stevens, the bookseller. Mr. Stevens announced his intention of sending them over to the British Museum. To prevent this and to secure them for Boston a number of Boston and Cambridge men, particularly Prof. Jared Sparks, Prof. Andrews Norton, Mr. George Livermore, and Mr. Charles Eliot Norton, who acted as Treasurer, undertook to solicit subscriptions, and raise the five thousand dollars which Stevens demanded for them, a sum which he afterwards reduced to three thousand eight hundred dollars. This amount and four hundred and fifty dollars beside was collected, the Athenæum itself contributing five hundred dollars; and at a meeting of the subscribers it was voted to place the books permanently in the Boston Athenæum, of which a majority of the subscribers were Proprietors. . . .

The collection of books bought from Stevens . . . comprises 455 volumes and about 750 pamphlets. Of these, 354 volumes (including 36 made up of pamphlets bound together) and several hundred unbound pamphlets may be assigned to General Washington's library, the large majority of them without question; the remaining 80 bound volumes and the rest of the pamphlets belonged to Judge Bushrod Washington or to other members of the Washington family. . . .

The remainder of Washington's library has been scattered, and no large number of his books now exists in any one place beside the Boston Athenæum . . . .

In order to show as far as possible how and when the several volumes in the Athenæum Collection were acquired by Washington, a careful examination of his published writings, and of the inedited material, account-books, letter-books, etc., in the Department of State, Washington, the Congressional Library, the Historical Society of Pennsylvania, the Massachusetts Historical Society (the Pickering papers), and the Lenox Library, was made, and a good deal of information gathered. Very many books, it is shown, he received by gift, especially during his public career, but he was also a constant buyer, mainly in practical lines, as appears by the orders to his agents, copies of which exist in his account-books preserved in the Department of State. . . .

★ ★ ★ ★ ★

ABERCROMBIE, Rev. James. 1758–1841.

A Sermon, preached in Christ Church and St. Peter's, Philadelphia: on Wednesday, May 9, 1798. Being the Day appointed by the President, as a Day of Fasting, Humiliation, and Prayer, throughout the United States of America. By James Abercrombie, A.M. One of the Assistant Ministers of Christ Church and St. Peter's. Published by Request.

Philadelphia: printed by John Ormrod (1798). Inscribed on the inside of the first cover, "To George Washington, Esqr From His most hble Servt. The Author."

The ARMINIAN Magazine: consisting of Extracts and original Treatises on General Redemption. Volume I., II. For the Year 1789, 1790.

Printed in Philadelphia, by Prichard & Hall . . . and sold by John Dickins. Washington's autograph on the title-pages.

BACKUS, Azel, D.D. 1765–1817.

Absalom's Conspiracy: A Sermon, preached at the General Election, at Hartford in the State of Connecticut, May 10th, 1798. By Azel Backus, A.M. Pastor of a Church in Bethlem.

Hartford, printed by Hudson and Goodwin. 1798.

BACKUS, Azel, D.D. 1765–1817.

A Sermon, delivered at the Funeral of His Excellency Oliver Wolcott, Governor of the State of Connecticut; who died 1st December 1797. By Azel Backus, A.M. Pastor of the Church in Bethlem.

Printed at Litchfield, by T. Collier. (1797).

BARCLAY, Robert. *English Quaker,* 1648–1690.

An Apology for the True Christian Divinity, being an Explanation and Vindication of the Principles and Doctrines of the People called Quakers. Written in Latin and English, by Robert Barclay, and since translated into High Dutch, Low Dutch, French, and Spanish, for the Information of Strangers. The eighth Edition in English.

Birmingham; printed by John Baskerville. (1765).

"Barclay's great book, 'The Apology,' is remarkable as the standard exposition of the principles of his sect, and is not only the first defence of those principles by a man of trained intelligence, but in many respects one of the most impressive theological writings of the century." —*Leslie Stephen.*

Washington's autograph is cut from the title-page.

BARTLETT, Josiah, M.D. *Signer of the Declaration of Independence,* 1729–1795.

A Discourse on the Origin, Progress and Design of Free Masonry. Delivered at the Meeting-House in Charlestown, in the Commonwealth of Massachusetts, on the Anniversary of St. John the Baptist. June 24, A.D. 1793. By Josiah Bartlett, M.B.

Boston: printed by Brother [sic] Thomas and John Fleet.

BELKNAP, Jeremy, D.D. *Historian,* 1744–1798.

A Sermon, delivered on the 9th of May, 1798, the Day of the national Fast, recommended by the President of the United States. By Jeremy Belknap, D.D. Minister of the Church in Federal-Street, Boston.

Printed by Samuel Hall. Boston, 1798.

BEND, Rev. Joseph.

A Discourse delivered in St. Paul's Church, Philadelphia, Sunday, July 25th, 1790, on Occasion of the Death of Mrs. Lucia Magaw, wife of the Rev. Samuel Magaw, D.D.: and now published at his Request. By Joseph Bend, A.M. Assistant Minister of Christ-Church and St. Peter's.

Philadelphia: printed by William Young. 1790.

BENEZET, Anthony. *Quaker philanthropist, born in France,* 1713–1784.

An earnest Address to such of the People called Quakers as are sincerely desirous of supporting and maintaining Christian Testimony of their Ancestors. Occasioned by a Piece, intituled, "The Testimony of the People called Quakers, given forth by a Meeting of the Representatives of said People, in Pennsylvania and New-Jersy [sic], held at Philadelphia the Twenty-fourth Day of the First Month, 1775."

Philadelphia, printed for John Douglas McDougal. 1775.

BERINGTON, Simon. *English Catholic divine*, 1679/80–1755.

Dissertations on the Mosaical Creation, Deluge, Building of Babel, and Confusion of Tongues, &c. . . . By S. Berington. London: printed for the Author: and sold by C. Davis, 1750.

Autograph of Washington written at the age of 17 or thereabouts on the title-page. "In these dissertations the author combats Infidels, and Hutchinsonians, La Pluche, Woodward, Sir Isaac Newton and many other writers." —*Gillow.*

BIRCH, Thomas Ledlie. *Irish Presbyterian minister, died* 1808.

The Obligations upon Christians, and especially Ministers, to be exemplary in their Lives; particularly at this important Period, when the Prophecies are seemingly about to be fulfilled in the Fall of Antichrist, as an Introduction to the Flowing in of Jew and Gentile into the Christian Church. A Sermon, preached before the very Reverend the General Synod of Ulster, at Lurgan, June 26th, 1793. By Thomas Ledlie Birch, A.M. Minister of the Gospel at Saintfield.

Belfast: printed by Hugh Dowell. 1794.

BLACKHALL, Offspring. *Bishop of Exeter*, 1654–1716.

The Sufficiency of a standing Revelation in General, and of the Scripture Revelation in Particular. Both as to the Matter of it, and as to the Proof of it; and that new Revelations cannot reasonably be desired, and would probably be unsuccessful. In eight Sermons, preach'd in the Cathedral-Church of St. Paul, London; at the Lecture founded by the Honourable Robert Boyle Esq; in the Year 1700. By Ofspring, late Lord Bishop of Exeter.

London: printed for Jer. Batley . . . and T. Warner. 1717.

Washington's autograph is written twice upon the title-page in a boyish hand. The signature is thought to be the earliest specimen of his writing extant, as it was probably written when he was eight or nine years of age.

BLAKE, Mark.

A Letter to the Clergy of the Church of Scotland. By Mark Blake, Esq.

London: printed for Daniel Isaac Eaton. 1794.

BLAND, Richard. *Virginia antiquary and writer*, 1710–1776.

A Letter to the Clergy of Virginia, in which the Conduct of the General-Assembly is vindicated, against the Reflexions contained in a Letter to the Lords of Trade and Plantations, from the Lord-Bishop of London. By Richard Bland, Esq; one of the Representatitves in Assembly for the County of Prince-George.

Williamsburg: printed by William Hunter, 1760.

The author of this tract, familiarly known as the "Antiquary," was a leading statesman and writer in pre-revolutionary times in Virginia. He wrote the first treatise on the relations of the Colonies with Great Britain, from an American standpoint, under the title, "Enquiries into the Rights of the British Colonies." This work made a decided impression, and Jefferson placed it above the *Farmer's Letters* in its logical presentation of the principles of colonial rights. . . .

The present tract is one of several controversial publications occasioned by the case of the Clergy against the Virginia Assembly, known as the "Parsons' Cause.". . .

Washington's autograph on the title-page and at the top of page iii.

BOYD, Rev. Adam, *Rector of the Church, Augusta, Georgia*.

Keep your Heart. A Sermon, occasioned by the Murder of the Federal Marshal of this State, Major Robert Forsyth: preached at the Desire of the District Society of Cincinnati at Augusta, and most respectfully inscribed to their President, Governor Mathews.

Augusta: printed by John Erdman Smith. 1794.

BRENT, Charles

Money Essay'd; or, the true Value of it tryed. In a Sermon preach'd before the Worshipful Society of Merchants, in the city of Bristol. By Charles Brent, M.A. Rector of Christ Church and of St. Werburge in the said City; and Canon Residentiary of St. David's.

London: printed for William and John Innys. 1728.

BROTHERS, Richard.

A Revealed Knowledge of the Prophecies and Times. Containing, with other great and remarkable Things not revealed to any other Person on Earth, the Restoration of the Jews to Jerusalem, by the Year 1798, under their revealed Prince and Prophet. Wrote by Himself. Book the First.

Philadelphia: printed by Francis & Robert Bailey. 1795.

BROTHERS, Richard.

A Revealed Knowledge of the Prophecies and Times, particularly of the present Time, the present War, and the Prophecy now fulfilling. Containing, with other great and remarkable Things not revealed to any other Person on Earth, the sudden and perpetual Fall of the Turkish, German & Russian Empires. Wrote under the Direction of the Lord God, and published by his Sacred Command; it being a Second Sign of Warning for the Benefit of all Nations; by the Man that will be revealed to the Hebrews as their Prince and Prophet. (Book II.) The Year of the World 5913.

Philadelphia: Francis & Robert Bailey. 1795.

BUCKMINSTER, Joseph, D.D. 1751–1812.

A Discourse, delivered at Portsmouth, New-Hampshire, November 1st, 1789. On Occasion of the President of the United States honoring that Capital with a Visit. By Joseph Buckminster, A.M. Pastor of the First Church in Portsmouth.

Portsmouth: New-Hampshire, printed and sold by John Melcher, 1789.

BURNABY, Andrew. *English divine and traveller,* 1734–1812.

Six occasional Sermons upon the following Subjects. Viz. Sermon I. Of the Necessity of religious Principles. II. Of the Degrees of Charity due to Men of different religious Persuasions. III. Of the Maintenance due to the Ministers of the Gospel. IV. Of the nature of Subscription to Articles of Religion. V. Of Things belonging to the Peace and Welfare of Nations. VI. Of Moral Advantages to be derived from Travelling in Italy. By the Rev. Andrew Burnaby, D.D. Vicar of Greenwich, and Late Chaplain to the British Factory at Leghorn.

London: Printed for J. Payne and son. 1777.

Washington's autograph on the title-page.

BURNET, Gilbert. *Bishop of Sarum,* 1643–1715.

An Exposition of the Thirty-nine Articles of the Church of England. Written by Gilbert Bishop of Sarum. The sixth Edition corrected.

London: printed for J. Knapton, C. Hitch. . . . 1759.

Washington's autograph on the title-page, with date of 1766.

Bought by Washington, as shown by an entry in the Invoice of Cary & Co. of London, March, 1766, preserved in the State Department at Washington.

CAMM, Rev. John. 1718–1779.

A Review of The Rector Detected: or the Colonel Reconnoitred. Part the First.

Williamsburg: Printed by Joseph Royle, 1764.

CARTER, Landon.

The Rector Detected: being a just Defence of the Twopenny Act, against the artful Misrepresentations of the Reverend John Camm, Rector of York-Hampton, in his Single and Distinct View. Containing also a plain Confutation of his several Hints, as a Specimen of the Justice and Charity of Colonel Landon Carter. By Landon Carter, of Sabine Hall.

Williamsburg: Printed by Joseph Royle. 1764.

CHANNING, Rev. Henry. *Yale College,* 1781, *died* 1840.

The Consideration of divine Goodness an argument for religious gratitude and obedience. A Sermon, delivered at New-London, November 27, 1794. Being the day appointed by Authority, for public Thanksgiving in the State of Connecticut. By Henry Channing, A.M. Pastor of the First Church in New-London.

New London: printed by Samuel Green. 1794.

The CHRISTIAN'S, Scholar's, and Farmer's Magazine; calculated, in an eminent Degree, to promote Religion; to disseminate useful Knowledge; to afford literary Pleasure and Amusement, and to advance the Interests of Agriculture. By a Number of Gentlemen. Vol. I. April, 1789–Mar. 1790.

Elizabeth-Town: printed and sold by Shepard Kollock. 1789.

Washington's autograph on the title-page.

COKE, Thomas, LL.D. *English Methodist Bishop in America,* 1747–1814.

The Substance of a Sermon, preached at Baltimore, in the State of Maryland, before the General Conference of the Methodist Episcopal Church, on the 27th of December, 1784, at the Ordination of the Rev. Francis Asbury, to the Office of a Superintendent. By Thomas Coke, L.L.D. Superintendent of the said Church. Published at the Desire of the Conference.

Baltimore, Maryland: printed by Goddard and Langworthy, 1785.

COMBER, Thomas, D.D. *Dean of Durham*, 1645–1699.

Short Discourses upon the whole Common-Prayer. Designed to inform the Judgment, and excite the Devotion of such as daily use the same. The fourth Edition. By Tho. Comber, D.D.

London, printed for J. Nicholson. 1712.

The first fly-leaf contains Washington's autograph when 13 years of age. . . .

COOMBE, Thomas, D.D. 1747–1822.

A Sermon, preached before the Congregations of Christ Church and St. Peter's, Philadelphia, on Thursday, July 20, 1775. Being the Day recommended by the Honorable Continental Congress for a General Fast throughout the twelve united Colonies of North-America. By Thomas Coombe, M.A. Chaplain to the Most Noble the Marquis of Rockingham. Published by Request.

Philadelphia: printed by John Dunlap. 1775.

Washington's autograph on the title-page.

CRUTWELL, Clement, *English author and compiler*, 1743–1808.

A Concordance of Parallels, collected from Bibles and Commentaries, which have been published in Hebrew, Latin, French, Italian, Spanish, English, and other Languages; with the Authorities of each. By the Rev. C. Cruttwell, Editor of Bishop Wilson's Works, &c.

Printed for the Author; and sold by the Booksellers in London, Bath, 1790.

Washington's autograph on the title-page.

DAVIDSON, Robert, D.D. 1750–1812.

A Sermon, on the Freedom and Happiness of the United States of America, preached in Carlisle, on the 5th Oct. 1794. And published at the Request of the Officers of the Philadelphia and Lancaster Troops of Light Horse. By Robert Davidson, D.D. Pastor of the Presbyterian Church in Carlisle, and One of the Professors in Dickinson College.

Philadelphia: printed by Samuel H. Smith for Robert Campbell. 1794.

DE BRAHM, John William Gerard. *Colonial surveyor for Southern District of North America.*

VII. Arm of the Tree of Knowledge, branching Sacred Chronology, through the six divine Labors in Mystic, Physic, Law, History, sacred and prophane, Gospel and Revelation.

Philadelphia: printed by Zachariah Poulson, junior. 1791.

DE BRAHM, John William Gerard. *Colonial surveyor for Southern District of North America.*

Apocalyptic Gnomon points out eternity's Divisibility rated with Time, pointed at Gnomons Sidereals.

Philadelphia: Francis & Robert Bailey. 1795.

Washington's autograph on title-page. Title on back is "End of Time.". . .

DODD, William, D.D. *English divine*, 1729–1777.

An earnest Address to his Parishioners, by a Minister of the Church of England, concerning the Necessity, Nature, Means, and Marks of true Faith in Christ Jesus. Design'd principally for the Poor. The second Edition.

London: printed for W. Faden. 1755.

DUCHÉ, Rev. Jacob. 1737–1798.

The Duty of standing fast in our spiritual and temporal Liberties, a Sermon preached in Christ-Church, July 7th, 1775. Before the First Battalion of the City and Liberties of Philadelphia; and now published at their Request. By the Reverend Jacob Duché, M.A.

Philadelphia. Printed and Sold by James Humphreys, Junior. 1775.

Given to Washington by the author. . . .

DWIGHT, Timothy, D.D. *President of Yale College*, 1752–1817.

The Nature, and Danger, of Infidel Philosophy, exhibited in two Discourses, addressed to the Candidates for the Baccalaureate, in Yale College. By the Rev. Timothy Dwight, D.D. President of Yale College; September 9th, 1797.

New Haven: printed by George Bunce, 1798.

ELIOT, John, D.D. *Historical writer*, 1754–1813.

A Sermon, delivered in the Chapel, Boston, before the Society of Antient and Honorable Free and Accepted Masons, on Monday, June 24, 1782. By John Eliot, A.M.

Boston: printed by Brother N. Willis. 1782.

ELY, REV. ZEBULON. 1759–1824.
The death of Moses the Servant of the Lord. A Sermon preached at the funeral Solemnity of His Excellency Jonathan Trumbull, Esq. L.L.D. Late Governor of the State of Connecticut, August 19, 1785. By Zebulon Ely, A.M. Pastor of the first church of Christ in Lebanon.
Hartford: Printed by Elisha Babcock, 1786.

EVANS, REV. ISRAEL. 1748–1807.
A Discourse, delivered at Easton, on the 17th of October, 1779, to the Officers and Soldiers of the Western Army, after their Return from an Expedition against the Five Nations of hostile Indians. By the Reverend Israel Evans, A.M. and Chaplain to General Poore's Brigade. Now published at the particular Request of the Generals and Field Officers of that Army.
Philadelphia: Printed by Thomas Bradford. 1779.

EVANS, REV. ISRAEL. 1748–1807.
An Oration, delivered at Hackinsack, on the Tenth of September, 1780. At the Interment of the Honorable Brigadier Enoch Poor, General of the New-Hampshire Brigade. By the Reverend Israel Evans, A.M. and Chaplain to the said Brigade. Published by Desire of the Officers of the New Hampshire Troops, and a Number of Gentlemen in Exeter.
Newbury-Port: printed and Sold by John Mycall. 1781.

EVANS, REV. ISRAEL. 1748–1807.
A Discourse delivered near York in Virginia, on the memorable Occasion of the Surrender of the British Army to the allied Forces of America and France, before the Brigade of New-York Troops and the Division of American Light-Infantry, under the Command of the Marquis de la Fayette. By Israel Evans, A.M., Chaplain to the Troops of New-Hampshire.
Philadelphia: printed by Francis Bailey. 1782.

EVANS, REV. ISRAEL. 1748–1807.
A Discourse, delivered in New-York, before a Brigade of Continental Troops, and a Number of Citizens, assembled in St. George's Chapel, on the 11th December, 1783. The Day set apart by the Recommendation of the United States in Congress, as a Day of Public Thanksgiving for the Blessings of Independence, Liberty and Peace, by the Rev. Israel Evans, A.M. Chaplain in the American Army.
Published, and Sold by John Holt, printer to the State of New-York. [1784?]

EVANS, REV. ISRAEL. 1748–1807.
A Sermon, delivered at Concord, before the Hon. General Court of the State of Newhampsire, at the annual Election, holden on the first Wednesday in June, 1791. By the Rev. Israel Evans, A.M. Pastor of the church in Concord.
Concord: printed by George Hough, for the Honourable General Court. 1791.
Washington's autograph on the title page.

FISH, REV. SAMUEL.
A Discourse, shewing the Certainty of Christ's personal Appearance and universal Reign at the head of his Zion, over all the Nations and Kingdoms in this lower World. [*Revelation 19:7.*]
Windham: printed for the Author. 1793.

FISH, REV. SAMUEL.
A Discourse, shewing the Certainty of Christ's spiritual Reign among all the Nations and Kingdoms in this lower World.
Windham: printed for the Author. 1793.

FISH, REV. SAMUEL.
An humble Address to every Christian of every Nation and Denomination of people under Heaven. Shewing an effectual Means to prevent Wars among all Nations of the Earth, and to maintain an everlasting Union, in Families, Societies, Churches, Towns, States, and in all the Kingdoms of this lower World.
Norwich: printed by John Trumbull, for the Author. 1793.

FISHER, MIERS. *Lawyer*, 1748–1819.
A Reply to the false Reasoning in the "Age of Reason." To which are added, some Thoughts on Idolatry; on the Devil; and the Origin of moral Evil; on educating Young Men for the Gospel Ministry; and on what is "The Word of God." All which refer, more or less, to Opinions advanced in Thomas Paine's "Investigations of true and fabulous Theology." By a Layman.
Philadelphia: printed by Henry Tuckniss, for the author. 1796.

G., N.
A Scriptural Comment on the Athanasian Creed.
Printed by Thomas Lang, Philadelphia. [1791.]
The author, who signed only the initials of his name, in presenting Washington with a copy of the book wrote as follows: — ". . . my situation in Life

forbids my appearing in person, but from my Humble Cot beg leave to present you with the inclosed performance upon the greatest and most sublime Mystery of our Holy Religion, being a short Scriptural Commentary on the ever Blessed Trinity, a work which engaged my attention at a time when to all Human appearances I was near the Gate of Death. . . ." N. G.

GORDON, Rev. William. *Historian*, 1730–1807.

A Sermon preached [July 19, 1775], before the Honorable House of Representatives, on the Day intended for the Choice of Counsellors, agreeable to the Advice of the Continental Congress. By William Gordon, Pastor of the Third Church in Roxbury.

Watertown: printed and sold by Benjamin Edes. 1775.

GORDON, Rev. William. *Historian*, 1730–1807.

The Separation of the Jewish Tribes, after the Death of Solomon, accounted for, and applied to the present Day, in a Sermon preached before the General Court, on Friday, July 4th, 1777. Being the Anniversary of the Declaration of Independency. By William Gordon. Pastor of the Third Church in Roxbury.

Boston: Printed by J. Gill, Printer to the General Assembly, 1777.

GREEN, Ashbel, D.D. 1762–1848.

A Sermon, delivered in the Second Presbyterian Church in the City of Philadelphia, on the 19th of February, 1795, being the Day of General Thanksgiving throughout the United States. By Ashbel Green, D.D. One of the Pastors of the aforesaid Church.

Philadelphia: printed by John Fenno, March, 1795.

HART, Rev. Oliver. 1723–1795.

America's Remembrancer, with Respect to her Blessedness and Duty. A Sermon, delivered in Hopewell, New Jersey, on Thanksgiving Day, November 26, 1789. By Oliver Hart, A.M.

Philadelphia: Printed by T. Dobson. 1791.

Washington's autograph on the title-page.

HENLEY, Rev. Samuel.

A candid Refutation of the Heresy imputed by Ro. C. Nicholas Esquire to the Reverend S. Henley.

Williamsburg, printed for B. White in London, D. Prince in Oxford, and J. Woodyer in Cambridge. 1774.

. . . .Bought by Washington as appears from the following:—

1774. June 15. By Henley's defence ag^{t}. y^{e}. cha: of Heresy 2/6

HINDMARSH, Robert. *English New Church writer*, 1759–1835.

A Short Account of the Honourable Emmanuel Swedenborg, and his theological Writings.

London, printed. Baltimore—Re-printed and sold by Samuel and John Adams. 1792.

HOMER, Jonathan, D.D. 1759–1843.

The Character and Duties of a Christian Soldier, considered and applied in a Sermon, preached before the Ancient and Honorable Company of Artillery on Monday, June 7, 1790; being the Anniversary of the Election of Officers. By Jonathan Homer, A.M. Pastor of the First Church in Newton.

Printed in Boston, By Benjamin Russell, 1790.

HOMER, Jonathan, D.D. 1759–1843.

The Succession of Generations among Mankind, illustrated and improved in a Century Sermon, preached at Newton, on Lord's day, Dec. 25, 1791; being the Commencement of a new Century, from the Incorporation of said Town. By Jonathan Homer, A.M. Pastor of the first Church in Newton.

Printed at the Apollo Press, in Boston, by Belknap and Young. 1792.

HORROCKS, Rev. James. *President of William & Mary College, died* 1772.

Upon the Peace. A Sermon. Preach'd at the Church of Petsworth, in the County of Gloucester, on August the 25th, the Day appointed by Authority for the Observance of that Solemnity. By the Reverend James Horrocks, A.M. Fellow of Trinity College, Cambridge, and Master of the Grammar School in William and Mary College.

Williamsburg: printed by Joseph Royle, 1763.

HURT, Rev. John. *Chaplain in the Continental Army.*

The Love of our Country. A Sermon, preached before the Virginia Troops in New-Jersey. By John Hurt, Chaplain.

Philadelphia: printed and sold by Styner and Cist. 1777.

JEBB, John, M.D. *English theological and political writer*, 1736–1786.

The Excellency of the Spirit of Benevolence, a

Sermon preached before the University of Cambridge, on Monday, December 28, 1772. By the Rev. John Jebb, M.A. Late Fellow of St. Peter's College.

Cambridge, printed in the year 1773.

London, Reprinted in the year 1782; and sold by J. Dixwell.

KEATINGE, GEORGE.

The Maryland Ahiman Rezon, of Free & Accepted Masons; containing the History of Masonry, from the Establishment of the Grand Lodge to the Present Time; with their ancient Charges, Addresses, Prayers, Lectures, Prologues, Epilogues, Songs, &c. Corrected from their old Records, faithful Traditions, & Lodge-Books. Compiled by Order of the Grand Lodge of Maryland, by Brother G. Keatinge, W.M.B.L.

Baltimore: printed by W. Pechin—for George Keatinge's Book-Store. 1797.

KENDAL, SAMUEL, D.D. 1753–1814.

A Sermon, delivered on the Day of National Thanksgiving, February 19, 1795. By Samuel Kendal, A.M. Pastor of the Congregational Church and Society in Weston.

Printed by Samuel Hall, Boston. 1795.

KIPPIS, ANDREW, D.D. *English biographer,* 1725–1795.

An Address, delivered at the Interment of the late Rev. Dr. Richard Price, on the twenty-sixth of April, 1791. By Andrew Kippis, D.D. F. R.S. and S.A.

London: printed for T. Cadell and J. Johnson, 1791.

KIRKLAND, JOHN THORNTON, D.D. *President of Harvard College,* 1770–1840.

A Sermon, delivered at the Interment of the Rev. Jeremy Belknap, D.D. Minister of the Church in Federal Street, Boston, June 22, 1798. By John Thornton Kirkland, Minister of the New South Church, Boston.

Boston: printed by Manning & Loring. [1798.]

LANGDON, SAMUEL, D.D. *President of Harvard College,* 1723–1797.

Government corrupted by Vice, and recovered by Righteousness. A Sermon preached before the Honorable Congress of the Colony of the Massachusetts-Bay in New-England, assembled at Watertown, on Wednesday the 31st Day of May, 1775. Being the Anniversary fixed by Charter for the Election of Counsellors. By Samuel Langdon, D.D. President of Harvard College in Cambridge.

Watertown: printed and sold by Benjamin Edes, 1775.

LANGDON, SAMUEL, D.D. *President of Harvard College,* 1723–1797.

The Co-incidence of Natural with Revealed Religion. A Sermon at the annual Lecture instituted in Harvard College by the last Will and Testament of the Honorable Paul Dudley, Esq; delivered November 1, 1775. By Samuel Langdon, D.D. President of Harvard College.

Boston: printed by Samuel Hall. 1776.

LANGDON, SAMUEL, D.D. *President of Harvard College,* 1723–1797.

The Republic of the Israelites an Example to the American States. A Sermon, preached at Concord, in the State of New Hampshire; before the Honorable General Court at the annual Election. June 5, 1788. By Samuel Langdon, D.D. Pastor of the Church in Hampton-Falls.

Exeter: printed by Lamson and Ranlet. 1788.

LANGDON, SAMUEL, D.D. *President of Harvard College,* 1723–1797.

A Correction of some great Mistakes committed by the Rev. John Cosens Ogden, a Presbyter in the Protestant Episcopal Church, in the United States of America, in his late Letters published at Boston. By Samuel Langdon, D.D. Minister of Hampton-Falls, in the State of New-Hampshire.

Portsmouth: printed by John Melcher, 1792.

LANGDON, SAMUEL, D.D. *President of Harvard College,* 1723–1797.

A Discourse on the Unity of the Church as a monumental Pillar of the Truth; designed to reconcile Christians of all Parties and Denominations in Charity and Fellowship, as one Body in Christ; delivered before the Association of Ministers convened at Portsmouth, October 12, 1791, and in Substance repeated at a Lecture in Hamptonfalls, January 26, 1792. By Samuel Langdon, D.D. Minister of the Church in Hamptonfalls, in the State of Newhampshire.

Printed at Exeter, by Henry Ranlet, 1792.

LATHROP, JOHN, D.D. 1740–1816.

A Discourse on the Peace; Preached on the Day of Public Thanksgiving, November 25, 1784. By John

Lathrop, A.M. Pastor of the Second Church in Boston.

Boston: printed by Peter Edes. 1784.

A LETTER from One of the Society of Friends, relative to the conscientious Scrupulousness of its Members to bear Arms.

From the Press, 1795.

LINN, William, D.D. 1752–1808.

The Blessings of America. A Sermon, preached in the Middle Dutch Church, on the Fourth July, 1791, being the Anniversary of the Independence of America: at the Request of the Tammany Society, or Columbian Order. By William Linn, D.D.

New-York—printed by Thomas Greenleaf. 1791.

LINN, William, D.D. 1752–1808.

A Discourse, delivered on the 26th of November, 1795; being the Day recommended by the Governor of the State of New-York to be observed as a Day of Thanksgiving and Prayer, on Account of the Removal of an Epidemic Fever, and for other national blessings. By William Linn, D.D. One of the ministers of the Reformed Dutch Church in the City of New-York.

New-York: printed by T. and J. Swords. 1795

LINN, William, D.D. 1752–1808.

A Discourse on national Sins: delivered May 9, 1798; being the Day recommended by the President of the United States to be observed as a Day of General Fast. By William Linn, D.D. One of the Ministers of the Reformed Dutch Church in the City of New-York.

New-York: printed by T. & J. Swords. 1798.

LOSKIEL, George Henry. *Moravian missionary,* 1740–1814.

History of the Mission of the United Brethren among the Indians in North America. In three Parts. By George Henry Loskiel. Translated from the German by Christian Ignatius La Trobe.

London: printed for the Brethren's Society for the furtherance of the Gospel. 1794.

Washington's autograph on the title-page.

McCORKLE, Samuel Eusebius, D.D. 1746–1811.

A Sermon, on the comparative Happiness and Duty of the United States of America, contrasted with other Nations, particularly the Israelites. Delivered in Salisbury, on Wednesday, February 18th; and at Thyatira, on Thursday, February 19th, 1795: Being the Day of General Thanksgiving and Prayer, appointed by the President of the United States. Published by the Request of the Hearers. By the Rev. Samuel E. McCorkle, D.D. Pastor of the Church at Thyatira and Salisbury, in Rowan County, North-Carolina.

Halifax: [N.C.]: Printed by Abraham Hodge. 1795.

MAGAW, Samuel, D.D. 1740–1812.

A Sermon preached in Christ-church, Dover, on Monday, December 27th, 1779, being the Anniversary of St. John the Evangelist; at the Request of and before the General Communication of Free and Accepted Masons of the Delaware State: By Samuel Magaw, M.A.

Philadelphia: printed by John Dunlap. [1780.]

Washington's autograph upon the title-page.

MAGAW, Samuel, D.D. 1740–1812.

A Sermon, preached in Christ-Church, Dover; before the General Communication of Free and Accepted Masons of the Delaware State: on Wednesday, December 27th, 1780. Being the Anniversary of St. John the Evangelist.

Philadelphia: printed by David C. Claypoole. 1781.

MAGAW, Samuel, D.D. 1740–1812.

Things Lovely and of good Report. A Sermon, delivered in St. Paul's Church, Philadelphia. On the 27th of December, 1793: being St. John the Evangelist's Day; in the Presence of the Grand Lodge of Pennsylvania: to which is prefixed a Prayer, before the Sermon. Published at their Request. By Samuel Magaw, D.D.

Philadelphia: printed by C. Oswald. 1794.

MANSFIELD, Rev. Isaac. 1750–1826.

A Sermon, preached in the Camp at Roxbury, November 23, 1775; being the Day appointed by Authority for Thanksgiving through the Province. By Isaac Mansfield, jun. A.M. Chaplain to General Thomas's Regiment in the Continental Army. Published at the Request of the Officers in said Regiment.

Boston: printed by S. Hall. 1776.

MASON, John Mitchell, D.D. 1770–1829.

A Sermon, preached September 20th, 1793; a Day set apart, in the City of New-York, for public Fasting, Humiliation and Prayer, on Account of a Malignant and Mortal Fever prevailing in the City of Philadelphia. By John Mitchel Mason, Minister of the Scotch Presbyterian Church in the City of New-York.

New-York: printed by Samuel Loudon & Son. 1793.

MASON, John Mitchell, D.D. 1770–1829.

Mercy remembered in Wrath. A Sermon, the Substance of which was preached on the 19th of February, 1795, observed throughout the United States, as a Day of Thanksgiving and Prayer. By John M. Mason, Pastor of the Scotch Presbyterian Church, in the City of New-York.

New-York: printed by J. Buel. 1795.

MATHER, Samuel, D.D. 1706–1785.

The Dying Legacy of an aged Minister of the everlasting Gospel, to the United States of North-America.

Boston: printed by Benjamin Edes and Sons. 1783.

MILLER, Samuel, D.D. 1791–1850.

A Sermon, preached in New-York, July 4th, 1793. Being the Anniversary of the Independence of America: at the Request of the Tammany Society, or Columbian Order. By Samuel Miller, A.M. One of the Ministers of the United Presbyterian Churches, in the city of New-York.

New-York—printed by Thomas Greenleaf. [1793.]

MILLER, Samuel, D.D. 1791–1850.

A Discourse delivered in the New Presbyterian Church, New-York: before the Grand Lodge of the State of New-York, and the Brethren of that Fraternity, assembled in General Communication, on the Festival of St. John the Baptist, June 24th, 1795. By Samuel Miller, A.M. One of the Ministers of the United Presbyterian Churches, in the City of New-York.

New-York:—Printed by F. Childs. 1795.

MILLER, Samuel, D.D. 1791–1850.

A Sermon, delivered in the New Presbyterian Church, New-York, July fourth, 1795, being the nineteenth Anniversary of the Independence of America: at the Request of, and before, the Mechanic, Tammany, and Democratic Societies, and the military Officers. By Samuel Miller, A.M. One of the Ministers of the United Presbyterian Churches, in the City of New-York.

New-York—printed by Thomas Greenleaf. 1795.

MORSE, Jedidiah, D.D. *Divine and author,* 1761–1826.

The present Situation of other Nations of the World, contrasted with our own. A Sermon, delivered at Charlestown, in the Commonwealth of Massachusetts, February 19, 1795; being the Day recommended by George Washington, President of the United States of America, for Public Thanksgiving and Prayer. By Jedidiah Morse, D.D. Minister of the Congregation in Charlestown.

Printed by Samuel Hall, Boston. 1795.

MORSE, Jedidiah, D.D. *Divine and author,* 1761–1826.

The Duty of Resignation under Afflictions, illustrated and enforced from the Example of Christ, in a Sermon preached at Charlestown, April 17, 1796. Occasioned by the Death of the Honourable Thomas Russell, Esquire, who died in Boston, April 8, 1796, aged Fifty-Six. By Jedidiah Morse, D.D. Minister of the Congregation in Charlestown. Published at the Request of the Mourners.

Printed by Samuel Hall, in Cornhill, Boston, 1796.

Washington's autograph on the title-page.

MORSE, Jedidiah, D.D. *Divine and author,* 1761–1826.

A Sermon, preached at Charlestown, November 29, 1798, on the anniversary Thanksgiving in Massachusetts. With an Appendix, designed to illustrate some Parts of the Discourse; exhibiting proofs of the early existence, progress, and deleterious effects of French intrigue and influence in the United States. By Jedidiah Morse, D.D. Pastor of the Church in Charlestown. Published by Request.

Printed by Samuel Hall, Boston. December, 1798.

Given to Washington by the author. Washington's letter of acknowledgment is here printed from the press copy preserved in the Lenox Library:—

"The Letter with which you were pleased to favour me, dated the first instant, accompanying your thanksgiving Sermon came duly to hand. —

"For the latter I pray you to accept my thanks. —I have read it, and the Appendix with pelasure, and wish the latter at least could meet with a more general circulation than it probably will have, for it contains important information, as little known out of a small circle as the dissemination of it would be useful if spread before the Community. Mt. Vernon 28 Feb. 1799."

MORSE, Jedidiah, D.D. *Divine and author,* 1761–1826.

A Sermon, exhibiting the present Dangers, and consequent Duties of the Citizens of the United States of America. Delivered at Charlestown, April 25, 1799. The Day of the National Fast. By Jedidiah Morse, D.D. Pastor of the Church in Charlestown. Published at the Request of the Hearers.

Charlestown: printed and sold by Samuel Etheridge. 1799.

MUIR, James, D.D. 1757–1820.

A Sermon preached in the Presbyterian Church at Alexandria, on the 9th of May, 1798, being the Day appointed for a General Fast. By the Revd. Doctor James Muir.

Philadelphia: published by William Cobbett. May 9, 1798.

NICOLLS, Samuel, LL.D. *Prebendary of St. Paul's, died* 1763.

A Sermon preach'd before the Society corresponding with the Incorporated Society in Dublin, for promoting English protestant Working-Schools in Ireland, at their General Meeting in the Parish-Church of St. Mary le Bow, on Tuesday, April 4th, 1749. By Samuel Nicolls, LL.D. Chaplain in Ordinary to His Majesty.

London: printed and sold by J. Oliver. 1749.

NISBET, Charles, D.D. *Scottish educator in America,* 1736–1804.

The Usefulness and Importance of human Learning, a Sermon preached before the Trustees of Dickinson College. Met at Carlisle, May 11, 1786; and published at their Desire. By Charles Nisbet, D.D. Principal of said College.

Carlisle: printed by Kline & Reynolds. [1786.]

OGDEN, Rev. John Cosens. 1755–1800.

A Sermon, delivered before His Excellency the President, the Honourable Senate, and the Honourable House of Representatives, of the State of Newhampshire, at the Annual Election, holden at Concord, on the first Wednesday in June, 1790. By John C. Ogden, A.M. Rector of Queen's chapel in Portsmouth.

Printed at Concord, by George Hough, for the General Court. 1790.

OGDEN, Rev. John Cosens. 1755–1800.

An Appeal to the Candid, upon the present State of Religion and Politics in Connecticut.

[Stockbridge? 1799?]

OGDEN, Rev. John Cosens. 1755–1800.

A View of the Calvinistic Clubs of the United States.

[Stockbridge? 1799?]

OGDEN, Rev. John Cosens. 1755–1800.

A View of the New England Illuminati: who are indefatigably engaged in destroying the Religion and Government of the United States; under a feigned Regard for their Safety—and under an impious Abuse of true Religion.

Philadelphia: printed by James Carey. 1799.

OGDEN, Rev. John Cosens. 1755–1800.

A short History of the late Ecclesiastical Oppressions in New-England and Vermont, by a Citizen. In which is exhibited a Statement of the Violation of religious Liberties, which are ratified by the Constitution of the United States.

Richmond: printed by James Lyon. 1799.

OGDEN, Uzal, D.D. 1744–1822.

A Sermon on practical Religion. Delivered at Newark, August 15, 1779. By the Rev. Uzal Ogden of Sussex County, New Jersey. Number II.

Chatham: printed by Shepard Kollock. 1780.

OGDEN, Uzal, D.D. 1744–1822.

A Sermon delivered at Roxbury, in Morris County, March 19, 1781, at the Funeral of Mrs. Elizabeth Hackett, Relict of Colonel John Hackett. By the Reverend Uzal Ogden, of Sussex County, New Jersey.

Chatham: printed by Shepard Kollock. 1781.

OGDEN, Uzal, D.D. 1744–1822.

A Sermon on Practical Religion. By the Reverend Uzal Ogden, at Sussex County, New Jersey. Number III.

Chatham: printed by Shepard Kollock. 1782.

OGDEN, Uzal, D.D. 1744–1822.

A Sermon delivered at Morris-Town, on Monday December 27, 1784, it being the Festival of St. John the Evangelist, before the Fraternity of Free and Accepted Masons, of Lodge No. 10, in the State of New-Jersey. By the Rev. Uzal Ogden. Published at the Request of the Lodge.

New-York: printed by J. McLean, and Co. 1785.

OGDEN, Uzal, D.D. 1744–1822.

An Address to those Persons at Elizabeth-Town, and Newark, and in their Vicinity, in the State of New Jersey, who have lately been seriously impressed with a Desire to obtain Salvation To which is annexed, a Prayer adapted to a Person in a State of Penitence. By the Reverend Uzal Ogden.

New-York: printed by J. McLean, and Co. 1785.

Washington's autograph on the title-page.

OGDEN, Uzal, D.D. 1744–1822.

Antidote to Deism. The Deist unmasked; or an ample Refutation of all the Objections of Thomas Paine, against the Christian Religion; as contained in a Pamphlet, intitled, The Age of Reason; addressed to the Citizens of these States. By the Reverend Uzal Ogden, Rector of Trinity Church, at Newark, in the State of New-Jersey. To which is prefixed, Remarks on Boulanger's Christianity unveiled. And to the Deist Unmasked, is annexed a Short Method with the Deists. By the Reverend Charles Leslie. In Two Volumes.

Newark, printed by John Woods. 1795. 2 vols. Vol. I, Vol. II.

Washington's autograph on the title-pages of both volumes.

OSGOOD, David, D.D. 1747–1822.

A Discourse, delivered February 19, 1795. The Day set apart by the President for a General Thanksgiving through the United States. By David Osgood, A.M. Pastor of the Church in Medford.

Printed by Samuel Hall, Boston. 1795.

PHIPPS, Joseph. *English Quaker*, 1708–1787.

The original and present State of Man, briefly considered: wherein is shewn, the Nature of his Fall, and the Necessity, Means and Manner of his Restoration, through the Sacrifice of Christ, and the sensible Operation of that Divine Principle of Grace and Truth, held forth to the World, by the People called Quakers. To which are added, some Remarks on the Arguments of Samuel Newton, of Norwich. By Joseph Phipps.

London, printed: New-York, re-printed by William Ross. 1788.

Washington's autograph on the title-page.

PORTEUS, Beilby. *Bishop of Chester, afterwards Bishop of London*, 1731–1808.

A Sermon preached before the Incorporated Society for the Propagation of the Gospel in Foreign Parts; at their anniversary Meeting in the Parish Church of St. Mary-le-Bow, on Friday, February 21, 1783. By the Right Reverend Father in God, Beilby Lord Bishop of Chester.

London: Printed for J. F. and C. Rivingtons. 1784.

PRIESTLEY, Joseph. *English divine and scientist*, 1733–1804.

Unitarianism, explained and defended, in a Disourse delivered in the Church of the Universalists, at Philadelphia, 1796. By Joseph Priestley, LL.D. F.R.S. &c. &c.

Philadelphia, printed by John Thompson. 1796.

PRIESTLEY, Joseph. *English divine and scientist*, 1733–1804.

Observations on the Increase of Infidelity. By Joseph Priestley, L.L.D. F.R.S. &c. &c. The third Edition. To which are added, Animadversions on the Writings of several modern Unbelievers, and especially the Ruins of Mr. Volney.

Philadelphia, printed for Thomas Dobson. 1797.

RAY, John. *English naturalist*, 1627–1704/5.

The Wisdom of God manifested in the Works of the Creation. In two Parts. Viz. The Heavenly Bodies, Elements, Meteors, Fossils, Vegetables, Animals, (Beasts, Birds, Fishes, and Insects) more particularly in the Body of the Earth, its Figure, Motion, and Consistency; and in the admirable Structure of the Bodies of Man and other Animals; as also in their Generation, &c. With Answers to some Objections. By John Ray, late Fellow of the Royal Society. The eleventh Edition, corrected.

London: printed for W. Innys. 1743.

Washington's autograph when seventeen years old or thereabouts, on the title-page.

אמת ואמונה

Reason and Faith, or, philosophical Absurdities, and the necessity of Revelation, intended to promote Faith among Infidels, and the unbounded Exercise of Humanity among all religious Men. By one of the Sons of Abraham to his Brethren.

Philadelphia: printed by F. Bailey. 1791.

Washington's autograph on the 3d page.

RICHARDS, William.

Reflections on French Atheism and on English Christianity. By William Richards, M.A. Member of the Pennsylvania Society for promoting the Abolition of Slavery.

Lynn: printed by William Turner, in the Year 1794.

RODGERS, John, D.D. 1727–1811.

The faithful Servant rewarded: a Sermon, delivered at Princeton, before the Board of Trustees of the College of New-Jersey May 6, 1795, occasioned by the Death of the Rev. John Witherspoon, D.D. L.L.D. By John Rodgers, D.D. Senior Minister of the United Presbyterian Churches, in the City of New York.

New-York—printed by Thomas Greenleaf. 1795.

ROGERS, William, D.D. 1751–1824.

An Oration, delivered July 4, 1789, at the Presbyterian church, in Arch Street, Philadelphia, by the Rev. William Rogers, A.M. Professor of English and Oratory, in the College and Academy of Philadelphia. To which is added, A Prayer delivered on the same Occasion, by the Rev. Ashbel Green, A.M. Junior Pastor of the Second Prebyterian Church. Published at the Request of the Pennsylvania Society of the Cincinnati.

Philadelphia: printed for T. Dobson. 1789.

SEABURY, Samuel, D.D. *Bishop of Connecticut,* 1729–1796.

An Address to the Ministers and Congregations of the Presbyterian and Independent Persuasions in the United States of America. By a Member of the Episcopal Church.

Printed in the Year 1790.

SENECA.

Seneca's Morals by way of abstract. To which is added, A Discourse under the Title of an After-Thought. By Sir Roger L'Estrange, Knt. The fifteenth Edition.

London: printed for G. Strahan. 1746.

Washington's autograph, written at the age of seventeen or thereabouts, on the title-page.

A SERMON, on the present Situation of the Affairs of America and Great Britain. Written by a Black, [anonymous], and printed at the Request of several Persons of distinguished Characters.

Philadelphia: printed by T. Bradford and P. Hall. 1782.

SHIPLEY, Jonathan. *Bishop of St. Asaph,* 1714(?)–1788.

A Speech intended to have been spoken on the Bill for altering the Charters of the Colony of Massachusett's Bay. The third Edition.

London, printed; Philadelphia; re-printed and sold, by William and Thomas Bradford. 1774.

SMITH, Samuel Stanhope, D.D., LL.D. 1750–1819.

A funeral Sermon, on the Death of the Hon. Richard Stockton, Esq. Princeton, March 2, 1781. By the Rev. Samuel S. Smith, A.M. Professor of Divinity and Moral Philosophy, in the College of New-Jersey.

Trenton: printed and sold by Isaac Collins. 1781.

SMITH, Samuel Stanhope, D.D., LL.D. 1750–1819.

A Discourse on the Nature and Reasonableness of Fasting, and on the existing Causes that call us to that Duty. Delivered at Princeton, on Tuesday the 6th January, 1795. Being the Day appointed by the Synod of New-York and New-Jersey, to be observed as a General Fast, by all the Churches of their Communion in those States; and now published in Compliance with the request of the Students of Theology and Law in Princeton. By Samuel Stanhope Smith, D.D. Vice-President and Professor of Moral Philosophy and Divinity, in the college of New-Jersey.

Philadelphia: printed by William Young. 1795.

SMITH, Samuel Stanhope, D.D., LL.D. 1750–1819.

The Divine Goodness to the United States of America. A Discourse on the Subjects of national Gratitude, delivered in the Third Presbyterian Church in Philadelphia, on Thursday the 19th of February, 1795, recommended by the President of the United States, to be observed throughout the Union as a Day of General Thanksgiving and Prayer. Published at the Request of the Committee of that Church. The second Edition. By Samuel Stanhope Smith, D.D. Vice-President and Professor of Moral Philosophy and Divinity, in the College of New-Jersey.

Philadelphia: printed by William Young, 1795.

SMITH, William, D.D. *Provost of the College and Academy of Philadelphia,* 1727–1803.

A Sermon on the present Situation of American Affairs. Preached in Christ-Church, June 23, 1775. At the Request of the Officers of the Third Battallion of the City of Philadelphia, and District of Southwark. By William Smith, D.D. Provost of the College in that City.

Philadelphia. Printed and Sold by James Humphreys, junior. 1775.

Æt. 13.

March 12th 1744/5

Geo Washington

Æt. 17.

Beginning this Eleventh Day of November 1749 —

GWashington

Æt. 25.

I am Sir, Yr. Most Obedt. Hble Servt.

Fort Loudoun 10th Septr. 1757 } — G:Washington

Æt. 44.

Yr Most affect. Brother,

G:Washington

New York 29th of April 1776.

Four days before his Death. Æt. 67.

Mount Vernon
December 10th
1799
G:Washington

George Washington's signature at ages thirteen, seventeen, twenty-five, forty-four, and sixty-seven, four days before his death.

SMITH, William, D.D. *Provost of the College and Academy of Philadelphia,* 1727–1803.

A Sermon preached in Christ-Church, Philadelphia, (for the Benefit of the Poor) by Appointment of and before the General Communication of Free and Accepted Masons of the State of Pennsylvania on Monday December 28, 1778. Celebrated, agreeable to their Constitution, as the Anniversary of St. John the Evangelist. By William Smith, D.D. Provost of the College and Academy of Philadelphia.

Philadelphia: printed by John Dunlap. 1779.

SMITH, William, D.D. *Provost of the College and Academy of Philadelphia,* 1727–1803.

Two Sermons, delivered in Christ-Church, Philadelphia, before the General Convention of the Protestant Episcopal Church of the States of New-York, New-Jersey, Pennsylvania, Delaware, Maryland, Virginia, and South-Carolina; viz. Serm. I. On Wednesday, July 29, 1789, at the Opening of the said Convention. Serm. II. On Tuesday, August 4, 1789, at the Funeral of the Rev. David Griffith, D.D. Late Bishop-elect of the said Church, in the State of Virginia. By William Smith, D.D. Provost of the College and Academy of Philadelphia. Both Sermons published at the Request and by Order of the Convention.

Philadelphia: printed by Dobson & Lang. 1789.

SMITH, William, D.D. *Provost of the College and Academy of Philadelphia,* 1727–1803.

A Sermon on temporal and spiritual Salvation, delivered in Christ-Church, Philadelphia, before the Pennsylvania Society of the Cincinnati. By William Smith, D.D. Provost of the College and Academy of Philadelphia. Prepared and published at the Request of the Society.

Philadelphia: from the Press of T. Dobson. 1790.

SMITH, William Pitt.

The Universalist. In Seven Letters to Amyntor; by William Pitt Smith. That God may be all in all.

New-York: printed by Francis Childs. 1788.

Washington's autograph on the title-page.

SPANGENBERG, August Gottlieb. *Moravian bishop,* 1704–1792.

An Account of the Manner in which the Protestant Church of the Unitas Fratrum or United Brethren, preach the Gospel, and carry on their Missions among the Heathen. Translated from the German of the Rev. August Gottlieb Spangenberg.

London: printed and sold by H. Trapp. 1788.

Washington's autograph on the title-page.

STEVENS, Benjamin, D.D. 1721–1791.

A Sermon occasioned by the Death of the Honourable Sir William Pepperell, Bart. Lieutenant-General in his Majesty's Service, &c. who died at his Seat in Kittery, July 6th, 1759, aged 63. Preached the next Lord's-Day after his Funeral. By Benjamin Stevens, A.M. Pastor of the First Church in Kittery.

Boston: printed by Edes and Gill. 1759.

STILES, Ezra, D.D. *President of Yale College,* 1727–1795.

The United States elevated to Glory and Honor. A Sermon, preached before His Excellency Jonathan Trumbull, Esq. L.L.D. Governor and Commander in Chief, and the Honorable the General Assembly of the State of Connecticut, convened at Hartford, at the Annual Election, May 8th, 1783. By Ezra Stiles, D.D. President of Yale-College.

New-Haven: printed by Thomas & Samuel Green. 1783.

STILLMAN, Samuel, D.D. 1737–1807.

Thoughts on the French Revolution. A Sermon, delivered November 20, 1794: being the Day of annual Thanksgiving. By Samuel Stillman, D.D. Pastor of the First Baptist Church in Boston.

Boston: printed by Manning & Loring. 1795.

STITH, William. *Historian, and President of W. & M. College,* 1689–1755.

A Sermon, preached before the General Assembly, at Williamsburg, March 2, 1745–6. By William Stith, A.M. Rector of Henrico Parish. Published at the Request of the House of Burgesses.

Williamsburg: printed and Sold by William Parks, 1745/6.

STITH, William. *Historian, and President of W. & M. College,* 1689–1755.

The Nature and Extent of Christ's Redemption. A Sermon preached before the General Assembly of Virginia: at Williamsburg, November 11th, 1753. By William Stith, A.M. President of William and Mary College. Published at the Request of the House of Burgesses.

Williamsburg: Printed and Sold by William Hunter. 1753.

Washington's autograph on the title-page.

STORY, Rev. Isaac. 1749–1816.

A Discourse, delivered February 15, 1795, at the Request of the Proprietors' Committee; as preparatory to the Collection, on the National Thanksgiving, the Thursday following, for the Benefit of our American Brethren in Captivity at Algiers. By Isaac Story, A.M. Pastor of the Second Congregational Society in Marblehead.

Printed by Thomas C. Cushing, Salem. 1795.

STORY, Rev. Isaac. 1749–1816.

A Sermon, preached February 19, 1795, (from Ecclesiastes ix. 18) being the Federal Thanksgiving, appointed by our beloved President, the illustrious George Washington, Esq. By Isaac Story, A.M. Pastor of the Second Congregational Society in Marblehead.

Printed by Thomas C. Cushing, Salem, 1795.

STORY, Rev. Isaac. 1749–1816.

A Sermon, preached August the 15th, 1798, at Hamilton, at the Ordination of the Rev. Daniel Story, to the pastoral Care of the Church in Marietta, and its Vicinity, in the Territory of the United States, North-West of the River Ohio. By his Brother, Isaac Story, Pastor of the Second Congregational church in Marblehead.

Printed by Thomas C. Cushing, Salem. 1798.

SWEDENBORG, Emanuel.

True Christian Religion; containing the univeral Theology of the New Church: which was foretold by the Lord in Daniel, Chap. vii. 5, 13, 14, and in the Apocalypse, Chap. xxi. 1, 2. By Emanuel Swedenborg, Servant of the Lord Jesus Christ. Translated from the original Latin [by John Clowes]. In two Volumes. The third Edition.

Philadelphia: printed by Francis Bailey. 1789.

SWEDENBORG, Emanuel.

Passages concerning the Lord's Prayer, and its internal Sense; Selected from the Writings of the Hon. Emanuel Swedenborg. Servant of the Lord Jesus Christ. For the Use of the Lord's New Church.

London: printed and sold by W. Chalklen. 1789.

TAPPAN, David, D.D. 1752–1803.

Christian Thankfulness explained and enforced. A Sermon, delivered at Charlestown, in the Afternoon of February 19, 1795. The Day of General Thanksgiving through the United States. By David Tappan, D.D. Hollisian Professor of Divinity in Harvard College.

Printed by Samuel Hall, Boston, 1795.

THACHER, Peter, D.D. 1752–1802.

A Sermon, preached to the Society in Brattle Sreet, Boston, November 14, 1790. And occasioned by the Death of the Hon. James Bowdoin, Esq. L.L.D.F.R.S. Lately Governor of the Commonwealth of Massachusetts. By Peter Thacher, A.M. Pastor of the Church in Brattle Street.

Printed at Boston, by I. Thomas and E. T. Andrews. 1791.

THACHER, Peter, D.D. 1752–1802.

A Sermon, preached to the Society in Brattle-Street, Boston, April 17, 1796; and occasioned by the Death of the Hon. Thomas Russell, Esq. By Peter Thacher, D.D. Pastor of the Church in Brattle-Street.

Boston; printed by Benjamin Sweetser. 1796.

THAYER, Rev. John. 1755(?)–1815.

A Discourse, delivered, at the Roman Catholic Church in Boston, on the 9th of May, 1798, a Day recommended by the President, for Humiliation and Prayer throughout the United States. By the Reverend John Thayer, Catholic Missioner. Printed at the pressing Solicitation of those who heard it.

Printed by Samuel Hall, Boston. 1798.

TRUMBULL, Benjamin, D.D. *Historian*, 1735–1820.

God is to be praised for the Glory of his Majesty, and for his mighty Works. A Sermon, delivered at North-Haven, December 11, 1783. The day appointed by the United States for a General Thanksgiving on Account of the Peace concluded with Great-Britain. By Benjamin Trumbull, A.M. Pastor of the Church in North-Haven. The second Edition.

New-Haven: Printed by Thomas and Samuel Green. 1784.

WADSWORTH, Benjamin, D.D. 1750–1826.

America invoked to praise the Lord. A Discourse delivered on the Day of Public Thanksgiving through the United States of America, February 19, 1795. By Benjamin Wadsworth, A.M. Pastor of the First Church in Danvers.

Printed at Salem, by Thomas C. Cushing. 1795.

WARE, Henry, D.D. 1764–1845.

The Continuance of Peace and increasing Propserity a Source of Consolation and just Cause of Gratitude to the Inhabitants of the United States. A Sermon, delivered February 19, 1795; being a Day set apart by the President, for Thanksgiving and Prayer through the United States. By Henry Ware, Pastor of a Church in Hingham.

Printed by Samuel Hall, Boston. 1795.

WESLEY, John.

Thoughts upon Slavery. By John Wesley, A.M.

London, printed: re-printed in Philadelphia, with notes, and sold by Joseph Crukshank. 1774.

WESLEY, John.

The Great Assize: a Sermon on Romans xiv. 10.

London: printed by John Paramore. 1783.

WESLEY, John.

A Sermon on Salvation by Faith.

London: printed by John Paramore. 1783.

WESLEY, John.

The Important Question: A Sermon on Matt. xvi. 26. by John Wesley, M.A.

London: printed by John Paramore, 1783.

WESLEY, John.

A Sermon on original Sin.

Bath: printed by S. Hazard. 1783.

WESLEY, John.

The Almost Christian. A Sermon on Acts xxvi. 28.

London: printed by J. Paramore. 1784.

WHITAKER, Nathaniel, D.D. 1732–1795.

An Antidote against Toryism, or the Curse of Meroz, and a Discourse on Judges 5th 23. By Nathaniel Whitaker D.D. Pastor of the Presbyterian Congregation in Salem, State of Massachusetts-Bay. Published at the Desire of many who heard it. Dedicated to his Excellency General Washington.

Newbury-Port: printed by John Mycall. 1777.

WHITE, William, DD. *Bishop of Pennsylvania,* 1748–1836.

The Case of the Episcopal Churches in the United States considered.

Philadelphia: printed by David C. Claypoole. 1782.

Washington's autograph on the title-page.

WHITE, William, DD. *Bishop of Pennsylvania,* 1748–1836.

A Sermon, on the reciprocal Influence of Civil Policy and Religious Duty. Delivered in Christ Church, in the City of Philadelphia, on Thursday, the 19th of February, 1795, being a Day of General Thanksgiving. By William White, D.D. Bishop of the Protestant Episcopal Church, in the Commonwealth of Pennsylvania.

Philadelphia: printed by Ormrod & Conrad. March 2d. 1795.

WHITE, William, DD. *Bishop of Pennsylvania,* 1748–1836.

A Sermon on the Duty of civil Obedience, as required in Scripture. Delivered in Christ Church and St. Peter's, April 25, 1799, being a day of general Humiliation, appointed by the President of the United States. By William White, D.D. Bishop of the Protestant Episcopal Church, in the Commonwealth of Pennsylvania.

Philadelphia: printed by John Ormrod. 1799.

WILMER, Rev. James Jones. *Born* 1749.

A Sermon, on the Doctrine of the New-Jerusalem Church: being the first promulgated within the United States of America. Delivered on the first Sunday in April, 1792, in the Court-House of Baltimore-Town, by James Wilmer, examined and approved for the Ministerial Office, by the late Dr. Terrick, Bishop of London.

Baltimore: printed and sold by William Goddard and James Angell. 1792.

WILMER, Rev. James Jones. *Born* 1749.

Consolation: being a Replication to Thomas Paine, and Others, on Theologics. By James Jones Wilmer, of Maryland.

Philadelphia: printed for the Author, by William W. Woodward. 1794.

WINCHESTER, Rev. Elhanan. 1751–1797.

Thirteen Hymns, suited to the present Times: Containing; the past, present, and future State of America; with Advice to Soldiers and Christians. Dedicated to the Inhabitants of the United Colonies. By Elhanan Winchester. The second Edition.

Baltimore: printed by M. K. Goddard. 1776.

WINCHESTER, Rev. Elhanan. 1751–1797.

Ten Letters addressed to Mr. Paine, in Answer to his Pamphlet, entitled the Age of Reason: containing some clear and satisfying Evidences of the Truth of Divine Revelation; and especially of the

Resurrection and Ascension of Jesus. By Elhanan Winchester. The second Edition.

New-York: printed and sold by Samuel Campbell. 1795.

YATES, PETER WALDRON. *Lawyer*, 1747–1826.

An Address. Delivered in the Lodge Room at Schenectady, the 27th December, 1783. On the Festival of St. John the Evangelist. In the Presence of the Officers and Brethren of Union Lodge No. 1, of the City of Albany, St. George's Lodge of Schenectady, and several visiting Brethren, of the Most Ancient and Honorable Society of Free and Accepted Masons. By Peter W. Yates, Esq; Counsellor at Law and Master of said Union Lodge.

Albany: printed by S. Balentine, 1784.

A

SERMON

PREACHED IN

CHRIST-CHURCH, PHILADELPHIA.

[For the Benefit of THE POOR]

BY APPOINTMENT OF AND BEFORE

THE GENERAL COMMUNICATION

OF

FREE AND ACCEPTED

MASONS

OF THE

STATE of PENNSYLVANIA,

On MONDAY December 28. 1778.

Celebrated, agreeable to their Conſtitution,
as the Anniverſary of

ST. JOHN THE EVANGELIST.

BY WILLIAM SMITH. D. D.
Provoſt of the College and Academy of Philadelphia.

PHILADELPHIA:
PRINTED BY JOHN DUNLAP.

MDCCLXXIX.

TO HIS EXCELLENCY

GEORGE WASHINGTON, ESQUIRE,

GENERAL AND COMMANDER IN CHIEF

OF THE

ARMIES OF THE UNITED STATES

OF

NORTH-AMERICA;

THE FRIEND

OF HIS COUNTRY AND MANKIND,

AMBITIOUS OF NO HIGHER TITLE

IF HIGHER WAS POSSIBLE;

THE FOLLOWING SERMON,

HONOURED WITH HIS PRESENCE WHEN DELIVERED,

IS DEDICATED,

IN TESTIMONY

OF THE

SINCEREST BROTHERLY AFFECTION

AND

ESTEEM OF HIS MERIT,

BY ORDER OF THE BRETHREN,

JOHN COATS, G. Sec. pro tem.

A Sermon

Dedicated to George Washington, Delivered in His Presence, and Included in His Library

A Sermon
Preached in Christ-Church, Philadelphia,
[For the Benefit of the Poor]
by appointment of and before
The General Communication of
Free and Accepted Masons
of the State of Pennsylvania,
On Monday, December 28, 1778.
Celebrated, agreeable to their Constitution,
as the Anniversary of
St. John the Evangelist.
By William Smith, D.D.
Provost of the College and
Academy of Philadelphia.

To His Excellency,
George Washington, Esquire,
General and Commander in Chief of the
Armies of the United States of North-America;
the Friend of his Country and Mankind,
ambitious of no higher title if higher was possible;
The following sermon,
honoured with his presence when delivered,
is dedicated in Testimony of the sincerest
Brotherly Affection and Esteem of his Merit,
by Order of the Brethren,
John Coats, G. Sec. pro tem.

William Smith, D.D., *Provost of the College and Academy of Philadelphia,* 1779

As Free, and not using your Liberty as a Cloak of Maliciousness; but as the Servants of God.
(1 Peter 2:16)

Liberty! Jewel of inestimable Price!

Liberty, evangelical and social! Jewel of inestimable Price! Thou Blessing, of all Blessings the first! Woo'd and courted by many; won and wedded by few! Ever near us; yet often at a distance fancied! Thro' all the *Modes of Faith*, by the Saint pursued; and, in every *Frame of Government*, by the Patriot sought! O thou cœlestial Good—or rather Thou who art the Author of all Good, terrestrial and cœlestial—Supreme Architect of the Universe; who, by our great and Spiritual Master thy Son, hast taught us the true Way of Liberty—the Way of being free and accepted thro' Him! May I now be enlightened and enlivened by a Ray from Thee, while I endeavour to shew, that the Doctrine delivered in my Text for the Enjoyment and Exercise of Liberty, among Christians in general, is what the Members of this Ancient Society (by whose appointment I appear in this place) have bound themselves by the strongest Obligations to follow, in the several Relations they sustain; viz.

Christ, the way of Liberty

Masons bound to promote Liberty

First, in all their Meetings and Communications with each other.

Secondly, in Society at large.

And Thirdly, in private Life, as Individuals glowing with the Love of their Species; and seeking to promote their Happiness, as far Opportunities can reach, or the wide Wish of Benevolence extend. Upon these Three Grand Pillars, founded on the adamantine Rock of Eternal Truth, we profess to support the Fabric of our Labors; convinced that other Foundation than what the great Master-Builder hath laid, can no Man lay. Did we presume to depart from this, or propose to cultivate a Science, which hath any thing less for its Object than the Contemplation and Imitation of that everlasting Order, Harmony and Proportion which ("in Measure, Number and Weight") He hath established through all his Works; I should consider our Foundations as laid in the Sand, and our Superstructures raised of Stubble. Whatever Curiosity might have at first prompted me to pry into the Secrets of this Science, the most solemn Obligations could not have engaged my Adherence to it, when found repugnant to antecedent Obligations, which are indispensible, and therefore more solemn.

"Other foundation can no man lay . . ." I Cor. 3:11

God's Order, Harmony and Proportion

These were my early* Declarations. Many Years have since roll'd over my Head. That Seriousness, which I ever wish'd to maintain on grave and serious Occasions, is now (thro' various Trials and Vicissitudes, public and private) become habitual to me. I would not, therefore, upon this Occasion, or in this sacred Place, rise up to indulge the wanton Sport of Imagination; but my Hope is that, in Discharge of the present Duty assigned me by the Brotherhood, I may be in some Degree instrumental, among all who honour us with their Attendance, in that best Office of a Christian Minister—the rendering God more feared and more adored, and Mankind more happy and more in Love with each other.

Duty of a Christian Minister

I proceed, then, to apply the Apostle's Doctrine to my first Head of Discourse; and, for that End, it is necessary to recite some preceding Parts of his sublime Charge. "Wherefore, says he, laying aside all Malice, and all Guile, and Hypocrisies, and Envies, and all Evil-Speaking"—be ye as "living Stones, built up a spiritual House—as Free, and not using your Liberty as a Cloak of Maliciousness, but as the Servants of God."

For the better understanding these Words it must be observed that, as in our modern Times; so likewise, from the first Stages of the Gospel, its true Purpose, respecting Liberty both spiritual and temporal, hath been misunderstood or misinterpreted by many.

Law of Christ's liberty misinterpreted

From the Power of Bigotry, the Strength of Prejudice, a strange Meanness and unhallowed Frame of Mind; some, who were first called into evangelic Freedom, had still, rooted in their Temper, a beggarly Hankering after the old abrogated Rites and Customs, both Jewish and Pagan.

Astonished at this, St. Paul, with his usual Fervor of Eloquence, cries out—"O foolish Galatians! who hath bewitched you?—After having known God, or rather are known of Him, how turn ye back to the weak and beggarly Elements, wherewith ye desire again to be united?"—Quit this Folly—be persuaded to "stand fast in the Liberty, wherewith Christ has made us Free—and be not entangled again with the Yoke of Bondage."

Galatians 3:1

Galatians 5:1

Others there were, and still are, in the contrary Extreme; so hardly do Men ever square their Conduct by the golden Rule, recommended in the Text.

The golden Rule

Such were many of the early Jewish Converts. The new Law of Christ, which promised them Liberty from the ancient spiritual Bondage, they interpreted into a Scheme of such unbounded Licentiousness, as dissolved all Obligations even of their own moral Law, which, he expressly told them, he "came not to destroy but to fulfil." Affecting to consider themselves as the peculiar Favorites of God, and under his sole Government, they sought an Exemption from the Authorities of this World, and were for trampling under Foot the Powers ordained, or permitted, by him.

Matthew 5:17

Thus, forgetting the Spirit of the Gospel, and blown up with the Pride of their own Spirit; they treated with Contempt all whom they considered as Unbelievers, or less righteous than themselves. In private Life, they thought that their superior professions of Sanctity and furious Zeal would atone for all Sorts of "Malice, Guile, Hypocrisy, Envies and Evil Speaking;" and, in public Life, would justify Seditions, Murders and the Destruction of their Brethren—

* Sermon preach'd on St. John Baptist's day, 1755.

Miserable Infatuation! as if the God of all Love and Goodness could be served, by extirpating from our Hearts not only those native Dictates of Humanity which were implanted to give us some Degree of Happiness in this World; but those nobler Lessons of Christian Charity, which are our best Preparation for the unbounded Happiness of the World to come!

The Apostle, in my Text, contends earnestly against this sad Mistake; teaching that it leads not to the Use but deplorable Abuse of true Liberty; making it a Covering for every wicked Purpose, and enslaving us more and more to those infernal Passions, from which our Divine Master came to set us Free.

Christ sets free from sin

To the like Purpose are we taught by another great and wise Master. —"Six Things," says Solomon, "doth the Lord hate; yea, Seven are an Abomination to Him," viz.

Proverbs 6:16

First—A proud Look.

Second—A lying Tongue.

Third—Hands that shed innocent Blood.

Fourth—A Heart that deviseth wicked Imaginations.

Fifth—Feet that be swift in running to Mischief.

Sixth—A false Witness that speaketh Lies.

Seventh—Him that soweth Discord among Brethren.

These seven Abominations of Solomon, comprehended also by St. Peter under the general Term Maliciousness, must ever be peculiarly hateful to Us, as a Society of Friends; linked together by a strong Tie of Brotherly Love, as well as by every other Tie of Religion and Law, for the Advancement of true Humanity, genuine good Humour, undissembled Virtue, rational Liberty and useful Science.

Principles uniting Masons

Indeed the whole Doctrine of the Text (calling us to consider ourselves "as the Servants of God," in the Use of every Thing which he offers for our Enjoyment here) must still be necessary among all Societies of Men, in a World wrapt up in false Peace; trusting too much to external Professions, and where Multitudes have yet to learn—That True Religion is something spiritual, and design'd to perfect the Soul in Holiness, thro' the Fear and Love of God—That she must lie deeper than in Ordinances and Professions—"Must reach the inner Parts, or rather take her Rise there, even in the hidden Man of the Heart, where Christ bruises the Serpent, subdues our natural Corruptions," erects his Throne within us, and consecrates us Temples of the Holy Ghost.

Christianity works from within

It is in this Sense only, that Men can be considered as living Stones, built up a spiritual House! It is in this Sense only that they can enjoy Liberty as the Servants of God; without "Maliciousness," and without Licentiousness!

As to you, Brethren! I hope I need not remind you that if none be accepted among us, but such as strive daily, thro' the Grace of Heaven, to lay aside those evil Passions, condemned by the Apostle; then shall the Lodge be truly denominated a "Spiritual House," and all its Members "Living Stones," hewn out of the Rock of Ages, and adorned with Jewels of unspeakable Value. Then shall they be free indeed! for the great Spiritual Master shall have set them free from the Turbulence of Passion, the Stings of Guilt and the Thraldom of Slavery, both of Body and Mind. In Wisdom, Strength and Beauty shall they ever appear—

Masons, living stones hewn out of Christ, The Rock, 1 Peter 2:5

That Wisdom which descends from on high—"a pure Influence flowing from the Glory of the Almighty—which is the Brightness of the everlasting Light, the unspotted Mirror of the Power of God, and the Image of his Goodness—more beautiful than the Sun and above all the Order of Stars—pure, peaceable, gentle and easy to be entreated—which whosoever findeth, findeth Life"—

That Strength, which depends not on the Arm of Flesh, nor delights in Oppression and Confusion; but is a Refuge to the Distress'd, a Band of Union among Brethren, and a Source of Comfort in our own Hearts—

That Beauty, which shines forth in the Ornaments of Holiness, the Jewels of Mercy, the Cloathing of Humility, and the Practice of all Religious, Moral and Social Duties.

In Conclusion, therefore, to this first Head of Discourse; let me, in the Fullness of my pledged Affection, exhort you to remember, in all your Meetings and Communications, that you are Brethren; although free, yet on the Level; bound to keep within the Compass of mutual Good-Will; and to frame your Conduct by the Square of Doing as you would be done by. Keep an open Heart to every suffering Brother, ready to receive him as a Tempest-driven Voyager into a Port of Safety; seeking among you that Relief and Shelter; which he sought in Vain, while toss'd upon the restless Ocean of common Life.

Free, yet bound

Be of one Mind. Avoid all Levity of Conversation. Be sober and temperate; abstaining from every Excess that would enervate the Body, debase the Understanding, cherish Strife and dishonour your Calling. Study to be quiet, and to do your own Business with your own Hands; as knowing that "a wise Brother's Delight is in the Work of his Craft." Learn when to be silent, and when to speak; for "a Babbler is an Abomination, because of the unspeakable Words, which a Man may not utter," but in a proper Place.

1 Thess. 4:11

These are fundamental Principles, and Practices of immutable Obligation in our Society. Flowing from the Fountain-head of Antiquity, they have roll'd down to us, in pure and uncorrupted Streams, through the Channels of Time; and, we trust, will still roll, broader and deeper, until the dread Order of this Terrestrial Fabric shall be consummated in the endless Order of Eternity. While we draw from such sacred Sources, our true Members, as in Times past, so likewise now and in Times to come, in different Climes and Ages, shall be able to silence "the Tribe of Scorners"; and to convince them that the only Qualities we wish to honour are those which form good Men and good Citizens; and the only Buildings we seek to raise, are Temples for Virtue and Dungeons for vice.

Principles and practices of Masonry

True Masons

The other Societies of this World—Empires, Kingdoms and Commonwealths—being of less perfect Constitutions, have been of less permanent Duration. Although men have busied themselves, thro' all Ages, in forming and reforming them, in casting down and building up; yet still their Labours have been in vain! The Reason was—hear it and be wise, ye Builders of the present Day—the Reason was, that they daub'd with untemper'd Mortar, and admitted into their Structures the base, discordant, heterogeneous Materials of Pride, Ambition, Selfishness, "Malice, Guile, Hypocrisies, Envies and Evil Speaking"—which we reject. Hence their Fabrics, unable to support themselves, tumbled to the Foundation, through internal Weakness, or were shaken to Pieces by external Violence.

Societies fall from internal weakness

The Egyptian, the Babylonian, the Assyrian, the Persian Empires; the Commonwealths of Athens, of Sparta, and of Rome, with many more of later Date—Where are they now? "Fall'n—Fall'n—Fall'n"—the weeping Voice of History replies! The Meteors of an Age, the Gaze of one part of the World; they rose—they blaz'd awhile on high—they burst and sunk again, beneath the Horizon, to that Place of Oblivion, where the pale Ghosts of departed Grandeur fleet about in sad Lamentation of their former Glory!

Rise and fall of nations from regard or neglect of principles

Such have been the Changes and Revolutions which, as a Fraternity, we have seen. From the Bosom of the Lodge (seated on an Eminence) its Foundations reaching the Center and its Summit the Sky; we have beheld, as upon a turbulent Ocean at an immense Distance beneath us, the States of this World alternately mounted up and cast down, as they have regarded or neglected the Principles described above; while, supported by them, the sublime Fabric of our Constitution has remained unshaken through Ages—and, thus supported, it shall still remain, while the Sun opens the Day to gild its Cloud-cap'd Towers, or the Moon leads on the Night to chequer its starry Canopy. The Current of Things may roll along its Basis; the Tide of Chance and Time may beat against its Walls; the stormy Gusts of Malice may assault its lofty Battlements, and the heavy Rains of Calumny may descend upon its spacious Roof—but all in vain. A Building, thus constructed and supported, is impregnable from without; and can then only be dissolved when the Pillars of the Universe shall be shaken, and "the great Globe itself, yea all which it inherit, shall, like the baseless Fabric of a Vision," pass away before the Almighty Architect!

Constitution of Masons

But altho' we have seen those Changes, Convulsions and Dissolutions; we have not seen them with Insensibility, nor without Heart-felt Grief and a sympathetic Tear. And this brings me to my—

Second Head, which was to shew—That our Love to God and Man leads us to cultivate the same rational and evangelic Use of Liberty in Society at large, as in our own subordinate Societies.

Christ's Two Commands

This, we know, is a more arduous Labor; because the same watchful Care cannot be so easily applied to the Admission, Rejection or Government of Members, in large Societies as in small. Nevertheless, if every Man, first in his own House, and then in all those lesser Societies of Brethren with whom he may be connected, would learn, in the Apostle's Use of Liberty, to subdue every evil and discordant Passion; the blessed Habit would easily be carried forth into Society at large.

America's Christian Principle of Christian self-government

Individual States would not only be happy, durable, and free from intestine Broils and Convulsions; but "Nation would no more rise against Nation" in dreadful Havoc and Oppression. The whole World would be as one Harmonious Lodge, knit together in Brotherly Love, and obedient to the Will of the great Heavenly Master!

Such a glorious Aera many believe to be promised, and hope it may yet come. Our Principles lead us to cherish this Hope; and, as the best Means, under Providence, for its accomplishment, to resist Violence, and to support Justice, Truth, Freedom and Happiness in the Governments to which we belong.

The Doctrine that One Man's Grandeur, or the Grandeur of a Few, is to be the Misery of All, can have no reception among us. We can acknowledge no absolute uncontroulable power upon Earth; and can form no Conjecture whence such power could come, or be pretended. From God, the supreme Fountain of all Power, it could not come; without supposing he granted it to dishonour his own Perfections, deface his Image in his Works, and debase his whole Creation. From Man it could not come; unless we suppose him, voluntarily and in his sober Senses, consenting to his own immediate Misery and Destruction.

In our Estimation, therefore, "no Government can be of divine Original, but as it resembles God's own Government; round whose eternal Throne, Justice and Mercy wait. And all Governments must be so far divine, as the Laws rule; and every Thing is ordered, under God, by free and common consent."

To contend for such Governments, with a holy, enlightened, and unquenchable zeal, is the highest temporal Glory. Wherefore, we dwell with Rapture upon the Records of former Renown, and contemplate with Veneration those transcendent Scenes of Heroism; in which we behold the Brave and the Free wearing upon their Swords the Fate of Millions—while the divine Genius of Victory, espousing their Cause, hovers o'er their Heads with expanded Wing; reaching forth the immortal Wreath that is to surround their triumphant Brow; and smiling upon the decisive Moment that is to fix the Happiness of future Generations!

Highest temporal glory

They who (from a Sense of Duty to God and their Country, seeking that Liberty and Peace which Heaven approves) have thus acted their Part, whether in more elevated or inferior Stations, form the first Class in the Roll of Worthies. And when they descend again into private Life, casting behind them vain Pomp and fastidious Pride, to mingle with their Fellow-Citizens in all the tender Charities and endearing Offices of Society and Humanity; their Characters, if possible, become still more Illustrious. Their very Maims and Scars are nobly Honourable. The Respect which they command, grows with their growing Years; and they approach the Horizon of Life, as the Sun in serene and setting Glory, with Orb more enlarged and mitigated, though less dazzling and splendid. Even their garrulous old Age, while it can only recount the Feats of former Days, will be listened to with Attention: Or should they survive all the active Powers both of Body and Mind, yet still, like some grand Structure, tottering and crumbling beneath the Hand of Time, they will be considered as majestic in Ruins, and venerable even in Decay!

And when at last the Messenger Death, who comes to all, shall come to them; undaunted they will obey the Summons; in conscious Hope of being speedily united and beatified with their Compatriots and Fore-runners, in the Mansions of endless Bliss!

Such, to name no more, was the Character of a Cincinnatus in ancient Times; rising "awful from the Plough" to save his Country; and, his Country saved, returning to the Plough again, with increased Dignity and Lustre. Such too, if we divine aright, will future Ages pronounce to have been the Character of a . . . ; but you all anticipate me in a Name, which Delicacy forbids me, on this occasion, to mention. Honoured with his Presence as a Brother, you will seek to derive Virtue from his Example; and never let it be said, that any Principles you profess, can render you Deaf to the calls of your Country; but, on the contrary, have animated you with intrepidity in the Hour of Danger, and Humanity in the Moments of Triumph.

American Cincinnatus

True Courage consists not in any Thing external to a Man—in the Trappings of Dress, the Parade of Office, the Pride of Looks, a quarrelsome Temper, or Loudsounding Boasts; but in a Soul serenely fixed on Duty, and unconscious of Guilt, as knowing that Death has no Terrors but what he derives from Sin. For it hath been well said on this Subject, that "Fire may as easily be struck out of Ice, as Valour out of Crimes; and he has the chance of most Valour who lives best."

True Religion, therefore, is a Man's Glory and Strong Hold in every situation of Life, whether Public or Private; and this brings me to my—

Third Head, Under which it was proposed briefly to remind you, as a Fraternity, of the Principles by which you profess to regulate your Conduct towards Individuals in private Life; which still having that great Commandment of our Heavenly Master, Brotherly Love, as the chief Corner-Stone; every Thing raised upon it should be superlatively Grand and Fair.

Hence, therefore, we must seek to expand our Souls to the whole human Species; ever striving to promote their Happiness to the utmost of our Power. Whatever is illiberal, partial and contracted—a selfish and unfeeling Heart, coiled up within its own scanty Orb—we must reject from among us. Looking far beyond the little Distinctions of Sect or Party (by which too many seek to know, and be known by, each other) we should labour to imitate the great Creator, in regarding those of every Nation, Religion, and Tongue, who "fear Him, and work Righteousness."

Masonic principles, Biblical, universal, and non-sectarian

Such Conduct becomes those who profess to believe that when our Master Christ shall come again to reward his faithful Workmen and Servants; He will not ask whether we were of Luther or of Calvin? Whether we prayed to him in White, Black, or Grey; in Purple, or in Rags; in fine Linen, or in Sack-cloth; in a woollen Frock, or peradventure in a Leather-Apron? Whatever is considered as most Convenient, most in Character, most for Edification, and infringes least on Spiritual Liberty, will be admitted as good in this Case.

Christ, the Measure of Good

But, although we may believe that none of these Things will be asked in that Great Day; let us remember that it will be assuredly asked—Were we of Christ Jesus? "Did we pray to him with the Spirit and with the Understanding?" Had we the true Marks of his Gospel in our Lives? Were we "meek and lowly of Heart?" Did we nail our rebellious Affections to his Cross, and strive to subdue our Spirits to the Rule of his Spirit? But above all, it will be asked us—Were we cloathed with the Wedding-garment of Love? Did we recognize our Heavenly Master in the Sufferings of those whom he died to save? Did we, for his sake, open our Souls wide, to the Cries of His distressed Poor? "When they were Hungry, did we give them Meat? When Thirsty, did we give them Drink? When Strangers, did we take them in? When Naked, did we clothe them? When Sick, did we visit them? When in Prison, did we come unto them," with Comfort and Relief?

Christ the Judge

This Day, my Brethren—nay, a few Moments hence—will furnish you with an Opportunity of laying up in your own Consciences, and sending before you to Heaven, an Answer to those important Questions, against the awful Day of final Retribution.

Hark! do you not this instant hear—amidst the unavoidable Calamities of your Country, the deep Distresses of War, the extreme Rigour of the Season, the unusual Price and Scarcity of the chief Necessaries of Life—Bread, Cloathing, and Fuel, —Hark! I say, Do you not, amidst these complicated Distresses, this instant, hear the loud Cries of many Hungry, Naked, Cold, Sick, and almost ready to Perish?—

I know you hear them, and have come, with open Heart and open Hand, to relieve them. This was the chief Purpose of the present Solemnity; and I have your Instructions to press it Home, as the best Exercise of those Principles, in which you profess most eminently to shine. Nor will your Practice, I trust, ever fall short of your Profession; or give Room to apply the Prophet's sarcastic Rebuke, either to yourselves, or your Preacher—"Lo! thou art unto them as a very lovely Song, of one that hath a pleasant Voice, and can play well upon an Instrument—for they hear thy Words, but they do them not." No, Brethren! you will never suffer this to be justly said of you; but, on the contrary, that you are always as ready to do as to hear.

Relieving the ravages of war

Many of you will remember, that the fourth Part of a Century—a Period that hath been big with important Events and Revolutions—hath passed away, since our last Meeting in this Place, on a similar Occasion. Let the Poor, then, have reason to consider our present Meeting, as a Jubilee to them rather than to us.

And while I address You on this Subject, I would, at the same time, beg leave to Address the whole of this numerous and respectable Auditory—for Charity is the concern of all; and we are peculiarly called to its highest Exercise at this particular Time.

Charity, the concern of all

But a few Days have past, since we were joining together in the Song of Angels; giving Thanks and "Glory to God in the "Highest" for the Birth of a Saviour, and the Spiritual Deliverance accomplished by Him. In a few Days* more, we are again, by special Appointment, to offer up Thanksgivings to

* The Thanksgiving Day appointed for Dec. 30th.

God for whatever temporal Blessings and Deliverances we have received through his Goodness. On both Accounts, one of the best Sacrifices of Thanksgiving which we can offer, is—to raise the drooping Mourner; cheer the lonely Heart of Woe; and be the Instruments of Heaven for encreasing the Number of the Thankful.

This is the Return of Gratitude which Christ peculiarly requires; namely, that, from the Consideration of his unbounded Love to us, our Heart should overflow with Love to each other. Such Love is justly stiled—"the fulfilling of the whole Law,"—the Sum and Substance of all Obedience. For true Religion being an Emanation from on high, cannot but shed Light upon the Understanding, and Love upon the Heart—even that Love, which, when genuine, will gradually consume every Thing that is gross and earthly within us; and mount up our Affections, at last, in a pure Flame, to the omnipotent Source of all Love.

Deeds of Love are the chief Employment of the Angels of God; and, into a Soul which overflows with Love and Charity, Heaven may be said to have descended, while on Earth. The other Virtues and Graces bring us nearer to God, as it were, by slow approaches; but, by the Divine Virtue of Charity, we are borne into his direct Presence, as in a fiery Chariot! This is the only Virtue which we can carry with us into the other World: Our Faith, after Death, shall be swallowed up in Sight, our Hope in Enjoyment; but our Charity, when we shake off this Mortality, shall then only begin to have its full Scope, enlarging itself into unbounded Dimensions, as the main Ingredient of our Happiness, in the Regions of Eternal Love!

Love fades not away

But I will detain you no longer, Brethren! You all pant to have a Foretaste of the Joy of Angels, by calling forth into immediate Exercise this heavenly Virtue of Charity; whereby you will give Glory* to the Thrice Blessed Three, Father, Son and Holy Ghost, one God over all!

(*At the Word "Glory," the Brethren rose together; and, in reverential Posture, on pronouncing the names of the Tri-une God, accompanied the same by a Correspondent Repetition of the Ancient Sign or Symbol of Divine Homage and Obeisance; concluding with the following Response—)

"Amen! So let it ever be!"

The End of the Sermon.

★

The following Short Account of the Procession of the Brethren to and from Church, &c. is recorded here by Desire.

At Nine o'Clock, A.M. near three hundred of the Body assembled at the College; where being properly cloathed—the Officers in the Jewels of their Lodges, and other Badges of their Dignity—the Procession began at 11 o'Clock, viz.

1. The Sword Bearer
2. Two Deacons, bearing wands, tipt with Gold.
3. The Three Orders, Doric, Ionic, and Corinthian; borne by three Brethren.
4. The Holy Bible and Book of Constitutions, on Crimson Velvet Cushions; borne by the Grand Treasurer and Grand Secretary.
5. A reverend Brother.
6. Four Deacons, bearing Wands.
7. His Excellency, our illustrious Brother George Washington, Esq.: supported by the Grand Master and his Deputy.
8. The Two Grand Wardens, bearing the proper Pillars.
9. The Past Masters of different Lodges.
10. The Present Masters of ditto.
11. The Senior Wardens,
12. The Junior Wardens,
13. The Secretaries,
14. The Treasurers,

   } Of different Private Lodges
15. Brother Proctor's Band of Music.
16. Visiting Brethren: and,
17. Members of different Lodges; two and two, according to Seniority.

The Procession entered the Church in the order of March; and being seated in the middle Isle, Prayers were read by the Rev. Mr. White; and the following Anthem Sung in its proper place by sundry of the Brethren, accompanied with the Organ and other Instrumental Music; viz.

A Grand Symphony

Chorus. Behold, how good and joyful a Thing it is, Brethren, to dwell together in Unity.

Solo. I will give Thanks unto Thee, O Lord! with my whole Heart. Secretly among the Brethren, and in the Congregation will I praise thee! I will speak the marvellous works of thy Hands; the Sun, the Moon and the Stars, which thou hast ordained.

Solo. The people that walked in Darkness have seen a great Light; and on them that dwelt in the Land of the Shadow of Death, doth the glorious Light of Jehovah shine.

Solo. Thou hast gathered Us from the East, and from the West, and from the North, and from the South—Thou hast made us Companions for the Mighty upon Earth—even for Princes of great Nations.

Trio. O! I AM! Inspire us with Wisdom and Strength to support us in all our Troubles, that we may worship Thee in the Beauty of Holiness!

★

After Sermon, near Four Hundred Pounds were collected for the Relief of the Poor. The Brethren then returned to the College in the same order as above described; from thence they departed to their several Lodges, and spent the Remainder of the Day with their usual good Harmony and Sociability.

The Dedication of the Washington National Monument

Jesus saith unto them, Did ye never read in the scriptures,
The stone which the builders rejected, the same is become the head of the corner:
this is the Lord's doing, and it is marvellous in our eyes?

Matthew 21:42

Now therefore ye are no more strangers and foreigners,
but fellow citizens with the saints, and of the household of God;
And are built upon the foundation of the apostles and prophets,
Jesus Christ himself being the chief corner stone;
In whom all the building fitly framed together groweth unto an holy temple in the Lord:
In whom ye also are builded together for an habitation of God through the Spirit.

Ephesians 2:19–22

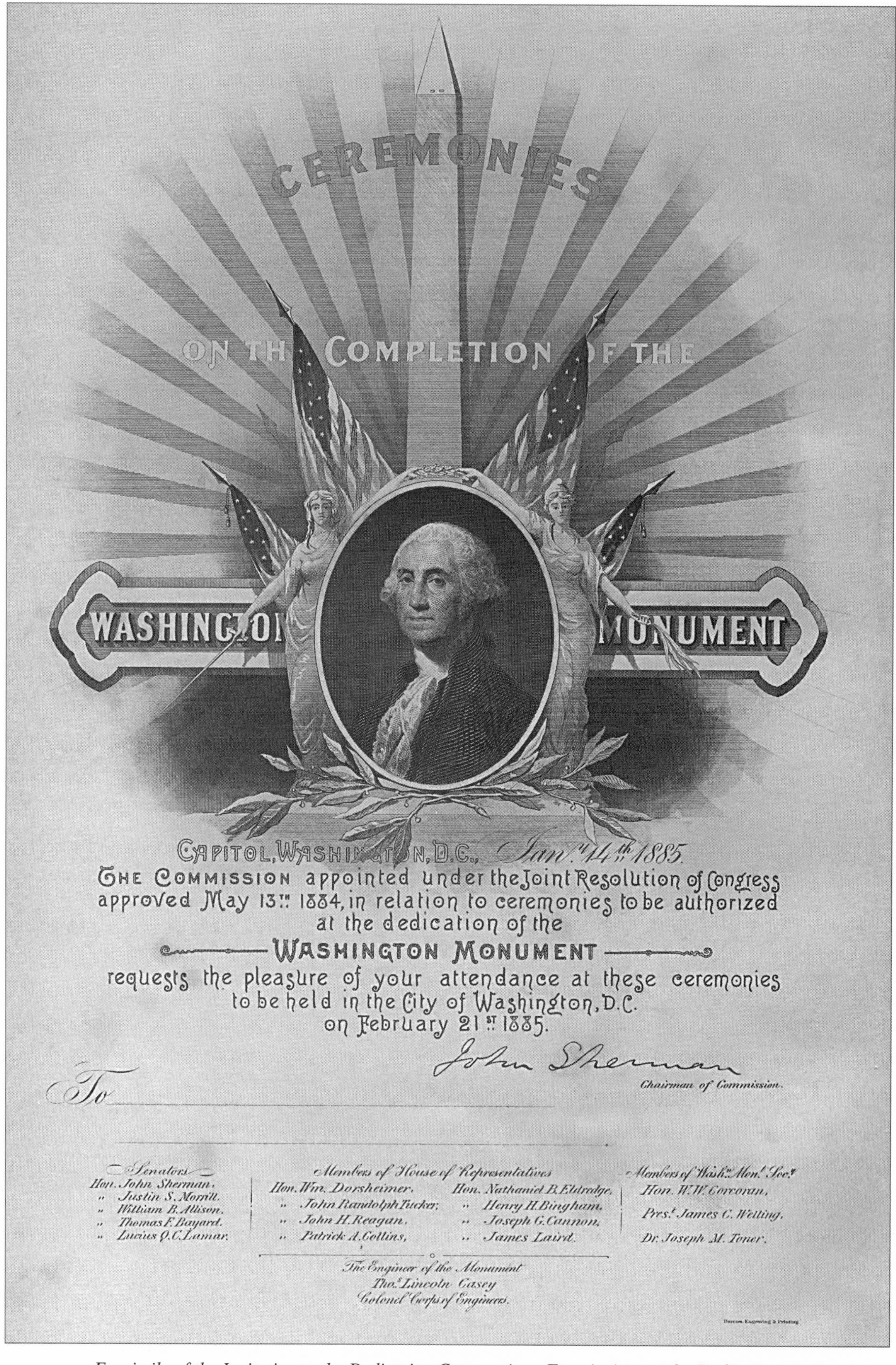

CEREMONIES

ON THE COMPLETION OF THE

WASHINGTON MONUMENT

CAPITOL, WASHINGTON, D.C., Jan. 14th 1885.

THE COMMISSION appointed under the Joint Resolution of Congress approved May 13th 1884, in relation to ceremonies to be authorized at the dedication of the

WASHINGTON MONUMENT

requests the pleasure of your attendance at these ceremonies to be held in the City of Washington, D.C. on February 21st 1885.

John Sherman
Chairman of Commission.

To ______________________

Senators
Hon. John Sherman,
" Justin S. Morrill.
" William B. Allison.
" Thomas F. Bayard.
" Lucius Q. C. Lamar.

Members of House of Representatives
Hon. Wm. Dorsheimer,
" John Randolph Tucker;
" John H. Reagan,
" Patrick A. Collins,
Hon. Nathaniel B. Eldredge,
" Henry H. Bingham,
" Joseph G. Cannon,
" James Laird.

Members of Washn. Monument Socy.
Hon. W. W. Corcoran,
Prest. James C. Welling,
Dr. Joseph M. Toner.

The Engineer of the Monument
Thos. Lincoln Casey
Colonel Corps of Engineers.

Bureau Engraving & Printing

Facsimile of the Invitation to the Dedication Ceremonies—Frontispiece to the Dedication Book

The Dedication of the Washington National Monument

"THE CONFESSION AND CREED OF WASHINGTON —WHICH CAN NEVER BE FORGOTTEN BY ANY CHRISTIAN PATRIOT"
(*Hon. Robert C. Winthrop*, February 21, 1885)

.... No one *can* rejoice more than I do at every step the people of this great Country take to preserve the Union, establish good order and government, and to render the Nation happy at home and respectable abroad. No Country upon Earth ever had it more in its power to attain these blessings than United America. Wondrously strange then, and much to be regretted indeed would it be, were we to neglect the means, and to depart from the road which Providence has pointed us to, so plainly; I cannot believe it will ever come to pass. The great Governor of the Universe has led us too long and too far on the road to happiness and glory, to forsake us in the midst of it. By folly and improper conduct, proceeding from a variety of causes, we may now and then get bewildered; but I hope and trust that there is good sense and virtue enough left to recover the right path before we shall be entirely lost. . . .
(Washington to Benjamin Lincoln, June 29, 1788)

.... No People can be bound to acknowledge and adore the invisible hand, which conducts the Affairs of men more than the People of the United States. Every step, by which they have advanced to the character of an independent Nation, seems to have been distinguished by some token of providential agency. . . . (*First Inaugural Address*, April 30, 1789)

Of all the dispositions and habits which lead to political prosperity, Religion and morality are indispensable supports. In vain would that man claim the tribute of Patriotism, who should labour to subvert these great Pillars of human happiness, these firmest props of the duties of Men and citizens....
(*Farewell Address*, September 19, 1796)

GEORGE WASHINGTON

The Writings of George Washington, Vols. 30 & 35, John C. Fitzpatrick, Editor, 1931

★

THE CHARACTER OF WASHINGTON!

Who can delineate it worthily? Who can describe that priceless gift of America to the world in terms which may do it any sort of justice, or afford any degree of satisfaction to his hearers or to himself?

Modest, disinterested, generous, just—of clean hands and a pure heart—self-denying and self-sacrificing, seeking nothing for himself, declining all remuneration beyond the reimbursement of his outlays, scrupulous to a farthing in keeping his accounts, of spotless integrity, scorning gifts, charitable

The Dedication of the Washington National Monument, February 21, 1885
Excerpt: ORATION OF ROBERT C. WINTHROP

to the needy, forgiving injuries and injustices, brave, fearless, heroic, with a prudence ever governing his impulses and a wisdom ever guiding his valor—true to his friends, true to his whole country, true to himself—fearing God, believing in Christ, no stranger to private devotion or public worship or to the holiest offices of the Church to which he belonged, but ever gratefully recognizing a Divine aid and direction in all that he attempted and in all that he accomplished—what epithet, what attribute could be added to that consummate character to commend it as an example above all other characters in merely human history! . . .

Nothing for himself

Recognizing a Divine aid and direction in all things attempted

. . . *[T]he Glory of Washington will remain unique and peerless until American Independence shall require to be again achieved, or the foundations of Constitutional Liberty to be laid anew. . . .* [*Italics added.*]

Where may the wearied eye repose
  When gazing on the great,
Where neither guilty glory glows,
  Nor despicable state!
Yes, One—the first, the last, the best,
The Cincinnatus of the West,
  Whom envy dared not hate—
Bequeathed the name of Washington,
To make men blush there was but One!

—Byron

. . . . In the words of our own poet Lowell:

Virginia gave us this imperial man,
Cast in the massive mould
Of those high-statured ages old
Which into grander forms our mortal metal ran;
She gave us this unblemished gentleman:
What shall we give her back but love and praise?

. . . . A celebrated philosopher of antiquity, who was nearly contemporary with Christ, but who could have known nothing of what was going on in Judea, and who alas! did not always "reck his own rede"—wrote thus to a younger friend, as a precept for a worthy life: "Some good man must be singled out and kept ever before our eyes, that we may live as if he were looking on, and do everything as if he could see it."

Let me borrow the spirit, if not the exact letter, of that precept, and address it to the young men of my Country: "Keep ever in your mind and before your mind's eye the loftiest standard of character. You have it, I need not say, supremely and unapproachably, in Him who spake as never man spake and lived as never man lived, and who died for the sins of the world. That character stands apart and alone. But of merely mortal men the monument we have dedicated to-day points out the one for all Americans to study, to imitate, and, as far as may be, to emulate. Keep his example and his character ever before your eyes and in your hearts. Live and act as if he were seeing and judging your personal conduct and your public career. Strive to approximate that lofty standard, and measure your integrity and your patriotism by your nearness to it or your departure from it. The prime meridian of universal longitude, on sea or land, may be at Greenwich, or at Paris, or where you will. But the prime meridian of pure, disinterested, patriotic, exalted human character will be marked forever by yonder Washington Obelisk!"

Loftiest standard of American Christian character

Yes, to the Young Men of America, under God, it remains, as they rise up from generation to generation, to shape the destinies of their Country's future—and woe unto them if, regardless of the great example which is set before them, they prove unfaithful to the tremendous responsibilities which rest upon them!

★

Dedication Book, pp. 3–113

PRELIMINARY PROCEEDINGS

The Congress of the United States, having received a notification from Hon. W. W. Corcoran, chairman of the Joint Commission for the completion of the Washington National Monument, that the shaft was approaching completion, passed the following joint resolution, which was reported to the Senate by the Hon. Justin S. Morrill, of Vermont:

JOINT RESOLUTION in relation to ceremonies to be authorized upon the completion of the Washington Monument.

Whereas the shaft of the Washington Monument is approaching completion, and it is proper that it should be dedicated with appropriate ceremonies, calculated to perpetuate the fame of the illustrious man who was "First in war, first in peace, and first in the hearts of his countrymen": Therefore,

Resolved by the Senate and House of Representatives of the United States of America in Congress assembled, That a commission to consist of five Senators appointed by the President of the Senate, eight Representatives appointed by the Speaker of the House of Representatives, three members of the Washington Monument Society, and the United States engineer in charge of the work, be, and the same is hereby, created, with full powers to make arrangements for—

First. The dedication of the Monument to the name and memory of George Washington, by the President of the United States, with appropriate ceremonies.

Second. A procession from the Monument to the Capitol, escorted by regular and volunteer corps, the Washington Monument Society, representatives of cities, States, and organizations which have contributed blocks of stone, and such bodies of citizens as may desire to appear.

Third. An oration in the Hall of the House of Representatives, on the twenty second day of February, anno Domini eighteen hundred and eighty-five, by the honorable Robert C. Winthrop, who delivered the oration at the laying of the cornerstone of the Monument in eighteen hundred and forty-eight, with music by the Marine Band.

Fourth. Salutes of one hundred guns from the navy-yard, the artillery headquarters, and such men-of-war as can be anchored in the Potomac.

And such sum of money as may be necessary to defray the expenses incurred under the above provisions, not exceeding two thousand five hundred dollars, is hereby appropriated, out of any money in the Treasury not otherwise appropriated.

Approved, May 13, 1884. . . .

THE DEDICATORY EXERCISES

The weather on Saturday, February 21, was clear and cold, the ground around the base of the Monument was covered with encrusted snow, and the keen wind, while it displayed the flags on every hand, made it rather uncomfortable for those who arrived before the appointed time. The regular troops and the citizen soldiery were massed in close column around the base of the Monument, the Freemasons occupied their allotted position, and in the pavilion which had been erected were the invited guests; the Executive, Legislative, and Judicial Officers; Officers of the Army, the Navy, the Marine Corps, and the Volunteers; the Diplomatic Corps, eminent Divines, Jurists, Scientists, and Journalists; venerable Citizens, representing former generations; the Washington National Monument Society, and a few Ladies who had braved the Arctic weather.

The Marine Band, stationed in front of the pavilion, enlivened the scene by the performance of admirable music.

Senator Sherman, precisely at 11 o'clock a.m., advanced to the front of the pavilion and commenced the dedicatory exercises with the following prefatory remarks:

Address by Hon. John Sherman

The Commission authorized by the two Houses of Congress to provide suitable ceremonies for the dedication of the Washington Monument direct me to preside and to announce the order of ceremonies deemed proper on this occasion.

I need not to say anything to impress upon you the dignity of the event you have met to celebrate. The Monument speaks for itself—simple in form, admirable in proportions, composed of enduring marble and granite, resting upon foundations broad and deep, it rises into the skies higher than any work of human art. It is the most imposing; costly, and appropriate monument ever erected in the honor of one man.

Foundations broad and deep

It had its origin in the profound conviction of the people, irrespective of party, creed, or race, not only of this country, but of all civilized countries, that the name and fame of Washington should be perpetuated by the most imposing testimonial of a nation's gratitude to its Hero, Statesman, and Father. This universal sentiment took form in a movement of private citizens associated under the name of the Washington National Monument Association, who, on the 31st day of January, 1848, secured from Congress an act authorizing them to erect the proposed Monument on this ground, selected as the most appropriate site by the President of the United States. Its cornerstone was laid on the 4th of July, 1848, by the Masonic fraternity, with imposing ceremonies, in the presence of the chief officers of the Government and a multitude of citizens. It was partially erected by the National Monument Association with means furnished by the voluntary contributions of the people of the United States.

Origin in the conviction of the people

Voluntary contributions

On the 5th day of July, 1876, one hundred years after the Declaration of American Independence, Congress, in the name of the people of the United States, formally assumed and directed the completion of the Monument. Since then the foundation has been strengthened, the shaft has been steadily advanced, and the now completed structure stands before you.

It is a fit memorial of the greatest character in human history. It looks down upon scenes most loved by him on earth, the most conspicuous object in a landscape full of objects deeply interesting to the American people. All eyes turn to it, and all hearts feel the inspiration of its beauty, symmetry, and grandeur. Strong as it is, it will not endure so long as the memory of him in whose honor it was built; but while it stands it will be the evidence to many succeeding generations of the love and reverence of this generation for the name and fame of George Washington—"First in war, first in peace, and first in the hearts of his countrymen." More even than this—the prototype of purity, manhood, and patriotism, for all lands and for all time.

Greatest character in human history

Prototype for all time and for all lands

Without further preface I proceed to discharge the duty assigned me.

After music by the Marine Band, prayer was offered by the Rev. Henderson Suter, Rector of Christ Church, Alexandria, Va., where Washington worshiped.

Prayer by Rev. Henderson Suter

Prayer by Rev. Henderson Suter

Almighty God, Ruler of nations and of men, by whose providence our fathers were led to this goodly land, and by whom they were guided and sustained in their efforts to secure their liberties, accept this day the grateful homage of us, the inheritors of their well-earned rights.

Them and their leaders Thou didst choose. With courage and patriotism Thou didst inspire all; but we to-day, while unmindful of none, are specially called to acknowledge as Thy gift George Washington.

Gift of God

In honor of him, Thy servant, the Nation of Thy planting and of his thoughts and prayers has built this Monument, and we today, in that Nation's behalf, speak to his God and ours in prayer and thanks.

Nation of God's planting

As we stand beneath the lofty height of this memorial work, and mark the symmetry of its form, we would remember Washington's high character and all the virtues which in him builded up the man.

A leader fearing God; a patriot unstained by self; a statesman wishing only the right, he has left us an example for whose following we supplicate Thy help for ourselves and for all who are now, and shall hereafter be, the instruments of Thy providence to this land and Nation.

Instrument of Providence

In so far as he followed the inspirations of wisdom and of virtue may we follow him, and may his character be to the latest generation a model for the soldier, for the civilian, and for the man; that in our armies may be trust in God, in our civilians integrity, and among our people that home life which extorteth praise; and so all those blessings which he coveted for his people and his kind be the heritage of us and of our children forever.

O God, the high and mighty Ruler of the universe, bless to-day and henceforth Thy servant the President of the United States and all others in authority.

To our Congress ever give wisdom. Direct and prosper all their consultations.

May our judges be able men, such as fear God, men of truth, governed in judgment only by the laws.

May our juries be incorruptible, ever mindful of the solemnity of the oath and of the great interests depending on its keeping.

May no magistrate or officer, having rights to maintain or order to secure, ever "wrest the judgment of the poor," or favor the rich man in his cause.

O God, throughout our land let amity continually reign. Bind ever the one part to the other part. Heal every wound opened by human frailty or by human wrong. Let the feeling of brotherhood have the mastery over all selfish ends, that with one mind and one heart, the North and the South, and the East and the West, may seek the good of the common country, and work out that destiny which has been allotted us among the nations of the earth.

Merciful Father, from whom "all good thoughts and good desires come," let the principles of religion and virtue find firm root and grow among our people. May they heed the words of their own Washington, and never "indulge the supposition that morality can be maintained without religion," or forget that "to political prosperity, religion and morality are indispensable supports." Deepen in them reverence for Thy character. Impress a sense of Thy power. Create a desire for Thy favor, and let it be realized that man's highest honor is to be a servant of God, and that to fear Him and keep His commandments is our whole duty.

O God, in all our relations with the nations of the earth let honor and justice rule us. May their wisdom be our guide and our good their choice.

Emulative only in the high purpose of bettering the condition of man, may they and we dwell together in unity and concord.

Honor and justice with other nations

Bless all efforts to widen the sphere of knowledge, that true wisdom may be garnered by our people and nature yield her secrets for man's good and Thy glory.

In all our seminaries of learning—our schools and colleges—may men arise who shall be able to hand down to the generations following all that time has given.

American Christian education

And look upon our land. Give us the rain and the fruitful season. Let no blight fall upon the tree, no disease upon the cattle, no pestilence upon man.

To honor Thee, O God, we this day yield our homage and offer our praise.

Our fathers, "cried unto Thee and were delivered."

"They trusted in Thee and were not confounded;" and we, their children, gathered by this Monument to-day, the silent reminder of Thy gifts, ask Thy blessing, O Ruler of nations and of men, in the name of Him through whom Thou hast taught us to pray; and may no private or public sins cause Thee to hide Thy face from us but from them turn Thou us and in our repentance forgive.

To our prayers we add our thanks—our thanks for mercies many and manifold.

Thou didst not set Thy love upon us and choose us because we were more in number than any people, but because Thou wouldst raise us up to be an asylum for the oppressed and for a light to those in darkness living.

America, an asylum and a light

For this great honor, O God, we thank Thee.

Not for our righteousness hast Thou upheld us hitherto and saved from those evils which wreck the nations, but because Thou hadst a favor unto us.

For this great mercy, O God, we thank Thee.

Not solely through man's wisdom have the great principles of human liberty been embodied for our Government, and every man become the peer of his fellow-man before the law; but because Thou hast ordered it.

For this great mercy, O God, we thank Thee.

And now, our Father, let this assembly, the representatives of the thousands whom Thou hast blessed, go hence to-day, their duty done, joyful and glad of heart for all the goodness that the Lord hath done for this great nation.

And for the generations to come, yet unborn, may this Monument which we dedicate to-day to the memory of George Washington stand as a witness for those virtues and that patriotism which, lived, shall secure for them Liberty and Union forever. *Amen.*

ADDRESS BY HON. W. W. CORCORAN

James C. Welling, L.L.D., President of Columbian University, then read the following address, which had been prepared by Hon. W. W. Corcoran, First Vice-President of the Washington National Monument Society:

It has been said that the fame of those who spend their lives in the service of their country is better preserved by the "unwritten memorials of the heart than by any material monument." The saying is pre-eminently true of the man whom the people of these United States must forever hold in grateful veneration as the one entitled above all others to the honored name of Pater Patriæ. Yet the instincts of the heart do not follow the impulses of our higher nature when, in honor of the mighty dead, they call for the commemorative column or the stately monument, not, indeed, to preserve the name and fame of an illustrious hero and patriot, but to signalize the gratitude of the generations for whom he labored.

And so on the 19th of December, 1799, the day after the mortal remains of George Washington had been committed to the tomb at Mount Vernon, John Marshall, of Virginia, destined soon afterward to fill with highest distinction the office of Chief Justice of the United States, rose in the House of Representatives and moved, in words penned by Henry Lee, of Virginia, that a committee of both Houses of Congress should be appointed "to report measures suitable to the occasion and expressive of the profound sorrow with which Congress is penetrated on the loss of a citizen first in war, first in peace, and first in the hearts of his countrymen."

It is through a long series of years, and through the ebbs and flows of much divergent opinion as to the monumental forms in which the national homage should most suitably express itself, that the American people have watched and waited for the grand consummation which we are this day met to celebrate. It is because the stream of the national gratitude was so full and overflowing that again and again it has seemed to sweep away the artificial banks prepared to receive it; but that, in all the windings and eddies of the stream, there has been a steady current of national feeling which has set in one given direction, the following historical memoranda will sufficiently demonstrate:

In pursuance of the resolution adopted by the House of Representatives on the motion of John Marshall, both Houses of Congress passed the following resolution on the 24th of December, 1799:

Resolved by the Senate and House of Representatives of the United States of America in Congress assembled, That a marble monument be erected by the United States in the Capitol at the City of Washington, and that the family of General Washington be requested to permit his body to be deposited under it; and that the monument be so designed as to commemorate the great events of his military and political life.

A copy of this proceeding having been transmitted to Mrs. Washington, she assented, in the following touching terms, to so much of the resolution as called for her concurrence:

"Taught by the great example which I have so long had before me never to oppose my private wishes to the public will, I need not, I cannot say what a sacrifice of individual feeling I make to a sense of public duty."

Mrs. Washington's tribute to his example

The select committee (Henry Lee, of Virginia, being chairman), which was appointed to carry into effect the foregoing resolution, made report on the 8th of May, 1800, directing that a marble monument be erected by the United States, at the capital, in honor of General Washington, to commemorate his services, and to express the feeling of the American people for their irreparable loss; and further directing that a resolution of the Continental Congress adopted August 7, 1783, which had ordered "That an equestrian statue of General Washington be erected at the place where the residence of Congress shall be established" should be carried into immediate execution.

This latter resolution had directed that the statue of Washington be supported by a "marble pedestal on which should be represented four principal events of the war in which he commanded in person," and which should also bear the following inscription:

"The United States, in Congress assembled, ordered this statue to be erected in the year of our Lord 1783, in honor of George Washington, the illustrious Commander-in-Chief of the Armies of the United States of America during the war which vindicated and secured their liberty, sovereignty, and independence."

Upon consideration of this resolution, that part relative to the erection of an equestrian statue was so amended as to provide that a "mausoleum of American granite and marble, in pyramidal form, one hundred feet square at the base, and of a proportional height" should be erected instead of it. An appropriation in pursuance of this end was not then made, but at a later day, on the 1st of January, 1801, a bill was passed by the House of Representatives appropriating two hundred thousand dollars in furtherance of this object.

In this measure the Senate failed to concur, for reasons easily found in the political excitements of that day, while absorbing public questions which ensued thereafter, and which finally issued in the war of 1812, sufficiently explain why the subject was dropped in Congress for many years.

In the month of February, 1816, the General Assembly of Virginia instructed the Governor of that State to open correspondence with Judge Bushrod Washington, at that time the proprietor of Mount Vernon, with a view to procure his assent to the removal of Washington's remains to Richmond, that a proper monument might there be erected to the memory of the Hero and Patriot. Immediately on the receipt of this intelligence in the Congress, then in session, Hon. Benjamin Huger, of South Carolina, who had been a member of the Congress of 1799, moved for the appointment of a joint committee of both Houses to take action in pursuance of the proceedings had at that time of Washington's death.

This joint committee recommended that a receptacle for the remains of Washington should be prepared in the foundation of the Capitol, and that a monument should there be erected to his memory. But the whole project fell through because, in the mean time, Judge Washington had declined to consent to the removal of Washington's remains, on the ground that they had been committed to the family vault at Mount Vernon in conformity with Washington's express wish.

His wish honored

"It is his own will," added Judge Washington, in replying to the Governor of Virginia, "and that will is to me a law which I dare not disobey."

To a similar proposition, as renewed by the

Congress of the United States in 1832, Mr. John Augustine Washington, who had then succeeded to the possession of Mount Vernon, made a similar reply, and since that date all thought of removing the remains of Washington from their hallowed resting place to the site of the proposed national Monument has been abandoned, and properly abandoned in view of the affecting natural considerations which had given a deep undertone of remonstrance even to Mrs. Washington's reluctant assent, as extorted from her by the ejaculations of the public grief in 1799.

It was precisely at this stage of our history, when all proceedings initiated in Congress had been frustrated by the failure to combine opinions on some preliminary condition held to be indispensable, that the people of this city, as if despairing of the desired consummation through the concerted action of both Houses of Congress, proceeded to initiate measures of their own looking in this direction.

Citizens accomplish what Congress is unable to do

In September, 1833, a paragraph appeared in the National Intelligencer of this city calling a meeting of the citizens of Washington to take the matter in hand.

In response to that call a meeting of citizens was held at the City Hall on the 26th of September, 1833, at which were present Daniel Brent, Joseph Gales, James Kearney, Joseph Gales, jr., Peter Force, W. W. Seaton, John McClelland, Pishy Thompson, Thomas Carberry, George Watterston, and William Cranch, afterwards Chief Justice of the Circuit Court of the District.

It was at this meeting that the Washington National Monument Society was formed, Chief Justice John Marshall, then seventy-eight years of age, having been elected its first President, and Judge Cranch the first Vice-President.

George Watterston, who deserves to be signalized as the originator of the movement, was the first secretary, and he served in that capacity from 1833 till his death in 1854, when he was succeeded by John Carroll Brent, who, in turn, was succeeded by Dr. John B. Blake, the successor of the latter being the Hon. Horatio King, the present secretary of the Society.

Upon the death of Chief Justice Marshall, in 1835, he was succeeded in the presidency of the Society by ex-President James Madison.

The plan adopted by the Society was to secure the assistance and unite the voluntary efforts of the people of the country in erecting a national monument to Washington.

Unite voluntary efforts of the people

At first, as if to give emphasis to the popular aims of the Society, all contributions were limited to the annual sum of one dollar from any one person, the contributors becoming, by that act, members of the Society. The collections on this plan had amounted in 1836 to the sum of twenty-eight thousand dollars, which was carefully placed at interest, the fund standing in the names of Nathan Towson, Thomas Munroe, and Archibald Henderson, as trustees.

In this year advertisements were published inviting designs for the Monument from American artists, but placing no limitation upon the form of the designs. It was recommended, however, that they should "harmoniously blend durability, simplicity, and grandeur."

The cost of the projected Monument was estimated at not less than one million dollars.

A great many designs were submitted, but the one selected was that of Mr. Robert Mills, comprising in its main features a vast stylobate surmounted by a tetrastyle pantheon, circular in form, and with an obelisk six hundred feet high rising from the center.

Design by Robert Mills

In 1846 the restriction upon the subscriptions was removed, and in 1847 the fund amounted to eighty-seven thousand dollars.

Regularly authorized and bonded collecting agents were appointed in all parts of the country, and appeals were made to the generosity of the public.

Mrs. James Madison, Mrs. John Quincy Adams, and Mrs. Alexander Hamilton, at the request of the Monument Society, effected an organization to assist in collecting funds through the women of the country.

In November, 1847, the Monument Society adopted a resolution that the corner-stone be laid on the 22d of February, 1848, provided a suitable site could be obtained.

In January, 1848, Congress passed a resolution granting a site on any of the unoccupied public grounds of the City of Washington, to be selected by the President of the United States and the Washington Monument Society. The site on Reservation 3 was accordingly selected, and title to the land was conveyed to the Society. On the 29th of January it was decided to postpone the laying of the cornerstone until the 4th of July, 1848. Objections in the mean time having been made to the plan for the Monument as proposed by Mr. Mills, the Society, pursuant to a report from its committee, in the month of April of that year, fixed upon a height of five hundred feet for the shaft, leaving in abeyance the surrounding pantheon and base.

The corner-stone was laid in accordance with this decision of the Society on the 4th of July, 1848, in the presence of the members of the executive, legislative, and judicial branches of the Government, foreign ministers and officers, and a vast concourse of citizens from all sections of the Union. The ceremonies—Masonic in character—were conducted under the direction of Hon. B. B. French, Grand Master of the Masonic fraternity for the District of Columbia, and were as interesting as they were impressive; the corner-stone being rested at the northeast angle of the foundation. The gavel used in this ceremony was the one used by General Washington in laying the corner-stone of the Capitol, and is now in the possession of Potomac Lodge, No. 5, of Free and Accepted Masons of the District of Columbia.

July 4, 1848

The prayer of consecration was offered by the Rev. Mr. McJilton, and the Oration of the day was pronounced by the Hon. Robert C. Winthrop, then Speaker of the House of Representatives. Profoundly regretting, as we all do, that this distinguished citizen cannot be with us to-day, because of recent illness, we still sincerely rejoice that he has sent to us the garland of his commanding eloquence, to be laid on the capstone of the Monument, amid the shoutings of the people as they cry, "Grace, grace unto it."

Hon. Robert C. Winthrop

Among the guests on the stand at the laying of the corner-stone were Mrs. Alexander Hamilton (then ninety-one years old), Mrs. Dolly Paine Madison, Mrs. John Quincy Adams, George Washington Parke Custis, Chief Justice Taney, Lewis Cass, Martin Van Buren, Millard Fillmore, and many others distinguished as well for their social eminence as for their public renown.

The work, when once begun, progressed steadily, until in 1854 the shaft had reached a height one hundred and fifty-two feet above the level of the foundation.

Subsequently, an addition of four feet was put upon the shaft, making its total height one hundred and fifty-six feet, the whole executed at a cost of about three hundred thousand dollars.

Under the auspices of the Society, as well in its earlier as in its later history, blocks of stone for insertion in the interior walls of the Monument, and bearing appropriate inscriptions, have been contributed by nearly every State and Territory, and by many foreign governments.

The treasury of the Society having now been exhausted, and all efforts to obtain further sums having proved unavailing, the Society presented a memorial to Congress, representing that they were unable to devise any plan likely to succeed, and, under the circumstances, asking that Congress should take such action as it might deem proper.

The memorial was referred in the House of Representatives to a select committee of thirteen, of which Mr. Henry May, of Maryland, was chairman, and this committee, on the 22d of February, 1855, made to the House an eloquent and able report, in which, after a careful examination of the whole subject, the proceedings of the Society in the past were reviewed and approved, and an appropriation of two hundred thousand dollars was recommended to be made by Congress "on behalf of the people of the United States to aid the funds" of the Society; but at this time complications of a political nature arose in the management of the Society, the appropriation recommended was not made, and, for the same reason, a stop was put to the active prosecution of the work on the Monument for a number of years.

On the 26th of February, 1859, the Congress gave to the Washington National Monument Society a formal charter of incorporation, the incorporators being Winfield Scott, Walter Jones, John J. Abert, James Kearney, Thomas Carberry, Peter Force, William A. Bradley, Philip R. Fendall, Walter Lennox, Matthew F. Maury, Thomas Blagden, J. B. H. Smith, W. W. Seaton, Elisha Whittlesey, B. Ogle Tayloe, Thomas H. Crawford, W. W. Corcoran, and John Carroll Brent.

The first meeting of this new board was held in the City Hall, March 22, 1859, at which meeting President Buchanan presided. The Society again went vigorously to work, issuing public appeals, making collections at the polls, and employing every means to secure funds for the completion of the Monument. But the condition of the country during the decade from 1860 to 1870 rendered their efforts futile. It was not until the year 1873 that the Society again presented a memorial to Congress, recommending the Monument to its favorable consideration.

Disunity disrupts completion

In the mean time the Society continued their

appeals to the country for aid according to a plan which contemplated the raising, by subscriptions from all chartered organizations, of a certain gross sum deemed sufficient to complete the Monument, the payment of the subscriptions into the hands of the treasurer of the Society being contingent upon the pledging of the entire sum. A measurable success met the efforts of the Society in this direction, a very considerable sum having been promised by responsible bodies, and the Society desisted from these efforts only when, on the 2d of August, 1876, an act of Congress, appropriating two hundred thousand dollars to continue the construction of the Monument, had become a law of the land.

This measure was introduced in the Senate by Hon. John Sherman, of Ohio, who properly presides at the high festival we hold this day at the base of the finished Monument. On the 5th of July, 1876 (the date is significant), he moved the adoption of a joint resolution declaring, after an appropriate preamble, that the Senate and House of Representatives in Congress assembled, "in the name of the people of the United States, at the beginning of the second century of the national existence, do assume and direct the completion of the Washington Monument, in the city of Washington." A bill in pursuance of this joint resolution was passed unanimously in the Senate on the 22d of July, in the House of Representatives without opposition on the 27th of July, and was signed by President Grant on the 2d of August, 1876.

Unanimity reached on behalf of the Monument

By this act, which gave a Congressional expression to the national gratitude, a Joint Commission was created, to consist of the President of the United States, the Supervising Architect of the Treasury Department, the Architect of the Capitol, the Chief of Engineers of the United States Army, and the First Vice-President of the Washington National Monument Society, under whose direction and supervision the construction of the Monument was placed.

Act of national gratitude

According to a provision of the same act, the Washington National Monument Society transferred and conveyed to the United States in due form all the property rights and easements belonging to it in the Monument, the conveyance being legally recorded in the proper court register.

By a further clause of this same act it was provided: That nothing therein should be so construed as to prohibit said Society from continuing its organization "for the purpose of soliciting and collecting money and material from the States, associations, and the people in aid of the completion of the Monument, and acting in an advisory and co-operative capacity" with the Commission named in the said act until the completion and dedication of the work.

Upon the death of President Madison, in 1836, the constitution of the Society had been so amended as to provide that the President of the United States should be *ex-officio* president of the Society. Andrew Jackson was the first *ex-officio* president. The mayors of Washington, and, at a later day, the Governors of the several States were made *ex-officio* vice-presidents.

The mayors of Washington thus connected with the work were John P. Van Ness, William A. Bradley, Peter Force, W. W. Seaton, Walter Lennox, John W. Maury, John T. Towers, William B. Magruder, Richard Wallach, James G. Berret, Sayles J. Bowen, and Matthew G. Emery.

In the roll of the Society's membership the following names are recorded:

Chief Justice John Marshall, Roger C. Weightman, Commodore John Rodgers, General Thomas S. Jesup, George Bomford, M. St. Clair Clarke, Samuel H. Smith, John McClelland, William Cranch, William Brent, George Watterston, Nathan Towson, Archibald Henderson, Thomas Munroe, Thomas Carberry, Peter Force, ex-President James Madison, John P. Van Ness, William Ingle, William L. Brent, General Alexander Macomb, John J. Abert, Philip R. Fendall, Maj. Gen. Winfield Scott, John Carter, General Walter Jones, Walter Lennox, T. Hartley Crawford, M. F. Maury, U.S. Navy, B. Ogle Tayloe, Thomas Blagden, John Carroll Brent, James Kearney, Elisha Whittlesey, W. W. Seaton, J. Bayard H. Smith, W. W. Corcoran, John P. Ingle, James M. Carlisle, Dr. John B. Blake, Dr. William Jones, William L. Hodge, Dr. James C. Hall, William B. Todd, James Dunlop, General U.S. Grant, George W. Riggs, Henry D. Cooke, Peter G. Washington, William J. McDonald, John M. Brodhead, General William T. Sherman, Dr. Charles H. Nichols, D. A. Watterston, Alexander R. Shepherd, Fitzhugh Coyle, James G. Berret, J. C. Kennedy, William A. Richardson, General O. E. Babcock, Edward Clark, Rear-Admiral L. M. Powell, Charles F. Stansbury, Frederick D. Stuart, Robert C. Winthrop, Joseph Henry, General William McKee Dunn, John C. Harkness, Horatio King, Daniel B. Clarke,

George W. McCrary, Dr. Joseph M. Toner, James C. Welling, George Bancroft, Rear-Admiral C. R. P. Rodgers.

In conclusion, let me say that I should be strangely wanting to my sense of the proprieties belonging to this time and place, if, standing here as the representative of the Washington National Monument Society, I should fail in this high presence and at this solemn moment to give emphatic expression to the profound gratitude which is due from the Society to the Legislative and Executive Departments of the Government, who have brought to a successful completion the patriotic work which the Society was not able to accomplish.

Well-balanced architecture

For the praise of the accomplished engineer of the Army, Col. Thomas Lincoln Casey, who has here built so solidly and so skillfully, we have only to look up to the finished work of his scientific hand, as that work stands before us to-day in the strong and even poise of its well-balanced architecture.

His actions put to the proof of time

The heraldic ensign of Washington bore for its motto the words *Exitus acta probat,* "Their issue puts actions to the proof." The actions of Washington, as put to the proof of time, have issued in a great nation made free and independent under his military leadership; in a constitutional polity, based on liberty regulated by law, as devised by the convention of statesmen over whose deliberations he presided; in the powerful Federal Government whose energies he first set in motion from the high seat of its Chief Executive; in the affectionate and grateful recollection of more than fifty millions of people who to-day find in his name and fame their choicest national legacy; and, finally, in the veneration and homage of all mankind, who, to the remotest ends of the world, have learned to honor in our illustrious countryman the best as well as the greatest of the sons of men.

Sacred national duty fulfilled

Surely, then, it is glory enough for the Washington National Monument Society that its pious labors, as put to the proof of time, have issued in the majestic structure which stands before us to-day, and it is glory enough for the Legislative and Executive Departments of the Government that in "assuming and directing the completion of the Monument" on the foundations laid by the people, they have at once redeemed a sacred national pledge, and fulfilled a sacred national duty, by giving to this great obelisk the culmination and crown with which it towers above earth and soars heavenward, like the fame it commemorates.

The Masonic Ceremonies

The Masonic dedicatory ceremonies were then performed by the Grand Lodge of Free and Accepted Masons of the District of Columbia, Myron M. Parker, Most Worshipful Grand Master. He was Assisted by Thomas P. Chifelle, R.W.D.G. Master; José M. Yznaga, R.W.S. Grand Warden; Jesse W. Lee, jr., R.W.J.G. Warden; William R. Singleton, R.W.G. Secretary; C. C. Duncanson, R.W.G. Treasurer; Joseph Hamacher, W.G. Lecturer; C. B. Smith, Rev. and W.G. Chaplain; H. Dingman, W.G. Marshal; Emmett C. Elmore, W.S.G. Deacon; Thomas F. Gibbs, W.J.G. Deacon; Orville Drown, W.G. Sword Bearer; O. S. Firmin, W.G. Pursuivant; Frank N. Carver, W.S.G. Steward; Edward Kern, W.J.G. Steward, and Thomas J. Edwards, Grand Tiler.

The following ritual, which is somewhat abridged from that used by the Order on similar occasions, was then recited.

Grand Master. R.W. Deputy Grand Master, what is the proper implement of your office?

Deputy Grand Master. The square, Most Worshipful.

Grand Master. What are its moral and Masonic uses?

Deputy Grand Master. To square our actions by the square of virtue, and prove our work when finished.

Grand Master. Have you applied the square to the Obelisk, and is the work squared?

Deputy Grand Master. I have, and I find the corners to be square; the workmen have done their duty.

Grand Master. R.W. Senior Grand Warden, what is the proper implement of your office?

Senior Grand Warden. The level, Most Worshipful.

Grand Master. What is its Masonic use?

Senior Grand Warden. Morally, it reminds us of equality, and its use is to prove horizontals.

Grand Master. Have you applied it, and are the courses level?

Senior Grand Warden. I have, and I find the courses to be level; the workmen have done their duty.

Grand Master. R.W. Junior Grand Warden, what is the proper implement of your office?

Junior Grand Warden. The plumb, Most Worshipful.

Grand Master. What is its Masonic use?

Junior Grand Warden. Morally, it teaches rectitude of conduct, and we use it to try perpendiculars.

Grand Master. Have you applied it, and have the walls been properly erected?

Junior Grand Warden. I have applied the plumb, and the walls have been skillfully erected according to rule; the workmen have done their duty.

Grand Master. The several grand officers having reported that this structure has been erected by the square, the level, and the plumb, the corner-stone of which having been laid July 4, 1848, by the Grand Master of Masons of the District of Columbia, I now, as the Grand Master, do pronounce this Obelisk to have been mechanically completed.

(*Junior Grand Warden presented the golden vessel of corn.*)

Grand Junior Warden. M.W. Grand Master, it has been the immemorial custom to scatter corn as an emblem of nourishment, I therefore present you with this golden vessel of corn.

Grand Master. I therefore now scatter this the *very* corn which was similarly used on the 22d of February, 1860, at the dedication of the equestrian statue of Washington, at the Circle in this city. In the name of the Great Jehovah, to whom be honor and glory, I now invoke a continuation of the great prosperity, and all those blessings which were then invoked at the laying of the corner-stone of this structure, July 4, 1848, and which have been ever since unceasingly bestowed upon the inhabitants of this city.

(*Senior Grand Warden presented the silver vessel of wine.*)

Senior Grand Warden. M.W. Grand Master, wine, the emblem of refreshment, having been used mystically by our ancient brethren, I present you with this silver vessel of wine.

Grand Master. In the name of the Holy Saints John, I pour out this wine to virtue; and may the Great Moral Governor of the Universe bless this whole people, and cause them to be distinguished for every virtue, as they are for their greatness.

(*Deputy Grand Master presented the silver vessel of oil.*)

Deputy Grand Master. M.W. Grand Master, I present to you, to be used according to ancient custom, this silver vessel of oil.

Grand Master. I pour out this oil, an emblem of joy, that joy which should animate the bosom of every Mason, on the completion of this Monument to our distinguished brother, George Washington.

Address by Grand Master Myron M. Parker

Address by Grand Master Myron M. Parker

It is eminently fitting, upon an occasion like the present, that we, as Masons, should associate with these ceremonies certain historic relics with which General Washington was intimately connected, some of them over a century ago.

His gavel

This gavel, prepared for the express purpose, was presented to Washington and used by him as President of the United States, and also as Grand Master *pro tempore* in laying the corner-stone of the Capitol of the Nation on the 18th day of September, 1793. Immediately thereafter he presented it to Potomac Lodge, No. 9, in whose possession it has ever since remained. It was used in laying the corner-stone of this Obelisk, July 4, 1848. Also the corner-stone of the equestrian statue of Washington at the Circle, and at its dedication, February 22, 1860. It was likewise used at the laying of the corner-stone of the extension of the Capitol, July 4, 1851; also by the Grand Master of the Grand Lodge of Virginia at the laying of the corner-stone of the Yorktown Monument, October 18, 1881, and at many other public buildings in various States.

Here behold the sacred volume, belonging to Fredericksburg Lodge, No. 4, of Virginia, upon which he took his first vows to Masonry, November 4, 1752, and here the constitution of that lodge signed by him.

The Bible

Here the sacred book, belonging to St. John's Lodge, No. 1, in the city of New York, upon which, on the 30th day of April, 1789, he took the oath of office as the first President of the United States.

Here the great light belonging to Alexandria Washington Lodge, No. 22, of Alexandria, Va., upon which he, as the Worshipful Master of that lodge, received the vows of the initiates made by him.

His apron made by Madame Lafayette

This is the apron worn by him, which was wrought by Madame La Fayette, and presented to him by that noble lady, the wife of the distinguished General Lafayette, Washington's compatriot, friend, and Masonic brother.

This golden urn contains a lock of Washington's hair, which was presented to the Grand Lodge of Massachusetts, in 1800, by Mrs. Washington, and has been transmitted by every Grand Master of that Grand Lodge to his successor immediately after his installation.

This lesser light is one of the three candles which was borne in Washington's funeral procession, by Alexandria Washington Lodge, No. 22, and was taken into the first tomb of Washington, at Mount Vernon, where, on December 18, 1799, his mortal remains were deposited.

Having thus briefly referred to a few of the historical relics with which Brother George Washington was associated, it is proper that as Grand Master I should advert for a few moments to his life as a Freemason, leaving all other phases to be eulogized by the distinguished gentlemen who are to conclude these ceremonies at the Capitol.

Life as a Freemason

George Washington's initiation into Masonry was during his minority, and was had under authority of the Grand Lodge of Scotland, which admits minors of eighteen to its mysteries. He was made a Fellow Craft March 3, and a Master Mason August 4, 1753. While Worshipful Master of Alexandria Lodge he received the Royal Arch degrees, according to the custom of those days, as a compliment to the Master.

When Commander-in-Chief of the Army, Washington occupied the chief place in the Masonic procession, on the occasion of St. John's (Evangelist) day, 1778, at Philadelphia.

It was after he had been Commander-in-Chief of the Army that our illustrious Brother received from Edmund Randolph (Governor of Virginia), as Grand Master, his commission as the first Master of Alexandria Lodge, No. 22, of Virginia.

When the Grand Lodge of Virginia was organized Washington was elected Grand Master, an honor he was compelled to decline, he not having at that time served as master of a lodge. In 1780 the Grand Lodge of Pennsylvania unanimously nominated General Washington as Grand Master of Masons of the United States, an office to which he would have been elected had not the sentiment and policy of Masonry at that time been opposed to a National Grand Lodge. From the latest writings of our distinguished Brother we find evidence of his love for and devotion to the principles of Masonry. On the 2d day of May, 1791, he wrote the Grand Lodge of South Carolina that he "recognized with pleasure" his "relations to the brethren" whose principles "lead to purity of morals and beneficence of action." Still later, in 1793, he wrote the Grand Lodge of Massachusetts, in response to its dedication to him of its "Book of Constitution," that it is "pleasing to know that the milder virtues of the heart are highly respected by the society whose liberal principles are founded on the immutable laws of truth and justice." Again, he wrote King David's Lodge, of Rhode Island, that Masonry promotes "private virtue and public prosperity," and that he should "always be happy to advance the interests of the society, and to be considered by them a deserving brother."

Sentiment of Masonry opposed to a national lodge

Founded on immutable Laws of truth and justice

In April, 1798, not three years before his death, he wrote the Grand Lodge of Massachusetts: "My attachment to the society will dispose me always to contribute my best endeavors to preserve the honor and interest of the Craft."

November 8, 1799, Washington wrote the Grand Lodge of Maryland, that "the principles and doctrines of Freemasonry are founded in benevolence and to be exercised for the good of mankind."

General Washington never forgot Masonry when a soldier. He encouraged and visited camp lodges and participated in their labor, frequently officiating as master. It was at the old Freeman's tavern, on the green of Morristown, N.J., in 1777, that General Washington himself made General La Fayette a Freemason. Upon one occasion, a detachment of the American Army overcoming a British force, captured from them the working tools, jewels, and clothing of a military lodge. General Washington, upon learning this, ordered restoration, declaring that "he waged no war against philanthropy and benevolence."

I have dwelt thus somewhat at length to show that General Washington was devoted to the humane principles of Freemasonry from his minority to his death, in public and private life, and to show that it is especially appropriate for the Masons of this country to participate in the imposing ceremonies of to-day. This ceremony is not ecclesiastical. It is the growth of a sentiment along the ages, and as such will command the respect and admiration of mankind long after this Monument shall have crumbled to the dust. Thus we find that the immortal Washington, himself a Freemason, devoted his hand, his heart, his sacred honor, to the cause of freedom of conscience, of speech, and of action, and from his successful leading has arisen this Nation. To him and the memory of his deeds, a grateful people have erected this memorial in the capital which he founded, and which will bear his name to remotest ages; a monument towering above other monuments as he towered above other men.

Grand Chaplain. May the Lord, the giver of every perfect gift, bless all who are assembled, and grant to each one, in needful supply, the corn of nourishment, wine of refreshment, and oil of joy: Amen! Amen! Amen!

The Most Worshipful Grand Master and the Brethren in unison responded: "So mote it be: Amen!"

STRUCTURE DELIVERED:

REMARKS OF COL. THOMAS LINCOLN CASEY, CHIEF ENGINEER

Col. Thomas Lincoln Casey, of the Corps of Engineers, U.S. Army, the Chief Engineer and Architect of the Monument, then formally delivered the structure to the President of the United States, in the following words:

Mr. Chairman: The duty has been assigned me of presenting the part taken by the General Government in the construction of this Monument, and of delivering it to the President of the United States.

You have heard from the First Vice-President of the Washington National Monument Society of the part taken by that distinguished body in the inception and partial construction of the Monument and of its appeals, both to the people of the country and to Congress, for assistance in the great work so bravely undertaken.

Whatever may have been the results of these appeals, no really effective proceedings were had in Congress, having in view the completion of the Monument, until July 5, 1876. On that day, Mr. Chairman, you introduced in the Senate a concurrent resolution, referring in terms to the Centennial of our National Independence and to the influence of George Washington in securing that independence, and closing as follows:

July 5, 1876

"Therefore, as a mark of our sense of honor due his name and his compatriots and associates, our Revolutionary fathers, we, the Senate and House of Representatives, in Congress assembled, in the name of the people of the United States, at this, the beginning of the second century of national existence, do assume and direct the completion of the Washington Monument in the City of Washington, and instruct the committees on appropriations of the respective Houses to propose suitable provisions of law to carry this resolution into effect."

Within two days from its introduction this resolution was passed unanimously by both Houses, and, in obedience to its instructions, a bill for the completion of the Washington Monument was at once reported in the House of Representatives, and became a law August 2, 1876. That statute appropriated two hundred thousand dollars for the completion of the Monument, to be expended in four equal annual installments; provided for a transfer to the United States of the ownership of the portion of the shaft then built, and created a Joint Commission to direct and supervise the construction of the Monument, which Commission was to make a report each year to Congress. The Commission was to consist of the President of the United States, the Supervising Architect of the Treasury Department, the Architect of the Capitol, the Chief of Engineers of the United States Army, and the First Vice-President of the Washington National Monument Society.

The act further required, "That, prior to commencing any work on the Monument, an examination should be made of its foundation, in order to thoroughly ascertain whether it was sufficient to sustain the weight of the completed structure, and, if the same should be found insufficient, then the further continuance of the work was not to be authorized by anything contained in the act until the further action of Congress."

Foundation to be examined

From the early days of the construction there had been apprehensions that the foundation was not of sufficient size to sustain the column if carried to the height originally designed. These apprehensions, which, just after the laying of the corner-stone, were shared by but few persons, had, as far back as 1853, become wide-spread, and were entertained by many intelligent people. In 1873, after a lapse of twenty years, the question of the sufficiency of the foundation was again the subject of discussion, at this time by a committee of the House of Representatives.

This was the select committee of thirteen, created to consider the practicability of completing the Washington Monument by the time of the Centennial Celebration of the Declaration of Independence, July 4, 1876. During their deliberations, they caused special investigations to be made concerning the stability of the existing structure. These investigations and the reports were made by capable engineers, and the conclusions drawn by them were to the effect that the existing foundation should not be subjected to any additional load whatever; in other words, that it would be unsafe to increase the height of the incomplete shaft.

It was hardly to be expected that the further examinations required by the act of August, 1876, would disclose anything different as to the condition of the foundation, nevertheless the Joint Commission secured the services of another board of experienced engineers, who, after careful borings, examinations, and tests of the earth of the site, and due deliberation, reported on the 10th of April and 15th of June, 1877, that the existing foundation was of insufficient spread and depth to sustain the weight of the completed structure, but that it was feasible to bring the foundation to the required stability by hooping-in the earth upon which it stood. These opinions were concurred in by most of the engineers who considered the subject, while they were quite as unanimous in the belief that to excavate beneath and put a new foundation under the old one would be hazardous in the extreme.

Congress authorizes expenditures

On the 8th of November, 1877, the Joint Commission made its first report to Congress, announcing the decision of the engineers, and this report led to the enactment of the joint resolution of June 14, 1878, authorizing the Joint Commission to expend the sum of thirty-six thousand dollars, if they deemed it advisable, in giving greater stability to the foundation.

Joint Commission authorized by Congress to spend $36,000

Two years had now elapsed since the creation of the Joint Commission. They at once secured the services of an engineer and his assistant, and directed the chief to prepare a project for strengthening the existing foundation so that the Obelisk could be carried to the desired height. This project, which necessarily included the form and dimensions of the finished Monument, was completed and approved October 1, 1878, and active operations were immediately commenced. The project contemplated first, the digging away of the earth from around and beneath the outer portions of the old foundation and replacing it with Portland cement concrete masonry; then, in removing a portion of the old masonry foundation itself from beneath the walls of the shaft and substituting therefor a continuous Portland cement concrete enlargement extending out over the new subfoundation. The weakness of the old foundation lay in the fact that it was too shallow and covered an area of ground insufficient to sustain the pressure of the completed work. The strengthening consisted in the enlargement of the foundation by spreading it over a greater area and sinking it a greater depth into the earth. The work of excavating beneath the Monument was commenced January 28, 1879, and the new foundation was finished May 29, 1880. It was impossible to properly enlarge the foundation with the funds granted in the joint resolution of June 14, 1878. A careful estimate of the cost, which accompanied the original project, amounted to about one hundred thousand dollars, and accordingly by the joint resolution of June 27, 1879, a further sum of sixty-four thousand dollars was granted to complete the foundation. This proved to be more than sufficient, as the foundation cost but ninety-four thousand four hundred and seventy-four dollars.

As completed, the new foundation covers two and a half times as much area and extends thirteen and a half feet deeper than the old one. Indeed, the bottom of the new work is only two feet above the level of high tides in the Potomac, while the water which permeates the earth of the Monument lot stands six inches above this bottom. The foundation now rests upon a bed of fine sand some two feet in thickness, and this sand stratum rests upon a bed of bowlders and gravel. Borings have been made in this gravel deposit for a depth of over eighteen feet without passing through it, and so uniform is the character of the material upon which the foundation rests that the settlements of the several corners of the shaft have differed from each other by only the smallest subdivisions of the inch. The pressures on the earth beneath the foundation are nowhere greater than the experiences of years have shown this earth to be able to sustain, while the strength of the masonry in the foundation itself is largely in excess of the strains brought upon it. The stability of this base is assured against all natural causes except earthquakes or the washing out of the sand bed beneath the foundation.

New foundation deeper

Having enlarged the foundation, the work upon the shaft was speedily commenced. The summer of 1880 was mostly taken up in building an iron frame within the shaft, preparing the hoisting machinery, and collecting the granite and marble needed in the construction. The first marble block was set in the shaft on the 7th of August, 1880, and the last stone was placed at the level five hundred on the 9th of August, 1884, thus consuming four seasons in finishing the shaft. The topmost stone of the pyramidion was set on the 6th of December, 1884, thus essentially completing the Obelisk. Minor additions and modifications in the details of the interior of the shaft are still to be made, and some filling, grading, and planting are required for the terrace, but no work is proposed that can change the existing appearance or proportions of the Monument.

The masonry constructed by the Government is the best known to the engineering art, and the weight is so distributed that, subjected to a wind pressure of one hundred pounds per square foot on any face, corresponding to a wind velocity of one hundred and forty-five miles per hour, the Monument would have a large factor of safety against overturning. The marble is of the same kind as that in the monolithic columns of the Capitol, has a fine grain, is close and compact in texture, free from disintegrating impurities, and in this climate will endure for ages.

There is not time, nor is this the occasion, to enter into the engineering details of the construction, to discuss all the strains and stresses in several parts of the work, or the factors of safety against destructive forces. It is sufficient to say, that although the dimensions of the foundation base were originally planned without due regard to the tremendous forces to be brought into play in building so large an obelisk, the resources of modern engineering science have supplied means for the completion of the grandest monumental column ever erected in any age of the world.

By means of modern engineering

In its proportions the ratios of the dimensions of the several parts of the ancient Egyptian obelisk have been carefully followed.

The entire height has been made slightly greater than ten times the breadth of base, producing an obelisk that, for grace and delicacy of outline, is not excelled by any of the larger Egyptian monoliths, while in dignity and grandeur it surpasses any that can be mentioned.

Mr. President: For and in behalf of the Joint Commission for the completion of the Washington Monument I deliver to you this column.

DEDICATION

PRESIDENT ARTHUR'S DEDICATORY ADDRESS

Senator Sherman then introduced "the President of the United States," and as Mr. Arthur stepped forward he was loudly applauded. When silence was restored he read the following remarks:

Fellow-Countrymen: Before the dawn of the century whose eventful years will soon have faded into the past, when death had but lately robbed this Republic of its most beloved and illustrious citizen, the Congress of the United States pledged the faith of the Nation that in this city, bearing his honored name, and then, as now, the seat of the General Government, a monument should be erected "to commemorate the great events of his military and political life."

The stately column that stretches heavenward from the plain whereon we stand bears witness to all who behold it that the covenant which our fathers made their children have fulfilled.

In the completion of this great work of patriotic endeavor there is abundant cause for national rejoicing; for while this structure shall endure it shall be to all mankind a steadfast token of the affectionate and reverent regard in which this people continue to hold the memory of Washington. Well may he ever keep the foremost place in the hearts of his countrymen.

Affectionate and reverent regard

The faith that never faltered, the wisdom that was broader and deeper than any learning taught in schools, the courage that shrank from no peril and was dismayed by no defeat, the loyalty that kept all selfish purpose subordinate to the demands of patriotism and honor, the sagacity that displayed itself in camp and cabinet alike, and above all that harmonious union of moral and intellectual qualities which has never found its parallel among men; these are the attributes of character which the intelligent thought of this century ascribes to the grandest figure of the last.

Attributes of character

But other and more eloquent lips than mine will to-day rehearse to you the story of his noble life and its glorious achievements.

To myself has been assigned a simpler and more formal duty, in fulfillment of which I do now, as President of the United States and in behalf of the people, receive this Monument from the hands of its builder, and declare it dedicated from this time forth to the immortal name and memory of George Washington.

President Arthur was frequently interrupted by applause, and when he had concluded the entire assemblage joined in repeated rounds of cheers, many waving their hats and handkerchiefs. It was with some difficulty that Senator Sherman could regain the attention of the audience, but when he did, he announced that the dedication ceremonies at the Monument were

Procession and Review

completed, and that those present would move in procession to the Hall of the House of Representatives, in the Capitol, where the orations would be delivered.

THE PROCESSION AND REVIEW

No sooner were the exercises concluded than the military were again formed in column, the invited guests entered their carriages, and the procession took up the line of march for the Capitol, bands playing, drums beating, colors and banners fluttering in the wind, while the cannon at the navy-yard, at the artillery headquarters, and at Fort Meyer fired minute guns. . . .

The procession moved from the Monument grounds through Seventeenth street to the new State, War, and Navy Department building, and thence in front of the Executive Mansion, through Fifteenth street into Pennsylvania avenue.

This national thoroughfare was decorated with flags and bunting, while many thousand spectators on stands and on the sidewalks formed a brilliant framework for the passing pageant. When the head of the column had reached the Capitol a halt was ordered, and the President of the United States, who occupied an open carriage drawn by four horses, passed the military to the Capitol. On his arrival there, after a brief delay, the President took his position on a reviewing stand which had been erected directly in front of the Capitol, where he was joined by the members of his Cabinet, several Senators, Representatives, and diplomats.

The column then passed in review, the officers saluting as they passed. General Sheridan, with his mounted staff, wheeled out after they had passed the reviewing stand and took their position opposite the President. It took upwards of an hour for the military and civic organizations to march past in review, and as each body left the Capitol Grounds it was dismissed to the command of its head.

EXERCISES AT THE CAPITOL

Exercises at the Capitol

The seats had been removed from the floor of the Hall of the House of Representatives, which was filled with chairs, assigned to the invited guests, viz: The Senators, Representatives, and Delegates composing the Forty-eighth Congress; the President of the United States, the President-elect, the Vice-President-elect, and the ex-Presidents; the Chief Justice and Associate Justices of the Supreme Court; the Cabinet officers, the Admiral of the Navy, the Lieutenant-General of the Army, and the officers of the Army and Navy who, by name, had received the thanks of Congress; the Chief Justice and Judges of the Court of Claims, and the Chief Justice and Associate Justices of the Supreme Court of the District of Columbia; the Diplomatic Corps; the Commissioners of the District, Governors of States and Territories, the general officers of the Society of the Cincinnati; the Washington National Monument Society, members and ex-members of the Joint Commission for the Completion of the Monument, engineers of the Monument, a detail of workmen, and other guests invited to the floor.

The Executive Gallery was reserved for the invited guests of the President, the families of the members of the Cabinet, and the families of the Supreme Court. The Diplomatic Gallery was reserved for the families of the members of the Diplomatic Corps. The Reporters' Gallery was reserved exclusively for the use of journalists, and the remaining galleries were thrown open to the holders of tickets thereto.

The Marine Band occupied the vestibule in the rear of the Speaker's chair, and performed a succession of patriotic airs.

The House of Representatives having been called to order by Mr. Speaker Carlisle, at a quarter past one o'clock p.m., Messrs. Dorsheimer, Tucker, and Cannon were appointed a committee to wait on the Senate and inform that body that the House was ready to receive it, and to proceed with the ceremonies which had been appointed to take place in the Hall of the House.

This duty was performed, and at half-past two o'clock the members of the Senate, following their President *pro tempore* and their Secretary, and preceded by their Sergeant-at-Arms, entered the Hall of the House of Representatives and occupied the seats reserved for them on the right and left of the main aisle.

The Hon. George F. Edmunds, a Senator from Vermont, President *pro tempore* of the Senate, occupied the Speaker's chair, the Speaker of the House sitting at his left. The Chaplain of the House, Rev. John S. Lindsay, D.D., and Rev. S. A. Wallis, of Pohick Church, near Mount Vernon, Virginia, sat at the Clerk's desk. The chairman of the Joint Committee of Arrangements, the orators, and the other officials designated were seated in accordance with the arrangements of the Joint Committee of Arrangements.

The President *pro tempore* of the Senate having rapped with his gavel, there was silence, and he said:

Gentlemen of the Senate and House of Representatives, you are assembled, pursuant to the concurrent order of the two Houses, to celebrate the completion of the Monument to the memory of the first President of the United States. It is not only a memorial but an inspiration that shall live through all the generations of our posterity, as we may hope, which we this day inaugurate and celebrate by the ceremonies that have been ordered by the two Houses.

Memorial for posterity

Rev. S. A. Wallis, of Pohick Church, near Mount Vernon, Virginia, then offered the following prayer:

Almighty and everlasting God, Lord of heaven and earth, who alone rulest over the nations of the world, and disposest of them according to Thy good pleasure, we praise Thy holy name for the benefits we commemorate this day.

Rulest over the nations

Wonderful things didst Thou for us in the days of our fathers, in the times of old. For they gat not the land in possession by their sword, neither did their own arm save them, but Thy right hand and the light of Thy countenance, because Thou hadst a favor unto them. Especially do we render Thee our hearty thanks for Thy servant George Washington, whom Thou gavest to be a commander and a governor unto this people, and didst by him accomplish for it a great and mighty deliverance. And as we are now gathered before Thee in these Halls, we bless Thee for the government and civil order Thou didst establish through him. Grant that it may be upheld by that righteousness which exalteth a nation, and that this place may evermore be the habitation of judgment and justice. Let Thy blessing rest upon our Chief Magistrate and his successors in all generations. Grant each in his time those heavenly graces that are requisite for so high a trust; that the laws may be impartially administered to the punishment of wickedness and vice, and to the maintenance of Thy true religion and virtue. We also humbly beseech Thee for our Senate and Representatives in Congress assembled that Thou wouldst be pleased to direct all their consultations to the advancement of Thy glory, the good of Thy Church, the safety, honor and welfare of Thy people, that all things may be so ordered and settled by their endeavors upon the best and surest foundations, that peace and happiness, truth and justice, religion and piety may be established among us for all generations. We pray Thee for our judges and officers that they may judge the people with just judgment, be no respecters of persons, and hear both the small and the great in his cause. O, Lord God of Hosts, be pleased to save and defend our Army and Navy, that each may be a safeguard to these United States, both by land and sea, until Thou dost fulfill Thy word, that nation shall not lift up sword against nation, neither shall they learn war any more. Be with those who have been appointed to speak unto us this day as they recount the deeds of old time, Thy marvelous works, and the judgments of Thy mouth. Give them grace to utter such words as may stir us up to emulate the virtues of our forefathers, so that we may transmit the Republic to our posterity high in praise and in name and in honor.

By Washington accomplished America's deliverance

Established government and civil order

Laws to maintain true religion

Congress to advance God's glory

Let Thy richest blessings rest upon our country at large; may we lend a true obedience to the laws cheerfully and willingly for conscience' sake. Let no causelesss divisions weaken us as a nation, but grant that we may be knit together more and more in the bonds of peace and unity. Preserve us from the dangers now threatening society, and enable each of us, high and low, rich and poor, to do his duty in that state of life unto which Thou hast called him. So we that are Thy people and sheep of Thy pasture shall give Thee thanks forever, and will always be showing forth Thy praise from generation to generation. These and all other benefits of Thy good providence we humbly beg in the name and through the mediation of Jesus Christ our most blessed Lord and Savior. *Amen.*

The President *pro tempore* of the Senate, after the Marine Band had played "Hail Columbia," said:

Gentlemen of the Senate and House of Representatives, the first proceeding in order is the oration by Hon. Robert C. Winthrop, of Massachusetts. The Chair is sorry to announce that Mr. Winthrop, from indisposition, is unable to attend. According to the arrangements of the committee the oration will be now read by Hon. John D. Long, a member of the House of Representatives from the State of Massachusetts.

Oration by Hon. Robert C. Winthrop

President Arthur, Senators and Representatives of the United States:

By a joint Resolution of Congress you have called upon me to address you in this Hall to-day on the completion of yonder colossal monument to the Father of his Country. Nothing less imperative could have brought me before you for such an effort. Nearly seven and thirty years have passed away since it was my privilege to perform a similar service at the laying of the corner-stone of that monument. In the prime of manhood, and in the pride of official station, it was not difficult for me to speak to assembled thousands in the open air, without notes, under the scorching rays of a midsummer sun. But what was easy for me then is impossible for me now. I am here to-day, as I need not tell you, in far other condition for the service you have assigned me—changed, changed in almost everything except an inextinguishable love for my Country, and its Union and an undying reverence for the memory of Washington. On these alone I rest for inspiration, assured that, with your indulgence, and the blessing of God, which I devoutly invoke, they will be sufficient to sustain me in serving as a medium for keeping up the continuity between the hearts and hands which laid the foundation of this gigantic structure and those younger hearts and hands which have at last brought forth the capstone with shoutings. It is for this you have summoned me. It is for this alone I have obeyed your call.

Cornerstone, July 4, 1848

Memory of Washington

Capstone, thirty-seven years later

Meantime I cannot wholly forget that the venerable Ex-President John Quincy Adams—at whose death-bed, in my official chamber beneath this roof, I was a privileged watcher thirty-seven years ago this very day—had been originally designated to pronounce the Corner-stone Oration, as one who had received his first commission, in the long and brilliant career at home and abroad which awaited him, from the hands of Washington himself. In that enviable distinction I certainly have no share; but I may be pardoned for remembering that, in calling upon me to supply the place of Mr. Adams, it was borne in mind that I had but lately taken the oath as Speaker at his hands and from his lips, and that thus, as was suggested at the time, the electric chain, though lengthened by a single link, was still unbroken. Let me hope that the magnetism of that chain may not even yet be entirely exhausted, and that I may still catch something of its vivifying and quickening power, while I attempt to bring to the memory of Washington the remnants of a voice which is failing and of a vigor which I am conscious is ebbing away!

It is now, Mr. President, Senators, and Representatives, more than half a century since a voluntary Association of patriotic citizens initiated the project of erecting a National Monument to Washington in the city which bears his name. More than a whole century ago, indeed—in that great year of our Lord which witnessed the Treaty of Peace and Independence, 1783—Congress had ordered an Equestrian Statue of him to be executed "to testify the love, admiration, and gratitude of his countrymen"; and again, immediately after his death, in 1799, Congress had solemnly voted a marble monument to him at the Capital, "so designed as to commemorate the great events of his military and political life." But our beloved country, while yet in its infancy, and I may add in its indigency, with no experience in matters of art, and heavily weighed down by the great debt of the Revolutionary War, knew better how to vote monuments than how to build them, or, still more, how to pay for them. Yorktown monuments and Washington monuments, and the statues of I know not how many heroes of our struggle for Independence, made a fine show on paper in our early records, and were creditable to those who ordered them; but their practical execution seems to have been indefinitely postponed.

America in its infancy

The Washington Monument Association, instituted in 1833, resolved that no such postponement should longer be endured, and proceeded to organize themselves for the work, which has at length been completed. They had for their first President the great Chief Justice John Marshall, the personal friend and chosen biographer of Washington, whose impressive image you have so recently and so worthily unveiled on yonder Western Terrace. They had for their second President the not less illustrious James Madison, the father of the Constitution of which Marshall was the interpreter, and whose statue might well have no inferior place on the same Terrace. Among the other officers and managers of that Association I cannot forget the names of William W. Seaton, whose memory

Chief Justice John Marshall

James Madison, Father of the Constitution

is deservedly cherished by all who knew him; of that grand old soldier and patriot Winfield Scott; of Generals Archibald Henderson and Nathan Towson; of Walter Jones, and Peter Force, and Philip R. Fendall, together with that of its indefatigable General Agent, honest old Elisha Whittlesey. To that Association our earliest and most grateful acknowledgments are due on this occasion. But of those whom I have named, and of many others whom I might name, so long among the honored and familiar figures of this metropolis, not one is left to be the subject of our congratulations. Meanwhile we all rejoice to welcome the presence of one of their contemporaries and friends, whose munificent endowments for Art, Education, Religion, and Charity entitle him to so enviable a place on the roll of American philanthropists—the venerable William W. Corcoran, now, and for many years past, our senior Vice-President.

Nearly fifteen years, however, elapsed before the plans or the funds of this Association were in a state of sufficient forwardness to warrant them even in fixing a day for laying the first foundation-stone of the contemplated structure. That day arrived at last—the 4th of July, 1848. And a great day it was in this capital of the nation. There had been no day like it here before, and there have been but few, if any, days like it here since. If any one desires a description of it, he will find a most exact and vivid one in the columns of the old National Intelligencer—doubtless from the pen of that prince of editors, the accomplished Joseph Gales. I recall among the varied features of the long procession Freemasons of every order, with their richest regalia, including the precious gavel and apron of Washington himself; Firemen, with their old-fashioned engines; Odd-Fellows from a thousand Lodges; Temperance Societies and other Associations innumerable; the children of the Schools, long ago grown to mature manhood; the military escort of regulars, marines, and volunteer militia from all parts of the country, commanded by Generals Quitman and Cadwalader and Colonel May, then crowned with laurels won in Mexico, which long ago were laid upon their graves. I recall, too, the masses of the people, of all classes, and sexes, and ages, and colors, gazing from the windows, or thronging the sidewalks, or grouped in countless thousands upon the Monument grounds. But I look around in vain for any of the principal witnesses of that imposing ceremonial: the venerable widows of Alexander Hamilton and James Madison; President Polk and his Cabinet, as then constituted—Buchanan, Marcy, John Y. Mason, Walker, Cave Johnson, and Clifford; Vice-President Dallas; George Washington Parke Custis, the adopted son of the great Chief; not forgetting Abraham Lincoln and Andrew Johnson, both then members of the House of Representatives, and for whom the liveliest imagination could hardly have pictured what the future had in store for them. Of that whole body there are now but a handful of survivors, and probably not more than two or three of them present here to-day—not one in either branch of Congress, nor one, as I believe, in any department of the national service.

To those of us who took part in the laying of that first stone, or who witnessed the ceremonies of the august occasion, and who have followed the slow ascent of the stupendous pile, sometimes with hope and sometimes with despair, its successful completion is, I need not say, an unspeakable relief, as well as a heartfelt delight and joy. I hazard little in saying that there are some here to-day, unwearied workers in the cause, like my friends Horatio King and Dr. Toner—to name no others—to whose parting hour a special pang would have been added had they died without the sight which now greets their longing eyes on yonder plain.

I dare not venture on any detailed description of the long intervening agony between the laying of the first stone and the lifting of the last. It would fill a volume, and will be sure hereafter to furnish material for an elaborate monograph, whose author will literally find "sermons in stones"—for almost every stone has its story if not its sermon. Every year of the first decade certainly had its eventful and noteworthy experiences. The early enthusiasm which elicited contributions to the amount of more than a quarter of a million dollars from men, women, and children in all parts of the land, and which carried up the shaft more than a hundred and fifty feet almost at a bound; the presentation and formal reception of massive blocks of marble, granite, porphyry, or freestone from every State in the Union and from so many foreign nations—beginning, according to the catalogue, with a stone from Bunker Hill and ending with one from the Emperor of Brazil; the annual assemblies at its base on each succeeding Fourth of July, with speeches by distinguished visitors; the sudden illness and sad death of that sterling patriot President Zachary Taylor, after an exposure to the midday heat at the gathering in 1850, when the well-remembered Senator Foote, of

Early enthusiasm

Mississippi, had indulged in too exuberant an address—these were among its beginnings; the end was still a whole generation distant.

Later on came the long, long disheartening pause, when—partly owing to the financial embarrassments of the times, partly owing to the political contentions and convulsions of the country, and partly owing to unhappy dissensions in the Association itself—any further contributions failed to be forthcoming, all interest in the Monument seemed to flag and die away, and all work on it was suspended and practically abandoned. A deplorable Civil War soon followed, and all efforts to renew popular interest in its completion were palsied.

Construction halts

How shall I depict the sorry spectacle which those first one hundred and fifty-six feet, in their seemingly hopeless, helpless condition, with that dismal derrick still standing as in mockery upon their summit, presented to the eye of every comer to the Capital for nearly a quarter of a century! No wonder the unsightly pile became the subject of pity or derision. No wonder there were periodical panics about the security of its foundation, and a chronic condemnation of the original design. No wonder that suggestions for tearing it all down began to be entertained in many minds, and were advocated by many pens and tongues. That truncated shaft, with its untidy surroundings, looked only like an insult to the memory of Washington. It symbolized nothing but an ungrateful country, not destined—as, God be thanked, it still was—to growth and grandeur and imperishable glory, but doomed to premature decay, to discord, strife, and ultimate disunion. Its very presence was calculated to discourage many hearts from other things, as well as from itself. It was an abomination of desolation standing where it ought not. All that followed of confusion and contention in our country's history seemed foreshadowed and prefigured in that humiliating spectacle, and one could almost read on its sides in letters of blood, "Divided! Weighed in the balance! Found wanting!"

Insult to the memory of Washington

And well might that crude and undigested mass have stood so forever, or until the hand of man or the operation of the elements should have crushed and crumbled it into dust, if our Union had then perished. An unfinished, fragmentary, crumbling monument to Washington would have been a fit emblem of a divided and ruined Country. Washington himself would not have had it finished. He would have desired no tribute, however imposing, from either half of a disunited Republic. He would have turned with abhorrence from being thought the Father of anything less than One Country, with one Constitution and one Destiny.

And how cheering and how inspiring the reflection, how grand and glorious the fact, that no sooner were our unhappy contentions at an end, no sooner were Union and Liberty, one and inseparable, once more and, as we trust and believe, forever reasserted and reassured, than this monument to Washington gave signs of fresh life, began to attract new interest and new effort, and soon was seen rising again slowly but steadily toward the skies—stone after stone, course upon course, piled up in peace, with foundations extended to the full demand of the enormous weight to be placed upon them, until we can now hail it as complete! Henceforth and forever it shall be lovingly associated, not only with the memory of him in whose honor it has been erected, but with an era of assured peace, unity, and concord, which would have been dearer to his heart than the costliest personal memorial which the toil and treasure of his countrymen could have constructed. The Union is itself the all-sufficient and the only sufficient monument to Washington. The Union was nearest and dearest to his great heart. "The Union in any event," were the most emphatic words of his immortal Farewell Address. Nothing less than the Union would ever have been accepted or recognized by him as a monument commensurate with his services and his fame. Nothing less ought ever to be accepted or recognized as such by us, or by those who shall rise up, generation after generation, to do homage to his memory!

Revival of interest

Union, nearest and dearest to Washington's heart

For the grand consummation which we celebrate to-day we are indebted primarily to the National Government, under the successive Presidents of the past nine years, with the concurrent action of the two branches of Congress, prompted by Committees so often under the lead of the veteran Senator Morrill, of Vermont. The wise decision and emphatic resolution of Congress on the 2d of August, 1876—inspired by the Centennial Celebration of American Independence, moved by Senator Sherman, of Ohio, and adopted, as it auspiciously happened, on the hundredth anniversary of the formal signing of the great Declaration—that the monument should no longer be left unfinished, with the appointment of a Joint Commission to direct and supervise its completion, settled the whole matter. To that Joint Commission, consisting of the President of the United States for the time being, the Senior Vice-President of the Monument Association, the Chief of Engineers of the United States Army, with the architects of the Capitol and the Treasury, the congratulations and thanks of us all may well be tendered. But I think they will all cordially agree with me that the main credit and honor of what has been accomplished belongs peculiarly and pre-eminently to the distinguished officer of Engineers who has been their devoted and untiring Agent from the outset. The marvellous work of extending and strengthening the foundations of a structure already weighing, as it did, not less than thirty-two thousand tons—sixty-four million pounds—an operation which has won the admiration of engineers all over the world, and which will always associate this monument with a signal triumph of scientific skill—was executed upon his responsibility and under his personal supervision. His, too, have been the ingenious and effective arrangements by which the enormous shaft has been carried up, course after course, until it has reached its destined height of five hundred and fifty-five feet, as we see it at this hour. To Col. Thomas Lincoln Casey, whose name is associated in three generations with valued military service to his country, the successful completion of the monument is due. But he would not have us forget his accomplished Assistant, Capt. George W. Davis, and neither of them would have us fail to remember Superintendent McLaughlin and the hard-handed and honest-hearted mechanics who have labored so long under their direction.

Sixty-four million pounds

Triumph of scientific skill

Finis coronat opus. The completion crowns the work. To-day that work speaks for itself, and needs no other orator. Mute and lifeless as it seems, it has a living and audible voice for all who behold it, and no one can misinterpret its language. Nor will any one, I think, longer cavil about its design. That design, let me add, originally prepared by the Washington architect, Robert Mills, of South Carolina, and adopted long before I had any relations to this Association, was commended to public favor by such illustrious names as Andrew Jackson, John Quincy Adams, Albert Gallatin, Henry Clay, and Daniel Webster. A colonnade encircling its base, and intended as a sort of Pantheon, was soon discarded from the plan. Its main feature, from the first, was an obelisk, after the example of that which had then been recently agreed upon for Bunker Hill. And so it stands to-day, a simple sublime obelisk of pure white marble, its proportions, in spite of its immense height, conforming exactly to those of the most celebrated obelisks of antiquity, as my accomplished and lamented friend, our late Minister to Italy, George P. Marsh, so happily pointed out to us. It is not, indeed, as were those ancient obelisks, a monolith, a single stone cut whole from the quarry; that would have been obviously impossible for anything so colossal. Nor could we have been expected to attempt the impossible in deference to Egyptian methods of construction. We might almost as well be called on to adopt as the emblems of American Progress the bronze Crabs which were found at the base of Cleopatra's Needle! America is certainly at liberty to present new models in art as well as in government, or to improve upon old ones; and, as I ventured to suggest some years ago, our monument to Washington will be all the more significant and symbolic in embodying, as it does, the idea of our cherished National motto, E Pluribus Unum. That compact, consolidated structure, with its countless blocks, inside and outside, held firmly in position by their own weight and pressure, will ever be an instructive type of the National strength and grandeur which can only be secured by the union of "many in one."

Liberty to present the new and improve upon the old

Had the Fine Arts indeed made such advances in our country forty years ago as we are now proud to recognize, it is not improbable that a different design might have been adopted; yet I am by no means sure it would have been a more effective and appropriate one. There will always be ample opportunity for the display of decorative art in our land. The streets and squares of this city and of all our great cities are wide open for the statues and architectural memorials of our distinguished statesmen and soldiers, and such monuments are everywhere welcomed and honored. But is not—I ask in all sincerity—is not the acknowledged pre-eminence of the Father of his Country, first without a second, more fitly and adequately represented by that soaring shaft, rising high above trees and spires and domes and all the smoke and stir of earth—as he ever rose above sectional prejudices and party politics and personal interests

Rose above prejudice, politics, and personal interests

—overtopping and dominating all its surroundings, gleaming and glistening out at every vista as far as human sight can reach, arresting and riveting the eye at every turn, while it shoots triumphantly to the skies? Does not—does not, I repeat, that Colossal Unit remind all who gaze at it, more forcibly than any arch or statue could do, that there is one name in American history above all other names, one character more exalted than all other characters, one example to be studied and reverenced beyond all other examples, one bright particular star in the clear upper sky of our firmament, whose guiding light and peerless lustre are for all men and for all ages, never to be lost sight of, never to be unheeded? Of that name, of that character, of that example, of that glorious guiding light, our Obelisk, standing on the very spot selected by Washington himself for a monument to the American Revolution, and on the site which marks our National meridian, will be a unique memorial and symbol forever.

To be studied and reverenced beyond all other examples

For oh, my friends, let us not longer forget, or even seem to forget, that we are here to commemorate not the Monument but the Man. That stupendous pile has not been reared for any vain purpose of challenging admiration for itself. It is not, I need not say it is not, as a specimen of advanced art, for it makes no pretension to that; it is not as a signal illustration of engineering skill and science, though that may confidently be claimed for it; it is not, certainly it is not, as the tallest existing structure in the world, for we do not measure the greatness of men by the height of their monuments, and we know that this distinction may be done away with here or elsewhere in future years; but it is as a Memorial of the pre-eminent figure in modern or in ancient history the world over—of the man who has left the loftiest example of public and private virtues, and whose exalted character challenges the admiration and the homage of mankind. It is this example and this character—it is the Man, and not the Monument—that we are here to commemorate!

The pre-eminent figure in modern or in ancient history

Assembled in these Legislative Halls of the Nation, as near to the Anniversary of his birth as a due respect for the Day of our Lord will allow, to signalize the long-delayed accomplishment of so vast a work, it is upon him in whose honor it has been upreared, and upon the incomparable and inestimable services he has rendered to his country and to the world, that our thoughts should be concentred at this hour. Yet what can I say, what can any man say, of Washington, which has not already been rendered as familiar as household words, not merely to those who hear me, but to all readers of history and all lovers of Liberty throughout the world? How could I hope to glean anything from a field long ago so carefully and lovingly reaped by such men as John Marshall and Jared Sparks, by Guizot and Edward Everett and Washington Irving, as well as by our eminent living historian, the venerable George Bancroft, happily here with us to-day?

Cotemporary Biographers

Others, many others, whom I dare not attempt to name or number, have vied with each other in describing a career of whose minutest details no American is ever weary, and whose variety and interest can never be exhausted. Every stage and step of that career, every scene of that great and glorious life, from the hour of his birth, one hundred and fifty-three years ago—"about ten in the morning of ye 11th day of February, 1731–2," as recorded in his mother's Bible—in that primitive Virginia farmhouse in the county of Westmoreland, of which the remains of the "great brick chimney of the kitchen" have been identified only within a few years past—every scene, I say, of that grand and glorious life, from that ever-memorable hour of his nativity, has been traced and illustrated by the most accomplished and brilliant pens and tongues of our land.

His childhood, under the loving charge of that venerated mother, who delighted to say that "George had always been a good son," who happily lived not only to see him safely restored to her after the exposures and perils of the Revolutionary struggle, but to see him, in her eighty-second year, unanimously elected to be the President in Peace of the country of which he had been the Saviour in War; his primary education in that "old-field schoolhouse," with Hobby, the sexton of the parish, for his first master; his early and romantic adventures as a land surveyor; his narrow escape from being a midshipman in the British Navy at fourteen years of age, for which it has been said a warrant had been obtained and his luggage actually put on board a man-of-war anchored in the river just below Mount Vernon; his still narrower and hair-breadth escapes from Indian arrows and from French bullets, and his survival—the only mounted officer not killed—at the defeat of Braddock, of whom he was an aide-de-camp; together with that most remarkable prediction of the Virginia pastor, Samuel

Davies, afterward President of Princeton College, pointing him out—in a sermon, in 1755, on his return, at the age of twenty-three, from the disastrous field of the Monongahela—as "that heroic youth, Colonel Washington, whom I cannot but hope Providence has preserved in so signal a manner for some important service to his country"; who has forgotten, who can ever forget these most impressive incidents of that opening career by which he was indeed so providentially preserved, prepared, and trained up for the eventful and illustrious future which awaited him?

Providentially preserved, prepared, and trained for service

Still less can any American forget his taking his seat, soon afterward, in the Virginia House of Burgesses—with the striking tribute to his modesty he won from the Speaker—and his subsequent election to the Continental Congress at Philadelphia, where on the 15th of June, 1775, at the instance of John Adams and on the motion of Thomas Johnson, afterward Governor of Maryland, he was unanimously appointed "General and Commander-in-Chief of such Forces as are, or shall be, raised for the maintenance and preservation of American Liberty." Nor can any of us require to be reminded of the heroic fortitude, the unswerving constancy, and the unsparing self-devotion with which he conducted through seven or eight years that protracted contest, with all its toils and trials, its vexations and vicissitudes, from the successful Siege of Boston, his first great triumph, followed by those masterly movements on the Delaware, which no less celebrated a soldier than Frederick the Great declared "the most brilliant achievements of any recorded in the annals of military action"—and so along—through all the successes and reverses and sufferings and trials of Monmouth and Brandywine and Germantown and Valley Forge—to the Siege of Yorktown, in 1781, where, with the aid of our generous and gallant allies, under the lead of Rochambeau and De Grasse and Lafayette, he won at last that crowning victory on the soil of his beloved Virginia.

Forces raised for America's liberty

Nor need I recall to you the still nobler triumphs witnessed during all this period—triumphs in which no one but he had any share—triumphs over himself; not merely in his magnanimous appreciation of the exploits of his subordinates, even when unjustly and maliciously contrasted with disappointments and alleged inaction of his own, but in repelling the machinations of discontented and mutinous officers at Newburgh, in spurning overtures to invest him with dictatorial and even Kingly power, and in finally surrendering his sword and commission so simply, so sublimely, to the Congress from which he had received them.

Triumphs over self

Or, turning sharply from this summary and familiar sketch of his military career—of which, take it for all in all, its long duration, its slender means, its vast theatre, its glorious aims and ends and results, there is no parallel in history—turning sharply from all this, need I recall him, in this presence, presiding with paramount influence and authority over the Convention which framed the Constitution of the United States, and then, with such consummate discretion, dignity, and wisdom, over the original administration of that Constitution, when the principles and precedents of our great Federal system of Government were molded, formed, and established?

Military career

Paramount influence

It was well said by John Milton, in one of his powerful Defences of the People of England, "War has made many great whom Peace makes small." But of Washington we may say, as Milton said of Cromwell, that, while War made him great, Peace made him greater; or rather that both war and peace alike gave opportunity for the display of those incomparable innate qualities which no mere circumstances could create or destroy.

But his sword was not quite yet ready to rest quietly in its scabbard. Need I recall him once more, after his retirement from a second term of the Chief Magistracy, accepting a subordinate position, under his successor in the Presidency, as Lieutenant-General of the American Armies in view of an impending foreign war, which, thank God, was so happily averted?

Nor can any one who hears me require to be reminded of that last scene of all, when, in his eight-and-sixtieth year, having been overtaken by a fatal shower of sleet and snow in the midst of those agricultural pursuits in which he so much delighted at Mount Vernon, he laid himself calmly down to die—"not afraid to go," as he whispered to his physician—and left his whole country in tears such as had never flowed before. "Mark the perfect man and behold the upright, for the end of that man is peace!"

Eighty-five years ago to-morrow—his sixty-eighth birthday—was solemnly assigned by Congress for a general manifestation of that overwhelming national sorrow, and for the commemoration, by eulogies, addresses, sermons, and religious rites, of the great life which had thus been closed. But long before that anniversary arrived, and one day only after the sad tidings had reached the seat of Government in Philadelphia, President John Adams, in reply to a message of the House of Representatives, had anticipated all panegyrics by a declaration, as true to-day as it was then, that he was "the most illustrious and beloved personage which this country ever produced"; while Henry Lee, of Virginia, through the lips of John Marshall, had summed up and condensed all that was felt, and all that could be or ever can be said, in those imperishable words, which will go ringing down the centuries, in every clime, in every tongue, till time shall be no more, "First in War, First in Peace, and First in the hearts of his Countrymen!"

But there are other imperishable words which will resound through the ages—words of his own not less memorable than his acts—some of them in private letters, some of them in official correspondence, some of them in inaugural addresses, and some of them, I need not say, in that immortal Farewell Address which an eminent English historian has pronounced "unequaled by any composition of uninspired wisdom," and which ought to be learned by heart by the children of our schools, like the Laws of the Twelve Tables in the schools of ancient Rome, and never forgotten when those children grow up to the privileges and responsibilities of manhood.

Farewell Address

It was a custom of the ancient Egyptians, from whom the idea of our Monument has been borrowed—I should rather say, evolved—to cover their obelisks with hieroglyphical inscriptions, some of which have to this day perplexed and baffled all efforts to decipher them. Neither Champollion, nor the later Lepsius, nor any of the most skillful Egyptologists, have succeeded in giving an altogether satisfactory reading of the legends on Pompey's Pillar and Cleopatra's Needle. And those legends, at their best—engraved, as they were, on the granite or porphyry, with the letters enameled with gold, and boasted of as illuminating the world with their rays—tell us little except the dates and doings of some despotic Pharaoh, whom we would willingly have seen drowned in the ocean of oblivion, as one of them so deservedly was in the depths of the Red Sea. Several of the inscriptions on Cleopatra's Needle, as it so strangely greets us in the fashionable promenade of our commercial capital, inform us in magniloquent terms, of Thothmes III, who lived in the age preceding that in which Moses was born, styling him a "Child of the Sun," "Lord of the Two Worlds," "Endowed and endowing with power, life, and stability." Other inscriptions designate him, or Rameses II—the great oppressor of the Israelites—as the "Chastiser of Foreign Nations," "The Conqueror," "The Strong Bull!"

Our Washington Needle, while it has all of the severe simplicity, and far more than all of the massive grandeur, which were the characteristics of Egyptian architecture, bears no inscriptions whatever, and none are likely ever to be carved on it. Around its base bas-reliefs in bronze may possibly one day be placed, illustrative of some of the great events of Washington's life; while on the terrace beneath may, perhaps, be arranged emblematic figures of Justice and Patriotism, of Peace, Liberty, and Union. All this, however, may well be left for future years, or even for future generations. Each succeeding generation, indeed, will take its own pride in doing whatever may be wisely done in adorning the surroundings of this majestic pile, and in thus testifying its own homage to the memory of the Father of his Country. Yet to the mind's eye of an American Patriot those marble faces will never seem vacant—never seem void or voiceless. No mystic figures or hieroglyphical signs will, indeed, be descried on them. No such vainglorious words as "Conqueror," or "Chastiser of Foreign Nations," nor any such haughty assumption or heathen ascription as "Child of the Sun," will be deciphered on them. But ever and anon, as he gazes, there will come flashing forth in letters of living light some of the great words, and grand precepts, and noble lessons of principle and duty which are the matchless bequest of Washington to his country and to mankind.

Can we not all read there already, as if graven by some invisible finger, or inscribed with some sympathetic ink—which it requires no learning of scholars, no lore of Egypt, nothing but love of our own land, to draw out and make legible—those masterly words of his Letter to the Governors of the States in 1783:

"There are four things which, I humbly conceive, are essential to the well-being—I may even venture to say, to the existence—of the United States as an independent Power: First, an indissoluble Union of the States under one Federal head; Second, a sacred regard to Public Justice; Third, the adoption of a proper Peace Establishment; and, Fourth, the prevalence of that pacific and friendly disposition among the People of the United States which will induce them to forget their local prejudices and policies, to make those mutual concessions which are requisite to the general prosperity, and, in some instances, to sacrifice their individual advantages to the interest of the Community. These are the Pillars on which the glorious fabric of our Independency and National Character must be supported."

Pillars of Independency and National Character

Can we not read, again, on another of those seemingly vacant sides, that familiar passage in his Farewell Address—a jewel of thought and phraseology, often imitated, but never matched—"The name of American, which belongs to you in your National capacity, must always exalt the just pride of patriotism more than any appellation derived from local discriminations?" and, not far below it, his memorable warning against Party Spirit—"A fire not to be quenched, it demands a uniform vigilance to prevent its bursting into a flame, lest, instead of warming, it should consume?"

The name American

Still again, terser legends from the same prolific source salute our eager gaze: "Cherish Public Credit;" "Observe good faith and justice towards all Nations; cultivate peace and harmony with all;" "Promote, as an object of primary importance, institutions for the general diffusion of Knowledge. In proportion as the structure of a Government gives force to public opinion, it is essential that public opinion should be enlightened."

Principles of Justice, peace, education, morality, and religion

And, above all—a thousand-fold more precious than all the rest—there will come streaming down from time to time, to many an eager and longing eye, from the very point where its tiny aluminium apex reaches nearest to the skies—and shining forth with a radiance which no vision of Constantine, no labarum for his legions, could ever have eclipsed—some of those solemnly reiterated declarations and counsels, which might almost be called the Confession and Creed of Washington, and which can never be forgotten by any Christian Patriot:

"When I contemplate the interposition of Providence, as it was visibly manifest in guiding us through the Revolution, in preparing us for the reception of the General Government, and in conciliating the good-will of the people of America toward one another after its adoption, I feel myself oppressed and almost overwhelmed with a sense of Divine munificence. I feel that nothing is due to my personal agency in all those wonderful and complicated events, except what can be attributed to an honest zeal for the good of my country." "No people can be bound to acknowledge and adore an Invisible Hand which conducts the affairs of men more than the people of the United States. Every step by which they have advanced to the character of an Independent Nation seems to have been distinguished by some token of Providential Agency." "Of all the dispositions and habits which lead to political prosperity, Religion and Morality are indispensable supports. In vain would that man claim the tribute of patriotism, who should labor to subvert these great pillars of human happiness, these firmest props of the duties of men and of citizens."

An invisible hand conducts the affairs of men and nations

Religion and morality

And thus on all those seemingly blank and empty sides will be read, from time to time, in his own unequaled language, the grand precepts and principles of Peace, Justice, Education, Morality, and Religion, which he strove to inculcate, while encircling and illuminating them all, and enveloping the whole monument, from corner-stone to cap-stone, will be hailed with rapture by every patriotic eye, and be echoed by every patriotic heart, "The Union, the Union in any event!"

But what are all the noble words which Washington wrote or uttered, what are all the incidents of his birth and death, what are all the details of his marvelous career from its commencement to its close, in comparison with his own exalted character as a Man? Rarely was Webster more impressive than when, on the completion of the monument at Bunker Hill, in describing what our Country had accomplished for the welfare of mankind, he gave utterance, with his characteristic terseness and in his inimitable tones, to the simple assertion, "America has furnished to the world the character of Washington!" And well did he add that, "if our American institutions had done nothing else, that alone would have entitled them to the respect of mankind."

The character of Washington! Who can delineate it worthily? Who can describe that priceless gift of America to the world in terms which may do it any sort of justice, or afford any degree of satisfaction to his hearers or to himself?

America's gift to the world

Modest, disinterested, generous, just—of clean hands and a pure heart—self-denying and self-sacrificing, seeking nothing for himself, declining all remuneration beyond the reimbursement of his outlays, scrupulous to a farthing in keeping his accounts, of spotless integrity, scorning gifts, charitable to the needy, forgiving injuries and injustices, brave, fearless, heroic, with a prudence ever governing his impulses and a wisdom ever guiding his valor—true to his friends, true to his whole country, true to himself—fearing God, believing in Christ, no stranger to private devotion or public worship or to the holiest offices of the Church to which he belonged, but ever gratefully recognizing a Divine aid and direction in all that he attempted and in all that he accomplished—what epithet, what attribute could be added to that consummate character to commend it as an example above all other characters in merely human history!

From first to last he never solicited or sought an office, military or civil. Every office stood candidate for him, and was ennobled by his acceptance of it. Honors clustered around him as if by the force of "first intention." Responsibilities heaped themselves on his shoulders as if by the law of gravitation. They could rest safely nowhere else, and they found him ever ready to bear them all, ever equal to discharge them all. To what is called personal magnetism he could have had little pretension. A vein of dignified reserve, which Houdon and Stuart have rightly made his peculiar characteristic in marble and on canvas, repressed all familiarities with him. His magnetism was that of merit—superior, surpassing merit—the merit of spotless integrity, of recognized ability, and of unwearied willingness to spend and be spent in the service of his country. That was sufficient to attract irresistibly to his support not only the great mass of the people, but the wisest and best of his contemporaries in all quarters of the Union, and from them he selected, with signal discrimination, such advisers and counselors, in War and in Peace, as have never surrounded any other American leader. No jealousy of their abilities and accomplishments ever ruffled his breast, and with them he achieved our Independence, organized our Constitutional Government, and stamped his name indelibly on the age in which he lived as the Age of Washington!

Dignified reserve

Spotless integrity

Well did Chief-Justice Marshall, in that admirable Preface to the biography of his revered and illustrious friend, sum up with judicial precision the services he was about to describe in detail. Well and truly did he say, "As if the chosen instrument of Heaven, selected for the purpose of effecting the great designs of Providence respecting this our Western Hemisphere, it was the peculiar lot of this distinguished man, at every epoch when the destinies of his country seemed dependent on the measures adopted, to be called by the united voice of his fellow-citizens to those high stations on which the success of those measures principally depended."

Instrument of Heaven

And not less justly has Bancroft said, when describing Washington's first inauguration as President: "But for him the Country could not have achieved its Independence; but for him it could not have formed its Union; and now but for him it could not set the Federal Government in successful motion."

I do not forget that there have been other men, in other days, in other lands, and in our own land, who have been called to command larger armies, to preside over more distracted councils, to administer more extended Governments, and to grapple with as complicated and critical affairs. Gratitude and honor wait ever on their persons and their names! But we do not estimate Miltiades at Marathon, or Pausanias at Platæa, or Themistocles at Salamis, or Epaminondas at Mantinea or Leuctra, or Leonidas at Thermopylæ, by the number of the forces which they led on land or on sea. Nor do we gauge the glory of Columbus by the size of the little fleet with which he ventured so heroically upon the perils of a mighty unknown deep. There are some circumstances which can not occur twice; some occasions of which there can be no repetition; some names which will always assert their individual pre-eminence, and will admit of no rivalry or comparison. The glory of Columbus can never be eclipsed, never approached, till our New World shall require a fresh discovery; and the glory of Washington will remain unique and peerless until American Independence shall require to be again achieved, or the foundations of Constitutional Liberty to be laid anew.

The glory of Washington

Think not that I am claiming an immaculate perfection for any mortal man. One Being only has ever walked this earth of ours without sin. Washington had his infirmities and his passions like the rest of us; and he would have been more or less than human had he never been overcome by them.

There were young officers around him, in camp and elsewhere, not unlikely to have thrown temptations in his path. There were treacherous men, also—downright traitors, some of them—whose words in council, or conduct in battle, or secret plottings behind his back, aroused his righteous indignation, and gave occasion for memorable bursts of anger. Now and then, too, there was a disaster, like that of St. Clair's expedition against the Indians in 1791, the first tidings of which stirred the very depths of his soul, and betrayed him into a momentary outbreak of mingled grief and rage, which only proved how violent were the emotions he was so generally able to control.

While, however, not even the polluted breath of slander has left a shadow upon the purity of his life, or a doubt of his eminent power of self-command, he made no boast of virtue or valor, and no amount of flattery ever led him to be otherwise than distrustful of his own ability and merits. As early as 1757, when only twenty-five years of age, he wrote to Governor Dinwiddie: "That I have foibles, and perhaps many of them, I shall not deny; I should esteem myself, as the world also would, vain and empty were I to arrogate perfection."

On accepting the command of the Army of the Revolution, in 1775, he said to Congress: "I beg it may be remembered by every gentleman in the room that I this day declare, with the utmost sincerity, I do not think myself equal to the command I am honored with."

And, in 1777, when informed that anonymous accusations against him had been sent to Laurens, then President of Congress, he wrote privately to beg that the paper might at once be submitted to the body to which it was addressed, adding these frank and noble words: "Why should I be exempt from censure—the unfailing lot of an elevated station? Merit and talents which I cannot pretend to rival have ever been subject to it. My heart tells me it has been my unremitted aim to do the best which circumstances would permit; yet I may have been very often mistaken in my judgment of the means, and may, in many instances, deserve the imputation of error."

And when at last he was contemplating a final retirement from the Presidency, and in one of the draughts of his Farewell Address had written that he withdrew "with a pure heart and undefiled hands," or words to that effect, he suppressed the passage and all other similar expressions, lest, as he suggested, he should seem to claim for himself a measure of perfection which all the world now unites in according to him. For I hazard little in asserting that all the world does now accord to Washington a tribute, which has the indorsement of the Encyclopædia Britannica, that "of all men that have ever lived, he was the greatest of good men, and the best of great men." Or, let me borrow the same idea from a renowned English poet, who gave his young life and brilliant genius to the cause of Liberty in modern Greece. "Where," wrote Byron—

> Where may the wearied eye repose
>   When gazing on the great,
> Where neither guilty glory glows,
>   Nor despicable state!
> Yes, One—the first, the last, the best,
> The Cincinnatus of the West,
>   Whom envy dared not hate—
> Bequeathed the name of Washington,
> To make men blush there was but One!

To what other name have such tributes ever been paid by great and good men abroad as well as at home? You have not forgotten the language of Lord Erskine in his inscription of one of his productions to Washington himself: "You are the only being for whom I have an awful reverence."

Tributes from abroad

You have not forgotten the language of Charles James Fox, in the House of Commons: "Illustrious Man, before whom all borrowed greatness sinks into insignificance."

You have not forgotten the language of Lord Brougham, twice uttered, at long intervals, and with a purpose, as Brougham himself once told me, to impress and enforce those emphatic words as his fixed and final judgment: "Until time shall be no more will a test of the progress which our race has made in Wisdom and Virtue be derived from the veneration paid to the immortal name of Washington!"

Nor can I fail to welcome the crowning tribute, perhaps, from our mother land—reaching me, as it has, at the last moment of revising what I had prepared for this occasion—in a published letter from Gladstone, her great Prime Minister, who, after saying in casual conversation that Washington was "the purest figure in history," writes deliberately, "that if, among all the pedestals supplied by history for public characters of extraordinary nobility and purity, I saw one higher than all the rest, and if I were required at a moment's notice to name the fittest occupant for it, I think my choice, at any time during the last forty-five years, would have

Purest figure in history

lighted, and it would now light, upon Washington!"

But if any one would get a full impression of the affection and veneration in which Washington was held by his contemporaries, let him turn, almost at random, to the letters which were addressed to him, or which were written about him, by the eminent men, military or civil, American or European, who were privileged to correspond with him, or who, ever so casually, found occasion to allude to his career and character. And let him by no means forget, as he reads them, that those letters were written a hundred years ago, when language was more measured, if not more sincere, than now, and before the indiscriminate use of the superlative, and the exaggerations and adulations of flatterers and parasites, sending great and small alike down to posterity as patterns of every virtue under Heaven, had tended to render such tributes as suspicious as they often are worthless.

Correspondence with the world's most eminent

What, for instance, said plain-speaking old Benjamin Franklin? "My fine crab-tree walking-stick, with a gold head curiously wrought in the form of the cap of Liberty,"—these are the words of his Will in 1789—"I give to my friend and the friend of mankind George Washington. If it were a sceptre, he has merited it, and would become it."

Benjamin Franklin

"Happy, happy America;" wrote Gouverneur Morris from Paris, in 1793, when the French Revolution was making such terrific progress—"happy, happy America, governed by reason, by law, by the man whom she loves, whom she almost adores! It is the pride of my life to consider that man as my friend, and I hope long to be honored with that title."

Gouverneur Morris

"I have always admired," wrote to him Count Herzburg, from Berlin, where he had presided for thirty years over the Ministry of Foreign Affairs, under Frederick the Great—"I have always admired your great virtues and qualities, your disinterested patriotism, your unshaken courage and simplicity of manners—qualifications by which you surpass men even the most celebrated of antiquity."

Count Herzburg, of Berlin

"I am sorry," wrote Patrick Henry, then Governor of Virginia, in allusion to the accusations of one of the notorious faction of 1777—"I am sorry there should be one man who counts himself my friend who is not yours."

Patrick Henry

Thomas Jefferson, who, we all know, sometimes differed from him, took pains, at a later period of his life, to say of him in a record for posterity: "His integrity was most pure; his justice the most inflexible I have ever known; no motives of interest or consanguinity, of friendship or hatred, being able to bias his decision. He was, indeed, in every sense of the word, a wise, a good, and a great man." And when it was once suggested to him, not long before his own death, that the fame of Washington might lessen with the lapse of years, Jefferson, looking up to the sky, and in a tone which betrayed deep emotion, is said to have replied: "Washington's fame will go on increasing until the brightest constellation in yonder heavens is called by his name!"

Thomas Jefferson

"If I could now present myself," wrote Edmund Randolph, who had made injurious imputations on Washington before and after his dismissal from the Cabinet in 1795 — "if I could now present myself before your venerated uncle," he wrote most touchingly to Judge Bushrod Washington in 1810, " it would be my pride to confess my contrition that I suffered my irritation, let the cause be what it might, to use some of those expressions respecting him, which, at this moment of indifference to the world, I wish to recall, as being inconsistent with my subsequent conviction. My life will, I hope, be sufficiently extended for the recording of my sincere opinion of his virtues and merit in a style which is not the result of a mind merely debilitated by misfortune, but of that Christian Philosophy on which alone I depend for inward tranquillity."

Edmund Randolph

And far more touching and more telling still is the fact that even Thomas Conway, the leader of that despicable cabal at Valley Forge, but who lived to redeem his name in other lands, if not in our own—when believing himself to be mortally wounded in a duel, in 1778, and "just able," as he said, "to hold the pen for a few minutes"—employed those few minutes in writing to Washington to express his "sincere grief for having done, written, or said anything disagreeable" to him, adding these memorable words: "You are, in my eyes, the great and good man. May you long enjoy the love, veneration, and esteem of these States, whose liberties you have asserted by your virtues!"

Thomas Conway

From his illustrious friend Alexander Hamilton I need not cite a word. His whole life bore testimony, more impressive than words, to an admiration and affection for his

Alexander Hamilton

great chief, which could not be exceeded, and which no momentary misunderstandings could shake.

But listen once more, and only once more, to Lafayette, writing to Washington from Cadiz, in 1783, when the glad tidings of the Treaty of Peace had just reached him: "Were you but such a man as Julius Cæsar, or the King of Prussia, I should almost be sorry for you at the end of the great tragedy where you are acting such a part. But, with my dear General, I rejoice at the blessings of a Peace in which our noble ends have been secured. . . . As for you, who truly can say you have done all this, what must your virtuous and good heart feel in the happy moment when the Revolution you have made is now firmly established!"

Lafayette

Rightly and truly did Lafayette say that his beloved General was of another spirit and of a different mould from Cæsar and Frederick. Washington had little, or nothing, in common with the great military heroes of his own or any other age—conquering for the sake of conquest—"wading through slaughter to a throne"—and overrunning the world, at a countless cost of blood and treasure, to gratify their own ambition, or to realize some mad dream of universal empire. No ancient Plutarch has furnished any just parallel for him in this respect. No modern Plutarch will find one. In all history, ancient and modern alike, he stands, in this respect, as individual and unique as yonder majestic Needle.

Unique even among the great

In his Eulogy on Washington before the Legislature of Massachusetts the eloquent Fisher Ames, my earliest predecessor in Congress from the Boston district, said, eighty-five years ago, that in contemplating his career and character, "Mankind perceived some change in their ideas of greatness. . . . The splendor of power, and even the name of Conqueror, had grown dim in their eyes. . . . They knew and felt that the world's wealth, and its empire too, would be a bribe far beneath his acceptance." Yes, they all saw that he bore ever in his mind and in his heart, as he said at Philadelphia on his way to Cambridge, in 1775, that "as the Sword was the last resort for the preservation of our liberties, so it ought to be the first thing laid aside when those liberties were firmly established." And they saw him lay down his sword at the earliest moment, and retire to the pursuits of peace, only returning again to public service at the unanimous call of his country; to preside for a limited period over a free Constitutional Republic, and then eagerly resuming the rank of an American Citizen. That was the example which changed the ideas of mankind as to what constituted real greatness. And that example was exhibited for all nations and for all ages, never to be forgotten or overlooked, by him who was born one hundred and fifty-three years ago to-morrow in that primitive little Virginia farm-house!

Fisher Ames

Changed the ideas of mankind

I am myself a New-Englander by birth, a son of Massachusetts, bound by the strongest ties of affection and of blood to honor and venerate the earlier and the later worthies of the old Puritan Commonwealth, jealous of their fair fame, and ever ready to assert and vindicate their just renown. But I turn reverently to the Old Dominion to-day, and salute her as the mother of the pre-eminent and incomparable American, the Father of his Country, and the foremost figure in all merely human history. In the words of our own poet Lowell:

Foremost figure in all merely human history

> Virginia gave us this imperial man,
> Cast in the massive mould
> Of those high-statured ages old
> Which into grander forms our mortal metal ran;
> She gave us this unblemished gentleman:
> What shall we give her back but love and praise?

Virginia has had other noble sons, whom I will not name, but whom I do not forget. When I remember how many they are, and how great they have been, and how much our country has owed them, I may well exclaim, *"Felix prole virûm."* But, as I think of her Washington—of our Washington, let me rather say—I am almost ready to add, *"Læta Deûm partu!"*

A celebrated philosopher of antiquity, who was nearly contemporary with Christ, but who could have known nothing of what was going on in Judea, and who alas! did not always "reck his own rede"—wrote thus to a younger friend, as a precept for a worthy life: "Some good man must be singled out and kept ever before our eyes, that we may live as if he were looking on, and do everything as if he could see it."

Let me borrow the spirit, if not the exact letter, of that precept, and address it to the young men of my Country: "Keep ever in your mind and before your mind's eye the loftiest standard of character. You have it, I need not say, supremely and unapproachably, in Him who spake as never man spake and lived as never man lived, and who died for the sins of the world. That character stands apart and alone. But of merely mortal men the monument we have dedicated to-day points out the one for all Americans to study, to imitate, and, as far as may be, to emulate. Keep his example and his character ever before your eyes and in your hearts. Live and act as if he were seeing and judging your personal conduct and your public career. Strive to approximate that lofty standard, and measure your integrity and your patriotism by your nearness to it or your departure from it. The prime meridian of universal longitude, on sea or land, may be at Greenwich, or at Paris, or where you will. But the prime meridian of pure, disinterested, patriotic, exalted human character will be marked forever by yonder Washington Obelisk!"

Yes, to the Young Men of America, under God, it remains, as they rise up from generation to generation, to shape the destinies of their Country's future—and woe unto them if, regardless of the great example which is set before them, they prove unfaithful to the tremendous responsibilities which rest upon them!

Yet, let me not seem even for a moment to throw off upon the children the rightful share of those responsibilities which belongs to their fathers. Upon us, upon us it devolves to provide that the advancing generations shall be able to comprehend and equal to meet the demands which are thus before them. It is ours—it is yours especially, Senators and Representatives—to supply them with the means of that Universal Education which is the crying want of our land, and without which any intelligent and successful Free Government is impossible.

Universal education essential

We are just entering on a new Olympiad of our national history—the twenty-fifth Olympiad since Washington first entered on the administration of our Constitutional Government. The will of the People has already designated under whom the first century of that Government is to be closed, and the best hopes and wishes of every patriot will be with him in the great responsibilities on which he is about to enter. No distinction of party or of section prevents our all feeling alike that our Country, by whomsoever governed, is still and always our Country, to be cherished in all our hearts, to be upheld and defended by all our hands!

Most happy would it be if the 30th of April, on which the first Inauguration of Washington took place in 1789, could henceforth be the date of all future inaugurations—as it might be by a slight amendment to the Constitution—giving, as it would, a much-needed extension to the short sessions of Congress, and letting the second century of our Constitutional History begin where the first century practically began.

April 30, 1789

But let the date be what it may, the inspiration of the Centennial Anniversary of that first great Inauguration must not be lost upon us. Would that any words of mine could help us all, old and young, to resolve that the principles and character and example of Washington, as he came forward to take the oaths of office on that day, shall once more be recognized and reverenced as the model for all who succeed him, and that his disinterested purity and patriotism shall be the supreme test and standard of American statesmanship! That standard can never be taken away from us. The most elaborate and durable monuments may perish. But neither the forces of nature, nor any fiendish crime of man, can ever mar or mutilate a great example of public or private virtue.

Supreme test of statesmanship

Our matchless Obelisk stands proudly before us to-day, and we hail it with the exultations of a united and glorious Nation. It may or may not be proof against the cavils of critics, but nothing of human construction is proof against the casualties of time. The storms of winter must blow and beat upon it. The action of the elements must soil and discolor it. The lightnings of Heaven may scar and blacken it. An earthquake may shake its foundations. Some mighty tornado, or resistless cyclone, may rend its massive blocks asunder and hurl huge fragments to the ground. But the character which it commemorates and illustrates is secure. It will remain unchanged and unchangeable in all its consummate purity and splendor, and will more and more command the homage of succeeding ages in all regions of the Earth.

God be praised, that character is ours forever!

The reading of Mr. Winthrop's oration, which was frequently interrupted by applause, was followed by music from the Marine Band.

Oration by Hon. John W. Daniel

The President of the Senate. Gentlemen, an oration will now be delivered by Hon. John W. Daniel, of Virginia.

Mr. President of the United States, Senators, Representatives, Judges, Mr. Chairman, and my Countrymen:

Alone in its grandeur stands forth the character of Washington in history; alone like some peak that has no fellow in the mountain range of greatness.

"Washington," says Guizot, "Washington did the two greatest things which in politics it is permitted to man to attempt. He maintained by Peace the independence of his country, which he had conquered by War. He founded a free government in the name of the principles of order and by re-establishing their sway."

Washington did indeed do these things. But he did more. Out of disconnected fragments he molded a whole and made it a country. He achieved his country's independence by the sword. He maintained that independence by peace as by war. He finally established both his country and its freedom in an enduring frame of constitutional government, fashioned to make Liberty and Union one and inseparable. These four things together constitute the unexampled achievement of Washington.

Unequaled achievements

The world has ratified the profound remark of Fisher Ames, that "he changed mankind's ideas of political greatness." It has approved the opinion of Edward Everett, that he was "the greatest of good men, and the best of great men." It has felt for him, with Erskine, "an awful reverence." It has attested the declaration of Brougham, that: "he was the greatest man of his own or of any age." It is a matter of fact to-day as when General Hamilton, announcing his death to the Army, said, "The voice of praise would in vain endeavor to exalt a name unrivaled in the lists of true glory." America still proclaims him, as did Col. Henry Lee, on the floor of the House of Representatives, "The man first in peace, first in war, and first in the hearts of his countrymen." And from beyond the sea the voice of Alfieri, breathing the soul of all lands and peoples, still pronounces the blessing, "Happy are you who have for the sublime and permanent basis of your glory the love of country demonstrated by deeds."

Ye who have unrolled the scrolls that tell the tale of the rise and fall of nations; before whose eyes has moved the panorama of man's struggles, achievements, and progression, find you anywhere the story of one whose life-work is more than a fragment of that which in his life is set before you? Conquerors, who have stretched your scepters over boundless territories; founders of empire, who have held your dominions in the reign of law; reformers, who have cried aloud in the wilderness of oppression; teachers, who have striven with reason to cast down false doctrine, heresy, and schism; statesmen, whose brains have throbbed with mighty plans for the amelioration of human society; scar-crowned Vikings of the sea, illustrious heroes of the land, who have borne the standards of siege and battle—come forth in bright array from your glorious fanes—and would ye be measured by the measure of his stature? Behold you not in him a more illustrious and more venerable presence?

Statesman, Soldier, Patriot, Sage, Reformer of Creeds, teacher of Truth and Justice, Achiever and Preserver of Liberty—the First of Men—Founder and Savior of his Country, Father of his People—this is HE, solitary and unapproachable in his grandeur, Oh! felicitous Providence that gave to America OUR WASHINGTON!

Providence gave Washington to America

High soars into the sky to-day—higher than the Pyramids or the dome of St. Paul's or St. Peter's—the loftiest and most imposing structure that man has ever reared—high soars into the sky where

> "Earth highest yearns to meet a star,"

the monument which "We the people of the United States" have erected to his memory.

It is a fitting monument, more fitting than any statue. For his image could only display him in some one phase of his varied character—as the Commander, the Statesman, the Planter of Mount Vernon, or the Chief Magistrate of his country. So Art has fitly typified his exalted life in yon plain lofty shaft. Such is his greatness, that only by a symbol could it be represented. As Justice must be blind in order to be whole in contemplation, so History must be silent, that by this mighty sign she may unfold the amplitude of her story.

It was fitting that the eminent citizen who thirty-seven years ago spoke at the laying of the corner-stone should be the orator at the consummation of the work which he inaugurated. It was Massachusetts that struck the first blow for independence; it was her voice that made the stones of Boston to "rise in mutiny"; it was her blessed blood that sealed the covenant of our salvation. The firmament of our national life she has thickly sown with deeds of glory. John Adams, of Massachusetts, was among the first to urge the name of Washington to the Continental Congress when it commissioned him as Commander-in-Chief of the American forces; it was upon her soil that he drew the sword which was sheathed at Yorktown, and there that he first

First blow for independence

gave to the battle-breeze the thirteen stripes that now float in new galaxies of stars. And meet it was that here in the Capitol of the Republic, at the distance of more than a century from its birth, the eloquent son of that illustrious State should span the chasm with his bridge of gold, and emblazon the final arch of commemoration.

And I fancy, too, that in a land where the factious tongues of the elder nations are being hushed at last, and all rival strains commingled in the blood of brotherhood, the accomplished mission of America finds fitting illustration in the Sage descended from the Pilgrims crowning the Hero sprung from the Cavaliers.

It has seemed fitting to you, Mr. Chairman and gentlemen of the Commission, that a citizen of the State which was the birthplace and the home of Washington—whose House of Burgesses, of which he was a member—made the first burst of opposition against the Stamp Act, although less pecuniarily interested therein than their New England brethren, and was the first representative body to recommend a General Congress of the Colonies; of the State whose Mason drew that Bill of Rights which has been called the Magna Charta of America; whose Jefferson wrote, whose Richard Henry Lee moved, the Declaration that these Colonies be "free and independent States"; whose Henry condensed the revolution into the electric sentence, "Liberty or Death;" of the State which cemented union with that vast territorial dowry out of which five States were carved, having now here some ninety representatives; of that State whose Madison was named "the Father of the Constitution," and whose Marshall became its most eminent expounder; of the State which holds within its bosom the sacred ashes of Washington, and cherishes not less the principles which once kindled them with fires of Heaven descended—it has seemed fitting to you, gentlemen, that a citizen of that State should be also invited to deliver an address on this occasion.

Magna Charta of America

Would, with all my heart, that a worthier one had been your choice. Too highly do I esteem the position in which you place me to feel aught but solemn distrustfulness and apprehension. And who indeed might not shrink from such a theater when a Winthrop's eloquence still thrilled all hearts with Washington the theme?

Yet, in Virginia's name, I thank you for the honor done her. She deserved it. Times there are when even hardihood is virtue; and to such virtue alone do I lay claim in venturing to abide your choice to be her spokesman.

None more than her could I offend did I take opportunity to give her undue exaltation. Her foremost son does not belong to her alone, nor does she so claim him. His part and her part in the Revolution would have been as naught but for what was so gloriously done by his brothers in council and in arms and by her sister Colonies, who kept the mutual pledge of "Life, Fortune, and Sacred Honor." New Hampshire, Massachusetts, Rhode Island, Connecticut, New York, New Jersey, Pennsylvania, Delaware, Maryland, North Carolina, South Carolina, Georgia, your comrade of the old heroic days, salutes you once again in honor and affection; no laurel could be plucked too bright for Virginia's hand to lay upon your brows. And ye, our younger companions, who have sprung forth from the wilderness, the prairie, and the mountain, and now extend your empire to the far slopes where your teeming cities light their lamps by the setting sun—what grander tribute to the past, what happier assurance of the present, what more auspicious omens of the future could Heaven vouchsafe us than those which live and move and have their being in your presence?

Virtue in the people

What heart could contemplate the scene today—grander than any of Old Rome, when her victor's car "climbed the Capitol"—and not leap into the exclamation, "I, too, am an American citizen!"

Yet may I not remind you that Washington was a Virginian before he became an American, to tell his countrymen that "the name of American, which belongs to you in your national capacity, must always exalt the just pride of patriotism more than any appellation derived from local discrimination?" And may I not seek the fountain from which sprang a character so instinct with love of country?

The Puritans of England, who from the landing at Plymouth in 1620 to the uprising against Charles I in 1640, "turned to the New World," in the language of Canning, "to redress the balance of the Old," were quickly followed to America by a new stream of immigration, that has left as marked an impress upon our civilization between the South Atlantic and the Mississippi as the sons of the Pilgrims have made between the North Atlantic and the Lakes.

When Charles I was beheaded in 1649, and when his son, the Second Charles, was beaten at Worcester in 1651, multitudes of the King's men turned their faces also to the new land of hope, the very events which checked the immigration of the

Puritans to New England giving impulse to the tide which moved the Cavaliers to the Old Dominion. Between 1650 and 1670 the Virginia Colony increased from fifteen thousand to forty thousand souls, and nearly one-half of this number thither came within the decade after the execution of the King and the establishment of Cromwell's commonwealth on the ruins of his throne.

Intense loyalists were these new Virginians, who "would defend the crown if it hung upon a bush"; and when indeed its substance vanished with the kingly head that wore it, these "faithful subjects of King and Church" held allegiance to its phantom and to the exiled claimant. But they were not inattentive to their liberties. And if Virginia was the last of all the countries belonging to England to submit to Cromwell, yet she was also "the first state in the world composed of separate boroughs, diffused over an extensive surface, where representation was organized on the principle of universal suffrage." And in the very terms of surrender to the commonwealth it was stipulated that "the people of Virginia" should have all the liberties of the free-born people of England; should intrust their business, as formerly, to their own grand Assembly; and should remain unquestioned for past loyalty to the King.

Loyalists, but attentive to their liberties

Representative government

As in New England the Pilgrim Colony grew apace, so in Virginia prospered that of the Cavaliers. With that love of landed estates which is an instinct of their race, they planted their homes in the fertile lowlands, building great houses upon broad acres, surrounded by ornamental grounds and gardens.

Love of landed estates

Mimic empires were these large estates, and a certain baronial air pervaded them. Trade with Europe loaded the tables of their proprietors with luxuries; rich plate adorned them. Household drudgeries were separated from the main dwelling. The family became a considerable government within itself—the mistress a rural queen, the master a local potentate, with his graziers, seedsmen, gardeners, brewers, butchers, and cooks around him. Many of the heads of families were traveled and accomplished men. The parishes were ministered to by the learned clergy of the Established Church. In the old college of William and Mary ere long were found the resources of classic education, and in the old capital town of Williamsburg the winter season shone resplendent with the entertainments of a refined society. Barges imported from England were resources of amusement and means of friendly visitations along the water-courses, and heavy coaches, drawn by four or six horses, became their mode of travel.

First sphere of government—the home

Learned clergy

"Born almost to the saddle and to the use of firearms, they were keen hunters, and when the chase was over they sat by groaning boards and drank confusion to the Frenchman and Spaniard abroad, and to Roundhead and Prelatist at home. When the lurking and predatory Indian became the object of pursuit, no speed of his could elude their fiery and gallantly mounted cavalry."

This was the Virginia, these the Virginians, of the olden time. If even in retrospect their somewhat aristocratic manners touch the sensitive nerve of a democratic people, it may at least be said of them that nothing like despotism, nihilism, or dynamite was ever found amongst them; that they cherished above all things Honor and Courage, the virtues preservative of all other virtues, and that they nurtured men and leaders of men well fitted to cope with great forces, resolve great problems, and assert great principles. And it is at least true that their habits of thought and living never proved more dangerous to "life, liberty, or the pursuit of happiness" than those of others who in later days corrupt the suffrage in the rank growth of cities; build up palaces and pile up millions amid crowded paupers; monopolize telegraphic and railway lines by corporate machinery; spurn all relations to politics, save to debauch its agencies for personal gain; and know no Goddess of Liberty and no Eagle of Country save in the images which satire itself has stamped on the Almighty Dollar.

Virginia developed capable leadership

In 1657, while yet "a Cromwell filled the Stuarts' throne," there came to Virginia with a party of Carlists who had rebelled against him John Washington, of Yorkshire, England, who became a magistrate and member of the House of Burgesses, and distinguished himself in Indian warfare as the first colonel of his family on this side of the water. He was the nephew of that Sir Henry Washington who had led the forlorn hope of Prince Rupert at Bristol in 1643, and who, with a starving and mutinous garrison, had defended Worcester in 1649, answering all calls for surrender that he "awaited his Majesty's commands."

Col. John Washington

And his progenitors had for centuries, running back to the conquest, been men of mark and fair renown. Pride and modesty of individuality alike forbid the seeking from any source of a borrowed luster, and the Washingtons were never studious or pretentious of ancestral dignities. But "we are quotations from our ancestors," says the philosopher of Concord—and who will say that in the loyalty to conscience and to principle, and to the right of self-determination of what is principle, that the Washingtons have ever shown, whether as loyalist or rebel, was not the germ of that deathless devotion to Liberty and Country which soon discarded all ancient forms in the mighty stroke for independence?

Two traits of the Anglo-Saxon have been equally conspicuous—respect for authority—resistance to its abuse. Exacting service from the one, even the Second Charles learned somewhat from the other. When pressed by James to an extreme measure, he answered: "Brother, I am too old to start again on my travels." James, becoming King, forgot the hint, was soon on his travels, with the Revolution of 1688 in full blast, and William of Orange upon his throne. The Barons of Runnymede had, indeed, written in the Great Charter that if the King violated any article thereof they should have the right to levy war against him until full satisfaction was made. And we know not which is most admirable, the wit or the wisdom of the English lawyer, John Selden, who, when asked by what law he justified the right of resistance, answered, "By the *custom* of England, which is part of the common law." Mountains and vales are natural correspondences.

Two traits of the Anglo-Saxon: respect for authority; resistence to its abuse

Resistance to tyranny is common law

A very Tempé had Virginia been, sheltering the loyal Cavaliers in their reverence for authority. The higher and manlier trait of the Anglo-Saxon was about to receive more memorable illustration, and she uprose, Olympus-like, in her resistance to its abuse.

And the Instrument of Providence to lead her people and their brethren, had he lived in the days when mythic lore invested human heroes with a God-like grace, would have been shrouded in the glory of Olympian Jove.

One hundred and fifty-three years ago, on the banks of the Potomac, in the county of Westmoreland, on a spot marked now only by a memorial stone, of the blood of the people whom I have faintly described, fourth in descent from the Col. John Washington whom I have named, there was born a son to Augustine and Mary Washington. And not many miles above his birthplace is the dwelling where he lived and now lies buried.

Augustine and Mary Washington

Borne upon the bosom of that river which here mirrors Capitol dome, and monumental shaft in its seaward flow, the river itself seems to reverse its current and bear us silently into the past. Scarce has the vista of the city faded from our gaze when we behold on the woodland height that swells above the waters—amidst walks and groves and gardens—the white porch of that old colonial plantation home which has become the shrine of many a pilgrimage.

Contrasting it as there it stands to-day with the marble halls which we have left behind us, we realize the truth of Emerson: "The atmosphere of moral sentiment is a region of grandeur which reduces all material magnificence to toys, yet opens to every wretch that has reason the doors of the Universe."

The quaint old wooden mansion, with the stately but simple old-fashioned mahogany furniture, real and ungarnished; the swords and relics of campaigns and scenes familiar to every school-boy now; the key of the Bastile hanging in the hall incased in glass, calling to mind Tom Paine's happy expression, "That the principles of the American Revolution opened the Bastile is not to be doubted, therefore the key comes to the right place;" the black velvet coat worn when the farewell address to the Army was made; the rooms all in nicety of preparation as if expectant of the coming host—we move among these memorials of days and men long vanished—we stand under the great trees and watch the solemn river, in its never-ceasing flow, we gaze upon the simple tomb whose silence is unbroken save by the low murmur of the waters or the wild bird's note—and we are enveloped in an atmosphere of moral grandeur which no pageantry of moving men nor splendid pile can generate. Nightly on the plain of Marathon the Greeks have the tradition, that there may yet be heard the neighing of chargers and the rushing shadows of spectral war. In the spell that broods over the sacred groves of Vernon, Patriotism, Honor, Courage, Justice, Virtue, Truth—seem bodied forth—the only imperishable realities of man's being.

Character—the only imperishable realities

There emerges from the shades the figure of a youth over whose cradle had hovered no star of destiny, nor dandled a royal crown—an ingenuous youth, and one who in his early days gave auguries of great powers; the boy whose strong arm could fling a stone across the Rappahannock; whose strong will could tame the most fiery horse; whose just spirit made him the umpire of his fellows; whose obedient heart bowed to a mother's yearning for her son and laid down the Midshipman's warrant in the British Navy which answered his first ambitious dream;

Boyhood and youth

the student transcribing mathematical problems, accounts, and business forms, or listening to the soldiers and seamen of vessels in the river as they tell of "hair breadth 'scapes by flood and field"; the early moralist in his thirteenth year compiling matured "Rules for behavior and conversation"; the surveyor of sixteen, exploring the wilderness for Lord Fairfax, sleeping on the ground, climbing mountains, swimming rivers, killing and cooking his own game, noting in his diary soils, minerals, and locations, and making maps which are models of nice and accurate draughtsmanship; the incipient soldier studying tactics under Adjutant Muse, and taking lessons in broadsword fence from the old soldier of fortune, Jacob Van Braam; the Major and Adjutant-General of the Virginia frontier forces at nineteen—we seem to see him yet as here he stood, a model of manly beauty in his youthful prime—a man in all that makes a man ere manhood's years have been fulfilled—standing on the threshold of a grand career, "hearing his days before him and the trumpet of his life."

The scene changes. Out into the world of stern adventure he passes, taking as naturally to the field and the frontier as the eagle to the air. At the age of twenty-one he is riding from Williamsburg to the French post at Venango, in western Pennsylvania, on a mission for Governor Dinwiddie, which requires "courage to cope with savages and sagacity to negotiate with white men"—on that mission which Edward Everett recognizes as "the first movement of a military nature which resulted in the establishment of American Independence." At twenty-two he has fleshed his maiden sword, has heard the bullets whistle, and found "something charming in the sound"; and soon he is colonel of the Virginia regiment in the unfortunate affair at Fort Necessity, and is compelled to retreat after losing a sixth of his command. He quits the service on a point of military etiquette and honor, but at twenty-three he reappears as Volunteer Aide by the side of Braddock in the ill-starred expedition against Fort DuQuesne, and is the only mounted officer unscathed in the disaster, escaping with four bullets through his garments, and after having two horses shot under him.

Out into the world at age twenty-one

Providentially preserved at Fort DuQuesne

The prophetic eye of Samuel Davies has now pointed him out as "that heroic youth, Colonel Washington, whom I can but hope Providence has hitherto preserved in so signal a manner for some important service to his country"; and soon the prophecy is fulfilled. The same year he is in command of the Virginia frontier forces. Arduous conflicts of varied fortunes are ere long ended, and on the 25th of November, 1759 [*sic*, 1758], he marches into the reduced fortress of Fort DuQuesne—where Pittsburgh now stands, and the Titans of Industry wage the eternal war of Toil—marches in with the advanced guard of his troops, and plants the British flag over its smoking ruins.

That self-same year Wolfe, another young and brilliant soldier of Britain, has scaled and triumphed on the Heights of Abraham—his flame of valor quenched as it lit the blaze of victory; Canada surrenders; the seven years' war is done; the French power in America is broken, and the vast region west of the Alleghanies, from the lakes to the Ohio, embracing its valley and tributary streams, is under the scepter of King George. America has been made whole to the English-speaking race, to become in time the greater Britain.

French power in America is broken

Thus, building wiser than he knew, Washington had taken no small part in cherishing the seed of a nascent nation.

Martha Washington George Washington

Miniatures painted by Charles Willson Peale, 1772.
Courtesy of The Mount Vernon Ladies' Association.

Mount Vernon welcomes back the soldier of twenty-seven, who has become a name. Domestic felicity spreads its charms around him with the "agreeable partner" whom he has taken to his bosom, and he dreams of "more happiness than he has experienced in the wide and bustling world."

Marriage and domestic felicity

Already, ere his sword had found its scabbard, the people of Frederick county had made him their member of the House of Burgesses. And the quiet years roll by as the planter, merchant, and representative superintends his plantation, ships his crop, posts his books, keeps his diary, chases the fox for amusement, or rides over to Annapolis and leads the dance at the Maryland capital—alternating between these private pursuits and serving his people as member of the Legislature and justice of the county court.

But ere long this happy life is broken. The air is electric with the currents of revolution. England has launched forth on the fatal policy of taxing her colonies without their consent. The spirit of liberty and resistance is aroused. He is loath to part with the Mother Land, which he still calls "home." But she turns a deaf ear to reason. The first Colonial Congress is called. He is a delegate, and rides to Philadelphia with Henry and Pendleton. The blow at Lexington is struck. The people rush to arms. The sons of the Cavaliers spring to the side of the sons of the Pilgrims. "Unhappy it is," he says, "that a brother's sword has been sheathed in a brother's breast, and that the once happy plains of America are to be either drenched in blood or inhabited by slaves. Sad alternative! But how can a virtuous man hesitate in his choice?" He becomes commander-in-chief of the American forces. After seven years' war he is the deliverer of his country. The old confederation passes away. The Constitution is established. He is twice chosen President, and will not consent to longer serve.

Return to Mount Vernon

Once again Mount Vernon's grateful shades receive him, and there—the world-crowned Hero now—becomes again the simple citizen, wishing for his fellow-men "to see the whole world in peace and its inhabitants one band of brothers, striving who could contribute most to the happiness of mankind"—without a wish for himself, but "to live and die an honest man on his farm." A speck of war spots the sky. John Adams, now President, calls him forth as Lieutenant-General and Commander-in-Chief to lead America once more. But the cloud vanishes. Peace reigns. The lark sings at Heaven's gate in the fair morn of the new nation. Serene, contented, yet in the strength of manhood, though on the verge of three-score years and ten, he looks forth—the quiet farmer from his pleasant fields, the loving patriarch from the bowers of home—looks forth and sees the work of his hands established in a free and happy people. Suddenly comes the mortal stroke with severe cold. The agony is soon over. He feels his own dying pulse—the hand relaxes—he murmurs, "It is well"; and Washington is no more. While yet Time had crumbled never a stone nor dimmed the lustrous surface, prone to earth the mighty column fell.

Death of Washington

Washington, the friend of Liberty, is no more!

The solemn cry filled the universe. Amidst the tears of his People, the bowed heads of kings, and the lamentations of the nations, they laid him there to rest upon the banks of the river whose murmurs were his boyhood's music—that river which, rising in mountain fastnesses amongst the grandest works of nature and reflecting in its course the proudest works of man, is a symbol of his history, which in its ceaseless and ever-widening flow is a symbol of his eternal fame.

Progress of man measured by freedom of the individual

No sum could now be made of Washington's character that did not exhaust language of its tributes and repeat virtue by all her names. No sum could be made of his achievements that did not unfold the history of his country and its institutions—the history of his age and its progress—the history of man and his destiny to be free. But, whether character or achievement be regarded, the riches before us only expose the poverty of praise. So clear was he in his great office that no ideal of the Leader or Ruler can be formed that does not shrink by the side of the reality. And so has he impressed himself upon the minds of men, that no man can justly aspire to be the chief of a great free people who does not adopt his principles and emulate his example. We look with amazement on such eccentric characters as Alexander, Cæsar, Cromwell, Frederick, and Napoleon; but when the serene face of Washington rises before us mankind instinctively exclaims, "This is the Man for the Nations to trust and reverence and for heroes and rulers to copy."

Drawing his sword from patriotic impulse, without ambition and without malice, he wielded it without vindictiveness and sheathed it without reproach. All that humanity could conceive he did to suppress the cruelties of war and soothe its sorrows. He never struck a coward's blow. To him age, infancy, and helplessness were ever sacred. He tolerated no extremity unless to curb the excesses of his enemy, and he never poisoned the sting of defeat by the exultation of the conqueror.

Peace he welcomed as the Heaven-sent herald

of Friendship; and no country has given him greater honor than that which he defeated; for England has been glad to claim him as the scion of her blood, and proud, like our sister American States, to divide with Virginia the honor of producing him.

Fascinated by the perfection of the man, we are loath to break the mirror of admiration into the fragments of analysis. But, lo! as we attempt it, every fragment becomes the miniature of such sublimity and beauty, that the destroying hand can only multiply the forms of immortality.

Grand and manifold as were its phases, there is yet no difficulty in understanding the character of Washington. He was no Veiled Prophet. He never acted a part. Simple, natural, and unaffected, his life lies before us, a fair and open manuscript. He disdained the arts which wrap power in mystery in order to magnify it. He practiced the profound diplomacy of truthful speech, the consummate tact of direct attention. Looking ever to the All-Wise Disposer of events, he relied on that Providence which helps men by giving them high hearts and hopes to help themselves with the means which their Creator has put at their service. There was no infirmity in his conduct over which Charity must fling its veil; no taint of selfishness from which Purity averts her gaze; no dark recess of intrigue that must be lit up with colored panegyric; no subterranean passage to be trod in trembling lest there be stirred the ghost of a buried crime.

Truthful speech

Reliance upon Divine Providence

A true son of nature was George Washington, of nature in her brightest intelligence and noblest mold; and difficulty, if such there be in comprehending him, is only that of reviewing from a single standpoint the vast procession of those civil and military achievements which filled nearly half-a-century of his life, and in realizing the magnitude of those qualities which were requisite to their performance—the difficulty of fashioning in our minds a pedestal broad enough to bear the towering figure, whose greatness is diminished by nothing but the perfection of its proportions. If his exterior—in calm, grave, and resolute repose—ever impressed the casual observer as austere and cold, it was only because he did not reflect that no great heart like his could have lived unbroken unless bound by iron nerves in an iron frame. The Commander of Armies, the Chief of a People, the Hope of Nations could not wear his heart upon his sleeve; and yet his sternest will could not conceal its high and warm pulsations. Under the enemy's guns at Boston he did not forget to instruct his agent to administer generously of charity to his needy neighbors at home. The sufferings of women and children, thrown adrift by war, and of his bleeding comrades, pierced his soul. And the moist eye and trembling voice with which he bade farewell to his veterans bespoke the underlying tenderness of his nature, even as the storm-wind makes music in its under-tones.

Underlying tenderness

Disinterested Patriot, he would receive no pay for his military services. Refusing gifts, he was glad to guide the benefaction of a grateful State to educate the children of his fallen braves in the institution at Lexington which yet bears his name. Without any of the blemishes that mark the tyrant, he appealed so loftily to the virtuous elements in man that he almost created the qualities of which his country needed the exercise; and yet he was so magnanimous and forbearing to the weaknesses of others, that he often obliterated the vices of which he feared the consequence. But his virtue was more than this. It was of that daring, intrepid kind that, seizing principle with a giant's grasp, assumes responsibility at any hazard, suffers sacrifice without pretense of martyrdom, bears calumny without reply, imposes superior will and understanding on all around it, capitulates to no unworthy triumph, but must carry all things at the point of clear and blameless conscience. Scorning all manner of meanness and cowardice, his bursts of wrath at their exhibition heighten our admiration for those noble passions which were kindled by the inspirations and exigencies of virtue.

Daring and intrepid virtue

Invested with the powers of a Dictator, the country bestowing them felt no distrust of his integrity; he, receiving them, gave assurance that, as the sword was the last resort of Liberty, so it should be the first thing laid aside when Liberty was won. And keeping the faith in all things, he left mankind bewildered with the splendid problem whether to admire him most for what he was or what he would not be. Over and above all his virtues was the matchless manhood of personal honor to which Confidence gave in safety the key of every treasure; on which Temptation dared not smile; on which Suspicion never cast a frown. And why prolong the catalogue? "If you are presented with medals of Cæsar, of Trojan, or Alexander, on examining their features you are still led to ask, what was their stature and the forms of their persons? but if you discover in a heap of ruins the head or the limb of an antique Apollo, be not curious about the other parts, but rest assured they were all conformable to those of a God."

Great as a Commander, it may not be said of him as of Marlborough, that "he never formed the plan of a campaign that he did not execute; never besieged a city that he did not take; never fought a battle that he did not gain." But it can be said of him that, at the head of raw volunteers, hungry to the edge of famine, ragged almost to nakedness, whose muniments of war were a burlesque of its necessities, he defeated the trained bands and veteran generals of Europe; and that, when he had already earned the name of the American Fabius, destined to save a nation by delay, he suddenly displayed the daring of a Marcellus. It may be said that he was the first general to employ large bodies of light infantry as skirmishers, catching the idea from his Indian warfare, and so developing it that it was copied by the Great Frederick of Prussia, and ere long perfected into the system now almost universal. It can be said of him, as testified by John Adams, that "it required more serenity of temper, a deeper understanding, and more courage than fell to the lot of Marlborough, to ride on the whirlwind" of such tempestuous times as Washington dealt with, and that he did "ride on the whirlwind and direct the storm." It can be said that he was tried in a crucible to which Marlborough was never subjected—adversity, defeat, depression of fortune bordering on despair. The first battle of his youth ended in capitulation. The first general engagement of the revolution at Long Island opened a succession of disasters and retreats. But with the energy that remolds broken opportunities into greater ones, with the firmness of mind that can not be unlocked by trifles but which when unlocked displays a cabinet of fortitude, he wrenched victory from stubborn fortune, compelling the reluctant oracle to exclaim as to Alexander, "My son, thou art invincible." So did he weave the net of war by land and sea, that at the very moment when an elated adversary was about to strike the final blow for his country's fall, he surrounded him by swift and far-reaching combinations, and twined the lilies of France with the Stars and Stripes of America over the ramparts of Yorktown. And if success be made the test of merit, let it be remembered that he conducted the greatest military and civil enterprises of his age, and left no room for fancy to divine greater perfection of accomplishment.

American Fabius

Capitulation at Fort Necessity

Yorktown

Great in action as by the council board, the finest horseman and knightliest figure of his time, he seemed designed by nature to lead in those bold strokes which needs must come when the battle lies with a single man—those critical moments of the campaign or the strife when, if the mind hesitates or a nerve flinches, all is lost. We can never forget the passage of the Delaware that black December night, amidst shrieking winds and great upheaving blocks of ice which would have petrified a leader of less hardy mold, and then the fell swoop at Trenton. We behold him as when at Monmouth he turns back the retreating lines, and galloping his white charger along the ranks until he falls, leaps on his Arabian bay, and shouts to his men: "Stand fast, my boys, the Southern troops are coming to support you!" And we hear Lafayette exclaim, "Never did I behold so superb a man!" We see him again at Princeton dashing through a storm of shot to rally the wavering troops; he reigns his horse between the contending lines, and cries: "Will you leave your general to the foe?" then bolts into the thickest fray. Colonel Fitzgerald, his aid, drops his reins and pulls his hat down over his eyes that he may not see his chieftain fall, when, through the smoke he reappears waving his hat, cheering on his men, and shouting: "Away, dear Colonel, and bring up the troops; the day is ours." "Cœur de Lion" might have doffed his plume to such a chief—for a great knight was he, who met his foes full tilt in the shock of battle and hurled them down with an arm whose sword flamed with righteous indignation.

Designed to lead

Battle of Trenton

Battle of Monmouth

Dashing through a storm of shot

As children pore over the pictures in their books ere they can read the words annexed to them so we linger with tingling blood by such inspiring scenes, while little do we reck of those dark hours when the aching head pondered the problems of a country's fate. And yet there is a greater theater in which Washington appears, although not so often has its curtain been uplifted.

For it was as a statesman that Washington was greatest. Not in the sense that Hamilton and Jefferson, Adams and Madison were statesmen; but in a larger sense. Men may marshal armies who can not drill divisions. Men may marshal nations in storm and

Greatest as statesman

travail who have not the accomplishments of their cabinet ministers. Not so versed as they was he in the details of political science. And yet as he studied tactics when he anticipated war, so he studied politics when he foresaw his civil *role* approaching, reading the history and examining the principles of ancient and modern confederacies, and making notes of their virtues, defects, and methods of operation.

Read and studied history

His pen did not possess the facile play and classic grace of their pens, but his vigorous eloquence had the clear ring of our mother tongue. I will not say that he was so astute, so quick, so inventive as the one or another of them—that his mind was characterized by the vivacity of wit, the rich colorings of fancy, or daring flights of imagination. But with him thought and action like well-trained coursers kept abreast in the chariot race, guided by an eye that never quailed, reined by a hand that never trembled. He had a more infallible discrimination of circumstances and men than any of his contemporaries. He weighed facts in a juster scale, with larger equity, and firmer equanimity. He best applied to them the lessons of experience. With greater ascendancy of character he held men to their appointed tasks; with more inspiring virtue he commanded more implicit confidence. He bore a truer divining-rod, and through a wilderness of contention he alone was the unerring Pathfinder of the People.

Pathfinder of the People

There can, indeed, be no right conception of Washington that does not accord him a great and extraordinary genius. I will not say he could have produced a play of Shakespeare or a poem of Milton, handled with Kant the tangled skein of metaphysics, probed the secrecies of mind and matter with Bacon, constructed a railroad or an engine like Stephenson, wooed the electric spark from Heaven to earth with Franklin, or walked with Newton the pathways of the spheres. But if his genius were of a different order, it was of as rare and high an order. It dealt with man in the concrete—with his vast concerns of business stretching over a continent and projected into the ages—with his seething passions; with his marvellous exertions of mind, body, and spirit to be free. He knew the materials he dealt with by intuitive perception of the heart of man—by experience and observation of his aspirations and his powers—by reflection upon his complex relations, rights, and duties as a social being. He knew just where, between men and States, to erect the monumental mark to divide just reverence for authority from just resistance to its abuse. A poet of social facts, he interpreted by his deeds the harmonies of justice.

Extraordinary genius

Practical yet exalted, not stumbling in the pit as he gazed upon the stars, he would "put no man in any office of consequence whose political tenets were opposed to the measures which the General Government were pursuing." Yet he himself, by the Kingliness of his nature, could act independently of party, return the confidence and affections, use the brains and have thrust upon him the unanimous suffrage of all parties—walking the dizzy heights of power in the perfect balance of every faculty, and surviving in that rarefied atmosphere which lesser frames could only breathe to perish.

Brilliant I will not call him, if the brightness of the rippling river exceed the solemn glory of old Ocean. Brilliant I will not call him, if darkness must be visible in order to display the light; for he had none of that rocket-like brilliancy which flames in instant corruscation across the black brow of night—and then is not. But if a steady, unflickering flame, slow rising to its lofty sphere, high hung in the Heavens of Contemplation, dispensing far and wide its rays, revealing all things on which it shines in due proportions and large relations, making Right, Duty, and Destiny so plain that in the vision we are scarce conscious of the light—if this be brilliancy—then the genius of Washington was as full-orbed and luminous as the god of day in his zenith.

This is genius in rarest manifestation; and, as life is greater than any theory of living, in so much does he who points the path of Destiny and brings great things to pass, exceed the mere dreamer of great dreams.

The work of Washington filled the rounded measure of his splendid faculties. Grandly did he illustrate the Anglo-Saxon trait of just resistance to the abuse of power—standing in front of his soldier-husbandmen on the fields of Boston, and telling the general of earth's greatest Empire, who stigmatized them as "rebels" and threatened them "with the punishment of the cord," that "he could conceive of no rank more honorable than that which flows from the uncorrupted choice of a brave and free People, the original and purest fountain of all power," and that, "far from making it a plea for cruelty, a mind of true magnanimity and enlarged ideas would comprehend and respect it."

Just resistance to the abuse of power

Victoriously did he vindicate the principle of the Declaration of Independence, that to secure the inalienable rights of man "governments are instituted amongst men, deriving their just powers from the consent of the governed, and that whenever any form of government becomes destructive of these ends, it is the right of the People to alter or abolish it, and to institute new government, laying its foundation on such principles, and organizing its power in such forms, as to them shall seem most likely to effect their safety and happiness." By these signs he conquered. And had his career ended here none other would have surpassed—whose could have equaled it? But where the fame of so many successful warriors has found conclusion, or gone beyond only to be tarnished, his took new flight upward.

Principle of the Declaration of Independence

If I might venture to discriminate, I would say that it was in the conflicts of opinion that succeeded the Revolution that the greatness of Washington most displayed itself; for it was then that peril thickened in most subtle forms; that rival passions burned in intestine flames; that crises came, demanding wider-reaching and more constructive faculties than may be exhibited in war, and higher heroism than may be avouched in battle.

When greatness was most displayed

And it was then that the soldier uplifted the visor of his helmet and disclosed the countenance of the sage, and passing from the fields of martial fame to the heights of civil achievement, still more resplendent, became the world-wide statesman, like Venus in her transit, sinking the light of his past exploits only in the sun of a new-found glory.

First to perceive, and swift to point out, the defects in the Articles of Confederation, they became manifest to all long before victory crowned the warfare conducted under them. Charged by them with the public defense, Congress could not put a soldier in the field; and charged with defraying expenses, it could not levy a dollar of imposts or taxes. It could, indeed, borrow money with the assent of nine States of the thirteen, but what mockery of finance was that, when the borrower could not command any resource of payment.

The States had indeed put but a scepter of straw in the legislative hand of the Confederation—what wonder that it soon wore a crown of thorns! The paper currency ere long dissolved to nothingness; for four days the Army was without food, and whole regiments drifted from the ranks of our hard-pressed defenders. "I see," said Washington, "one head gradually changing into thirteen; I see one army gradually branching into thirteen, which, instead of looking up to Congress as the supreme controlling power, are considering themselves as dependent upon their respective States." While yet his sword could not slumber, his busy pen was warning the statesmen of the country that unless Congress were invested with adequate powers, or should assume them as matter of right, we should become but thirteen States, pursuing local interests, until annihilated in a general crash—the cause would be lost—and the fable of the bundle of sticks applied to us.

Warned of the weaknesses of the Confederation

In rapid succession his notes of alarm and invocations for aid to Union followed each other to the leading men of the States, North and South. Turning to his own State, and appealing to George Mason, "Where," he exclaimed, "where are our men of abilities? Why do they not come forth and save the country?" He compared the affairs of this great continent to the mechanism of a clock, of which each State was putting its own small part in order, but neglecting the great wheel, or spring, which was to put the whole in motion. He summoned Jefferson, Wythe, and Pendleton to his assistance, telling them that the present temper of the States was friendly to lasting union, that the moment should be improved and might never return, and that "after gloriously and successfully contending against the usurpation of Britain we may fall a prey to our own folly and disputes."

Foresaw the coming evil of follies and disputes

How keen the prophet's ken, that through the smoke of war discerned the coming evil; how diligent the Patriot's hand, that amidst awful responsibilities reached futureward to avert it!

By almost a miracle the weak Confederation, "a barrel without a hoop," was held together perforce of outside pressure; and soon America was free.

But not yet had beaten Britain concluded peace—not yet had dried the blood of Victory's field ere "follies and disputes" confounded all things with their Babel tongues and intoxicated Liberty gave loose to license. An unpaid Army with unsheathed swords clamored around a poverty-stricken and helpless Congress. And grown at last impatient even with their chief, officers high in rank plotted insurrection and circulated an anonymous address, urging it "to appeal from the justice to the fears of government, and suspect the man who would advise to longer forbearance." Anarchy was about to wreck the Arch of Triumph—poor, exhausted, bleeding, weeping America lay in agony upon her bed of laurels.

Not a moment did Washington hesitate. He convened his officers, and going before them he read them an address, which, for home-thrust argument, magnanimous temper, and the eloquence of persuasion which leaves nothing to be added, is not exceeded by the noblest utterances of Greek or Roman. A nobler than Coriolanus was before them, who needed no mother's or wife's reproachful tears to turn the threatening steel from the gates of Rome. Pausing, as he read his speech, he put on his spectacles and said: "I have grown gray in your service, and now find myself growing blind." This unaffected touch of nature completed the master's spell. The late fomenters of insurrection gathered to their chief with words of veneration—the storm went by—and, says Curtis in his History of the Constitution, "Had the Commander-in-Chief been other than Washington, the land would have been deluged with the blood of civil war."

But not yet was Washington's work accomplished. Peace dawned upon the weary land, and parting with his soldiers, he pleaded with them for union. "Happy, thrice happy, shall they be pronounced," he said, "who have contributed anything in erecting this stupendous fabric of freedom and empire; who have assisted in protecting the rights of human nature, and establishing an asylum for the poor and oppressed of all nations and religions." But still the foundations of the stupendous fabric trembled, and no cement held its stones together. It was then, with that thickening peril, Washington rose to his highest stature. Without civil station to call forth his utterance, impelled by the intrepid impulse of a soul that could not see the hope of a nation perish without leaping into the stream to save it, he addressed the whole People of America in a *Circular to the Governors of the States*: "Convinced of the importance of the crisis, silence in me," he said, "would be a crime. I will, therefore, speak the language of freedom and sincerity." He set forth the need of union in a strain that touched the quick of sensibility; he held up the citizens of America as sole lords of a vast tract of continent; he portrayed the fair opportunity for political happiness with which Heaven had crowned them; he pointed out the blessings that would attend their collective wisdom; that in their fate was involved that of unborn millions; that mutual concessions and sacrifices must be made; and that supreme power must be lodged somewhere to regulate and govern the general concerns of the Confederate Republic, without which the union would not be of long duration. And he urged that happiness would be ours if we seized the occasion and made it our own.

Federal union

In this, one of the very greatest acts of Washington, was revealed the heart of the man, the spirit of the hero, the wisdom of the sage—I might almost say the sacred inspiration of the prophet.

But still the wing of the eagle drooped; the gathering storms baffled his sunward flight. Even with Washington in the van, the column wavered and halted—States straggling to the rear that had hitherto been foremost for permanent Union, under an efficacious Constitution. And while three years rolled by amidst the jargon of sectional and local contentions, "the half-starved government," as Washington depicted it, "limped along on crutches, tottering at every step." And while monarchical Europe with saturnine face declared that the American hope of Union was the wild and visionary notion of romance, and predicted that we would be to the end of time a disunited people, suspicious and distrustful of each other, divided and subdivided into petty commonwealths and principalities, lo! the very earth yawned under the feet of America, and in that very region whence had come forth a glorious band of orators, statesmen, and soldiers to plead the cause and fight the battles of Independence—lo! the volcanic fires of Rebellion burst forth upon the heads of the faithful, and the militia were leveling the guns of the Revolution against the breasts of their brethren. "What, gracious God! is man?" Washington exclaimed: "It was but the other day that we were shedding our blood to obtain the Constitutions under which we live, and now we are unsheathing our swords to overturn them."

But see! there is a ray of hope, Maryland and Virginia had already entered into a commercial treaty for regulating the navigation of the rivers and great bay in which they had common interests, and Washington had been one of the Commissioners in its negotiation. And now, at the suggestion of Maryland, Virginia had called on all the States to meet in convention at Annapolis, to adopt commercial regulations for the whole country. Could this foundation be laid, the eyes of the Nation-builders foresaw that the permanent structure would ere long rise upon it. But when the day of meeting came, no State north of New York or south of Virginia was represented; and in

Annapolis Convention

their helplessness those assembled could only recommend a Constitutional Convention, to meet in Philadelphia in May, 1787, to provide for the exigencies of the situation.

And still thick clouds and darkness rested on the land, and there lowered upon its hopes a night as black as that upon the freezing Delaware; but through its gloom the dauntless leader was still marching on to the consummation of his colossal work, with a hope that never died; with a courage that never faltered; with a wisdom that never yielded that "all is vanity."

It was not permitted the Roman to despair of the Republic, nor did he—our Chieftain. "It will all come right at last," he said. It did. And now let the historian, Bancroft, speak: "From this state of despair the country was lifted by Madison and Virginia." Again he says: "We come now to a week more glorious for Virginia beyond any in her annals, or in the history of any Republic that had ever before existed."

It was that week in which Madison, "giving effect to his own long-cherished wishes, and still earlier wishes of Washington," addressing, as it were, the whole country, and marshaling all the States, warned them "that the crisis had arrived at which the People of America are to decide the solemn question, whether they would, by wise and magnanimous efforts reap the fruits of Independence and of Union, or whether by giving way to unmanly jealousies and prejudices, or to partial and transitory interests, they would renounce the blessings prepared for them by the Revolution," and conjuring them "to concur in such further concessions and provisions as may be necessary to secure the objects for which that Government was instituted, and make the United States as happy in peace as they had been glorious in war."

In such manner, my countrymen, Virginia, adopting the words of Madison, and moved by the constant spirit of Washington, joined in convoking that Constitutional Convention, in which he headed her delegation, and over which he presided, and whose deliberations resulted in the formation and adoption of that instrument which the Premier of Great Britain pronounces "the most wonderful work ever struck off at a given time by the brain and purpose of man."

In such manner the State which gave birth to the Father of his Country, following his guiding genius to the Union, as it had followed his sword through the battles of Independence, placed herself at the head of the wavering column.

Presided over the Constitutional Convention

In such manner America heard and hearkened to the voice of her chief; and now closing ranks, and moving with reanimated step, the Thirteen Commonwealths wheeled and faced to the front, on the line of the Union, under the sacred ensign of the Constitution.

Thus at last was the crowning work of Washington accomplished. Out of the tempests of war, and the tumults of civil commotion, the ages bore their fruit, the long yearning of humanity was answered. "Rome to America" is the eloquent inscription on one stone contributed to yon colossal shaft—taken from the ancient Temple of Peace that once stood hard by the Palace of the Cæsars. Uprisen from the sea of Revolution, fabricated from the ruins of the battered Bastiles, and dismantled palaces of unhallowed power, stood forth now the Republic of Republics, the Nation of Nations, the Constitution of Constitutions, to which all lands and times and tongues had contributed of their wisdom. And the Priestess of Liberty was in her Holy Temple.

The crowning work of Washington

When Salamis had been fought and Greece again kept free, each of the victorious generals voted himself to be first in honor; but all agreed that Themistocles was second. When the most memorable struggle for the rights of human nature, of which time holds record, was thus happily concluded in the muniment of their preservation, whoever else was second, unanimous acclaim declared that Washington was first. Nor in that struggle alone does he stand foremost. In the name of the people of the United States—their President, their Senators, their Representatives, and their Judges, do crown to-day, with the grandest crown that veneration has ever lifted to the brow of glory, Him whom Virginia gave to America—whom America has given to the world and to the ages—and whom mankind with universal suffrage has proclaimed the foremost of the founders of empire in the first degree of greatness; whom Liberty herself has anointed as the first citizen in the great republic of Humanity.

Encompassed by the inviolate seas stands to-day the American Republic which he founded—a freer Greater Britain—uplifted above the powers and principalities of the earth, even as his monument is uplifted over roof and dome and spire of the multitudinous city.

Long live the Republic of Washington! Respected by mankind, beloved of all its sons, long may it be the asylum of the poor and oppressed of

Courtesy of the Pennsylvania Academy of the Fine Arts, Philadelphia. Bequest of William Bingham.

GEORGE WASHINGTON
by Gilbert Stuart, 1796

all lands and religions—long may it be the citadel of that Liberty which writes beneath the Eagle's folded wings, "We will sell to no man, we will deny to no man, Right and Justice."

Long live the United States of America! Filled with the free, magnanimous spirit, crowned by the wisdom, blessed by the moderation, hovered over by the guardian angel of Washington's example; may they be ever worthy in all things to be defended by the blood of the brave who know the rights of man and shrink not from their assertion—may they be each a column, and altogether, under the Constitution, a perpetual Temple of Peace, unshadowed by a Cæsar's palace; at whose altar may freely commune all who seek the union of Liberty and Brotherhood.

Long live our Country! Oh, long through the undying ages may it stand, far removed in fact as in space from the Old World's feuds and follies—alone in its grandeur and its glory—itself the immortal monument of Him whom Providence commissioned to teach man the power of Truth, and to prove to the nations that their Redeemer liveth.

America, a monument to Christ

The delivery of the above was repeatedly interrupted with loud applause.

The President of the Senate. In accordance with the programme, Benediction will now be pronounced by Rev. Dr. Lindsay, Chaplain of the House of Representatives.

The Rev. John S. Lindsay, D.D., *then pronounced this benediction:*

The blessing of God Almighty, the Father, the Son, and the Holy Ghost, be among you and remain with you always. *Amen.*

At 5 o'clock p.m. the President of the United States, the Supreme Court, the Senate, and the invited guests retired from the Hall.

Mark the perfect man, and behold the upright;
for the end of that man is peace.
Psalm 37:37

Photo by and Courtesy of National Park Service, National Capitol Region, Parks and History Association

Rebuilding the Foundations

Verna M. Hall

As we consider and ponder the Christian qualities of character of the men and women who won for us our civil freedom, we can see how disappointed and grieved they would be if they could see how in two hundred years, American Christians have allowed the world's first Christian republic to drift into a socialist state. But infinitely more serious, is how we have grieved the Holy Spirit by our forgetfulness, our disinterestedness in the unique government He brought about in America for His glory.

As American Christians begin the third century and look at the world's attitude toward them, and the attitude of many of the people in our own nation, we are not presented with a very encouraging sight, yet when viewed against the backdrop of America's Christian history, the American Christians of 1976 [and 1999] are seen to have been given by God as unique a challenge and opportunity in relation to God's Law of Liberty as He gave to Mr. Boudinot and the other colonists 200 years ago. It is our turn to walk by faith and not by sight (II Cor. 5:7), faith to look back to what the Arm of the Lord hath done "in the ancient days, in the generations of Old," (Isa. 51:9) faith enough in Christ to know that even if America becomes surrounded by communist or pro-communist nations, they are not just against America, but are against America's God, who will not share His glory with another. America from the days of creation has been for God's glory and for His people, and if His people will be willing to learn what He has done for them in days past, repent and ask God's forgiveness for forgetting what He had done in bringing America into being, God will deal with their enemies within and without.

(*The Christian History of the American Revolution: Consider and Ponder*, "Introduction," Verna M. Hall, 1975, pp. XXXIV–XXXV; insert by editor.)

APPENDIX

A

B

Rules of Civility & Decent Behaviour In Company and Conversation

1st Every Action done in Company, ought to be with Some Sign of Respect, to those that are Present.

2 When in Company, put not your Hands to any Part of the Body, not usualy Discovered.

3 Shew Nothing to your Freind that may affright him.

4 In the Presence of Others Sing not to yourself with a humming Noise, nor Drum with your Fingers or Feet.

5 If You Cough, Sneeze, Sigh, or Yawn, do it not Loud but Privately; and Speak not in your Yawning, but put your handkercheif or Hand before your face and turn aside.

6th Sleep not when others Speak, Sit not when others stand, Speak not when you Should hold your Peace, walk not on when others Stop.

7 Put not off your Cloths in the presence of Others, nor go out your Chamber half Drest.

8th At Play and at Fire its Good manners to give Place to the last Commer, and affect not to Speak Louder than Ordinary.

9th Spit not in the Fire, nor Stoop low before it neither Put your Hands into the Flames to warm them, nor Set your Feet upon the Fire especially if there be meat before it.

10th When you Sit down, Keep your Feet firm and Even; without putting one on the other or Crossing them.

11th Shift not yourself in the Sight of others nor Gnaw your nails.

12th Shake not the head, Feet, or Legs rowl not the Eys lift not one eyebrow higher than the other wry not the mouth, and bedew no mans face with your Spittle, by appr

George Washington's Rules of Civility,
Facsimile of First and Last Page

104th It belongs to ye Chiefest in Company to unfold his Napkin and fa[ll to]
Meat first But he ought then to Begin in time & to Dispatc[h]
with Dexterity that ye Slowest may have time allowed him
105th Be not Angry at Table whatever happens & if you have reas[on]
to be so, Shew it not but on a Chearfull Countenance especially if
there be Strangers for Good Humour makes one Dish of Meat a Fe[ast]
106th Set not yourself at ye upper of ye Table but if it be your Due
or that ye Master of ye house will have it so, Contend not least
you Should Trouble ye Company
107th If others talk at Table be attentive but talk not with
Meat in your Mouth
108th When you Speak of God or his Atributes, let it be Seriously & in
Reverence. Honour & Obey your Natural Parents altho they be Poor
109th Let your Recreations be Manfull not Sinfull.
110th Labour to keep alive in your Breast that Little Spark of Celes
tial fire Called Conscience

Finis

17

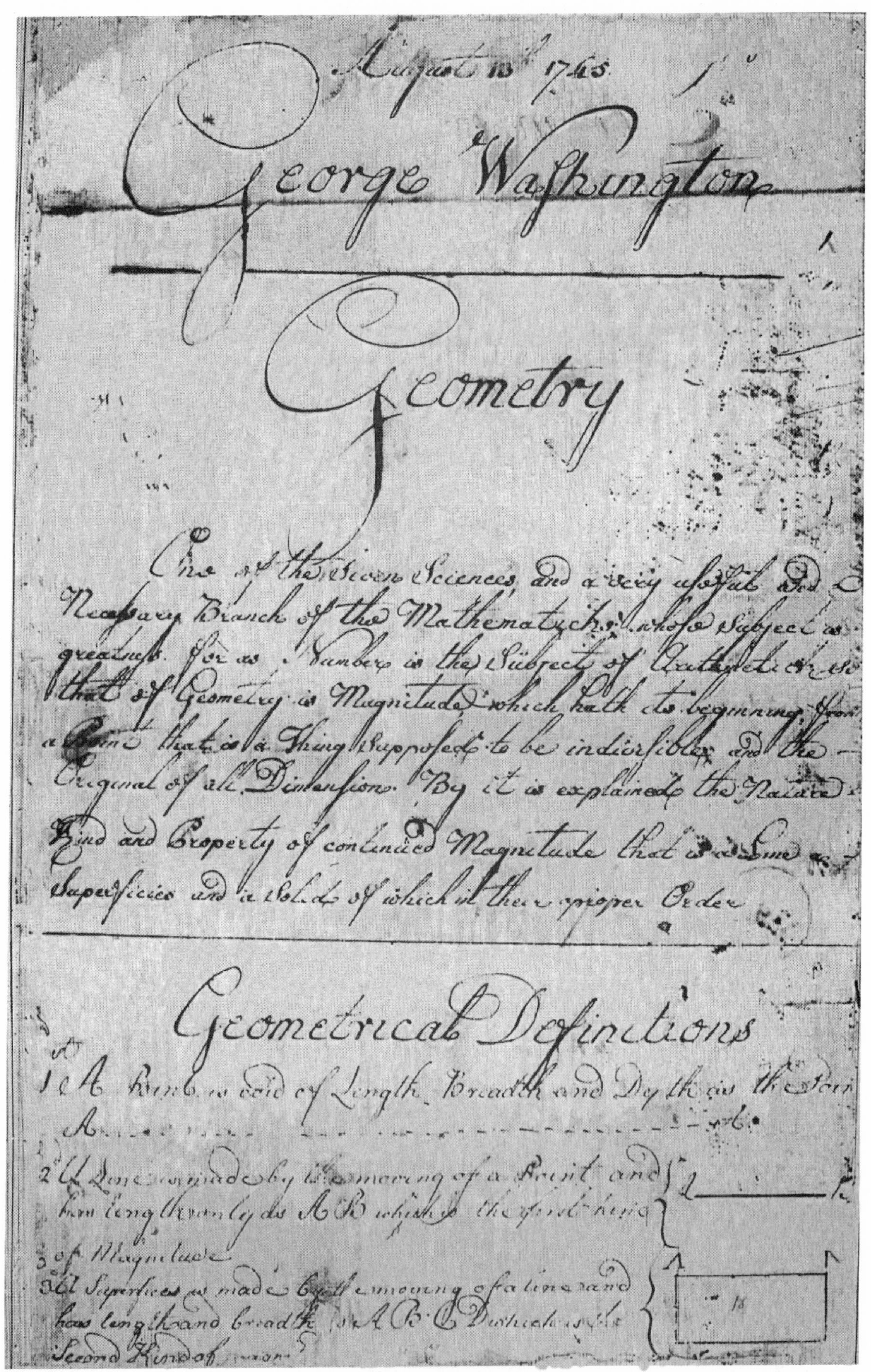

August 13th 1745

George Washington

Geometry

One of the Seven Sciences, and a very useful and Necessary Branch of the Mathematicks, whose Subject is greatness. For as Number is the Subject of Arithmetick so that of Geometry is Magnitude which hath its beginning from a Point that is a Thing Supposed to be indivisible and the Original of all Dimensions. By it is explained the Nature Kind and Property of continued Magnitude that is a Line Superficies and a Solid of which in their proper Order

Geometrical Definitions

1 A Point is void of Length Breadth and Depth as the Point A

2 A Line is made by the moving of a Point and hath length only as A B which is the first kind of Magnitude

3 A Superficies is made by the moving of a line and has length and breadth as A B C D which is the Second Kind of Magnitude

GEORGE WASHINGTON'S SCHOOL COPYBOOK, 1745
Selected Facsimile Pages

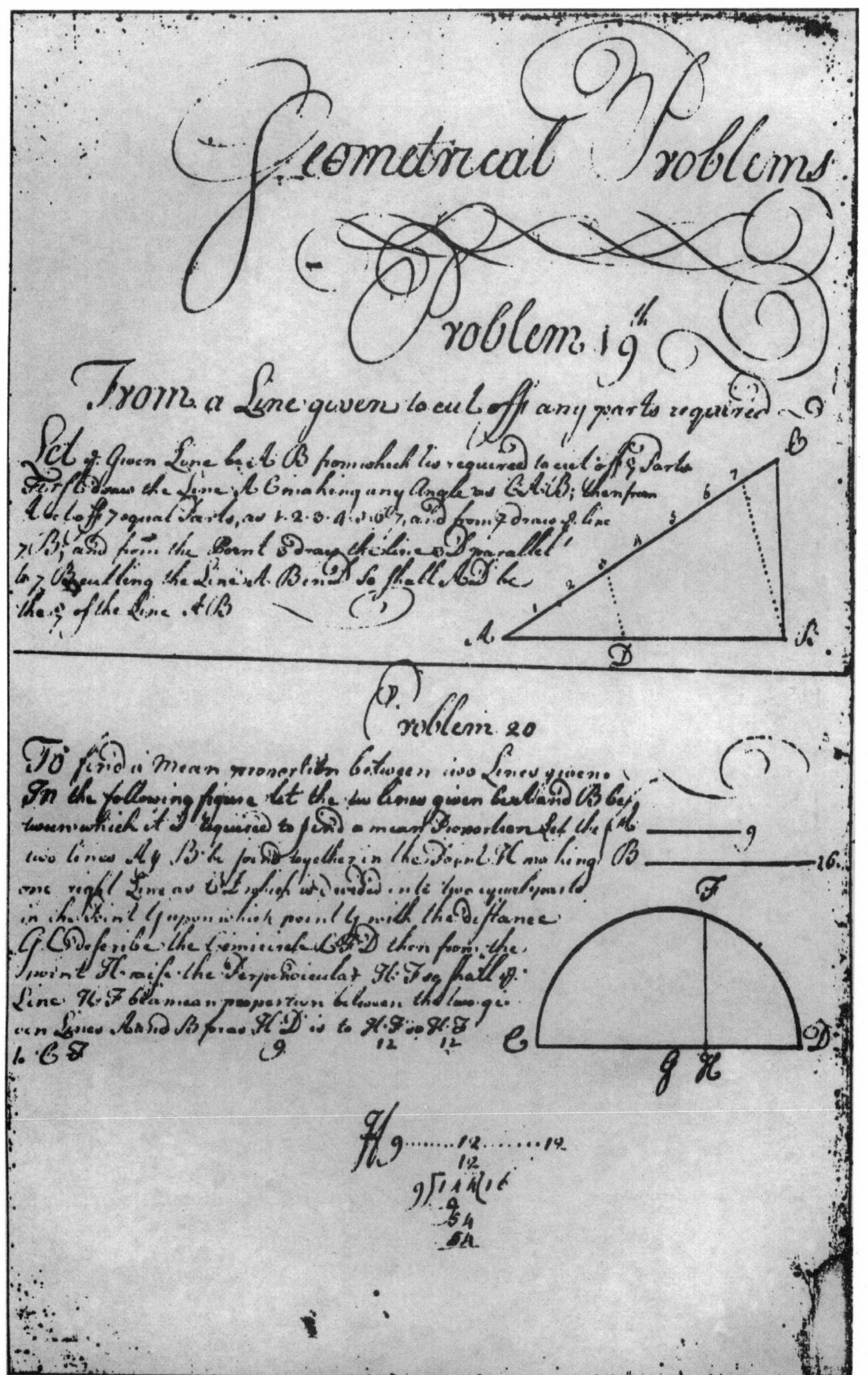
Geometrical Problems
Problem 19th
From a Line given to cut off any parts required
Let ye Given Line be A B from which tis required to cut off 3/7 Parts
First draw the Line A C making any Angle as CAB; then from
A set off 7 equal Parts, as 1·2·3·4·5·6·7, and from 7 draw ye line
7 B; and from the Point 3 draw the Line 3 D parallel
to 7 B cutting the Line A B in D. So shall AD be
the 3/7 of the Line AB
A
B
C
D
Problem 20
To find a Mean proportion between two Lines given.
In the following figure let the two lines given be A and B between which it is required to find a mean Proportion. Let the
two lines A & B be joined together in the Point H making
one right Line as CD which is divided into two equal parts
in the Point G upon which point G with the distance
G C describe the Semicircle CFD then from the
point H raise the Perpendicular H F so shall ye
Line H F be a mean proportion between the two given Lines A and B for as H D is to H F so H F
to C D
9
12
12
A
9
B
16
F
C
D
G H
H 9 .... 12 16
12
9) 144 (16
9
54
54
A–5

Plain Trigonometry Geometrical and Logarithmetical

Exm: 1st The Hypothenuse AC 121 Leagues & ye Leg AB 69 Leagues what is ye leg BC by ye Square Root?

Hypoten. 121
121
121
242
121
sq 14641
square 4761 of Perpen.
99880 (99.390 Leg BC
81
189) 1780
1701
1983) 7900
5949
19869) 195100
178820
198780) 1627.00
1590304
37596

Perpen 69
69
621
414
4761

Ans. 99.390

Exam 2d The leg AB is 90 Miles & the leg BC 69 Miles given. What is ye Hypothenuse AC by ye Square Root

Perpend. 90
90
8100
sq. 8100 of Perpen
sq. 4761 of Base
12861 (113.405 Hypoten.
1
21) 28
21
223) 761
669
2260) 9200
9004
22265) 19600
..

Base 69
69
621
414
4761

Concerning Simple Interest

1st When Money pertaining or belonging to one Person is in the Hands, Possession or Keeping, or is lent to another, & the Debter payeth or alloweth to the Creditor, a Certain sum in consideration of forbearance for certain Time; such consideration for Forbearance, is called Interest, Loan, or Use Money; & the Money so lent, & forborne, is called the Principal

2 Interest is either Simple or Compound

3 When for a sum of Money lent there is Loan or Interest allowed, & the same is not paid when it becomes Due, & if such Interest doth not then become a Part of the Principal it is called simple Interest

Exm If £ 100 gain £ 6 in 12 Months what will £ 75 gain in the same Time?

If £ 100 ...... £ 6 ...... £ 75
6
100 | 450 | £ 4
50
20
100 | 1000 | 10
0

Answer £ 4 . 10 . 00 S D

Or thus
£ 75
6
£ - - 4.5 0
20
S - - 10.00

61

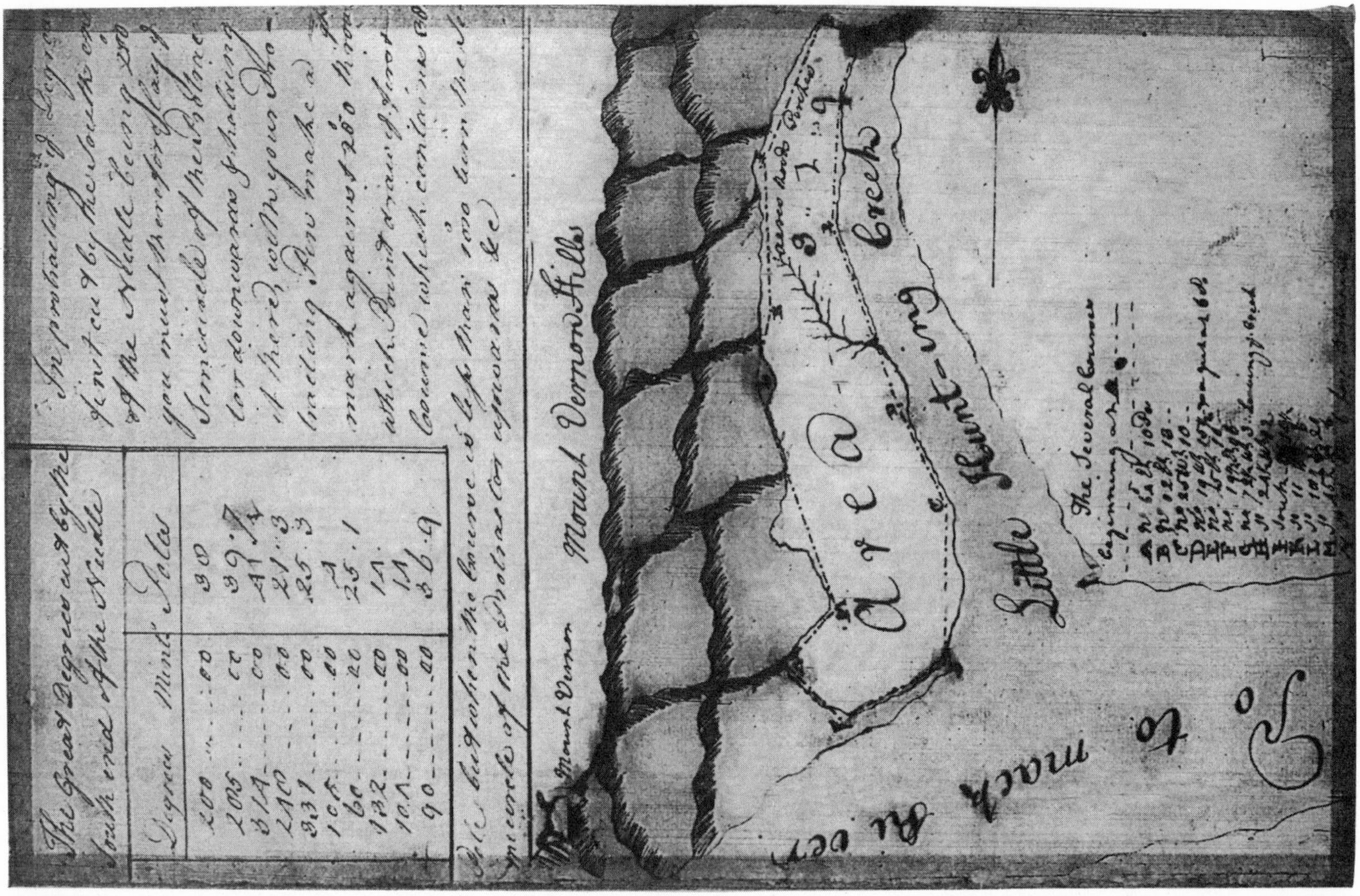

Surveying

A Plan of Major Law: Washington's Turnip Field as Surveyd by me

This 27 Day of February 1747/8

GW

Area

Acres R. Perch
5 " 3 " 37

Garden Wall

The Great Degrees cut by the South end of the Needle

Degrees	Mint.	Poles
200	00	30
205	00	39.7
314	00	41.4
240	00	21.3
331	00	25.3
105	00	4
60	00	25.1
132	00	14
104	00	14
90	00	36.9

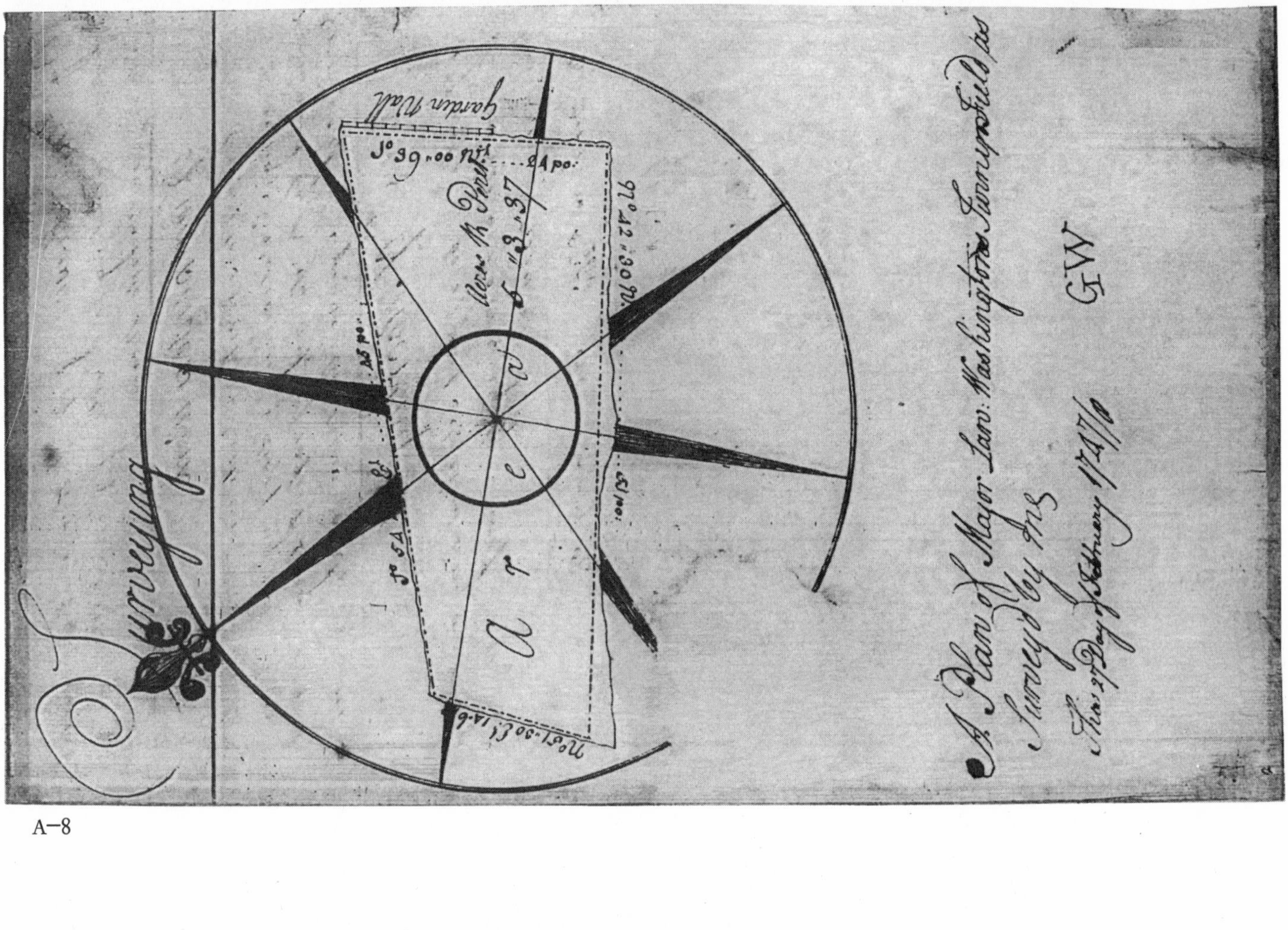

In protracting ye Degrees first cut by the South end of the Needle being 200 you must therefore lay ye Semicircle of the Protractor downwards & holding it there, with your Protracting Pen make a mark against 200 through which Point draw ye first Course which contains 30 Pole but when the Course is less than 180 turn the Semicircle of the Protractor upwards &c

Mount Vernon

Mount Vernon Hills

Area

Acres Roods Perches
3 " 2 " 9

Little Hunt-ing Creek

Go to mach River

The Several Courses beginning at

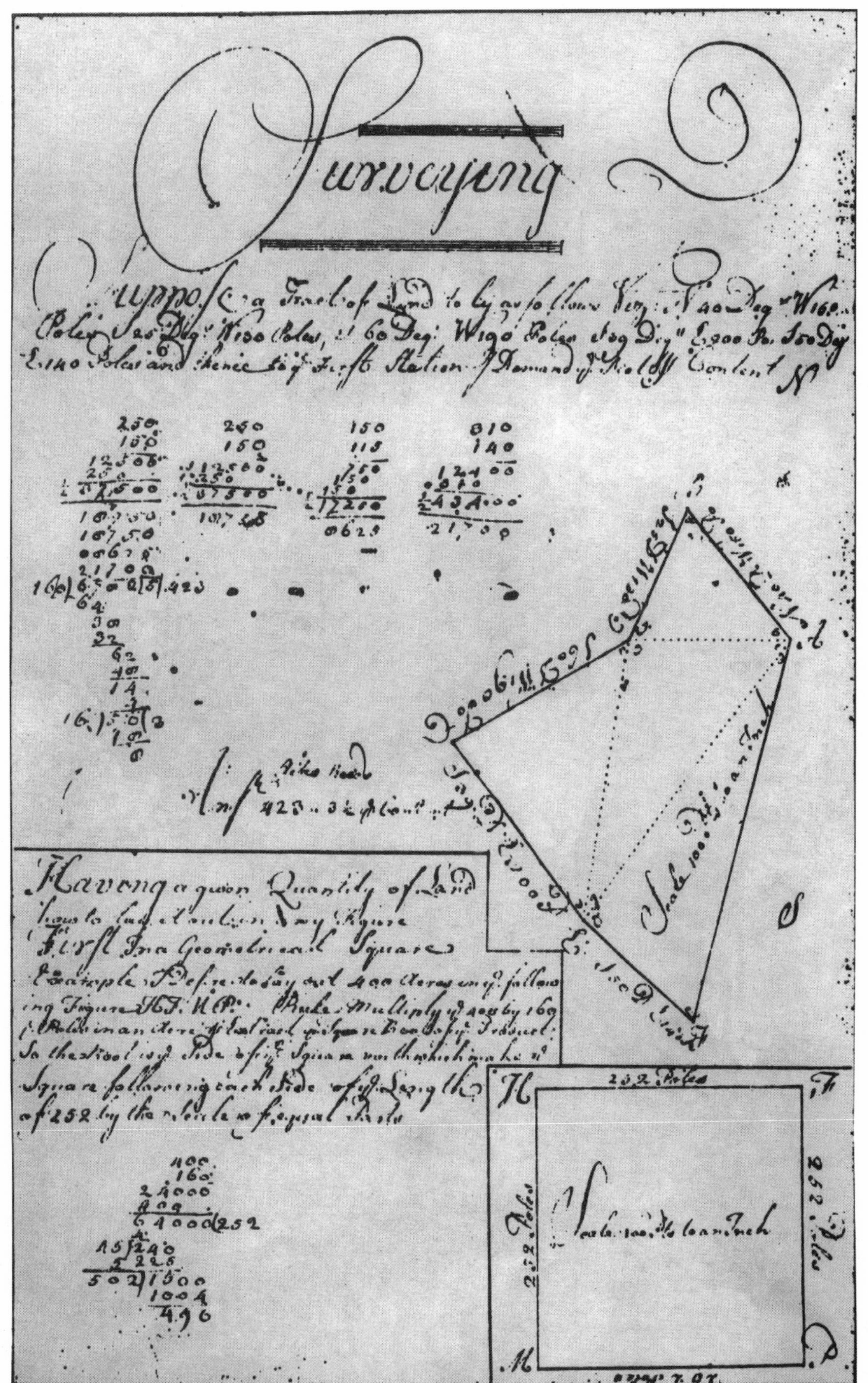

Surveying

Suppose a Tract of Land to lye as follows Viz: N 40 Deg W 160 Poles S 20 Deg W 130 Poles, S 60 Deg W 90 Poles S 9 Deg E 200 Po. S 50 Deg E 140 Poles and thence to ye First Station I Demand ye Solid Content

Ans 423 . 3 . 2

Having a given Quantity of Land how to lay it out in any Figure

First In a Geometrical Square

Example I Desire to lay out 400 Acres in ye following Figure H.F.N.P. Rule. Multiply ye 400 by 160 ye Pole in an Acre [illegible] Square [illegible] of 252 by the Scale [illegible]

THE

JOURNAL

OF

Major *George Waſhington*,

SENT BY THE

Hon. *ROBERT DINWIDDIE*, Eſq;
His Majeſty's Lieutenant-Governor, and
Commander in Chief of *VIRGINIA*,

TO THE

COMMANDANT

OF THE

FRENCH FORCES

ON

OHIO.

TO WHICH ARE ADDED, THE
GOVERNOR's LETTER;
AND A TRANSLATION OF THE
FRENCH OFFICER's ANSWER.

WILLIAMSBURG:
Printed by WILLIAM HUNTER. 1754.

ADVERTISEMENT.

AS it was thought adviſeable by his Honour the Governor to have the following Account of my Proceedings to and from the French *on* Ohio, *committed to Print; I think I can do no leſs than apologize, in ſome Meaſure, for the numberleſs Imperfections of it.*

There intervened but one Day between my Arrival in Williamſburg, *and the Time for the Council's Meeting, for me to prepare and tranſcribe, from the rough Minutes I had taken in my Travels, this Journal; the writing of which only was ſufficient to employ me cloſely the whole Time, conſequently admitted of no Leiſure to conſult of a new and proper Form to offer it in, or to correct or amend the Diction of the old; neither was I appriſed, or did in the leaſt conceive, when I wrote this for his Honour's Peruſal, that it ever would be publiſhed, or even have more than a curſory Reading; till I was informed, at the Meeting of the preſent General Aſſembly, that it was already in the Preſs.*

There is nothing can recommend it to the Public, but this. Thoſe Things which came under the Notice of my own Obſervation, I have been explicit and juſt in a Recital of:——Thoſe which I have gathered from Report, I have been particularly cautious not to augment, but collected the Opinions of the ſeveral Intelligencers, and ſelected from the whole, the moſt probable and conſiſtent Account.

G. WASHINGTON.

FACSIMILE OF FIRST FOUR PAGES
(from printed version)

THE JOURNAL, &c.

Wedneſday, October 31ſt, 1753,

I WAS commiſſioned and appointed by the Honourable *Robert Dinwiddie*, Eſq; Governor, &c. of *Virginia*, to viſit and deliver a Letter to the Commandant of the *French* Forces on the *Ohio*, and ſet out on the intended Journey the ſame Day; the next, I arrived at *Frederickſburg*, and engaged Mr. *Jacob Vanbraam*, to be my *French* Interpreter; and proceeded with him to *Alexandria*, where we provided Neceſſaries; from thence we went to *Wincheſter*, and got Baggage, Horſes, &c. and from thence we purſued the new Road to *Wills*-Creek, where we arrived the 14th of *November*.

Here I engaged Mr. *Giſt* to pilot us out, and alſo hired four others as Servitors, *Barnaby Currin*, and *John MacQuire*, Indian Traders, *Henry Steward*, and *William Jenkins*, and in Company with thoſe Perſons, left the Inhabitants the Day following.

The exceſſive Rains and vaſt Quantity of Snow that had fallen, prevented our reaching Mr. *Frazier*'s an Indian Trader, at the Mouth of *Turtle*-Creek, on *Monongahela*, till *Thurſday* the 22d. We were informed here, that Expreſſes were ſent a few Days ago to the Traders down the River, to acquaint them with the *French* General's Death, and the Re-

turn of the major Part of the *French* Army into Winter Quarters.

The Waters were quite impaſſable, without ſwimming our Horſes; which obliged us to get the Loan of a Canoe from *Frazier*, and to ſend *Barnaby Currin*, and *Henry Steward*, down *Monongahela*, with our Baggage, to meet us at the Forks of *Ohio*, about 10 Miles, to croſs *Aligany*.

As I got down before the Canoe, I ſpent ſome Time in viewing the Rivers, and the Land in the Fork, which I think extremely well ſituated for a Fort, as it has the abſolute Command of both Rivers. The Land at the Point is 20 or 25 Feet above the common Surface of the Water, and a conſiderable Bottom of flat, well-timbered Land all around it, very convenient for Building: The Rivers are each a Quarter of a Mile, or more, acroſs, and run here very near at right Angles: *Aligany* bearing N. E. and *Monongahela* S. E. the former of theſe two is a very rapid and ſwift running Water, the other deep and ſtill, without any perceptible Fall.

About two Miles from this, on the South Eaſt Side of the River, at the Place where the *Ohio* Company intended to erect a Fort, lives *Shingiſs*, King of the *Delawares*; we call'd upon him, to invite him to Council at the *Loggs*-Town.

As I had taken a good deal of Notice Yeſterday of the Situation at the *Forks*, my Curioſity led me to examine this more particularly, and I think it greatly inferior, either for Defence or Advantages; eſpecially the latter; for a Fort at the *Forks* would be equally well ſituated on *Ohio*, and have the entire Command of *Monongahela*, which runs up to our Settlements and is extremely well deſign'd for Water Carriage, as it is of a deep ſtill Nature; beſides, a Fort at the *Fork* might be built at a much leſs Expence, than at the other Place.——

Nature has well contrived the lower Place, for Water Defence; but the Hill whereon it muſt ſtand being about a

Copy of His Honour the Governor's Letter, to the Commandant of the French Forces on the Ohio, sent by Major George Washington

Sir,

The Lands upon the River *Ohio*, in the Western Parts of the Colony of *Virginia*, are so notoriously known to be the Property of the Crown of *Great-Britain*; that it is a Matter of equal Concern and Surprize to me, to hear that a Body of French Forces are erecting Fortresses, and making Settlements upon that River, within his Majesty's Dominions.

The many and repeated Complaints I have received of these Acts of Hostility, lay me under the Necessity, of sending, in the Name of the King my Master, the Bearer hereof, *George Washington*, Esq; one of the Adjutants General of the Forces of this Dominion; to complain to you of the Encroachments thus made, and of the Injuries done to the Subjects of *Great-Britain*, in open Violation of the Law of Nations, and the Treaties now subsisting between the two Crowns.

If these Facts are true, and you shall think fit to justify your Proceedings, I must desire you to acquaint me, by whose Authority and Instructions you have lately marched from *Canada*, with an armed Force; and invaded the King of *Great-Britain*'s Territories, in the Manner complained of? that according to the Purport and Resolution of your Answer, I may act agreeably to the Commission I am honoured with, from the King my Master.

However Sir, in Obedience to my Instructions, it becomes my Duty to require your peaceable Departure; and that you would forbear prosecuting a Purpose so interruptive of the Harmony and good Understanding, which his Majesty is desirous to continue and cultivate with the most Christian King.

I persuade myself you will receive and entertain Major *Washington* with the Candour and Politeness natural to your Nation; and it will give me the greatest Satisfaction, if you return him with an Answer suitable to my Wishes for a very long and lasting Peace between us. I have the Honour to subscribe myself,

Sir,

Your most obedient,

Humble Servant,

Robert Dinwiddie.

Williamsburgh, in *Virginia*,
October 31st, 1753

Translation of a Letter from Mr. Legardeur de St. Piere, a principal French Officer, to Robert Dinwiddie, esq., in Answer to the Governor's Letter.

Sir,

As I have the Honour of commanding here in Chief, Mr. *Washington* delivered me the Letter which you wrote to the Commandant of the *French* Troops.

I should have been glad that you had given him Orders, or that he had been inclined to proceed to *Canada*, to see our General; to whom it better belongs than to me to set-forth the Evidence and Reality of the Rights of the King, my Master, upon the Lands situated along the River *Ohio*, and to contest the Pretensions of the King of *Great-Britain* thereto.

I shall transmit your Letter to the Marquis Duguisne. His Answer will be a Law to me; and if he shall order me to communicate it to you, Sir, you may be assured I shall not fail to dispatch it to you forthwith.

As to the Summons you send me to retire, I do not think myself obliged to obey it. Whatever may be your Instructions. I am here by Virtue of the Orders of my General; and I intreat you, Sir, not to doubt one Moment, but that I am determin'd to conform myself to them with all the Exactness and Resolution which can be expected from the best Officer.

I don't know that in the Progress of this Campaign any Thing has passed which can be reputed an Act of Hostility, or that is contrary to the Treaties which subsist between the two Crowns; the Continuation whereof as much interests, and is as pleasing to us, as the *English*. Had you been pleased, Sir, to have descended to particularize the Facts which occasioned your Complaint, I should have had the Honour of answering you in the fullest, and, I am persuaded, most satisfactory Manner.

I made it my particular Care to receive Mr. *Washington*, with a Distinction suitable to your Dignity, as well as his own Quality and great Merit. I flatter myself that he will do me this Justice before you, Sir; and that he will signify to you in the Manner I do myself, the profound Respect with which I am,

Sir,

Your most humble, and

most obedient Servant,

Legardeur de St. Piere.

From the Fort sur La Riviere au Beuf,
the 15th *of* December 1753.

(*George Washington in the Ohio Valley,* by Hugh Cleland, University of Pittsburgh Press, Pittsburgh, 1955)

BIBLIOGRAPHY

Acton, Lord. *The Cambridge Modern History*, VOL. XVIII, 1904.

Adams, John, Letter to Mrs. Adams, September 16, 1774. *Letters of the Members of the Continental Congress*, Edmund C. Burnett, Editor, 1921.

American Archives, Fourth Series Vol. I, Peter Force, 1837.

Arthur, President Chester A., Address; see *The Dedication of the Washington National Monument.*

Bancroft, Aaron, D.D. *The Life of George Washington, Commander of the American Army*, 1807, 1826.

Byron, Lord. Verses quoted by Winthrop.

Casey, Col. Thomas Lincoln, Chief Engineer, Washington National Monument, Remarks; see *The Dedication of the Washington National Monument.*

Cleland, Hugh, *Washington in the Ohio Valley,* Pittsburgh: University of Pittsburgh Press, 1955.

Corcoran, Hon. W. W. Address; see *The Dedication of the Washington National Monument.*

Daniel, Hon. John W. Oration; see *The Dedication of the Washington National Monument.*

The Dedication of the Washington National Monument, February 21, 1885. Government Printing Office, Washington, 1885.

Ellet, Elizabeth F. *The Women of the American Revolution*, 1849.

Enclycopædia Britannica, Eleventh Edition, Vol. 19–20.

Fitzpatrick, John C., Editor. *The Diaries of George Washington*, Vols. 1–5. The Mount Vernon Ladies' Association, 1925.

Fitzpatrick, John C., Editor. *The Writings of George Washington*, Vols. 1–30,37. U.S. Government Printing Office, 1931.

Foljambe, Rev. S. W., *Annual Election Sermon: The Hand of God in American History,* Boston, Mass., January 5, 1876.

Greenberg, Allan. *George Washington, Architect,* Andreas Papadakis Publisher, 1999.

Griffin, Appleton P. C., compiler. A Catalogue of the Washington Collection in *The Boston Athenæum.* University Press, John Wilson and Son, Cambridge, U.S.A, 1897.

Journals of the Continental Congress, Vol. XXV, 1783.

Hale, Sir Matthew, Knight and Chief Justice of the King's Bench. *Contemplations, Moral and Divine.* London, 1679.

Hall, Verna M., Compiler. *The Christian History of the American Revolution: Consider and Ponder*, 1975.

Hall, Verna M., Compiler. *The Christian History of the Constitution of the United States of America,* Vol. I: *Christian Self-Government*, 1960.

Headley, Joel Tyler. *Washington and his Generals*, 1847.

Holy Bible, King James Version.

Hooker, Rev. Thomas. Sermon May 31, 1638, which inspired The Fundamental Orders of Connecticut. *Christian History*, Vol. 1, compiled by Verna M. Hall, 1960.

Hoover, Herbert. Foreword, *The Writings of George Washington,* edited by John C. Fitzpatrick, 1931; Inaugural Address, March 4, 1929, *Public Papers of the Presidents of the United States,* 1929.

Irving, Washington. *The Life of George Washington,* Vol. 1., 1856.

Knapp, Samuel L. *The History and Topography of the United States*, 1834.

Lee, Henry. George Washington Eulogy, *Orations of American Orators*, Vol. 1. The Colonial Press, 1900.

Lowell, James Russell. Verses quoted by Slaughter and Winthrop.

Marshall, John. *The Life of George Washington*, Vols. 1&5, 1826, 1832.

McGuire, E. C. *The Religious Opinions and Character of Washington*, 1836.

Muhlenberg, Rev. Henry Melchior. "Oration at Valley Forge, 1778." *Christian History,* Vol. 1, compiled by Verna M. Hall, 1960.

Parker, Grand Master Myron M., Address; see *The Dedication of the Washington National Monument.*

Parkman, Francis, *Montcalm and Wolfe: France and England in North America,* 1904.

Paulding, James K. *A Life of Washington*, Vol. 1, 1782.

Ramsay, David, M.D. *Life of George Washington, Commander in Chief of the Armies of the United States of America, throughout the War which Established Their Independence; and First President of the United States,* Second Edition, 1811.

Ribblett, David L. *Nelly Custis: Child of Mount Vernon.* The Mount Vernon Ladies' Association, 1993.

Sherman, Hon. John. Address, *Dedication of the Washington National Monument.*

Slaughter, Philip, D.D. *Christianity, the Key to the Character and Career of Washington*, 1886.

Smith, William, D.D. *A Sermon*, preached in Christ Church, Philadelphia, 1779.

Sparks, Jared. *The Life of George Washington*, one volume separate edition, 1902; (originally part of *The Writings of Washington*, 1837).

Sparks, Jared, Editor. *The Writings of Washington*, 12 vols., 1837.

Suter, Rev. Henderson, Prayer, *The Dedication of the Washington National Monument.*

Upham, C. W., Ed., *The Life of General Washington*, 1851.

Wallis, Rev. S. A., Prayer; see *The Dedication of the Washington National Monument.*

Washington, George. *The Journal of Major George Washington*; Selected Letters, Addresses, and Diary excerpts; Rules of Civility; School Copy-Book pages.

Wilbur, Gen. William H., *The Making of George Washington*, 1st Edition.

Winthrop, Hon. Robert C., Oration; see *The Dedication of the Washington National Monument*.

BIOGRAPHIES OF THE WRITERS

Prepared by
Mary-Elaine
Swanson

AARON BANCROFT
1755–1839

The father of historian George Bancroft, Aaron Bancroft was a minister and writer of whom it has been said that he "embodied the finest traits of New England Puritanism."

He was born on November 10, 1755 in Reading, Massachusetts, studied at Harvard College between 1774–1778. His studies were interrupted, however, when war broke out and he marched with the Minute Men of Reading to Lexington and Bunker Hill.

After graduation from Harvard he was a teacher and then studied theology under his pastor, Thomas Haven. When he was licensed to preach, he spent five years as a missionary in Yarmouth, Nova Scotia, returning to Worcester in 1783. In 1788 he was ordained a minister of the Congregational Church and shortly thereafter became the pastor of a new church in Worcester. He remained its pastor for fifty years. Rev. Bancroft's doctrinal views, and those of his Congregation, were Arminian, rather than Calvinist, and this involved him in frequent controversy. His church did not accept written creeds but relied only upon the Bible as its sufficient guide to faith and the godly life.

His congregation published a volume of his sermons in 1822 and, in 1836, he published a discourse on his fifty-year ministry in Worcester. But he was better known to the general public as the author of a *Eulogy on Washington* (1800) and a *Life of George Washington . . .* (1807) which were widely read and admired.

At age seventy, although disliking the idea of division in the Church, he allowed himself to be persuaded by younger pastors to join in forming the American Unitarian Association which he served as President until 1836. He died in Worcester on August 19, 1839.

(See the excerpt from his *Life of George Washington . . .* on pp. 11–12.)

EDMUND C. BURNETT
1864–1949

Edmund C. Burnett, university professor, historical researcher and writer, was born in Henry County, Alabama in 1864; attended Brown University, Providence, Rhode Island, where he received an A.M. in 1890 and a PH.D in 1897. He began his teaching career there as assistant professor of mathematics, 1890–91. He then taught Greek and modern languages at Carson and Newman College, 1891–94.

He became professor of Greek, at Brown University, 1894–95, and history instructor, 1895–99; professor of English, Bethel College, Russellville, Kentucky, 1899–1900. From 1900–05 he was professor of history at Mercer University, Macon, Georgia. In 1907 he joined the staff of the Carnegie Institute as a historical researcher. Here he remained until 1936.

Burnett wrote many books, among which were: *The Name "United States of America"* (1925); *Perquisites of the Presidents of The Continental Congress* (1929); *Who was the First President of the United States?* (1932); and *The Continental Congress* (1941) which won the Loubat Prize in 1943. He edited *Letters of Members of The Continental Congress*, Vols. 1 to 8, (1921–36). (A letter from John Adams to his wife, Abigail, from Volume I, appears in this volume on pages 110–11.) He was also a contributor to *Cyclopedia of American Government, American Historical Record*, and *The Dictionary of American Biography*.

Burnett made his home in Del Rio, Tennessee and upon his death in 1949, was buried in Union Cemetery, Newport, Tennessee.

John W. Daniel
1842–1910

Lawyer, legislator, and orator, John Warwick Daniel was born on September 5, 1842 in Lynchburg, Virginia, the son of William and Sarah Anne Warwick Daniel. He attended a classical school in Virginia. Then, hardly nineteen years old, he enlisted in the Confederate Army as a private in May 1861. By age twenty he was a major, but in May 1864 he was severely wounded in the Battle of the Wilderness. This ended his army career and left him on crutches and often in pain for the rest of his life.

He spent a year at the University of Virginia in 1865–66, and then began practicing law with his father in Lynchburg. Making his way in the legal profession slowly but steadily, he became known for his eloquent oral arguments before the state supreme court. In 1869, he married a neighbor, Julia E. Munnell.

He entered politics as a member of the House of Delegates in 1871, and served as a state senator (1875–79). In 1881, after several attempts, he was nominated for governor, but was defeated. From 1884 until his death, however, he served in Congress beginning as a Congressman and going on to serve in the United States Senate from 1887. He was also a member of every Democratic national convention until his death. An eloquent orator, he was often called upon to speak at important events, such as the Dedication of the Washington National Monument on February 21, 1885.

His oration may be found on pp. 312–26.

Elizabeth F. Ellet
1818–1877

Elizabeth Fries Lummis Ellet, historian and poet, was born in October 1818 at Sodus Point, Lake Ontario, N.Y. Her parents were Dr. William Nixon Lummis and Sarah Maxwell Lummis. Her father was from New Jersey, but practiced medicine in Philadelphia. After purchasing an estate at Sodus Point, however, he became involved in the development of western New York. As the daughter of an affluent father, she was educated at the Aurora Female Seminary, Aurora, N.Y., then headed by Susanna Marriott, an English Quaker. She began to write when she was fifteen years old, and throughout her life she found her greatest happiness in writing. Her favorite studies were: American and European history and literature and foreign languages. (She learned French, German, and Italian so as to translate the legends of these peoples and wrote criticism of various foreign works.)

Her poetry appeared in the *American Ladies' Magazine* when she was only a teenager. Her first book was a translation from the Italian of Silvio Pellico's tragedy, *Euphemio of Messina.* It was published in 1834 when she was only sixteen. Her *Poems Translated and Original* were published the following year. Throughout her life she was to contribute many stories, poems and sketches to various literary publications including the *Southern Quarterly,* the *North American Review,* and the *American Quarterly Review.*

In 1835, she married William Henry Ellet, a professor of chemistry at Columbia College, New York City. The couple moved to Columbia, South Carolina, when William became a professor at South Carolina College. While living in Columbia, she wrote two books on German literature: *The Characters of Schiller* (1839) and *Evenings at Woodlawn* (1849), an adaptation of German legends never before translated into English. She also wrote *Rambles about the Country* (1840), a book intended to introduce young Americans to a variety of scenes around the United States. In that same year, she wrote a historical novel, *Scenes in the Life of Joanna of Sicily.*

Novelettes of the Musicians came out in 1852 and *Women Artists in all Ages and Countries* in 1859. The latter work is still an excellent source for the history of women in the arts.

Most valuable to the student of American history, however, are the books she wrote on women in our history and culture: *Women of the American Revolution* (1848) (See her chapter on Mary Washington on pp. 119–22.); *A Domestic History of the American Revolution* (1850); *Pioneer Women of the West* (1852); *Queens of American Society* (1867); and *Court Circles of the Republic* (1869). She also wrote a book on domestic economy, *The Practical Housekeeper*, published in 1857.

It is said that Elizabeth Ellet was the first historian of the revolutionary period to use private documents and personal interviews with participants in the events she described. The major theme in these books is the significant influence of women on the civil life of the nation—an influence effected without departing from their role as wives and mothers. Although she deemed the influence of women important to American life, she was not a feminist. She declined to join the women who met at Seneca Falls in 1848 to agitate for women's rights, because she was convinced that a woman's most important role was in the home. Here the moral and intellectual education she gave to her children was crucial to the future of the Republic. Here, too, she could provide her husband with support, advice, and encouragement in regard to public affairs. She was also convinced that women's role in the Republic, though different from that of men, was no less important.

Mrs. Ellet and her husband moved back to New York City in 1849. After his death in 1859, she remained in the city where she took an active part in several charities aiding needy women and children. An Episcopalian for most of her life, she became a Roman Catholic in her later years. She died at her home on Twelfth Street in New York City on June 3, 1877.

John C. Fitzpatrick
1876–1940

This historian and archivist was born August 10, 1876 in Washington, D.C. He received his A.M. degree from St. Mary's college, Pennsylvania in 1918, an L.H.D from George Washington University in 1926, and a Litt.D. from Washington and Lee University in 1932. In 1922 he married Elizabeth V. Kelly by whom he had one daughter, Elizabeth Laney.

Beginning in 1897 he joined the staff of the Library of Congress, becoming assistant chief of the manuscript division in 1902, a post he held until 1928 when he resigned to pursue other editorial and historical research work.

Much of Fitzpatrick's writing and research concerned George Washington. He was editor of *The Writings of George Washington* (1931) from which excerpts appear in this volume on pp. 172–238, 240. He also edited and compiled *The Complete Diaries of George Washington* (1925) from which excerpts appear on pp. 242–253, and was the author of *Washington's Expenses as Commander-in-Chief* (1917), *George Washington, Colonial Traveler* (1927), and *George Washington Himself* (1933).

He died at his home in Washington, D.C. on February 10, 1940.

Appleton P. C. Griffin
1852–1926

Appleton Prentiss Clark Griffin, noted librarian and bibliographer, was born in Wilton, New Hampshire on July 24, 1852 but grew up in Medford, Massachusetts where his family moved in 1854. His parents were Moses Porter Griffin and Charlotte Helen (Clark) Griffin. He had a distinguished ancestry which included Hugh Griffin, the first town clerk of Sudbury, Massachusetts; Samuel Appleton, of Ipswich, Massachusetts, who was a commander in King Philip's War and a staunch opponent of Sir Edmond Andros; Roger Conant, the first governor of the Cape Ann Colony, 1625–26; Henry Prentiss, who planted Cambridge in 1640; and John Rogers, the first president of Harvard College.

Although descended from a long line of Harvard graduates, he went to work as a "runner" for the Boston Public Library immediately after leaving the Medford public school in December, 1865. From then on his education consisted of his library research and help from private tutors from time to time. He advanced by degrees at the Boston Public Library from runner, to Custodian of the Shelves, Custodian of the Building and, at last, to Keeper of the Books. This latter post entailed selecting, ordering, and classifying some 25,000 volumes of fine literature added annually to one of the finest collections of books in the United States. Over a fifteen year period he became known as one of the best bibliographers in the country.

On October 23, 1878, Griffin was married to Emily Call Osgood of Cambridge, Massachusetts by whom he had four children.

His association of twenty-eight years with the Boston Public Library came to an end in September 1894. For the next three years he was engaged in research at the Lenox Library in New York and the Boston Athenæum. It was for the Athenæum that he prepared his highly valuable *Catalogue of the Washington Collection* in 1897. (Excerpts selected by Verna Hall from the *Washington Collection* appear in this volume on pp. 254–71.)

Other significant contributions from his scholarship include his *Bibliography of the Historical Publications of the New England States* (1895) for the Colonial Society of Massachusetts and biographical sketches of Philip Freneau, Robert Fulton, Thomas Gage, and Nathanael Greene for *Appletons' Cyclopedia of American Biography.*

When a staff was being developed for the Library of Congress in 1897, he was chosen as an assistant. In 1900 he was appointed chief bibliographer of the newly created division of bibliography. Here he remained for eight years, publishing more than fifty important bibliographic lists. In 1908, he became chief assistant librarian of Congress which entailed advising the librarian on the selection of worthwhile books for this nationally important research library.

Griffin's wife died in 1924 and he died in 1926 after a short illness. He was buried in Mount Auburn, Cambridge, beside his wife and daughter.

Sir Matthew Hale
1609–1676

During the English Civil Wars (1642–1646) this eminent English jurist was renowned as an incorruptible judge who refused to be the tool of either King or Parliament. Hale was born in Alderley, Gloucestershire, in 1609, the son of Robert Hale, a retired barrister. Orphaned at the tender age of five, he was put into the care of a Puritan vicar with whom he lived until age sixteen when he was enrolled in Magdalen College, Oxford. It was intended that he be prepared to take holy orders, but he soon abandoned the life of a scholar for a life of pleasure, spending his time fencing and gambling and attending theatrical entertainments. Then he decided to leave the university and go to the Netherlands to volunteer for the army of the Prince of Orange.

Before he could put his plan into action, however, he was summoned to London to defend his rights in a lawsuit aimed at depriving him of his inheritance. So impressed was his legal counsel by his client's ability to grasp legal questions that he prevailed upon him to give up the idea of becoming a soldier in favor of entering the legal profession.

In 1628 Hale began his legal studies at Lincoln's Inn in London under John Selden, one of the finest jurists of the period. Under Selden's tutelage, Hale not only studied law but also English history and mathematics, and he delved into physics and chemistry, anatomy and architecture. Admitted to the bar in 1637, he rose rapidly in his profession. It was a critical period in England with King and Parliament locked in a struggle over Charles I's attempts to tax the people without the consent of Parliament. Hale was wooed by both the Royalists and the Puritan Parliament but was determined to steer a middle course between the contending parties believing that in order to be an impartial jurist he must hold himself aloof from both factions.

Hale would have defended Charles I had the King submitted to trial by Parliament. On the other hand, when Parliament became supreme, Hale signed the Solemn League and Covenant with the Scots. He also became a member of the assembly which, in 1644, drew up plans at Westminster to reform the Church of England. He preferred the Presbyterian form of church government but accepted the modified Episcopal form proposed by Archbishop Usher.

In 1649 he took the oath of fidelity to the republican Commonwealth. He was active in the movement to reform the English legal system heading a committee of advisors to Parliament on the subject in 1651–1652. The year 1654 saw him appointed a judge in the Court of Common Pleas.

When Oliver Cromwell died Hale stepped down as judge and became a member of Parliament for Oxford. In the proceedings of the Convention Parliament, he played a prominent role in promoting the return of the monarchy under Charles II, but he disapproved of the lack of written restrictions on the monarchy. After the Restoration in 1660, Hale was knighted and made Chief Baron of the Exchequer. In 1671 he became Chief Justice of the King's Bench, a post he occupied until failing health caused him to retire in 1676. He died at Alderley in December of that year.

Although a judge of integrity and impartiality, Hale is better known as a jurist whose indefatigable research into the common law resulted in his best known legal work, *History of the Pleas of the Crown*, finally published in 1736. This work is still one of the great authorities on the common law in relation to criminal offenses. He also wrote on both constitutional and civil law. When William Blackstone wrote his *Commentaries on the Laws of England* (1765–1769) he relied on Hale's "Analysis of the Civil Part of the Law."

Hale was a sincere Christian who retained his Puritan sympathies but was also friendly with dissenters from the Church of England such as Richard Baxter, a well-known nonconformist. He wrote several works on religion and is well-known today for his *Contemplations, Moral and Divine*. The *Contemplations* were not written for publication but were simply the thoughts he wrote down each Sunday after Church, the better to fix them in his mind that "they might not be lost by forgetfulness or other interventions."[1]

It was this book which Mary Washington used to instruct her children. Washington Irving observes in his biography of George Washington that "the admirable maxims therein contained for outward action as well as self-government, sank deep into the mind of George, and, doubtless had great influence in forming his character. They certainly were exemplified in his conduct throughout his life."[2]

One study from the *Contemplations, Moral and Divine*, The Great Audit & The Account of the Good Steward was selected by Verna Hall for this book, and appears on pp. 124–43.)

---

[1] See Preface to the *Contemplations, Moral and Divine* (1679) by Dr. Antonius Saunders.

[2] See extracts from Irving's biography of George Washington in this volume.

Joel Tyler Headley
1813–1897

Minister, legislator, and highly popular historical writer, Joel Tyler Headley was born in 1813 at Walton, Delaware County, New York, the son of a minister. He graduated from Union College in 1839 going on to study for the ministry at Auburn Theological Seminary. He was licensed to preach in New York but when called to a large church, he turned down the offer on his physician's advice because of poor health. Instead, he accepted the call of a small congregation in Stockbridge, Massachusetts. In 1842, however, his health broke down completely and he went to Italy to recover his strength. While there he wrote a series of letters on his travels which were published in a New York newspaper and reprinted in a book titled *Italy and Italians* (1844).

On his return, finding that his health was not much improved, he reluctantly gave up the ministry and devoted himself to writing. In 1846 his book *Napoleon and His Marshals* appeared. In that same year he accepted an offer to become associate editor of the *New York Tribune*. In 1847 his work on *Washington and His Generals* was published.

In 1850, Headley married Anna Alston Russel and moved to Newburgh, N.Y. There he served a term in the New York Assembly followed by a term as Secretary of State (1855–1858) after which he returned to writing and editing at his home where he died in 1897.

Joel Tyler Headley wrote more than thirty histories, biographies, and travel books which, in 1853, reached total sales of 200,000. Among them were *A History of the Second War between England and the United States* (1853) and an excellent study of *The Chaplains and Clergy of the Revolution* (1861). His two-volume work on *Washington and His Generals* (excerpt here on p. 4), became so popular that the *New York Nation* estimated that it was one of the five secular books most often found in the typical America's home library.

Washington Irving
1783–1859

On a day in 1789, when the First Congress under the new Federal Constitution was meeting in New York City, a little boy was out for a walk with a Scottish maid servant employed by his family. Suddenly, the maid servant saw the nation's new president, George Washington, entering a shop. Quickly she took her small charge's hand and ran into the store where she breathlessly exclaimed, "Please, your honor, here's a bairn that was named after you!"[1] Washington knew what the nurse wanted and, putting his hand on the boy's head, gave him his blessing. No one in that shop could know that one day there would be more than this fleeting connection between the great general and his little namesake, that the little boy named after him was destined to write what many still consider the finest biography of George Washington.

Washington Irving was born in Manhattan on April 8, 1783, two years after the victory at Yorktown which effectively brought the War of Independence to a close and in the year of the treaty between Great Britain and the United States formally ending the war. He was the last of eleven children born to William Irving, who had come to New York from the Isle of Orkney off the Northern Coast of Scotland, and his wife, Sara Sanders of Plymouth, England. It was Sarah's wish that the baby be named after the great general whose tireless exertions had finally brought victory.

Although Washington Irving's father was an austere Scottish Presbyterian, "his household was more literary and intellectual than that of many of his neighbors, and young Irving's artistic tendencies benefited by the influence."[2] His mother's gentle, kind disposition made her the confidante of her children and greatly loved by her youngest child. Although in later life Irving acknowledged that the principles he learned from his father were an enduring influence on him, he left William Irving's severe Presbyterianism and became a member of the Episcopal Church.

Irving left school at sixteen and soon began the study of the law in the office of Judge Josiah Hoffman. He was, however, far more interested in literature. In 1802, he wrote some humorous pieces under the name of "Jonathan Oldstyle, Gent." which appeared in *The Morning Chronicle*, a newspaper owned by one of his brothers.

He early displayed a keen interest in travel and took a long arduous trip with Judge Hoffman into the Canadian wilderness. On his return his family was alarmed by the decline in his health owing to the rigors of the journey and packed him off to Europe to recover. By the time he reached France the sea air of the voyage had completely restored his health and he enjoyed sight-seeing in Italy, France, Switzerland, and England. Returning to New York on January 17, 1806, he resumed his law studies. In the autumn he was admitted to the bar, but his real interest lay in writing. Before long he contributed a series of twenty papers on politics, theater, and fiction to a new magazine, *The Salmagundi Papers*. (Salmagundi referred to a popular, highly-seasoned mixed salad of chopped chicken, veal, or turkey.)

A lively, handsome, and witty man, Irving shone in society. Soon he courted Judge Hoffman's daughter, Matilda, who had blossomed from a child of fourteen when he left for Europe into a beautiful and sweet-tempered young lady of sixteen upon his return. In 1808 they were engaged to be married. Early the next year, however, Matilda caught a severe cold which turned into lung disease from which she died two months later. Irving was prostrated with a grief from which he never fully recovered. Matilda's death is believed to be the reason he never married.

Irving was so full of melancholy that he could not return to his work in the law office. In order to distract him from his grief, his family urged him to finish a book on which he had been working before Matilda's death. It purported to be a serious history of old New Amsterdam by one Diedrich Knickerbocker, but in reality was a rollicking satire on the life and customs of the old Dutch city. When it appeared in 1809, Irving became an instant celebrity. The book delighted all who read it except a few of the old Dutch families who were not amused by Irving's satirical style, even though it was genial and good humored. Irving was lionized by society in New York, Baltimore, and Washington, D.C. When he attended one of Dolley Madison's soirees, she told him how much she and the President were enjoying reading the *Knickerbocker History* together.

When the war of 1812 broke out, Irving enlisted and became Governor Daniel B. Tompkins' aide-de-camp. The war brought financial disaster to the Irving's import/export firm which had relied heavily on its clients in Great Britain. Irving was sent to the Liverpool office to help his ailing brother, Peter, cope with its financial problems. He did his best but, knowing little about the business, he was unable to stave off bankruptcy which came in 1818.

Freed from the cares of the business world for which he believed himself unsuited, Irving took up his pen in hopes of supporting himself by writing. The result was *The Sketch Book of Geoffrey Crayon, Esq.* (1820) which became a great success in both England and America. It owed its publication largely to Sir Walter Scott whom Irving had visited at Abbotsford in 1817 and who recommended Irving's book to a well-known London publisher. This volume of essays and short stories, mostly on English themes, was followed by another volume,

Bracebridge Hall (1822), a continuation of the story of the English family introduced in his Christmas stories in *The Sketch Book*. It was also a success. Therefore, it was a great shock to Irving when his *Tales of a Traveler* (1824) was a complete failure on both sides of Atlantic. Deeply wounded by the adverse criticism it received, he abandoned fiction for other literary forms.

This was a providential turning point in Irving's career because shortly afterwards he was led to the field of biography in which he was to excel. It was Archibald Constable, a Scottish publisher who, in July 1825, suggested he do a biography of his famous countryman, George Washington. Irving, however, was not yet ready for such an undertaking. He replied that the task "would require a great deal of reading and research, and that too of a troublesome and irksome kind among public documents and state papers; for Washington's life was more important as Statesman than as a General." He also said that he felt himself incapable of executing his idea of the task explaining that "It is one that I dare not attempt lightly. I stand in too great awe of it."[3]

So, although the seed was planted, it was many years before Irving finally embarked on his *Life of Washington*. In the meantime, he was being prepared for the task when, in 1826, he accepted a post at the American Legation in Madrid, offered to him at the request of Edward Everett, American Minister to Spain. He had always longed to visit Spain and had already begun to study Spanish. Irving was delighted that the purpose of his appointment was to make an English translation of the Fernandez de Navarretes papers on the voyage of Columbus. From this assignment came his own book, *The Life and Voyages of Columbus* (1828), which is still a standard authority on the subject.

Irving discovered that biographical writing required many hours of research before the actual writing could begin, and he usually began work at 6:00 a.m. This period in Spain was a very productive one for him. In addition to his fine volume on Columbus, he also wrote *The Conquest of Granada* (1829) and *Tales of The Alhambra* (1832).

In 1829, Irving left Spain regretfully to take up an appointment as Secretary of the American Legation in London. Because of the illness of a superior, he took charge of the legation from June 1831 to April 1832 conducting trade negotiations with the English on the British West Indies. While in England, he received a gold medal from the Royal Society and a Degree of Doctor of Civil Laws from Oxford University.

When he left home for England in 1815 he little dreamed that he would be away from his native land for seventeen years but it was not until April 1832 when he was forty-nine years old that he finally returned to America. Here he discovered that he had become a famous citizen. Many entertainments were given in New York in honor of his return.

Eager to acquaint himself with the rapidly growing new nation, Irving took a tour of the Oklahoma Territory, traveling by coach and steamboat, then by horseback when leaving Independence, Missouri for Indian country. He wrote of his experiences on the frontier in "A Tour of the Prairies," which appeared in his *Crayon Miscellany* (1835). John Jacob Astor suggested that he write about the fur trade in the Pacific Northwest which resulted in *Astoria* (1836). This was followed in 1837 by a volume on *The Adventures of Captain Bonneville* using the explorer's papers. Edward Wagenecht, one of Irving's biographers, remarks that "With these works, the man who created American literature in the consciousness of European readers reached out to possess himself of what was afterwards to be called the 'farthest reach' of American civilization upon this continent."[4]

After many years of travel Irving yearned for a quiet retreat and, in 1835, he purchased an old Dutch farmhouse on the Hudson River near Tarrytown, N.Y. which he named "Sunnyside." Here he entertained his nephews and nieces and began to experience the joys of family life. In 1840, when he was fifty-seven years old, he began work on his *Life of Washington*. But in 1842 the project was unexpectedly interrupted when Secretary of State Daniel Webster appointed Irving Ambassador to Spain. He was astounded to receive such an offer to represent his country abroad and considered it the greatest honor he ever received.

Irving was in Spain from 1842 to 1845 when it was going through a period of political turmoil between rival parties. The young queen, Isabella II, was under age and required a regent to govern in her stead. While Irving was in Spain three regents came and went each one being toppled from power. Finally Madrid was under siege in a battle between two opposing political parties. The situation greatly complicated Irving's negotiations with Spain concerning Cuba which the United States wished to buy from Spain. He wrote a long paper addressed to the Spanish premier on America's conduct of the Mexican War, which reveals his talents as a highly experienced diplomat. Because of his efforts to protect Queen Isabella during the siege of Madrid, he was greatly esteemed by the Spanish people.

Irving's last service abroad came to an end in 1846 when he returned to America, never to leave it again. Before settling down to work on his *Life of Washington*, he produced a *Life of Oliver Goldsmith* (1849), one of his most charming biographies, and *Mahomet and His Successors* (1850). Irving was now sixty-seven years old. As he worked on his Washington biography, he wondered if his strength would hold out long enough for him to do justice to the great canvas upon which he toiled. He wrote to his nephew Pierre, "All I fear is to fail in health, and fail in completing this work at the same time. If I can only live to finish it, I would be willing to die the next moment. I think I can make it a most interesting book—can give interest and strength to many points, without any prostration of historic dignity."[5]

In 1853, while doing research on Washington at the State Department, he wrote to Pierre, "I am making a longer sojourn in Washington than I intended, but it takes time to make the necessary researches in the archives of state. . . . I cannot say that I find much that is new among the manuscripts of Washington, Sparks having published the most interesting; but it is important to get facts from the fountainhead, not at second hand through his publications."[6]

In June, Irving, who had already visited Mount Vernon twice, visited other sites connected with Washington's life. Meanwhile, his nephew Pierre remained at Sunnyside going over his uncle's manuscript which had nearly arrived at Washington's presidency. In reply to a letter from Pierre praising the book Irving wrote on July 18, "I now feel my mind prodigiously relieved, and begin to think I have not labored in vain. . . . I rejoice that I have arrived at a good stopping-place."[7] According to his nephew, Irving intended to end his story here and was happy to do so because of deteriorating health.

Author Charles Neider, editor of a one-volume condensation of Irving's biography of Washington (1976), observes that "The reception of the work as it issued from the press in single volumes [beginning in 1855], printed in clean, large type with ample margins, greatly heartened the ailing, distracted author. Above all, the work's vividness and anecdotal qualities were praised, for a Washington of fits of temper and, to one's sense of relief, of a capacity for laughter to the point of tears, was seen to be emerging form the time-honored, enigmatic, super self-controlled figure. . . . But after all, Irving unlike previous biographers of Washington, was a literary genius who had a special feel for the living tissue. . . . "[8]

As Neider also points out, Irving's own experiences contributed to the effectiveness of his writing. His personal knowledge of the frontier gained from his tour of the Oklahoma Territory helped him to describe Washington's experiences on the frontier.

Irving received accolades for his work from American historians. George Bancroft wrote of the writer's style as "masterly, clear, easy, and graceful . . . . You do everything rightly, as if by grace; and I am in no fear of offending your modesty, for I think you were elected and foreordained to excell your contemporaries."[9] Perhaps most indicative of the reaction to Irving's style is seen in William Prescott's comments in a letter to Irving in 1856: "You have done with Washington just as I thought you would, and, instead of a cold, marble statue of a demigod, you have made him a being of flesh and blood, like ourselves—one with whom we can have sympathy. The general sentiment of the country has been too decidedly expressed for you to doubt for a moment that this is the portrait of him which is to hold a permanent place in the national gallery."[10]

In a note to Volume III, Irving explained that it had been his intention to complete the work in three volumes, but that "his theme has unexpectedly expanded under his pen, and he now lays his third volume before the public, with his task yet unaccomplished."[11] There were two more volumes to come before Irving's task was completed in 1859. The labor involved was made all the more difficult for him because of his rapidly declining health. Irving lingered on for some months after the publication of Volume V, finally passing away November 28, 1859.

Washington Irving has been called the first American author to earn his living by writing, the first to win fame in Europe, and the first to write a great humorous work (*The Knickerbocker History*). He has also been called "the Father of the American Short Story." It is, however, by his title of "The Father of American Literature," that we think of him when considering his masterly biography of

George Washington, "the Father of his country." Excerpts on Washington's early life from Volume I are found from pp. 17–118.

---

[1] Pierre Irving, *The Life and Letters of Washington Irving*, Vol. I, 1863, pp. 26–27.

[2] Charles Neider, "Introduction," *George Washington, A Biography* by Washington Irving, edited and abridged by Charles Neider (Garden City, New York: Doubleday and Company, Inc., 1976), p. xviii.

[3] Ibid., p. xxx.

[4] Edward Wagenknecht, *Washington Irving: Moderation Displayed*, 1962, p. 20.

[5] Charles Neider, p. xxxi.

[6] *Ibid.*

[7] *Ibid.*, p. xxxii.

[8] *Ibid.*, p. xxxiii.

[9] *Ibid.*, p. xxxiii.

[10] *Ibid.*, p. xxxiv.

[11] *Ibid.*, p. xxxv.

John Marshall
1755–1835

As Chief Justice of the Supreme Court of the United States from 1801–1835, John Marshall exercised a decisive influence on the development of American constitutional law. He also made his mark as a soldier in the War of Independence, a legislator at the state and national levels, and in a brief but significant role as a diplomat in France. The man who became best known as "the great Chief Justice" was born in Prince William County (now Fauquier County), Virginia, September 24, 1755, in a humble log cabin. He was the eldest son of Thomas Marshall, a soldier who fought in the French and Indian War and in the expedition of General Braddock. John's mother was Mary Keith, the daughter of an Episcopalian minister.

When John was ten years old, the growing Marshall family (there were to be fifteen children) moved thirty miles to the west to an area of the Blue Ridge called "the Hollow," and in 1773 moved a few miles to the east. Brought up on the Virginia frontier and living a rugged outdoor life strengthened young John's physique. He learned patience early in life as he was kept busy helping to take care of his younger brothers and sisters.

John Marshall was blessed with exceptional parents who saw to it that his character and intellect were properly developed. Thomas Marshall was highly esteemed by his neighbors and represented Fauquier County in the Virginia House of Burgesses at various times between 1761 and 1776. He also served as county sheriff and principal vestryman of his parish. Since the family lived in the wilderness, John's education and that of his six brothers and eight sisters was in the capable hands of his parents who transmitted to their children their strong religious convictions and high moral and ethical standards. Their educational efforts were supplemented by a Scottish tutor, a Reverend Thompson, who came to live with the family when John was about twelve. When John turned fourteen, his parents sent him to an academy in Westmoreland County run by the Reverend Archibald Campbell. Here George Washington had been a pupil, and one of John's fellow students was James Monroe. He studied at this academy for about a year, then returned home to be tutored once again by Reverend Thompson who put him to work studying the works of Horace and Livy, which he enjoyed so much that later he continued to study them by himself with the help of a dictionary.

The main influence on his education, however, was from his father who superintended his reading in the field of English literature for which young John soon developed a lifelong devotion, particularly to the works of Alexander Pope. Then, in 1772, his father bought for him a copy of the first American edition of Blackstone's *Commentaries on the Laws of England.* Soon John began to teach himself the law using Blackstone's famous book. John was very close to his father to whom he later attributed "the solid foundation" of all his achievements.

From childhood, he heard his father talk of the importance of unity among the colonies in order to fend off attacks from the Indians and perhaps even from the English if they persisted in trying to take away from the colonists their rights as Englishmen. John knew that his father's good friend, George Washington, shared many of the same views. Born in the same county, Thomas Marshall and George Washington became friends as children. Later, when Washington was a surveyor for Lord Fairfax, he asked John's father to be his assistant. So it was that Thomas Marshall traveled with Washington for three years surveying the western portion of the Fairfax lands. From his father, John learned to admire and respect Washington. In 1775, after Lexington and Concord, both Thomas Marshall and George Washington heartily supported Patrick

Henry in his speech at St. John's Church, Richmond, and were stirred by its concluding words, "Give me liberty, or give me death!" Thomas Marshall later wrote that Henry's speech was "one of the most bold, animated and vehement pieces of eloquence that had ever been delivered." [1]

He told his nineteen-year-old son of the resolves for defense. Both father and son knew the manual of arms and now began to instruct and drill their patriotic neighbors. John first saw action at Greatbridge, Virginia, in the fall of 1775. He went on to fight at the siege of Norfolk as one of the Culpeper Minute men. Just weeks after the Declaration of Independence was signed, John and his father joined the Continental Army led by General George Washington, John as a lieutenant in the third Virginia Regiment. During his years of service he rose to the rank of Captain and fought in the battles of Brandywine, Germantown and Monmouth, as well as participating in the capture of Stony Point.

Perhaps the most instructive experience of his time in the army was the winter that he spent at Valley Forge which reinforced his conviction that a strong national government was an urgent necessity. Day by day, he had the spectacle before his eyes of starving, ill-clad troops who remained unpaid and underfed throughout that long, cold winter. The lack of response to Washington's pleadings to Congress for help showed Marshall that without a national government with the power to tax the states, rather than merely *request* their aid, the United States would never become a nation but would soon dissolve into an increasingly ineffectual league of states. As Albert J. Beveridge remarked in his biography of Marshall, "Thus it is that, in his service as a soldier in the War for our Independence, we find the fountainhead of John Marshall's national thinking. . . . "[2]

When Marshall's term of enlistment was up, he went to Williamsburg in hopes of raising another Virginia regiment. In May and June of 1780, while working on this plan, he attended a series of lectures on the law at William and Mary College given by its distinguished chancellor George Wythe. This period of about a month was to be the only law instruction he ever received. Despite this short time, he evidently demonstrated his ability and was admitted to the bar on August 29. It was during this time in Richmond that he fell in love with Mary Willis Ambler, the daughter of the state treasurer. Despite Mary's attractions and the prospect of becoming a lawyer in her home town, he set off for Philadelphia on foot, having failed to raise a new Virginia regiment. When he arrived, his clothes were in tatters and he was suffering from malnutrition. He eagerly returned to duty, however, and served under Baron Von Steuben who took him back to Virginia. He continued to serve until late January 1781 when he resigned his commission and, no new one being offered him, returned home.

The next year he was elected to the Virginia House of Delegates which met in Richmond, the new capital of Virginia. Here he married Mary Ambler on January 3, 1783 and set up his law practice in Richmond. Success in his profession was soon in coming to the homespun looking young lawyer even though the field was already full of distinguished members of the bar, such as Patrick Henry and Edmund Randolph.

When Marshall first served in the Virginia legislature, governmental power was still in the hands of the states which began to engage in commercial wars among themselves and quarrels over land boundaries. Marshall's experience in his state legislature once again showed him that the only remedy to the reigning disunity was a strong, well-organized "general government," and he joined George Washington and James Madison in their call for a strengthened union. In 1784 he was reelected to the state legislature and again in 1787 when he urged a Ratifying Convention be held to consider the new Constitution crafted in Philadelphia. He was elected to serve at this convention held the following year and took a leading part in the debates, ably seconding James Madison's efforts for ratification.

When concern was expressed during the debates about the possible actions of the national legislature, it is significant that Marshall insisted that if Congress tried to "make a law not warranted by any of the powers enumerated . . . they [the judges] would declare it void."[3] Here is a clear statement of the doctrine of judicial review which he was to assert later as Chief Justice of the United States Supreme Court. He was not, however, the originator of the idea. At the Constitutional Convention in Philadelphia, it was generally viewed as a legitimate part of the judicial process. Indeed, James Madison, "the Father of the Constitution," endorsed judicial review at the Convention, as well as subsequently in *The Federalist Papers* and at the Virginia Ratifying Convention, although he never saw the federal judiciary as the only branch of the government to rule on the constitutionality of laws.

Marshall continued to serve in the Virginia legislature until the spring of 1791. He was shocked to find it necessary to defend the policies of President Washington who was being violently attacked by the Democratic Republicans. These opponents of the President's policy of neutrality wanted the United States to run to the aid of the French Revolution, while the President believed this revolution to be very different from our own and that the United States, still in a precarious financial situation, should not intervene. So abusive was the language of the President's opponents that Marshall was so disgusted he refused to run for reelection in 1791. In 1795, however, he returned to the legislature in time to defend Washington once again. The President was under attack for the treaty on commerce and navigation rights which John Jay had negotiated with Great Britain in 1794.

When the President sent John Jay to England to negotiate a treaty, Great Britain still held frontier forts in the Northwest and brazenly seized loaded American ships at sea bound for France with whom England was at war and confiscated their cargoes. British vessels also frequently seized American sailors and forced them into their navy. President Washington saw war looming on the horizon and, if possible, wished to avoid it as the United States needed the tariff revenues from trade with Great Britain. Washington believed that if trade were cut off in retaliation for British acts at sea, this would be devastating to the American economy.

When the Treaty arrived in Washington in March 1795, the President was disappointed. It secured peace, but the United States was forced to yield on many points. On the plus side, it provided for the withdrawal of English troops from the forts they still occupied in the Northwest. It also called for the establishment of a joint commission to settle claims regarding the illegal seizure of American ships since the United States was a neutral in England's contest with France; it dealt with the disputed boundaries between Maine and Canada; and trade between the two nations was to become reciprocal. But the rights of neutral nations were not made clear and, worst of all, one clause on American trade with the West Indies was put under so many restrictions as to be unacceptable to both President Washington and the Senate. Accordingly, this clause was struck from the Treaty before the Senate would ratify it. Even so, the President's opponents in Virginia were up in arms against the treaty which the Democratic Republican press depicted in the darkest hues. Marshall vigorously defended the President and the treaty in the Virginia legislature. It must have taken considerable courage to take such a strong stand in the face of so much opposition. But courage John Marshall had in abundance and he continued to stand stoutly for the Treaty and for the wisdom of President Washington. His eloquence was acknowledged, but the legislators remained unconvinced.

At length, on April 25, 1796, Marshall spoke in defense of the Treaty at a large public meeting of citizens held in Richmond. The object was to gain signatures on a petition to the United States House of Representatives (now in the hands of the Democratic Republicans) urging them to give their support to the Treaty. Marshall's eloquence won over a majority of those present and so many petitions favorable to the Treaty flooded the House, that it finally voted in favor of appropriating the necessary monies in order to put the Treaty into effect.

Marshall's courage, skill, and determination lifted him higher than ever in the eyes of the President and other Federalist leaders. The President had offered him the post of Attorney General in 1795, but Marshall had turned it down. In 1796, he offered him an appointment as Minister to France which Marshall again refused reluctantly because of personal financial problems which he believed made it necessary for him to continue his lucrative law practice.

After John Adams became president, Marshall finally was prevailed upon to accept an appointment as one of three envoys to France. They were to try to straighten out a serious rupture with France over the Jay Treaty with England which France claimed was a violation of American neutrality and used as an excuse to seize 316 American vessels between 1796 and 1797. Charles Cotesworth Pinckney had been sent to France in 1796 as American Minister, but the French government had refused to receive him. John Marshall and his co-envoys, Elbridge Gerry and Pinckney (who had remained in Europe) arrived at the French court, only to be similarly rebuffed by the French who would not receive them officially. The French Foreign Minister, Talleyrand, merely sent three "agents" to talk with them. (These anonymous agents became known as X, Y and Z in the American press.) They brazenly announced that before any negotiations could begin, President Adams must issue an apology for statements he was alleged to have made to Congress, a loan of 32 million florins must be paid to the French government and, in addition, a payment of 1,200,000 lives which the three envoys quickly recognized as a bribe.

They indignantly refused, saying that the American government would not pay even six pence! Marshall prepared a stern *Memorial* rebuffing these attempts at bribery and telling Talleyrand that the attitude of the government of France violated the laws and customs of civilized nations. Upon his return home, Marshall was received warmly by his fellow Americans for his courageous rebuke of the insults France had offered him and his companions. A public dinner honoring him was held by the two houses of Congress.

In 1798, John Adams tried to appoint Marshall an associate justice of the United States Supreme Court, but Marshall declined. In 1799, however, he yielded to pleas from George Washington and Patrick Henry to run for Congress. He was elected to the House of Representatives where he became a primary spokesman for the Federalists. In May 1800, Adams again attempted to give Marshall an appointment, this time as his Secretary of War, but again he declined. A few days later, however, when Adams beseeched him to accept appointment as Secretary of State, Marshall accepted. That autumn, after defeat in his bid for reelection as President, Adams had another important appointment to fill before he turned over the reins of government to the next president in February 1801. The Chief Justice of the Supreme Court, Oliver Ellsworth, had resigned because of illness and Adams finally decided that his Federalist ally, John Marshall, was the man for the job. Marshall was startled because he had recommended Judge William Patterson. But, as he wrote in his 1827 autobiographical sketch: "I had never before heard myself named for the office and had not even thought of it. I was pleased as well as surprised, and bowed in silence."[4] In January 1801 President Adams sent the nomination to the Senate which confirmed it on January 27, 1801. Thus began thirty-five years of service as Chief Justice in which Marshall's views of the constitutional role of the United States Supreme Court were indelibly impressed on the American judicial system.

Before Marshall was appointed Chief Justice, the Supreme Court had not played a large role in the new federal system of government. It had not nullified any acts of Congress, although it was generally admitted that the Court might legally do so and might play a role in interpreting the Constitution. Still, a respectable body of opinion held that the legislative and executive branches could also rule on the constitutionality of proposed laws. Both Jefferson and Madison held to this view. In the early years of the republic, Congress and the Chief Executive decided many issues involving how the Constitution should be interpreted. As late as 1817, when Congress presented President Madison with a bill to improve roads and canals, the president vetoed it as unconstitutional. Thomas Jefferson held that each of the three branches of government—legislative, executive and judicial—had the right to decide for itself the constitutionality of proposed laws. The Jeffersonians in Congress adhered to this view.

Marshall made his position clear in his first decision in *Marbury vs. Madison* (1803). Here he laid out the Court's rights to judicial review and to disregard Federal statutes the Court deemed unconstitutional. In 1816, the Court found in *Hunter's Lessee* (1816) and *Cohens v. Virginia* in 1821 a right to overrule a state court on a federal matter. In *McCullough v. Maryland* (1819) the Court proposed the doctrine of "implied powers," i.e., powers suggested by the language of the Constitution. *Fletcher v. Peck* (1810) and *Dartmouth College v. Woodward* (1819) declared the inviolability of a state's contracts. And *Gibbons v. Ogden* (1824) upheld the right of the Federal Government to regulate interstate commerce even if this meant overriding a state law.

Although these landmark decisions of the Court increased the powers of the national government, it is not to be thought that they were woven merely out of Marshall's personal convictions regarding the primacy of the Union. His ability to persuade his fellow justices to adopt his views in case after case was the result of a finely honed logic applied to the language of the Constitution and his obvious reverence for the document.

Like most Americans, Marshall viewed the Constitution as a higher law binding on lesser laws. He wrote in *Marbury* that "all those who have framed constitutions contemplate them as forming the fundamental and paramount law of the nation, and consequently, the theory of every such government must be that an act of the legislature, repugnant to the Constitution, is void."[5] In *Ogden v. Saunders* Marshall also stated flatly that what the Constitution says is not to be "extended to objects not . . . contemplated by its framers."[6] Like other Americans, Marshall and the Court were thoroughly familiar with the idea of a higher law. They were accustomed, for example to being ruled under the English Constitution and colonial charters. Beyond that, however, the justices, like most Americans, believed that the divine law of the Holy Scriptures was higher than all man-made laws and was the pattern for constitutions and laws.

Marshall's respect for the Constitution and the intentions of its Framers grew out of his understanding of the higher law. Thus, in adjudicating the cases that came before them he always wanted the Court to remember that "it is a *constitution* we are expounding."[7] Not surprisingly, Marshall's view of "implied powers" was far more carefully held within the bounds of the Constitution than has been the case with later courts.

Three important premises lay at the bottom of his approach to the law: 1) That a judge must have no will of his own except the will of the law; 2) that the meaning of the Constitution, like that of the Bible, was perfectly clear when construed properly; and 3) the proper way to construe the Constitution may be found by consulting the purposes of the Framers as revealed in such writings as *The Federalist Papers.*[8]

Marshall's great influence over his fellow justices during his long career may seem remarkable in view of his scant formal legal training and his personal appearance. He was loose-limbed and ungainly and his plain homespun clothing certainly lent his figure no elegance. But he possessed to an extraordinary degree the power to convince his fellow justices by his clear exposition of the facts of a case and by using his meticulous logical discourse to persuade them rather than bombastic appeals to emotion. His personal character, too, impressed them.

All who knew him well admired his devotion to his family. His wife suffered from a severe nervous affliction for many years and he spent much time reading aloud to her, as they both shared a love of reading books together. Ten children were born of their union, but four died early deaths. Since the Supreme Court sat for only one term per year, of about seven or eight weeks, plus circuit court duties for each justice, Marshall had time to devote to his beloved wife and children.

He also had time to accomplish a task which his fellow justice, Bushrod Washington, gave him. Justice Washington served on the Supreme Court between 1798 and 1829 and, as George Washington's nephew, he was a close friend of the Chief Justice and consistently supported him on all the constitutional issues that arose in the first twenty-five years of the nineteenth century. It was to Marshall that he entrusted the letters, private papers and documents that George Washington had bequeathed to him so that Marshall could write a biography of Washington. He could not have made a more appropriate choice than Marshall, Washington's friend and defender for so many years and one who had fought with him in the Revolution.

It took Marshall seven years to produce the first edition of his five-volume *Life of George Washington* which appeared between 1804 and 1807. Part of the work was reprinted in 1824 and eight years after that, the whole work reappeared in a revised and condensed edition.

Marshall had a strong physique and enjoyed good health until 1831 when he was operated on for the removal of kidney stones. He appeared to be recovering well, but the death of his wife on Christmas Day of that year was a blow from which he never quite recovered. In the spring of 1835, a stagecoach in which he was riding overturned. He suffered from the effects of the accident and in June went to Philadelphia for medical help. He died there on July 6, 1835. When the Liberty Bell was tolled as a mark of respect for his loss, it suddenly cracked as though it, too, mourned the loss of "the great Chief Justice." Marshall's body was taken to Richmond for burial, for here was his home, here he had met his wife, and here he had begun his legal career.

Excerpts from his *Life of George Washington* are on pp. 10–11.

---

1 Albert J. Beveridge, *The Life of John Marshall,* 2 Vols. (Boston: 1916), Vol. 1. p. 65.

2 Beveridge, Vol. 1, p. 147.

3 Jonathan Elliott, *The Debates on the Adoption of the Federal Constitution,* 1828, Vol. II, p. 404.

4 *Dictionary of American Biography,* (New York: Charles Scribner's Sons: 1965), Vol. VI, p. 319.

5 Cited in William F. Swindler, *The Constitution and Chief Justice Marshall(* (New York: Dodd, Mead & Company), p. 141.

6 *Ogden v. Saunders,* 25 U.S. (12 Wheat.), 213, 332 (1827), Cited in John W. Whitehead, *The Second American Revolution* (Elgin, Illinois—Weston, Ontario: David C. Cook Publishing Co., 1982), p. 208.

7 See *McCulloch v. Maryland,*, 1819, in William F. Swindler, *The Constitution and Chief Justice Marshall* (New York: Dodd, Mead & Company, 1978), p. 309.

8 See the discussion of this point in the biography of John Marshall in *The Dictionary of American Biography,* (New York: Charles Scribners Sons, 1964), Vol. 6, p. 323.

E. C. McGuire
1793–1858

Born in Frederick County, Virginia, in July 1793, Edward C. McGuire began his studies for the ministry on January 1, 1812 under the Reverend William Meade, then rector of Christ Church, Alexandria, and a future bishop of the Protestant Episcopal Church of Virginia. Reverend Meade moved away within a few months and McGuire continued his theological studies with the Reverend William H. Wilmer, rector of St. Paul's Church, Alexandria, followed by a year under the Reverend George Dashiell of Baltimore. In September 1813, McGuire received a call from St. George's Episcopal Church in Fredericksburg, Virginia, and preached his first sermon there on October 3. He was shocked to discover that the church had dwindled to only eight or ten people and the 75-year-old church building was very dark and dismal. Young and inexperienced as he was, he nevertheless threw himself into the business of working with the trustees to build a new edifice. A loan was taken out to construct the new building, and plans were set in motion to dispose of the old building and apply the proceeds to the funds for the new one. The cornerstone of the new church was laid in 1814 and, on October 16, 1815, the day after the Church's consecration by Bishop Richard Channing Moore, the pews were sold for a sum in excess of the cost of the new building.

Through their new pastor's faithful teaching of the fundamentals of the Christian faith, the congregation steadily grew from under a dozen when Reverend McGuire first came to Fredericksburg, to sixty souls by 1815, the year the new church was built. (By 1832, there were two hundred and twenty-eight communicants, a higher number than those of any Episcopal church in Richmond. It was said that this large increase was the result of a revival in this church. By 1859, St. George's Church had two hundred and fifty-one members.)

On April 17, 1816, Reverend McGuire married Judith C. Lewis, who was in his first confirmation class. She was related to George Washington, being the granddaughter of his sister Betty who married Colonel Fielding Lewis. Judith's father, Robert Lewis, was mayor of Fredericksburg for eight years.

Although Reverend McGuire struggled with illness for several years, he continued to work hard for his parishioners. He believed that goodness should be active and not passive. In April 1823 he was happy to note that some of his parishioners attended services as often as six or seven times a week. He taught a Bible class at night in the Church through the month of February 1830 and the following month taught a Bible class for women. At this time, some fifty teachers taught Sunday School for about two hundred and fifty children.

Early in 1825, the Marquis de LaFayette visited Fredericksburg and attended services at Reverend McGuire's church, and also visited the McGuire's home in the afternoon. In 1825 Virginia was afflicted by a serious and prolonged drought. On Sunday, October 23, Reverend McGuire prayed publicly for rain at the morning service. The following week "the Lord was pleased to send a gracious and refreshing shower," as Reverend McGuire joyfully commented at Church the next Sunday as he gave thanks for answered prayer.

Reverend McGuire was also active in the affairs of the community and endeavored to improve the treatment of black people. After a visit to New England, he came to believe that it was voluntary, rather than involuntary labor which overcame the difficulties of farming with which New Englanders were faced. He implied that free laborers could achieve the same thing in the South. By 1835, he was also active in the Temperance movement.

Through his wife's connection with the Washington family, he became greatly interested in George Washington, particularly in his religious convictions, which he believed had not been sufficiently discussed. Therefore, he set about writing a book which he titled, *The Religious Opinions and Character of Washington*; see excerpts pp. 159d–166a, 169d–170. In the Advertisement preceding his work, which was published in 1836, he wrote that he had been "at much pains to acquire the requisite materials for his present undertaking. . . . Besides the ordinary sources of information, he has enjoyed the advantages of access to some, not heretofore thrown open to others. . . . It may be added, that in search of matter, there has been a studious refusal of whatever could be regarded as apocryphal or fanciful—care being taken to employ only such facts as can be proved authentic, or bear the indubitable marks of being so."[1] In describing his motives for writing his book, he explained in the Preface that, while Washington's life and character had been discussed in other works in great detail, little had been written about his religious convictions. He noted that:

"The qualities of the hero and statesman, universally attractive as they are, have been those on which the most have chiefly delighted to dwell. . . . In the mean time other important peculiarities of disposition and habit, have been suffered to pass unnoticed, or with only a reluctant and impatient glance. Among these may be especially numbered the religious views and character of this illustrious man. These, indeed, have not been entirely unobserved by the public, and no doubt have much engaged the attention of some. But they have not shared a due proportion of interest, or their merited pre-eminence in the constellation of his virtues."[2]

Reverend McGuire's talents and abilities as a minister gradually became well-known outside his home state. In 1839, Kenyon College, Gambier, Ohio, gave him an honorary doctorate. By 1846, Reverend McGuire's congregation was so large that it was rapidly outgrowing the church edifice. Accordingly, funds for a new, larger building were solicited. The new edifice was consecrated on Sunday, April 22, 1849, by Bishop William Meade. Again, the pews were sold on the following day, and the proceeds were sufficient to pay off the remaining debt. The lovely new building was partially destroyed by fire in 1854, but repairs and improvements were completed the following year.

In 1858, there was a great revival at St. George's Church. Dr. McGuire was overjoyed to see over one hundred new members join his church. Although his physical powers were ebbing away, he preached his forty-fifth anniversary sermon on October 3, 1858. Five days later he died. When his funeral was held on October 11, all the church bells in the city tolled for him. Reverend Philip Slaughter officiated at the funeral, and Bishop Johns delivered the eulogy. His saintly character was extolled and his leadership in the revival of the Episcopal Church in Virginia praised. Dr. McGuire was buried in a grave behind the church he loved and had served for so long.

---

1 E. C. McGuire, *The Religious Opinions and Character of Washington* (New York: Harper & Brothers, 1836), p. vii.

2 *Ibid.*, p. v.

Francis Parkman
1823–1893

Francis Parkman, American historian, was born in Boston, Massachusetts, of an old New England family. His father, the Reverend Francis Parkman, was descended from Elias Parkman who had settled at Dorchester around 1633. His mother, born Caroline Hall, was a descendent of the Reverend John Cotton. His grandfather, Samuel Parkman, was a wealthy Boston merchant, whose bequest to Francis enabled him to pursue his historical writing without having to worry about earning a living. As a boy, his health was so delicate that when he was eight years old his parents sent him to live in the country with his maternal grandfather, Nathaniel Hall, of Medford. Here he remained for the next five years attending a small school run by John Angier. The country life agreed with him, and being able to explore a wild forest nearby developed his taste for outdoor life and exploration. When he was thirteen years old he returned to his parents in Boston and began attending a famous private school run by Gideon Thayer. Here he was given excellent instruction in English literature and composition. Through these two experiences, learning to explore and learning to write well, he was providentially prepared for his future career.

In 1840, he entered Harvard where, providentially, one of his professors was American historian Jared Sparks from whom he must have learned much about the art of historical writing and research. During school vacations he made several long trips by foot and canoe through the White Mountains, up the Magalloway River and around Lakes George and Champlain. He also traveled in Europe from November 1843 to June 1844. He graduated from Harvard in 1844 and enrolled in its law school. After two years of study, he made a momentous journey which changed his life.

On April 28, 1846, he and his cousin, Quincy Adams Shaw, left for St. Louis to go into the Wyoming Territory. They were gone until October, exploring the California and Oregon Trail, going from St. Louis to Fort Laramie, camping and hunting with the Sioux tribe and studying Indian tribal life. The ostensible reason for Parkman's trip was to improve his health, but along the way he encountered so many physical hardships that he returned home worn out and ill. He would never forget this wilderness experience, however, and wrote a series of articles on *The Oregon Trail* which ran in the *Knickerbocker Magazine* between February 1847 and February 1849. His eyesight became very bad so that he had to dictate some parts of the work to cousin Quincy while recuperating in Brattleboro, Vermont. It was published in book form in 1849 under the title *The California and Oregon Trail.* It was to become one of his most popular books.

In 1848, despite suffering from several disabilities—failing eyesight, frequent severe headaches, and a nervous disorder that at times prevented him from sustained and close concentration—he nevertheless began his *History of the Conspiracy of Pontiac,* the first of a series of volumes dealing with the power struggle on the American continent between England and France. Despite his many physical ailments and his reliance upon a reader to read to him all the needed research materials, the first book was completed within two and a half years and was published in 1851.

In 1850, Parkman married Catherine Scollay Bigelow, the daughter of Boston physician, Dr. Jacob Bigelow. They had three children. In 1853, his nervous disability increased and he was forced to abandon his research and historical writing for several years. For relaxation he wrote *Vassal Morton,* a semi-autobiographical novel. Published in 1856, it proved unsuccessful, and quietly passed into oblivion. Needing something to keep up his interest in life, Parkman took to raising new varieties of flowers, especially lilies and roses. His unexpected success in the field of horticulture led to his becoming president of the Massachusetts Horticultural Society and—many years later (in 1871)—becoming professor of horticulture at Harvard.

In 1858, just as he appeared to be recovering his health, his wife and his only son died within a year of each other. These tragic events so prostrated him that he went to Paris to consult a specialist who, however, could do little for him. It was about four years before his powers of concentration were restored. Finally, he decided to make an effort to continue his former book project on the French in America and, in 1865, he published *Pioneers of France in the New World.* This volume earned him a solid reputation as a historian. Two years later, his *Jesuits in America* was published, followed by *The Discovery of the Great West* (later known by the title *La Salle and the Discovery of the Great West,* 1879 edition). And still the volumes came—*The Old Regime in Canada* in 1874 and *Count Frontenac and New France under Louis XIV* in 1877.

Twenty-eight years had passed and Parkman was anxious to finish the story before he died, so he broke the time sequence and jumped into *Montcalm and Wolfe* which was published in 1884 in two volumes. He finally finished the long saga in 1892 with *A Half-Century of Conflict*, also in two volumes. A few months after he had finally brought this monumental task to its conclusion, he suffered a severe attack of pleurisy from which he barely recovered, only to die less than a year later from appendicitis.

One should not think of the life of this acclaimed American historian as one of continuous gloom and struggle against infirmity, for there was much sunlight in his life, too, not least the sunny temperament he himself manifested when even partially well. Parkman had many interests and many devoted friends. Although sometimes isolated from his friends when his nervous illness was at its worst, he always thought of them with affection and dedicated his book *La Salle,* to his college class of 1844, and his *Montcalm and Wolfe* to Harvard College.

Parkman's books shine not only as history, but also as literature. His vivid descriptions of the landscape of the American wilderness and of the characters that filled that wilderness in the years of conflict between England and France—mountain men, trappers and *voyageurs*, the American Indian, and the soldier-heroes—Champlain, Frontencac, La Salle, Pontiac, Wolfe, and Washington—give his great historical canvas color and vibrancy. But his volumes are not only literature, they are painstakingly documented history. He visited Canada nine times to do research and traveled to England and France six times to gather the original sources upon which his historical writing relies. An extensive collection of transcripts of these documents is now in the Massachusetts Historical Society.

Parkman loved the heroic in human nature, which is not surprising, for he manifested heroism himself over a period of many years. Illness vanquished him at times, but did not prevent him from accomplishing his life's work of depicting an important period in America's past.

An excerpt from *Montcalm and Wolfe*, Vol. I, is found on pp. 39–40.

David Ramsay
1749–1815

"The political creed of an American colonist was short, but substantial. He believed that God made all mankind originally equal; that he endowed them with the rights of life, property, and as much liberty, as was consistent with the rights of others; that he had bestowed on his vast family of the human race, the earth for their support; and that all government was a political institution between men naturally equal, not for the aggrandizement of one, or a few, but for the general happiness of the whole community. Impressed with sentiments of this kind, they grew up, from their earliest infancy, with that confidence which is well calculated to inspire a love for liberty, and a prepossession in favour of independence."[1]

These words of David Ramsay aptly describe not only the views of the American colonists in general, but his own deeply held convictions. As an ardent patriot active in the defense of South Carolina in the War of Independence, he served his country in three capacities—as physician, historian, and legislator.

He was born on April 2, 1749 in Drumore Township, Lancaster County, Pennsylvania, the son of James Ramsay, an Irish emigrant and farmer, and Jane Montgomery Ramsay. After graduating from the College of New Jersey in 1765 he tutored in a Maryland family for two years, then studied medicine receiving his degree from the College of Pennsylvania in 1772. He practiced medicine there for a year and then, in 1773, went to Charleston, South Carolina, bearing a letter from his teacher, Dr. Benjamin Rush, which declared him to be "far superior to any person we ever graduated at our college." [2]

Dr. Ramsay soon had a flourishing practice. But in 1776, after war had broken out between Great Britain and her North American colonies, he was elected to represent Charlestown in the state legislature. He also served as a surgeon during the war at the siege of Savannah. When the British captured Charleston in 1780, they imprisoned Ramsay along with thirty-two other patriots in St. Augustine. Upon his release a year later, he returned to Charleston and in 1782 he was a delegate to the Continental Congress. He attended its sessions regularly and was in favor of strengthening the powers of the general government.

From 1784–1790 (with the exception of 1785–1786 when he was President of the Continental Congress) he served in the South Carolina House of Representatives. For three terms (1792, 1794, and 1796) he was President of the state Senate. He opposed paper money and the importation of slaves and was known for his ability and integrity.

Dr. Ramsay's personal life was marked by early tragedy. In 1775, he married Sabina Ellis, the daughter of a Charleston merchant. After only a year of marriage she died. In 1783, he married Frances Witherspoon, a daughter of Dr. John Witherspoon, President of the College of New Jersey and a signer of the Declaration of Independence. Frances died in childbirth in 1784. Though much saddened by these losses, Dr. Ramsay retained his deep Christian faith. On the death of Frances, he wrote to Dr. Witherspoon of his conviction that she had "exchanged earth for heaven."[3]

In 1787, Dr. Ramsay married Martha Laurens, the daughter of Henry Laurens, statesman, diplomat, and President of Congress in 1777. He lived happily with Martha for the next twenty-four years. After her death in 1811, he published a tribute to her in *Memoirs of the Life of Martha Laurens Ramsay* (1812).

Despite his contributions to his country as physician and legislator, David Ramsay is best known for his historical writings. "A ready writer and a careful observer, of encyclopedic memory and intense patriotism, he early set himself to the work for which his gifts and position fitted him."[4] His impartiality and his acquaintance with many of the leading figures of the Revolution made him peculiarly well qualified to write in this historical field.

The first historical work to come from his pen was his two-volume *History of the Revolution of South Carolina* (1785). Next came his *History of the American Revolution*, 2 vols., (1790), and in 1816 *History of the United States.* In it he wrote of George Washington:

"The integrity of Washington was incorruptible. His principles were free from the contamination of selfish and unworthy passions. . . . He was a statesman without guile, and his professions, both to his fellow-citizens and to foreign nations, were always sincere. . . . He was an example of the distinction which exists between wisdom and cunning; and his manly, open conduct, was an illustration of the soundness of the maxim—'that honesty is the best policy.'" [5]

He also wrote a popular *Life of George Washington* (1807). It had the ring authenticity, as it was written by one who knew and admired the great General. Dr. Ramsay's perceptive study of Washington was followed in 1808 by a *History of South Carolina*.

On May 6, 1815, Dr. Ramsay's life was brought to a sudden and unexpected close by a maniac's gun shot. His remaining historical works were posthumously issued. In 1816, a three-volume *History of the United States* (1607–1808) was published from his manuscript with additions by the Reverend S. Smith. In 1819, his last great historical work appeared, an eight-volume *Universal History,* on which he had worked for many years.

Excerpts from Ramsay's *Life of George Washington*, can be found on pp. 5–9.

---

[1] David Ramsay, *History of the United States*, 1816, Verna M. Hall, Compiler, *The Christian History of the American Revolution: Consider and Ponder* (San Francisco: Foundation for American Christian Education, 1976), p. 436.

[2] *Dictionary of American Biography*, (New York: Charles Scribners' Sons, 1964), Vol. VIII, p. 338.

[3] Martha Lou Lemmon Stohlman, *John Witherspoon: Parson, Politician, Patriot* (Louisville, Kentucky: John Knox Press, 1976), p. 155.

[4] *Dictionary of American Biography*, Vol. 8, p. 338.

[5] David Ramsay, *History of the American Revolution*, 1790, Verna M. Hall, Compiler; *George Washington: The Character and Influence of One Man*, (San Francisco: Foundation for American Christian Education, 1999), p. 6.

Philip Slaughter
1802–1890

An Episcopal clergyman and historian who wrote much on the old parishes and families of Virginia, Philip Slaughter was born in the family home, "Springfield," in Culpeper County, Virginia, on November 21, 1802. His father, Philip Slaughter, was a captain in the American Revolution and his mother, Elizabeth, was the daughter of Col. Thomas Towles, of Lancaster County, Virginia, and the widow of William Brock. Young Philip's formal education began in an academy in Winchester, Virginia. His studies there were followed by courses at the University of Virginia (1825–1828).

After completing his university studies, he took up the law, but after practicing for five years, he decided to study for the ministry at the Theological Seminary of the Protestant Episcopal Church at Alexandria. He was ordained a deacon in 1834 and in that same year married Anne Sophia, daughter of Dr. Thomas Semmes of Alexandria. Ordained a priest in July 1835, he was active as a minister for twelve years, serving at several churches and concluding this period with five years at St. Paul's Church, Petersburg.

Rev. Slaughter became well known as an eloquent evangelical preacher and gave sermons at many churches and rural parishes. It was said of him that he had "all the personal magnetism, the fire and spiritual power of Whitefield. Great crowds attended on his ministry and conversions were numbered by the hundred."[1]

His short, brilliant career as a preacher was brought to a close by illness. After traveling to Europe in 1848 in an unsuccessful attempt to regain his health, he returned to Virginia in 1850 realizing that he must give up the ministry. He wanted to be active in some way, however, and in that year he began a periodical on the colonization of the slaves in Africa (*The Virginia Colonizationist*). It appeared for five years and aroused great interest and support for the colonization movement in Virginia.

Still yearning to preach, however, he returned to his home on Slaughter's Mountain in Culpeper County and put up a church on his father's farm where he preached whenever he was well enough to do so. During the Civil War the church was destroyed and he and his family were forced to flee to Petersburg. While he was there he began publishing the *Army and Navy Messenger*, a religious newspaper that was distributed to the soldiers of the Confederate Army.

When the war ended, Rev. Slaughter returned to his home and decided to pursue his early interest in Virginia parish history. Before the war, he had published *A History of Bristol Parish* (1846) and *A History of St. George's Parish* (1847). They aroused interest in preserving early records of other parishes. But Rev. Slaughter wanted to write a more extensive book on the old parishes and families of Virginia and collected a good deal of material for this work. Worsening health, however, finally prompted him to give this material to Bishop William Meade who continued the research he had begun and, in 1857, published his *Old Churches, Ministers, and Families of Virginia.* Rev. Slaughter was able to write *A History of St. Mark's Parish* (1877) and almost completed *The History of Truro Parish*, before his death on June 12, 1890. In 1908, it was published by Rev. Edward L. Goodwin.

Other writings on church history which Rev. Slaughter produced include a paper on the historic churches of Virginia, published in W. S. Perry's *The History of the American Episcopal Church* (1885); "The Colonial Church in Virginia," in *Addresses and Historical Papers before the Centennial Council of the Protestant Episcopal Church in Virginia* (1885) and a biography of the Rt. Rev. William Meade, in *Memorial Biographies of the New England Historic and Genealogical Society* (Vol. IV, 1885).

While primarily a church historian, Rev. Slaughter wrote other historical books, pamphlets, and addresses. Among the best of these was his *Christianity the Key to the Character and Career of Washington* (1886). In this eloquent work, he wrote that through faith in Christ, Washington "conquered not only the independence of his country—but he conquered himself, thus realizing the proverb of Solomon, 'He who ruleth his own spirit, is better than he who taketh a city.'"

Excerpts can be found on pp. 153–59.

[1] See *Dictionary of American Biography*, (New York: Charles Scribners' Sons, 1964) Vol. IX, p. 207.

William Smith
1726–1803

This Episcopalian clergyman and educator was born in Aberdeen, Scotland where he was graduated from the University of Aberdeen in 1747. Emigrating to New York two years later, he became tutor to Governor Martin's family. Deeply interested in education, he prepared and published in 1753 a plan for a college. He addressed it to the trustees the legislature had appointed to study proposals for establishing a college in New York. Smith's plan outlined his ideas for the kind of college he believed would be suitable for a new country. The goal was to produce men and citizens of good character. The plan, which emphasized religion, history, and agriculture, also was meant to meet the needs of those who would eventually follow the "mechanic profession" for whom Smith believed a knowledge of Latin and Greek would be unnecessary.

Smith sent a copy of his plan to Benjamin Franklin and to the Reverend Richard Peters, who were trustees of the Academy and Charitable School of Philadelphia. Franklin was so pleased with Smith's ideas that he invited him to visit Philadelphia. On his visit, Smith was so impressed by what the Academy had accomplished that he dashed off an enthusiastic Poem on Visiting the Academy of Philadelphia, June 1753. The result of his visit was an invitation to teach at the Academy. Smith accepted with alacrity. Before taking up his post, however, he went to England to be ordained a deacon in the Church of England on December 21, 1753 and, two days later, a priest. Returning to Philadelphia the following May, he taught logic, rhetoric and natural and moral philosophy at the Academy.

When asked by the trustees in 1754 to draft a clause for the school's charter giving the Academy the power to bestow degrees, Reverend Smith and the rector, Francis Allison, ended by drawing up a new charter, adding the word "college" to the Academy's name. The charter was approved in 1755 and Smith was then made provost of "the College, Academy and Charitable School of Philadelphia." The next year the trustees requested of him a curriculum which he was able to give them promptly as he had prepared one two years earlier. It has been called "one of the most comprehensive schemes of education which up to that time had been devised for any American college."[1]

Active though he was as provost and teacher at the College, Reverend Smith had many other interests and gradually became influential in many areas of Pennsylvania life—from the religious, social and scientific to the literary and political. He was deeply concerned about the Germans in the colony who spoke little English and wanted to integrate them into the colony. He asked the Society for the Propagation of the Gospel to set up educational facilities throughout Pennsylvania especially for the German population. When the Society set up a board of trustees to develop schools for the German settlers, Smith was appointed its secretary.

Reverend Smith was very active in the Anglican Church and was anxious for advancement. He ardently hoped that an American bishopric would be set up by the Church of England and that he would be asked to fill that high position. He was also very active in the Masonic order as were many other prominent leaders in Philadelphia.

During the French and Indian Wars, he criticized the Assembly for not pursuing a more vigorous military opposition and published a pamphlet on the subject in 1755. It caused much controversy as, among other measures, he urged an oath of allegiance to the King be taken by all members of the Assembly promising not to refuse to defend their country against all the King's enemies. He also urged withdrawing the right to vote from the German population of Pennsylvania until they knew English well enough to understand the issues facing the colony. His character was attacked in the press but was vindicated by the trustees of the College who refused to fire him.

In 1757, the controversial provost began *The American Magazine and Monthly Chronicle of the British Colonies*. It vigorously supported the Crown against France but also ran many religious and scientific papers. It encouraged the work of poets like Francis Hopkinson and brought the young American artist Benjamin West to the attention of the public. Smith also wrote a series of religious articles for the magazine. The publication only lasted a year, however, for in December 1757 he was accused of publishing a libelous article concerning the General Assembly. He was imprisoned in January 1758, released in April and, after a trip to England in December 1758 to appeal his case to the King, was vindicated and returned to Philadelphia in May 1759.

While in England he received a Doctor of Divinity degree from Oxford University and also a doctorate from the University of Aberdeen. He returned to England briefly in 1762 on a highly successful fund-raising trip for the College. While abroad, he visited Dublin where the University honored him with a degree of Doctor of Divinity in 1763. At home again, Reverend Smith became rector of Trinity Church, Oxford, Pennsylvania, where he served from 1766 to 1777. In 1768, he was elected to membership in the American Philosophical Society.

As contention grew between Great Britain and her North American colonies, Reverend Smith found himself in an awkward situation: He opposed the Stamp Act, declaring it to be "contrary to the faith of charters and the inherent rights of Englishmen," but he could not favor independence from Great Britain. In 1775 he preached before Congress a *Sermon on the Present Situation of American Affairs* at Christ Church, Philadelphia. His sermon created a great stir, for while he staunchly opposed the Stamp Act, he also spoke of the need for "a return to the Halcyon-days of harmony with the Mother Country." In 1776, he issued a pamphlet signed Candidus declaring that the idea of American independence was "illusory, ruinous, and impracticable." When General Howe was marching to Philadelphia, Smith's authorship of this pamphlet caused him to be arrested for "conduct and conversation inimical to the American cause." He was allowed to retire to an island belonging to an estate he had purchased on the Schuylkill. Once the patriot army had evacuated the city in October 1777 and General Howe had taken possession of it for the British, he returned to Philadelphia and to his College duties.

The British evacuated Philadelphia in 1778 and in 1779 the General Assembly appointed a committee to look into some questions that had arisen with regard to the College. The Committee's majority opinion was that the college corporation had shown hostility to the government and constitution of the state and had not lived up to its original principles which required that it give equal privileges to all religious denominations. On November 27, 1779, the Assembly voided the charter of the College and created a new corporation known as "the Trustees of the University of the State of Pennsylvania."

Reverend Smith then left Philadelphia for Maryland where he became rector of Chester Parish, Chestertown, in Kent County. Here he established a school which in 1782 was chartered as Washington College. Smith was its president. An indefatigable fund raiser, Smith raised more than 10,000 pounds for the new college. He remained active in the Episcopal Church and was elected president of every convention of the Church held in Maryland while he lived there. He was also sent as a delegate to the General Conventions. Here he led in organizing the new American Episcopal Church and is credited with giving it its new name—the Protestant Episcopal Church.

It was his dream to be made bishop of the new Church, and the Maryland Convention of 1783 did elect him Bishop, but the General Convention did not confirm him in the office. The reason seems to have been that at the Convention in New York in October 1784, where he was the presiding officer, Smith appeared in a drunken condition. The long coveted post denied him, he continued to try to get the rights of his old College restored. Finally, in 1789, the Assembly declared the act of 1779 "repugnant to justice" and restored the old charter. In July of that year Smith returned to his position as Provost. But in 1791 the College was merged with the University of the State of Pennsylvania with John Ewing named as provost.

Reverend Smith spent his last years at his estate at the Falls of the Schuylkill, where he slowly sank into alcoholism. He died in Philadelphia survived by five children by his wife Rebecca, daughter of his friend Judge William Moore.

Despite the sad ending to his life, it has been said of him "the importance of his service for practically a quarter of a century during the formative period of what is now the University of Pennsylvania is incalculable, and his contribution to education in general, not inconsiderable. He imparted literary enthusiasm to a notable group of young men, aided in the publication of their work, and helped to make Philadelphia a literary center."[2]

It is also important to remember that while Reverend Smith was with the Loyalists regarding American independence from Great Britain, he still loved liberty and in the end rejoiced to see it established in an independent nation. In the Masonic Sermon he gave in Christ Church, Philadelphia, on St. John's Day, December 28, 1778, before the Masons of Pennsylvania and with George Washington in attendance, he praised evangelical and social liberty rooted in "the true Way of Liberty—the Way of being free and accepted thro' Him!"

See the facsimile title page and text of his sermon on pp. 272–80, and listing as part of Washington's library on p. 268.

---

[1] *Dictionary of American Biography* (New York: Charles Scribner's Sons, 1964), Vol. IX, p. 354.

[2] *Ibid.*, p. 357.

Jared Sparks
1789–1866

A versatile New Englander—active as clergyman, editor, and historian—Sparks was born in Willingon, Connecticut, on May 10, 1789. He was the son of Eleanor Orcutt and Joseph Sparks, a farmer. Jared's early life was unsettled as, in the mid-1790s, he was sent away to live with an aunt and uncle in Camden, New York, in order to lessen the financial burden of the many children then in the family. In 1805, he went to live with another uncle in Tolland, Connecticut. He was apprenticed to a carpenter and also taught school for awhile.

Early in life he discovered three subjects that greatly interested him: theology, literature, and American history. In 1809 he received a scholarship to attend Phillips Exeter Academy in New Hampshire. Here began his life-long friendship with John Palfrey, who was to make a name as a New England historian. While at Phillips Exeter, Sparks began writing articles for the local press on various subjects as disparate as education and astronomy. In 1811 he entered Harvard College. When he graduated in 1815, he received the Bowdoin Prize for an essay on Isaac Newton. After graduation, he stayed on at Harvard to study theology.

He had left college briefly, between May 1812 and June 1813, because of lack of finances. He went to Maryland to tutor a family in Havre de Grace. While there he saw a British naval bombardment which he wrote up and got published in *The North American Review*. This contact resulted in his becoming the editor of the *Review* from May 1817 to March 1818. In 1819 he received his master's degree in theological studies from Harvard and accepted a call to the ministry from a Baltimore Unitarian church. He also served as the chaplain of Congress in 1821, but was not happy in Baltimore or the District of Columbia. His situation was complicated by illness and perhaps concerns about whether the ministry was his calling. In any event, he returned to Boston in 1823. After recovering his energies, he was given an opportunity to buy *The North American Review*. He seized the chance and edited this periodical until 1830. By then he succeeded in making it the leading journal of its kind in the country.

It was in 1820, however, that he found his real life work. A publisher asked him to recommend someone to edit and publish the papers of George Washington. Sparks had visited Mount Vernon in 1815 and greatly admired Washington. He decided to undertake the project himself. It was only after extensive negotiations with Washington's nephew, Bushrod Washington, that he got permission, in 1827, to examine Washington's papers at Mount Vernon. While still negotiating with Washington's nephew, he realized that the project would entail a great deal of research. So he went South to examine the public records covering the period of the War of Independence. In an article he wrote for *The North American Review*, he insisted that in order to write a history of the United States, many historical manuscripts had to be made available and assembled. Not content with the materials available here, Sparks journeyed to England and the Continent to consult historical records concerning America. In 1829–1830 he published twelve volumes of *The Diplomatic Correspondence of the American Revolution.*

In 1832 he married Frances Ann Allen by whom he had one child. In this happy year, he brought out a three-volume *Life of Gouverneur Morris.* His most important work, *The Life and Writings of George Washington*, in twelve volumes, finally appeared between 1834 and 1837. In 1835, in the midst of his work on Washington, his wife died. Sparks married again in 1839. His wife was Mary Crowninshield Silsbee. They had five children, of whom four survived infancy.

While still laboring on the writings of Washington, he started working on the writings of Benjamin Franklin and, between 1833 and 1840, he put out ten volumes, entitled *The Works of Benjamin Franklin; with Notes and a Life of the Author*. An indefatigable worker, he also found time to oversee the publication between 1833–1849 of a 25-volume *Library of American Biography*. In all of his documentary work, Sparks showed his great love and admiration for his country and his conviction that original documents told the story of the nation in the most compelling way.

These publications made him a member of that select group of leading nineteenth-century historians that included George Bancroft and William Prescott. In 1838, he was appointed McLean Professor of Ancient and Modern History at his *alma mater*, Harvard College. In 1849, he became President of the College. While President, he rearranged and reclassified the early records of the college. In 1853, he published his *Correspondence of the American Revolution* in four volumes. This was also the year which saw his retirement from his professorship at Harvard, after which he traveled in Europe for a year and continued to gather materials for his history of the American Revolution. Death came on March 14, 1866, before he finished this work.

Sparks was a staggeringly prolific historian who published more than sixty volumes of historical writings in a thirty-year period, a time also crammed with many other activities, such as his work on *The North American Review,* and his professorship and presidency at Harvard.

See excerpts from Sparks's *The Life of George Washington*, on pp. 27, 34–36, 39, and Washington's addresses to churches from Sparks's *Writings of George Washington*, on pp. 238–241.

C. W. Upham
1802–1875

Charles Wentworth Upham, a New England minister, congressman and historian, was born in St. John, New Brunswick, Canada on May 4, 1802. He was the son of Joshua Upham, a lawyer, and Mary Chandler Upham. He was descended from John Upham who, in 1635, emigrated to Massachusetts from Weymouth, England. Joshua was born in Brookfield, Massachusetts, and was a graduate of Harvard. He fought on the British side in the American Revolution. After the war he moved to New Brunswick where he was a judge of the supreme court. Despite the honor of his position as judge, the remuneration was not great. As a consequence, his wife and son were left impoverished after his death in 1808.

Charles attended school in St. John but, at age ten, he went to work for an apothecary shop, mixing medicines. He taught himself how to be a pharmacist by studying a pharmacology textbook. At age twelve, however, we find him working as a day laborer on a farm in Annapolis, Nova Scotia. In 1816, his cousin, Phineas Upham, a prosperous Boston merchant, came to the rescue and took him on as his apprentice. He soon discovered, however, that Charles had exceptional intellectual abilities and was of a very studious nature. He decided to place him under the tutelage of Deacon Samuel Greele, and, in 1817, he sent him to Harvard College. Charles graduated in 1821, second in his class. After graduation, he went on to three years study in the Cambridge Divinity School. Here he was instructed in liberal theology which came to be known as Unitarian. In December of 1824, he was ordained associate pastor of the First Church of Salem. In 1826, he married Ann Susan, daughter of the Reverend Abiel Holmes of Cambridge, and sister of Oliver Wendell Holmes. They had fourteen children. Unhappily, only three survived to adulthood. Upham remained the pastor of First Church for twenty years after which he resigned because of a chronic bronchial illness.

In 1848, after partially recovering from his illness, he turned his attention to Whig politics and, in 1849, was elected to the Massachusetts House of Representatives. In 1850–51, he served in the state senate and again in 1857 and 1858. He also served as Mayor of Salem in 1852. He was a strong supporter of President Zachary Taylor and was selected by the town authorities to deliver a eulogy on Taylor after the President's death in 1850. In 1853, Upham was a delegate to the state constitutional convention and, between 1853–55, he was a member of the thirty-third Congress.

As a Congressman, he opposed the Kansas-Nebraska Act insisting that the Ordinance of 1787 that prohibited slavery in the new territories was still valid. In 1856, he actively supported the newly organized Republican Party and wrote a biography of its first presidential candidate, titled *Life, Explorations and Public Services of John Charles Frémont*, published in 1856.

Upham retired from politics in 1860 and devoted himself to history, a subject that had long interested him. His best known historical work is *Salem Witch-*

craft (2 vols., 1867). Historians still find this work useful to consult. Upham died in Salem on June 15, 1875.

"The character and influence of one man," is quoted from *The Life of General Washington,* edited by C. W. Upham, found here on pp. 3–4.

Robert C. Winthrop
1809–1894

Statesman, orator, and author, Robert C. Winthrop was born in Boston, Massachusetts, at the home of his great-uncle, James Bowdoin. He was the son of the state's then Lieutenant Governor, Thomas Lindall Winthrop and Elizabeth Temple Winthrop. He was sixth in descent from John Winthrop (1588–1649), the first governor of the Massachusetts Bay Colony. After graduating from Harvard University in 1828, he studied law under Daniel Webster, the great American statesman and orator. He was admitted to the bar in 1831, then served in the state legislature for six years beginning in 1834. He was Speaker for the last three years of his term. It was during this period that Winthop began to be known as an eloquent orator.

In November 1840 he was elected a member of Congress, but in 1842 he resigned because his wife had become very ill. He did not return to public office until after her death when he was once again elected a member of Congress serving between 1843–50. He was Speaker between 1847–9 and was criticized by the anti-slavery members as not taking a strong enough stand against slavery. He was defeated by the "Free-Soilers" in his bid for a second term. In 1850–1 he served in the United States Senate, having been appointed initially to fill out the unexpired term of his old law teacher, Daniel Webster, who had resigned. Charles Sumner, a strong Abolitionist, defeated him in his run for the Senate in 1851. Winthrop then withdrew from politics and devoted the rest of his life to educational and historical interests.

Winthrop was much in demand as an orator for special commemorative occasions such as the laying of the cornerstone for the Washington National Monument in 1848 and its dedication in 1885. On this last occasion, his health did not permit him to deliver the talk he had written and it was read instead by the Honorable John D. Long, member of the House of Representatives from the State of Massachusetts.

Among his many other commemorative addresses, there is his moving address on the Pilgrim Fathers given at Plymouth, Massachusetts, December 21, 1870 and his impressive *Oration on the Hundredth Anniversary of the Surrender of Cornwallis,* given before Congress in 1881 at the invitation of both houses.

Winthrop was a member of the Massachusetts Historical Society 1839–1894 and its president for thirty of those years. As a devout Christian, well versed in history, he was deeply concerned about his country's future as a nation based on Christian principles. In an address given at the annual meeting of the Massachusetts Bible Society in Boston, he gave a warning as timely for our day as when he delivered it in 1849.

"All societies of men must be governed in some way or other. The less they may have of stringent State Government, the more they must have of individual self-government. The less they rely on public law or physical force, the more they must rely on private moral restraint. Men, in a word, must necessarily be controlled, either by a power within them, or by a power without them: either by the word of God, or by the strong arm of man; either by the Bible or by the bayonet. It may do for other countries and other governments to talk about the State supporting religion. Here, under our own free institutions, it is Religion which must support the State.

"And never more loudly than at this moment have these institutions of ours called for such support. . . . Who does not perceive in all these circumstances that our country is threatened, more seriously than it ever has been before, with that moral deterioration, which has been the unfailing precursor of political downfall? And who is so bold a believer in any system of human checks and balances as to imagine, that dangers can be effectively counteracted or averted in any other way than by bringing the mighty moral and religious influences of the Bible to bear in our defences."[1]

Winthrop's Oration read at the Dedication of the Washington Monument appears on pp. 300–312.

---

[1] See extended extracts of this address; Verna M. Hall, Compiler, *The Christian History of the American Revolution: Consider and Ponder* (San Francisco: Foundation for American Christian Education, 1975), p. 20.

BIOGRAPHIES OF THE ARTISTS

Prepared by
Mary-Elaine
Swanson

EDWIN AUSTIN ABBEY
1852–1911

It has been said of this illustrator and painter that "it would be difficult to name another living artist who has given so much delight, and a delight so keen and so wholesome."[1] His illustrations for volumes of poetry and his illustrated Shakespeare were highly popular with the public of his day. Abbey was born in Philadelphia, the son of Maxwell Abbey, a commercial broker and Margery Ann Kiple Abbey. He studied briefly in 1868 at the Pennsylvania Academy of Fine Arts taking night classes under Christian Schussele just at the time when Thomas Eakins (1844–1916) began to assist Schussele. According to E. P. Richardson, however, "his real teachers were the illustrations in English books by artists like Millais, Rossetti, Houghton, Keene, which he saw in Philadelphia bookstores and antique shops."[2]

In 1871, Abbey went to work for Harper & Brothers as an illustrator. The relationship between publisher and artist was to last a lifetime. It was an excellent time to be an illustrator, as all the popular magazines were using illustrations, not only for their fiction but for news stories and feature articles. At the beginning of his career, Harper's was using wood engraving for its drawings. To be a successful illustrator required the artist to be a highly skilled draftsman. Abbey perfected his ability with his pen, and the illustrations he produced were "little jewels of impressionist pen drawing."[3] A charming example was his first drawing done to accompany Robert Herrick's poem "Corinna's Going A-May-ing," published in Harper's New Monthly Magazine (May, 1874). This work also became the subject of his first oil painting done in 1890. It heralded a change that would occur in his work later when he shifted from illustration to oil painting. But in 1875, when he did the illustrations for an edition of *Charles Dickens Christmas Stories*, he was known and admired for his work as an illustrator.

Harper's sent Abbey to England in 1828 to illustrate an article on Stratford-on-Avon. Here he became acquainted with fellow American artists James McNeill Whistler (1834–1903) and John Singer Sargent (1856–1925). He also came under the influence of the mid-nineteenth-century English painters known as the Pre-Raphaelites. He took a particularly keen interest in the England of the seventeenth and eighteenth centuries and illustrated a volume of Herrick's poems (1882) for Harper's and a popular edition of Goldmith's *She Stoops to Conquer* (1887). For the rest of his life he lived mainly in England.

In 1888 Harper's gave him his largest commission—to illustrate all of Shakespeare's plays. He traveled throughout Europe to see the plays in their various settings and collected period costumes and furniture to recreate scenes in his Gloucestershire studio. The Shakespeare comedies were completed and published with his illustrations in 1896. Again, his work as illustrator inspired him to do two of his finest oil paintings—*The Play Scene in Hamlet* (1897) and *King Lear's Daughters* (1898). Known primarily as an illustrator, it was a surprise when the Boston Public Library commissioned him, in 1890, to do a large mural depicting the story of the Holy Grail. The work, done in a twelfth-century French setting, was completed in 1902.

In that year, Abbey received another commission from his native land: to decorate the new state capitol in Harrisburg, Pennsylvania. This was his last major commission and its scope entailed hiring several assistants, making hundreds of figure drawings, and using lantern slides to transfer his drawings to very large canvases. The largest painting, *Apotheosis of Pennsylvania*, is 35 feet tall and is in the Pennsylvania House of Representatives. His historical paintings, *Penn's Treaty with the Indians* and *The Reading of the Declaration of Independence*, completed the group. In the Rotunda he worked on lunettes representing "the treasures of the state," from its landscape to its religious liberty and to its workers in iron and steel. Abbey did not live to see the completion of this commission. After his death in London on August 1, 1911, his friend John Singer Sargent was brought in to oversee its completion.

While Abbey's large paintings were much admired, his real fame rests on his being one of the leading illustrators of the period who "made the last quarter of the nineteenth century the golden age of this branch of American art." [4]

Painting: *The Camp of the American Army at Valley Forge, 1778*, p. 192.

---

[1] Samuel Isham, *The History of American Painting* (New York: The Macmillan Company, 1936), p. 420.

[2] E. P. Richardson, *Painting in America*, (New York: Thomas Y. Crowell, 1956), p. 354.

[3] *Ibid.*

[4] *Ibid.*, p. 324.

Alonzo Chappel
1828–1887

He was born in New York City on March 1, 1828 of a family of French Huguenot descent. His father, William Pelton Chappel, was a tinsmith and amateur artist, and his mother was Maria Louise Howes. Alonzo early showed artistic talent and when only nine years old did a painting for the American Institute Fair titled *The Father of His Country*. His family's financial situation must have been poor, because he was painting on the streets of New York City when he was twelve years old charging his customers five or ten dollars to do their portraits. A couple of years later he left school to learn two artistic trades: japanning and window shade painting. After two more years, in 1844, he was listed as an artist in the New York City Directory. He now charged twenty-five dollars to paint a portrait. In 1845, he attended the National Academy of Design. Here he studied anatomy by drawing from the casts of antique statues. As far as can be discovered, this was the only instruction in the arts that he ever received.

In 1848, he was apparently settled in Brooklyn as a portrait artist and also picked up work as a painter of stage scenery. At this time he also married Almira Stewart by whom he had four children. As a genre painter dealing with scenes of everyday life, he displayed his paintings at the American Art-Union, the National Academy of Design and for a distinguished firm, Goupil and Company. At this period he painted *The Strolling Minstrels* (1849); *A Militia Cavalryman Preparing His Mount for a Fourth of July Parade* (1854) now in the West Point Museum, U.S. Military Academy, West Point, N.Y.); and other work.

Chappel met New York publisher Henry Johnson in 1856 through the Reverend Elias Magoon, a well-known collector of American art, who introduced the two men. It was a fortunate introduction, for Johnson commissioned Chappel to illustrate John Frederick Schroeder's *Life and Times of George Washington*, which was published by Johnson, Fry and Company in 1857. This was the beginning of a long and fruitful association with the Johnson firm which employed him to do the illustrations for many books on American history. Among the books he illustrated were: Henry B. Dawson's *Battles of the United States* and Jesse Ames Spencer's *History of the United States*, both published in 1858; Evert A.

Duyckinck's *National Portrait Gallery of Eminent Americans* (1862), *National History of the War for the Union* (1861–1865), *History of the World, Ancient and Modern* (1871), and *Portrait Gallery of Eminent Men and Women of Europe and America* (1872–1873).

Chappel was adept at painting both portraits and historical events. Moreover, his pictures were the result of painstaking research. "He did not rely solely on the books he was illustrating to provide information on the subject at hand; he consulted other sources as well in order to ensure that his depictions were as accurate as possible."[1] As an illustrator, he did not paint from life but based his own work on already available life portraits, engravings, or photographs. His portrait of a friend, the artist William Marshall Swayne, which he painted from life between 1864–1866, shows that he could have been a very successful portrait painter. His time was entirely taken up, however, with his work as an illustrator.

He usually worked in oils, but sometimes in chalk or crayon. Some of his oil paintings are in color, but most are in grisaille, that is in grey or a grayish monotone. This was done to help the engraver whose task it was to translate the artist's work into black-and-white engravings. In the 1860s, several of Chappel's illustrations were exhibited at the National Academy of Design and the Brooklyn Art Association. Chappel also did a number of historical paintings, such as *The Last Hours of Lincoln* (1865–1868).

Several years after the death of his wife in 1863, Chappel married Abby J. Briggam, a widow with one son. He continued to be active in the Brooklyn art world and, in the 1860s, he participated in creating the Brooklyn Art Association. In 1869, he bought some land in Middle Island, Long Island, on a body of water which was later renamed "Artist's Lake" in his honor. Here he built a home and continued to be active for about fifteen years. He retired in 1885 and died two years later on Middle Island. He is buried in the local Presbyterian cemetery.

Engravings of Chappel's illustrations are still being used to illustrate both popular and scholarly works. They have also been used on postage stamps. His surviving original illustrations have been used also in books and on television. Some of his paintings, such as *The Capture of Fort Ticonderoga, The Battle of Long Island* (in the Brooklyn Historical Society); *The Battle of Bennington* (Bennington Museum, Vermont); and *The Death of Captain Lawrence: Don't Give Up the Ship* (Franklin D. Roosevelt National Historic Site, Hyde Park, N.Y.) "have become the best known, even definitive, depictions of these events."[2]

In 1992, the Brandywine River Museum presented the first retrospective exhibition of Chappel's work which was also seen at the Maryland Historical Society in Baltimore and the Virginia Historical Society in Richmond. The largest collections of his original paintings is in the Chicago Historical Society. Others are in private collections, as in the Virginia Historical Society, Richmond; the National Portrait Gallery, Washington, D.C.; the National Museum of American Art, Washington; the U.S. Naval Academy Museum, Annapolis, Md.; the Brandywine River Museum, Chadds Ford, Pa.; the New-York Historical Society, New York City; the Museum of Fine Arts, Boston; and the Museum of Art, Rhode Island School of Design, Providence.

Illustrations: *Washington's Interview with His Mother*, p. 21; *Washington on His Mission to the Ohio, 1753*, p. 42; *Washington's First Interview with Mrs. Custis*, p. 87; *The Marquis de Lafayette*, p. 195; *The First Cabinet*, p. 233.

---

1 *American National Biography* (New York and Oxford: Oxford University Press, 1999), Vol. 4, p. 717.

2 *Ibid.*, p. 718.

JAMES EDWARD KELLY
1855–1933

Born in New York City on July 30, 1855, he is best known as a sculptor, but began as a magazine illustrator whose work benefited from the new strides being made in engraving which utilized "white lines, flocks or dots to suggest the painter's atmospheric colors and gradations of tone."[1] Kelly's wash drawing, *The Gillie Boy*, in *Scribner's Magazine* for August 1877, is thought to have been the first woodcut executed completely in the new manner. E. A. Richardson writes that "the new style, once found, made possible the most brilliant period of American illustration, which lasted from 1877 until the literary monthlies were driven out of the field by a cheaper mass journalism at the end of the century."[2]

Kelly's Scottish-born father and Irish mother recognized and encouraged his artistic talents, and it was his mother who inspired him with a love of America. He became intensely interested in American history and read everything he could find on this subject. His earliest pictures were on historical subjects, and he decided early in life that he would work as an artist on American subjects exclusively.

In 1871, Kelly's formal education as an artist began at the National Academy of Design. He later became one of the founders of the Art Students League of New York. After working in the art department of Harper & Brothers he and Edwin Austin Abbey opened a studio in 1873 and began doing illustrations for magazines.

Because of his keen interest in American history, Kelly began to look for men who had fought with distinction in the Civil War, interviewing them and doing sketches of them from life. He produced a series of sketches accompanied by the men's stories just as they had related them to him. Most of his subjects approved of his accounts and signed them. This was a unique venture and came at a time when firsthand information on the Civil War was fast disappearing.

Kelly was an illustrator for Scribner's, Harper's, and St. Nicolas, until 1881 when he abandoned magazine illustration for sculpture. His first work as a sculptor was a statuette of *Sheridan's Ride* which he modeled in wax after receiving a few instructions from a sculptor friend. He used sketches he had made of Sheridan and his own knowledge of horses. His first big assignment as a sculptor was to do five bas-reliefs around the base of the "Monmouth Battle Monument." His designs were chosen over those of sixty competitors. The five subjects were: *Ramsey Defending His Guns; Washington Rallying His Troops; Molly Pitcher; The Council of War at Hopewell*; and *Wayne's Charge.*

In 1904 he executed his most famous work, the beautiful bas-relief, *Washington in Prayer at Valley Forge* which was originally in the New York West Side Y.M.C.A. but was later moved to the East front of the U.S. Sub-Treasury Building, Wall and Broad Streets, New York City, at the direction of President Theodore Roosevelt. There it was ceremonially unveiled on February 22, 1907. Before undertaking this bas-relief, Kelly thoroughly researched all the narratives he could find on the encampment at Valley Forge in 1777–78 so as to be sure of the historical accuracy of the accounts of Washington at prayer. The whole country took a great interest in this bas-relief and he received and supplied many requests for facsimiles from various institutions, such as churches, schools, colleges, and historical societies.

Among his many outstanding sculptures are: an equestrian statue of General Sherman; *Col. Roosevelt at San Juan Hill; Paul Revere's Ride; General Grant at Donelson*; and *Knowlton at Harlem Heights*, at Columbia College for the Sons of the Revolution.

Bas-Relief: *George Washington in Prayer at Valley Forge*, p. 243.

---

[1] E. P. Richardson, *Painting in America* (New York: Thomas Y. Crowelll, 1956), p. 326.

[2] *Ibid.*

Emanuel G. Leutze
1816–1868

Emanuel Leutze, portrait and historical painter, was born in Gmünd, Württemberg, Germany, the son of artisan Gottlieb Leutze and his wife, whose name is unknown. The family moved to the United States when Emanuel was nine years old and settled first in Fredericksburg, Virginia, then in Philadelphia, not far from the story of Washington's crossing of the Delaware. Young Emanuel became fascinated with this story and perhaps dreamed of one day painting this scene, for he early decided to become an artist. It is said that after his father's death when Emanuel was still a boy, he began to sell his drawings to support his mother and the other children in the family. He studied art in Philadelphia with Rubens Smith in 1834 and later was hired to do likenesses for James Barton Longacre's and James Herring's *National Portrait Gallery of Distinguished Americans.* By age twenty he could confidently call himself a professional artist.

In 1837, his task for the *National Portrait Gallery* completed, he was earning his living painting portraits in the area around Frederickburg, Virginia. In 1840, Edward L. Carey and Edward Seal, wealthy art patrons in Philadelphia, made it possible for him to go to Germany to study art. He enrolled in the Düsseldorf Art Academy which was then considered to be no less distinguished that those in Paris, Florence and Munich. Here he studied under Karl Friedrich Lessing and learned to do figure painting with much realistic detail. He also learned historical painting, an important aspect of the teaching at the Academy.

An important turning point in his life came in 1843, when he traveled to Italy on the southern route from Germany. This turned out to be an unforgettable experience which shaped his future. He wrote:

"The romantic ruins of what were once free

cities . . . led me to think how glorious had been the course of freedom from those small isolated manifestations of the love of liberty to where it has unfolded all its splendor in the institutions of our own country. Nearly crushed and totally driven from the old world it could not be vanquished, and found a new world for its home. This course represented itself in pictures to my mind, forming a long cycle, from the first dawning of free institutions in the middle ages, to the Reformation and revolution in England . . . to the Revolution and Declaration of Independence [in the United States.]"[1]

Returning to Düsseldorf he was inspired by his vision to begin a series of historical paintings. He had already painted *Columbus Before the Council of Salamanca* which was thought to be so fine that it was bought by the Art Union of Düsseldorf. Now, he painted and sent back to the United States *Columbus Before the Queen* (1843), which is now in the Brooklyn Museum. This was quickly followed by several scenes from English history, such as *Cromwell and Milton* (now in the Corcoran Gallery, Washington, D.C.).

Leutze did not intend to remain in Düsseldorf, but his marriage in 1845 to Juliane Lottner, a German woman, resulted in his remaining in Europe until 1859. He and Juliane had a daughter in 1846 and a son in 1847. Leutze soon became deeply involved in the art scene and in politics. He became president of the Union of Düsseldorf Artists and also co-founded, along with his former professor Karl Friedrich Lessing and other painters and poets, the Malkasten, a club with democratic views which favored efforts to unite the German states into one democratic state.

A number of American artists, some afterwards well known, came to Düsseldorf to study painting and draftsmanship. "They congregated around Leutze, who taught them or found them instructors, introduced them to the Malkasten membership, advised them, lent them money, sent them on long tours of the Rhine, and behaved in every way toward them as a father and a friend."[2] Among America painters who enjoyed Leutze's guidance while in Düsseldorf were Albert Bierstadt, Eastman Johnson, Charles Wimar and John Adams Elder.

Although now considered a German artist, America was constantly in his mind. In 1849 he began a painting of the dramatic moment of the attack on the Hessian soldiers camped on the New Jersey side of the Delaware river on Christmas Eve of 1776. The American victory over the Hessians revived the flagging spirits of the American patriots and showed Washington's bold leadership and keen understanding of strategy. "Not surprisingly, the encounter had attracted earlier artists, such as John Trumbull and Thomas Sully, but only Leutze's image has attained lasting and almost universal recognition."[3] Unfortunately, the painting was damaged by a fire in 1850. Repaired and exhibited in several German cities *Washington Crossing the Delaware* was bought by the Bremen Kunstalle which was destroyed in 1943 by Allied bombings. A second and larger canvas, however, depicting the same scene was purchased by Goupil and Company for the International Art Union in March 1851. It was exhibited in New York in September. In 1852 it was exhibited in the United States Capitol, where art collector Marshall Roberts saw it and purchased it. It remained in his collection until 1897 when John S. Kennedy bought it and gave it to the Metropolitan Museum. It became his best-known painting and has been reproduced widely.

After completing this, his greatest work, Leutze painted another scene of *Washington Rallying the Troops at the Battle of Monmouth*. The story behind the painting is this: In 1778, at Freehold in New Jersey, Washington discovered American soldiers fleeing before the enemy. He denounced their commanding officer, Major General Charles Lee, and then gathered the troops together and led them to a victory against the British. After *Washington Rallying the Troops at Monmouth* was exhibited in Berlin and Brussels, it was purchased by a private collector and is now in the University of California, Berkeley.

The pull of America must have been strong for Leutze, so interested was he in American subjects. In 1858, he returned to America and settled in Washington, D.C. and here he remained for the rest of his life except for one trip to Düsseldorf. Here in America he continued to produce historical paintings. In 1861 Congress commissioned Leutze to paint a 20 x 30-foot mural on the pioneer spirit and the development of the Far West for the walls of the Great Stairway in the House of Representatives. He traveled to the Rocky Mountains to study the country he was to depict and then painted *Westward the Course of Empire Takes Its Way* (1862). Leutze painted it directly on the way on a layer of cement made of lime and crushed stone. The colors were then applied to this background and fixed with a spray of water-glass solution. Congress paid Leutze $20,000 for this mural. Leutze also did many portraits of distinguished Americans, among them: Chief Justice Roger B. Taney (1859), portrait now at Harvard Law School, Cambridge, Massachusetts; William Seward (1859), now in the Union League Club, New York; Nathaniel Hawthorne (1863), now in the National Portrait Gallery, Washington, D.C.; and Frederick Church (1865), owned by a private collector. Leutze continued to paint until his death in Washington, D.C. in July 1868. Left on his easel was a sketch for a large painting he had titled *The Emancipation of the Slaves*. Although Leutze spent so many years abroad, he was an American patriot. Both his son and grandson became Admirals in the United States Navy.

Washington Rallying the Troops at Monmouth, p. 194.

---

[1] Henry T. Tuckerman, *Artist Life*, 1847, p. 177.

[2] *American National Biography* (New York: Oxford University Press, 1999), Vol. 13, p. 533.

[3] *Ibid.*

Benson John Lossing
1813–1891

This American author, editor and wood engraver was born on February 12, 1813 in Beekman, Dutchess County, N.Y. He was the son of John Lossing and Miriam Dorland Lossing. The name Lossing is derived from that of a Dutch ancestor—Pietre Pieterse Lassingh—who emigrated to Albany about 1648. Benson's father had a small farm and died when Benson was a baby. When Benson was about twelve years old his mother died. After her death he was apprenticed to a Poughkeepsie watchmaker.

Despite being alone in the world and leading a hard early life, he did not give up hope for his future. He became interested in history and spent most of his free time reading books on historical subjects. When he was only twenty-two years old he became a joint editor and proprietor of the *Poughkeepsie Telegraph*. Later he became a joint editor of a literary journal, the *Poughkeepsie Casket*. Here he met J. A. Adams, who illustrated the magazine. From him, he learned how to engrave on wood. In 1838, he went to New York City and set himself up as a wood-engraver. From June 1839 to May 1841 he also edited and illustrated *The Family Magazine*. In his spare time he wrote *An Outline History of the Fine Arts* which Harpers' Family Library published in 1840.

In 1848, Lossing came up with a highly original idea for a different kind of publication: a pictorial as well as narrative history devoted to scenes and events of the American Revolution. Harper & Brothers was sufficiently impressed to advance him the money to write and illustrate what became *The Pictorial Field Book of the Revolution*. It was published in parts between 1850–1852 and later in two octavo volumes.

It took Lossing five years to complete the book and more than eight thousand miles of travel in the United States and Canada. Everywhere he went he made sketches of the places and events of the Revolution which he later made into drawings on the engraver's block. His book was a great success and was followed by more than forty historical and biographical works, such as *Our Countrymen*, or *Brief Memoirs of Eminent Americans* (1855); *Pictorial Field Book of the War of 1812* (1868); *Pictorial History of the Civil War* (3 vols., 1866–68); *Our Country* (2 vols., 1876–78); *A Biography of James Garfield* (1882); *History of New York City* (1884); and *The Empire State* (1887).

Between 1872–74 he edited a magazine titled the *American Historical Record and Repertory of Notes and Queries*. He was also the author of an important paper, *Memorial of Alexander Anderson, M.D.*, the *First Engraver on Wood in America* which he read at a meeting of the New York Historical Society in 1870 and which was published in 1872. Lossing made valuable contributions to our knowledge of American history, but his *Pictorial Field Book of the American Revolution* remains his finest work. "It was an original idea well executed, and the antiquarian of today turns to it for details which cannot be found elsewhere."[1]

Lossing married Alice Barritt in 1833. After her death, he married Helen Sweet in 1856. Their home, "The Ridge," was in Dover Plains, N.Y., near the Connecticut Boundary. Here Lossing died in 1891.

Sketches: *Washington's Boyhood Home*, p. 16; *Washington and Fairfax at a War Dance*, p. 25; *Washington and Gist Visit Queen Aliquippa, p. 50; Washington Reading Prayers in Camp, p. 59; Raising the British Flag at Fort DuQuesne, p. 90; Mount Vernon*, p. 96; *Washington Taking Command, p. 116; Pohick Church*, p. 247; *Christ Church*, p. 249; *Trinity Church*, p. 251.

---

[1] *Dictionary of American Biography* (New York: Charles Scribners' Sons, 1961), Vol. VI, p. 422.

Tompkins H. Matteson
1813–1884

Tompkins Harrison Matteson is known today for his patriotic historical paintings which were extremely popular in his time through the many reproductions of them which were widely circulated. He was born in Peterboro, N.Y. on May 9, 1813. His father was a politician in the Democratic party and named his son for New York Governor Tompkins. Young Tompkins early manifested a strong interest in drawing and painting. His first art lessons came about in a most unusual way: His father was deputy sheriff of Madison County and allowed him to visit an Indian prisoner in the Morrisville Jail who was well known for his drawings and carvings. After lessons with the Indian prisoner, Tompkins continued to pursue his art studies with great tenacity. Having obtained a paint-box, he experimented with it in his spare time between work in a tailor's shop and a pharmacy. He copied prints and cut out silhouettes. There must have been some opposition to his pursuit of art, because he ran away to Albany, thinking he could support himself by crayon drawings of the people he met along the way. When he reached Albany, however, his money ran out; he was exhausted and turned his feet homeward. But he didn't stay there for long, preferring to wander the area doing portraits in Manlius, Cazenovia, Hamilton and other places near Peterboro.

The year 1834 found him in Sherburne, New York, with a company of strolling players. Here, when the star became suddenly ill, he made an appearance as Othello. Next he went to New York City where he got into the National Academy school. He then opened a studio. In 1839 he returned to Sherburne to marry Elizabeth Merrill. In 1841 he moved to Geneva, N.Y. where he did a series of highly successful patriotic historical paintings. His *Spirit of Seventy-six* was bought by the Art Union. Other works included: *Signing the Compact on the Mayflower, The First Sabbath of the Pilgrims, Perils of the Early Colonists, Washington's Inaugural*, and *Eliot Preaching to the Indians*. He was made an associate of the National Academy where his work was often exhibited.

He retired to Sherburne in 1850 where he lived for the rest of his life. He and Elizabeth had a large family, and he was active in the community, serving in many public offices including president of the agricultural society, foreman of the fire department, president of the school board, and as a member of the state legislature. He continued to paint and teach art. He also conducted drawing classes in the schools. When he died in 1884, the National Academy paid tribute to his character and talents. Today the Sherburne Public Library owns his celebrated painting, *Washington Crossing the Delaware*, as well as his *King Lear*. The Essex Institute, Salem, Massachusetts, owns his *Trial of George Jacobs for Witchcraft*.

Painting: *The First Prayer in Congress*, p. 110.

Charles Willson Peale
1741–1827

Peale was an outstanding example of the versatile colonist of eighteenth century America. Necessity caused many creative answers to needs that the colonist had to supply for himself. But it was more than necessity that drove Charles Willson Peale; he had an observant and endlessly curious mind; he also had single-minded perseverance in the pursuit of knowledge and proficiency in the variety of fields in which he became engaged. He began his working life as a saddler, went on to work as an upholsterer, harness maker, silversmith, sign painter, watch and clock repairer and, finally, as a painter and engraver. As if this were not enough, he served his country as a soldier, politician, taxidermist, scientist, naturalist, proprietor of his own art gallery and a natural history museum, and writer on several subjects. He can truly be classed with such versatile geniuses as Benjamin Franklin and Thomas Jefferson, both of whom he came to know and with whom he corresponded.

He was born in St. Paul's parish, Queen Anne County, Maryland, the eldest of five children. His father, Charles Peale (1709–1750) was a native of Rutlandshire, England, and had received a classical education. His mother was Margaret Mathews of Annapolis, Maryland. After emigrating to Maryland, Charles Peale became a teacher in the public school at Annapolis and later at two other schools. Charles Willson remembered his father as a fine teacher. "Education within a family context became, therefore, an influential ideal in Peale's intellectual life, along with the conviction that family members were responsible for and to each other."[1]

When Charles Peale died in 1750, many responsibilities fell on the shoulders of his eldest son, then eight years old. Charles Willson's mother moved the family back to Annapolis where she eked out a living for her family as a dressmaker. Charles was recruited to make "patterns for the ladies to work after." He soon developed an interest in drawing and painting. His earliest signed work was a painting of Adam and Eve which he did as a schoolboy. His schooling ended at age thirteen, however, when his mother apprenticed him to a saddler for seven years. It was a time of "bondage," he noted later. When he was twenty, his master released him from his apprenticeship as a reward for his conscientious work. He then set up in business for himself, thanks to money advanced to him by Judge James Tilghman and materials his former master gave him on credit. Having made this promising start, he married Rachel Brewer (1744–1790) the daughter of an Anne Arundel County landowner and merchant.

Paying off his debts to his former master proved to be more difficult than he had imagined and caused him much anxiety. He narrowly missed being sent to debtor's prison on one occasion. He later wrote that he had "engaged in so many labors of body and mind with my several mechanical undertakings, that I allowed myself no time for reflections of any kind. I did not seem to regard the future being wholly occupied with the present, or feared danger until I was overtaken with difficulties."[2] He made heroic efforts to pay his debts, but when he joined the Sons of Freedom during the Stamp Act crisis in 1764, he incurred the ire of his Loyalist creditors who forced him out of business. (In the end he finally paid off his debts, but it took him eleven years to do so.) This seemingly disastrous turn of events, however, turned into a blessing for Peale, as he acknowledged later in his *Memoirs*, for it resulted in his becoming a professional artist.

His interest in art had been aroused earlier through a visit to Norfolk, Virginia, to purchase leather to make saddles. Here he ran across a portrait and some "miserably done" landscapes and was sure that, given paints and a paintbrush, he could do better. He followed his conviction by painting a landscape and several portraits of members of his family. He also began a sign painting business. At first, he had no idea of how to prepare a painter's palette (never having seen one) or how to apply the colors, so he had to work it out by trial and error, as when he designed his own tools for watchmaking and silversmithing. Although he received several commissions to paint portraits, he soon realized that he needed more knowledge. On a trip to Philadelphia he visited several artists' studios and bought a book on painting (*The Handmaid to the Arts*, 1758, by Robert Dossie). He also traded a saddle for some lessons in portrait painting with John Hesselius (1728–1778).

In 1765 he was forced to flee his creditors and took passage on a merchant vessel owned by his brother-in-law. The vessel was bound for Boston but made a stop at Newburyport where he had the opportunity to paint several portraits. Upon arrival in Boston, he met John Singleton Copley (1738–1815), a prominent American artist, who graciously gave him a portrait to copy. He also saw some paintings by John Smibert (1688–1751) which impressed him as being "in a stile superior to any I had seen before." While in Boston, Peale assisted the leaders of the opposition to the Stamp Act by designing patriotic emblems protesting the Act. On his way home he stopped off in Virginia and got several portrait commissions which kept him there for a year.

When he finally returned to Annapolis in 1766, his works gained the notice of several merchants and planters who were so impressed with his talents that they set up a fund to send Peale to England to study art with Benjamin West (1738–1820), the highly successful American artist who lived and worked in London. On his arrival in London in February 1767, he went at once to see West. Always gracious to young artists from the colonies who came to London and wanted to study with him, West accepted him as a pupil, found him lodgings and helped him in many ways during his stay in London. Peale never forgot West's many kindnesses to him during the three years he studied in London. As an American patriot, however, he was not comfortable in England and worked as hard and fast as he could in order to return to America as soon as possible.

During the London years (1767–1769), Peale's artistic versatility became evident. He excelled at both the painstaking art of miniature painting, done in water color on ivory, and full-sized oil portraits, sculpture, and mezzotint engraving. He did a full-length portrait of Lord Chatham—that great friend of the colonies—which was sent to Virginia in 1768 and from which he did his first engravings. He also exhibited paintings at the exhibitions of the Society of Artists, and twice posed for portraits done by West. As an American patriot who believed passionately that the colonies should be free to develop their own manufactures, he made it a point to take no English-made clothes with him when he left England in 1769.

On his return to Annapolis, he was an artist thoroughly trained in the English style of portrait painting, which he taught to his brothers and his children, adding his own ideas. The English school at that time placed the subject in an open-air setting, sometimes beside a fountain, a statue, or perhaps a vase. Peale used beautiful landscapes as his backgrounds, or used some incident connected with the sitter, perhaps an interesting personal item that would add color and interest. His early canvases were very large, full-length portraits, and sometimes group portraits, such as the one he did of his own family around 1770. *The Peale Family* was an important painting to him. It realized beautifully what he had set out to do, and that was to illustrate the beauty of family life. It was indeed a happy family joined together in love and harmony, and this is clearly seen in the faces of his subjects. Included in the painting were his wife Rachel, his mother, her friend and companion Peggy Durgan, Peale's brother St. George, who was a register for the Land Office for Western Maryland, and his brother James, then a carpenter's apprentice, but soon to become an artist under his brother's tutelage. Later on, Peale inserted his sister Margaret Jane who, after being widowed, came to live with his family. Peale did not complete this work until 1808 when only two of the subjects were still alive. One can imagine with what nostalgia he undertook lovingly to finish the work that had been laid aside for so many years because of other demands upon his time. When John Adams saw the painting on a visit to Peale's studio in 1776, he was impressed with its atmosphere. "There was a pleasant, a happy cheerfulness in their countenances, and a familiarity in their air towards each other."[3]

Peale's reputation as an artist soon brought him many commissions in Maryland and Virginia. In 1772, he went to Mount Vernon to paint George Washington's portrait. It was the first time Washington sat for a painter and it became one of Peale's best known paintings. The three-quarter length portrait showed Washington as a colonel in the Virginia militia. Peale also did a miniature of Martha Washington set in a gold frame in a pendant for Washington to wear around his neck. It is said that he wore it until his last days. In 1776, Peale did another three-quarter length portrait of Washington in Continental uniform. This was painted for George Hancock in Philadelphia. Next he did a miniature on ivory of Washington in 1777. This was followed by a portrait bust, which the artist is said to have begun at Valley Forge.

In 1779, the Supreme Executive Council of Pennsylvania commissioned a Continental portrait of Washington placed before a background of Nassau Hall at Princeton. Washington's left hand is placed on a cannon. It has been said that this painting represents the Washington of the Revolution "more truthfully than do later portraits by others, even by so great a master as Stuart, who never saw Washington until four years before his death"[4] and so painted a man whose face was much changed by the cares he had borne. In 1787, Peale did another bust portrait of Washington during the Constitutional Convention at Philadelphia. Finally, in 1795, he painted a bust of him as President.

Peale moved to Philadelphia in December 1775 just when the city was actively preparing for war, the shipyards humming with activity and the militia being organized. Peale painted flags for several volunteer companies and other public designs for displays such as celebratory arches. He even experimented with gun powder manufacturing and telescopic sights for rifles. In December 1776 a diary entry of his reads: "Entered as a common soldier in Captain Peter's company of militia. Went on guard that night."[5] Within a couple of months he was made lieutenant. After being promoted captain in June 1777, he served with General Washington's army at both Trenton and Princeton. He was a resourceful and ingenious officer who foraged for food for his men and cooked them their meals; seeing the tattered state of many of his men's shoes, he made them fur-lined moccasins. At Valley Forge he painted miniatures on ivory of forty officers to send home to their families. He also painted Washington, Lafayette, Nathaniel Greene, and many other leaders using bed ticking in place of canvas.

As soon as the British evacuated Philadelphia he returned and plunged into the city's political life. This had an unexpected consequence: his wealthy Tory patrons were offended and gave him no more business. But he persevered in his patriotic activities and in 1778 was elected to the Assembly where he became either chairman or member of thirty-two legislative committees. At the end of his term, however, he decided not to seek reelection, writing in his autobiography that he felt he had been in a "dangerous and troublesome Political Sea" and that "the difference of opinion here made me enemies of those whom before I had considered my friends."[6] Since most of his former Tory friends were members of the Church of England which opposed the war, he withdrew from it and joined the Presbyterian Church whose members mainly supported the War of Independence. His son Rembrandt was christened in the Presbyterian Church on August 26, 1779.

In the post-war years, he had to think of ways to support his large family at a time when economic conditions did not favor portrait painting. He and his wife Rachel had six children, most named for famous painters. There was Raphaelle (1774–1825) ; Angelica Kauffmann (1775–1853); Rembrandt (1778–1860); Titian Ramsay (1780-1798); Rubens (1784–1865); and Sophonisba Angusciola (1786–1859). He was also bringing up the three children of his deceased sister Elizabeth Polk. Peale took great pains to teach his children all he could about painting with the thought that they would then be prepared to follow some branch of the arts and become useful members of society.

Ever ingenious and resourceful, he experimented with the creation of a public entertainment that consisted of a series of scenes portraying the naval battle between the Bon Homme and the Serapis. He called these "moving pictures" because they were mechanically moved and operated by Peale backstage with suitable sound effects. He tried his hand at making mezzotints of portraits of figures from history to sell to the public. He also made for exhibition transparencies which were oil paintings on paper lit from behind by many candles. From time to time he traveled to Maryland's Eastern Shore and to Baltimore to paint portraits. Perhaps most important, he proceeded to paint life-size portraits of the revolutionary heroes he had portrayed in small pictures done in the field of war. He exhibited these life-size paintings in what was the first public picture gallery in the country.

In 1786 he decided to expand his picture gallery into a museum of natural history. His interest in natural history was aroused by some recently discovered bones of a mastodon of which he was asked to make drawings. This led to his becoming keenly interested in the natural world around him. Soon he was collecting examples of birds and animals. He taught himself taxidermy and used his experience as a sculptor to model the bodies into natural looking positions. Then he placed them in natural looking settings. He was the first to do this. He searched the countryside for plants, fossils, and minerals.

In 1790, Peale suffered the loss of his wife, Rachel, and evidently was soon overcome by the needs of his large brood of children and his own loneliness, for he married Elizabeth De Peyster (1765–1804) of New York City in 1791 and stopped traveling in order to concentrate his attention on his Philadelphia Museum. He decided it should be a public rather than private institution and so it was governed by a Society of Visitors. In 1794, it was moved to the hall of the American Philosophical Society. Then, in 1802, the Pennsylvania Assembly granted the use of the second floor of Independence Hall for the use of the museum. Eventually, it became the Philadelphia Museum and was directed by a board of trustees. By then it was one of the notable museums of the time.

As was typical of Peale, the museum was a family affair. "The family lived in the museum building —Philosophical Hall . . . the children were initiated into the art of taxidermy and museum management; his son—Benjamin Franklin—was born and named there, and the museum became not only 'a world in miniature' for the public, but Peale's private world as well."[7] One of the museum's most popular exhibits was the skeleton of a mastodon that he had assembled after helping excavate it in Ulster County, New York, in 1801.

Another interest Peale had was to start an Academy to show the work of Philadelphia artists. So, in 1795, he helped to found the Columbianum, or American Academy of Fine Arts, in Philadelphia, an organization to provide training for young artists as well as to encourage patronage of the arts. The whole family and others displayed their work in what they hoped would be the first of many exhibitions. The venture only lasted a year, however, because of wrangling among its various members. It did, however, lead to his being one of the Founders of the Pennsylvania Academy of Fine Arts in 1805.

In 1803, Peale's son Rembrandt returned from studying with Benjamin West in London. He brought back with him new techniques which he shared with his father. Peale had been so busy with his museum and naturalist studies, that he had not painted for six years. Now, his interest in painting revived and he was not too proud to take daily lessons from his son. At age seventy, he made a major change in style as the result of another trip abroad of Rembrandt's, this time to Paris. Peale began to use the new techniques of pupils of Jacques Louis David. To some critics, the paintings he did in his later years were his best. He was eighty when he began one of his largest paintings, *Christ Healing the Sick at the Pool of Bethesda*, on a canvas eight feet wide and more than six feet high. It was adapted from a print by Christian Wilhelm Ernst Dietrich, and Peale finished it in three months, despite falling off a scaffold and breaking some ribs.

Peale's second wife, Elizabeth, died in 1804. She had borne him six children of which two, Benjamin Franklin and Titian Ramsay (who was given the name of his deceased half-brother), became naturalists. In 1805, Peale married Hannah Moore, a Quaker lady. With her he moved to Belfield, a farm near Philadelphia and retired from active management of the Philadelphia Museum. Here he began to take a great interest in agriculture, but an idea for a new kind of museum would not go away. Before long he designed a lovely "pleasure garden" which attracted many visitors from Philadelphia and other areas. So passed ten tranquil years with Hannah. When she died in 1821, he returned to Philadelphia, took up his work at the museum, and once more returned to his first love, painting.

Peale was eighty-six years old when he died, a distinguished artist and naturalist. Somehow he also had found time in his busy life for a few inventions: an improved kitchen chimney; a stove that consumed its own smoke; a steam bath; and an improved polygraph for copying documents. He also was an author who wrote *An Essay on Building Wooden Bridges* (1797); *A Discourse Introductory to a Course of Lectures on the Science of Nature* (1800); *Introduction to a Course of Lectures on Natural History* (1800) given at the University of Pennsylvania; *An Epistle to a Friend on the Means of Preserving Health* (1803); *An Essay to Promote Domestic Happiness* (1812); and an *Address to the Corporation and Citizens of Philadelphia* (1816). He left behind a prosperous family of artists and naturalists, all carefully trained by a loving father. Throughout his long life his family was always uppermost in his mind, and his own successes never blinded him to their needs. He set out to prepare them "to be industrious and careful," so that they would become "useful members of the community." In this, perhaps his dearest ambition, he was also eminently successful.

Paintings: *George Washington as Colonel of the Virginia Regiment*, Frontispiece; *Martha Washington*, p. 9; *George Washington* and *Martha Washington*, miniatures, p. 317.

---

1 Lillian B. Miller, ed., The *Peale Family: Creation of a Legacy*, 1770–1870 (New York: Abbeville Press in Association with the Trust for Museum Exhibitions, The National Portrait Gallery, and the Smithsonian Institution, 1996), p. 18.

2 Charles Coleman Sellers, *Charles Willson Peale* (Charles Scribners' Sons, New York, 1969), p. 43.

3 *Familiar Letters of John Adams and his Wife, Abigail Adams during the Revolution*, New York, 1876, p. 215.

4 *Dictionary of American Biography*, (Charles Scribners' Sons, 1964), Vol. X, p. 347.

5 *James Thomas Flexner, America's Old Masters* (New York: Dover Publications, Inc.), 1967, p. 194.

6 *Sellers*, p. 171.

7 Lillian B. Miller, "Biography of A Family" in *The Peale Family*, p. 25.

Rembrandt Peale
1778–1860

The son of a famous American artist, Charles Willson Peale, and Rachel Brewer Peale, he was born on February 22, 1778, in Bucks County, Pennsylvania. It was here that his father—then a captain of a volunteer company at Valley Forge—found a farm house to shelter his wife and children, who had fled from the British forces then occupying Philadelphia. As soon as the British evacuated the city, the family returned to Philadelphia.

Rembrandt early showed great talent for drawing and painting. At the age of thirteen he did an excellent self-portrait in oils which he proudly signed "Rembrandt Peale, 1791/artist." As the son of a hardworking artist father, Rembrandt Peale also applied himself diligently to his art and was quick to grasp new ideas. He studied with his father, painstakingly copying some of his paintings, and also studied prints and paintings in various art collections in Philadelphia.

In 1795, he contributed no less than five portraits and a city-scape to an exhibition at the Columbianum, a fine arts academy that his father had helped found in Philadelphia that year. It was to be a very important year for Rembrandt, because at last he would meet George Washington, the man whose birthday he shared and whom he idolized for his character and leadership during the War of Independence. Rembrandt not only met Washington, he also was allowed to paint him from life, as his father had done before him and was now to do for the last time. An amusing account of the event relates how the seventeen-year-old Rembrandt shared this honor, not only with his father, but with his brother, Raphaelle Peale (1774–1825) and his uncle, James Peale (1749–1831), a fine painter in his own right.

"Rembrandt worked in front, slightly to the sitter's left, his father taking a three-quarters view on Wash-ing-ton's left and Rembrandt's right hand. James on the other side, began a three-quarters view on ivory, and beyond him, on Washington's right, Raphaelle began a profile on paper. Gilbert Stuart (1755–1828), for whom the President had just previously sat, was told by Mrs. Washington of the scene. He replied by warning her earnestly to take good care of her husband, for he stood in danger of being 'Pealed all around.'"[1]

Rembrandt's portrait of the President was "a strong unidealized likeness." He took his painting of Washington with him to Charleston, S.C. Here he made ten copies of it and also painted a portrait of Dr. David Ramsay, the physician and historian, for the elder Peale's art gallery. He also did portraits of the Generals Gadsden and Sumter. That year and in 1796, Rembrandt and his brother, Raphaelle, displayed their *Portraits of Patriots* in Charleston, their paintings, copies of some of their father's paintings, and natural history exhibits that lasted for about two years. After that, Rembrandt worked for awhile in New York City on portrait commissions, returning to Philadelphia in June 1798 to marry Eleanor May Short, by whom he had seven daughters and two sons. Since he was barely twenty when he married, and was still being partially supported by his father, he was anxious to stand on his own feet financially. Therefore, he traveled to Baltimore and along the Eastern Shore of Maryland seeking portrait commissions. At this time "his paintings grew in technical and expressive refinement, and under the influence of Gilbert Stuart he developed a mastery of three-dimensional effects and a dramatic use of light that became a hallmark of his style."[2]

In 1802, Rembrandt made his first trip across the Atlantic in company with his wife and two children in order to help his brother Rubens set up an exhibition of the mastodon that he and his father excavated in Ulster County, New York. He wrote a pamphlet to accompany the exhibit, entitled *An Historical Disquisition on the Mammoth*, or *Great American Incognitum*. While in London he had the priceless opportunity to see great art and to study with Benjamin West. Here he met such painters as Sir Thomas Lawrence (1769–1830) and fellow American Washington Allston (1779–1843). He also exhibited several paintings at the Royal Academy in 1803 and painted portraits of the poet Robert Bloomfield and Sir Joseph Banks, president of the Royal Society, for his father's art gallery.

Returning to America in 1803, Rembrandt opened a studio in Philadelphia. He was now a painter of some renown and was so sought after to do portraits of prominent people that he could hardly keep up with the demands on his time. In 1805, he became one of the founders of the Pennsylvania Academy of the Fine Arts. Despite his success, he was eager for more artistic knowledge and sailed for France in June 1808. At the Louvre he closely studied certain works which struck him with their style and excellence, in particular the works of Rubens, Raphael, Titian, Van Dyck, Correggio, and Veronese. He "selected their beauties, noticed their defects, methodized their systems and formed a union of their various excellences."[3] He also studied and adopted some aspects of the French style of painting which emphasized modeling and outline. He admired the work of such French artists of his own time as Jacques-Louis David, Francois Gerard, and Robert Lefevre. On his return to Philadelphia with seven portraits he had done of prominent people, his father was so pleased that he sent him back to Paris in 1809 to do fifty portraits of "the most eminent men." Accompanied by his wife and children, Rembrandt left for Paris in the autumn of 1809 and remained there for a year.

Always interested in the new techniques, he experimented with encaustic which mixes heated wax with the paint to fix the colors. The result is color of an enamel-like brilliance. It has been noted that "intensification of color, greater linear definition, and a remarkable luminosity in the depiction of flesh were the stylistic legacy of his French studies."[4] His work during this time and for the following decade is considered the peak of his artistic achievement. His stay in France also fired his interest in historical painting in the "grand manner."

After returning to Philadelphia in November 1810, his father urged him to confine his efforts to portrait painting and exhibiting his works in Philadelphia. He wanted to establish a museum and art gallery of his own, however, and chose Baltimore as the site. Unlike his father's museum in Philadelphia, his had a separate art gallery. Exhibits of such American artists as John Vanderlyn (1775–1852), Thomas Sully (1783–1872), and others were part of changing displays. In 1815, an organ was installed, and the following year the museum was lit by gaslight.

Rembrandt painted portraits and many large-scale historical paintings, such as his *Ascent of Elijah*, for exhibition in his gallery. He also did an historical painting twenty-four feet long and thirteen feet high, with 23 full-sized figures, called *The Court of Death* (1820). It was an allegory taken from a poem by Beilby Porteus, an English bishop. This painting was the largest done in America at that time. It was a mural painting without a wall, because it was to be taken on tour. It was seen by 32,000 people over a period of its thirteen-month tour of the principal cities on the East Coast and earned the artist more than $9,000. In New York City, many Pastors recommended it to their congregations, and the City Corporation went as a body to view it. Soon other artists were also painting large-scale canvases depicting moral or Biblical themes.

In 1822, he sold his museum to his brother, Rubens, and moved to New York City. Rubens managed it until 1830 when the city bought it. Now restored, it is The Peale Museum once again, making it the oldest museum building in the United States.

He worked in New York in 1822–23, then returned to Philadelphia and reopened his studio. Here he set to work to create what he hoped would be the "standard likeness" of George Washington revealing his virtue. In 1824, after sixteen attempts, he exhibited what he believed was this likeness. He called it *Patriae Pater*, and it was a composite of his and his father's 1795 portraits. Widely exhibited and promoted, it was bought for the United States Capitol in 1832. He did many variations on this work over the next thirty years. Because he made some 76 copies of this work, it is his best-known painting. Another well-known work, also done in 1824, was his large and complex *Washington at Yorktown*, an equestrian painting showing Washington giving a gesture of command.

In 1825, Rembrandt Peale succeeded John Trumbull (1756-1843) as President of the American Academy of Fine Arts. In 1826, he became a founding member of the National Academy of Design in New York City. He then moved to Boston where he worked on perfecting his lithographic skills. Over the next thirty years he produced many fine prints. In 1827, his *Patriae Pater* won the Franklin Institute's award for the best American lithograph. Late in 1828, he and his son Angelo left for Italy because he felt that he should not become an old man and die without seeing that land. He returned to America in 1830, having stopped off at Paris and London. He brought with him copies he had made of the old masters which he wanted to use to educate Americans in the great art of Europe. Sadly, his displays of his Italian paintings were unsuccessful, but his *Notes on Italy* (1831) became popular.

In the 1830s Peale did considerable work as a writer. His *Graphics: A Manual of Drawing and Writing for the Use of Schools and Families* (1834) was highly successful, going through four editions and nineteen printings between 1834 and 1866. Although his work as an artist, which entailed much traveling, left him little time for teaching, he did tutor his niece Mary Jane Peale and his cousin Sarah Miriam Peale in the art of painting. His wife died in April 1836, and in 1840 he married Harriet Cany who was also an artist.

In his late years he continued painting in Philadelphia and made many copies of his *Patriae Pater* in reduced size to fulfill what he called his "Vocation to multiply the Countenance of Washington." In the late 1850s he delivered a lecture "Washington and His Portraits" in cities from Massachusetts to Virginia, promoting these reproductions. He shared with his audience his memories of Washington and displayed a variety of portraits of the great man. According to the press of the time, he spoke with "vigor and enthusiasm" and he was described as "a living link between the past and present." His "Reminiscences" appeared in the periodical *The Crayon* (1855–1856). In 1860, Rembrandt Peale, died, one of the most respected and admired artists of his time.

Painting: *George Washington at Patriae Pater*, 1829, p. 152.

---

[1] See John Grossman's biography of Rembrandt Peale in Verna M. Hall, Compiler, *The Christian History of the American Revolution: Consider and Ponder*, (San Francisco: Foundation for American Christian Education, 1975), p. 584.

[2] *American National Biography* (New York: Oxford University Press, 1999), Vol. 17, p. 200.

[3] *Ibid.*

[4] *Ibid.*

Allan Ramsay
1713–1784

This Scottish-born artist became one of the foremost portrait painters of his day. Born in Edinburgh, he studied drawing at the Academy of St. Luke before moving to London in 1733 where he studied art at the St. Martin's Lane Academy. From 1736 to 1738 he studied painting in Italy. His portraits of *Samuel Torriano* and *Francis, second Duke of Buccleuch*, both done at this time, already show his mastery of the "grand style" in which the sitters were posed in a classical manner.

By 1739 Ramsay was once again in London. Here he remained throughout the remainder of his career except for frequent visits to Scotland. He soon became the most popular painter among the English aristocracy. His 1746 full-length painting of *Dr. Mead,* which he gave to the Founding Hospital, is an excellent example of the classic style he was pursuing, as is one he did in 1748 of *Norman, 22nd Chief of Macleod*, which reminds the viewer of the Apollo Belvedere.

Another aspect of Ramsay's painting at this time are several he did of women, such as *Jean Nisbet* (1748). The style is engaging by its simplicity and naturalness. Early in the 1750s, Ramsay began to take an interest in using landscape settings for his portraits as in *William, 17th Earl of Sutherland* (1753). He also began to show a flair for the portrayal of character as in his early portrait of *David Hume*. When Joshua Reynolds (1723–1792) returned to England from Italy in 1753, Ramsay had his first real rival. He must have felt so sure of his own popularity, however, that he left for Rome in 1754 where he studied drawing at the French Academy and did studies of the Comenichino frescoes at the Church of San Luigi dei Francesi. He also studied the work of the Italian masters while he was in Rome, making note of their particular styles and their finesse as artists, which he could then embody in his own work. Ramsay's best portrait from this period, considered by some as his masterpiece, is that of his second wife, Margaret Lindsay, whom he married in 1752. (His first wife Anne, died in 1743.) This picture has all the exquisite delicacy of a French portrait and is infused with the artist's affection for his subject.

Ramsay's success as a portrait painter continued after his return to London. Between 1754 and 1766, he painted his finest full-length portraits, most of which were commissioned by the Earl of Bute. A most important commission from the Earl was to do the painting now known as *George III as Prince of Wales*, (1757). This portrait pleased the prince so much that when he became king in 1760, he appointed Ramsay as Painter-in-Ordinary, a post many had thought would go to Joshua Reynolds. Thereafter, George III was loyal to his favorite painter and was unwilling to sit for any other. He brushed aside Lord Eglinton's plea to let Reynolds paint him with the remark, "Mr. Ramsay is my painter, my Lord." Ramsay painted the King and Queen in their coronation robes. Other fine paintings of this period include *John Stuart, 3d Earl of Bute* and *Lady Mary Coke.*

In 1766, Ramsay did a portrait of *Jean-Jacques Rousseau* and a second one of *Hume.* Both are shrewd portrayals of character. Strangely enough, Ramsay's interest in painting waned at this time and he did not submit any of his portraits to the Royal Academy when it was established in 1768. He turned rather to literary pursuits and wrote essays on a variety of subjects and several books, such as *The Constitution of England* (1766) which is his best-known work. By the time he died he was better known as an author than a painter. Yet he had painted some 1,000 outstanding portraits, among which most critics consider the following as the best: *George III* (see p. 114), *Queen Charlotte, Lord Chesterfield, Dr. Mead, David Hume,* and, of course, the *Portrait of the Artist's Wife*, perhaps the finest of them all.

Edward Savage
1761–1817

Edward Savage, an artist known both for portrait and landscape painting, was born in Princeton, Massachusetts, the second child of Seth and Lydia Craige Savage. He was a grandson of Edward Savage, of a Huguenot family living in Ireland, who emigrated to Massachusetts in 1696. Young Edward learned the goldsmith's trade and then became a painter and engraver. By 1789 he had become a painter of sufficient stature to be commissioned to do a portrait of George Washington for Harvard College. This is his earliest recorded work. George Washington noted in a diary entry for December 21, 1789: "Sat from ten to one o'clock for a Mr. Savage, to draw my Portrait for the University of Cambridge, in the State of Massachusetts." Savage delivered the portrait to Harvard around August

1790. About this time, while on a visit to New York, Savage also painted another portrait of Washington for John Adams.

Although a successful artist, he evidently felt the need for more training. So, like so many other American artists of the period, he headed for London, in 1791, to study with the distinguished American artist, Benjamin West. It has been said that around such leaders as West there "grew up a school of neoclassic portraiture that is one of the solid and distinctive achievements of American painting."[1] Savage was to be of this school. After three years of study under West, he went to Italy and studied there for awhile before returning to America.

Upon his return to America, he married Sara Seaver and moved to Philadelphia where his brother John was a successful merchant. In 1795, he exhibited there a large panorama of London and Westminster which he had painted while in London. In 1796 he executed his most famous painting, a life-size group portrait of *The Washington Family*, done from life sketches he had made in 1789. This painting is now in the National Gallery of Art in Washington, D.C. He also did portraits of George and Martha Washington, now in the Boston Museum of Fine Arts, and oil portraits of Gen. Anthony Wayne, Dr. Benjamin Rush, and Thomas Jefferson.

About 1801, he left Philadelphia to join with Daniel Bowen in opening the New York Museum which exhibited works of art and curiosities. The museum's contents were later moved to the Columbian Museum in Boston. This museum, however, was damaged by fire in 1803, re-erected, but burned again in 1807. Finally, it was absorbed by the New England Museum. By 1805, Savage seems to have returned to Princeton, Massachusetts, for it was here that his sixth child was born on August 22, and two more children thereafter. Here Savage was to spend the rest of his life. He became greatly interested in mechanics and invention and, in 1809, became a partner in the Poignaud and Plant Cotton Factory in the nearby town of Lancaster.

Two portraits of Savage exist, a full-face self-portrait and an effective profile by C. B. J. de Saint-Mémin. The self-portrait may be seen in the Worcester Art Museum, which also has the best-preserved examples of his engravings. The Massachusetts Historical Society has a large collection of the artist's miniature portraits, engravings and various family souvenirs. Another painting of George Washington is in The Chicago Art Institute. It is recorded as having been done in 1793. If so, Savage painted this picture while still living in England.

Painting: *The Washington Family*, p. 220.

[1] E. P. Richardson, *Painting in America*, (New York: Thomas Y. Crowell, 1956), p. 120.

Frank E. Schoonover
1877–1972

This painter and illustrator was born in Oxford, New Jersey on August 19, 1877. He studied art at the Drexel Institute, Philadelphia, under Howard Pyle. As an illustrator, his specialty was painting American Indians and Canadian Trappers. He illustrated and wrote a number of books between 1912–18 and illustrated children's classics between 1920–30. He was also a designer of stained glass windows. From 1937 he was primarily a landscape artist. His work is represented in this volume by one of his illustrations from the book *George Washington* by Lucy Foster Madison.

Painting: *George Washington, The Surveyor*, p. 29.

J. B. Stearns
1810–1885

Junius Brutus Stearns, painter of American historical subjects was born on July 2, 1810 in Arlington, Vermont. He was a pupil at the National Academy of Design where he became an Associate in 1848 and an Academician the following year. His five paintings depicting George Washington as citizen, farmer, soldier, statesman, and Christian are considered his finest works. His painting *Millennium* is in the New York Academy of Design and several of his portraits are in the New York City Hall. He died in Brooklyn, N.Y. on September 17, 1885.

Painting: *The Wedding of George Washington and Martha Custis*, p. 92.

Gilbert Stuart
1755–1828

Gilbert Stuart is preeminent in the history of American portraiture, and his work rivals that of the great English portrait painters of his time. He painted one thousand portraits during his long career, but is most remembered today for his portraits of George Washington. His beginnings, however, gave little indication of the remarkable future that lay before him. His father, also named Gilbert Stuart, was a millwright from Perth Scotland who emigrated to Rhode Island. He married Elizabeth Anthony, daughter of a wealthy land owner in Middleton, and became a manufacturer of snuff.

Gilbert was born on December 3, 1755 in North Kingstown, Kings (later Washington) County, in the living quarters over the mill his father and two business partners built to produce snuff. When the business failed in 1761, his father sold his share of the mill to his partners. The family moved to Newport where they lived in what Gilbert later recalled as "a hovel on Bannister's Wharf." Here he spent his early years, a ragged urchin roaming the Newport docks. He was a charity scholar at a school founded by Nathaniel Kay, collector of customs during the reign of Queen Anne. In 1734, Kay bequeathed a fund to Trinity Church "to teach ten poor boys their grammar and the mathematics gratis."[1] Stuart early showed a talent for drawing. He started to copy pictures when he was about thirteen; when scarcely older, he began drawing portraits in black lead.

When Cosmo Alexander, a Scottish itinerant painter, set up a studio in Newport, the fourteen-year-old Gilbert begged to be taken on as a student. He was so eager to learn and so willing to make himself useful in Alexander's studio that the painter consented to make him his apprentice. Stuart went with his teacher on his journeys throughout the colonies in search of commissions and, finally, to Edinburgh, Scotland. There, in 1772, his master died leaving the sixteen-year-old boy alone and almost penniless. He tried bravely to support himself by painting, but was unable to eke out more than a precarious living. In 1773 or 1774, he accepted defeat and decided to go home. Since he had no money for the voyage, he worked out his passage as a seaman on a vessel bound for Nova Scotia.

When he returned to America, Stuart had learned a good deal about painting portraits, enough to please many Newport merchants. Several of these men were so impressed with his talent that they paid for his passage back to England in June 1775. Arriving in London in November, Stuart settled in cheap lodgings and tried to find clients. He received so little money for the few commissions he succeeded in obtaining that once again he soon found himself in dire financial straits. He knew that Benjamin West (1738–1820) was the acknowledged leader of historical painting in England and that he had a studio in London. Still he had been too proud to ask his fellow American for help. Desperation, however, finally caused him to send a note to West detailing his plight.

"Destitute of the means of acquiring knowledge, my hopes from home blasted, and incapable of returning thither, pitching headlong into misery, I have only this hope—I pray that it may not be too great—to live and learn without being a burden. Should Mr. West in his abundant kindness think of aught for me, I shall esteem it an obligation which shall bind me forever with gratitude."[2]

When West received this *cri de coeur*, he responded at once. Stuart was accepted as his student, moved to an address close to West's studio and, around 1777, moved into West's own household. He remained with him for almost five years as chief apprentice. These were happy and productive years that saw the young painter become thoroughly grounded in his art. Although Stuart admired his master, he had little interest in West's chosen field of historical painting.

From the beginning, Stuart seemed destined to be a portrait painter. He exhibited portraits at the Royal Academy exhibitions in 1777, 1779, and 1781. He became noted not only for the technical merits of his portraits but for his remarkable likenesses. Although his portraits were greatly admired, some critics said that Stuart could not paint a body "below the fifth button." Aware of this charge, Stuart produced *The Skater*, a full-length painting of his friend, William Grant, skating in St. James's Park with Westminster Abbey in the background. It is a fine portrait of a skater who appears to be executing a figure eight. This painting made Stuart's name in London and led him to set up his own studio. He received many commissions from the London elite. Soon, his work rivaled in popularity that of the great English portrait painters—Reynolds, Romney, and Gainsborough. A London print seller also commissioned him to do fifteen portraits of leading painters and engravers of the time for sale to the public.

All in all, Stuart was riding on a tide of success. Now financially affluent, he married Charlotte Coates, a young girl of eighteen, the daughter of a physician from Berkshire. Dr. Coates opposed the marriage, but it turned out to be a happy one. Two of the couple's twelve children, (Charles Gilbert and Jane, his youngest daughter) inherited some of their father's artistic talent. Unfortunately, Stuart never learned how to manage money. He spent on a grand scale at his fashionable London house. Employing a French chef to give his guests elegant meals, he also hired professional musicians to entertain them. Sometimes he would join the musicians, for he was an excellent keyboard artist. In his early days in London he had been a substitute organist for a church in Foster Lane (probably Saint Vedast's). Stuart's daughter Jane tried to excuse her father's prodigality by asserting that his position as a fashionable London artist required the purchase of expensive clothes and costly elegant dinners and entertainments for his fashionable clientele. In any event, he seems to have been entirely heedless of his expenses until his debts were too great to meet.

In 1787, he left England without warning and sailed for Ireland leaving his debts behind him. Daughter Jane insisted, though, that he went to Dublin at the Duke of Rutland's request to paint his portrait as Lord Lieutenant of Ireland. When Stuart arrived in Dublin, however, it was to find that his new patron had died and his funeral was to be held that day. Nothing daunted by this setback, Stuart set out to conquer Dublin, which he did. In a very short time, he became the city's most successful portrait painter. He painted numerous portraits of the most noted figures in Dublin's public life. Once again, however, his love of social life and his desire to please the city's elegant society led him to spend beyond his means. Jane Stuart wrote that in later years it gave her mother much pain to remember her husband's reckless extravagances during those Dublin years.

In 1792 or 1793, Stuart left for New York, probably because of his debts. He was so low on funds that he paid his way over by painting a portrait of the ship owner. He said that when he got back to America he hoped to earn enough to pay his English and Irish creditors by painting portraits of George Washington. He leased a studio in New York City. Soon many prominent New Yorkers came to him to have their portraits done. By the end of 1794, he moved to Philadelphia where Congress then met, and opened a studio at the southwest corner of Fifth and Chestnut Streets. Philadelphia was then the largest city in the United States. Stuart made it his business to meet all the leaders in politics and fashionable society.

Here he realized his dream of painting George Washington who sat for two portraits. The first one, painted in 1795 and known as the *Vaughn Type*, shows Washington from the right side of his face. Thirty-two subscribers ordered copies of this work. In 1796, Washington began sitting for the second portrait known as the *Lansdowne Type*. A full-length portrait, it shows Washington standing with his right arm extended, as if addressing an audience.

Because Stuart's paintings attracted so many visitors to his studio, he was often delayed in completing his commissions, so he moved to Germantown. Here he set up his studio in a barn belonging to the Wister Mansion. In the autumn of 1796, at Mrs. Washington's request, the president sat for a third portrait, a bust showing the left side of his face. This is known as the *Athanæm Head* and it is on every dollar bill. The original is now in the Boston Museum of Fine Arts. Of the qualities he discerned in Washington, Stuart wrote: "There were features in his face totally different from what I had observed in any other human being. The sockets of the eyes, for instance, were larger than what I ever met with before, and the upper part of the nose broader. All his features were indicative of the strongest passions; yet like Socrates his judgement and self-command made him appear a man of different cast in the eyes of the world."[3]

In 1803, Stuart opened a studio in Washington D.C. Here he painted Jefferson, Madison, Monroe and other political leaders. In 1805, he moved again, this time to Boston where he remained until his death in 1828. As in other cities he was very successful, but in the fall of 1825 his health began to fail. His left arm was partly paralyzed, but he continued trying to paint. In the spring of 1828 he came down with gout and died on July 9.

Aside from his ability to produce remarkable likenesses, Stuart's work had several distinguishing characteristics. Among them was his "mastery of the use of what may be called transparent color which gave his portraits their lifelike quality and luminous effect, and it is in this quality that they stand supreme among American paintings."[4] Another characteristic was his unique vision. His old master, Benjamin West, paid tribute to his former pupil's ability to see below the surface when he said: "It is of no use to steal Stuart's colors; if you want to paint as he does you must steal his eyes."[5] Stuart himself said: "I wish to find out what nature is for myself and see her with my own eyes." Stuart certainly wanted to see his subjects with his own eyes and to delve below the surface to their innermost character.

Stuart's students—among them John Neagle, Thomas Sully, John Vanderlyn, and Washington Allston—all gained from their studies with Stuart, although it was difficult for him to communicate his own distinctive technique of portrait painting. "Stuart proceeded on the principle that it is simplest to explore first the general nature of a phenomenon, and only afterwards inquire into its particular characteristics. He would begin with a vague blob of a head seen in a dim, dark mirror. The image always had precisely the color of the sitter's flesh, and usually all the other colors in the picture would be keyed to that."[6] Chatting all the while with his sitter, he would gradually round out the blob until the features took form. "Then a few bold highlights and shadows, laid on smartly with no fuss, brought the subject to actuality, as if the sitter suddenly popped up in the cloudy cube of space that Stuart conceived his canvases to be. A swift final glaze added the blush of life."[7]

Paintings: *George Washington*, p. 9; *George Washington*, 1796, p. 325.

---

1 *Dictionary of American Biography* (New York: Charles Scribners' Sons, 1964), Vol. IX, p. 164.

2 Alexander Eliot, *Three Hundred Years of American Painting* (New York: Time, Inc., 1957), p. 34.

3 *Ibid.*, p. 39.

4 *Dictionary of American Biography*, Vol. IX, p. 168.

5 *Ibid.*

6 *Three Hundred Years of American Painting*, p. 38.

7 *Ibid.*

John Trumbull
1756–1843

John Trumbull is rightly known as "the Painter of the Revolution," but he was also a soldier and aide-de-camp to General Washington who is featured in two of his finest historical paintings, *The Battle of Trenton* and *The Resignation of General Washington*. Trumbull's career is encapsulated in the words on a memorial tablet in the Yale Gallery of Fine Arts: "Patriot and Artist, Friend and Aid of Washington. . . . To his Country he gave his SWORD and his PENCIL." Trumbull was born on June 6, 1756, in Lebanon, New London County, Connecticut, the youngest of six children. His father was Jonathan Trumbull, the governor of Connecticut who became famous during the War of Independence. His mother was Faith Robinson Trumbull, a descendent of the Pilgrim's pastor, Rev. John Robinson.

Soon after his birth John developed convulsions caused by overlapping bones in his cranium, but the physicians were able to restore the natural form of his head by the time he was three. When he was about five years old, he severely injured his left eye in a fall down a flight of stairs causing a permanent loss of vision in that eye. This did not deter him from being enrolled in a prestigious local school run by Nathan Tisdale. Here he proved a precocious child who learned to read Greek at age six. He also developed a lively interest in drawing.

When he finished his studies with Tisdale at age fifteen, he begged his father to send him to study painting under John Singleton Copley (1738–1815), but his father, by then governor of Connecticut, had other plans for him. He wanted to send his son to Harvard to prepare for a career as a minister or a lawyer. Art was of no interest to the elder Trumbull and he believed it would be of no use to his son. In 1772, John set off for Harvard with a heavy heart. On his way to Cambridge he decided to stop in Boston to visit Copley. He was amazed by the beauty of his paintings and later wrote that they "riveted, absorbed my attention, and renewed all my desire to enter upon such a pursuit."[1] Instead, he sadly finished his journey to Cambridge, passed his examination, and was admitted to the junior class at Harvard. Here he taught himself all he could about the fine arts by studying the art works that hung on the college walls and searching the library for books on the arts. He found a study on perspective which he copied. He also copied several engravings and learned French through his own study, supplemented by frequent visits to a French family living in Cambridge. Soon he was fluent in the language which was to be important to him in the future. He graduated from Harvard in July 1773, the youngest boy in his class.

At home in Lebanon, he taught school that winter, continued his study of painting, and copied engravings. On December 16, 1773, came the Boston Tea Party and, like his father, John became deeply committed to the cause of the colonists in their quarrel with the Mother Country. "I sought for military information," he wrote in his *Reminiscences*, "acquired what knowledge I could, soon formed a small company from among the young men of the school and the village, taught them, or more properly we taught each other, to use the musket and to march, and military exercises and studies became the favorite occupation of the day."[2]

In 1775, shortly after the Battle of Lexington, Trumbull became an adjutant of the First Regiment of Connecticut stationed in Roxbury under the command of General Joseph Spencer. From Roxbury, he witnessed the Battle of Bunker Hill through his field glasses. He was brought to General Washington's attention through the accurate drawings he had made of the British position at Boston Neck. This led to his appointment as second aide-de-camp to the General. He saw action at Dorchester Heights the following March and saw the British evacuate Boston before the army moved on to New York.

In June of 1776, he was given the rank of colonel by General Gates, now commander of the Army in the Northern Department, and was appointed adjutant to the regiment bound for Fort Ticonderoga. His most significant contribution to this campaign was his plan for strengthening the Fort which he developed with the engineer Thaddeus Kosciusko. He served at Crown Point and Ticonderoga and, after the British retreated from Ticonderoga, he accompanied General Gates to Newtown, Pennsylvania, to join General Washington.

In all this time he had been without a commission, while other junior officers received their commissions thus making them equal in rank with him, although he was doing the work of a higher ranking officer. When his long-awaited commission finally arrived, he discovered it was dated from September 12, 1776 instead of June 28 when Gates had appointed him adjutant. When his efforts to get the matter corrected proved of no avail, the impetuous twenty-one-year-old abruptly resigned on February 22, 1777.

At home in Lebanon he returned to his art studies painting several scenes from Biblical and ancient history, as well as portraits of himself, and friends and relations. The family atmosphere did not prove conducive to his art studies, however, for his father still viewed a career as an artist unsuitable for his son. So Trumbull moved to Boston and hired a studio which had been the painting room of the artist, John Smibert. Here he was elated to find several copies of famous European paintings which he found very helpful in his studies. In 1778, however, he left off painting to volunteer to be an aide-de-camp to General Sullivan in the Rhode Island campaign where he acquitted himself well. He then returned to Boston and halfheartedly joined his brothers' tea and rum business. In the autumn of 1779, however, he gained permission through his father's English friend John Temple, who later became English Consul-General in the United States, to study painting in London. In May of 1780 he sailed for France. Here he met with Benjamin Franklin who earlier had offered him a post as his secretary. Seeing that Trumbull's heart was set on painting, Franklin kindly gave him a letter of introduction to American painter Benjamin West (1738–1820) who lived and taught painting in London.

Although determined to pursue his goal of becoming a painter, he had agreed to manage a family financial project in Europe involving the investment of American securities, and was supposed to study with West only in his spare-time. (It was plain his family still thought of painting as a sort of hobby which he could pursue as time permitted.) It is thought that Trumbull also may have become involved in a secret mission from Congress to Franklin, something relating to the conflict in the West Indies between the Netherlands, France, and England. When he arrived in Paris he learned, undoubtedly with mixed emotions, that his family's business project had collapsed, because the crushing defeat of the colonists at Charleston, South Carolina, had made the public securities worthless.

Leaving for London in July 1780, armed with his letter of introduction to West, he was cordially welcomed by the great painter who asked him if he had brought any of his paintings with him. When Trumbull answered in the negative, West sent him into a room where Gilbert Stuart (1755–1828), then a pupil of West's, was painting and asked him to choose a painting to copy. Trumbull chose a copy of Raphael's "Madonna della sedia." West said that if he did a good job of copying this painting, he would think well of him. Such must have been the case, for during the next four months Trumbull worked closely with Gilbert Stuart on joint exercises West gave them to do. Although their temperaments were very different, Stuart and Trumbull worked well together and soon became friends.

The time passed uneventfully with the two artists working diligently at their easels when Trumbull was suddenly arrested on November 19, 1780 and charged with "suspicion of treason." He was imprisoned in Tothill Fields, Bridewell. A London magazine cited items of his correspondence as evidence of treason. It is true that his letters home contained expressions of anti-British sentiments with regard to the war. It soon became apparent, however, that the real reason for his arrest was retaliation for the American execution of Major Andre who had plotted to put West Point into British hands. Trumbull was duly put on trial and, according to a London reporter, conducted himself with fortitude. He argued that he had resigned from the military and was in London only to study painting. He also added, as a veiled threat, that he was the son of the Governor of Connecticut and had been an aide-de-camp to General Washington. "I am entirely in your power," he acknowledged, "and, after the hint which I have given you, treat me as you please, always remembering, that as I may be treated, so will your friends in America be treated by mine."[3]

Trumbull was treated courteously but was not released. Benjamin West went to King George III and said he would vouch for Trumbull if he were released and reiterated Trumbull's declaration that he was only in England to study painting. The King assured West that his protege's life was in no danger, but said that he could do nothing in the matter. Edmund Burke next took an interest in the case and, after many letters of appeal, got the Privy Council to free Trumbull on condition that he leave England within thirty days and have nothing to say until that time. Trumbull complied and left for the Netherlands immediately upon his release on June 12—after eight months in prison. In Amsterdam, he tried to negotiate a loan for Connecticut through M. de Neufville & Son, his father's bankers, for whom he painted a full-length portrait of George Washington. Valentine Green made an engraving of it and published it the next year (1781). Trumbull's was the first authentic painting of Washington to appear in Europe.

In January 1782, Trumbull finally arrived in New York after six months at sea owing to bad weather. He made his way home at once, exhausted and dejected because of the failure of his attempts to transact business for his family and the failure of his promising career as an artist. "My reflections were painful—I had thrown away two of the most precious years of life—had encountered many dangers, and suffered many inconveniences, to no purpose. I was seized with a serious illness, which confined me to my bed, and endangered my life; and it was autumn before I had recovered strength sufficient to attempt any occupation."[4]

His father continued to urge a career in the law as the ideal profession in a republic. But Trumbull continued to urge the arts as the only profession for him, talking eloquently about the great honors paid to artists in the glory days of Athens, to which his father replied, "You appear to forget, sir, that Connecticut is not Athens."[5] In 1783, however, his father gave in and got him a letter of introduction to the Earl of Dartmouth discussing his desire to return to England to work further with Benjamin West. Trumbull arrived in London in January 1784 where West greeted him warmly. Trumbull's plan was to study with West for two years and then to spend the following year in Rome. While studying with West, Trumbull followed a strict schedule, beginning at 5 a.m. with the study of anatomy, followed by breakfast at eight, then painting for the rest of the day, with a break for lunch at around 2 o'clock. His evenings were spent attending classes at the Royal Academy where he frequently sat with Thomas Lawrence (1769–1830). His generous teacher was happy to introduce Trumbull to many artists, diplomats and members of the aristocracy. Sometimes, he and West went to Windsor Castle to sketch. Still, Trumbull continued to feel ill at ease in England and pined for Lebanon. But he was eager to visit Italy before returning home. A letter to his brother tells of the field of arts that particularly interested him. Although he knew he could make a respectable living painting portraits, his great desire was to paint the principal events of the War of Independence. He doubted that it would earn him much monetary profit, but was sure that it would require great artistic skill, which he hoped to attain before leaving Europe for home.

He met Thomas Jefferson in London in 1785 and later, in July 1786, visited him in Paris where Trumbull showed him two historical paintings he had completed—*The Death of General Warren at the Battle of Bunker's Hill* and *The Death of General Montgomery at Quebec*. Jefferson and John Adams made suggestions for ten other subjects to be painted. In the end, Trumbull completed eight of these which are now in the Yale University library. While staying with Jefferson, Trumbull met many prominent artists, such as architect Charles Bulfinch, (1765–1844) and French painter Jacques-Louis David (1748–1825). He attended social gatherings at the home of Madame Marie Vigee-Lebrun (1755–1842), another well-known French portrait painter and close friend of the Queen, Marie Antoinette.

His time in Paris was not only filled with pleasant social events. It was also a time of work. He made a sketch of *The Declaration of Independence* at

Jefferson's house in 1786, with Jefferson giving him a drawing of the room and telling him about the event. Back in London, he completed its composition, although he left out the heads which were to be painted from life as the opportunity arose. (While still in West's studio, he also completed *The Surrender of Lord Cornwallis, The Battle of Trenton* and *The Battle of Princeton.*)

An opportunity soon presented itself to begin painting some of the subjects' heads from life when he again visited Jefferson in the fall. He now painted Jefferson's portrait on the canvas of the *Declaration* as well as the faces of the French officers on the canvas of *The Surrender of Lord Cornwallis*. He also painted John Adams's head in London in the autumn 1787 and commented that just prior to leaving the Court, Adams combed the powder out of his hair and that its color and natural curl were beautiful. He immediately seized the opportunity of painting his head into the *Declaration of Independence*. It was to take him eight years to complete the painting with all the heads of the signers completed, thirty-six of the forty-eight from life, the rest from portraits or from Trumbull's memory. The painting is not strictly accurate, however, because thirteen signers were not included and four non-signers were included. Still, "this brilliant and dignified achievement remains the most important visual record of the heroic period of American history. . . . "[6]

Late in 1787, Trumbull painted a scene that showed British heroism: *The Sortie Made by the Garrison of Gibraltar.* He undertook to do this painting because his revolutionary war scenes were not popular in England. The Sortie turned out to be "a little masterpiece." Its exhibition in 1789, had only limited success, however, leaving Trumbull very depressed. Just at this time Jefferson offered him a post as his private secretary at 300 pounds a year. It was a tempting offer, but Trumbull resolved to remain true to his objective—to become the artistic chronicler of the Revolution. To fulfill this dream, it now seemed the time to return to America.

December 1789 found him in New York where Congress was then meeting. His intention was to paint portraits from the four historical paintings he had already done and to obtain subscriptions for engravings he had procured of two of them. George Washington ordered four sets and also sat for Trumbull. The artist went on to paint heads for his paintings and to collect subscribers to the engravings as he traveled throughout New England, Pennsylvania, Virginia, and South Carolina. He also did many small portraits on wood of many of the distinguished men of the time to be used in the historical paintings he planned to do later. Fifty-eight of these are now in the Yale Gallery of Fine Arts, at Yale University. In order to better portray them in his paintings, he visited several historic sites, including Yorktown.

In 1792, he was again in Philadelphia. Here he painted a large portrait of Washington *Before the Battle of Princeton* (engraved later in stipple by Thomas Cheesman) for Charleston, South Carolina. But the picture was rejected and he had to paint another. This was a blow to him. Also, subscriptions to his engravings dwindled and he failed in his efforts to get the federal government to extend financial backing for his series of paintings on the Revolution. Deeply discouraged, Trumbull turned his back on his painting career. Instead, in 1794, he set out for England as private secretary to John Jay, envoy extraordinary to Great Britain. The mission was to draw up a treaty to settle the commercial and frontier differences between the United States and Great Britain. The negotiations for the Treaty went on until November when "Jay's Treaty," as it came to be known, was completed. Trumbull committed the Treaty to memory and, in 1795, was sent to Paris to repeat its provisions to James Monroe, United States Minister to France. Unfortunately, he had been given a proviso which was that the information he transmitted to Monroe would not be shared with the French. Monroe refused to agree, and the message was never delivered. While he waited for his next instruction, Trumbull became unwelcome in diplomatic circles. He kept himself busy, however, with his artist friends who helped him to buy paintings by the old masters from aristocratic families now fallen into poverty because of the French Revolution of 1789.

In 1796 his brother Jonathan asked him to come home and join him in a business venture, but Trumbull had earned some money from investments he had made in Germany and England and was now anxious to see how the engravings of his *Bunker's Hill, Gibraltar*, and *Quebec* paintings was progressing in Stuttgart. In 1797, engravings of the three works were published.

In that year, Trumbull was also appointed to serve on a commission to carry out the seventh article of the Jay Treaty which was the settlement of claims made by American and British shippers in regard to captured ships and their cargoes. As a courier to the American envoys in Paris, Trumbull became embroiled in what was later known at the "XYZ Affair," which involved French Foreign Minister Talleyrand's attempt to extort $250,000 from the envoys in order to assure the cooperation of the French. The envoys, including Trumbull, were told they could not leave France without permission from the French government. Trumbull wrote to Talleyrand from Calais asking for a passport. Receiving no answer he returned to Paris where Talleyrand interrogated him minutely regarding information on his political activities. He evidently thought that Trumbull's artistic and business activities were a cover-up for political spying, and he refused to give Trumbull leave to leave France. It was only after enlisting the help of the celebrated French painter, Jacques-Louis David, that Trumbull was finally allowed to leave for England. Here he decided to return to his first love, painting. He was dismayed, however, to discover how much he had lost of his former artistic skills. He determined to regain his ability and thought of little else for months.

In October 1800 Trumbull, now age forty-four, surprised his family and friends by marrying Sarah Hope Harvey, a young Englishwoman of twenty-six whose background was shrouded in mystery and about whom there was much conjecture. She had great beauty, and Trumbull did the first of three portraits of her. By 1803, Trumbull decided he should return to America although he was apprehensive about his ability to earn money through painting. In 1804, his work on the Jay Treaty Commission now completed, he returned to the United States with his wife. He went first to New York but, failing to arouse interest in his work, he moved to Boston. There, too, the reception he received was tepid. Learning that his old friend Gilbert Stuart had been invited to settle in Boston, he concluded that there would not be enough work for two rival artists and returned to New York where he became established as the first artist of the city. Between 1805–06 he painted portraits of Boston's prominent citizens. But the economic consequences of the Embargo Act of 1808, prohibiting all international trade with American ports, resulted in dwindling commissions for Trumbull.

Trumbull not only had money concerns but his deteriorating eyesight caused him to return to England for treatment. In London, because war with the United States seemed imminent, Trumbull won very few commissions. Trumbull's desire to return to America was cut short by the outbreak of the War of 1812. He appealed to the government for permission to move to Bath which was finally granted. Despite the adverse conditions under which he labored, several of his paintings on literary and religious subjects were shown at the Royal Academy. In 1815, the Trumbulls finally returned to the United States where they settled permanently in New York. Here, in 1816, Trumbull exhibited twenty paintings at the first exhibition of the American Academy. Afterwards, the Academy bought four of his paintings for $10,000. They failed to raise this sum, however, and Trumbull agreed to accept an annuity of $900 a year.

He found himself falling into debt, however, and wrote to Jefferson and Adams of his dream that the government would choose him to decorate the new U.S. Capitol with his American historical paintings. He succeeded in getting his paintings exhibited in the House of Representatives in 1816. In February 1817, Congress at last commissioned him to do four paintings in the Rotunda which were to be: *The Surrender of General Burgoyne at Saratoga*, *The Surrender of Lord Cornwallis at Yorktown*, *The Declaration of Independence*, and *The Resignation of Washington*. Congress agreed to pay Trumbull $8,000 for each painting. President Madison decided that the figures should be as large as life. This proved to be a very difficult task for the aging painter who, even in his youth, had never excelled at large painting.

In 1824, he finished the task of painting the large versions (twelve feet by eighteen feet) of the twenty-by-thirty inch miniature paintings he had done so exquisitely years before. The results were disappointing to those who had seen the originals. They seemed heavy-handed and he seemed to have lost the ability to reproduce the likenesses that had been so successful in the originals. Nevertheless, his reputation as an artist rests upon his earlier work as a miniaturist. "No schoolboy but sees the Revolution through his eyes. His 250 to 300 faithful representations, drawn from life, of the principal actors and actions of the Revolution make him at once the chief, the most prolific, and the most competent visual recorder of that heroic period."[7]

In 1824, the year he finally completed his paintings for the Capitol Rotunda, Trumbull lost his wife, "who," he wrote, "had been the faithful and beloved companion of all the vicissitudes of twenty-four years. She was the perfect personification of truth and sincerity."[8] His late years were also clouded by increasing financial difficulties and by his failure to persuade Congress to commission him to fill the four remaining niches in the Capitol Rotunda with his historical paintings. In 1831, Trumbull decided to approach the Trustees of Yale College, through his nephew-in-law, Dr. Benjamin Silliman, concerning his desire to giving the eight original paintings of the events of the Revolution to the college in exchange for an annuity of $1,000. Included would also be his miniature portraits of patriot leaders of the Revolution. The Trustees accepted Trumbull's offer and, in the summer of 1831 he began to work on the design of the Trumbull Gallery. He arranged to have installed a crypt beneath the Gallery where he and his wife would be buried. The Gallery opened to the public in October 1832. It was the first college museum in the country and a unique one, for only in this museum can one find so many original portraits of prominent figures of the American Revolution. They total about 250 and show the student of history what these men really looked like. This collection is therefore a most important source of original historical information.

In 1841, the *Autobiography, Letters, and Reminiscences of John Trumbull from 1756 to 1841* was published in New Haven, New York and London. His was the first autobiography written by an American artist. In 1843, John Trumbull died at the age of eighty-seven. His funeral was held at Yale College Chapel and, as he had wished, he was buried next to his wife in the Trumbull Gallery underneath his full-length portrait of George Washington.

Painting: *The Resignation of George Washington*, p. 212.

---

1 Col. J. Trumbull, *Reminiscences of His Own Times from 1756 to 1841* (New York, 1841), p. 11.

2 Trumbull, *Reminiscences*, p. 15–16.

3 Trumbull, *Reminiscences*, pp. 71–72.

4 *Ibid.*, 87–88.

5 *Ibid*, p. 88–89.

6 *Dictionary of American Biography* (New York: Charles Scribners' Sons, 1964), Vol. X, p. 13.

7 *Dictionary of American Biography*, Vol. X, p. 15.

8 Trumbull, *Reminiscences*, p. 276.

John Wollaston
d. 1770

This English painter was active from about 1736 to 1767 and painted portraits in America from 1749 to 1758. It is believed that he began as an assistant to a better-known English painter, or painters. The job of assistants to prominent painters in England was to paint the background details and accessories in a painting, such as draperies, and sometimes the costumes the sitter was wearing. They were known as "drapery painters."

In America, however, Wollaston became a successful portrait painter who painted portraits from New York to South Carolina. His work utilized brilliant colors and was elegant and graceful. One of his best-known paintings is that of John Bartram, the botanist. It is in the National Portrait Gallery, Washington, D.C. Bartram is seen pointing to the Lady Petre pear he had propagated in 1758 from seeds sent to him by his patroness. Such details of a sitter's life were often used in portraits.

Wollaston returned to England around 1759 where he continued to paint until about 1767. He died in 1770 in the fashionable city of Bath where aristocrats and well-to-do merchants and their families came "to take the waters."

An engraving of his painting of Martha Dandridge Custis from life at age 26 appears in this volume on p. 86.

---

1 Henry T. Tuckerman, *Artist Life* , 1847, p. 177.

2 *American National Biography* (New York: Oxford University Press, 1999), Vol. 13, p. 533

3 *Ibid.*

4 *Ibid.*, p. 534.

SCRIPTURE REFERENCES*

This section of the volume will serve to help the reader appreciate the Biblical scholarship of George Washington and his fellow-citizens—the American pastors, historians, and statesmen of the eighteenth and nineteenth centuries. Those who best knew and understood the worth of George Washington's Christian character and its importance to the very existence of America as the first nation founded upon the Christian liberty of the individual, were those who knew and revered what the Scriptures taught about men and nations, liberty and law, and church and civil government.

The reader must be attentive to the fact that in reading, "*The Great Audit & The Account of the Good Steward*," pp. 124–43, or "*A Sermon*, Dedicated to George Washington, by William Smith, D.D.," (pp. 272–80), he is imbibing from the whole, original work. These are not abridgements nor a series or collection of excerpts. Bringing the entire work to the reader is intentional so that he might be able to follow adept reasoning from Biblical principles in its fulness and beauty, and to comprehend the ability to view and the agility to explain external effects from internal, spiritual causes, thus, to deal with all subjects from a Biblical standpoint.

Because of the Biblical education George Washington and those of his generation received from within their homes and from the pastors in their churches, this kind of scholarly thinking, teaching and speaking was typical of the times. The reader will come to realize that American Christianity in that time was characterized by a high level of Biblical knowledge and the ability to apply it to the nature and actions of a nation in its civil government and constitutions! The content of public orations and speeches were once, typically, Scriptural in theme and in ideas, and these ideas were fundamentally well understood and well received.

The level of Biblical education belonging to the Founding Father generations was high and superior to what is generally claimed as Christian education in the present generation. The historical records have not, however, been erased and the standard of scholarship remains to be reclaimed and restored to the national life of America. May American Christians of today return to the Bible as their Original Resource, and, thereby, to give God's Word predominance in everything related to life and living, of both men and nations.

—Katherine Dang

INDEXING KEY: Letters a, b, c, d following page numbers indicate first, second, third, fourth quarters of page—

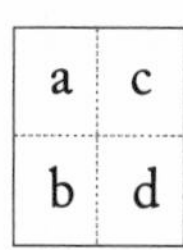

* The King James Version of the Bible is used in this volume.

Genesis

Exodus

Leviticus

Deuteronomy

Joshua

Judges

I Kings

I Chronicles

II Chronicles

Esther

Job

Psalms

Proverbs

Ecclesiastes

Isaiah

Ezekiel

Daniel

Joel

Amos

Micah

Habakkuk

Zechariah

Malachi

Chronological Tables

of English and American History, 1649–1775, as They Relate to the Providential Preparation of George Washington, Commander-in-Chief of the Continental Armed Forces of America

Compiled by Verna M. Hall

England:	*The Christian History of the American Revolution: Consider and Ponder*. Selections from Chronological Annals of English History, p. 259–262
America:	*The Christian History of the United States of America,* Vol. I: *Christian Self-Government.* Selections from Chronological Table, page 420–426
Washington:	*George Washington: The Character and Influence of One Man*

England	America	The Washingtons
1649 Execution of Charles I, Jan. 30 Scotland proclaims Charles II. England proclaims itself a Commonwealth.	1649 A part of Virginia is granted to Lord Culpepper and others.	1649 Sir Henry Washington, who fought for Prince Rupert at Bristol in 1643, defended Worcester in 1649.
1651 Union with Scotland and Ireland Hobbe's "*Leviathan*"		1650–1670 The Virginia Colony increased from fifteen thousand to forty thousand. Virginia was loyal to the exiled monarch and the Anglican Church, and became a favorite resort to the Cavaliers.
1654 Oliver Cromwell, Lord Protector Peace concluded with Holland.		
1657 Cromwell refuses title of King.		1657 John and Andrew Washington arrive in Virginia and purchase lands in Westmoreland County. John marries Miss Anne Pope; settles at Bridges Creek; becomes a Magistrate and a member of the House of Burgesses; distinguishes himself as the first colonel of the Washington family in America. He was the nephew of Sir Henry Washington.
1658 Death of Cromwell, Sept. 3. Richard Cromwell, Lord Protector		
1660 Charles the Second		
1662 Puritan clergy driven out.		
1669 Lord Ashley shrinks back from toleration to Catholics	1669 John Locke assists in drawing up "The Fundamental Constitution of Carolina."	
1673 War between England and Holland	1673 The Dutch take New York.	
1674 Charles makes peace with Holland.	1674 New York restored to the English. Andros appointed Governor of New York.	
	1675–1676 King Philip's War	

England	America	The Washingtons
1677 Prince of Orange marries Mary, daughter of the future James II.	1677 Virginia obtains a charter. Massachusetts purchases Maine.	
1679 Habeas Corpus Act passed.		
	1681 Penn receives from Charles II a Grant of Pennsylvania.	
	1678–1684 LaSalle, under the patronage of the king of France, discovers the country along the Mississippi and the lakes, which is called Louisiana.	
	1684 A treaty of peace is concluded with the Five Nations. Massachusetts deprived of her charter.	
1685–1686 James the Second Test Act dispensed with by Royal authority. Ecclesiastical Commission set up.	1686 James II appoints Sir Edmund Andros governor general of New England.	
1687 Newton's "*Principia*" Declaration of Indulgence, protested by William of Orange	1687 Andros attempts to take the charter of Connecticut; the government is surrendered to him.	
1688 William of Orange lands at Torbay. Flight of James II	1688 General suppression of charter governments	
1689 Convention Parliament: Declaration of Rights William and Mary made King and Queen. Toleration Bill Bill of Rights War between England and France	1689 Andros is imprisoned, and the government of Massachusetts in the hands of a committee of safety. Connecticut and Rhode Island resume their charters.	
1690 Locke's *Of Civil Government*	1690 French Protestants settle in Carolina and Virginia.	
1694 Bank of England set up. Death of Mary		1694 John Washington's grandson, Augustine, the father of George Washington, born in Westmoreland County.

England	America	The Washingtons
1702 Queen Anne Great Britain at War with France and Spain		
1713 Treaty of Utrecht ends war.		
1714 George the First Ministry of Townshend and Walpole		
1715 Jacobite Revolt under Lord Mar.	1715 Indian war in South Carolina	1715 Augustine Washington marries Jane, daughter of Caleb Butler, by whom he has four children, of whom only Lawrence and Augustine survive childhood.
1727 War with Austria and Spain George the Second	1727 A fort is erected at Oswego, N.Y.	
		1728 Jane Washington, wife of Augustine Washington, dies November 24.
	1729 North and South Carolina purchased by the crown.	
1730 Free exportation of American rice allowed.		1730 On March 6, Augustine Washington marries Mary, the Daughter of Colonel Ball. By her he has four sons, George, Samuel, John Augustine, and Charles, and two daughers, Elizabeth, or Betty, and Mildred, who died in infancy.
		1732 George Washington born on the 22nd of Feb. (11th, o.s.), in the homestead on Bridges Creek, Westmoreland Co., Va.
		1734–1735 Augustine Washington moves his family to Huntington Creek Estate, now known as Mt. Vernon. George's half-brothers, Lawrence and Augustine, are sent to school in England.
1739 War between England and Spain		1739 Augustine Washington moves his family to "Ferry Farm" on the Rappahannock River, opposite Fredericksburg. Here George is taught rudiments of education.

England	America	The Washingtons
1740 War of the Austrian Succession	1740 Oglethorpe invades Florida, and makes an unsuccessful attempt on St. Augustine. The French conclude a peace with the Chickasaws.	1740 Lawrence returns from England, obtains a captain's commission in a newly raised regiment, and embarks with it for the West Indies. He serves in the joint expeditions of Admiral Vernon and General Wentworth.
1742 Resignation of Walpole	1742 A Spanish fleet invades Georgia, but retires with loss.	1742 Lawrence Washington returns home from the campaign in impaired health.
1743 Ministry of Henry Pelham Battle of Dettingen, June 27		1743 George's father dies suddenly April 12. Lawrence inherits the Huntington Creek Estate (Mt. Vernon); George inherits the lands on the Rappahannock. July. Lawrence Washington marries Anne Fairfax, daughter of the Hon. William Fairfax of Belvoir Manor; they settle at Mt. Vernon, named after British Admiral Vernon. George studies at brother Augustine's at Wakefield.
1744 War proclaimed between England and France.		
1745 Charles Edward lands in Scotland, reaches Derby, Dec. 4.	1745 The colonists, under Col. Pepperell, take Louisburg and Cape Breton from the French.	1745 George copies out the Rules of Civility, returns to his mother's at Pine Grove, and studies at the parish school at Fredericksburg.
1746 Battle of Falkirk, Jan. 23 Battle of Culloden, April 16	1746 The French send a fleet to destroy the colonies.	1746 George obtains a midshipman's warrant in the English navy, but yields to his mother's entreaties to stay at home.
		1747 George takes final leave of school in the autumn and goes to live with his brother Lawrence at Mount Vernon. He becomes acquainted with Thomas, Lord Fairfax, who has come to Virginia to develop his extensive lands.
1748 Peace of Aix-la-Chapelle, leaves undefined the boundaries between French and English possessions in America.		1748 In March, George, now sixteen, sets out on horseback on his first expedition into the wilderness to survey Lord Fairfax's lands. He notes in his diary soils, minerals, and locations and makes accurate and neatly drafted maps.

England	America	The Washingtons
	1750 The French make encroachments. A large tract of land in the Ohio river area is granted to the Ohio company, which erects trading houses; but the French consider this as invading their territories.	1748–1750 Washington appointed public surveyor, a post he holds for three years.
	1751 Virginia is divided into military districts, each with an adjutant general with the rank of major.	1751 Lawrence Washington seeks and obtains post of adjutant general for George. At age nineteen, George becomes Major and Adjutant General of the Virginia frontier forces. September. Lawrence ill with severe pulmonary symptoms. On doctor's advice, he sails for Barbadoes, taking George with him. They make landfall Nov. 3.
1752 France moves to defend Ohio territory.	1752 Georgia becomes a royal province.	1752 Lawrence arranges for George to return to Virginia and bring his wife to Barbadoes. On Dec. 22 George sails for Virginia, arriving Feb. 1. His health rapidly worsening, Lawrence returns to Mount Vernon in time to die under his own roof on July 26. Mount Vernon goes to Lawrence's infant daughter, who dies within the year. It then goes to George.
1753 England is concerned that France controls Canada and the country west of the Mississippi and is building a chain of forts between the shores of Lake Erie and the Alleghany River. Both England and France claim the upper Ohio Valley.	1753 Washington sent from Dinwiddie with a letter to the French requiring them to quit the English territories.	1753 Washington receives Masonic degrees. On October 30, George, age twenty-one, sets out from Williamsburg to the French post at Venango in Western Pennsylvania. His *Journal* of this trip is published and creates great interest.
	1754 The French erect fort DuQuesne. Washington is sent to maintain the rights of the English; he is attacked at Fort Necessity by a French force, and capitulates. A congress of delegates from seven provinces meets at Albany and proposes a plan of union for the colonies, which is rejected.	1754 Washington and his officers receive a vote of thanks for their bravery in defending the rights of their country. Washington commands Virginia troops at victorious skirmish at Great Meadows, first hostilities leading to the Seven Years War and, in America, the French and Indian War.

England	America	The Washingtons
1755 The Seven Years War	1755 June. Nova Scotia taken from the French. July. General Braddock leads an expedition against Fort DuQuesne, falls into an ambuscade, and is totally defeated. July. Treaty with the Cherokees Sept. 8. The French are repulsed at lake George.	1755 Washington resigns his commission, disengages himself from public affairs, and returns to Mount Vernon. General Braddock invites Washington to join his staff and he accepts the invitation. At twenty-three, as a volunteer aide to General Braddock in the expedition against Fort DuQuesne, he is the only mounted officer unscathed in the battle, although four bullets go through his coat and two horses are shot under him.
1756 Formal declaration of war between England and France		1756 Feb. To settle disputes when the claims of two governments collide, Washington is sent to Boston to obtain a decision from Gov. Shirley on the disputed point and a regulation to prevent difficulties in the future. He visits Philadelphia, New York, and Boston, and is treated as the hero of the battle at Fort DuQuesne.
1757 Ministry of William Pitt	1757 Aug. 8. The French, under Montcalm, capture Fort William Henry.	1757 Washington is stationed at Winchester. Part of his force is detached to South Carolina and he is left with 700 men to defend a frontier of more than 350 miles. The troubles he experiences are heightened by misunderstandings with Governor Dinwiddie. He suffers repeated attacks of dysentery and fever, but continues to perform his duties. His illness increasing, he is induced by Dr. Craik, the army surgeon, to give up his post toward the end of the year and return to Mount Vernon.
	1758 July 6. Louisburg taken by the English. Nov. 25. Fort DuQuesne is retaken by the English.	1758 April. Washington's health improved, he is again in command at Fort Loudoun. He proposes marriage to Martha Custis and is accepted, their marriage to take place after the campaign against Fort DuQuesne is ended. Nov. 25. Washington, with the advance guard, marches in and plants the English flag on the smoking ruins of Fort DuQuesne which is renamed Fort Pitt in honor of the statesman whose support aided the campaign.

England	America	The Washingtons
	1759 July 27. Gen. Amherst takes Fort Ticonderoga. Aug. 4. Crown Point surrenders to the English. Sept. 18. Qubec surrenders to the English.	1759 Jan. 6. Washington marries Martha Custis at her home. He also enters the House of the Burgesses.
1760 George III	1760 April 28. Battle near Quebec Sept. 8. Canada surrenders to Great Britain.	
1761 Ministry of Lord Bute	1761 Cherokees are subdued.	
1762 England at war with Spain Plans are made to change the government of the colonies		
1763 Treaty of Paris ends the war.	1763 Detroit under siege from the Indians commanded by Pontiac.	1763 Washington's retirement from the army prevents him from being entangled in this savage war.
1764 Great Britain determines to tax the colonies, and accordingly lays additional duties on sugar, molasses, and other articles.		
1765 Stamp Act passed by Parliament. Ministry of Lord Rockingham	1765 Great opposition to the Act in the colonies is led by Virginia and Massachusetts.	1765 Washington disapproves of the Act, but does not participate in agitation on the issue.
1766 March. Stamp Act repealed but Parliament declares right to bind the colonies.	1766 Rejoicing in the colonies	1766 Washington is pleased that the Act has been repealed and declares in a letter that "all . . . who were instrumental in procuring the repeal, are entitled to the thanks of every British subject."
1767 Parliament imposes new taxes on the colonies.		
1768 Ministry of the Duke of Grafton	1768 Massachusetts requests the co-operation of the other colonies in resisting British oppression. Her assembly has been dissolved. Sept. 28. British troops are stationed in Boston.	

England	America	The Washingtons
1769 Letters of *Junius*	1769 The colonies enter into non-importation agreements.	1769 April 5. Washington and Mason draft a plan of association and non-importation. Washington presents it to the House of Burgesses in May. All present sign the instrument which is then circulated throughout the country and is soon adopted universally. Washington adheres to the agreement rigorously, ordering his London agent to send him nothing subject to taxation.
1770 Ministry of Lord North Parliament removes the duties imposed on the colonies except the tax on tea.	1770 March 5. The Boston Massacre	1770 Washington makes an expedition to the Ohio with Dr. Craik on behalf of the soldiers' claims.
	1773 A correspondence is established between the colonies. Attempts made to import tea into the colonies; the cargoes of three ships are thrown overboard in Boston harbor.	
1774 March. A bill to close the Port of Boston is passed by Parliament.	1774 The Port of Boston is closed. May 24. The Virginia House of Burgesses sets June 1 as a day of fasting and prayer. Aug. 1. General Convention of the colony of Virginia is held at Williamsburg and passes resolutions similar to those of Fairfax County affirming their rights to be governed by laws to which they have given their assent through their own legislative bodies, not to be subject to taxation by Parliament, and to enter into non-importation agreements.	1774 June. Washington presided as moderator at a meeting of the inhabitants of Fairfax County. He is appointed Chairman of a Committee to draw up resolutions to present at a general meeting of the country. June 18. Washington presents the Fairfax County Resolutions at the Alexandria Court House. The Resolutions are passed and Washington is chosen to be a delegate to represent the county at the General Convention at Williamsburg. Washington is one of seven delegates chosen to represent Virginia in the First Continental Congress.

England	America	The Washingtons
1775 Parliament rejects Chatham's plan of conciliation with the colonies.	1775 Feb. 26. British attempt to take field pieces at Salem April 19. War begins at Lexington. May 10. Ticonderoga and Crown Point are taken by the Americans. May 10. The Second Continental Congress assembles at Philadelphia. Royal governments are laid aside in the southern colonies. June 12. General Gage, commander-in-chief of the British forces in America, calls for martial law in the province of Massachusetts. June 12. Congress calls for a day of prayer and fasting for July 20.	1775 Washington is made chairman of all committees for military affairs and drafts most of the rules and regulations for the army. June 15. Congress elects Washington as commander-in-chief of the Continental army.

INDEX

OF

ARTICLES, SUBHEADINGS,

MARGINAL NOTES, AND

COMPILER VERNA M. HALL'S

EDITORIAL COMMENTS

GENERAL INDEX

WITH EMPHASIS ON THE PROVIDENCE OF GOD

IN THE LIFE OF GEORGE WASHINGTON

INDEXING KEY: Letters a, b, c, d following page numbers indicate first, second, third, fourth quarters of page—

a	c
b	d

INDEX

ARTICLES, SUBHEADINGS, MARGINAL NOTES, AND COMPILER VERNA M. HALL'S EDITORIAL COMMENTS

THE CHARACTER OF GEORGE WASHINGTON

GEORGE WASHINGTON: HIS PROVIDENTIAL PREPARATION, 15–150

Psalm 71:17, Proverbs 23:12, Matthew 5:16, 15

The Life of George Washington, Vol. I, by Washington Irving, 1856:

MARGINAL NOTES by Katherine Dang

INDEXING KEY: Letters a, b, c, d following page numbers indicate first, second, third, fourth quarters of page—

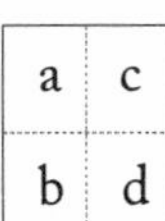

Washington's Attendance at Various Churches, 242–253

From George Washington's *Diaries*, 1748–1799

GEORGE WASHINGTON'S RELIGIOUS LIBRARY
Catalogued in the *Boston Athenæm*
by Appleton P. C. Griffin, 1897, 254–271:

A Sermon,

Dedicated to George Washington, Delivered in His Presence, and Included in His Library, 272–280

The Dedication of the Washington National Monument, 281–326

GENERAL INDEX

WITH EMPHASIS ON THE PROVIDENCE OF GOD IN THE LIFE OF GEORGE WASHINGTON

Prepared by Dorothy Dimmick

INDEXING KEY: Letters a, b, c, d following page numbers indicate first, second, third, fourth quarters of page—

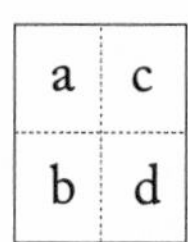

A

C

D

E

F

G

M

N

O

P

Q

R

S

T

U

V

W

Y